Hyundai Excel & Accent Automotive Repair Manual

by Mike Stubblefield, L. Alan LeDoux and John H Haynes
Member of the Guild of Motoring Writers

Models covered:
All Hyundai Excel and Accent models
1986 through 2009

(43015-7Q3-2)   ABC

Haynes Publishing Group
Sparkford Nr Yeovil
Somerset BA22 7JJ England

Haynes North America, Inc
861 Lawrence Drive
Newbury Park
California 91320 USA

Acknowledgements

We are grateful for the help and cooperation of the Hyundai Motor Company for assistance with technical information. Technical writers who contributed to this project include Larry Warren, Bob Henderson and Ken Freund.

A book in the Haynes Automotive Repair Manual Series

Printed in the U.S.A.

ISBN-13: 978-1-56392-804-8
ISBN-10: 1-56392-804-3

Library of Congress Control Number: 2010920956

While every attempt is made to ensure that the information in this manual is correct, no liability can be accepted by the authors or publishers for loss, damage or injury caused by any errors in, or omissions from, the information given.

Contents

Haynes photographer, mechanic and author with Hyundai Excel

About this manual

Its purpose

The purpose of this manual is to help you get the best value from your vehicle. It can do so in several ways. It can help you decide what work must be done, even if you choose to have it done by a dealer service department or a repair shop; it provides information and procedures for routine maintenance and servicing; and it offers diagnostic and repair procedures to follow when trouble occurs.

We hope you use the manual to tackle the work yourself. For many simpler jobs, doing it yourself may be quicker than arranging an appointment to get the vehicle into a shop and making the trips to leave it and pick it up. More importantly, a lot of money can be saved by avoiding the expense the shop must pass on to you to cover its labor and overhead

costs. An added benefit is the sense of satisfaction and accomplishment that you feel after doing the job yourself.

Using the manual

The manual is divided into Chapters. Each Chapter is divided into numbered Sections, which are headed in bold type between horizontal lines. Each Section consists of consecutively numbered paragraphs.

At the beginning of each numbered Section you will be referred to any illustrations which apply to the procedures in that Section. The reference numbers used in illustration captions pinpoint the pertinent Section and the Step within that Section. That is, illustration 3.2 means the illustration refers to Section 3 and Step (or paragraph) 2 within that Section.

Procedures, once described in the text, are not normally repeated. When it's necessary to refer to another Chapter, the reference will be given as Chapter and Section number. Cross references given without use of the word "Chapter" apply to Sections and/or paragraphs in the same Chapter. For example, "see Section 8" means in the same Chapter.

References to the left or right side of the vehicle assume you are sitting in the driver's seat, facing forward.

Even though we have prepared this manual with extreme care, neither the publisher nor the author can accept responsibility for any errors in, or omissions from, the information given.

NOTE

A **Note** provides information necessary to properly complete a procedure or information which will make the procedure easier to understand.

CAUTION

A **Caution** provides a special procedure or special steps which must be taken while completing the procedure where the Caution is found. Not heeding a Caution can result in damage to the assembly being worked on.

WARNING

A **Warning** provides a special procedure or special steps which must be taken while completing the procedure where the Warning is found. Not heeding a Warning can result in personal injury.

Introduction to the Hyundai Excel and Accent

Hyundai Excel models are available in 2 and 4-door hatchback and 4-door sedan body styles. Hyundai Accent models are available in 2 door hatchback and 4-door sedan body styles. The 2 door hatchback is often referred to as the 3-door model.

These vehicles are powered by either a 1.5L Single Overhead Camshaft (SOHC) engine, a 1.5L Dual Overhead Camshaft (DOHC) engine, or a 1.6L DOHC engine. The

engine drives the front wheels through either a 4 or 5-speed manual or 3-speed or 4-speed automatic transaxle via independent front-drive driveaxles.

The front suspension is a MacPherson strut design. The rear suspension on 1994 and earlier models uses a solid rear axle with trailing arms, coil springs and shock absorbers. The rear suspension on 1995 through 2005 is fully independent, using trailing arms,

lateral links and strut/coil spring assemblies. On 2006 and later models, a solid rear axle with trailing arms, coil springs and shock absorbers is used.

The brakes are disc at the front and either drums or disc at the rear, with power assist standard. 1995 and later models are equipped with Anti-Lock Brakes (ABS) and an airbag Supplemental Restraint System (SRS).

Vehicle identification numbers

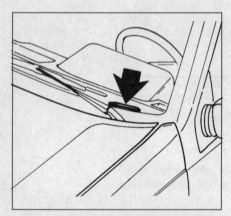

The Vehicle Identification Number (VIN) (arrow) is visible from outside the vehicle through the driver's side of the windshield

Modifications are a continuing and unpublicized process in vehicle manufacturing. Since spare parts lists are compiled on a numerical basis, the individual vehicle numbers are essential to correctly identify the component required.

Vehicle Identification Number (VIN)

This very important identification number is stamped on a plate attached to the left side cowling just inside the windshield on the driver's side of the vehicle (see illustration). The VIN also appears on the Vehicle Certificate of Title and Registration. It contains information such as where and when the vehicle was manufactured, the model year and the body style.

Manufacturers Plate

This plate is attached to the engine compartment firewall on the driver's side (see illustration). It contains information on the vehicle model, engine and transaxle as well as the paint code.

Vehicle Certification Plate

The Vehicle Certification Plate (VC label) is affixed to the left front door pillar. The plate contains the name of the manufacturer, the month and year of production, the Gross Vehicle Weight Rating (GVWR) and the certification statement.

Engine ID number

The engine number is stamped into a machined pad located at the front of the engine block (see illustration).

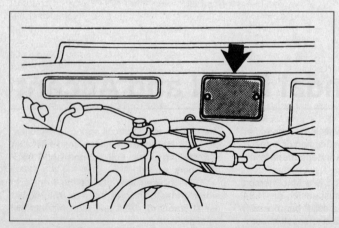

The Manufacturers Plate (arrow) is located on the firewall in the engine compartment

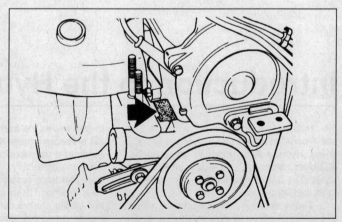

The engine ID number (arrow) is located at the front of the engine block - typical

Buying parts

Replacement parts are available from many sources, which generally fall into one of two categories - authorized dealer parts departments and independent retail auto parts stores. Our advice concerning these parts is as follows:

Retail auto parts stores: Good auto parts stores will stock frequently needed components which wear out relatively fast, such as clutch components, exhaust systems, brake parts, tune-up parts, etc. These stores often supply new or reconditioned parts on an exchange basis, which can save a considerable amount of money. Discount auto parts stores are often very good places to buy materials and parts needed for general vehicle maintenance such as oil, grease, filters, spark plugs, belts, touch-up paint, bulbs, etc. They also usually sell tools and general accessories, have convenient hours, charge lower prices and can often be found not far from home.

Authorized dealer parts department: This is the best source for parts which are unique to the vehicle and not generally available elsewhere (such as major engine parts, transmission parts, trim pieces, etc.).

Warranty information: If the vehicle is still covered under warranty, be sure that any replacement parts purchased - regardless of the source - do not invalidate the warranty!

To be sure of obtaining the correct parts, have engine and chassis numbers available and, if possible, take the old parts along for positive identification.

Maintenance techniques, tools and working facilities

Maintenance techniques

There are a number of techniques involved in maintenance and repair that will be referred to throughout this manual. Application of these techniques will enable the home mechanic to be more efficient, better organized and capable of performing the various tasks properly, which will ensure that the repair job is thorough and complete.

Fasteners

Fasteners are nuts, bolts, studs and screws used to hold two or more parts together. There are a few things to keep in mind when working with fasteners. Almost all of them use a locking device of some type, either a lockwasher, locknut, locking tab or thread adhesive. All threaded fasteners should be clean and straight, with undamaged threads and undamaged corners on the hex head where the wrench fits. Develop the habit of replacing all damaged nuts and bolts with new ones. Special locknuts with nylon or fiber inserts can only be used once. If they are removed, they lose their locking ability and must be replaced with new ones.

Rusted nuts and bolts should be treated with a penetrating fluid to ease removal and prevent breakage. Some mechanics use turpentine in a spout-type oil can, which works quite well. After applying the rust penetrant, let it work for a few minutes before trying to loosen the nut or bolt. Badly rusted fasteners may have to be chiseled or sawed off or removed with a special nut breaker, available at tool stores.

If a bolt or stud breaks off in an assembly, it can be drilled and removed with a special tool commonly available for this purpose. Most automotive machine shops can perform this task, as well as other repair procedures, such as the repair of threaded holes that have been stripped out.

Flat washers and lockwashers, when removed from an assembly, should always be replaced exactly as removed. Replace any damaged washers with new ones. Never use a lockwasher on any soft metal surface (such as aluminum), thin sheet metal or plastic.

Fastener sizes

For a number of reasons, automobile manufacturers are making wider and wider use of metric fasteners. Therefore, it is important to be able to tell the difference between standard (sometimes called U.S. or SAE) and metric hardware, since they cannot be interchanged.

All bolts, whether standard or metric, are sized according to diameter, thread pitch and length. For example, a standard 1/2 - 13 x 1 bolt is 1/2 inch in diameter, has 13 threads per inch and is 1 inch long. An M12 - 1.75 x 25 metric bolt is 12 mm in diameter, has a thread pitch of 1.75 mm (the distance between threads) and is 25 mm long. The two bolts are nearly identical, and easily confused, but they are not interchangeable.

In addition to the differences in diameter, thread pitch and length, metric and standard bolts can also be distinguished by examining the bolt heads. To begin with, the distance across the flats on a standard bolt head is measured in inches, while the same dimension on a metric bolt is sized in millimeters (the same is true for nuts). As a result, a standard wrench should not be used on a metric bolt and a metric wrench should not be used on a standard bolt. Also, most standard bolts have slashes radiating out from the center of the head to denote the grade or strength of the bolt, which is an indication of the amount of torque that can be applied to it. The greater the number of slashes, the greater the strength of the bolt. Grades 0 through 5 are commonly used on automobiles. Metric bolts have a property class (grade) number, rather than a slash, molded into their heads to indicate bolt strength. In this case, the higher the number, the stronger the bolt. Property class numbers 8.8, 9.8 and 10.9 are commonly used on automobiles.

Strength markings can also be used to distinguish standard hex nuts from metric hex nuts. Many standard nuts have dots stamped into one side, while metric nuts are marked with a number. The greater the number of dots, or the higher the number, the greater the strength of the nut.

Metric studs are also marked on their ends according to property class (grade). Larger studs are numbered (the same as metric bolts), while smaller studs carry a geometric code to denote grade.

It should be noted that many fasteners, especially Grades 0 through 2, have no distinguishing marks on them. When such is the case, the only way to determine whether it is standard or metric is to measure the thread pitch or compare it to a known fastener of the same size.

Standard fasteners are often referred to as SAE, as opposed to metric. However, it should be noted that SAE technically refers to a non-metric fine thread fastener only. Coarse thread non-metric fasteners are referred to as USS sizes.

Grade 1 or 2   Grade 5   Grade 8

Bolt strength marking (standard/SAE/USS; bottom - metric)

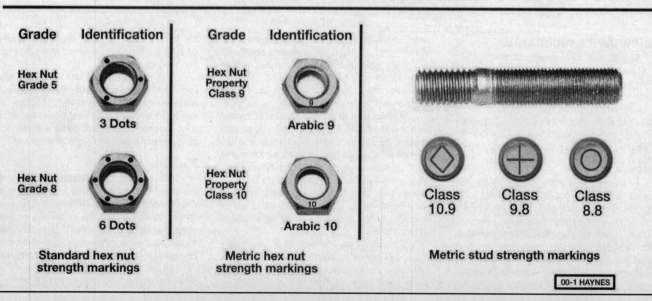

Grade	Identification
Hex Nut Grade 5	3 Dots
Hex Nut Grade 8	6 Dots

Standard hex nut strength markings

Grade	Identification
Hex Nut Property Class 9	Arabic 9
Hex Nut Property Class 10	Arabic 10

Metric hex nut strength markings

Class 10.9   Class 9.8   Class 8.8

Metric stud strength markings

Since fasteners of the same size (both standard and metric) may have different strength ratings, be sure to reinstall any bolts, studs or nuts removed from your vehicle in their original locations. Also, when replacing a fastener with a new one, make sure that the new one has a strength rating equal to or greater than the original.

Tightening sequences and procedures

Most threaded fasteners should be tightened to a specific torque value (torque is the twisting force applied to a threaded compo-

nent such as a nut or bolt). Overtightening the fastener can weaken it and cause it to break, while undertightening can cause it to eventually come loose. Bolts, screws and studs, depending on the material they are made of and their thread diameters, have specific torque values, many of which are noted in the Specifications at the beginning of each Chapter. Be sure to follow the torque recommendations closely. For fasteners not assigned a specific torque, a general torque value chart is presented here as a guide. These torque values are for dry (unlubricated) fasteners threaded into steel or cast iron (not alumi-

num). As was previously mentioned, the size and grade of a fastener determine the amount of torque that can safely be applied to it. The figures listed here are approximate for Grade 2 and Grade 3 fasteners. Higher grades can tolerate higher torque values.

Fasteners laid out in a pattern, such as cylinder head bolts, oil pan bolts, differential cover bolts, etc., must be loosened or tightened in sequence to avoid warping the component. This sequence will normally be shown in the appropriate Chapter. If a specific pattern is not given, the following procedures can be used to prevent warping.

Metric thread sizes	Ft-lbs	Nm
M-6	6 to 9	9 to 12
M-8	14 to 21	19 to 28
M-10	28 to 40	38 to 54
M-12	50 to 71	68 to 96
M-14	80 to 140	109 to 154

Pipe thread sizes		
1/8	5 to 8	7 to 10
1/4	12 to 18	17 to 24
3/8	22 to 33	30 to 44
1/2	25 to 35	34 to 47

U.S. thread sizes		
1/4 - 20	6 to 9	9 to 12
5/16 - 18	12 to 18	17 to 24
5/16 - 24	14 to 20	19 to 27
3/8 - 16	22 to 32	30 to 43
3/8 - 24	27 to 38	37 to 51
7/16 - 14	40 to 55	55 to 74
7/16 - 20	40 to 60	55 to 81
1/2 - 13	55 to 80	75 to 108

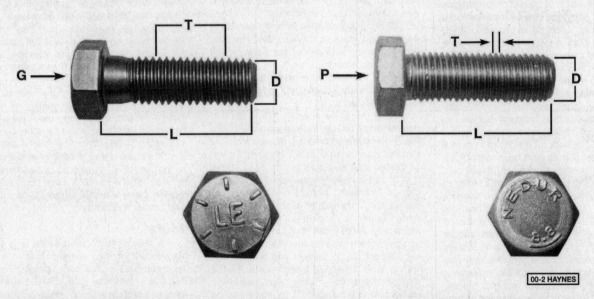

00-2 HAYNES

Standard (SAE and USS) bolt dimensions/grade marks

G   Grade marks (bolt strength)
L   Length (in inches)
T   Thread pitch (number of threads per inch)
D   Nominal diameter (in inches)

Metric bolt dimensions/grade marks

P   Property class (bolt strength)
L   Length (in millimeters)
T   Thread pitch (distance between threads in millimeters)
D   Diameter

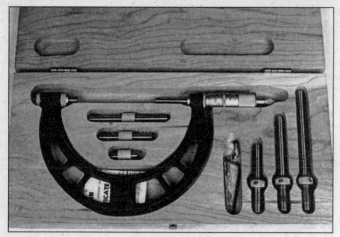

Micrometer set

Dial indicator set

Initially, the bolts or nuts should be assembled finger-tight only. Next, they should be tightened one full turn each, in a criss-cross or diagonal pattern. After each one has been tightened one full turn, return to the first one and tighten them all one-half turn, following the same pattern. Finally, tighten each of them one-quarter turn at a time until each fastener has been tightened to the proper torque. To loosen and remove the fasteners, the procedure would be reversed.

Component disassembly

Component disassembly should be done with care and purpose to help ensure that the parts go back together properly. Always keep track of the sequence in which parts are removed. Make note of special characteristics or marks on parts that can be installed more than one way, such as a grooved thrust washer on a shaft. It is a good idea to lay the disassembled parts out on a clean surface in the order that they were removed. It may also be helpful to make sketches or take instant photos of components before removal.

When removing fasteners from a component, keep track of their locations. Sometimes threading a bolt back in a part, or putting the washers and nut back on a stud, can prevent mix-ups later. If nuts and bolts cannot be returned to their original locations, they should be kept in a compartmented box or a series of small boxes. A cupcake or muffin tin is ideal for this purpose, since each cavity can hold the bolts and nuts from a particular area (i.e. oil pan bolts, valve cover bolts, engine mount bolts, etc.). A pan of this type is especially helpful when working on assemblies with very small parts, such as the carburetor, alternator, valve train or interior dash and trim pieces. The cavities can be marked with paint or tape to identify the contents.

Whenever wiring looms, harnesses or connectors are separated, it is a good idea to identify the two halves with numbered pieces of masking tape so they can be easily reconnected.

Gasket sealing surfaces

Throughout any vehicle, gaskets are used to seal the mating surfaces between two parts and keep lubricants, fluids, vacuum or pressure contained in an assembly.

Many times these gaskets are coated with a liquid or paste-type gasket sealing compound before assembly. Age, heat and pressure can sometimes cause the two parts to stick together so tightly that they are very difficult to separate. Often, the assembly can be loosened by striking it with a soft-face hammer near the mating surfaces. A regular hammer can be used if a block of wood is placed between the hammer and the part. Do not hammer on cast parts or parts that could be easily damaged. With any particularly stubborn part, always recheck to make sure that every fastener has been removed.

Avoid using a screwdriver or bar to pry apart an assembly, as they can easily mar the gasket sealing surfaces of the parts, which must remain smooth. If prying is absolutely necessary, use an old broom handle, but keep in mind that extra clean up will be necessary if the wood splinters.

After the parts are separated, the old gasket must be carefully scraped off and the gasket surfaces cleaned. Stubborn gasket material can be soaked with rust penetrant or treated with a special chemical to soften it so it can be easily scraped off. A scraper can be fashioned from a piece of copper tubing by flattening and sharpening one end. Copper is recommended because it is usually softer than the surfaces to be scraped, which reduces the chance of gouging the part. Some gaskets can be removed with a wire brush, but regardless of the method used, the mating surfaces must be left clean and smooth. If for some reason the gasket surface is gouged, then a gasket sealer thick enough to fill scratches will have to be used during reassembly of the components. For most applications, a non-drying (or semi-drying) gasket sealer should be used.

Hose removal tips

Warning: *If the vehicle is equipped with air conditioning, do not disconnect any of the A/C hoses without first having the system depressurized by a dealer service department or a service station.*

Hose removal precautions closely parallel gasket removal precautions. Avoid scratching or gouging the surface that the hose mates against or the connection may leak. This is especially true for radiator hoses. Because of various chemical reactions, the rubber in hoses can bond itself to the metal spigot that the hose fits over. To remove a hose, first loosen the hose clamps that secure it to the spigot. Then, with slip-joint pliers, grab the hose at the clamp and rotate it around the spigot. Work it back and forth until it is completely free, then pull it off. Silicone or other lubricants will ease removal if they can be applied between the hose and the outside of the spigot. Apply the same lubricant to the inside of the hose and the outside of the spigot to simplify installation.

As a last resort (and if the hose is to be replaced with a new one anyway), the rubber can be slit with a knife and the hose peeled from the spigot. If this must be done, be careful that the metal connection is not damaged.

If a hose clamp is broken or damaged, do not reuse it. Wire-type clamps usually weaken with age, so it is a good idea to replace them with screw-type clamps whenever a hose is removed.

Tools

A selection of good tools is a basic requirement for anyone who plans to maintain and repair his or her own vehicle. For the owner who has few tools, the initial investment might seem high, but when compared to the spiraling costs of professional auto maintenance and repair, it is a wise one.

To help the owner decide which tools are needed to perform the tasks detailed in this manual, the following tool lists are offered: *Maintenance and minor repair, Repair/overhaul* and *Special*.

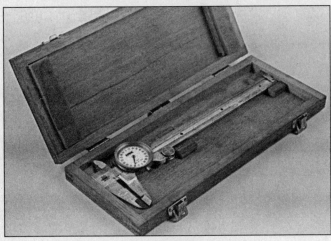

Dial caliper

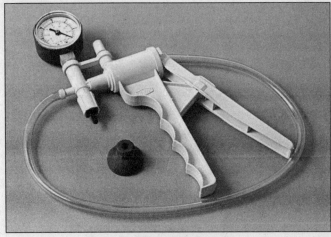

Hand-operated vacuum pump

Timing light

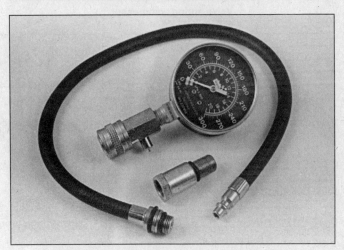

Compression gauge with spark plug hole adapter

Damper/steering wheel puller

General purpose puller

Hydraulic lifter removal tool

The newcomer to practical mechanics should start off with the *maintenance and minor repair* tool kit, which is adequate for the simpler jobs performed on a vehicle. Then, as confidence and experience grow, the owner can tackle more difficult tasks, buying additional tools as they are needed. Eventually the basic kit will be expanded into the *repair and overhaul* tool set. Over a period of time, the experienced do-it-yourselfer will assemble a tool set complete enough for most repair and overhaul procedures and will add tools from the special category when it is felt that the expense is justified by the frequency of use.

Maintenance and minor repair tool kit

The tools in this list should be considered the minimum required for performance of routine maintenance, servicing and minor repair work. We recommend the purchase of combination wrenches (box-end and open-

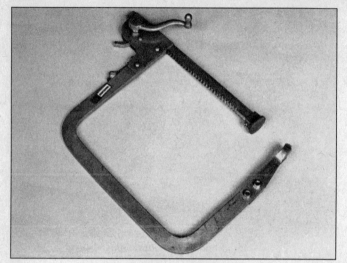

Valve spring compressor

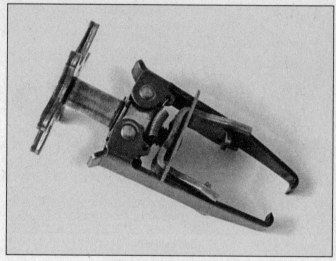

Valve spring compressor

Ridge reamer

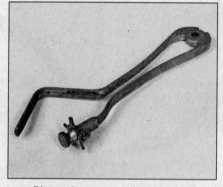

Piston ring groove cleaning tool

Ring removal/installation tool

end combined in one wrench). While more expensive than open end wrenches, they offer the advantages of both types of wrench.

> Combination wrench set (1/4-inch to
>   1 inch or 6 mm to 19 mm)
> Adjustable wrench, 8 inch
> Spark plug wrench with rubber insert
> Spark plug gap adjusting tool
> Feeler gauge set
> Brake bleeder wrench
> Standard screwdriver (5/16-inch x
>   6 inch)
> Phillips screwdriver (No. 2 x 6 inch)
> Combination pliers - 6 inch
> Hacksaw and assortment of blades
> Tire pressure gauge
> Grease gun
> Oil can
> Fine emery cloth
> Wire brush
> Battery post and cable cleaning tool
> Oil filter wrench
> Funnel (medium size)
> Safety goggles
> Jackstands (2)
> Drain pan

Note: *If basic tune-ups are going to be part of routine maintenance, it will be necessary to purchase a good quality stroboscopic timing*

light and combination tachometer/dwell meter. Although they are included in the list of special tools, it is mentioned here because they are absolutely necessary for tuning most vehicles properly.

Repair and overhaul tool set

These tools are essential for anyone who plans to perform major repairs and are in addition to those in the maintenance and minor repair tool kit. Included is a comprehensive set of sockets which, though expensive, are invaluable because of their versatility, especially when various extensions and drives are available. We recommend the 1/2-inch drive over the 3/8-inch drive. Although the larger drive is bulky and more expensive, it has the capacity of accepting a very wide range of large sockets. Ideally, however, the mechanic should have a 3/8-inch drive set and a 1/2-inch drive set.

> Socket set(s)
> Reversible ratchet
> Extension - 10 inch
> Universal joint
> Torque wrench (same size drive as
>   sockets)
> Ball peen hammer - 8 ounce
> Soft-face hammer (plastic/rubber)

Ring compressor

> Standard screwdriver (1/4-inch x 6 inch)
> Standard screwdriver (stubby -
>   5/16-inch)
> Phillips screwdriver (No. 3 x 8 inch)
> Phillips screwdriver (stubby - No. 2)
> Pliers - vise grip
> Pliers - lineman's
> Pliers - needle nose
> Pliers - snap-ring (internal and external)
> Cold chisel - 1/2-inch

Cylinder hone

Brake hold-down spring tool

Scribe
Scraper (made from flattened copper tubing)
Centerpunch
Pin punches (1/16, 1/8, 3/16-inch)
Steel rule/straightedge - 12 inch
Allen wrench set (1/8 to 3/8-inch or 4 mm to 10 mm)
A selection of files

Torque angle gauge

Wire brush (large)
Jackstands (second set)
Jack (scissor or hydraulic type)
Note: *Another tool which is often useful is an electric drill with a chuck capacity of 3/8-inch and a set of good quality drill bits.*

Special tools

The tools in this list include those which are not used regularly, are expensive to buy, or which need to be used in accordance with their manufacturer's instructions. Unless these tools will be used frequently, it is not very economical to purchase many of them. A consideration would be to split the cost and use between yourself and a friend or friends. In addition, most of these tools can be obtained from a tool rental shop on a temporary basis.

This list primarily contains only those tools and instruments widely available to the public, and not those special tools produced by the vehicle manufacturer for distribution to dealer service departments. Occasionally, references to the manufacturer's special tools are included in the text of this manual. Generally, an alternative method of doing the job without the special tool is offered. However,

sometimes there is no alternative to their use. Where this is the case, and the tool cannot be purchased or borrowed, the work should be turned over to the dealer service department or an automotive repair shop.

Valve spring compressor
Piston ring groove cleaning tool
Piston ring compressor
Piston ring installation tool
Cylinder compression gauge
Cylinder ridge reamer
Cylinder surfacing hone
Cylinder bore gauge
Micrometers and/or dial calipers
Hydraulic lifter removal tool
Balljoint separator
Universal-type puller
Impact screwdriver
Dial indicator set
Stroboscopic timing light (inductive pick-up)
Hand operated vacuum/pressure pump
Tachometer/dwell meter
Universal electrical multimeter
Cable hoist
Brake spring removal and installation tools
Floor jack

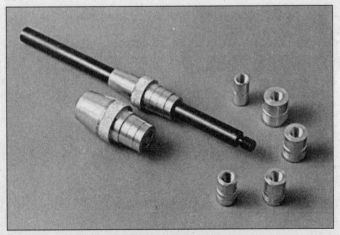

Clutch plate alignment tool

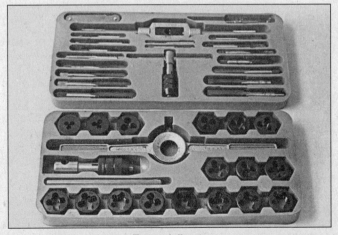

Tap and die set

Buying tools

For the do-it-yourselfer who is just starting to get involved in vehicle maintenance and repair, there are a number of options available when purchasing tools. If maintenance and minor repair is the extent of the work to be done, the purchase of individual tools is satisfactory. If, on the other hand, extensive work is planned, it would be a good idea to purchase a modest tool set from one of the large retail chain stores. A set can usually be bought at a substantial savings over the individual tool prices, and they often come with a tool box. As additional tools are needed, add-on sets, individual tools and a larger tool box can be purchased to expand the tool selection. Building a tool set gradually allows the cost of the tools to be spread over a longer period of time and gives the mechanic the freedom to choose only those tools that will actually be used.

Tool stores will often be the only source of some of the special tools that are needed, but regardless of where tools are bought, try to avoid cheap ones, especially when buying screwdrivers and sockets, because they won't last very long. The expense involved in replacing cheap tools will eventually be greater than the initial cost of quality tools.

Care and maintenance of tools

Good tools are expensive, so it makes sense to treat them with respect. Keep them clean and in usable condition and store them properly when not in use. Always wipe off any dirt, grease or metal chips before putting them away. Never leave tools lying around in the work area. Upon completion of a job, always check closely under the hood for tools that may have been left there so they won't get lost during a test drive.

Some tools, such as screwdrivers, pliers, wrenches and sockets, can be hung on a panel mounted on the garage or workshop wall, while others should be kept in a tool box or tray. Measuring instruments, gauges, meters, etc. must be carefully stored where they cannot be damaged by weather or impact from other tools.

When tools are used with care and stored properly, they will last a very long time. Even with the best of care, though, tools will wear out if used frequently. When a tool is damaged or worn out, replace it. Subsequent jobs will be safer and more enjoyable if you do.

How to repair damaged threads

Sometimes, the internal threads of a nut or bolt hole can become stripped, usually from overtightening. Stripping threads is an all-too-common occurrence, especially when working with aluminum parts, because aluminum is so soft that it easily strips out.

Usually, external or internal threads are only partially stripped. After they've been cleaned up with a tap or die, they'll still work. Sometimes, however, threads are badly damaged. When this happens, you've got three choices:

1) *Drill and tap the hole to the next suitable oversize and install a larger diameter bolt, screw or stud.*

2) *Drill and tap the hole to accept a threaded plug, then drill and tap the plug to the original screw size. You can also buy a plug already threaded to the original size. Then you simply drill a hole to the specified size, then run the threaded plug into the hole with a bolt and jam nut. Once the plug is fully seated, remove the jam nut and bolt.*

3) *The third method uses a patented thread repair kit like Heli-Coil or Slimsert. These easy-to-use kits are designed to repair damaged threads in straight-through holes and blind holes. Both are available as kits which can handle a variety of sizes and thread patterns. Drill the hole, then tap it with the special included tap. Install the Heli-Coil and the hole is back to its original diameter and thread pitch.*

Regardless of which method you use, be sure to proceed calmly and carefully. A little impatience or carelessness during one of these relatively simple procedures can ruin your whole day's work and cost you a bundle if you wreck an expensive part.

Working facilities

Not to be overlooked when discussing tools is the workshop. If anything more than routine maintenance is to be carried out, some sort of suitable work area is essential.

It is understood, and appreciated, that many home mechanics do not have a good workshop or garage available, and end up removing an engine or doing major repairs outside. It is recommended, however, that the overhaul or repair be completed under the cover of a roof.

A clean, flat workbench or table of comfortable working height is an absolute necessity. The workbench should be equipped with a vise that has a jaw opening of at least four inches.

As mentioned previously, some clean, dry storage space is also required for tools, as well as the lubricants, fluids, cleaning solvents, etc. which soon become necessary.

Sometimes waste oil and fluids, drained from the engine or cooling system during normal maintenance or repairs, present a disposal problem. To avoid pouring them on the ground or into a sewage system, pour the used fluids into large containers, seal them with caps and take them to an authorized disposal site or recycling center. Plastic jugs, such as old antifreeze containers, are ideal for this purpose.

Always keep a supply of old newspapers and clean rags available. Old towels are excellent for mopping up spills. Many mechanics use rolls of paper towels for most work because they are readily available and disposable. To help keep the area under the vehicle clean, a large cardboard box can be cut open and flattened to protect the garage or shop floor.

Whenever working over a painted surface, such as when leaning over a fender to service something under the hood, always cover it with an old blanket or bedspread to protect the finish. Vinyl covered pads, made especially for this purpose, are available at auto parts stores.

Booster battery (jump) starting

Observe the following precautions when using a booster battery to start a vehicle:

a) *Before connecting the booster battery, make sure the ignition switch is in the Off position.*

b) *Turn off the lights, heater and other electrical loads.*

c) *Your eyes should be shielded. Safety goggles are a good idea.*

d) *Make sure the booster battery is the same voltage as the dead one in the vehicle.*

e) *The two vehicles MUST NOT TOUCH each other.*

f) *Make sure the transmission is in Neutral (manual transaxle) or Park (automatic transaxle).*

g) *If the booster battery is not a maintenance-free type, remove the vent caps and lay a cloth over the vent holes.*

Connect the red jumper cable to the positive (+) terminals of each battery.

Connect one end of the black cable to the negative (-) terminal of the booster battery. The other end of this cable should be connected to a good ground on the engine block **(see illustration)**. Make sure the cable will not come into contact with the fan, drivebelts or other moving parts of the engine.

Start the engine using the booster battery, then, with the engine running at idle speed, disconnect the jumper cables in the reverse order of connection.

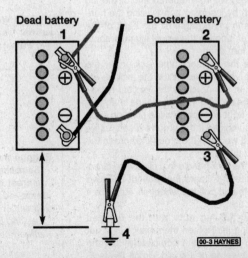

Make the booster battery cable connections in the numerical order shown (note that the negative cable of the booster battery is NOT attached to the negative terminal of the dead battery)

Jacking and towing

Jacking

Warning: *The jack supplied with the vehicle should only be used for changing a tire or placing jackstands under the frame. Never work under the vehicle or start the engine while this jack is being used as the only means of support. Also, do not change a wheel where you risk being hit by another vehicle - try to stop away from traffic and be aware of passing vehicles while changing the wheel. Use hazard warning flashing lights.*

The vehicle should be on firm, level ground. Place the shift lever in Park, if you have an automatic, or Reverse if you have a manual transaxle. Block the wheel diagonally opposite the wheel being changed. Set the parking brake. Chock the wheel diagonally opposite the one being removed - large stones will do if no other objects are available.

Remove the spare tire and jack from stowage. Unscrew the spare wheel retainer and remove it from the storage compartment.

Remove the wheel cover and trim ring (if so equipped) with the tapered end of the lug nut wrench by inserting and twisting the handle and then prying against the back of the wheel cover. Loosen the wheel lug nuts about 1/4-to-1/2 turn each.

Place the scissors-type jack under the side of the vehicle and adjust the jack height until it fits in the notch in the vertical rocker panel flange nearest the wheel to be changed. There is a front and rear jacking point on each side of the vehicle. If the ground is soft, use a flat piece of wood on the ground to spread the load under the jack.

Turn the jack handle in a clockwise direction until the tire clears the ground. Remove the lug nuts and pull the wheel off. Replace it with the spare.

Install the lug nuts with the beveled edges facing in. Tighten them snugly. Do not attempt to tighten them completely until the vehicle is lowered or it could slip off the jack. Turn the jack handle counterclockwise to lower the vehicle. Remove the jack and tighten the lug nuts in a diagonal pattern.

Install the wheel cover (and trim ring, if used), making sure the tire air valve protrudes through the wheel cover properly. Be sure the wheel cover is snapped into place all the way around.

Stow the tire, jack and wrench. Unblock the wheels.

Check the tire pressure - if it is low, drive slowly to the nearest garage to inflate the tire. Have the damaged tire repaired as soon as possible.

Towing

Vehicles with a manual transaxle

As a general rule, the vehicle should be towed with the front (drive) wheels off the ground. Be sure to release the parking brake. If the vehicle is being towed with the front wheels on the ground, place the transmission in Neutral. Also, the ignition key must be in the ACC position, since the steering lock mechanism isn't strong enough to hold the front wheels straight while towing.

Vehicles with an automatic transaxle

Caution: *Never tow a vehicle with an automatic transaxle from the rear with the front wheels on the ground. If the vehicle must be towed from the rear, place the front wheels on a towing dolly.*

Vehicles equipped with an automatic transaxle can be towed from the front only with all four wheels on the ground, provided that speeds don't exceed 30 mph and the distance is not over 50 miles. Before towing, check the transmission fluid level (see Chapter 1). If the level is below the HOT mark on the dipstick, add fluid or use a towing dolly. Release the parking brake, put the transaxle in Neutral and place the ignition key in the ACC position. A driver must be in the towed vehicle to steer and operate the brakes.

All vehicles

Equipment specifically designed for towing should be used. It should be attached to the main structural members of the vehicle, not the bumpers or brackets.

Safety is a major consideration when towing and all applicable state and local laws must be obeyed.

A safety chain must be used at all times. Remember that power steering and brakes won't work with the engine off.

Engage the jack head with the rocker panel flange nearest the wheel to be removed. Note: *On 1989 and earlier models, the front jacking point is located **ahead** of the front wheel*

Automotive chemicals and lubricants

A number of automotive chemicals and lubricants are available for use during vehicle maintenance and repair. They include a wide variety of products ranging from cleaning solvents and degreasers to lubricants and protective sprays for rubber, plastic and vinyl.

Cleaners

Carburetor cleaner and choke cleaner is a strong solvent for gum, varnish and carbon. Most carburetor cleaners leave a dry-type lubricant film which will not harden or gum up. Because of this film it is not recommended for use on electrical components.

Brake system cleaner is used to remove brake dust, grease and brake fluid from the brake system, where clean surfaces are absolutely necessary. It leaves no residue and often eliminates brake squeal caused by contaminants.

Electrical cleaner removes oxidation, corrosion and carbon deposits from electrical contacts, restoring full current flow. It can also be used to clean spark plugs, carburetor jets, voltage regulators and other parts where an oil-free surface is desired.

Demoisturants remove water and moisture from electrical components such as alternators, voltage regulators, electrical connectors and fuse blocks. They are non-conductive and non-corrosive.

Degreasers are heavy-duty solvents used to remove grease from the outside of the engine and from chassis components. They can be sprayed or brushed on and, depending on the type, are rinsed off either with water or solvent.

Lubricants

Motor oil is the lubricant formulated for use in engines. It normally contains a wide variety of additives to prevent corrosion and reduce foaming and wear. Motor oil comes in various weights (viscosity ratings) from 0 to 50. The recommended weight of the oil depends on the season, temperature and the demands on the engine. Light oil is used in cold climates and under light load conditions. Heavy oil is used in hot climates and where high loads are encountered. Multi-viscosity oils are designed to have characteristics of both light and heavy oils and are available in a number of weights from 0W-20 to 20W-50.

Gear oil is designed to be used in differentials, manual transmissions and other areas where high-temperature lubrication is required.

Chassis and wheel bearing grease is a heavy grease used where increased loads and friction are encountered, such as for wheel bearings, balljoints, tie-rod ends and universal joints.

High-temperature wheel bearing grease is designed to withstand the extreme temperatures encountered by wheel bearings in disc brake equipped vehicles. It usually contains molybdenum disulfide (moly), which is a dry-type lubricant.

White grease is a heavy grease for metal-to-metal applications where water is a problem. White grease stays soft under both low and high temperatures (usually from -100 to +190-degrees F), and will not wash off or dilute in the presence of water.

Assembly lube is a special extreme pressure lubricant, usually containing moly, used to lubricate high-load parts (such as main and rod bearings and cam lobes) for initial start-up of a new engine. The assembly lube lubricates the parts without being squeezed out or washed away until the engine oiling system begins to function.

Silicone lubricants are used to protect rubber, plastic, vinyl and nylon parts.

Graphite lubricants are used where oils cannot be used due to contamination problems, such as in locks. The dry graphite will lubricate metal parts while remaining uncontaminated by dirt, water, oil or acids. It is electrically conductive and will not foul electrical contacts in locks such as the ignition switch.

Moly penetrants loosen and lubricate frozen, rusted and corroded fasteners and prevent future rusting or freezing.

Heat-sink grease is a special electrically non-conductive grease that is used for mounting electronic ignition modules where it is essential that heat is transferred away from the module.

Sealants

RTV sealant is one of the most widely used gasket compounds. Made from silicone, RTV is air curing, it seals, bonds, waterproofs, fills surface irregularities, remains flexible, doesn't shrink, is relatively easy to remove, and is used as a supplementary sealer with almost all low and medium temperature gaskets.

Anaerobic sealant is much like RTV in that it can be used either to seal gaskets or to form gaskets by itself. It remains flexible, is solvent resistant and fills surface imperfections. The difference between an anaerobic sealant and an RTV-type sealant is in the curing. RTV cures when exposed to air, while an anaerobic sealant cures only in the absence of air. This means that an anaerobic sealant cures only after the assembly of parts, sealing them together.

Thread and pipe sealant is used for sealing hydraulic and pneumatic fittings and vacuum lines. It is usually made from a Teflon compound, and comes in a spray, a paint-on liquid and as a wrap-around tape.

Chemicals

Anti-seize compound prevents seizing, galling, cold welding, rust and corrosion in fasteners. High-temperature ant-seize, usually made with copper and graphite lubricants, is used for exhaust system and exhaust manifold bolts.

Anaerobic locking compounds are used to keep fasteners from vibrating or working loose and cure only after installation, in the absence of air. Medium strength locking compound is used for small nuts, bolts and screws that may be removed later. High-strength locking compound is for large nuts, bolts and studs which aren't removed on a regular basis.

Oil additives range from viscosity index improvers to chemical treatments that claim to reduce internal engine friction. It should be noted that most oil manufacturers caution against using additives with their oils.

Gas additives perform several functions, depending on their chemical makeup. They usually contain solvents that help dissolve gum and varnish that build up on carburetor, fuel injection and intake parts. They also serve to break down carbon deposits that form on the inside surfaces of the combustion chambers. Some additives contain upper cylinder lubricants for valves and piston rings, and others contain chemicals to remove condensation from the gas tank.

Miscellaneous

Brake fluid is specially formulated hydraulic fluid that can withstand the heat and pressure encountered in brake systems. Care must be taken so this fluid does not come in contact with painted surfaces or plastics. An opened container should always be resealed to prevent contamination by water or dirt.

Weatherstrip adhesive is used to bond weatherstripping around doors, windows and trunk lids. It is sometimes used to attach trim pieces.

Undercoating is a petroleum-based, tar-like substance that is designed to protect metal surfaces on the underside of the vehicle from corrosion. It also acts as a sound-deadening agent by insulating the bottom of the vehicle.

Waxes and polishes are used to help protect painted and plated surfaces from the weather. Different types of paint may require the use of different types of wax and polish. Some polishes utilize a chemical or abrasive cleaner to help remove the top layer of oxidized (dull) paint on older vehicles. In recent years many non-wax polishes that contain a wide variety of chemicals such as polymers and silicones have been introduced. These non-wax polishes are usually easier to apply and last longer than conventional waxes and polishes.

Conversion factors

Length (distance)

Inches (in)	X	25.4	= Millimeters (mm)	X 0.0394	= Inches (in)
Feet (ft)	X	0.305	= Meters (m)	X 3.281	= Feet (ft)
Miles	X	1.609	= Kilometers (km)	X 0.621	= Miles

Volume (capacity)

Cubic inches (cu in; in^3)	X	16.387	= Cubic centimeters (cc; cm^3)	X 0.061	= Cubic inches (cu in; in^3)
Imperial pints (Imp pt)	X	0.568	= Liters (l)	X 1.76	= Imperial pints (Imp pt)
Imperial quarts (Imp qt)	X	1.137	= Liters (l)	X 0.88	= Imperial quarts (Imp qt)
Imperial quarts (Imp qt)	X	1.201	= US quarts (US qt)	X 0.833	= Imperial quarts (Imp qt)
US quarts (US qt)	X	0.946	= Liters (l)	X 1.057	= US quarts (US qt)
Imperial gallons (Imp gal)	X	4.546	= Liters (l)	X 0.22	= Imperial gallons (Imp gal)
Imperial gallons (Imp gal)	X	1.201	= US gallons (US gal)	X 0.833	= Imperial gallons (Imp gal)
US gallons (US gal)	X	3.785	= Liters (l)	X 0.264	= US gallons (US gal)

Mass (weight)

Ounces (oz)	X	28.35	= Grams (g)	X 0.035	= Ounces (oz)
Pounds (lb)	X	0.454	= Kilograms (kg)	X 2.205	= Pounds (lb)

Force

Ounces-force (ozf; oz)	X	0.278	= Newtons (N)	X 3.6	= Ounces-force (ozf; oz)
Pounds-force (lbf; lb)	X	4.448	= Newtons (N)	X 0.225	= Pounds-force (lbf; lb)
Newtons (N)	X	0.1	= Kilograms-force (kgf; kg)	X 9.81	= Newtons (N)

Pressure

Pounds-force per square inch (psi; lbf/in^2; lb/in^2)	X	0.070	= Kilograms-force per square centimeter (kgf/cm^2; kg/cm^2)	X 14.223	= Pounds-force per square inch (psi; lbf/in^2; lb/in^2)
Pounds-force per square inch (psi; lbf/in^2; lb/in^2)	X	0.068	= Atmospheres (atm)	X 14.696	= Pounds-force per square inch (psi; lbf/in^2; lb/in^2)
Pounds-force per square inch (psi; lbf/in^2; lb/in^2)	X	0.069	= Bars	X 14.5	= Pounds-force per square inch (psi; lbf/in^2; lb/in^2)
Pounds-force per square inch (psi; lbf/in^2; lb/in^2)	X	6.895	= Kilopascals (kPa)	X 0.145	= Pounds-force per square inch (psi; lbf/in^2; lb/in^2)
Kilopascals (kPa)	X	0.01	= Kilograms-force per square centimeter (kgf/cm^2; kg/cm^2)	X 98.1	= Kilopascals (kPa)

Torque (moment of force)

Pounds-force inches (lbf in; lb in)	X	1.152	= Kilograms-force centimeter (kgf cm; kg cm)	X 0.868	= Pounds-force inches (lbf in; lb in)
Pounds-force inches (lbf in; lb in)	X	0.113	= Newton meters (Nm)	X 8.85	= Pounds-force inches (lbf in; lb in)
Pounds-force inches (lbf in; lb in)	X	0.083	= Pounds-force feet (lbf ft; lb ft)	X 12	= Pounds-force inches (lbf in; lb in)
Pounds-force feet (lbf ft; lb ft)	X	0.138	= Kilograms-force meters (kgf m; kg m)	X 7.233	= Pounds-force feet (lbf ft; lb ft)
Pounds-force feet (lbf ft; lb ft)	X	1.356	= Newton meters (Nm)	X 0.738	= Pounds-force feet (lbf ft; lb ft)
Newton meters (Nm)	X	0.102	= Kilograms-force meters (kgf m; kg m)	X 9.804	= Newton meters (Nm)

Vacuum

Inches mercury (in. Hg)	X	3.377	= Kilopascals (kPa)	X 0.2961	= Inches mercury
Inches mercury (in. Hg)	X	25.4	= Millimeters mercury (mm Hg)	X 0.0394	= Inches mercury

Power

Horsepower (hp)	X	745.7	= Watts (W)	X 0.0013	= Horsepower (hp)

Velocity (speed)

Miles per hour (miles/hr; mph)	X	1.609	= Kilometers per hour (km/hr; kph)	X 0.621	= Miles per hour (miles/hr; mph)

Fuel consumption*

Miles per gallon, Imperial (mpg)	X	0.354	= Kilometers per liter (km/l)	X 2.825	= Miles per gallon, Imperial (mpg)
Miles per gallon, US (mpg)	X	0.425	= Kilometers per liter (km/l)	X 2.352	= Miles per gallon, US (mpg)

Temperature

Degrees Fahrenheit = (°C x 1.8) + 32   Degrees Celsius (Degrees Centigrade; °C) = (°F - 32) x 0.56

*It is common practice to convert from miles per gallon (mpg) to liters/100 kilometers (l/100km), where mpg (Imperial) x l/100 km = 282 and mpg (US) x l/100 km = 235

DECIMALS to MILLIMETERS

Decimal	mm	Decimal	mm
0.001	0.0254	0.500	12.7000
0.002	0.0508	0.510	12.9540
0.003	0.0762	0.520	13.2080
0.004	0.1016	0.530	13.4620
0.005	0.1270	0.540	13.7160
0.006	0.1524	0.550	13.9700
0.007	0.1778	0.560	14.2240
0.008	0.2032	0.570	14.4780
0.009	0.2286	0.580	14.7320
		0.590	14.9860
0.010	0.2540		
0.020	0.5080		
0.030	0.7620		
0.040	1.0160	0.600	15.2400
0.050	1.2700	0.610	15.4940
0.060	1.5240	0.620	15.7480
0.070	1.7780	0.630	16.0020
0.080	2.0320	0.640	16.2560
0.090	2.2860	0.650	16.5100
		0.660	16.7640
0.100	2.5400	0.670	17.0180
0.110	2.7940	0.680	17.2720
0.120	3.0480	0.690	17.5260
0.130	3.3020		
0.140	3.5560		
0.150	3.8100		
0.160	4.0640	0.700	17.7800
0.170	4.3180	0.710	18.0340
0.180	4.5720	0.720	18.2880
0.190	4.8260	0.730	18.5420
		0.740	18.7960
0.200	5.0800	0.750	19.0500
0.210	5.3340	0.760	19.3040
0.220	5.5880	0.770	19.5580
0.230	5.8420	0.780	19.8120
0.240	6.0960	0.790	20.0660
0.250	6.3500		
0.260	6.6040		
0.270	6.8580	0.800	20.3200
0.280	7.1120	0.810	20.5740
0.290	7.3660	0.820	21.8280
		0.830	21.0820
0.300	7.6200	0.840	21.3360
0.310	7.8740	0.850	21.5900
0.320	8.1280	0.860	21.8440
0.330	8.3820	0.870	22.0980
0.340	8.6360	0.880	22.3520
0.350	8.8900	0.890	22.6060
0.360	9.1440		
0.370	9.3980		
0.380	9.6520		
0.390	9.9060	0.900	22.8600
0.400	10.1600	0.910	23.1140
0.410	10.4140	0.920	23.3680
0.420	10.6680	0.930	23.6220
0.430	10.9220	0.940	23.8760
0.440	11.1760	0.950	24.1300
0.450	11.4300	0.960	24.3840
0.460	11.6840	0.970	24.6380
0.470	11.9380	0.980	24.8920
0.480	12.1920	0.990	25.1460
0.490	12.4460	1.000	25.4000

FRACTIONS to DECIMALS to MILLIMETERS

Fraction	Decimal	mm	Fraction	Decimal	mm
1/64	0.0156	0.3969	33/64	0.5156	13.0969
1/32	0.0312	0.7938	17/32	0.5312	13.4938
3/64	0.0469	1.1906	35/64	0.5469	13.8906
1/16	0.0625	1.5875	9/16	0.5625	14.2875
5/64	0.0781	1.9844	37/64	0.5781	14.6844
3/32	0.0938	2.3812	19/32	0.5938	15.0812
7/64	0.1094	2.7781	39/64	0.6094	15.4781
1/8	0.1250	3.1750	5/8	0.6250	15.8750
9/64	0.1406	3.5719	41/64	0.6406	16.2719
5/32	0.1562	3.9688	21/32	0.6562	16.6688
11/64	0.1719	4.3656	43/64	0.6719	17.0656
3/16	0.1875	4.7625	11/16	0.6875	17.4625
13/64	0.2031	5.1594	45/64	0.7031	17.8594
7/32	0.2188	5.5562	23/32	0.7188	18.2562
15/64	0.2344	5.9531	47/64	0.7344	18.6531
1/4	0.2500	6.3500	3/4	0.7500	19.0500
17/64	0.2656	6.7469	49/64	0.7656	19.4469
9/32	0.2812	7.1438	25/32	0.7812	19.8438
19/64	0.2969	7.5406	51/64	0.7969	20.2406
5/16	0.3125	7.9375	13/16	0.8125	20.6375
21/64	0.3281	8.3344	53/64	0.8281	21.0344
11/32	0.3438	8.7312	27/32	0.8438	21.4312
23/64	0.3594	9.1281	55/64	0.8594	21.8281
3/8	0.3750	9.5250	7/8	0.8750	22.2250
25/64	0.3906	9.9219	57/64	0.8906	22.6219
13/32	0.4062	10.3188	29/32	0.9062	23.0188
27/64	0.4219	10.7156	59/64	0.9219	23.4156
7/16	0.4375	11.1125	15/16	0.9375	23.8125
29/64	0.4531	11.5094	61/64	0.9531	24.2094
15/32	0.4688	11.9062	31/32	0.9688	24.6062
31/64	0.4844	12.3031	63/64	0.9844	25.0031
1/2	0.5000	12.7000	1	1.0000	25.4000

Safety first!

Regardless of how enthusiastic you may be about getting on with the job at hand, take the time to ensure that your safety is not jeopardized. A moment's lack of attention can result in an accident, as can failure to observe certain simple safety precautions. The possibility of an accident will always exist, and the following points should not be considered a comprehensive list of all dangers. Rather, they are intended to make you aware of the risks and to encourage a safety conscious approach to all work you carry out on your vehicle.

Essential DOs and DON'Ts

DON'T rely on a jack when working under the vehicle. Always use approved jackstands to support the weight of the vehicle and place them under the recommended lift or support points.

DON'T attempt to loosen extremely tight fasteners (i.e. wheel lug nuts) while the vehicle is on a jack - it may fall.

DON'T start the engine without first making sure that the transmission is in Neutral (or Park where applicable) and the parking brake is set.

DON'T remove the radiator cap from a hot cooling system - let it cool or cover it with a cloth and release the pressure gradually.

DON'T attempt to drain the engine oil until you are sure it has cooled to the point that it will not burn you.

DON'T touch any part of the engine or exhaust system until it has cooled sufficiently to avoid burns.

DON'T siphon toxic liquids such as gasoline, antifreeze and brake fluid by mouth, or allow them to remain on your skin.

DON'T inhale brake lining dust - it is potentially hazardous (see *Asbestos* below).

DON'T allow spilled oil or grease to remain on the floor - wipe it up before someone slips on it.

DON'T use loose fitting wrenches or other tools which may slip and cause injury.

DON'T push on wrenches when loosening or tightening nuts or bolts. Always try to pull the wrench toward you. If the situation calls for pushing the wrench away, push with an open hand to avoid scraped knuckles if the wrench should slip.

DON'T attempt to lift a heavy component alone - get someone to help you.

DON'T *rush or take unsafe shortcuts to finish a job.*

DON'T allow children or animals in or around the vehicle while you are working on it.

DO wear eye protection when using power tools such as a drill, sander, bench grinder, etc. and when working under a vehicle.

DO keep loose clothing and long hair well out of the way of moving parts.

DO make sure that any hoist used has a safe working load rating adequate for the job.

DO get someone to check on you periodically when working alone on a vehicle.

DO carry out work in a logical sequence and make sure that everything is correctly assembled and tightened.

DO keep chemicals and fluids tightly capped and out of the reach of children and pets.

DO remember that your vehicle's safety affects that of yourself and others. If in doubt on any point, get professional advice.

Steering, suspension and brakes

These systems are essential to driving safety, so make sure you have a qualified shop or individual check your work. Also, compressed suspension springs can cause injury if released suddenly - be sure to use a spring compressor.

Airbags

Airbags are explosive devices that can **CAUSE** injury if they deploy while you're working on the vehicle. Follow the manufacturer's instructions to disable the airbag whenever you're working in the vicinity of airbag components.

Asbestos

Certain friction, insulating, sealing, and other products - such as brake linings, brake bands, clutch linings, torque converters, gaskets, etc. - may contain asbestos or other hazardous friction material. Extreme care must be taken to avoid inhalation of dust from such products, since it is hazardous to health. If in doubt, assume that they do contain asbestos.

Fire

Remember at all times that gasoline is highly flammable. Never smoke or have any kind of open flame around when working on a vehicle. But the risk does not end there. A spark caused by an electrical short circuit, by two metal surfaces contacting each other, or even by static electricity built up in your body under certain conditions, can ignite gasoline vapors, which in a confined space are highly explosive. Do not, under any circumstances, use gasoline for cleaning parts. Use an approved safety solvent.

Always disconnect the battery ground (-) cable at the battery before working on any part of the fuel system or electrical system. Never risk spilling fuel on a hot engine or exhaust component. It is strongly recommended that a fire extinguisher suitable for use on fuel and electrical fires be kept handy in the garage or workshop at all times. Never try to extinguish a fuel or electrical fire with water.

Fumes

Certain fumes are highly toxic and can quickly cause unconsciousness and even death if inhaled to any extent. Gasoline vapor falls into this category, as do the vapors from some cleaning solvents. Any draining or pouring of such volatile fluids should be done in a well ventilated area.

When using cleaning fluids and solvents, read the instructions on the container carefully. Never use materials from unmarked containers.

Never run the engine in an enclosed space, such as a garage. Exhaust fumes contain carbon monoxide, which is extremely poisonous. If you need to run the engine, always do so in the open air, or at least have the rear of the vehicle outside the work area.

The battery

Never create a spark or allow a bare light bulb near a battery. They normally give off a certain amount of hydrogen gas, which is highly explosive.

Always disconnect the battery ground (-) cable at the battery before working on the fuel or electrical systems.

If possible, loosen the filler caps or cover when charging the battery from an external source (this does not apply to sealed or maintenance-free batteries). Do not charge at an excessive rate or the battery may burst.

Take care when adding water to a non maintenance-free battery and when carrying a battery. The electrolyte, even when diluted, is very corrosive and should not be allowed to contact clothing or skin.

Always wear eye protection when cleaning the battery to prevent the caustic deposits from entering your eyes.

Household current

When using an electric power tool, inspection light, etc., which operates on household current, always make sure that the tool is correctly connected to its plug and that, where necessary, it is properly grounded. Do not use such items in damp conditions and, again, do not create a spark or apply excessive heat in the vicinity of fuel or fuel vapor.

Secondary ignition system voltage

A severe electric shock can result from touching certain parts of the ignition system (such as the spark plug wires) when the engine is running or being cranked, particularly if components are damp or the insulation is defective. In the case of an electronic ignition system, the secondary system voltage is much higher and could prove fatal.

Hydrofluoric acid

This extremely corrosive acid is formed when certain types of synthetic rubber, found in some O-rings, oil seals, fuel hoses, etc. are exposed to temperatures above 750-degrees F (400-degrees C). The rubber changes into a charred or sticky substance containing the acid. *Once formed, the acid remains dangerous for years. If it gets onto the skin, it may be necessary to amputate the limb concerned.*

When dealing with a vehicle which has suffered a fire, or with components salvaged from such a vehicle, wear protective gloves and discard them after use.

Troubleshooting

Contents

This section provides an easy reference guide to the more common problems which may occur during the operation of your vehicle. These problems and possible causes are grouped under various components or systems; i.e. Engine, Cooling System, etc., and also refer to the Chapter and/or Section which deals with the problem.

Remember that successful troubleshooting is not a mysterious black art practiced only by professional mechanics. It's simply the result of a bit of knowledge combined with an intelligent, systematic approach to the problem. Always work by a process of elimination, starting with the simplest solution and working through to the most complex - and never overlook the obvious. Anyone can forget to fill the gas tank or leave the lights on overnight, so don't assume that you are above such oversights.

Finally, always get clear in your mind why a problem has occurred and take steps to ensure that it doesn't happen again. If the electrical system fails because of a poor connection, check all other connections in the system to make sure that they don't fail as well. If a particular fuse continues to blow, find out why - don't just go on replacing fuses. Remember, failure of a small component can often be indicative of potential failure or incorrect functioning of a more important component or system.

Engine

1 Engine will not rotate when attempting to start

1 Battery terminal connections loose or corroded. Check the cable terminals at the battery. Tighten the cable or remove corrosion as necessary.
2 Battery discharged or faulty. If the cable connections are clean and tight on the battery posts, turn the key to the On position and switch on the headlights and/or windshield wipers. If they fail to function, the battery is discharged.
3 Automatic transaxle not completely engaged in Park or Neutral or clutch pedal not completely depressed.
4 Broken, loose or disconnected wiring in the starting circuit. Inspect all wiring and connectors at the battery, starter solenoid and ignition switch.
5 Starter motor pinion jammed in flywheel ring gear. If manual transaxle, place transaxle in gear and rock the vehicle to manually turn the engine. Remove starter and inspect pinion and flywheel at earliest convenience (Chapter 5).
6 Starter solenoid faulty (Chapter 5).
7 Starter motor faulty (Chapter 5).
8 Ignition switch faulty (Chapter 12).

2 Engine rotates but will not start

1 Fuel tank empty.
2 Fault in the carburetor (Chapter 4).
3 Battery discharged (engine rotates slowly). Check the operation of electrical components as described in the previous Section.
4 Battery terminal connections loose or corroded (see previous Section).
5 Faulty fuel pump or fuel pump circuit (Chapter 4).
6 Fuel injection system faulty (fuel-injected models) (chapter 4).
7 Excessive moisture on, or damage to, ignition components (Chapter 5).
8 Worn, faulty or incorrectly gapped spark plugs (Chapter 1).
9 Broken, loose or disconnected wiring in the starting circuit (see previous Section).
10 Distributor loose, causing ignition timing to change. Turn the distributor as necessary to start the engine, then set the ignition timing as soon as possible (Chapter 1).
11 Broken, loose or disconnected wires at the ignition coil or faulty coil (Chapter 5).
12 Broken or stripped timing belt (Chapter 2A)

3 Starter motor operates without rotating engine

1 Starter pinion sticking. Remove the starter (Chapter 5) and inspect.
2 Starter pinion or flywheel teeth worn or broken. Remove the flywheel/driveplate access cover and inspect.

4 Engine hard to start when cold

1 Battery discharged or low. Check as described in Section 1.
2 Fault in the fuel or electrical systems (Chapters 4 and 5).
3 Carburetor/fuel injection system in need of repair or overhaul (Chapter 4).
4 Distributor rotor carbon tracked and/or damaged (Chapters 1 and 5).
5 Choke control stuck or inoperative (Chapters 1 and 4).

5 Engine hard to start when hot

1 Air filter clogged (Chapter 1).
2 Fault in the fuel or electrical systems (Chapters 4 and 5).
3 Fuel not reaching the carburetor or fuel injection system (see Section 2).

6 Starter motor noisy or excessively rough in engagement

1 Pinion or flywheel gear teeth worn or broken. Remove the cover at the rear of the engine (if so equipped) and inspect.
2 Starter motor mounting bolts loose or missing.

7 Engine starts but stops immediately

1 Loose or faulty electrical connections at distributor, coil or alternator.
2 Fault in the fuel or electrical systems (Chapters 4 and 5).
3 Insufficient fuel reaching the carburetor/fuel injector(s). Check the fuel pump (Chapter 4).
4 Vacuum leak at the gasket surfaces of the intake manifold, or carburetor. Make sure all mounting bolts/nuts are tightened securely and all vacuum hoses connected to the carburetor and manifold are positioned properly and in good condition.

8 Engine lopes while idling or idles erratically

1 Vacuum leakage. Check the mounting bolts/nuts at the carburetor/throttle body and intake manifold for tightness. Make sure all vacuum hoses are connected and in good condition. Use a stethoscope or a length of fuel hose held against your ear to listen for vacuum leaks while the engine is running. A hissing sound will be heard. A soapy water solution will also detect leaks.
2 Fault in the fuel or electrical systems (Chapters 4 and 5).
3 Leaking EGR valve or plugged PCV valve (see Chapters 1 and 6).
4 Air filter clogged (Chapter 1).
5 Fuel pump not delivering sufficient fuel to the carburetor/fuel injector(s) (see Chapter 4).
6 Carburetor out of adjustment (Chapter 4).
7 Leaking head gasket. Perform a compression check (Chapter 2).
8 Camshaft lobes worn (Chapter 2).

9 Engine misses at idle speed

1 Spark plugs worn or not gapped properly (Chapter 1).
2 Fault in the fuel or electrical systems (Chapters 4 and 5).
3 Faulty spark plug wires (Chapter 1).

10 Engine misses throughout driving speed range

1 Incorrect ignition timing (Chapter 1).
2 Check for cracked distributor cap, disconnected distributor wires and damaged distributor components (Chapter 1).
3 Defective spark plug wires (Chapter 1).
4 Check for defective ignition coil (Chapter 5).

5   Faulty emissions system components (Chapter 6).

6   Low or uneven cylinder compression pressures. Remove the spark plugs and test the compression with a gauge (Chapter 2).

7   Weak or faulty ignition system (Chapter 5).

8   Vacuum leaks at the carburetor/throttle body, intake manifold or vacuum hoses (see Section 8).

9   Faulty fuel injector (fuel injected modes) (Chapter 4).

11 Engine stalls

1   Idle speed incorrect. Refer to the VECI label and Chapter 1.

2   Fuel filter clogged and/or water and impurities in the fuel system (Chapter 1).

3   Distributor or ignition coil components damp or damaged (Chapter 5).

4   Fault in the fuel system or sensors (Chapters 4 and 6).

5   Faulty emissions system components (Chapter 6).

6   Faulty or incorrectly gapped spark plugs (Chapter 1). Also check the spark plug wires (Chapter 1).

7   Vacuum leak at the carburetor/fuel injection unit(s), intake manifold or vacuum hoses. Check as described in Section 8.

12 Engine lacks power

1   Incorrect ignition timing (Chapter 1).

2   Fault in the fuel or electrical systems (Chapters 4 and 5).

3   Excessive play in the distributor shaft. At the same time, check for a damaged rotor, faulty distributor cap, wires, etc. (Chapters 1 and 5).

4   Faulty or incorrectly gapped spark plugs (Chapter 1).

5   Carburetor not adjusted properly or excessively worn (Chapter 4).

6   Faulty coil (Chapter 5).

7   Brakes binding (Chapter 1).

8   Automatic transaxle fluid level incorrect (Chapter 1).

9   Clutch slipping (Chapter 8).

10   Fuel filter clogged and/or impurities in the fuel system (Chapter 1).

11   Emissions control system not functioning properly (Chapter 6).

12   Use of substandard fuel. Fill the tank with the proper octane fuel.

13   Low or uneven cylinder compression pressures. Test with a compression tester, which will detect leaking valves and/or a blown head gasket (Chapter 2).

13 Engine backfires

1   Emissions system not functioning properly (Chapter 6).

2   Fault in the fuel or electrical systems (Chapters 4 and 5).

3   Ignition timing incorrect (Chapter 1).

4   Faulty secondary ignition system (cracked spark plug insulator, faulty plug wires, distributor cap and/or rotor) (Chapters 1 and 5).

5   Carburetor in need of adjustment or worn excessively (Chapter 4).

6   Vacuum leak at the carburetor/throttle body, intake manifold or vacuum hoses. Check as described in Section 8.

7   Valves sticking (Chapter 2).

14 Pinging or knocking engine sounds during acceleration or uphill

1   Incorrect grade of fuel. Fill the tank with fuel of the proper octane rating.

2   Fault in the fuel or electrical systems (Chapters 4 and 5).

3   Ignition timing incorrect (Chapter 1).

4   Carburetor in need of adjustment (Chapter 4).

5   Improper spark plugs. Check the plug type against the VECI label located in the engine compartment. Also check the plugs and wires for damage (Chapter 1).

6   Worn or damaged distributor components (Chapter 5).

7   Faulty emissions system (Chapter 6).

8   Vacuum leak. Check as described in Section 9.

9   Knock sensor not functioning (Chapter 4).

15 Engine diesels (continues to run) after switching off

1   Idle speed too high. Refer to Chapter 1.

2   Fault in the fuel or electrical systems (Chapters 4 and 5).

3   Ignition timing incorrectly adjusted (Chapter 1).

4   Thermo-controlled air cleaner heat valve not operating properly (Chapters 1 and 6).

5   Excessive engine operating temperature. Probable causes of this are a malfunctioning thermostat, clogged radiator, faulty water pump (Chapter 3).

Engine electrical system

16 Battery will not hold a charge

1   Alternator drivebelt defective or not adjusted properly (Chapter 1).

2   Electrolyte level low or battery discharged (Chapter 1).

3   Battery terminals loose or corroded (Chapter 1).

4   Alternator not charging properly (Chapter 5).

5   Loose, broken or faulty wiring in the charging circuit (Chapter 5).

6   Short in the vehicle wiring causing a continual drain on battery (refer to Chapter 12 and the Wiring Diagrams).

7   Battery defective internally.

17 Ignition light fails to go out

1   Fault in the alternator or charging circuit (Chapter 5).

2   Alternator drivebelt defective or not properly adjusted (Chapter 1).

18 Ignition light fails to come on when key is turned on

1   Instrument cluster warning light bulb defective (Chapter 12).

2   Alternator faulty (Chapter 5).

3   Fault in the instrument cluster printed circuit, dashboard wiring or bulb holder (Chapter 12).

Fuel system

19 Excessive fuel consumption

1   Dirty or clogged air filter element (Chapter 1).

2   Incorrectly set ignition timing (Chapter 1).

3   Choke sticking or improperly adjusted (Chapter 1).

4   Emissions system not functioning properly (Chapter 6).

5   Fault in the fuel or electrical systems (Chapters 4 and 5).

6   Carburetor internal parts excessively worn or damaged (Chapter 4).

7   Low tire pressure or incorrect tire size (Chapter 1).

20 Fuel leakage and/or fuel odor

1   Leak in a fuel feed or vent line (Chapter 4).

2   Tank overfilled. Fill only to automatic shut-off.

3   Evaporative emissions system canister clogged (Chapter 6).

4   Vapor leaks from system lines (Chapter 4).

5   Carburetor internal parts excessively worn or out of adjustment (Chapter 4).

Cooling system

21 Overheating

1   Insufficient coolant in the system (Chapter 1).

2   Water pump drivebelt defective or not adjusted properly (Chapter 1).
3   Radiator core blocked or radiator grille dirty and restricted (Chapter 3).
4   Thermostat faulty (Chapter 3).
5   Fan blades broken or cracked (Chapter 3).
6   Radiator cap not maintaining proper pressure. Have the cap pressure tested by gas station or repair shop.
7   Ignition timing incorrect (Chapter 1).

22   Overcooling

Thermostat faulty (Chapter 3).

23   External coolant leakage

1   Deteriorated or damaged hoses or loose clamps. Replace hoses and/or tighten the clamps at the hose connections (Chapter 1).
2   Water pump seals defective. If this is the case, water will drip from the weep hole in the water pump body (Chapter 3).
3   Leakage from radiator core or header tank. This will require the radiator to be professionally repaired (see Chapter 3 for removal procedures).
4   Engine drain plug leaking (Chapter 1) or water jacket core plugs leaking (see Chapter 2).

24   Internal coolant leakage

Note: *Internal coolant leaks can usually be detected by examining the oil. Check the dipstick and inside of the cylinder head cover for water deposits and an oil consistency like that of a milkshake.*
1   Leaking cylinder head gasket. Have the cooling system pressure tested.
2   Cracked cylinder bore or cylinder head. Dismantle the engine and inspect (Chapter 2).

25   Coolant loss

1   Too much coolant in the system (Chapter 1).
2   Coolant boiling away due to overheating (see Section 15).
3   External or internal leakage (see Sections 23 and 24).
4   Faulty radiator cap. Have the cap pressure tested.

26   Poor coolant circulation

1   Inoperative water pump. A quick test is to pinch the top radiator hose closed with your hand while the engine is idling, then let it loose. You should feel the surge of coolant if the pump is working properly (Chapter 1).
2   Restriction in the cooling system. Drain, flush and refill the system (Chapter 1). If necessary, remove the radiator (Chapter 3) and have it reverse flushed.
3   Water pump drivebelt defective or not adjusted properly (Chapter 1).
4   Thermostat sticking (Chapter 3).

Clutch

27   Fails to release (pedal pressed to the floor shift lever does not move freely in and out of Reverse)

1   On cable-operated models, worn or stretched cable. On hydraulically operated models, low hydraulic fluid level (Chapter 1) or leaking seal in the master cylinder (Chapter 8).
2   Clutch plate warped or damaged (Chapter 8).
3   Worn or dry clutch release shaft bushing (Chapter 8).

28   Clutch slips (engine speed increases with no increase in vehicle speed)

1   Linkage out of adjustment (Chapter 8).
2   Clutch plate oil soaked or lining worn. Remove clutch (Chapter 8) and inspect.
3   Clutch plate not seated. It may take 30 or 40 normal starts for a new one to seat.

29   Grabbing (chattering) as clutch is engaged

1   Oil on clutch plate lining. Remove (Chapter 8) and inspect. Correct any leakage source.
2   Worn or loose engine or transaxle mounts. These units move slightly when the clutch is released. Inspect the mounts and bolts (Chapter 2).
3   Worn splines on clutch plate hub. Remove the clutch components (Chapter 8) and inspect.
4   Warped pressure plate or flywheel. Remove the clutch components and inspect.

30   Squeal or rumble with clutch fully disengaged (pedal depressed)

1   Worn, defective or broken release bearing (Chapter 8).
2   Worn or broken pressure plate springs (or diaphragm fingers) (Chapter 8).

31   Clutch pedal stays on floor when disengaged

Linkage or release bearing binding. Inspect the linkage or remove the clutch components as necessary.

Manual transaxle

32   Noisy in Neutral with engine running

1   Input shaft bearing worn.
2   Damaged main drive gear bearing.
3   Worn countershaft bearings.
4   Worn or damaged countershaft end play shims.

33   Noisy in all gears

1   Any of the above causes, and/or:
2   Insufficient lubricant (see the checking procedures in Chapter 1).

34   Noisy in one particular gear

1   Worn, damaged or chipped gear teeth for that particular gear.
2   Worn or damaged synchronizer for that particular gear.

35   Slips out of high gear

1   Transaxle loose on clutch housing (Chapter 7).
2   Shift rods (1986 through 1989 models) or shift cables (1990 and later models) interfering with the engine mounts or clutch lever (Chapter 7).
3   Shift rods or cables not working freely (Chapter 7).
4   Dirt between the transaxle case and engine or misalignment of the transaxle (Chapter 7).
5   Worn or improperly adjusted linkage (Chapter 7).

36   Difficulty in engaging gears

1   Clutch not releasing completely (see clutch adjustment in Chapter 1).
2   Loose, damaged or out-of-adjustment shift linkage. Make a thorough inspection, replacing parts as necessary (Chapter 7).

37   Oil leakage

1   Excessive amount of lubricant in the transaxle (see Chapter 1 for correct checking

procedures). Drain lubricant as required.
2   Driveaxle oil seal or speedometer oil seal in need of replacement (Chapter 7).

Automatic transaxle

Note: *Due to the complexity of the automatic transaxle, it's difficult for the home mechanic to properly diagnose and service this component. For problems other than the following, the vehicle should be taken to a dealer service department or a transmission shop.*

38 General shift mechanism problems

1   Chapter 7 deals with checking and adjusting the shift linkage on automatic transaxles. Common problems which may be attributed to poorly adjusted linkage are:
  Engine starting in gears other than Park or Neutral.
  Indicator on shifter pointing to a gear other than the one actually being selected.
  Vehicle moves when in Park.
2   Refer to Chapter 7 to adjust the linkage.

39 Transaxle will not downshift with accelerator pedal pressed to the floor

Chapter 7 deals with adjusting the throttle cable to enable the transaxle to downshift properly.

40 Transaxle slips, shifts rough, is noisy or has no drive in forward or reverse gears

1   There are many probable causes for the above problems, but the home mechanic should be concerned with only one possibility fluid level.
2   Before taking the vehicle to a repair shop, check the level and condition of the fluid as described in Chapter 1. Correct fluid level as necessary or change the fluid and filter if needed. If the problem persists, have a professional diagnose the probable cause.

41 Fluid leakage

1   Automatic transaxle fluid is a deep red color. Fluid leaks should not be confused with engine oil, which can easily be blown by air flow to the transaxle.
2   To pinpoint a leak, first remove all built-up dirt and grime from around the transaxle. Degreasing agents and/or steam cleaning will achieve this. With the underside clean, drive the vehicle at low speeds so air flow will not blow the leak far from its source. Raise the

vehicle and determine where the leak is coming from. Common areas of leakage are:
  a) *Pan: Tighten the mounting bolts and/or replace the pan gasket as necessary (see Chapter 7).*
  b) *Filler pipe: Replace the rubber seal where the pipe enters the transaxle case.*
  c) *Transaxle oil lines: Tighten the connectors where the lines enter the transaxle case and/or replace the lines.*
  d) *Vent pipe: Transaxle overfilled and/or water in fluid (see checking procedures, Chapter 1).*
  e) *Speedometer connector: Replace the O-ring where the speedometer cable enters the transaxle case (Chapter 7).*

Driveaxles

42 Clicking noise in turns

Worn or damaged outer joint. Check for cut or damaged seals. Repair as necessary (Chapter 8).

43 Knock or clunk when accelerating after coasting

Worn or damaged inner joint. Check for cut or damaged seals. Repair as necessary (Chapter 8)

44 Shudder or vibration during acceleration

1   Excessive joint angle. Have checked and correct as necessary (Chapter 8).
2   Worn or damaged CV joints. Repair or replace as necessary (Chapter 8).
3   Sticking CV joint assembly. Correct or replace as necessary (Chapter 8).

Rear axle

45 Noise

1   Road noise. No corrective procedures available.
2   Tire noise. Inspect tires and check tire pressures (Chapter 1).
3   Rear wheel bearings loose, worn or damaged (Chapter 1).

Brakes

Note: *Before assuming that a brake problem exists, make sure that the tires are in good condition and inflated properly (see Chapter 1), that the front end alignment is correct and that the vehicle is not loaded with weight in an unequal manner.*

46 Vehicle pulls to one side during braking

1   Defective, damaged or oil contaminated disc brake pads on one side. Inspect as described in Chapter 9.
2   Excessive wear of brake pad material or disc on one side. Inspect and correct as necessary.
3   Loose or disconnected front suspension components. Inspect and tighten all bolts to the specified torque (Chapter 10).
4   Defective caliper assembly. Remove the caliper and inspect for a stuck piston or other damage (Chapter 9).

47 Noise (high-pitched squeal with the brakes applied)

Disc brake pads worn out. The noise comes from the wear sensor rubbing against the disc (does not apply to all vehicles) or the actual pad backing plate itself if the material is completely worn away. Replace the pads with new ones immediately (Chapter 9). If the pad material has worn completely away, the brake discs should be inspected for damage as described in Chapter 9.

48 Excessive brake pedal travel

1   Partial brake system failure. Inspect the entire system (Chapter 9) and correct as required.
2   Insufficient fluid in the master cylinder. Check (Chapter 1), add fluid and bleed the system if necessary (Chapter 9).
3   Rear brakes not adjusting properly. Make a series of starts and stops while the vehicle is in Reverse. If this does not correct the situation, remove the drums and inspect the self-adjusters (Chapter 9).

49 Brake pedal feels spongy when depressed

1   Air in the hydraulic lines. Bleed the brake system (Chapter 9).
2   Faulty flexible hoses. Inspect all system hoses and lines. Replace parts as necessary.
3   Master cylinder mounting bolts/nuts loose.
4   Master cylinder defective (Chapter 9).

50 Excessive effort required to stop vehicle

1   Power brake booster not operating properly (Chapter 9).
2   Excessively worn linings or pads. Inspect and replace if necessary (Chapter 9).
3   One or more caliper pistons or wheel cyl-

inders seized or sticking. Inspect and rebuild as required (Chapter 9).

4   Brake linings or pads contaminated with oil or grease. Inspect and replace as required (Chapter 9).

5   New pads or shoes installed and not yet seated. It will take a while for the new material to seat against the drum (or rotor).

51 Pedal travels to the floor with little resistance

Little or no fluid in the master cylinder reservoir caused by leaking wheel cylinder(s), leaking caliper piston(s), loose, damaged or disconnected brake lines. Inspect the entire system and correct as necessary.

52 Brake pedal pulsates during brake application

1   Caliper improperly installed. Remove and inspect (Chapter 9).

2   Disc or drum defective. Remove (Chapter 9) and check for excessive lateral runout and parallelism. Have the disc or drum resurfaced or replace it with a new one.

3   Anti-lock brakes (ABS) engaged during hard braking (Chapter 9).

Suspension and steering systems

53 Vehicle pulls to one side

1   Tire pressures uneven (Chapter 1).

2   Defective tire (Chapter 1).

3   Excessive wear in suspension or steering components (Chapter 10).

4   Front end in need of alignment.

5   Front brakes dragging. Inspect the brakes as described in Chapter 9.

54 Shimmy, shake or vibration

1   Tire or wheel out-of-balance or out-of-round. Have professionally balanced.

2   Loose, worn or out-of-adjustment rear wheel bearings (Chapter 1).

3   Shock absorbers and/or suspension components worn or damaged (Chapter 10).

55 Excessive pitching and/or rolling around corners or during braking

1   Defective shock absorbers. Replace as a set (Chapter 10).

2   Broken or weak springs and/or suspension components. Inspect as described in Chapter 10.

56 Excessively stiff steering

1   Lack of fluid in power steering fluid reservoir (Chapter 1).

2   Incorrect tire pressures (Chapter 1).

3   Front end out of alignment.

57 Excessive play in steering

1   Excessive wear in suspension or steering components (Chapter 10).

2   Steering gearbox damaged (Chapter 10).

58 Lack of power assistance

1   Steering pump drivebelt faulty or not adjusted properly (Chapter 1).

2   Fluid level low (Chapter 1).

3   Hoses or lines restricted. Inspect and replace parts as necessary.

4   Air in power steering system. Bleed the system (Chapter 10).

59 Excessive tire wear (not specific to one area)

1   Incorrect tire pressures (Chapter 1).

2   Tires out of balance. Have professionally balanced.

3   Wheels damaged. Inspect and replace as necessary.

4   Suspension or steering components excessively worn (Chapter 10).

60 Excessive tire wear on outside edge

1   Inflation pressures incorrect (Chapter 1).

2   Excessive speed in turns.

3   Front end alignment incorrect (excessive toe in). Have professionally aligned.

4   Suspension arm bent or twisted (Chapter 10).

61 Excessive tire wear on inside edge

1   Inflation pressures incorrect (Chapter 1).

2   Front end alignment incorrect. Have professionally aligned.

3   Loose or damaged steering components (Chapter 10).

62 Tire tread worn in one place

1   Tires out of balance.

2   Damaged or buckled wheel. Inspect and replace if necessary.

3   Defective tire (Chapter 1). Make the booster battery cable connections in the numerical order shown (note that the negative cable of the booster battery is NOT attached to the negative terminal of the dead battery).

Notes

Notes

Chapter 1
Tune-up and routine maintenance

Contents

Specifications

Recommended lubricants and fluids

Note: *The fluids and lubricants listed here are those recommended by the manufacturer at the time this manual was printed. Vehicle manufacturers occasionally upgrade their fluid and lubricant specifications. Check with your local parts store for the most current fluid and lubricant recommendations for your vehicle.*

Engine oil
- Type .... API "certified for gasoline engines"
- Viscosity .... See accompanying chart
- Capacity * .... 3.3 to 3.6 quarts (including oil filter)

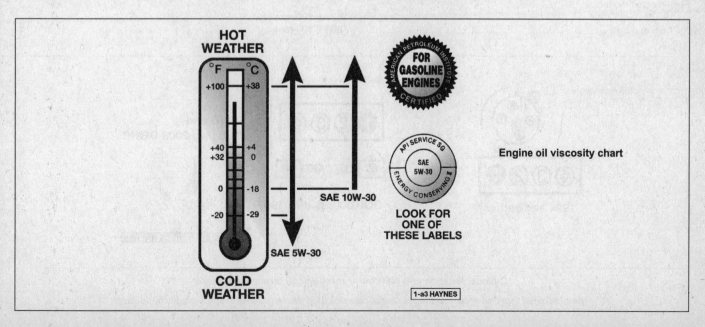

HOT WEATHER

°F   °C
+100 +38

+40   +4
+32   0

0   -18   SAE 10W-30

-20   -29

                SAE 5W-30

COLD WEATHER

FOR GASOLINE ENGINES — AMERICAN PETROLEUM INSTITUTE — CERTIFIED

API SERVICE SG
SAE 5W-30
ENERGY CONSERVING II

LOOK FOR ONE OF THESE LABELS

Engine oil viscosity chart

1-a3 HAYNES

Recommended lubricants and fluids (continued)

Engine coolant
    Type .... 50/50 mixture of ethylene glycol based antifreeze and water
    Capacity* .... 7 quarts
Automatic transmission fluid
    Type
        1985 through 1989 models .... DEXRON II or equivalent
        1990 through 1996 models .... Mopar ATF Plus Type 7176 or equivalent
        1997 through 1999 models .... Hyundai SP-II or equivalent
        2000 and later models .... Hyundai SP-III or equivalent
    Capacity (dry fill)*
        1986 to 1989 models .... 6.0 quarts
        1990 to 1994 models .... 6.4 quarts
        1995 and later models .... 6.8 quarts
Manual transmission lubricant
    Type
        1994 and earlier models .... API-GL-5 or SAE 75W/85W gear oil
        1995 and later models .... API-GL-4S or SAE 75W/85W gear oil
    Capacity*
        1986 to 1989 models .... 2.2 quarts
        1990 to 1994 models .... 1.9 quarts
        1995 and later models .... 2.3 quarts
Brake and clutch fluid .... DOT 3 brake fluid
Power steering system fluid
    Type
        1999 and earlier models .... DEXRON II automatic transmission fluid or equivalent
        2000 and later models .... Hyundai PSF-III or equivalent
    Capacity* .... 1.0 quart
Rear wheel bearing grease .... NLGI No. 2 EP wheel bearing grease

All capacities approximate. Add as necessary to bring up to the appropriate level.

Ignition system

Spark plug type and gap
    1994 and earlier .... Champion RN9YC @ 0.044 inch
    1995 and later .... Champion RC10YC4 @ 0.044 inch
Ignition timing .... See Chapter 5
Firing order 1-3-4-2

Idle speed

Carbureted models
    1988 and earlier
        Manual transaxle .... 700 ± 100 rpm
        Automatic transaxle .... 750 ± 100 rpm
    1989 .... 800 ± 100 rpm
    1990 through 1994 .... 700 ± 50 rpm
Fuel-injected models
    1990 through 1994 .... 825 ± 100 rpm
    1995 and later .... 800 ± 100 rpm

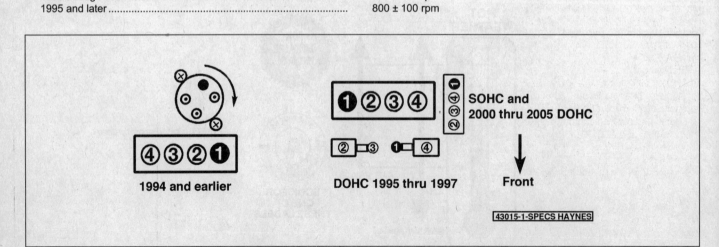

Cylinder location and distributor rotation/coil terminal position

The blackened terminal shown on the distributor cap indicated the Number One spark plug wire position

Valve clearance (engine hot)

1994 and earlier models
    Intake .... 0.006 inch
    Exhaust .... 0.010 inch
    Jet valve .... 0.010 inch
1995 and later models .... No adjustment required
    (hydraulic lifters)

Drivebelt deflection

Alternator and engine water pump
    1994 and earlier models .... 9/32 to 5/16 inch
    1995 and later models .... 11/32 to 13/32 inch
Power steering pump .... 9/32 to 13/32 inch
Air conditioning compressor .... 5/16 to 13/32 inch

Cooling system

Thermostat rating
    Starts to open .... 190-degrees F
    Fully open .... 212-degrees F

Clutch pedal

Cable-operated models
    Clutch pedal freeplay .... 1 inch
    Adjusting nut-to-insulator clearance .... 1/4 inch
Hydraulically operated models
    Clutch pedal clevis pin freeplay .... 0.04 to 0.10 inch
    Clutch pedal freeplay .... 1/4 to 1/2 inch

Brakes

Disc brake pad lining thickness (minimum) .... 1/8 inch
Drum brake shoe lining thickness (minimum) .... 3/32 inch

Steering and suspension

Steering wheel freeplay limit .... 1.0 inch
Balljoint allowable movement .... 0 inch

Torque specifications

Ft-lbs (unless otherwise indicated)

Note: *One foot-pound (ft-lb) of torque is equivalent to 12 inch-pounds (in-lbs) of torque. Torque values below approximately 15 ft-lbs are expressed in inch-pounds, since most foot-pound torque wrenches are not accurate at these smaller values.*

Automatic transaxle
    Pan bolts .... 96 in-lbs
    Filter bolts .... 60 in-lbs
    Drain plug 25
Alternator mounting bolts
    Lower bolt 18
    Upper (adjustment) bolt .... 120 in-lbs
Power steering pump mounting bolts 20
Manual transaxle drain and filler plugs 25
Engine oil pan drain plug 32
Fuel filter banjo bolts (fuel-injected models) 22
Spark plugs 18
Wheel lug nuts
    Steel wheel 54
    1987 to 1990 aluminum wheel 68
    1991 and later aluminum wheel 74
Rear wheel spindle nut (1994 and earlier models)
    Castellated nut (1986 through 1989)
        Step 1 15
        Step 2 .... loosen to 0
        Step 3 .... 48 in-lbs
    Self-locking nut (1990 through 1994) 130

Engine compartment maintenance items (1986 through 1989 models)

1	Secondary air control valve	6	Clutch cable	11	Power steering fluid reservoir
2	Battery	7	Air cleaner wingnut	12	Oxygen sensor
3	Coolant reservoir	8	Distributor	13	Air cleaner housing
4	Windshield washer reservoir	9	Engine oil dipstick	14	Radiator cap
5	Brake fluid reservoir	10	Engine drivebelt		

Front underside maintenance items (1986 through 1989 models)

1	Front suspension radius arm	6	Brake caliper
2	Front suspension stabilizer bar	7	Driveshaft rubber boot
3	Engine oil pan	8	Driveshaft
4	Exhaust front downpipe	9	Steering tie rod end
5	Engine oil drain plug	10	Steering gear rubber boot

11	Exhaust intermediate pipe
12	Steering gear
13	Automatic transaxle drain plug
14	Automatic transaxle fluid pan

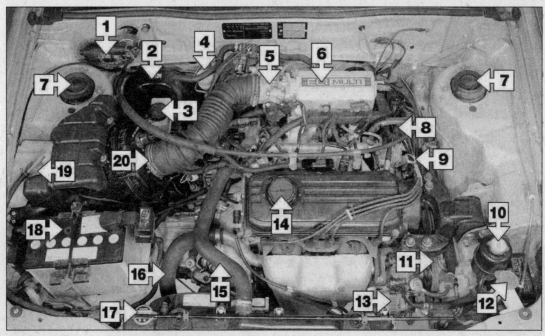

Engine compartment maintenance items (1990 through 1994 models)

1	Windshield wiper motor	8	Distributor	15	Upper radiator hose
2	Power brake booster	9	Engine oil dipstick	16	Lower radiator hose
3	Brake fluid reservoir	10	Power steering fluid reservoir	17	Radiator filler cap
4	Clutch fluid reservoir	11	Power steering pump and drivebelt	18	Battery
5	Throttle housing	12	Windshield washer fluid reservoir	19	Coolant reservoir
6	Intake manifold/plenum	13	Alternator	20	Airflow meter/air cleaner cover
7	Suspension strut upper mounting	14	Engine oil filler cap		

Front underside maintenance items (1990 through 1994 models)

1	Radiator	5	Drivebelt	9	Front suspension lower arm
2	Longitudinal crossmember	6	Engine oil drain plug	10	Engine torque rod
3	Exhaust front downpipe	7	Brake caliper	11	Transaxle drain plug
4	Oil filter	8	Driveaxle		

Engine compartment maintenance items (typical 1995 through 2005 models - SOHC engine shown)

1	Windshield wiper motor	8	Ignition coils/spark plug wires	15	Upper radiator hose
2	Power brake booster	9	Engine oil level dipstick	16	Lower radiator hose
3	Brake fluid reservoir	10	Power steering fluid reservoir	17	Radiator filler cap
4	Clutch fluid reservoir	11	Power steering pump and drivebelt	18	Battery
5	Throttle body	12	Windshield washer fluid reservoir	19	Coolant reservoir
6	Upper intake manifold/plenum	13	Alternator (not visible in photo)	20	Air cleaner cover
7	Suspension strut upper mounting	14	Engine oil filler cap	21	Underhood fuse box

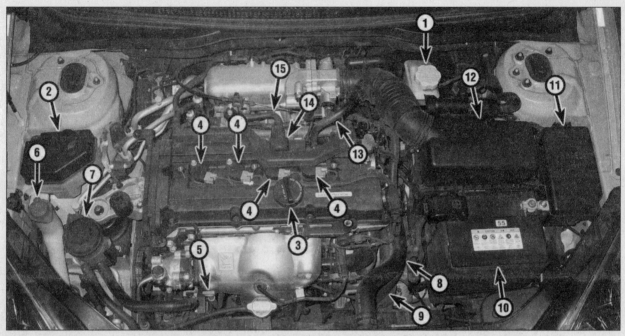

Engine compartment maintenance items (2006 and later models)

1	Brake fluid reservoir	7	Power steering fluid reservoir	12	Air filter housing
2	Coolant reservoir	8	Upper radiator hose	13	PCV fresh air inlet hose
3	Oil filler cap	9	Lower radiator hose	14	PCV valve
4	Ignition coils	10	Battery	15	PCV crankcase ventilation hose
5	Engine oil level dipstick	11	Engine compartment fuse and		(PCV hose)
6	Windshield washer fluid reservoir		relay box		

Front underside maintenance items (typical 1995 through 2005 models)

1	Radiator	5	Drivebelt	8	Driveaxle
2	Longitudinal crossmember	6	Engine oil drain plug	9	Front suspension lower arm
3	Exhaust front downpipe	7	Brake caliper	10	Transaxle drain plug
4	Oil filter				

Front underside maintenance items (2006 and later models)

1	Radiator drain plug	4	Transaxle lubricant drain plug	7	Front brake calipers
2	Oil filter	5	Inner CV joint boots	8	Automatic transaxle fluid pan
3	Engine oil drain plug	6	Outer CV joint boots		drain plug

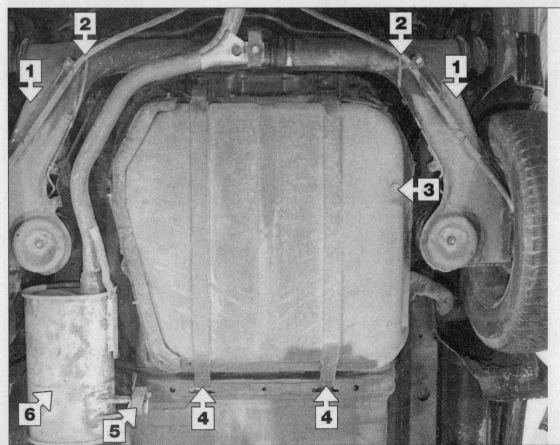

Rear underside maintenance items - 1994 and earlier models (typical)

1 Suspension trailing arms
2 Parking brake cable
3 Fuel tank
4 Fuel tank retaining straps
5 Exhaust system hanger
6 Muffler

Rear underside maintenance items - 1995 through 2005 models

1	Rear suspension lateral link (4 links)	3	Parking brake cable	5	Exhaust tail pipe and muffler
2	Rear suspension trailing arm	4	Fuel tank		

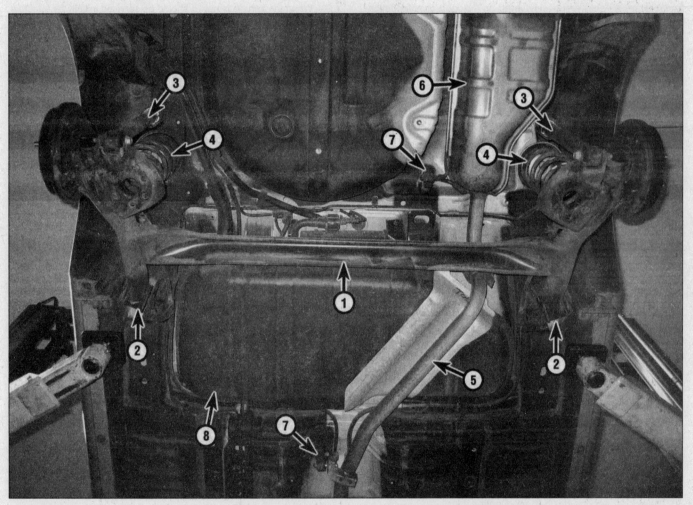

Rear underside maintenance items (2006 and later models)

1 Rear axle beam
2 Rear axle trailing arm bushings
3 Rear shock absorbers
4 Rear coil springs
5 Exhaust pipe
6 Muffler
7 Exhaust pipe hangers
8 Fuel tank

1 Maintenance schedule

The following maintenance intervals are based on the assumption that the vehicle owner will be doing the maintenance or service work, as opposed to having a dealer service department do the work. Although the time/mileage intervals are loosely based on factory recommendations, most have been shortened to ensure, for example, that such items as filters, lubricants and fluids are checked/changed at intervals that promote maximum engine/driveline service life. Also, subject to the preference of the individual owner interested in keeping his or her vehicle in peak condition at all times, and with the vehicle's ultimate resale in mind, many of the maintenance procedures may be performed more often than recommended in the following schedule. We encourage such owner initiative.

When the vehicle is new it should be serviced initially by a factory authorized dealer service department to protect the factory warranty. In many cases the initial maintenance check is done at no cost to the owner (check with your dealer service department for more information).

Every 250 miles or weekly, whichever comes first

Check the engine oil level (Section 4)
Check the engine coolant level (Section 4)
Check the windshield washer fluid level (Section 4)
Check the water (electrolyte) in the battery (Section 4)
Check the brake fluid level (Section 4)
Check the tires and tire pressures (Section 5)

Every 3500 miles or 3 months, whichever comes first

All items listed above plus . . .
Check the power steering fluid level (Section 6)
Check the automatic transaxle fluid level (Section 7)
Change the engine oil and oil filter (Section 8)

Every 7500 miles or 6 months, whichever comes first

Inspect/replace the windshield wiper blades (Section 9)
Check/adjust the clutch pedal freeplay (Section 10)
Check and service the battery (Section 11)
Check/adjust the engine drivebelts (Section 12)
Inspect/replace all underhood hoses (Section 13)
Check the cooling system (Section 14)
Rotate the tires (Section 15)
Inspect the brakes (Section 16)

Every 15,000 miles or 12 months, whichever comes first

All items listed above plus . . .
Check/replace the air and PCV filters (Section 17)
Check the throttle position sensor system (Section 18)
Check/adjust the valve clearances on 1986 through 1994 models (Section 19)

Check/adjust the engine idle speed (Section 20)
Replace the fuel filter (Section 21)
Inspect the fuel system (Section 22)
Inspect the steering and suspension components (Section 23)*
Check the driveaxle boots (Section 24)*
Inspect the exhaust system (Section 25)
Check the manual transaxle lubricant level (Section 26)

Every 30,000 miles or 24 months, whichever comes first

Check/replace the spark plugs (Section 27)
Inspect/replace the spark plug wires, distributor cap and rotor, where applicable (Section 28)*
Check the carburetor choke (Section 29)
Check the thermostatically controlled air cleaner on carbureted engines (Section 30)
Replace the drivebelts for the water pump and alternator (Section 12)
Drain, flush and refill the cooling system (Section 31)
Check/repack the rear wheel bearings (Section 32)
Drain the brake system and refill it with new fluid (Section 33)
If the vehicle is equipped with an automatic transaxle, change the fluid and filter (Section 34)**
If the vehicle is equipped with a manual transaxle, drain and refill it with new lubricant (Section 35)

Every 50,000 miles or 40 months, whichever comes first

Inspect the evaporative emissions control system and replace the canister (1986 through 1993 models) (Section 36)
Check/adjust the ignition timing, where applicable (Section 37)
Check/replace the PCV valve (Section 38)
Replace the oxygen sensor (1986 through 1990 models) (Section 39)

Every 60,000 miles or 48 months, whichever comes first

Install a new timing belt (Chapter 2A)
*This item is affected by "severe" operating conditions as described below. If the vehicle in question is operated under "severe" conditions, perform all maintenance indicated with an asterisk (*) at 7500 mile/6 month intervals. Consider the conditions "severe" if most driving is done . . .
   In dusty areas*

   When towing a trailer
   At low speeds or with extended periods of engine idling
   When outside temperatures remain below freezing and most trips are less than four miles
**If most driving is done under one or more of the following conditions, change the automatic transaxle fluid every 15,000 miles:
   In heavy city traffic where the outside temperature regularly reaches 90-degrees F (32-degrees C) or higher
   In hilly or mountainous terrain
   Frequent trailer pulling*

2 Introduction

This Chapter is designed to help the home mechanic maintain the Hyundai Excel and Accent with the goals of maximum performance, economy, safety and reliability in mind.

Included is a master maintenance schedule, followed by procedures dealing specifically with each item on the schedule. Visual checks, adjustments, component replacement and other helpful items are included. Refer to the accompanying illustrations of the engine compartment and the underside of the vehicle for the locations of various components.

Adhering to the mileage/time maintenance schedule and following the step-by-step procedures, which is simply a preventive maintenance program, will result in maximum reliability and vehicle service life. Keep in mind that it is a comprehensive program - maintaining some items but not others at the specified intervals will not produce the same results.

As you service the vehicle, you will discover that many of the procedures can - and should - be grouped together because of the nature of the particular procedure you're performing or because of the close proximity of two otherwise unrelated components to one another.

For example, if the vehicle is raised for chassis lubrication, you should inspect the exhaust, suspension, steering and fuel systems while you're under the vehicle. When you're rotating the tires, it makes good sense to check the brakes, since the wheels are already removed. Finally, let's suppose you have to borrow or rent a torque wrench. Even if you only need it to tighten the spark plugs, you might as well check the torque of as many critical fasteners as time allows.

The first step in this maintenance program is to prepare yourself before the actual work begins. Read through all the procedures you're planning to do, then gather up all the parts and tools needed. If it looks like you might run into problems during a particular job, seek advice from a mechanic or an experienced do-it-yourselfer.

3 Tune-up general information

The term tune-up is used in this manual to represent a combination of individual operations rather than one specific procedure.

If, from the time the vehicle is new, the routine maintenance schedule is followed closely and frequent checks are made of fluid levels and high wear items, as suggested throughout this manual, the engine will be kept in relatively good running condition and the need for additional work will be minimized.

More likely than not, however, there will be times when the engine is running poorly due to lack of regular maintenance. This is even more likely if a used vehicle, which has not received regular and frequent maintenance checks, is purchased. In such cases, an engine tune-up will be needed outside of the regular routine maintenance intervals.

The first step in any tune-up or diagnostic procedure to help correct a poor running engine is a cylinder compression check (see Chapter 2). This check will help determine the condition of internal engine components and should be used as a guide for tune-up and repair procedures. For instance, if a compression check indicates serious internal engine wear, a conventional tune-up will not improve the performance of the engine and would be

a waste of time and money. Because of its importance, the compression check should be done by someone with the right equipment and the knowledge to use it properly.

The following procedures are those most often needed to bring a generally poor running engine back into a proper state of tune.

Minor tune-up
Check all engine related fluids (Section 4)
Clean, inspect and test the battery (Section 11)
Check and adjust the drivebelts (Section 12)
Replace the spark plugs (Section 27)
Inspect the distributor cap and rotor where applicable (Section 28)
Inspect the spark plug and coil wires (Section 28)
Check and adjust the idle speed where applicable (Section 20)
Check the PCV valve (Section 38)
Check the air filter (Section 17)
Check the cooling system (Section 14)
Check all underhood hoses (Section 13)

Major tune-up
All items listed under Minor tune-up, plus . . .
Check the EGR system (Chapter 6)
Check the ignition system (Chapter 5)
Check the charging system (Chapter 5)
Check the fuel system (Chapter 4)
Replace the air filter (Section 17)
Replace the distributor cap and rotor (Section 28)
Replace the spark plug wires (Section 28)

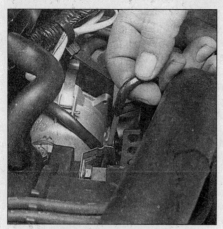

4.2a On 1986 through 1994 models, the engine oil dipstick is located at the left end of the engine

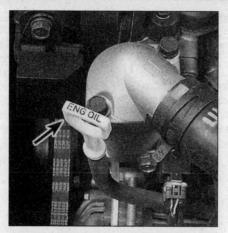

4.2b On 1995 and later models, the engine oil dipstick is located at the right end of the engine

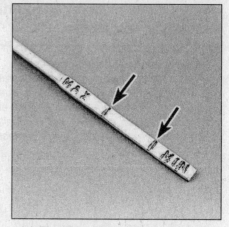

4.4 The oil level should be between the MIN and MAX marks. Later models use "F" (full) and "L" (low) instead of MAX and MIN

4.6 Rotate the oil filler cap half a turn to remove it - always make sure the area around the opening is clean before unscrewing the cap; this prevents dirt from contaminating the engine

4   Fluid level checks

Note: *The following fluid level checks should be done on a 250 mile or weekly basis. Additional fluid level checks can be found in specific maintenance procedures which follow. Regardless of intervals, be alert for fluid leaks under the vehicle which would indicate a leak to be fixed immediately.*

1   Fluids are an essential part of the lubrication, cooling, brake and windshield washer systems. Because the fluids gradually become depleted and/or contaminated during normal operation of the vehicle, they must be periodically replenished. See *Recommended lubricants and fluids* at the beginning of this Chapter before adding fluid to any of the following components. **Note:** *The vehicle must be on level ground when fluid levels are checked.*

Engine oil

Refer to illustrations 4.2a, 4.2b, 4.4 and 4.6

2   The engine oil level is checked with a dipstick located at the front (drivebelt) end of the engine **(see illustrations)**. It extends through a tube and into the oil pan at the bottom of the engine.

3   The oil level should be checked before the vehicle has been driven, or about five minutes after the engine has been shut off. If the oil is checked immediately after driving the vehicle, some of the oil will remain in the upper engine components, resulting in an inaccurate reading on the dipstick.

4   Pull the dipstick out and wipe all the oil off the end with a clean rag or paper towel. Insert the clean dipstick all the way back into the tube, then pull it out again. Note the oil at the end of the dipstick. Add oil as necessary to keep the level between the MIN mark and the MAX mark on the dipstick **(see illustration)**.

5   Don't overfill the engine by adding too much oil, since it may result in oil fouled spark plugs, oil leaks or oil seal failures.

6   Oil is added to the engine after removing the cap from the valve cover **(see illustration)**. A funnel will help to reduce spills.

7   Checking the oil level is an important preventive maintenance step. A consistently low oil level indicates oil leakage through damaged seals, defective gaskets or past worn rings or valve guides. If the oil looks milky in color or has water droplets in it, the cylinder head gasket may be blown or the head or block may be cracked. The engine should be checked immediately. The condition of the oil should also be noted. Whenever you check the oil level, slide your thumb and index finger up the dipstick before wiping off the oil. If you see small dirt or metal particles clinging to the dipstick, the oil should be changed (see Section 8).

Engine coolant

Refer to illustration 4.8

Warning: *Do not allow antifreeze to come in contact with your skin or painted surfaces of the vehicle. Flush contaminated areas immediately with plenty of water. Don't store new coolant or leave old coolant lying around where it's accessible to children or pets - they're attracted by its sweet smell. Ingestion of even a small amount of coolant can be fatal! Wipe up garage floor and drip pan coolant spills immediately. Keep antifreeze containers covered and repair leaks in your cooling system as soon as they are noted.*

8   All vehicles covered by this manual are equipped with a coolant recovery system. A white plastic coolant reservoir is connected by a hose to the radiator filler neck **(see illustration)**. If the engine overheats, coolant escapes through a valve in the radiator cap and travels through the hose into the reservoir. As the engine cools, the coolant is automatically drawn back into the cooling system to maintain the correct level.

4.8 Make sure the engine coolant level in the reservoir is between the LOW and FULL marks

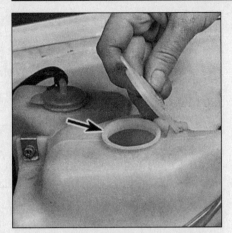

4.14a The windshield washer fluid reservoir is located on the right side of the engine compartment, next to the coolant reservoir on early models - be careful not to confuse these two reservoirs!

4.14b Windshield washer fluid reservoir (typical 1995 and later model)

4.17 On conventional batteries, remove the cell caps to check the electrolyte level of the battery - if the level is too low, add distilled water only

9   The coolant level in the reservoir should be checked regularly. **Warning:** *Do not remove the radiator cap to check the coolant level when the engine is warm. The level in the reservoir varies with the temperature of the engine. When the engine is cold, the coolant level should be at or slightly above the LOW mark on the reservoir. Once the engine has warmed up, the level should be at or near the FULL mark. If it isn't, allow the engine to cool, then remove the cap from the reservoir and add a 50/50 mixture of ethylene glycol-based antifreeze and water.*

10   Drive the vehicle and recheck the coolant level. If only a small amount of coolant is required to bring the system up to the proper level, water can be used. However, repeated additions of water will dilute the antifreeze and water solution. In order to maintain the proper ratio of antifreeze and water, always top up the coolant level with the correct mixture. An empty plastic milk jug or bleach bottle makes an excellent container for mixing coolant. Do not use rust inhibitors or additives.

11   If the coolant level drops consistently, there may be a leak in the system. Inspect the radiator, hoses, filler cap, drain plugs and water pump (see Section 14). If no leaks are noted, have the radiator cap pressure tested by a service station.

12   If you have to remove the radiator cap, wait until the engine has cooled, then wrap a thick cloth around the cap and turn it to the first stop. If coolant or steam escapes, let the engine cool down longer, then remove the cap.

13   Check the condition of the coolant as well. It should be relatively clear. If it's brown or rust colored, the system should be drained, flushed and refilled. Even if the coolant appears to be normal, the corrosion inhibitors wear out, so it must be replaced at the specified intervals.

Windshield washer fluid

Refer to illustrations 4.14a and 4.14b

14   Fluid for the windshield washer system is located in a plastic reservoir in the engine compartment **(see illustrations)**.

15   In milder climates, plain water can be used in the reservoir, but it should be kept no more than 2/3 full to allow for expansion if the water freezes. In colder climates, use windshield washer system antifreeze, available at any auto parts store, to lower the freezing point of the fluid. Mix the antifreeze with water in accordance with the manufacturer's directions on the container. **Caution:** *Don't use cooling system antifreeze - it will damage the vehicle's paint.*

16   To help prevent icing in cold weather, warm the windshield with the defroster before using the washer.

Battery electrolyte

Refer to illustration 4.17

17   All vehicles with which this manual is concerned are equipped with a battery which is permanently sealed (except for vent holes) and has no filler caps. Water doesn't have to be added to these batteries at any time. If an aftermarket maintenance-type battery is installed, the caps on top of the battery should be removed periodically to check for a low water level **(see illustration)**. This check is most critical during the warm summer months.

Brake and clutch fluid

Refer to illustrations 4.19a and 4.19b

18   The brake master cylinder is mounted on the front of the power booster unit in the engine compartment. The smaller clutch master cylinder (1990 and later models) is normally located next to the brake master cylinder.

19   The fluid inside is readily visible. The level should be between the MIN and MAX marks on the reservoir **(see illustrations)**. If

4.19a The brake fluid level should be kept between the MAX and MIN lines on the translucent plastic reservoir - unscrew the cap to add fluid

4.19b Clutch master cylinder fluid reservoir (typical)

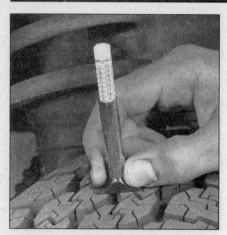

5.2 A tire tread depth indicator should be used to monitor tire wear - they are available at auto parts stores and service stations and cost very little

a low level is indicated, be sure to wipe the top of the reservoir cover with a clean rag to prevent contamination of the hydraulic system before removing the cover.

20   When adding fluid, pour it carefully into the reservoir to avoid spilling it onto surrounding painted surfaces. Be sure the specified fluid is used, since mixing different types of brake fluid can cause damage to the system. See *Recommended lubricants and fluids* at the front of this Chapter or your owner's manual. **Warning:** *Brake fluid can harm your eyes and damage painted surfaces, so use extreme caution when handling or pouring it. Do not use brake fluid that has been standing open or is more than one year old. Brake fluid absorbs moisture from the air. Excess moisture can cause a dangerous loss of braking effectiveness.*

21   At this time the fluid and master cylinder can be inspected for contamination. The system should be drained and refilled if deposits, dirt particles or water droplets are seen in the fluid (see Section 33).

22   After filling the reservoir to the proper level, make sure the cover is on tight to prevent fluid leakage.

23   The brake fluid level in the master cylinder will drop slightly as the pads and the brake shoes at each wheel wear down during normal operation. If the master cylinder requires repeated additions to keep it at the proper level, it's an indication of leakage in the brake system, which should be corrected immediately. Check all brake lines and connections (see Section 16 for more information).

24   The level in the clutch reservoir should remain relatively constant. If the level drops, there's a leak (see Chapter 8).

25   If, upon checking the master cylinder fluid level, you discover the reservoir empty or nearly empty, the hydraulic system should be bled (see Chapter 9).

5   Tire and tire pressure checks

Refer to illustrations 5.2, 5.3, 5.4a, 5.4b and 5.8

1   Periodic inspection of the tires may spare you the inconvenience of being stranded with a flat tire. It can also provide you with vital information regarding possible problems in the steering and suspension systems before major damage occurs.

2   The original tires on this vehicle are equipped with 1/2-inch wide bands that will appear when tread depth reaches 1/16-inch, at which point the tires can be considered worn out. Tread wear can be monitored with a simple, inexpensive device known as a tread depth indicator **(see illustration)**.

3   Note any abnormal tread wear **(see illustration)**. Tread pattern irregularities such as cupping, flat spots and more wear on one side than the other are indications of front end

UNDERINFLATION

CUPPING

Cupping may be caused by:
- **Underinflation and/or mechanical irregularities such as out-of-balance condition of wheel and/or tire, and bent or damaged wheel.**
- **Loose or worn steering tie-rod or steering idler arm.**
- **Loose, damaged or worn front suspension parts.**

OVERINFLATION

INCORRECT TOE-IN OR EXTREME CAMBER

FEATHERING DUE TO MISALIGNMENT

5.3 This chart will help you determine the condition of your tires, the probable cause(s) of abnormal wear and the corrective action necessary

5.4a If a tire loses air on a steady basis, check the valve core first to make sure it's snug (special inexpensive wrenches are commonly available at auto parts stores)

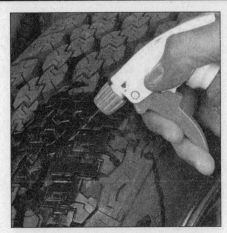

5.4b If the valve core is tight, raise the corner of the vehicle with the low tire and spray a soapy water solution onto the tread as the tire is turned - slow leaks will cause small bubbles to appear

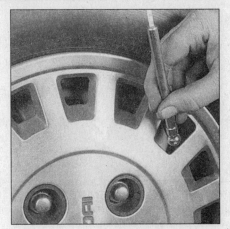

5.8 To extend the life of the tires, check the air pressure at least once a week with an accurate gauge (don't forget the spare!)

alignment and/or balance problems. If any of these conditions are noted, take the vehicle to a tire shop or service station to correct the problem.

4   Look closely for cuts, punctures and embedded nails or tacks. Sometimes a tire will hold air pressure for a short time or leak down very slowly after a nail has embedded itself in the tread. If a slow leak persists, check the valve stem core to make sure it's tight **(see illustration)**. Examine the tread for an object that may have embedded itself in the tire or for a "plug" that may have begun to leak (radial tire punctures can sometimes be repaired with a plug that's installed in a puncture). If a puncture is suspected, it can be easily verified by spraying a solution of soapy water onto the suspected area **(see illustration)**. The soapy solution will bubble if there's a leak. Unless the puncture is unusually large, a tire shop or service station can usually repair the tire.

5   Carefully inspect the inner sidewall of each tire for evidence of brake fluid. If you see

any, inspect the brakes immediately.

6   Correct air pressure adds miles to the lifespan of the tires, improves mileage and enhances overall ride quality. Tire pressure cannot be accurately estimated by looking at a tire, especially if it's a radial. A tire pressure gauge is essential. Keep an accurate gauge in the vehicle. The pressure gauges attached to the nozzles of air hoses at gas stations are often inaccurate.

7   Always check tire pressure when the tires are cold. Cold, in this case, means the vehicle has not been driven over a mile in the three hours preceding a tire pressure check. A pressure rise of four to eight pounds is not uncommon once the tires are warm.

8   Unscrew the valve cap protruding from the wheel or hubcap and push the gauge firmly onto the valve stem **(see illustration)**. Note the reading on the gauge and compare the figure to the recommended tire pressure shown on the label attached to the inside of the glove compartment door. Be sure to rein-

stall the valve cap to keep dirt and moisture out of the valve stem mechanism. Check all four tires and, if necessary, add enough air to bring them up to the recommended pressure.

9   Don't forget to keep the spare tire inflated to the specified pressure (refer to your owner's manual or the tire sidewall).

6   Power steering fluid level check

Refer to illustrations 6.2a, 6.2b and 6.5

Warning: *The electric cooling fan can activate at any time, even when the ignition is in the Off position. Disconnect the fan motor or negative battery cable when working in the vicinity of the fan.*

1   Unlike manual steering, the power steering system relies on fluid which may, over a period of time, require replenishing.

2   The fluid reservoir for the power steering pump is located near the front of the engine compartment **(see illustrations)**.

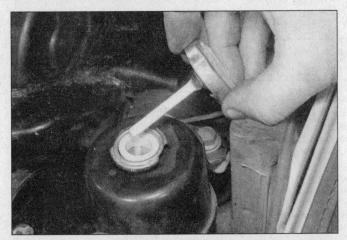

6.2a The power steering fluid filler cap/dipstick (typical 1986 through 1994 model) - unscrew the cap to check the dipstick and/ or add fluid

6.2b On 1995 and later models, the power steering fluid reservoir has marks on the reservoir instead of a dipstick

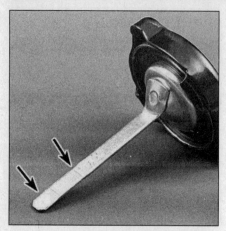

6.5 The power steering fluid level should be kept between the MIN and MAX lines on the dipstick (1986 through 1994 models)

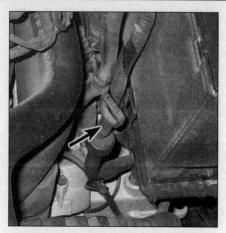

7.4 The automatic transmission dipstick is located near the battery (typical)

7.6 Check the fluid with the transaxle at normal operating temperature - the level should be kept in the HOT range (between the two lines)

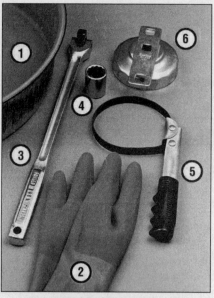

8.3 These tools are required when changing the engine oil and filter

1   **Drain pan** - *It should be fairly shallow in depth, but wide in order to prevent spills*
2   **Rubber gloves** - *When removing the drain plug and filter it is inevitable that you will get oil on your hands (the gloves will prevent burns)*
3   **Breaker bar** - *Sometimes the oil drain plug is pretty tight and a long breaker bar is needed to loosen it*
4   **Socket** - *To be used with the breaker bar or a ratchet (must be the correct size to fit the drain plug)*
5   **Filter wrench** - *This is a metal band-type wrench, which requires clearance around the filter to be effective*
6   **Filter wrench** - *This type fits on the bottom of the filter and can be turned with a ratchet or breaker bar (different size wrenches are available for different types of filters)*

3   For the check, the front wheels should be pointed straight ahead and the engine should be off.
4   Use a clean rag to wipe off the reservoir cap and the area around the cap. This will help prevent any foreign matter from entering the reservoir during the check.
5   On 1986 through 1994 models, remove the cap and note the dipstick attached to it. Wipe off the fluid with a clean rag, reinsert the dipstick, then withdraw it and read the fluid level. The level should be between the MIN and MAX marks **(see illustration)**. Never allow the fluid level to drop below the MIN mark.
6   On 1995 and later models, simply note the level of the fluid inside the translucent reservoir **(see illustration 6.2b)**. It should be between the MIN and MAX marks. Don't let the fluid level drop below the MIN mark.
7   If additional fluid is required, pour the specified type directly into the reservoir, using a funnel to prevent spills.
8   If the reservoir requires frequent fluid additions, all power steering hoses, hose connections and the power steering pump should be carefully checked for leaks.

7   Automatic transaxle fluid level check

Refer to illustrations 7.4 and 7.6
Warning: *The electric cooling fan can activate at any time, even when the ignition is in the Off position. Disconnect the fan motor or negative battery cable when working in the vicinity of the fan.*
1   The level of the automatic transaxle fluid should be carefully maintained. Low fluid level can lead to slipping or loss of drive, while overfilling can cause foaming, loss of fluid and transaxle damage.
2   The transaxle fluid level should only be checked when the engine is at normal operating temperature. **Caution:** *If the vehicle has just been driven for a long time at high speed*

or in city traffic in hot weather, or if it has been pulling a trailer, an accurate fluid level reading cannot be obtained. Allow the fluid to cool down for about 30 minutes.
3   Park on level ground, apply the parking brake and start the engine. While the engine is idling, depress the brake pedal and move the selector lever through all the gear ranges, beginning and ending in Neutral.
4   With the engine still idling, remove the dipstick **(see illustration)**.
5   Wipe the fluid off the dipstick with a clean rag and reinsert it until the cap seats.
6   Pull the dipstick out again. The fluid level should be in the HOT range **(see illustration)**. If the level is at the low side of the range, add the specified automatic transmission fluid through the dipstick tube with a funnel.
7   Add the fluid a little at a time and keep checking the level until it's correct.
8   The condition of the fluid should also be checked along with the level. If the fluid at the end of the dipstick is black or a dark reddish/brown color, or if it smells burned, the fluid should be changed (see Section 34). If you're in doubt about the condition of the fluid, purchase some new fluid and compare the two for color and odor.

8   Engine oil and filter change

Refer to illustrations 8.3, 8.9a, 8.9b, 8.14 and 8.18
1   Frequent oil changes are the most important preventive maintenance procedures that can be done by the home mechanic. As engine oil ages, it becomes diluted and contaminated, which leads to premature engine wear.
2   Although some sources recommend oil filter changes every other oil change, a new filter should be installed every time the oil is changed.
3   Gather all necessary tools and materials before beginning this procedure **(see illustration)**.

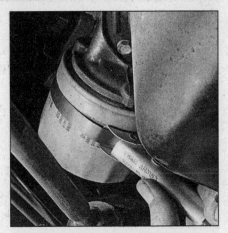

8.9a Use the proper size box-end wrench or socket to remove the oil drain plug to avoid rounding it off (early model with stamped-steel oil pan)

8.9b Location of the engine oil drain plug on a later model with a cast aluminum oil pan

8.14 The oil filter is usually on very tight and will require a special wrench for removal - DO NOT use the wrench to tighten the new filter

4   You should have plenty of clean rags and newspapers handy to mop up any spills. Access to the underside of the vehicle is greatly improved if the vehicle can be lifted on a hoist, driven onto ramps or supported by jackstands. **Warning:** *Do not work under a vehicle which is supported only by a bumper, hydraulic or scissors-type jack.*

5   If this is your first oil change, and familiarize yourself with the locations of the oil drain plug and the oil filter. The engine and exhaust components will be warm during the actual work, so note how they are situated to avoid touching them when working under the vehicle.

6   Warm the engine to normal operating temperature. If the new oil or any tools are needed, use this warm-up time to gather everything necessary for the job. Refer to *Recommended lubricants and fluids* at the beginning of this Chapter for the type of oil required.

7   With the engine oil warm (warm engine oil will drain better and more built-up sludge will be removed with it), raise and support the vehicle. Make sure it's safely supported!

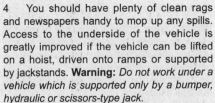

8.18 Lubricate the gasket with clean oil before installing the filter on the engine

8   Move all necessary tools, rags and newspapers under the vehicle. Set the drain pan under the drain plug. Keep in mind that the oil will initially flow from the pan with some force; position the pan accordingly.

9   Being careful not to touch any of the hot exhaust components, use a wrench to remove the drain plug near the bottom of the oil pan **(see illustrations)**. Depending on how hot the oil is, you may want to wear gloves while unscrewing the plug the final few turns.

10   Allow the old oil to drain into the pan. It may be necessary to move the pan as the oil flow slows to a trickle.

11   After all the oil has drained, wipe off the drain plug with a clean rag. Small metal particles may cling to the plug and would immediately contaminate the new oil.

12   Clean the area around the drain plug opening and reinstall the plug. Tighten it securely with the wrench. If a torque wrench is available, use it to tighten the plug.

13   Move the drain pan into position under the oil filter.

14   Use the filter wrench to loosen the oil filter **(see illustration)**. Chain or metal band filter wrenches may distort the filter canister, but it doesn't matter since the filter will be discarded anyway.

15   Completely unscrew the old filter. Be careful; it's full of oil. Empty the oil inside the filter into the drain pan.

16   Compare the old filter with the new one to make sure they're the same type.

17   Use a clean rag to remove all oil, dirt and sludge from the area where the oil filter mounts to the engine.

18   Apply a light coat of clean oil to the rubber gasket on the new oil filter **(see illustration)**.

19   Attach the new filter to the engine, following the tightening directions printed on the filter canister or packing box. Most filter manufacturers recommend against using a wrench due to the possibility of overtightening the filter and damaging the seal.

20   Remove all tools, rags, etc. from under

the vehicle, being careful not to spill the oil in the drain pan, then lower the vehicle.

21   Move to the engine compartment and locate the oil filler cap.

22   Pour three quarts of new engine oil into the engine. Wait a few minutes to allow the oil to drain into the pan, then check the level on the oil dipstick (see Section 4 if necessary). If the oil level is above the MIN mark, start the engine and allow the new oil to circulate.

23   Run the engine for only about a minute and then shut it off. Immediately look under the vehicle and check for leaks at the oil pan drain plug and around the oil filter.

24   With the new oil circulated and the filter now completely full, recheck the level on the dipstick after approximately five minutes and add more oil as necessary.

25   During the first few trips after an oil change, make it a point to check frequently for leaks and proper oil level.

26   The old oil drained from the engine cannot be reused in its present state and should be disposed of. Check with your local auto parts store, service station, refuse disposal company or environmental agency to see if they will accept the oil for recycling. Don't pour used oil into drains or onto the ground. After the oil has cooled it can be drained into a container (capped plastic jugs, topped bottles, milk cartons, etc.) for transport to a disposal site.

9   Windshield wiper blade inspection and replacement

Refer to illustrations 9.5 and 9.6

1   The windshield wiper and blade assembly should be inspected periodically for damage, loose components and cracked or worn blade elements.

2   Road film can build up on the wiper blades and affect their efficiency, so they should be washed regularly with a mild detergent solution.

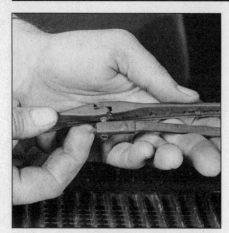

9.5 Lift up on the release lever and slide the blade assembly pin out of the arm (typical earlier model)

9.6 Use a small screwdriver to pry the lock up and over the end of the blade insert, then slide the insert out of the wiper arm, away from the lock (typical earlier model)

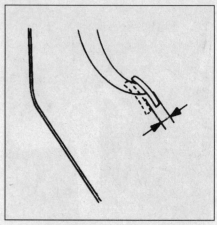

10.1 To check clutch pedal freeplay, measure the distance between the natural resting place of the pedal and the point at which you encounter resistance

3   The action of the wiping mechanism can loosen bolts, nuts and fasteners, so they should be checked and tightened, as necessary, at the same time the wiper blades are checked.

4   If the wiper blade elements are cracked, worn or warped, or no longer clean adequately, they should be replaced with new ones.

Earlier models

5   Lift the arm assembly away from the glass for clearance, lift up on the release lever and detach the blade assembly from the arm **(see illustration)**.

6   Pry the metal lock on the end of the wiper arm up with a small screwdriver until it clears the metal tab on the end of the insert, then slide the insert away from the lock, out of the arm **(see illustration)**.

7   Slide the new insert into place until the hole in the end snaps over the tab.

Later models

8   On later models, several different versions of wiper arm blades are used and each type is installed in a slightly different manner than the typical earlier unit shown here. Follow the removal and installation instructions included with the new wiper blades.

---

10   Clutch pedal freeplay check and adjustment

Cable-operated models

Refer to illustrations 10.1 and 10.2

1   Push down on the clutch pedal and use a small steel ruler to measure the distance that it moves freely before the clutch resistance is felt **(see illustration)**. The freeplay should be within the specified limits. If it isn't, it must be adjusted.

2   Working within the engine compartment,

turn the outer cable adjusting nut (located at the point where the cable enters the firewall until the specified nut-to-insulator clearance is achieved **(see illustration)**.

3   Recheck the freeplay. Repeat the adjustment as necessary.

Hydraulically operated models

Refer to illustration 10.5

Caution: *When adjusting the clutch pedal clevis freeplay, be careful not to force the pushrod toward the master cylinder.*

4   Push down on the clutch pedal and measure the distance that it moves freely before the clutch resistance is felt **(see illustration 10.1)**. The clevis pin freeplay should be within the specified limits. If it isn't, it must be adjusted.

5   Loosen the locknut and turn the master cylinder pushrod in either direction until clearance is achieved **(see illustration)**. Tighten the locknut. Repeat the adjustment if necessary.

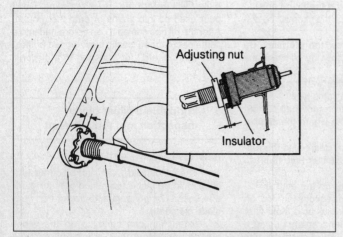

10.2 Adjust the clutch pedal freeplay by turning the cable adjusting nut until the specified clearance (C) is achieved

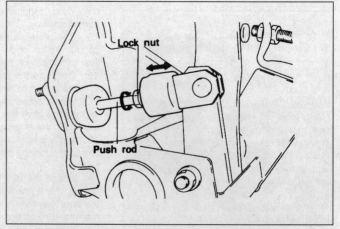

10.5 Loosen the locknut and turn the master cylinder pushrod in either direction (hydraulically operated models)

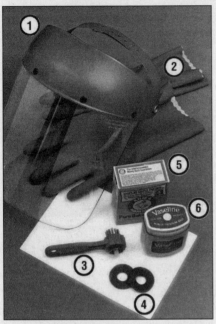

11.1 Tools and materials required for battery maintenance

1   *Face shield/safety goggles* - When removing corrosion with a brush, the acidic particles can easily fly up into your eyes

2   *Rubber gloves* - Another safety item to consider when servicing the battery - remember that's acid inside the battery!

3   *Battery terminal/cable cleaner* - This wire brush cleaning tool will remove all traces of corrosion from the battery and cable

4   *Treated felt washers* - Placing one of these on each terminal, directly under the cable end, will help prevent corrosion (be sure to get the correct type for side-terminal batteries)

5   *Baking soda* - A solution of baking soda and water can be used to neutralize corrosion

6   *Petroleum jelly* - A layer of this on the battery terminal bolts will help prevent corrosion

11   Battery check and maintenance

Refer to illustrations 11.1, 11.5, 11.6a, 11.6b and 11.6c

Warning: *Certain precautions must be followed when checking and servicing the battery. Hydrogen gas, which is highly flammable, is always present in the battery cells, so keep lighted tobacco and all other open flames and sparks away from the battery. The electrolyte inside the battery is actually dilute sulfuric acid, which will cause injury if splashed on your skin or in your eyes. It will also ruin clothes and painted surfaces. When removing the battery cables, always detach the negative cable first and hook it up last!*

1   Battery maintenance is an important pro-

11.5 Use a wrench to check the tightness of battery cable bolts; when removing corroded bolts, it may be necessary to use special battery pliers

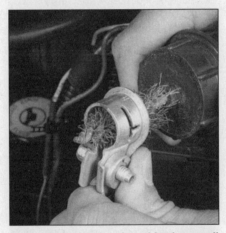

11.6b When cleaning the cable clamps, all corrosion must be removed (the inside of the clamp is tapered to match the taper on the post, so don't remove too much material)

cedure which will help ensure that you aren't stranded because of a dead battery. Several tools are required for this procedure **(see illustration).**

2   When checking/servicing the battery, always turn the engine and all accessories off.

3   A sealed (sometimes called maintenance-free), battery is standard equipment on these vehicles. The cell caps cannot be removed, no electrolyte checks are required and water cannot be added to the cells.

4   The external condition of the battery should be checked periodically. Look for damage such as a cracked case.

5   Check the tightness of the battery cable bolts **(see illustration)** to ensure good electrical connections. Inspect the entire length of each cable, looking for cracked or abraded insulation and frayed conductors.

6   If corrosion (visible as white, fluffy deposits) **(see illustration)** is evident, remove the cables from the terminals, clean them with a

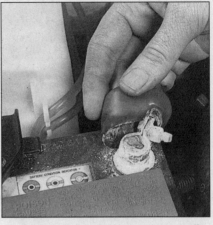

11.6a Battery terminal corrosion usually appears as a white fluffy powder

11.6c Regardless of the type of tool used to clean the battery posts, a clean, shiny surface should result

battery brush and reinstall them **(see illustrations).** Corrosion can be kept to a minimum by applying a layer of petroleum jelly or grease to the terminals.

7   Make sure the battery carrier is in good condition and the holddown clamp is tight. If the battery is removed (see Chapter 5 for the removal and installation procedure), make sure that no parts remain in the bottom of the carrier when it's reinstalled. When reinstalling the hold-down clamp, don't overtighten the nuts.

8   Corrosion on the carrier, battery case and surrounding areas can be removed with a solution of water and baking soda. Apply the mixture with a small brush, let it work, then rinse it off with plenty of clean water.

9   Any metal parts of the vehicle damaged by corrosion should be coated with a zinc-based primer, then painted.

10   Additional information on the battery, charging and jump starting can be found in the front of this manual and in Chapter 5.

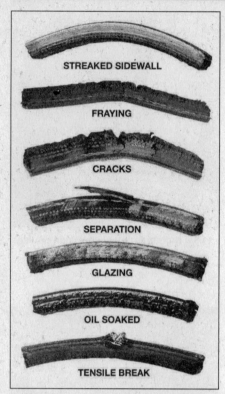

12.3a Here are some of the more common problems associated with V-belts - check the belts very carefully to prevent an untimely breakdown

---

12   Drivebelt check, adjustment and replacement

Warning: *The electric cooling fan can activate at any time, even when the ignition is in the Off position. Disconnect the fan motor or negative battery cable when working in the vicinity of the fan.*

Check

Refer to illustrations 12.3a, 12.3b and 12.5

1   The alternator and air conditioning compressor drivebelts, also referred to as V-belts (early models), V-ribbed belts (later models) or simply "fan" belts, are located at the front (timing belt) end of the engine. The condition and proper adjustment of the drivebelts is critical to the operation of the engine. Since they stretch and deteriorate as they get older, they must be inspected periodically.

2   The number of belts used on a particular vehicle depends on the accessories installed. One belt transmits power from the crankshaft to the alternator and water pump. If the vehicle is equipped with air conditioning, the air conditioning compressor is driven by another belt.

3   With the engine off, open the hood and locate the drivebelts. With a flashlight, check each belt for separation of the adhesive rubber on both sides of the core, core separation from the belt side, a severed core, separation of the ribs from the adhesive rubber, cracking

or separation of the ribs, and torn or worn ribs or cracks in the inner ridges of the ribs **(see illustrations)**. Also check for fraying and glazing, which gives the belt a shiny appearance. Both sides of the belt should be inspected, which means you will have to twist the belt to check the underside. Use your fingers to feel the belt where you can't see it. If any of the above conditions are evident, replace the belt (go to Step 8).

4   To check the tension of each belt in accordance with factory specifications, install a belt tension gauge on the belt. Measure the tension in accordance with the manufacturer's instructions and compare your measurement to the specified drivebelt tension for either a used or new belt. **Note:** *A "used" belt is defined as any belt which has been operated more than five minutes on the engine; a "new" belt is one that has been used for less than five minutes.*

5   If you don't have either of the special tools, and cannot borrow one, the following rule of thumb method is recommended: Push firmly on the belt with your thumb at a distance halfway between the pulleys and note how far the belt can be moved (deflected). Measure the deflection with a ruler **(see illustration)** and compare the deflection with the values listed in this Chapter's Specifications. Adjust the belt as necessary

Adjustment

6   If the alternator or power steering pump belt must be adjusted, loosen the adjustment bolt that secures the alternator or power steering pump to the slotted bracket and pivot the alternator or power steering pump (away from the engine block to tighten the belt, toward the block to loosen the belt). It's helpful to lever the alternator or power steering pump with a large prybar when adjusting the belt because the prybar enables you to precisely position the component until the adjuster bolt is tightened. Be very careful not to damage the aluminum housing of the alternator or power steering pump. Recheck the belt tension using one of the above methods. Repeat this Step until the alternator or power steering pump drivebelt tension is correct.

12.3b Small cracks in the underside of a V-ribbed drivebelt are acceptable - lengthwise cracks, or missing pieces are cause for replacement

7   If the air conditioning compressor drivebelt must be adjusted, locate the idler pulley, just above the compressor. Turn the idler pulley adjuster bolt. Measure the belt tension in accordance with one of the above methods. Repeat this step until the air conditioning compressor drivebelt is adjusted.

Replacement

8   To replace a belt, follow the above procedures for drivebelt adjustment but slip the belt off the crankshaft pulley and remove it. If you're replacing the alternator belt, you'll have to remove the air conditioning compressor belt first because of the way they're arranged

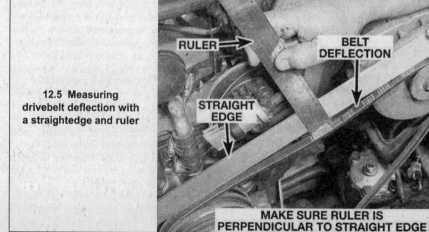

12.5 Measuring drivebelt deflection with a straightedge and ruler

on the crankshaft pulley. Because of this and because belts tend to wear out more or less together, it's a good idea to replace both belts at the same time. Mark each belt and its appropriate pulley groove so the replacement belts can be installed in the proper positions.

9 Take the old belts to the parts store in order to make a direct comparison for length, width and design.

10 After replacing a V-ribbed drivebelt (1995 and later models), make sure that it fits properly in the ribbed grooves in the pulleys. It's essential that the belt be properly centered.

11 Adjust the belt(s) as described above.

13 Underhood hose check and replacement

Warning: *Replacement of air conditioning hoses must be left to a dealer service department or air conditioning shop that has the equipment to depressurize the system safely. Never remove air conditioning components or hoses until the system has been depressurized.*

General

1 High temperatures in the engine compartment can cause the deterioration of the rubber and plastic hoses used for engine, accessory and emission systems operation. Periodic inspection should be made for cracks, loose clamps, material hardening and leaks.

2 Information specific to the cooling system hoses can be found in Section 14.

3 Some, but not all, hoses are secured to the fittings with clamps. Where clamps are used, check to be sure they haven't lost their tension, allowing the hose to leak. If clamps aren't used, make sure the hose has not expanded and/or hardened where it slips over the fitting, allowing it to leak.

Vacuum hoses

4 It's quite common for vacuum hoses, especially those in the emissions system, to be color coded or identified by colored stripes molded into them. Various systems require hoses with a different wall thickness, collapse resistance and temperature resistance. When replacing hoses, be sure the new ones are made of the same material.

5 Often the only effective way to check a hose is to remove it completely from the vehicle. If more than one hose is removed, be sure to label the hoses and fittings to ensure correct installation.

6 When checking vacuum hoses, be sure to include any plastic T-fittings in the check. Inspect the fittings for cracks and the hose where it fits over the fitting for distortion, which could cause leakage.

7 A small piece of vacuum hose (1/4-inch inside diameter) can be used as a stethoscope to detect vacuum leaks. Hold one end of the hose to your ear and probe around vacuum hoses and fittings, listening for the "hissing"

sound characteristic of a vacuum leak. **Warning:** *When probing with the vacuum hose stethoscope, be very careful not to come into contact with moving engine components such as the drivebelts, cooling fan, etc.*

Fuel hose

Warning: *There are certain precautions which must be taken when inspecting or servicing fuel system components. Work in a well ventilated area and do not allow open flames (cigarettes, appliance pilot lights, etc.) or bare light bulbs near the work area. Mop up any spills immediately and do not store fuel soaked rags where they could ignite.*

8 Check all rubber fuel lines for deterioration and chafing. Check especially for cracks in areas where the hose bends and just before fittings, such as where a hose attaches to the fuel filter.

9 High quality fuel line, designed specifically for fuel systems, must be used for fuel line replacement. On fuel-injected models, hose specifically designed for fuel-injection systems must be used. Never, under any circumstances, use unreinforced vacuum line, clear plastic tubing or water hose for fuel lines.

10 Spring-type clamps are commonly used on fuel lines. These clamps often lose their tension over a period of time, and can be "sprung" during removal. Replace all spring-type clamps with screw clamps whenever a hose is replaced.

Metal lines

11 Sections of metal line are often used for fuel line between certain components. Check carefully to be sure the line has not been bent or crimped and that cracks have not started in the line.

12 If a section of metal fuel line must be replaced, only seamless steel tubing should be used, since copper and aluminum tubing don't have the strength necessary to withstand normal engine vibration.

13 Check the metal brake lines where they enter the master cylinder and brake proportioning unit (if used) for cracks in the lines or loose fittings. Any sign of brake fluid leakage calls for an immediate thorough inspection of the brake system.

14 Cooling system check

Refer to illustration 14.4

1 Many major engine failures can be attributed to a faulty cooling system. If the vehicle is equipped with an automatic transmission, the cooling system also cools the transmission fluid and thus plays an important role in prolonging transmission life.

2 The cooling system should be checked with the engine cold. Do this before the vehicle is driven for the day or after the engine has been shut off for at least three hours.

3 Remove the radiator cap by turning it to the left until it reaches a stop. If you hear a hissing sound (indicating there is still pressure

Check for a chafed area that could fail prematurely.

Check for a soft area indicating the hose has deteriorated inside.

Overtightening the clamp on a hardened hose will damage the hose and cause a leak.

Check each hose for swelling and oil-soaked ends. Cracks and breaks can be located by squeezing the hose.

14.4 Hoses, like drivebelts, have a habit of failing at the worst possible time - to prevent the inconvenience of a blown radiator or heater hose, inspect them carefully

in the system), wait until it stops. Now press down on the cap with the palm of your hand and continue turning to the left until the cap can be removed. Thoroughly clean the cap, inside and out, with clean water. Also clean the filler neck on the radiator. All traces of corrosion should be removed. The coolant inside the radiator should be relatively transparent. If it's rust colored, the system should be drained and refilled (Section 31). If the coolant level isn't up to the top, add additional antifreeze/coolant mixture (see Section 4).

4 Carefully check the large upper and lower radiator hoses along with the smaller diameter heater hoses which run from the engine to the firewall. Inspect each hose along its entire length, replacing any hose which is cracked, swollen or shows signs of deterioration. Cracks may become more apparent if the hose is squeezed **(see illustration)**. Regardless of condition, it's a good idea to replace hoses with new ones every two years.

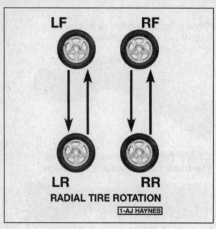

15.2 The recommended tire rotation pattern for these vehicles

16.5 You will find an inspection hole like this in each caliper - placing a ruler across the hole should enable you to determine the thickness of the remaining pad material for both inner and outer pads

16.12 The rear brake shoe lining thickness is measured from the outer surface of the lining to the metal shoe

5   Make sure that all hose connections are tight. A leak in the cooling system will usually show up as white or rust colored deposits on the areas adjoining the leak. If wire-type clamps are used at the ends of the hoses, it may be a good idea to replace them with more secure screw-type clamps.

6   Use compressed air or a soft brush to remove bugs, leaves, etc. from the front of the radiator or air conditioning condenser. Be careful not to damage the delicate cooling fins or cut yourself on them.

7   Every other inspection, or at the first indication of cooling system problems, have the cap and system pressure tested. If you don't have a pressure tester, most gas stations and repair shops will do this for a minimal charge.

15   Tire rotation

Refer to illustration 15.2

1   The tires should be rotated at the specified intervals and whenever uneven wear is noticed. Since the vehicle will be raised and the tires removed anyway, check the brakes (see Section 16) at this time.

2   Radial tires must be rotated in a specific pattern **(see illustration)**.

3   Refer to the information in *Jacking and towing* at the front of this manual for the proper procedures to follow when raising the vehicle and changing a tire. If the brakes are to be checked, do not apply the parking brake as stated. Make sure the tires are blocked to prevent the vehicle from rolling.

4   Preferably, the entire vehicle should be raised at the same time. This can be done on a hoist or by jacking up each corner and then lowering the vehicle onto jackstands placed under the frame rails. Always use four jackstands and make sure the vehicle is firmly supported.

5   After rotation, check and adjust the tire pressures as necessary and be sure to check the lug nut tightness.

6   For further information on the wheels and tires, refer to Chapter 10.

16   Brake check

Note: *For detailed photographs of the brake system, refer to Chapter 9.*

1   In addition to the specified intervals, the brakes should be inspected every time the wheels are removed or whenever a defect is suspected. Any of the following symptoms could indicate a potential brake system defect: The vehicle pulls to one side when the brake pedal is depressed; the brakes make squealing or dragging noises when applied; brake travel is excessive; the pedal pulsates; brake fluid leaks, usually onto the inside of the tire or wheel.

2   Loosen the wheel lug nuts.

3   Raise the vehicle and place it securely on jackstands.

4   Remove the wheels (see *Jacking and towing* at the front of this book, or your owner's manual, if necessary).

Disc brakes

Refer to illustration 16.5

5   There are two pads - an outer and an inner - in each caliper. The pads are visible through small inspection holes in each caliper **(see illustration)**.

6   Check the pad thickness by looking at each end of the caliper and through the inspection hole in the caliper body. If the lining material is less than the specified thickness, replace the pads. **Note:** *Keep in mind that the lining material is riveted or bonded to a metal backing plate and the metal portion is not included in this measurement.*

7   If it is difficult to determine the exact

thickness of the remaining pad material by the above method, or if you are at all concerned about the condition of the pads, remove the caliper(s), then remove the pads from the calipers for further inspection (refer to Chapter 9).

8   Once the pads are removed from the calipers, clean them with brake cleaner and re-measure them with a small steel pocket ruler or a vernier caliper.

9   Check the disc. Look for score marks, deep scratches and burned spots. If these conditions exist, the hub/disc assembly will have to be removed (see Chapter 9).

10   Before installing the wheels, check all brake lines and hoses for damage, wear, deformation, cracks, corrosion, leakage, bends and twists, particularly in the vicinity of the rubber hoses at the calipers. Check the clamps for tightness and the connections for leakage. Make sure that all hoses and lines are clear of sharp edges, moving parts and the exhaust system. If any of the above conditions are noted, repair, reroute or replace the lines and/or fittings as necessary (refer to Chapter 9).

Rear drum brakes

Refer to illustrations 16.12 and 16.14

11   Refer to Section 32 and remove the rear brake drums. **Warning:** *Brake dust produced by lining wear and deposited on brake components is hazardous to your health. DO NOT blow it out with compressed air and DO NOT inhale it! DO NOT use gasoline or solvents to remove the dust. Brake system cleaner should be used to flush the dust into a drain pan. After the brake components are wiped clean with a damp rag, dispose of the contaminated rag(s) and solvent in a covered and labeled container. Try to use non-asbestos replacement parts whenever possible.*

12   Note the thickness of the lining material on the rear brake shoes **(see illustration)** and

look for signs of contamination by brake fluid and grease. If the lining material has worn down to the minimum lining thickness listed in this Chapter's Specifications, replace the brake shoes with new ones. **Note:** *Some linings are bonded to the brake shoe; others are riveted. On riveted linings, measure from the tops of the rivet heads to the surface of the lining.* The shoes should also be replaced if they are cracked, glazed (shiny lining surfaces) or contaminated with brake fluid or grease. See Chapter 9 for the replacement procedure.

13   Check the shoe return and hold-down springs and the adjusting mechanism to make sure they're installed correctly and in good condition. Deteriorated or distorted springs, if not replaced, could allow the linings to drag and wear prematurely.

14   Check the wheel cylinders for leakage by carefully peeling back the rubber boots **(see illustration)**. If brake fluid is noted behind the boots, the wheel cylinders must be replaced (see Chapter 9).

15   Check the drums for cracks, score marks, deep scratches and hard spots, which will appear as small discolored areas. If imperfections cannot be removed with emery cloth, the drums must be resurfaced by an automotive machine shop (see Chapter 9 for more detailed information).

16   Refer to Chapter 9 and install the brake drums.

17   Install the wheels and lug nuts.

18   Remove the jackstands and lower the vehicle.

19   Tighten the wheel lug nuts to the torque listed in this Chapter's Specifications.

Parking brake

20   A simple method of checking the parking brake is to first park the vehicle on a level surface, and chock the wheels. Then fully release the parking brake lever, apply the brake pedal several times and release the brake pedal to establish correct shoe-to-rear brake drum clearance, then apply and release the parking brake lever several times to ensure that the self-adjust mechanism is fully adjusted. Grasp

16.14   Peel the wheel cylinder boot back carefully and check for leaking fluid, indicating the cylinder must be replaced or rebuilt

the parking brake handle and apply moderate force pulling upward to the fully applied position, counting the number of clicks heard from the ratchet mechanism. If adjustment is correct, there should be between 5 and 7 clicks to fully apply the parking brake (see Chapter 9). When finished checking the parking brake, leave the parking brake set and remove the wheel chocks.

21   Another method is to stop the vehicle on a steep hill, set the parking brake with the transmission in Neutral (be sure to stay in the vehicle for this test). If the parking brake cannot prevent the vehicle from rolling, the parking brake is in need of adjustment (see Chapter 9).

17   Air filter and PCV filter replacement

Carbureted models

Refer to illustrations 17.2, 17.4 and 17.7

Warning: *The electric cooling fan can activate at any time, even when the ignition is in*

17.2   The air filter cover is removed by releasing the clips on the sides and unscrewing the wing nut on the top (carbureted models)

the Off position. Disconnect the fan motor or negative battery cable when working in the vicinity of the fan.

1   At the specified intervals, the air filter and PCV filter (if equipped) should be replaced with new ones. The engine air cleaner also supplies filtered air to the PCV system.

2   The filter is located on top of the carburetor and is replaced by unscrewing the wing nut, detaching the clips from the top of the filter housing and lifting off the cover **(see illustration)**.

3   While the top plate is off, be careful not to drop anything down into the carburetor or air cleaner assembly.

4   Lift the air filter element out of the housing **(see illustration)** and wipe out the inside of the air cleaner housing with a clean rag.

5   Place the new filter in the air cleaner housing. Make sure it seats properly in the bottom of the housing.

6   The PCV filter is also located inside the air cleaner housing. Remove the top plate and air filter as previously described, then locate the PCV filter on the inside of the housing.

7   Remove the old filter **(see illustration)**.

17.4   Lift out the air filter element and wipe out the inside of the air cleaner housing with a clean rag

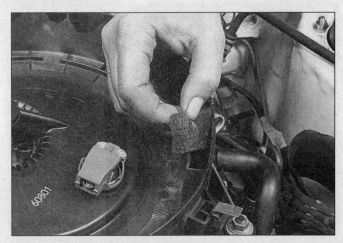

17.7   Removing the PCV filter (carbureted models)

17.13 On 1990 through 1994 fuel-injected models, the air filter is inside this drum-shaped housing - release the clips to remove the filter

17.14a On 1995 through 1999 fuel-injected models, remove the air cleaner housing cover by removing the cover screws and lifting up on the cover to expose the filter element

8   Install the new PCV filter and the new air filter.

9   Install the top plate and any hoses which were disconnected. Don't overtighten the wing nut.

Fuel-injected models

Refer to illustrations 17.13, 17.14a, 17.14b and 17.14c

Caution: Use care when removing the air filter cover, since it contains the airflow sensor (which can be damaged easily).

10   At the specified intervals, the air filter element should be replaced with a new one.

11   The air filter housing is attached to the right-hand inner fender panel; loosen the air intake hose clamp screw and disconnect the hose from the air filter cover on 1994 and earlier models.

12   Unplug the electrical connector from the airflow sensor.

13   Release the clips and remove the air filter cover on 1994 and earlier models, then lift

the air filter element out of the housing and wipe out the housing with a clean rag (see illustration).

14   On 1995 and later models, remove the housing cover screws or clips and lift out the filter (see illustrations).

15   Place the new filter element in the housing. Make sure it seats properly in the housing.

16   Install the cover and secure. Install the air intake hose and tighten the hose clamp screw securely. Plug in the electrical connector.

18   Throttle position sensor check (carbureted models)

Refer to illustrations 18.3 and 18.4

1   The throttle position sensor and linkage must work properly or vehicle driveability will be affected.

2   Have an assistant open and close the

throttle while you watch the sensor and linkage.

3   On 1986 and 1987 models, the cam-shaped actuator must move smoothly throughout its arc, progressively depressing and releasing the throttle position sensor (see illustration).

4   On 1988 and later models, check the lever for smooth operation and make sure the two retaining screws are tight (see illustration).

5   If the linkage or the sensor bind, refer to Chapter 4 for more information on the throttle position sensor.

19   Valve clearance check and adjustment (1986 through 1994 SOHC models)

Refer to illustrations 19.5, 19.7 and 19.12

Warning: The electric cooling fan can activate at any time, even when the ignition is in

17.14b On 2000 and later models, remove the air filter housing cover by flipping open these four clips

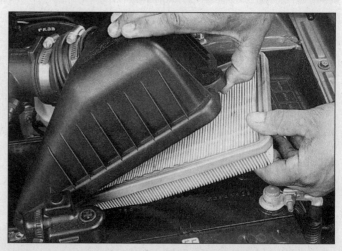

17.14c Pull out the air cleaner while lifting the filter housing cover

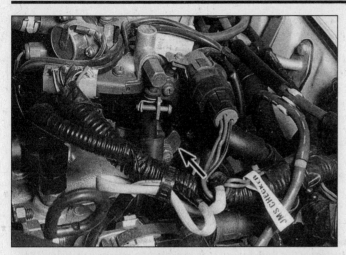

18.3 On 1986 and 1987 models, the cam-shaped actuator on the left side of the carburetor (arrow) must move smoothly through its arc and press progressively on the throttle position sensor, located directly to the rear of the actuator

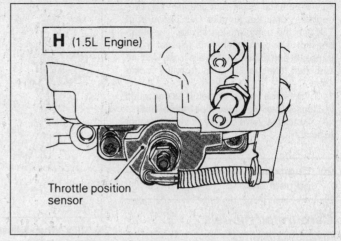

18.4 On 1988 and later models, check the lever for smooth operation and make sure the two retaining screws are tight

the Off position. Disconnect the fan motor or negative battery cable when working in the vicinity of the fan.

1   The valve clearances are checked and adjusted with the engine at normal operating temperature.

2   Remove the air cleaner assembly (see Chapter 4).

3   Remove the valve cover (see Chapter 2).

4   Place the number one piston at Top Dead Center (TDC) on the compression stroke (see Chapter 2A). The number one cylinder rocker arms (closest to the timing belt end of the engine) should be loose (able to move up and down slightly) and the camshaft lobes should be facing away from the rocker arms.

5   With the crankshaft in this position, the valves labeled A (plus the jet valves adjacent to the intake valves) can be checked and adjusted **(see illustration)**. Always check and adjust the jet valve clearance first.

6   The intake valve and jet valve adjust-

ing screws are located on a common rocker arm. Make sure the intake valve adjusting screw has been backed off two full turns, then loosen the locknut on the jet valve adjusting screw.

7   On models so equipped, turn the jet valve adjusting screw counterclockwise and insert the appropriate size feeler gauge between the valve stem and the adjusting screw. Carefully tighten the adjusting screw until you can feel a slight drag on the feeler gauge as you withdraw it from between the stem and adjusting screw **(see illustration)**.

8   On models so equipped, use special care not to force the jet valve open, since the jet valve spring is relatively weak. Be particularly careful if the adjusting screw is hard to turn. Hold the adjusting screw with a screwdriver (to keep it from turning) and tighten the locknut. Recheck the clearance to make sure it hasn't changed.

9   Next, check and adjust the intake valve

clearance. Insert the appropriate size feeler gauge between the intake valve stem and the adjusting screw. Carefully tighten the adjusting screw until you can feel a slight drag on the feeler gauge as you withdraw it from between the stem and adjusting screw.

10   Hold the adjusting screw with a screwdriver (to keep it from turning) and tighten the locknut. Recheck the clearance to make sure it hasn't changed.

11   Loosen the locknut on the exhaust valve adjusting screw. Turn the adjusting screw counterclockwise and insert the appropriate size feeler gauge between the valve stem and the adjusting screw. Carefully tighten the adjusting screw until you can feel a slight drag on the feeler gauge as you withdraw it from between the stem and adjusting screw.

12   Hold the adjusting screw with a screwdriver (to keep it from turning) and tighten the locknut **(see illustration)**. Recheck the clearance to make sure it hasn't changed.

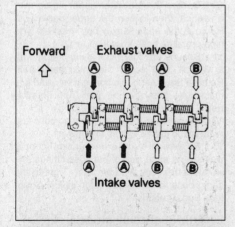

19.5 With the number one piston at Top Dead Center (TDC), adjust the valves marked (A) - with the number four piston at TDC, adjust the valves marked (B)

19.7 There should be a slight drag as the feeler gauge is pulled between the valve adjustment screw and the valve stem

19.12 To make sure the adjusting screw doesn't move when the locknut is tightened, use a box-end wrench and have a good grip on the screwdriver

13   Rotate the crankshaft one full turn (360-degrees) until the number four piston is at TDC on the compression stroke. The number four cylinder rocker arms (closest to the transaxle end of the engine) are loose with the camshaft lobes facing away from the rocker arms.
14   Adjust the valves labeled B as described in Steps 4 through 8 (see illustration 19.5).
15   Install the valve cover and the air cleaner assembly.

20   Engine idle speed check and adjustment

Carbureted models

Refer to illustration 20.8

1   Engine idle speed is the speed at which the engine operates when no accelerator pedal pressure is applied, as when stopped at a traffic light. This speed is critical to the performance of the engine itself, as well as many engine subsystems.
2   Set the parking brake firmly and block the wheels to prevent the vehicle from rolling. Put the transaxle in Neutral.
3   Connect a hand held tachometer.
4   Start the engine and allow it to reach normal operating temperature.
5   Check, and adjust if necessary, the ignition timing (see Section 37).
6   Allow the engine to idle for two minutes.
7   Check the engine idle speed on the tachometer and compare it to the value listed in this Chapters Specifications. **Note:** *If the Emission Control Information label indicates a different idle speed than that listed in this Chapter's Specifications, use the specification on the label.*
8   If the idle speed is too low or too high, turn the speed adjusting screw (SAS 1) **(see illustration)** until the specified idle speed is obtained. Turn only the SAS 1 screw, as the other adjustment screws are preset at the factory and require special equipment for proper adjustment.

21.2 On carbureted models, unsnap the fuel filter from the clip and pull it out for better access to the hoses

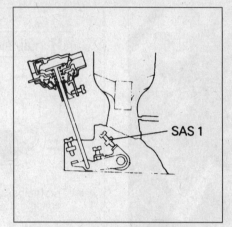

20.8 When adjusting the engine idle speed, make sure to turn only the SAS 1 screw - the other screws are preset at the factory and require special equipment for proper adjustment

Fuel-injected models

9   The engine idle speed on fuel-injected models requires several pieces of calibrated test equipment; therefore, the adjustment should be made by a dealer service department or qualified automotive repair facility.

21   Fuel filter replacement

Warning: *Gasoline is extremely flammable, so take extra precautions when you work on any part of the fuel system. Don't smoke or allow open flames or bare light bulbs near the work area, and don't work in a garage where a gas-type appliance (such as a water heater or a clothes dryer) is present. Since gasoline is carcinogenic, wear latex gloves when there's a possibility of being exposed to fuel, and, if you spill any fuel on your skin, rinse it off immediately with soap and water. Mop up any spills immediately and do not store fuel-soaked rags where they could ignite. The fuel system on fuel-injected models is under constant pressure, so, if any fuel lines are to be disconnected, the fuel pressure in the system must be relieved first (see Chapter 4). When you perform any kind of work on the fuel system, wear safety glasses and have a Class B type fire extinguisher on hand.*

Carbureted models

Refer to illustrations 21.1 and 21.2

1   The fuel filter is located on the firewall, near the emissions canister **(see illustration)**.
2   For easier access, pull the filter out of the spring clip so both fittings can be reached **(see illustration)**.
3   Release the hose clamps at the filter fittings and slide them back up the hoses.
4   Disconnect the hoses and remove the filter. Now would be a good time to replace the hoses if they're deteriorated.

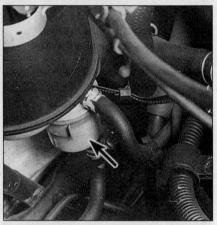

21.1 On carbureted models, the fuel filter is mounted on the firewall, below the evaporative mission system canister

5   Push the hoses onto the new filter and position the clamps approximately 1/4-inch back from the ends.
6   Push the filter back into the spring clip. Check to make sure it is held securely and the hoses are not kinked.
7   Start the engine and check for fuel leaks at the filter.

Fuel-injected models
1990 through 1999 models

Refer to illustration 21.11

Warning: *Fuel pressure must be released prior to disconnecting any component of the fuel injection system to prevent pressurized fuel from being sprayed when the lines are disconnected (see Chapter 4).*

8   The fuel filter is located on the firewall, next to the air filter inlet hose.
9   Relieve the fuel pressure (see Chapter 4). Place a rag over the top hose connection of the fuel filter to prevent fuel from splashing out when the upper fitting is loosened.
10   Secure the fuel filter upper fitting with a wrench, then loosen the upper banjo bolt. Remove the upper banjo bolt, gaskets and high-pressure hose from the fuel filter.
11   Secure the fuel filter lower fitting with a wrench, then loosen the lower banjo bolt. Remove the lower banjo bolt, gaskets and fuel main hose from the fuel filter **(see illustration)**.
12   Remove the fuel filter mounting bolts and remove the fuel filter from the firewall.
13   Be sure to install a new gasket (copper washer) on each side of the hose fittings and install both hoses onto the filter. Tighten the banjo bolts to the torque listed in this Chapter's Specifications.

2000 through 2002 models

14   Relieve the fuel system pressure (see Chapter 4).
15   Disconnect the cable from the negative battery terminal (see Chapter 5).

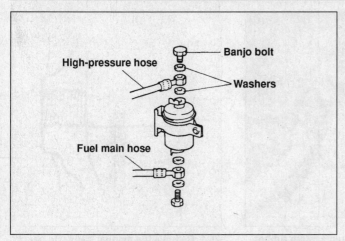

21.11 Fuel filter installation details (1990 through 1999 fuel injected models)

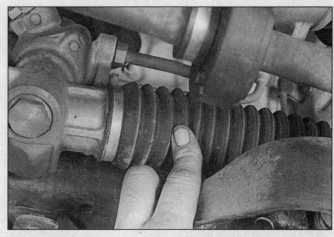

23.6 Push on the steering gear boots to check for cracks and lubricant leaks

16   Remove the back seat cushion (see Chapter 11).

17   Remove the access panel from the floor.

18   Place shop rags under both ends of the fuel filter and disconnect the fuel line fittings from the filter. Put a wrench on the hex on each end of the fuel filter to hold the filter so that you can break loose each fuel line banjo bolt. Discard the old sealing washers.

19   Remove the upper part of the fuel filter clamp and remove the fuel filter from the lower part of the clamp.

20   Installation is the reverse of removal. Be sure to use new sealing washers and tighten the fuel supply line banjo bolts to the torque listed in this Chapter's Specifications.

2003 and later models

21   The fuel filter is an integral component of the fuel pump/fuel level sending unit module, which is located inside the fuel tank. Although the manufacturer specifies that the filter be changed every 52,500 miles, in-tank filters are virtually trouble-free and rarely need to be changed. If you own one of these models, we recommend that you consult your dealer for guidance before changing this filter, because it will mean changing the fuel pump/fuel level sending unit module.

---

22   Fuel system check

Warning: *Certain precautions should be observed when inspecting or servicing the fuel system components. See the* **Warning** *in Section 21.*

1   If you smell gasoline while driving, after refueling or after the vehicle has been sitting in the sun, inspect the fuel system immediately.

2   Remove the gas filler cap and inspect if for damage and corrosion. The gasket should have an unbroken sealing imprint. If the gasket is damaged or corroded, replace the cap.

3   Inspect the fuel feed and return lines for cracks. Check the metal fuel line connections to make sure they are tight.

4   Since some components of the fuel system - the fuel tank and part of the fuel feed and return lines, for example - are underneath the vehicle, they can be inspected more easily with the vehicle raised on a hoist. If that's not possible, raise the vehicle and secure it on jackstands.

5   With the vehicle raised and safely supported, inspect the gas tank and filler neck for punctures, cracks and other damage. The connection between the filler neck and the tank is particularly critical. Sometimes a rubber filler neck will leak because of loose clamps or deteriorated rubber. These are problems a home mechanic can usually rectify. **Warning:** *Do not, under any circumstances, try to repair a fuel tank (except rubber components). A welding torch or any open flame can easily cause fuel vapors inside the tank to explode.*

6   Carefully check all rubber hoses and metal lines leading away from the fuel tank. Check for loose connections, deteriorated hoses, crimped lines and other damage. Carefully inspect the lines from the tank to the carburetor or fuel rail. Repair or replace damaged sections as necessary.

---

23   Steering and suspension check

Note: *For detailed illustrations of the steering and suspension components, refer to Chapter 10.*

With the wheels on the ground

1   With the vehicle stopped and the front wheels pointed straight ahead, rock the steering wheel gently back and forth. If freeplay is excessive, a front wheel bearing, main shaft yoke, intermediate shaft yoke, lower arm balljoint or steering system joint is worn or the steering gear is out of adjustment or worn out. Refer to Chapter 10 for the appropriate repair procedure.

2   Other symptoms, such as excessive vehicle body movement over rough roads, swaying (leaning) around corners and binding as the steering wheel is turned, may indicate faulty steering and/or suspension components.

3   Check the shock absorbers by pushing down and releasing the vehicle several times at each corner. If the vehicle does not come back to a level position within one or two bounces, the shocks/struts are worn and must be replaced. When bouncing the vehicle up and down, listen for squeaks and noises from the suspension components. Additional information on suspension components can be found in Chapter 10.

With the vehicle raised

Refer to illustration 23.6

4   Raise the vehicle and support it securely on jackstands. See *Jacking and towing* at the front of this book for the proper jacking points.

5   Check the tires for irregular wear patterns and proper inflation (see Section 5).

6   Inspect the universal joint between the steering shaft and the steering gear housing. Check the steering gear housing for grease leakage or oozing. Make sure that the dust seals and boots are not damaged and that the boot clamps are not loose **(see illustration)**. Check the steering linkage for looseness or damage. Check the tie-rod ends for excessive play. Look for loose bolts, broken or disconnected parts and deteriorated rubber bushings on all suspension and steering components. While an assistant turns the steering wheel from side to side, check the steering components for free movement, chafing and binding. If the steering components do not seem to be reacting with the movement of the steering wheel, try to determine where the slack is located.

7   Inspect the balljoint boots for damage and leaking grease. Replace the boots with new ones if they are damaged (see Chapter 10).

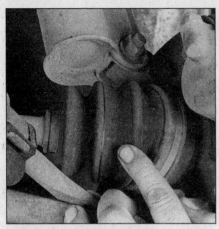

24.2 Flex the driveaxle boots by hand to check for cracks or leaking grease

25.2 Check the exhaust system rubber hangers for cracks and deterioration - replace any that are in poor condition

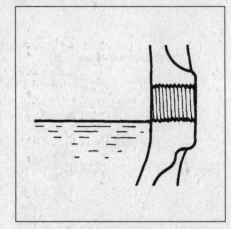

26.1 Remove the manual transaxle check/ fill plug - the oil level must be at the lower edge of the hole

24   Driveaxle boot check

Refer to illustration 24.2

1   The driveaxle boots are very important because they prevent dirt, water and foreign material from entering and damaging the constant velocity (CV) joints. External oil and grease can cause the boot material to deteriorate prematurely, so it's a good idea to wash the boots with soap and water.

2   Inspect the boots for tears and cracks as well as loose clamps **(see illustration)**. If there is any evidence of cracks or leaking lubricant, they must be replaced as described in Chapter 8.

25   Exhaust system check

Refer to illustration 25.2

1   With the engine cold (at least three hours after the vehicle has been driven), check the complete exhaust system from its starting point at the engine to the end of the tailpipe. This should be done on a hoist where unrestricted access is available, or with the vehicle raised on jackstands.

2   Check the pipes and connections for evidence of leaks, severe corrosion or damage. Make sure that all brackets and hangers are in good condition and tight **(see illustration)**.

3   At the same time, inspect the underside of the body for any holes, corrosion, open seams, etc. which may allow exhaust gases to enter the passenger compartment. Seal all body openings with silicone or body putty.

4   Rattles and other noises can often be traced to the exhaust system, especially the mounts and hangers. Try to move the pipes, muffler and catalytic converter. If the components can come in contact with the body or suspension parts, secure the exhaust system with new mounts.

5   Check the running condition of the engine by inspecting inside the end of the tail-

pipe. The exhaust deposits here are an indication of engine state-of-tune. If the pipe is black and sooty or coated with white deposits, the engine is in need of a tune-up, including a thorough fuel system inspection and adjustment.

26   Manual transaxle lubricant level check

Refer to illustration 26.1

1   The manual transaxle does not have a dipstick. To check the lubricant level, raise the vehicle and support it securely on jackstands. On the lower right front of the transaxle housing, you will see a plug. Remove it. If the lubricant level is correct, it should be up to the lower edge of the hole **(see illustration)**.

2   If the transaxle needs more lubricant (if the level is not up to the hole), use a syringe to add more. Stop filling the transaxle when the lubricant begins to run out the hole.

3   Install the plug and tighten it securely. Drive the vehicle a short distance, then check for leaks.

27   Spark plug replacement

Refer to illustrations 27.1, 27.4a, 27.4b, 27.6, 27.8 and 27.10

1   Spark plug replacement requires a spark plug socket which fits onto a ratchet wrench. This socket is lined with a rubber grommet to protect the porcelain insulator of the spark plug and to hold the plug while you insert it into the spark plug hole. You will also need a wire-type feeler gauge to check and adjust the spark plug gap and a torque wrench to tighten the new plugs to the specified torque **(see illustration)**.

2   When replacing the plugs, purchase the new plugs in advance, adjust them to the proper gap and then replace each plug one at a time. **Note:** *When buying new spark*

plugs, it's essential that you obtain the correct plugs for your specific vehicle. This information can be found on the Vehicle Emissions Control Information (VECI) label located on the underside of the hood or in the owner's manual. If these two sources specify different plugs, purchase the spark plug type specified on the VECI label because that information is provided specifically for your engine.

3   Inspect each of the new plugs for defects. If there are any signs of cracks in the porcelain insulator of a plug, don't use it.

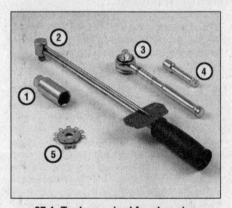

27.1 Tools required for changing spark plugs

1   *Spark plug socket - This will have a rubber grommet inside to protect the spark plug porcelain insulator*

2   *Torque wrench - Although not mandatory, use of this tool is the best way to ensure that the plugs are tightened properly*

3   *Ratchet - Standard hand tool to fit the plug socket*

4   *Extension - Depending on model and accessories, you may need special extensions and universal joints to reach one or more of the plugs*

5   *Wire-type feeler gauge - This gauge for checking the gap comes in a variety of styles. Make sure the gap for your engine is included*

27.4a Spark plug manufacturers recommend using a wire-type gauge when checking the gap - if the wire does not slide between the electrodes with a slight drag, adjustment is required

27.4b To change the gap, bend the side electrode only, as indicated by the arrows, and be very careful not to crack or chip the porcelain insulator surrounding the center electrode

4   Check the electrode gaps of the new plugs. Check the gap by inserting the wire gauge of the proper thickness between the electrodes at the tip of the plug **(see illustration)**. The gap between the electrodes should be identical to that specified on the VECI label. If the gap is incorrect, use the notched adjuster on the feeler gauge body to bend the curved side electrode slightly **(see illustration)**.

5   If the side electrode is not exactly over the center electrode, use the notched adjuster to align them. **Caution:** *If the gap of a new plug must be adjusted, bend only the base of the ground electrode - do not touch the tip.*

6   To prevent the possibility of mixing up spark plug wires on 1986 through 2005 models, work on one spark plug at a time. Remove the wire and boot from one spark plug. Grasp the boot - not the cable - give it a half twisting motion and pull it off **(see illustration)**.

7   On 2006 and later models, remove the ignition coils (see Chapter 5).

8   If compressed air is available, blow any dirt or foreign material away from the spark plug area before proceeding. Remove the spark plug **(see illustration)**.

9   Compare each old spark plug with those shown on the inside back cover of this manual to determine the overall running condition of the engine.

10   It's often difficult to insert spark plugs into their holes without cross-threading them. To avoid this possibility, fit a short piece of rubber hose over the end of the spark plug **(see illustration)**. The flexible hose acts as a universal joint to help align the plug with the plug hole. Should the plug begin to cross-thread, the hose will slip on the spark plug, preventing thread damage. Tighten the plug securely.

11   Attach the plug wire to the new spark plug, again using a twisting motion on the boot until it is firmly seated on the end of the spark plug.

12   Follow the above procedure for the remaining spark plugs, replacing them one at a time to prevent mixing up the spark plug wires.

28 Spark plug wire, distributor cap and rotor check and replacement

Refer to illustrations 28.11a, 28.11b and 28.12

1   On 1986 through 2005 models, the spark plug wires should be checked whenever new spark plugs are installed.

2   Begin this procedure by making a visual check of the spark plug wires while the engine is running. In a darkened garage (make sure there is ventilation) start the engine and observe each plug wire. Be careful not to come into contact with any moving engine

27.6 When removing the spark plug wires, pull only on the boot and use a twisting/pulling motion

TWIST AND PULL

27.8 To remove the spark plugs on DOHC models, you'll need a long extension

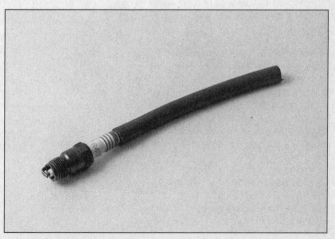

27.10 A length of rubber hose will save time and prevent damaged threads when installing the spark plugs

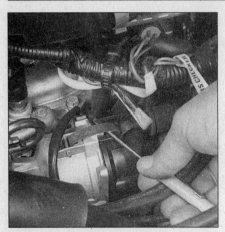

28.11a Use a small screwdriver to pry off the distributor cap retaining clips (1994 and earlier models)

parts. If there is a break in the wire, you will see arcing or a small spark at the damaged area. If arcing is noticed, make a note to obtain new wires, then allow the engine to cool and check the distributor cap and rotor.

3   The spark plug wires should be inspected one at a time to prevent mixing up the order, which is essential for proper engine operation. Each original plug wire should be numbered to help identify its location. If the number is illegible, a piece of tape can be marked with the correct number and wrapped around the plug wire.

4   Disconnect the plug wire from the spark plug. A removal tool can be used for this purpose or you can grasp the rubber boot, twist the boot half a turn and pull the boot free. Do not pull on the wire itself **(see illustration 27.6)**.

5   Check inside the boot for corrosion, which will look like a white crusty powder.

6   Push the wire and boot back onto the

end of the spark plug. It should fit tightly onto the end of the plug. If it doesn't, remove the wire and use pliers to carefully crimp the metal connector inside the wire boot until the fit is snug.

7   Using a clean rag, wipe the entire length of the wire to remove built-up dirt and grease. Once the wire is clean, check for burns, cracks and other damage. Do not bend the wire sharply, because the conductor within the wire might break.

8   Disconnect the wire from the distributor or ignition coil. Again, pull only on the rubber boot. Check for corrosion and a tight fit. Press the wire back into the distributor or ignition coil.

9   Inspect the remaining spark plug wires, making sure that each one is securely fastened at the distributor and spark plug when the check is complete.

10   If new spark plug wires are required, purchase a pre-cut wire set with the boots installed for your specific engine model. Remove and replace the wires one at a time to avoid mix-ups in the firing order.

11   On 1994 and earlier models, detach the distributor cap by prying off the two cap retaining clips **(see illustration)**. Look inside it for cracks, carbon tracks and worn, burned or loose contacts **(see illustration)**.

12   Pull the rotor off the distributor shaft and examine it for cracks and carbon tracks **(see illustration)**. Replace the cap and rotor if any damage or defects are noted.

13   It is common practice to install a new cap and rotor whenever new spark plug wires are installed, but if you wish to continue using the old cap, clean the terminals first.

14   When installing a new cap, remove the wires from the old cap one at a time and attach them to the new cap in the exact same location - do not simultaneously remove all the wires from the old cap or firing order mix-ups may occur.

29   Carburetor choke check

Refer to illustration 29.3

Warning: *The electric cooling fan can activate at any time, even when the ignition is in the Off position. Disconnect the fan motor or negative battery cable when working in the vicinity of the fan.*

1   The choke operates only when the engine is cold, so this check should be performed before the engine has been started for the day.

2   Take off the top plate of the air cleaner assembly. It's held in place by a wing nut at the top and clips on the side. If any vacuum hoses must be disconnected, make sure you tag the hoses for reinstallation in their original positions. Place the top plate and wing nut aside, out of the way of moving engine components.

3   Look at the center of the air cleaner housing. You will notice a flat plate at the carburetor opening **(see illustration)**.

4   Press the accelerator pedal to the floor. The plate should close completely. Start the engine while you watch the plate at the carburetor. Don't position your face near the carburetor, as the engine could backfire, causing serious burns. When the engine starts, the choke plate should open slightly.

5   Allow the engine to continue running at an idle speed. As the engine warms up to operating temperature, the plate should slowly open, allowing more air to enter through the top of the carburetor.

6   After a few minutes, the choke plate should be fully open to the vertical position. Snap the throttle to make sure the fast idle cam disengages.

7   You'll notice that the engine speed corresponds with the plate opening. With the plate fully closed, the engine should run at a fast idle speed. As the plate opens and the throttle

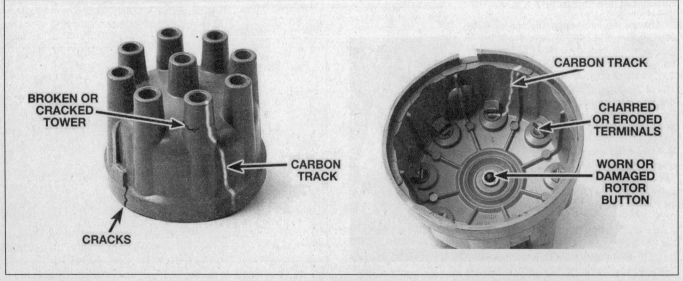

28.11b Some common defects to look for when inspecting the distributor cap (if in doubt about its condition, install a new one)

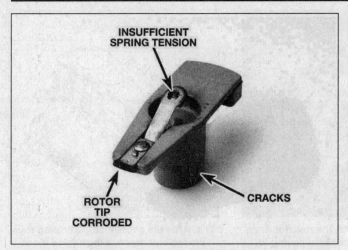

28.12 The ignition rotor on 1986 through 1989 models should be checked for wear and corrosion as indicated here (if in doubt about its condition, buy a new one)

29.3 The choke plate is located in the carburetor throat

is moved to disengage the fast idle cam, the engine speed will decrease.

8   Refer to Chapter 4 for specific information on adjusting and servicing the choke components.

30 Thermostatically controlled air cleaner check (carbureted models)

Refer to illustration 30.3

Warning: *The electric cooling fan can activate at any time, even when the ignition is in the Off position. Disconnect the fan motor or negative battery cable when working in the vicinity of the fan.*

1   All engines are equipped with a thermostatically controlled air cleaner which draws air to the carburetor from different locations, depending on engine temperature.

2   This is a visual check, requiring the use of a small mirror.

3   When the engine is cold, locate the air control valve inside the air cleaner assembly. It's inside the long snorkel of the air cleaner housing **(see illustration)**.

4   There is a flexible air duct attached to the end of the snorkel, leading to an area behind the headlight. Disconnect it at the snorkel. This will enable you to look through the end of the snorkel and see the air control valve inside.

5   Start the engine and look through the snorkel at the valve, which should move up to block off the air cleaner snorkel. With the valve closed, air cannot enter through the end of the snorkel, but instead enters the air cleaner through the flexible duct attached to the exhaust manifold and the heat stove passage.

6   As the engine warms up to operating temperature, the valve should move down to allow air to be drawn through the snorkel end. Depending on outside temperature, this may

take 10-to-15 minutes. To speed up this check you can reconnect the snorkel air duct, drive the vehicle, then check to see if the valve is completely open.

7   If the thermostatically controlled air cleaner isn't operating properly, see Chapter 6 for more information.

31 Cooling system servicing (draining, flushing and refilling)

Warning: *Antifreeze is a corrosive and poisonous solution, so be careful not to spill any of the coolant mixture on the vehicle's paint or your skin. If this happens, rinse immediately with plenty of clean water. Consult local authorities regarding proper disposal procedures for antifreeze before draining the cooling system. In many areas, reclamation centers have been established to collect used oil and coolant mixtures. The electric cooling fan can activate at any time, even when the ignition is in the Off position. Disconnect the fan*

motor or negative battery cable when working in the vicinity of the fan.

1   Periodically, the cooling system should be drained, flushed and refilled to replenish the antifreeze mixture and prevent formation of rust and corrosion, which can impair the performance of the cooling system and cause engine damage. When the cooling system is serviced, all hoses and the radiator cap should be checked and replaced if necessary.

Draining

Refer to illustrations 31.4a, 31.4b and 31.5

Warning: *Wait until the engine is completely cool before beginning this procedure.*

2   Apply the parking brake and block the wheels. If the vehicle has just been driven, wait several hours to allow the engine to cool down before beginning this procedure.

3   Once the engine is completely cool, remove the radiator cap.

4   Remove the splash cover located beneath the radiator. Then move a large container under the radiator drain to catch the

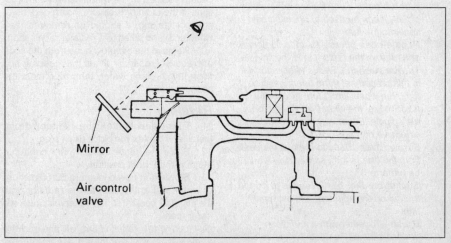

30.3 Use a mirror to observe movement of the air control valve

31.4a On most models you will have to remove a cover for access to the radiator drain fitting located at the bottom of the radiator - before opening the valve, push a short section of rubber hose onto the fitting to prevent the coolant from splashing as it drains

31.4b On later models, the radiator drain plug is accessible without having to remove any covers (2006 model shown)

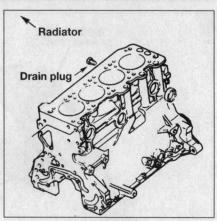

31.5 After the coolant stops flowing from the radiator, remove the engine block coolant drain plug and allow the coolant to drain from the engine block (typical)

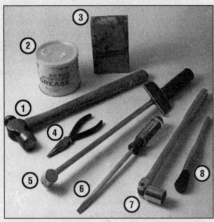

32.1 Tools and materials needed for rear wheel bearing maintenance

1   **Hammer** - A common hammer will do just fine
2   **Grease** - Grease which is formulated specially for wheel bearings should be used
3   **Wood block** - If you have a scrap piece of 2x4, it can be used to drive the new seal into the hub
4   **Needle-nose pliers** - Used to straighten and remove the cotter pin in the spindle
5   **Torque wrench** - This is very important in this procedure; if the bearing is too tight, the wheel won't turn freely - if it is too loose, the wheel will wobble on the spindle. Either way, it could mean extensive damage
6   **Screwdriver** - Used to remove the seal from the hub (a long screwdriver would be preferred)
7   **Socket/breaker bar** - Needed to loosen the nut on the spindle if it is extremely tight
8   **Brush** - Together with some clean solvent, this will be used to remove old grease from the hub and spindle

coolant. Attach a 3/8-inch inner diameter hose to the drain fitting to direct the coolant into the container (some models are already equipped with a hose), then open the drain fitting (a pair of pliers may be required to turn it) **(see illustrations)**.
5   After the coolant stops flowing out of the radiator, move the container under the engine block drain plug **(see illustration)**. Loosen the plug and allow the coolant in the block to drain.
6   While the coolant is draining, check the condition of the radiator hoses, heater hoses and clamps (refer to Section 14 if necessary).
7   Replace any damaged clamps or hoses.

Flushing

8   Once the system is completely drained, flush the radiator with fresh water from a garden hose until water runs clear at the drain. The flushing action of the water will remove sediments from the radiator but will not remove rust and scale from the engine and cooling tube surfaces.
9   These deposits can be removed by the chemical action of a cleaner. Follow the procedure outlined in the manufacturer's instructions. If the radiator is severely corroded, damaged or leaking, it should be removed (see Chapter 3) and taken to a radiator repair shop.
10   Remove the overflow hose from the coolant recovery reservoir. Drain the reservoir and flush it with clean water, then reconnect the hose.

Refilling

11   Close and tighten the radiator drain. Install and tighten the block drain plug.
12   Place the heater temperature control in the maximum heat position.
13   Slowly add new coolant (a 50/50 mixture of water and antifreeze) to the radiator until it's full. Add coolant to the reservoir up to the lower mark.
14   Leave the radiator cap off and run the engine in a well-ventilated area until the thermostat opens (coolant will begin flowing

through the radiator and the upper radiator hose will become hot).
15   Turn the engine off and let it cool. Add more coolant mixture to bring the level back up to the lip on the radiator filler neck.
16   Squeeze the upper radiator hose to expel air, then add more coolant mixture if necessary. Replace the radiator cap.
17   Start the engine, allow it to reach normal operating temperature and check for leaks.

32 Rear wheel bearing check, repack and adjustment (1994 and earlier models)

Note: *This procedure applies only to 1994 and earlier models - 1995 and later models use sealed bearings (see Chapter 10).*

Check

Refer to illustration 32.1

1   In most cases the rear wheel bearings will not need servicing until the brake shoes are changed. However, the bearings should be checked whenever the rear of the vehicle is raised for any reason. Several items, including a torque wrench and special grease, are required for this procedure **(see illustration)**.
2   With the vehicle securely supported on jackstands, spin each wheel and check for noise, rolling resistance and freeplay.
3   Grasp the top of each tire with one hand and the bottom with the other. Move the wheel in-and-out on the spindle. If there's any noticeable movement, the bearings should be checked and then repacked with grease or replaced if necessary.

Repack

Refer to illustrations 32.6, 32.7a, 32.7b, 32.8, 32.9, 32.11 and 32.15

4   Remove the wheel.
5   If necessary, back off the parking brake adjuster (Chapter 9).

32.6 Pry the dust cap out of the hub

32.7a Wire cutters are useful for pulling the cotter pin out

32.7b Remove the nut lock from the spindle nut

6   Pry the dust cap out of the drum/hub assembly using a screwdriver or hammer and chisel **(see illustration)**.

7   On models with a castellated spindle nut, straighten the bent ends of the cotter pin, then pull the cotter pin out of the nut lock then discard the cotter pin and use a new one during reassembly; remove the nut lock **(see illustrations)**. **Note:** *If no cotter pin is present, the vehicle is equipped with a self-locking nut. Obtain a new nut for reassembly.*

8   Remove the spindle nut and washer from the end of the spindle **(see illustration)**.

9   Pull the drum/hub assembly out slightly, then push it back into its original position; this should force the outer bearing off the spindle enough so it can be removed **(see illustration)**.

10   Pull the drum/hub off the spindle.

11   Use a seal puller or screwdriver to pry the seal out of the rear of the drum/hub **(see illustration)**. As this is done, note how the seal is installed.

12   Remove the inner wheel bearing from the drum/hub.

13   With the bearings removed, use solvent

to remove all traces of the old grease from the bearings, hub and spindle. A small brush may prove helpful; however make sure no bristles from the brush embed themselves inside the bearing rollers. Allow the parts to air dry.

14   Carefully inspect the bearings for cracks, heat discoloration, worn rollers, etc. Check the bearing races inside the hub for wear and damage. If the bearing races are defective, the hubs should be taken to a machine shop with the facilities to remove the old races and press new ones in. Note that the bearings and races come as matched sets and old bearings should never be installed on new races.

15   Use wheel bearing grease to pack the bearings. Work the grease completely into the bearings, forcing it between the rollers, cone and cage from the back side **(see illustration)**.

16   Apply a thin coat of grease to the spindle at the outer bearing seat, inner bearing seat, shoulder and seal seat.

17   Put a small quantity of grease inboard of each bearing race inside the hub. Using your finger, form a dam at these points to provide extra grease availability and to keep thinned

32.8 Remove the washer with a small screwdriver (the spindle nut has been removed in this illustration)

grease from flowing out of the bearing.

18   Place the grease-packed inner bearing into the rear of the drum/hub and put a little more grease outboard of the bearing.

32.9 Remove the outer wheel bearing after pulling the drum/hub out slightly to dislodge it

32.11 Pry the seal out of the hub with a screwdriver or hooked seal puller such as this one (available at auto parts stores)

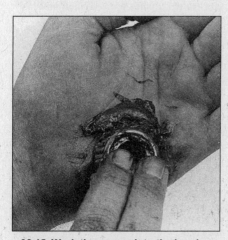

32.15 Work the grease into the bearing rollers from the back side of the bearing race

32.27 Tap the grease cap into place with a large punch and a hammer, working around the outer circumference

34.7a Use a box-end wrench to remove the automatic transaxle drain plug without rounding it off (early models)

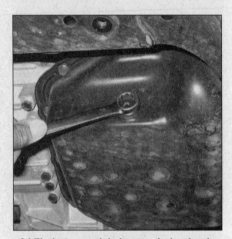

34.7b Later models have a drain plug in the fluid pan

19   Place a new seal over the inner bearing and tap the seal evenly into place with a hammer and block of wood until it is flush with the hub.

20   Carefully place the drum/hub assembly onto the spindle and push the grease-packed outer bearing into position.

Adjustment

Refer to illustration 32.27

Note: *The adjustment procedure applies to a castellated nut only, if equipped with a self-locking nut, install a new nut and tighten it to the torque listed in this Chapter's Specifications, then proceed to Step 27.*

21   Install the washer and spindle nut. Tighten the nut only slightly (no more than 15 ft-lbs of torque).

22   Spin the drum/hub in a forward direction to seat the bearings and remove any grease or burrs which could cause excessive bearing play later.

23   Check to see that the tightness of the spindle nut is still approximately 15 ft-lbs.

24   Loosen the spindle nut until it is just

loose, and no more.

25   Tighten the nut until it's snug (approximately 48 in-lbs). Install the nut lock, then install a new cotter pin through the hole in the spindle and the slots in the nut lock. If the slots do not line up, loosen the nut slightly until they do. The nut should not be loosened more than one-half flat to install the cotter pin.

26   Bend the ends of the cotter pin until flat against the nut. Cut off any extra length which could interfere with the dust cap.

27   Install the dust cap, tapping it into place with a hammer and a large punch **(see illustration)**.

28   Install the wheel on the drum/hub and tighten the lug nuts.

29   Grasp the top and bottom of the tire and check the bearings in the manner described earlier in this Section.

30   Lower the vehicle and tighten the lug nuts to the torque listed in this Chapter's Specifications.

33   Brake fluid replacement

1   Because brake fluid absorbs moisture which could ultimately cause corrosion of the brake components, and which could boil as fluid temperatures rise (which would render the brakes useless), the fluid should be replaced at the specified intervals. This job can be accomplished for a nominal fee by a properly equipped brake shop using a pressure bleeder. The task can also be done by the home mechanic with the help of an assistant. To bleed the air and old fluid and replace it with new fluid from sealed containers, refer to the brake bleeding procedure in Chapter 9.

2   If there is any possibility that incorrect fluid has been used in the system, drain all the fluid and flush the system with brake system cleaner. If this has happened, it will also be necessary to replace all piston seals and cups in the brake system (or install new or rebuilt components), as they will be affected and could possibly fail under pressure.

34   Automatic transaxle fluid and filter change

Refer to illustrations 34.7a, 34.7b, 34.9 and 34.11

1   At the specified time intervals, the automatic transaxle fluid should be drained and replaced.

2   Before beginning work, purchase the specified transmission fluid (see *Recommended lubricants and fluids* in this Chapter's Specifications).

3   Other tools necessary for this job include jackstands to support the vehicle in a raised position, a drain pan capable of holding at least eight quarts, newspapers and clean rags.

4   The fluid should be drained immediately after the vehicle has been driven. Hot fluid is more effective than cold fluid at removing built up sediment. **Warning:** *Fluid temperature can exceed 350-degrees in a hot transaxle. Wear protective gloves.*

5   After the vehicle has been driven to warm up the fluid, raise it and place it on jackstands for access to the transaxle drain plug.

6   Move the necessary equipment under the vehicle, being careful not to touch any of the hot exhaust components.

7   Place the drain pan under the drain plug in the transaxle and remove the drain plug **(see illustrations)**. Be sure the drain pan is in position, as fluid will come out with some force. Once the fluid is drained, reinstall the drain plug securely.

8   Remove the transaxle pan bolts, carefully pry the pan loose with a screwdriver and remove it.

9   Remove the filter retaining bolts, and detach the filter from the transaxle **(see illustration)**. Be careful when lowering the filter as it contains residual fluid.

10   Place the new filter in position and install the bolts. Tighten the bolts to the specified torque.

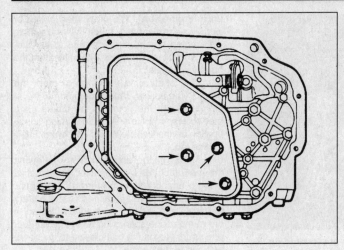

34.9 Remove the four bolts (arrows) and detach the filter (typical)

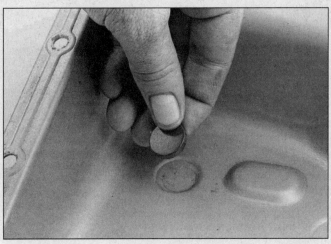

34.11 Be sure to reinstall the magnet in the fluid pan recess

11   Carefully clean the gasket surfaces of the fluid pan, removing all traces of old gasket material. Wash the pan in clean solvent and dry it with compressed air. Be sure to clean and reinstall the magnet **(see illustration)**.

12   Install a new gasket, place the fluid pan in position and install the bolts. Tighten the bolts to the specified torque.

13   Lower the vehicle.

14   With the engine off, add 3-1/2 to 4 quarts of new fluid to the transaxle through the dipstick tube (see *Recommended lubricants and fluids* for the recommended fluid type). Use a funnel to prevent spills. It is best to add a little fluid at a time, continually checking the level with the dipstick (see Section 7). Allow the fluid time to drain into the pan.

15   Start the engine and shift the selector into all positions from Park through Low, then shift into Park and apply the parking brake.

16   With the engine idling, check the fluid level. Add fluid up to the HOT level on the dipstick.

35   Manual transaxle lubricant change

Refer to illustration 35.1

1   After the vehicle has been driven to warm up the fluid, raise the vehicle and place it securely on jackstands for access to the transaxle drain plug. Remove the drain plug and drain the lubricant **(see illustration)**.

2   Reinstall the drain plug. Tighten it to the torque listed in this Chapter's Specifications.

3   Add new oil until it begins to run out of the filler hole (see Section 26). See *Recommended lubricants and fluids* for the specified lubricant type.

36   Evaporative emissions control system check and canister replacement (1986 through 1993 models)

Refer to illustration 36.2

Note: *This procedure applies only to models equipped with a carburetor; it does not apply to fuel-injected models.*

1   The function of the evaporative emissions control system is to draw fuel vapors from the gas tank and fuel system, store them in a charcoal canister and route them to the intake manifold during normal engine operation.

2   The most common symptom of a fault in the evaporative emissions system is a strong fuel odor in the engine compartment. If a fuel odor is detected, inspect the charcoal canister, located in the engine compartment **(see illustration)**. Check the canister and all hoses

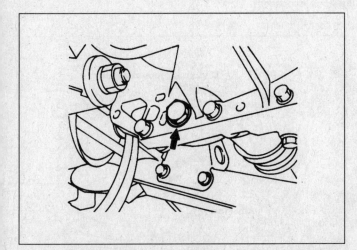

35.1 The manual transaxle drain plug is located on the side of the case - typical

36.2 On 1986 through 1989 models, the canister is mounted on the firewall (shown). On 1990 through 1993 models it's mounted in the lower right front corner of the engine compartment, ahead of the right front wheel

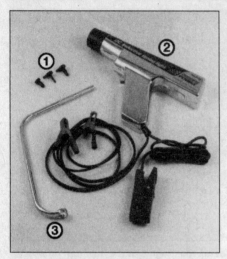

37.1 Tools needed to check and adjust the ignition timing

1 *Vacuum plugs - Vacuum hoses will, in most cases, have to be disconnected and plugged. Molded plugs in various shapes and sizes are available for this*
2 *Inductive pick-up timing light - Flashes a bright concentrated beam of light when the number one spark plug fires. Connect the leads according to the instructions supplied with the light*
3 *Distributor wrench - On some models, the hold-down bolt for the distributor is difficult to reach and turn with conventional wrenches or sockets. A special wrench like this must be used*

for damage and deterioration.

3   At the specified intervals, the charcoal canister must be replaced with a new one. Disconnect the hoses, release the spring clip and lift the canister from the engine compartment. Installation is the reverse of removal.

4   The evaporative emissions control system is explained in more detail in Chapter 6.

37.3 The timing marks are located on the drivebelt end of the engine - highlight the notch in the crankshaft pulley and the appropriate mark on the timing plate

37 Ignition timing check and adjustment (1986 through 1994 models)

Refer to illustrations 37.1, 37.3, 37.7 and 37.11

Note: *If the information in this Section differs from the Vehicle Emission Control Information label in the engine compartment of your vehicle, the label should be considered correct.*

1   Some special tools are required for this procedure **(see illustration)**. The engine must be at normal operating temperature and the air conditioner must be Off. Make sure the idle speed is correct (see Section 20).

2   Apply the parking brake and block the wheels to prevent movement of the vehicle. The transmission must be in Park (automatic) or Neutral (manual).

3   Locate the timing marks at the drivebelt end of the engine (they should be visible from above after the hood is opened)

(see illustration). The crankshaft pulley or vibration damper has a notch in it and a plate with raised numbers is attached to the timing cover. Clean the plate with solvent so the numbers are visible.

4   Use chalk or white paint to mark the notch in the pulley/vibration damper.

5   Highlight the point on the timing plate that corresponds to the ignition timing specification on the Vehicle Emission Control Information label.

6   Hook up the timing light by following the manufacturer's instructions (an inductive pick-up timing light is preferred). Generally, the power leads are attached to the battery terminals and the pick-up lead is attached to the number one spark plug wire. The number one spark plug is the one closest to the drivebelt end of the engine.

7   On carbureted models, disconnect the vacuum hose from the distributor and plug the hose. On fuel injected models, connect a jumper wire between the terminal for ignition timing adjustment and ground **(see illustration)**.

8   Make sure the timing light wires are routed away from the drivebelts and fan, then start the engine.

9   Allow the idle speed to stabilize, then point the flashing timing light at the timing marks - be very careful of moving engine components!

10   The mark on the pulley/vibration damper will appear stationary. If it's aligned with the specified point on the timing plate, the ignition timing is correct.

11   If the marks aren't aligned, adjustment is required. Loosen the distributor mounting nut and turn the distributor very slowly until the marks are aligned **(see illustration)**.

12   Tighten the nut and recheck the timing.

13   Turn off the engine and remove the timing light. Reconnect the vacuum hose to the distributor or remove the jumper wire from the timing adjustment connector, as applicable.

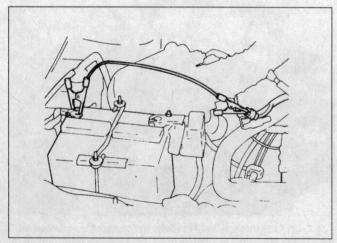

37.7 On fuel injected models, ground the timing adjustment terminal before checking or adjusting the timing

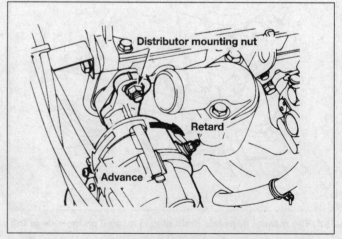

37.11 After loosening the mounting nut, rotate the distributor housing to adjust the ignition timing

38.1 On 1986 through 1989 models, the PCV valve is screwed into the right end of the valve cover and is connected to the air cleaner by a hose

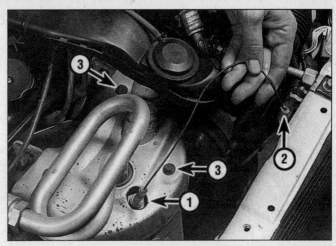

39.1 Prior to removing the oxygen sensor (1), unplug the wire at the connector (2), unscrew the bolts (3) and remove the exhaust manifold heat shield

38   Positive Crankcase Ventilation (PCV) valve check and replacement (1986 through 1990 models)

Refer to illustrations 38.1

1   The PCV valve is located at the valve cover **(see illustration)**.
2   Disconnect the hose, remove the PCV valve from the cover, then reconnect the hose.
3   With the engine idling at normal operating temperature, place your finger over the valve opening. If there's no vacuum at the valve, check for a plugged hose or valve. Replace any plugged or deteriorated hoses.
4   Turn off the engine. Remove the PCV valve from the hose. Blow through the valve from the threaded end. If air will not pass through the valve in this direction, replace it with a new one.
5   When purchasing a replacement PCV valve, make sure it's for your particular vehicle and engine size. Compare the old valve with the new one to make sure they're the same.

39   Oxygen sensor replacement (1986 through 1990 models)

Refer to illustration 39.1

Warning: *The electric cooling fan can activate at any time, even when the ignition is in the Off position. Disconnect the fan motor or negative battery cable when working in the vicinity of the fan.*

Note: *For more information about oxygen sensors, refer to Section 17 in Chapter 4.*
1   Unplug the oxygen sensor wire at the connector located directly behind the top left corner of the radiator and remove the exhaust manifold heat shield bolts **(see illustration)**.
2   Lift the heat shield up for access and unscrew the oxygen sensor. **Note:** *Do not touch the tip of the oxygen sensor or allow it to be contaminated by any oil or grease during removal and installation.*
3   Screw the new oxygen sensor into the exhaust manifold. Tighten the sensor securely.
4   Place the heat shield in position and install the retaining bolts. Tighten the bolts securely.
5   Plug in the electrical connector.

Notes

Chapter 2 Part A
Engines

Contents

Specifications

General
Firing order ... 1-3-4-2
Cylinder numbers (drivebelt end-to-transaxle end) ... 1-2-3-4

Cylinder head
Warpage limit
1994 and earlier ... 0.004 inch
1995 and later ... 0.002 inch

Camshaft
Camshaft endplay
1994 and earlier ... 0.002 to 0.008 inch
1995 and later
SOHC ... 0.003 to 0.011 inch
DOHC ... 0.004 to 0.008 inch

Cylinder location and distributor rotation/coil terminal positions

The blackened terminal shown on the distributor cap indicates the Number One spark plug wire position

1994 and earlier

SOHC and 2000 thru 2005 DOHC

DOHC 1995 thru 1997

Front

43015-1-SPECS HAYNES

Camshaft (continued)

Camshaft lobe height
   1989 and earlier
      Intake .... 1.500 inches
      Exhaust .... 1.504 inches
   1990 through 1994
      Carbureted models
         Intake .... 1.5318 inches
         Exhaust .... 1.5216 inches
      Fuel injected models
         Intake .... 1.5318 inches
         Exhaust .... 1.5344 inches
   1995 through 1999
      SOHC
         Intake .... 1.6873 inches
         Exhaust .... 1.6825 inches
      DOHC
         Intake .... 1.7027 inches
         Exhaust .... 1.7263 inches
   2000 through 2005
      SOHC
         Intake .... 1.6873 inches
         Exhaust .... 1.6825 inches
      DOHC
         Intake .... 1.7106 inches
         Exhaust .... 1.7263 inches
   2006 and later
      Intake .... 1.7224 to 1.7302 inches
      Exhaust .... 1.7381 to 1.7460 inches
   Wear limit (all) .... 0.020 inch
Camshaft journal diameter
   1994 and earlier .... Not available
   1995 through 2005
      SOHC .... 1.181 inches
      DOHC .... 1.063 inches
   2006 and later (DOHC only) .... 1.0616 to 1.0622 inches
Camshaft bearing oil clearance
   1994 and earlier .... 0.0020 to 0.0035 inch
   1995 through 2005
      SOHC .... 0.0020 to 0.0035 inch
      DOHC .... 0.0014 to 0.0028 inch
   2006 and later (DOHC only) .... 0.0008 to 0.0024 inch

Timing belt

Timing belt deflection .... 0.28 to 0.35 inch
Clearance between timing belt and seal line .... 0.55 inch (approximate)

Oil pump

Clearance
   1994 and earlier
      Outer rotor-to-housing .... 0.0039 to 0.0079 inch
      Outer rotor-to-crescent .... 0.0087 to 0.0134 inch
      Inner rotor-to-crescent .... 0.0083 to 0.0126 inch
      Rotor endplay .... 0.0016 to 0.0039 inch
   1995 through 2005
      Outer rotor-to-housing .... 0.0047 to 0.0070 inch
      Outer and inner rotor tip clearance .... 0.0010 to 0.0027 inch
      Rotor endplay .... 0.0016 to 0.0033 inch
   2006 and later
      Side clearance
         Inner rotor .... 0.0016 to 0.0033 inch
         Outer rotor .... 0.0016 to 0.0035 inch
      Body clearance .... 0.0024 to 0.0035 inch
Pressure regulator spring free length
   1994 and earlier .... 1.850 inches
   1995 and later .... 1.835 inches

Torque specifications

Ft-lbs (unless otherwise indicated)

Note: *One foot-pound (ft-lb) of torque is equivalent to 12 inch-pounds (in-lbs) of torque. Torque values below approximately 15 ft-lbs are expressed in inch-pounds, since most foot-pound torque wrenches are not accurate at these smaller values.*

Valve cover bolts
  1994 and earlier models .... 16 in-lbs
  1995 through 1999 models .... 72 to 84 in-lbs
  2000 through 2005 models
    SOHC engine .... 132 to 180 in-lbs
    DOHC engine .... 72 to 84 in-lbs
  2006 and later models .... 70 to 86 in-lbs
Intake and exhaust manifold fasteners
  SOHC models (carbureted and fuel-injected) .... 156 in-lbs
  DOHC models
    Intake manifold fasteners .... 132 to 180 in-lbs
    Exhaust manifold fasteners .... 18 to 22
Throttle body bolts/nuts .... 156 in-lbs
Camshaft sprocket bolt
  1994 and earlier 52
  1995 and later 68
Camshaft idler pulley bolt (DOHC) 35
Camshaft bearing cap bolts (DOHC) .... 120 in-lbs
Cylinder head bolts
  1986 through 1999
    Cold engine 53
    Warm engine 61
  2000 and 2001
    SOHC
      Step 1 .... 17 to 20
      Step 2 .... Tighten an additional 60 degrees
      Step 3 .... Tighten an additional 60 degrees
    DOHC
      Step 1 .... 26, then tighten an additional 75 degrees
      Step 2 .... Back-off until loose
      Step 3 .... 26, then tighten an additional 75 degrees
  2002 and later
    SOHC
      Step 1 .... 17 to 20
      Step 2 .... Tighten an additional 60 degrees
      Step 3 .... Tighten an additional 60 degrees
    DOHC
      Step 1 .... 22, then tighten an additional 90 degrees
      Step 2 .... Back-off until loose
      Step 3 .... 22, then tighten an additional 90 degrees
Crankshaft pulley/sprocket center bolt
  1994 and earlier 63
  1995 and later 105
Oil pump-to-block bolts
  1986 through 2001 (DOHC and SOHC) .... 120 in-lbs
  2002 and later
    SOHC .... 120 in-lbs
    DOHC .... 204 in-lbs
Oil pan bolts
  1986 through 1994
    SOHC .... 72 in-lbs
    DOHC .... 84 in-lbs
  1995 and later
    SOHC .... 144 in-lbs
    DOHC .... 96 in-lbs
Flywheel/driveplate bolts
  SOHC .... 96 to 101
  DOHC
    All except 2006 on .... 89 to 96
    2006 on .... 87 to 94
Rocker arm shaft bolts (SOHC) 18
Timing belt tensioner bolt 18

1   General information

Chapter 2A covers in-vehicle engine repair procedures for all engines. Information concerning engine removal and installation and engine overhaul can be found in Chapter 2B. The following repair procedures are based on the assumption that the engine is installed in the vehicle with all accessories connected. If the engine has been removed from the vehicle and mounted on a stand, the preliminary disassembly information which precedes each operation may be ignored.

Engine description

The engines are in-line four-cylinder units with either a single-overhead camshaft (SOHC) or a double-overhead camshaft (DOHC). They are mounted transversely in one of two arrangements: On 1994 and earlier models, the front of the engine faces the left-hand side of the vehicle and the transaxle is mounted on the right-hand side of the vehicle. On 1995 and later models, the front of the engine faces the right-hand side of the vehicle and the transaxle is mounted on the left-hand side.

On SOHC engines, the camshaft actuates the valves by rocker arms mounted on two shafts (intake and exhaust) which are bolted to the cylinder head above the camshaft. On DOHC engines, the valves are actuated directly by the camshafts.

2   Repair operations possible with the engine in the vehicle

Warning: *Some of the models covered by this manual are equipped with airbags. Always disable the airbag system before working around impact sensors, the steering column or the instrument panel to avoid the accidental deployment of the airbag, which could cause personnel injury (see Chapter 12).*

Many major repair operations can be accomplished without removing the engine from the vehicle. Clean the engine compartment and the exterior of the engine with degreaser before any work is done to make the job easier and help keep dirt out of the internal areas of the engine.

It may be helpful to remove the hood to improve access to the engine as repairs are performed (see Chapter 11). Cover the fenders to prevent damage to the paint.

If vacuum, exhaust, oil or coolant leaks develop, indicating a need for gasket or seal replacement, the repairs can usually be made with the engine in the vehicle. The intake and exhaust manifold gaskets, oil pan gasket, crankshaft oil seals and cylinder head gasket are all accessible with the engine in place.

Exterior engine components, such as the intake and exhaust manifolds, oil pan (and oil pump), water pump, starter motor, alternator, distributor and fuel system components can be removed for repair with the engine in place.

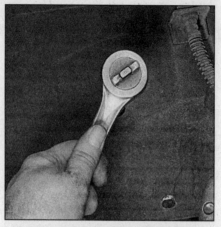

3.4 The crankshaft may be turned by placing a socket on the crankshaft pulley center bolt and slipping an extension through the left inner fender panel (remove the front wheel for additional clearance)

Since the camshaft and cylinder head can be removed without pulling the engine, valve component repair/renewal can also be accomplished with the engine in the vehicle. Replacement of the timing belt and sprockets is also possible with the engine in the vehicle.

Lack of the proper equipment may necessitate repair or replacement of piston rings, pistons, connecting rods and rod bearings with the engine in the vehicle. However, this is not recommended because of the cleaning and preparation work that must be done to the components involved.

3   Top Dead Center (TDC) for number one piston - locating

Refer to illustrations 3.4, 3.6, 3.8, 3.9a, 3.9b, 3.9c and 3.9d

1   Top Dead Center (TDC) is the highest point in the cylinder that each piston reaches as it travels up-and-down. Each piston reaches TDC on the compression stroke and again on the exhaust stroke, but TDC usually refers to piston position on the compression stroke.

2   Positioning the piston(s) at TDC is an essential part of many procedures such as rocker arm removal, camshaft removal, timing belt/sprocket removal and distributor removal.

3   Before beginning this procedure, be sure to place the transaxle in Neutral and apply the parking brake or block the rear wheels. Also, if method b) or c) will be used to rotate the engine in the next step, disable the ignition system by detaching the coil wire from the center terminal of the distributor cap and grounding it on the block with a jumper wire (1994 and earlier models) or disconnecting the electrical connector from the ignition coil pack (1995 and later models), and, on fuel-injected models, disable the fuel system (see Chapter 4, Section 14). **Note:** *Remove all four spark plugs to make the engine easier to turn (see Chapter 6).*

3.6 Align the notch in the pulley with the "T" on the timing indicator (early SOHC engine)

4   In order to bring any piston to TDC, the crankshaft must be turned using one of the methods outlined below. When looking at the drivebelt end of the engine, normal crankshaft rotation is clockwise.

a) *The preferred method is to turn the crankshaft with a socket and ratchet attached to the bolt in the drivebelt end of the crankshaft* **(see illustration).**
b) *A remote starter switch, which may save some time, can also be used. Follow the instructions included with the switch. Once the piston is close to TDC, use a socket and ratchet as described in paragraph a).*
c) *If a helper is available to turn the ignition switch to the Start position in short bursts, you can get the piston close to TDC without a remote starter switch. Make sure your helper is out of the vehicle, away from the ignition switch, then use a socket and ratchet (see Step a) to complete the procedure.*

5   Remove the upper timing belt cover (see Section 7).
6   Turn the crankshaft (see Step 4) until the notch in the crankshaft pulley is aligned with the T on the timing indicator (located on the lower timing belt cover) **(see illustration).**
7   Look at the camshaft sprocket timing marks (see Section 7); they should be aligned. If the marks are 180-degrees off, turn the crankshaft one complete turn (360-degrees) clockwise; the marks should now be aligned. **Note:** *If it's impossible to align the timing marks, the timing belt may have jumped teeth on the sprockets or may have been installed incorrectly.*
8   On 1994 and earlier models (equipped with a distributor), remove the distributor cap. The rotor should be pointing at a point corresponding to the number one spark plug wire terminal on the distributor cap when the ignition timing marks are aligned and the number one piston is at TDC on the compression stroke **(see illustration).**
9   On 1995 and later models, which are not equipped with a distributor, remove the spark plugs (see Chapter 1) and install a compres-

3.8 When the number one piston is at Top Dead Center on the compression stroke, the distributor rotor should point at the number one spark plug wire terminal (1994 and earlier models)

3.9a On engines without a distributor, use a compression gauge in the number one spark plug hole to help you find TDC

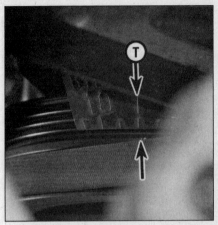

3.9b When compression begins to register on the gauge, rotate the engine until the notch on the crankshaft pulley is aligned with the timing mark for TDC ("T")

sion gauge in the number one cylinder (see illustration). Turn the crankshaft clockwise with a socket and breaker bar. When the piston approaches TDC, note the compression reading on the compression gauge. Continue turning the crankshaft until the notch in the crankshaft damper pulley is aligned with the TDC mark on the front cover (see illustration). At this point, the number one cylinder is at TDC. If the marks are aligned, but there is no compression, the piston is on the exhaust stroke. Rotate the crankshaft another 360 degrees (one turn) and line up the timing marks again. The compression gauge should now indicate compression. **Note:** *If a compression gauge is not available, you can also find TDC for the No. 1 piston by simultaneously aligning the hole in the camshaft timing belt sprocket with the mark on the cylinder head* (see illustrations) *and the marks on the crankshaft damper with the TDC mark on the front cover.*

10   After the number one piston has been positioned at TDC on the compression stroke, TDC for any of the remaining pistons can be located by turning the crankshaft in 180-degree increments and following the firing order.

4   Valve cover - removal and installation

SOHC models
Removal

Refer to illustration 4.3

1   Disconnect the cable from the negative terminal of the battery.
2   On carbureted models, remove the air cleaner assembly (see Chapter 4).
3   Remove the spark plug wires and cable brackets from the valve cover (see illustration).

3.9c To verify that the engine is on TDC on the compression stroke, remove the upper timing belt cover . . .

3.9d . . . and make sure that the timing hole in the camshaft timing belt sprocket is aligned with the timing mark on the cylinder head

4.3 Detach the spark plug wires and cable bracket

4.8 Place a new gasket on the valve cover

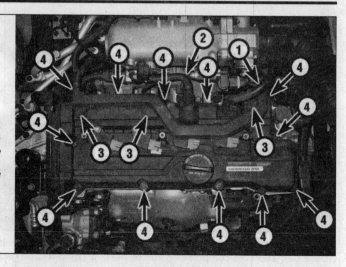

4.14 Valve cover details - DOHC models

1 PCV fresh air inlet hose
2 PCV crankcase ventilation hose
3 Harness cover bolts (2006 and later models)
4 Valve cover bolts

4   Unbolt the accelerator cable support bracket from the cylinder head.
5   Label and disconnect emission hoses which connect to or cross over the valve cover.
6   Remove the valve cover bolts and lift the cover off. If the cover sticks to the cylinder head, tap on it with a soft-face hammer or place a block of wood against the cover and tap on the wood with a hammer.

Installation

Refer to illustration 4.8

7   Clean the valve cover and remove all traces of old gasket material.
8   Place a new gasket on the cover, using RTV to hold it in place **(see illustration)**. Place the cover on the engine and install the cover bolts.
9   Working from the center out, tighten the bolts to the torque specified in this Chapter's Specifications.
10   Installation is the reverse of removal.
11   Run the engine and check for oil leaks.

DOHC models

Refer to illustration 4.14

12   Disconnect the cable from the negative terminal of the battery.
13   Disengage the accelerator cable from any cable guides or clips on the valve cover.
14   Disconnect the PCV fresh air inlet hose and the crankcase breather hose (PCV hose) from the valve cover **(see illustration)**.
15   On models with a single ignition coil pack, remove the spark plug wire cover from the valve cover.
16   On models with a single ignition coil pack, disconnect the spark plug wires from the spark plugs.
17   On 2006 and later models, remove the ignition coils (see Chapter 5).
18   Remove the valve cover bolts and remove the valve cover.
19   Remove the valve cover gasket. Inspect the old gasket. If it's cracked, torn or deteriorated, replace it.
20   Installation is the reverse of removal.

Tighten the valve cover bolts to the torque listed in this Chapter's Specifications.

5   Rocker arm assembly (SOHC engines) - removal, inspection and installation

Removal

Refer to illustration 5.4

1   Remove the valve cover (see Section 4).
2   Position the number one piston at Top Dead Center (see Section 3).
3   Check each rocker arm assembly for identification marks. Mark the position of each assembly to ensure correct installation. **Note:** *The rear assembly is Intake and the front assembly is Exhaust.*
4   Working on each assembly in turn, progressively loosen the bolts until the valve spring pressure is relieved; do not remove the bolts from the shafts, they will hold the rocker arms in position when the shaft assembly is removed **(see illustration)**. On 1995 and later models, wrap a short section of vinyl tape around the rocker arm and hydraulic lash adjuster so the adjuster doesn't fall out when the rocker arm assembly is removed.
5   Lift the rocker arm assemblies away from

the top of the cylinder head with the retaining bolts and washers in place.

Inspection

Refer to illustrations 5.7, 5.8a and 5.8b

6   Mark the shafts on the timing belt end and identify them as Intake and Exhaust. The timing belt end of the shafts have larger chamfered edges than the opposite end.
7   With the bolts removed from the shafts, slide off the rocker arms and springs one at a time until they are all removed. Keep the components in order so that you can reassemble them in the same positions. On 1994 and earlier models, note that the springs on the exhaust rocker shaft are shorter than those on the intake rocker shaft. The free length of the exhaust shaft springs is 1.85 inches, and the intake shaft springs is 3.0 inches **(see illustration)**. Rocker arm shaft spring free length is not available for 1995 and later engines.
8   Clean the components and inspect them for wear or damage **(see illustrations)**. On 1994 and earlier models, check the rocker arm faces that contact the camshaft and the adjusting screw tips that contact the valve stems; the screw tips can be replaced separately. On models equipped with jet valves, also check the jet valve contact faces. On 1995 and later models, check the rocker arm

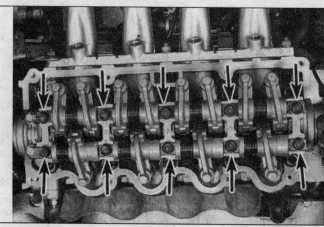

5.4 Rocker arm shaft mounting bolts

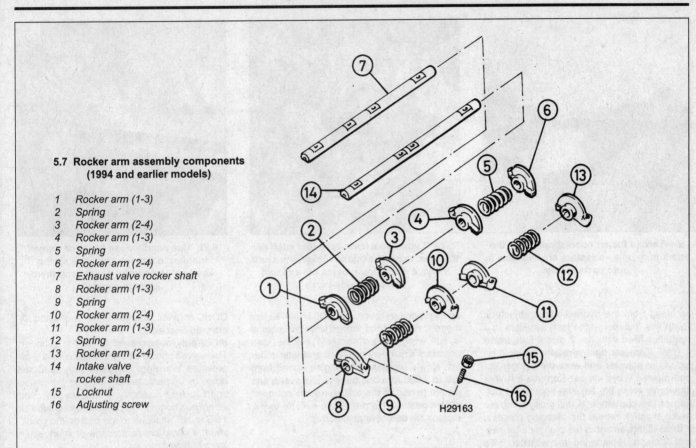

5.7 Rocker arm assembly components (1994 and earlier models)

1   Rocker arm (1-3)
2   Spring
3   Rocker arm (2-4)
4   Rocker arm (1-3)
5   Spring
6   Rocker arm (2-4)
7   Exhaust valve rocker shaft
8   Rocker arm (1-3)
9   Spring
10 Rocker arm (2-4)
11 Rocker arm (1-3)
12 Spring
13 Rocker arm (2-4)
14 Intake valve
    rocker shaft
15 Locknut
16 Adjusting screw

tip, roller and lash adjuster pocket for wear. Inspect each lash adjuster carefully for signs of wear or damage, particularly on the ball tip that contacts the rocker arm. The hydraulic lash adjusters frequently become clogged; replace them if you're concerned about their condition or if the engine is exhibiting valve tapping noises. Replace any components that are damaged or excessively worn. Also, make sure that the oil holes in the shafts and rocker arms are clear of any debris by blowing air through them.

Installation

Refer to illustration 5.10

9   Lubricate the bearing surfaces of all the components with engine assembly lube or clean engine oil, then reassemble the shafts in the reverse order of disassembly **(see illustration 5.4)**. When installing the rocker arms, shafts and springs, note the markings and the difference between the left and right side parts. Note that the rocker arms themselves are angled, and are identified with

cylinder numbers. For example, a rocker arm with numbers "2-4" on it must be installed on the valves for cylinders 2 and 4. If any of the rocker arms have been replaced, make sure the correct one has been purchased. Insert the bolts in their holes to keep the components on the shafts.
10   On 1994 and earlier models, loosen the locknuts and back off the adjusters until they protrude approximately 0.04 inch **(see illustration)**.
11   On 1995 and later models, the air must

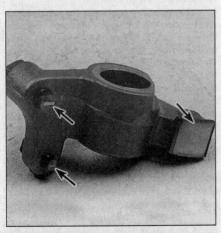

5.8a On 1994 and earlier models, check the contact faces and adjusting screw tips (jet valve model shown)

HYDRAULIC LASH ADJUSTER

5.8b On 1995 and later models, inspect the hydraulic lash adjuster and the roller for signs of wear or damage

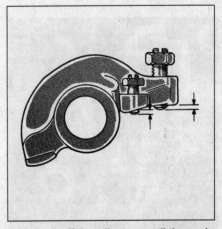

5.10 Back off the adjusters until they only protrude 0.04 inch (jet valve model shown)

6.4 Thread the air hose adapter into the spark plug hole - adapters are available in auto parts stores

6.7a If you use a lever-type tool such as this one, leave the intake rocker arm shaft in place while you replace the exhaust seals and vice-versa

6.7b Use needle-nose pliers or a small magnet to remove the valve spring keepers - be careful not to drop them into the engine!

be bleed from the hydraulic lash adjusters. To do this, submerge the lash adjusters in a container filled with no. 2 diesel fuel. Insert a small diameter rigid wire into the hole on top of the adjuster and work the plunger up-and-down several times. Remove the wire and firmly press the adjuster against the bottom of the container. If the plunger moves (even slightly), repeat the bleeding process. If there is movement in the plunger after several attempts, replace the lash adjuster. If it's necessary to store a fully bled lash adjuster/ rocker arm assembly for any length of time, make sure the oil hole it kept up so the diesel fuel doesn't leak out.

12   Position the rocker arm assemblies on the cylinder head and alternately tighten the bolts until the shafts are fully seated, then tighten the bolts in several stages to the torque listed in this Chapter's Specifications.

13   On 1994 and earlier models, adjust the valve clearances (cold) (see Chapter 1).

14   Install the remaining parts in the reverse order of removal.

15   Run the engine and check for oil leaks

6.8 Remove the valve seal from the valve guide with a pair of needle-nose pliers

and proper operation. On 1994 and earlier models, readjust the valves while the engine is still warm (see Chapter 1). If the lash adjusters are noisy on 1995 and later models, slowly increase the engine speed from idle to 3,000 rpm and back to idle over a one minute period. If the adjuster(s) do not quiet after repeating this procedure several times, replace the defective adjuster(s).

6   Valve springs, retainers and seals - replacement

Refer to illustrations 6.4, 6.7a, 6.7b, 6.8, 6.13 and 6.15

Note: *Broken valve springs and defective valve stem seals can be replaced without removing the cylinder heads. Special tools and a compressed air source are normally required to perform this operation. Read this Section carefully and rent or buy the tools before beginning the job.*

1   Remove the valve cover (see Section 4).

2   Remove the spark plug from the cylinder which has the defective component. If all of the valve stem seals are being replaced, all of the spark plugs should be removed.

3   Turn the crankshaft until the piston in the affected cylinder is at Top Dead Center on the compression stroke (see Section 3). If you're replacing all the valve stem seals, begin with cylinder number one and work on the valves one cylinder at a time. Move from cylinder-to-cylinder following the firing order sequence (see this Chapter's *Specifications*).

4   Thread an adapter into the spark plug hole **(see illustration)** and connect an air hose from a compressed air source to it. Most auto parts stores can supply the air hose adapter. **Note:** *Many cylinder compression gauges utilize a screw-in fitting that may work with your air hose quick-disconnect fitting.*

5   On SOHC engines, remove the rocker arm shafts (see Section 5) (unless you are using a lever-type tool - see Step 7). On

DOHC engines remove the camshafts and lifters (see Section 9).

6   Apply compressed air to the cylinder. The valves should be held in place by the air pressure. **Warning:** *The piston may be forced down by compressed air, causing the crankshaft to turn suddenly. If the wrench used when positioning the number one piston at TDC is still attached to the bolt on the crankshaft, it could cause damage or injury when the crankshaft moves.*

7   Use an appropriate valve spring compressor to compress the spring and remove the valve keepers with small needle-nose pliers or a magnet **(see illustrations)**. **Note:** *Several different types of tools are available for compressing the valve springs with the cylinder head in place. One type grips the lower spring coils and presses on the retainer as the knob is turned, while the other type utilizes the rocker arm shaft or camshaft for leverage. Both types work very well, although the lever type is usually less expensive. If your working on a DOHC engine, a special adapter will also be needed because the valve springs are recessed into the cylinder head.*

8   Release the pressure on the valve spring and remove the spring and retainer. Remove the valve seal from the valve guide **(see illustration)**. **Note:** *If air pressure fails to hold the valve in the closed position during this operation, the valve face and/or seat is probably damaged. If so, the cylinder head will have to be removed for additional repair operations.*

9   Wrap a rubber band or tape around the top of the valve stem so the valve doesn't fall into the combustion chamber, then release the air pressure.

10   Inspect the valve stem for damage. Rotate the valve in the guide and check the end for eccentric movement, which indicates that the valve is bent.

11   Move the valve up-and-down in the guide and make sure it doesn't bind. If the valve stem binds, either the valve is bent or the guide is damaged. In either case, the head will have to be removed for repair.

12   Reapply air pressure to the cylinder to retain the valve in the closed position, then remove the tape or rubber band from the valve stem.

13   Lubricate the valve stem with engine oil and install a new guide seal **(see illustration)**.

14   Install the spring and retainer in position over the valve.

15   Compress the valve spring and carefully position the valve keepers in the groove. If necessary, apply a small dab of grease to the inside of each keeper to hold it in place **(see illustration)**.

16   Remove the pressure from the valve spring compressor. Make sure the keepers are seated by tapping on the end of the valve stem with a soft-faced hammer.

17   Disconnect the air hose and remove the adapter from the spark plug hole.

18   Install the rocker arm shafts (see Section 5) or the camshafts and lifters (see Section 9).

19   Install the spark plug(s) and the spark plug wire(s).

20   Install the valve cover (see Section 4).

21   Start and run the engine, then check for oil leaks and unusual sounds coming from the valve cover area.

6.13 Gently tap the seal into place with a hammer and deep socket or equivalent tool

6.15 Apply a small dab of grease to each keeper before installation to hold it in place on the valve stem until the spring is released

7   Timing belt and sprockets - removal, inspection and installation

Removal

Refer to illustrations 7.8, 7.9, 7.10a, 7.10b, 7.11a, 7.11b, 7.12, 7.13, 7.16 and 7.17

Caution 1: *The timing system is complex. Severe engine damage will occur if you make any mistakes. Do not attempt this procedure unless you are highly experienced with this type of repair. If you are at all unsure of your abilities, consult an expert. Double-check all*

your work and be sure everything is correct before you attempt to start the engine.
Caution 2: *If the timing belt failed with the engine operating, damage to the valves may have occurred. Perform an engine compression check to confirm damage.*
Caution 3: *Do not attempt to turn the crankshaft with the camshaft sprocket bolt and do not rotate the crankshaft counterclockwise.*

1   Disconnect the cable from the negative terminal of the battery.

2   On carbureted models, remove the air cleaner assembly and associated hoses (see Chapter 4).

3   Set the parking brake and block the rear wheels. Raise the front of the vehicle and support it securely on jackstands.

4   Remove the left engine mount (see Section 17).

5   Loosen the four water pump pulley bolts, then remove the drivebelts (see Chapter 1).

6   Unbolt and remove the water pump pulley.

7   Remove the splash pan from beneath the drivebelt end of the engine.

8   Remove the four crankshaft pulley bolts and the crankshaft pulley **(see illustration)**. **Note:** *On later models, the crankshaft pulley may be removed without removing the crankshaft sprocket bolt. The sprocket bolt and sprocket need only be removed if replacing the oil seal, oil pump, etc. On early models, the crankshaft sprocket bolt must be removed before removing the pulley.*

9   Remove the large center bolt from the crankshaft pulley. It's very tight, so to break it loose, wrap a rag around the pulley and attach a chain wrench. Slip a socket onto the bolt, then fit an extension through the hole in the inner fender. Carefully turn the extension with a breaker bar **(see illustration)**.

10   If you are unable to loosen the bolt due to the chain wrench slipping, you can prevent the crankshaft from turning by having an assistant wedge a flat-blade screwdriver in the

7.8 Remove the crankshaft pulley bolts

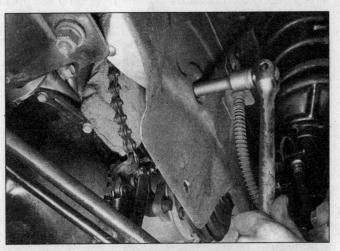

7.9 Wrap a protective cloth around the pulley and attach a chain wrench - loosen the crankshaft pulley center bolt with a socket, extension and breaker bar

7.10a Remove these bolts and the flywheel/driveplate cover for access . . .

7.10b . . . and wedge a flat-blade screwdriver in the ring gear teeth at the right corner of the engine block

7.11a Remove the bolts retaining the upper timing belt cover . . .

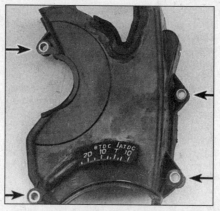

7.11b . . . and the lower timing belt cover (1994 and earlier model shown, other models similar)

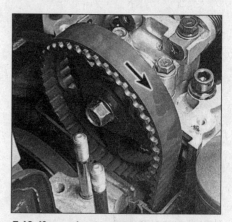

7.12 If you plan to reuse the belt, paint an arrow on it to indicate direction of rotation (clockwise)

flywheel/driveplate ring gear teeth (see illustrations). To do this, you must first remove the flywheel/driveplate cover (see transaxle removal procedures in Chapter 7).

11   Remove the bolts retaining the timing

7.13 Loosen the timing belt tensioner bolt and pry the tensioner towards the water pump

belt cover(s) and remove the cover(s) (see illustrations).

12   Temporarily install the crankshaft sprocket bolt (if removed) and rotate the crankshaft clockwise until the timing marks on the crankshaft and camshaft sprockets align with their respective marks (see illustrations 7.21a and 7.21b). At this location, the engine will be positioned with the number one piston at TDC on the compression stroke. If you plan to reuse the timing belt, paint an arrow on it (see illustration) to indicate the direction of rotation (clockwise).

13   Loosen the adjusting bolt and move the timing belt tensioner towards the water pump as far as possible (see illustration). Temporarily secure the tensioner by tightening the bolt.

14   On some models, the engine mounting bracket that secures the timing belt end of the engine must be unbolted before you can remove the timing belt (see Section 17).

15   Slip the timing belt off the camshaft and crankshaft sprockets and set it aside. Do not alter the position of the camshaft or crankshaft sprockets with the timing belt removed.

16   To remove the camshaft, remove the camshaft sprocket bolt and pull the sprocket

off; a large screwdriver inserted through a hole in the sprocket will keep it from turning while you remove the bolt (see illustration).

17   To replace the crankshaft front oil seal, remove the crankshaft sprocket bolt and pull the crankshaft sprocket off the crankshaft. If the sprocket is difficult to remove, a bolt-type puller (such as a steering wheel puller) may be used. Remove the timing belt guide flange located behind the crankshaft sprocket. When removing the flange, note how it's installed (the chamfered side faces out) (see illustration).

Inspection

Refer to illustrations 7.18 and 7.19

18   Rotate the tensioner pulley by hand and move it from side-to-side to detect roughness or excess play (see illustration). Inspect the sprockets for signs of damage and wear. Replace parts as necessary. **Note:** *The timing belt should be replaced, regardless of age, if it appears to be defective in any manner or if it has been in contact with water, oil or steam.*

19   Inspect the timing belt for cracks, separation, wear, missing teeth and oil contamina-

7.16 Slip a large screwdriver through the sprocket to prevent the camshaft from turning - be sure to protect the gasket surface to prevent damage to the cylinder head

7.17 When removing the belt guide, note how it's installed - the chamfered side faces out

7.18 Turn the tensioner pulley by hand to detect roughness and excess play

tion **(see illustration)**. Replace the belt if it is in poor condition.

Installation

Refer to illustrations 7.20, 7.21a, 7.21b, 7.22a, 7.22b, 7.28 and 7.30

Caution: *Before starting the engine, carefully rotate the crankshaft by hand through at least two full revolutions (use a socket and breaker bar on the crankshaft pulley center bolt). If you feel any resistance, STOP! There is something wrong - most likely, valves are contacting the pistons. You must find the problem before proceeding. Check your work and see if any updated repair information is available.*

20 Reinstall the timing belt sprockets, if they were removed **(see illustration)**. Note that the camshaft sprocket is indexed by a dowel. Slip the belt guide flange onto the crankshaft

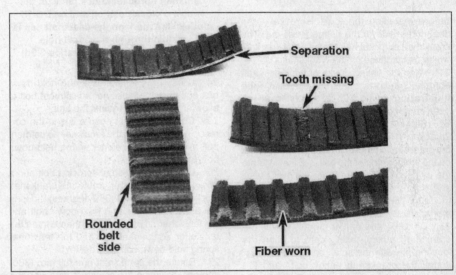

7.19 Carefully inspect the timing belt for the conditions described here

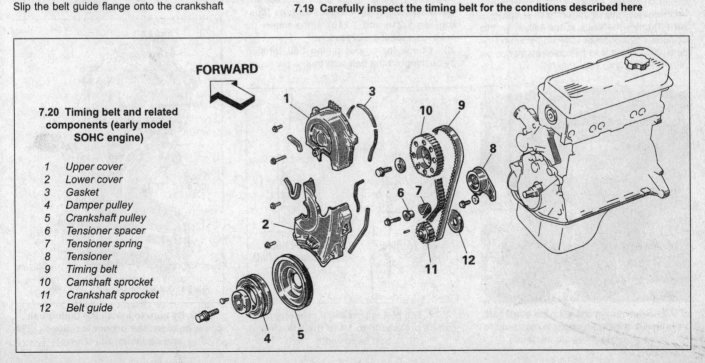

FORWARD

7.20 Timing belt and related components (early model SOHC engine)

1 Upper cover
2 Lower cover
3 Gasket
4 Damper pulley
5 Crankshaft pulley
6 Tensioner spacer
7 Tensioner spring
8 Tensioner
9 Timing belt
10 Camshaft sprocket
11 Crankshaft sprocket
12 Belt guide

7.21a Align the timing mark or dowel on the crankshaft sprocket with the stationary mark on the oil pump housing

7.21b Align the triangular mark on the camshaft sprocket with the stationary mark on the cylinder head - note that the camshaft sprocket knock pin is in the twelve o'clock position and on DOHC models, the mark on the camshaft cap is visible through the small hole in the sprocket (see illustration 3.9d)

7.22a Maintain tension on the side opposite of the timing belt tensioner during installation

before installing the lower sprocket - the chamfered side of the flange faces out. The crankshaft sprocket has two different size flats which match those on the crankshaft.

21   Align the timing marks of the crankshaft sprocket and the camshaft sprocket **(see illustrations)** with the No. 1 piston at top dead center of its compression stroke.

22   Slip the timing belt onto the crankshaft sprocket. While maintaining tension between the crankshaft sprocket and camshaft sprocket on the tension side of the belt, slip the belt onto the camshaft sprocket (under the idler pulley and onto the camshaft sprocket on DOHC models). Recheck that the sprocket timing marks are still aligned **(see illustrations)**.

23   On 1994 and earlier models, install the crankshaft pulley, taking care to align the locating pin with the small hole in the pulley. Install the crankshaft pulley bolts and the center crankshaft sprocket bolt. On 1995 and later models, Install the crankshaft sprocket bolt. Tighten the bolts to the torque in this Chapter's Specifications. When tightening the bolts, be sure to hold the crankshaft securely (see Steps 12 and 13).

24   Loosen the tensioner spring hold-down bolt and then the tensioner adjustment bolt to allow spring tension against the belt.

25   Check the belt to ensure it is in the correct position. Tighten the tensioner adjustment bolt and then the tensioner spring hold-down bolt, in order.

26   Using the crankshaft sprocket bolt and a socket and breaker bar, rotate the crankshaft clockwise one full turn (360-degrees). Loosen the tensioner coil spring hold-down bolt and the tensioner adjustment bolt, then tighten the tensioner adjustment bolt and the tensioner spring hold-down bolt, in order.

27   Rotate the crankshaft one full turn (360-degrees), aligning the camshaft sprocket and crankshaft sprocket timing marks **(see illustrations 7.21a and 7.21b)**. If the marks do not align, repeat the procedure.

28   Check for proper timing belt tension by pushing on the belt with thumb pressure.

It should deflect to 1/4 of adjuster bolt head width **(see illustration)**. If it is too tight or too loose, loosen the tensioner bolts and adjust the tensioner.

29   Tighten the tensioner bolts to the specified torque, starting with the adjustment bolt; then tighten the tension spring hold-down bolt.

30   Reinstall the remaining parts in the reverse order of removal. Note that the timing belt cover bolts are different lengths **(see illustration)**.

31   Start the engine, set the ignition timing (see Chapter 1) and road test the vehicle.

7.22b Since you must view the camshaft sprocket marks at an angle, it may help to use a pointer to avoid mistakes

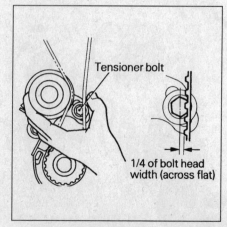

7.28 The belt is tensioned properly if it can be pressed in to 1/4 of the adjustment bolt head width

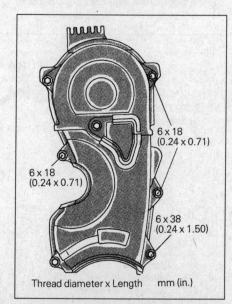

7.30 Be sure to install the timing belt cover bolts to their proper locations (1994 and earlier model shown)

8.2a Carefully drill two holes in the oil seal and screw in self-tapping screws . . .

8.2b . . . then pull out the oil seal with a pair of pliers

8.2c If a small screwdriver is used to remove the oil seal, take care not to damage the surface of the camshaft

8 Camshaft oil seal - replacement

Refer to illustrations 8.2a, 8.2b, 8.2c and 8.4

1 Remove the camshaft sprocket (see Section 7).

2 Make a note of the correct installed depth of the seal then drill two small holes opposite each other in the oil seal. Screw a self-tapping screw into each hole and pull on the screws with pliers to extract the seal **(see illustrations)**. An alternate method is to use small screwdriver may be used to pry out the oil seal (be careful not to damage the surface of the camshaft) **(see illustration)**.

3 Clean the seal housing and polish off any burrs or raised edges which may have caused the seal to fail in the first place.

4 Lubricate the lips of the new seal with clean engine oil and push it into position on the end of the shaft. Press the seal into its housing until it is positioned at the same depth as the original, prior to removal. If necessary,

a tubular drift, such as a socket, which bears only on the hard outer edge of the seal can be used to tap the seal into position **(see illustration)**. Take care not to damage the seal lips during installation and make sure that the seal lips face inwards. If the surface of the shaft is badly scored, press the new seal slightly less into its housing so that its lip is running on an unmarked area of the shaft.

5 Install and adjust the camshaft sprocket and timing belt (see Section 7).

9 Camshaft - removal, inspection and installation

SOHC models

Removal

Refer to illustrations 9.8a, 9.8b, 9.9a and 9.9b

1 Disconnect the cable from the negative terminal of the battery.

2 Drain the cooling system (see Chapter 1) and disconnect the upper radiator hose from the thermostat housing. Place the hose to one side away from the end of the cylinder head.

3 Remove the valve cover (see Section 4).

4 On SOHC engines, remove the rocker arm assemblies (see Section 5).

5 On 1994 and earlier models, remove the distributor. On 1995 and later models, remove the ignition coil assembly (see Chapter 5).

6 On carburetor models, remove the fuel pump (see Chapter 4).

7 Remove the timing belt and the camshaft sprocket (see Section 7).

8 On 1994 and earlier models, remove the retaining screws and the rear cover from the end of the cylinder head **(see illustration)**. Remove the gasket and discard it, a new one is required for cover plate installation. Remove the camshaft thrust case retaining bolt from the top of the cylinder head **(see illustration)**.

9 On 1994 and earlier models, slide the

8.4 Tap the new seal into position using a hammer and suitable socket

9.8a Remove the lower bolts (A) first and set the bracket aside, then the upper bolts (B) and finally the thrust case retaining bolt (C)

9.8b Grip the camshaft between the third and fourth exhaust lobes and remove the thrust case-to-camshaft bolt

9.9a Pull the thrust case out of the cylinder head - if it's stuck, slide the camshaft back and forth slightly to push it out

9.9b Guide the camshaft out of the cylinder head - be careful not to damage the camshaft journal bores in the cylinder head

camshaft and thrust case out from the end of the cylinder head **(see illustrations)**. Where necessary, unbolt and move the windshield washer reservoir to one side to provide additional clearance.

10   On 1995 and later models, remove the camshaft bearing caps, noting the location from which each bearing cap was removed for correct reinstallation later. Lift out the camshaft(s); on DOHC models, separate the rear timing chain from the camshafts The hydraulic lifters may be removed from the cylinder head if necessary.

11   Remove the camshaft oil seal.

Inspection

Refer to illustrations 9.14a, 9.14b and 9.16

12   Thoroughly clean the camshaft(s), all removed components, and gasket surfaces. Examine the camshaft bearing surfaces and lobes for wear ridges, pitting or scoring. Replace the camshaft if it is damaged.

13   Examine the camshaft bearing surfaces

in the cylinder head. Deep scoring or other damage means that the cylinder head must be replaced.

14   Using a micrometer, measure the camshaft lobe heights and camshaft journal diameters and compare them to this Chapter's Specifications **(see illustrations)**. If measurements are not within limits in this Chapter's Specifications, the camshaft must be replaced.

15   On SOHC engines, inspect the rocker arms and hydraulic lash adjusters (see Section 5).

16   On 1994 and earlier models, use feeler gauges to measure the endplay clearance between the end of the camshaft and the camshaft thrust case **(see illustration)**. On 1995 and later models, install the camshaft in the cylinder head and measure the endplay clearance at the bearing cap thrust surface. If the measurement is not within the endplay range given in this Chapter's Specifications, the thrust case and its retaining washer or bearing caps must be replaced. On 1994 and

earlier models, replace the thrust case and retaining washer by gripping the camshaft in a vise between blocks of wood, then loosening and removing the thrust case retaining bolt and washer; then install the new thrust case and washer and securely tighten the retaining bolt.

Installation

17   Lubricate the camshaft bearings with clean engine oil.

18   On 1994 and earlier models, slide the camshaft into position in the cylinder head and align the thrust case threaded hole with the cylinder head hole. Install the thrust case retaining bolt and tighten it securely. On 1995 and later models, position the camshaft(s) in the cylinder head and install the bearing caps, tightening them to the torque listed in this Chapter's Specifications. **Note:** *On DOHC engines, check the bearing cap markings for intake (I) and exhaust (E) identification and cap number.*

9.14a Measure the camshaft lobe heights

9.14b Measure the camshaft journal diameters

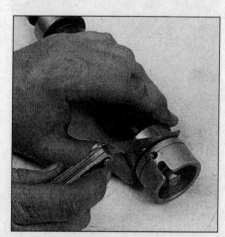

9.16 Measure camshaft endplay with a feeler gauge (1994 and earlier models)

9.31a Starting at the center of the cylinder head and working your way toward the ends of the head, gradually and evenly loosen the camshaft bearing cap bolts in a criss-cross fashion

9.31b When you get to the bolts for the last two caps, remove the upper chain guide

19 Ensure all cover mating surfaces are clean and dry. On 1994 and earlier models, install the cylinder head end cover plate using a new gasket, and securely tighten the retaining bolts.

20 Install a new camshaft oil seal (see Section 8).

21 Rotate the camshaft so that the camshaft sprocket locating pin hole is on top; this will position the camshaft correctly with the No 1 cylinder at TDC on its compression stroke.

22 On carbureted models install the fuel pump (see Chapter 4).

23 Install the camshaft sprocket(s) and timing belt (see Section 7).

24 Install the distributor (see Chapter 5) where equipped.

25 On SOHC engines, install the rocker arm assemblies (see Section 5). On 1994 and earlier models, check and adjust the valve clearances (cold) before installing the valve cover.

26 The remaining installation is the reverse of removal. Refill the cooling system (see Chapter 1).

27 Reconnect the cable to the negative terminal of the battery.

28 Warm the engine up to its normal operating temperature and on 1994 and earlier models, recheck the valve clearances with the engine hot.

DOHC models

Note 1: *The camshaft and lifters should always be thoroughly inspected before installation and camshaft endplay should always be checked prior to camshaft removal. Although the hydraulic lifters are self-adjusting and require no periodic service, there is an in-vehicle procedure for checking excessively noisy hydraulic lifters.*

Note 2: *2006 and later models use the Continuously Variable Valve Timing (CVVT) system. This consists of a CVVT unit,*

attached to the end of the exhaust camshaft, which drives the intake camshaft via a timing chain. This increases performance by automatically changing the intake camshaft timing while running.

Hydraulic lifters - in-vehicle check

29 Noisy valve lifters can be checked for wear without disassembling the engine by following the procedure outlined below:

a) *Run the engine until it reaches normal operating temperature.*

b) *Remove the valve cover (see Section 4).*

c) *Set the No.1 piston to TDC on the compression stroke (see Section 3).*

d) *Insert a feeler gauge between the camshaft lobe and the lifter to measure the clearance. If the clearance exceeds 0.008 inch (0.2 mm), the lifter and/or the camshaft lobe has worn beyond its limits.*

e) *If no clearance exists, depress the lifter to force it to bleed down, then check the clearance again.*

f) *Lifter clearance on the remaining cylinders can be checked by following the firing order sequence and positioning each of the remaining pistons at TDC.* **Note:** *Lifter clearance can also be checked on any lifter whose cam lobe is pointing upward.*

g) *If the clearance is beyond the maximum allowed, inspect the camshaft as described in Step 40.*

h) *If the camshaft is OK, the lifters are faulty and must be replaced.*

Removal

Refer to illustrations 9.31a, 9.31b, 9.33, 9.34, 9.35, 9.37a and 9.37b

30 Remove the valve cover (see Section 4), then remove the timing belt cover, the timing belt and the camshaft timing belt sprocket (see Section 5). Before removing the

camshafts, check the camshaft endplay (see Step 42).

31 Starting in the middle of the cylinder head, at bearing cap No. 3 on the intake camshaft or at cap No. 4 on the exhaust cam, loosen the camshaft bearing caps, working your way out toward the ends of the head in a criss-cross fashion **(see illustration)**. Loosen the cap bolts gradually and evenly, in two or three passes. After removing the two inner bolts for the two rear caps, remove the upper chain guide **(see illustration)**.

32 Remove the bearing caps. Keep the intake and exhaust cam caps separated. They must be installed at the same location from which they were removed. To prevent confusion, the caps are marked "I" (intake) or "E" (exhaust) and are numbered (1, 2, 3, etc.).

33 Remove the intake and exhaust camshafts and the camshaft timing chain as a single assembly **(see illustration)**. Remove the old camshaft seal from the exhaust cam and discard it.

9.33 Remove the camshafts and the timing chain together

9.34 To detach the lower timing chain guide, remove these two bolts

9.35 Mark the positions of the hydraulic lifters (I-1, I-2, E-1, E-2, etc.) so they can be reinstalled in their original locations

9.37a Check the chain rollers and the teeth on the camshaft sprockets (2003 and earlier non-CVVT shown, 2004 and later similar)

34   Remove the lower chain guide **(see illustration)**.

35   Wipe off the tops of the lifters, then mark them with a marking pen (I-1, I-2, E-1, E-2, etc.), or mark strips of tape and affix them to the top of each lifter **(see illustration)**.

36   Remove the lifters from the cylinder head. Keep the intake and exhaust lifters separated, and keep them in order.

37   Thoroughly clean the cam timing chain and the timing chain sprockets on the camshafts with fresh solvent and a stiff brush and inspect the timing chain and the sprockets **(see illustration)**. Make sure that the bearing surfaces (the shiny parts) of the chain rollers are in good condition and that the chain isn't stiff. If the chain is excessively worn or damaged, replace it. Make sure that the teeth on the camshaft timing chain sprockets are in good condition. If any of the teeth are broken or excessively worn, replace the camshaft(s). Also inspect the timing chain guides **(see illustration)**. Make sure that the friction sur-faces of the guides are still in good condition. If either guide is excessively worn, replace it.

38   Inspect the camshafts and the lifters (see Chapter 2B).

Camshafts, lifters and bearings - inspection

Refer to illustrations 9.39, 9.42, 9.43a and 9.43b

39   Inspect the camshaft bearing surfaces **(see illustration)** for pitting, score marks, galling and abnormal wear. If the bearing surfaces are damaged, replace the cylinder head.

40   Compare the camshaft lobe height by measuring each lobe with a micrometer **(see illustration 9.14a)**. Measure each of the intake lobes and record the measurements and relative positions. Then measure each of the exhaust lobes and record the measurements and relative positions also. This will let you compare all of the intake lobes to one another and all of the exhaust lobes to one another. If the difference between the lobes exceeds 0.005 inch, the camshaft should be replaced. Do not compare intake lobe heights to exhaust lobe heights as lobe lift may be different. Only compare intake lobes-to-intake lobes and exhaust lobes-to exhaust lobes for this comparison.

41   Measure the outside diameter of each camshaft bearing journal **(see illustration 9.14b)**, record your measurements, then compare them to specified journal outside diameter listed in this Chapter's Specifications. Then measure the inside diameter of each corresponding camshaft bearing and record those measurements. To calculate the oil clearance for each bearing, subtract each journal outside diameter from its corresponding cam bearing bore inside diameter. Compare the results to the journal-to-bearing clearance listed in this Chapter's Specifications. If any of the measurements fall outside the standard specified wear limits in this Chapter, either the camshaft(s) or the cylinder head, or both, must be replaced.

9.37b Also inspect the friction surfaces of the timing chain guides

9.39 Inspect the camshaft bearing surfaces in the cylinder head for pits, score marks and abnormal wear. If there's damage, replace the cylinder head

9.42 Mount a dial indicator as shown to measure camshaft endplay. Pry the camshaft forward and back, then read the indicated endplay on the dial

42   Measure the camshaft endplay by placing a dial indicator with the stem in line with the camshaft and touching the snout (**see illustration**). Push the camshaft all the way to the rear and zero the dial indicator. Next, pry the camshaft to the front as far as possible and check the reading on the dial indicator. The distance it moves is the endplay. If it's greater than the value listed in this Chapter's Specifications, check the bearing caps for wear. If the bearing caps are worn, the cylinder head must be replaced.

43   Inspect the contact and sliding surfaces of each lifter for wear and scratches (**see illustrations**). **Note:** *If the lifter pad is worn, it's a good idea to double-check the corresponding camshaft lobe. Do not lay the lifters on their side or upside down, or air can become trapped inside and the lifter will have to be bled. The lifters can be laid on their side only if they are submerged in a pan of clean engine oil until reassembly.*

44   Verify that each lifter moves up and down freely in its bore. If it doesn't, the valve may stick open and cause internal engine damage.

45   Make sure all the parts, new or old, have been thoroughly inspected before reassembly.

Installation

Refer to illustrations 9.48a, 9.48b, 9.48c and 9.50

46   Apply clean engine oil to the walls of the lifters and insert the lifters into their respective bores in the cylinder head. Push down the lifters until they contact the valves, then lubricate the top surfaces.

47   Lubricate the camshaft and cylinder head bearing journals with clean engine oil or camshaft installation lubricant.

48   Install the camshaft timing chain on the camshaft sprockets.

   1999 and earlier models: Align the timing marks on the cam chain sprockets with the centers of the two colored side plates, with four links in between (**see illustration**).

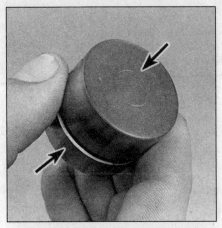

9.43a Inspect the top (contact surface) and the walls (sliding surface) of each lifter for signs of excessive wear . . .

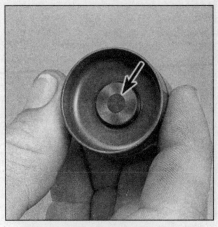

9.43b . . . then inspect the valve stem contact surface underneath for wear

   2000 through 2005 models: Align the timing mark on the exhaust camshaft sprocket between the two colored side plates that are next to each other, and the timing mark on the intake camshaft sprocket with the other colored side plate (**see illustration**).

   2006 and later models: Align the timing marks on the cam chain sprockets with the centers of the two colored side plates, with five links in between (**see illustration**).

49   Clean the oil seal bore and the sealing surface of the nose (forward end) of the camshaft, lubricate the lip of the new camshaft oil

9.48a Camshaft sprocket and chain alignment details - 1999 and earlier models

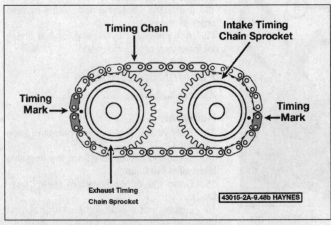

9.48b Camshaft sprocket and chain alignment details - 2000 through 2005

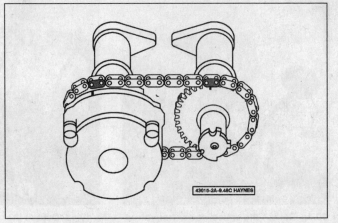

9.48c Camshaft sprocket and chain alignment details - 2006 and later models

9.50 Slide the new cam seal over the nose of the cam, place the cam in position in the head and gently push the seal onto the nose of the cam until the chamfered edge around the face of the seal bore is exposed

10.4a Label the wires and hoses with masking tape and a marking pen

10.4b Disconnect the solenoid control valve connector (carbureted models)

seal with clean engine oil and slide it over the nose of the camshaft.

50   Carefully lower the camshafts and timing chain into position on the cylinder head with the camshaft lobes for the No. 1 cylinder facing up (180 degrees from the cylinder head mating surface). Gently push the seal onto the nose of the cam until the chamfered edge around the face of the cam seal bore is visible **(see illustration)**. Oil the upper surfaces of the camshaft bearing journals, then install the bearing caps over the camshafts. Then, working in a criss-cross fashion from the ends of the head toward the center, gradually and evenly tighten the cap retaining bolts to the torque listed in this Chapter's Specifications.

51   Install the timing belt sprocket on the exhaust camshaft (see Section 5).

52   Install the timing belt (see Section 5). When installing the timing belt, make sure the crankshaft is at TDC for the No. 1 cylinder (see Section 3), the camshaft sprocket marks are aligned with the upper edge of the

cylinder head **(see illustration 5.7)**. and the crankshaft sprocket mark is aligned with the stationary index mark on the oil pump housing **(see illustration 5.22)**.

53   The remainder of installation is the reverse of removal.

10   Intake manifold - removal and installation

Carbureted models

Refer to illustrations 10.4a, 10.4b, 10.4c and 10.4d

Removal

1   Disconnect the cable from the negative terminal of the battery.

2   Drain the cooling system (see Chapter 1).

3   On carbureted models, remove the air cleaner (see Chapter 4).

4   Clearly label **(see illustration)** and disconnect all hoses, wires, brackets and emis-

sion lines which run to the carburetor and intake manifold. Several components may be slipped out of brackets and laid over the carburetor **(see illustrations)**.

5   Disconnect the fuel lines from the carburetor and cap the fittings to prevent leakage (see Chapter 4).

6   Disconnect the throttle cable from the carburetor (see Chapter 4).

7   Detach the cable which runs from the carburetor to the transaxle (automatic transaxle only) and the cruise control cable, on vehicles so equipped.

8   Unbolt the intake manifold and remove it from the engine. If it sticks, tap the manifold with a soft-face hammer. **Caution:** *Do not pry between gasket sealing surfaces or damage the carburetor.*

9   If necessary, remove the carburetor and components from the manifold. Thoroughly clean the manifold and cylinder head mating surfaces, remove all traces of gasket material.

Installation

10   Install the manifold, using a new gasket. Tighten the nuts in several stages, working from the center out, to the torque listed in this Chapter's Specifications.

11   Install the remaining parts in the reverse order of removal.

12   Add coolant, run the engine and check for leaks and proper operation.

Fuel-injected models

Refer to illustrations 10.27 and 10.32

Removal

13   Relieve the fuel system pressure (see Chapter 4).

14   Disconnect the cable from the negative terminal of the battery.

15   Drain the cooling system (see Chapter 1).

16   Disconnect the air temperature sensor electrical connector, air hose and the MAF sensor electrical connector, as applicable from the air intake duct, then loosen the

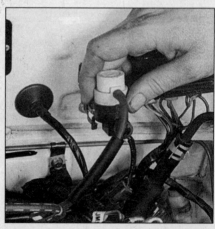

10.4c Detach the emission control valves from the brackets (carbureted models)

10.4d Detach the solenoid (A) from the firewall and disconnect the hose from the back of the valve (B) (carbureted models)

10.27 Remove the intake air plenum from the intake manifold (1995 through 1999 SOHC and DOHC models; 2000 and later models use a one-piece manifold)

10.32 Remove the intake manifold bolts/nuts and detach the intake manifold from the cylinder head (1995 through 1999 SOHC and DOHC models; 2000 and later models use a one-piece manifold)

clamps and disconnect the air duct from the air cleaner and throttle body (see Chapter 4).

17   Remove the intake duct from the engine compartment.

18   Carefully mark and disconnect all hoses and wiring connectors from the upper intake manifold (plenum) and throttle body.

19   On 1995 through 2005 models, disconnect the electrical connector from the Idle Speed Actuator (ISA), which is bolted to the throttle body. On 2006 and later models, remove the ISA from the intake manifold.

20   Loosen the bolts and disconnect the accelerator cable from the throttle body (see Section 4). Remove the cable from the intake plenum mounting bracket and place the accelerator cable to one side.

21   Remove the throttle body from the intake plenum (see Chapter 4).

22   Loosen the clamps and disconnect the positive crankcase ventilation hose and brake servo vacuum hose from the intake manifold.

23   Mark, then disconnect any remaining vacuum hoses or electrical connectors.

24   Disconnect the fuel feed and return lines from the fuel rail (see Chapter 4). Disconnect the electrical connectors from the fuel injectors.

25   Remove the fuel rail, fuel injectors and fuel pressure regulator as an assembly (see Chapter 4). Tape over, plug, or cover all fuel hoses and injector holes to prevent dust and dirt intrusion.

26   Unbolt and remove the intake plenum support bracket from the intake manifold.

27   Remove the intake plenum and gasket **(see illustration)**.

28   Loosen the clamp and disconnect the heater hose from the intake manifold.

29   On 1994 and earlier models, disconnect the wiring from the two engine temperature sensors on the right-hand end of the intake manifold.

30   On 1994 and earlier models, remove the thermostat (see Chapter 3).

31   On 1994 and earlier models, remove the distributor, ignition coil and the power transistor (see Chapter 5).

32   Unscrew the nuts or bolts and remove the intake manifold from the engine **(see illustration)**. Remove the gasket.

Installation

33   Installation is the reverse of the removal procedures, noting the following:

a) *Prior to installation, examine the manifold studs for signs of damage and corrosion; remove all traces of corrosion, and repair or replace any damaged studs.*

b) *Ensure that the manifold and cylinder head mating surfaces are clean and dry, and install a new gasket. Install the manifold, and tighten its retaining nuts and bolts to the torque listed in the Specifications.*

c) *Install the stay bracket, tighten the bracket bolts by hand, then tighten them to the torque listed in the Specifications.*

d) *Ensure that hoses are reconnected to their original positions, and are held by their retaining clamps.*

e) *Refill the cooling system (see Chapter 1).*

f) *Reconnect and adjust the accelerator cable (see Section 4). Adjust the kickdown cable (if required) (see Chapter 7B).*

---

11   Exhaust manifold - removal and installation

Carbureted models

Refer to illustrations 11.3, 11.6, 11.7, 11.8 and 11.12

Warning: *Allow the engine to cool completely before following this procedure.*

Removal

1   Disconnect the cable from the negative terminal of the battery.

2   Set the parking brake and block the rear wheels. Raise the vehicle and support it securely on jackstands.

3   Working from under the vehicle, remove the nuts retaining the exhaust downpipe to the exhaust manifold **(see illustration)**. Apply penetrating oil to the threads to make removal easier. Lower and support the exhaust pipe. Remove the gasket.

4   Remove the air cleaner assembly (see Chapter 4).

5   Disconnect the oxygen sensor electrical connector, if equipped (see Chapter 6). Remove the oxygen sensor, if necessary.

6   Apply penetrating oil and unscrew the flare nuts on the air injection tube, if equipped

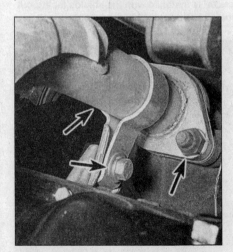

11.3 Working under the vehicle, apply penetrating oil to the threads and remove the nuts - note that one is hidden from view (carbureted models)

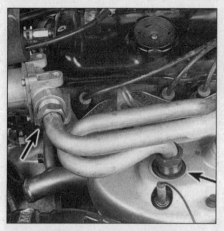

11.6 Apply penetrating oil and unscrew the air injection tube flare nuts (carbureted models)

11.7 Remove the bolts from the heat shield (carbureted models)

Installation

10   Clean and inspect all threaded fasteners and repair as necessary.

11   Remove any traces of gasket material from the mating surfaces and inspect them for wear and cracks.

12   Install a new gasket (see illustration), install the manifold and tighten the nuts in stages, working from the center out, to the torque listed in this Chapter's Specifications.

13   Install the remaining parts in the reverse order of removal.

14   Run the engine and check for exhaust leaks.

Fuel injected models

Refer to illustrations 11.16a, 11.16b, 11.17, 11.19a and 11.19b

15   Raise the vehicle and place it securely on jackstands. Remove any engine splash shields.

16   Remove the flange bolts and nuts that secure the lower end of the exhaust manifold to the rest of the exhaust system (see illustrations). Lower the vehicle.

17   Locate the oxygen sensor (see Chap-

(see illustration). Remove the tube from the manifold.

7   Remove the three bolts that hold the heat shield to the exhaust manifold (see illustration). Lift off the heat shield.

8   Apply penetrating oil to the threads and remove the exhaust manifold mounting nuts (see illustration), brackets and emission components.

9   Slide the manifold off the studs and remove it from the engine compartment.

11.8 Remove the exhaust manifold mounting nuts (1986 through 1993 carbureted model shown)

11.12 The exhaust gasket is installed with the shields facing out as shown here (1986 through 1993 model shown)

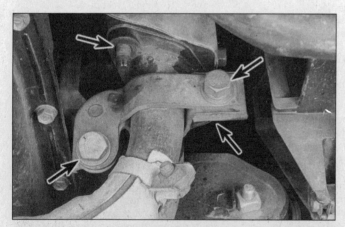

11.16a Typical connection between the exhaust manifold and the downpipe on 1998 and earlier models. Remove the clamp bolts and clamp, then remove the two manifold flange nuts (one flange nut not visible)

11.16b Typical 1996 and later connection between the exhaust manifold (which includes the catalytic converter) and the exhaust system. Simply remove the two exhaust manifold flange nuts

11.17 Disconnect the oxygen sensor electrical connector, then remove the heat shield retaining bolts

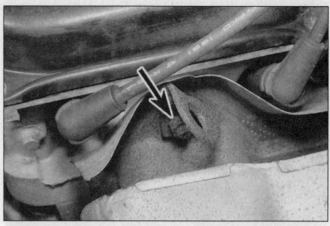

11.19a Before removing the exhaust manifold on 1990 through 1995 fuel-injected models, note the location of the engine lifting bracket. When you install the exhaust manifold, don't forget to install this bracket on the same manifold stud

ter 6), trace the sensor electrical lead to the connector (see illustration) and disconnect it.

18 Unbolt and remove the heat shield from the exhaust manifold.

19 Note the location of the engine lifting bracket, if installed, on the exhaust manifold (see illustration). Don't forget to install this bracket at the same location when installing the exhaust manifold. Remove the exhaust manifold nuts (see illustration) and remove the manifold. Remove and discard the old exhaust gasket.

Installation

20 Installation is the reverse of the removal procedure, note the following:

a) Examine all the exhaust manifold studs for signs of damage and corrosion; remove all traces of corrosion, and repair or replace any damaged studs.

b) Ensure that the manifold and cylinder head mating surfaces are clean and flat, and install the new manifold gasket with the gasket shields facing out. Install the lifting bracket and tighten the manifold

retaining nuts to the torque listed in the Specifications.

c) Reconnect the front downpipe to the manifold, using a new gasket and retaining nuts.

12 Cylinder head - removal and installation

Caution: Allow the engine to cool completely before following this procedure.

Removal

Refer to illustration 12.10

Note: To aid installation, note the locations of all brackets and the routing of hoses and cables before removing them.

1 Position the number one piston at Top Dead Center (see Section 3).

2 Disconnect the cable from the negative terminal of the battery.

3 Drain the cooling system and remove the spark plugs (see Chapter 1).

4 Remove the intake manifold (see Section 10).

5 Remove the exhaust manifold (see Section 11).

6 Remove the distributor or ignition coil pack, including the spark plug wires (see Chapter 5).

7 On carbureted models, remove the air cleaner assembly and intake duct, then remove the fuel pump (see Chapter 4).

8 Remove the timing belt (see Section 7).

9 Remove the valve cover (see Section 4).

10 Loosen the cylinder head bolts, 1/4-turn at a time, in the sequence shown (see illustration) until they can be removed by hand.

11 Carefully lift the cylinder head straight up and place the head on wooden blocks to prevent damage to the sealing surfaces. If the head sticks to the engine block, dislodge it by placing a block of wood against the head casting and tapping the wood with a hammer. Cylinder head disassembly and inspection procedures are covered in Chapter 2B. It's a good idea to have the head checked for warpage, even if you're just replacing the gasket.

11.19b To detach the exhaust manifold from the cylinder head, remove the manifold retaining nuts (typical DOHC model shown)

12.10 Cylinder head bolt loosening sequence (DOHC model shown, SOHC models same)

12.13 Install the new head gasket dry (no sealer) as shown - it can
only go on one way due to the dowels

12.14a Cylinder head bolt tightening sequence (DOHC model
shown, SOHC models same)

12.14b On 2000 and later models, an
angle-measuring gauge is needed to
angle-torque the cylinder head bolts

Installation

Refer to illustrations 12.13, 12.14a and 12.14b

12   Remove all traces of gasket material from the block and head. Do not allow
anything to fall into the engine. Clean and
inspect all threaded fasteners and be sure the
threaded holes in the block are clean and dry.

13   Place a new gasket and the cylinder
head in position (see illustration).

14   Tighten the cylinder head bolts progressively, and in the correct sequence to the
torque listed in this Chapter's Specifications
(see illustrations).

15   Install the timing belt (see Section 7).

16   Install the remaining parts in the reverse
order of removal.

17   Be sure to refill the cooling system and
check all fluid levels. Rotate the crankshaft
clockwise slowly by hand through two complete revolutions. Recheck the camshaft timing marks (see Section 7).

18   Start the engine and set the ignition
timing (see Chapter 1). Run the engine until
normal operating temperature is reached.
Check for leaks and proper operation. Shut
off the engine, Remove the valve cover and
re-tighten the cylinder head bolts, unless the
gasket manufacturer states otherwise. On
1994 and earlier models, recheck the valve
adjustment.

13   Oil pan - removal and Installation

Removal

Refer to illustrations 13.5a and 13.5b

1   Disconnect the cable from the negative
terminal of the battery.

2   Set the parking brake and block the rear
wheels. Raise the front of the vehicle and support it securely on jackstands.

3   Remove the splash shield under the drive-

13.5a To detach the oil pan, remove all bolts from the perimeter of
the pan (stamped-steel oil pan shown, cast aluminum
pans similar)

13.5b Strike the oil pan with a rubber mallet to break the seal

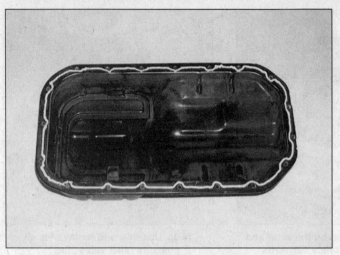

13.8 Apply a 3/16-inch wide bead of RTV sealant to the oil pan flange

14.1a Unscrew the retaining bolts . . .

belt end of the engine, then remove the dipstick and drain the engine oil (see Chapter 1).

4   Unbolt the exhaust downpipe from the exhaust manifold (see Section 11).

5   Remove the bolts and lower the oil pan from the vehicle **(see illustrations)**. If the pan is stuck, tap it with a soft-face hammer or place a block of wood against the pan and tap the wood with a hammer.

6   While the oil pan is removed, take the opportunity to check the oil pump pick-up/strainer for signs of clogging or splitting. If necessary, unbolt the pick-up/strainer and remove it from the base of the oil pump housing along with its gasket. The strainer can then be cleaned easily in solvent or replaced.

Installation

Refer to illustration 13.8

7   Thoroughly clean the oil pan and sealing surfaces. Remove all traces of old gasket

material. On models with a stamped-steel oil pan, check the oil pan sealing surface for distortion (straighten or replace as necessary).

8   If the oil pan was sealed with RTV sealant only (no gasket), apply a 1/8 to 3/16 inch bead of RTV sealant as shown **(see illustration)**. If you are using a gasket, apply a thin coat of gasket sealer to the oil pan flange and attach the gasket.

9   Place the oil pan in position and install the bolts finger tight. Working side-to-side from the center out, tighten the bolts to the torque listed in this Chapter's Specifications.

10   Install the remaining parts in the reverse order of removal.

11   Refill the crankcase with the proper quantity and grade of oil and run the engine, checking for leaks. Road test the vehicle and check for leaks again.

14   Oil pump - removal, inspection and installation

Removal

Refer to illustrations 14.1a, 14.1b and 14.4

1   Remove the oil pan (see Section 13), then unbolt and remove the oil pump pick-up strainer from the bottom of the oil pump housing. Remove the gasket **(see illustrations)**.

2   Remove the oil filter (see Chapter 1).

3   Remove the timing belt, timing belt tensioner pulley, the crankshaft sprocket and timing belt guide flange (see Section 7).

4   Loosen and remove the oil pump retaining bolts, note the location of each bolt (the bolts are of different lengths) **(see illustration)**.

5   Slide the oil pump assembly off the end of the crankshaft. Remove the gasket and discard it.

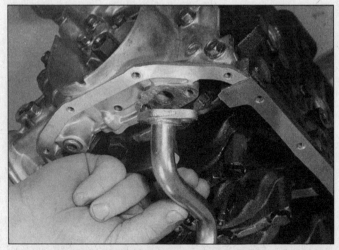

14.1b . . . and remove the oil pump pick-up strainer and gasket

14.4 Oil pump retaining bolt locations - 1994 and earlier models

1   Short bolts (20 mm)   3   Long bolts (60 mm)
2   Medium bolts (30 mm)

14.6 Remove the oil pump cover retaining screws

14.7 The indentations on the inner and outer rotors must face outwards

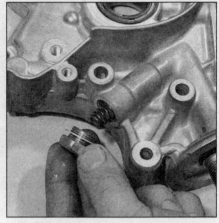

14.9a Unscrew and remove the oil pressure relief valve plug . . .

Inspection

Refer to illustrations 14.6, 14.7, 14.9a, 14.9b, 14.11a, 14.11b, 14.11c, 14.11d and 14.11e

6   Remove the retaining screws and lift the oil pump cover from the rear of the oil pump housing **(see illustration)**.

7   Check if the rotor positions are marked; they should have indentations on their outside surfaces. If not, use a marking pen to mark the surface of both the pump inner and outer rotors **(see illustration)**.

8   Lift the inner and outer rotors from the oil pump housing.

9   Unscrew the oil pressure relief valve plug from the top of the oil pump housing and remove its seal. Remove the spring and plunger from the oil pump housing, note how the plunger is installed **(see illustrations)**.

10   Clean the components, and carefully examine the rotors, pump body and relief valve plunger for signs of scoring or wear. Individual components are available but it is highly recommended that the complete pump is replaced if it is excessively worn.

11   If the components are repairable, measure the clearances given in this Chapter's

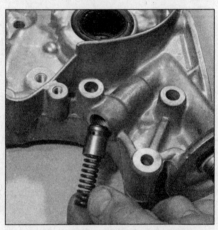

14.9b . . . and remove the spring and plunger

Specifications using feeler gauges. Also measure the rotor endplay, and check the flatness of the end cover **(see illustrations)**. If any clearance exceeds the tolerance listed in this Chapter's Specifications, the oil pump must be replaced.

14.11b On 1994 and earlier models, check the inner rotor-to-crescent clearance . . .

14.11a Using a feeler gauge to measure the outer rotor-to-housing clearance

12   If the oil pump is satisfactory, reassemble the components in the reverse order of removal, tightening the cover screws to the torque listed in this Chapter's Specifications. Prime the oil pump by filling it with clean engine oil while rotating the inner rotor.

14.11c . . . and the outer rotor-to-crescent clearance

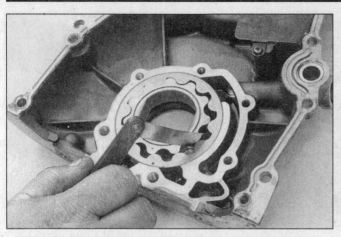

14.11d On 1995 and later models, check the clearance between the inner and outer rotor tips

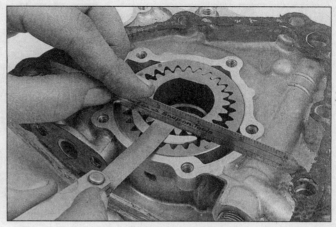

14.11e . . . Use a precision straightedge and feeler gauge to measure the rotor endplay

Installation

Refer to illustration 14.13a, 14.13b, 14.14 and 14.15

13   Prior to installation, note the correct installed depth of the crankshaft oil seal then carefully pry out the seal using a flat-bladed screwdriver. Install a new oil seal, making sure its sealing lip is facing inwards, and press it squarely into the housing using a socket which bears only on the hard outer edge of the seal **(see illustrations)**.

14   Make sure the locating dowels are in position, then wipe the mating faces of the oil pump housing and cylinder block clean and place a new gasket on the cylinder block face **(see illustration)**.

15   Carefully maneuver the oil pump housing into position, engaging the inner rotor with the flats on the crankshaft, take care not damage the oil seal lip **(see illustration)**.

16   Install the oil pump housing retaining bolts in their original locations and tighten them to the torque listed in this Chapter's Specifications.

17   Install the oil pick-up strainer on the bot-

tom of the oil pump housing, install a new gasket and tighten the mounting bolts to the torque listed in this Chapter's Specifications.

18   Install the oil pan and a new gasket (see Section 13).

19   Install the timing belt tensioner pulley, the crankshaft sprocket and timing belt guide flange (together with the timing belt) (see Section 7).

20   Install the oil filter and refill the engine with clean oil (see Chapter 1).

---

15   Flywheel/driveplate - removal and installation

Removal

Flywheel (manual transaxle models)

Refer to illustration 15.3

1   Remove the transaxle (see Chapter 7A) then remove the clutch assembly (see Chapter 6).

14.13a Prior to installation, carefully pry out the oil seal . . .

2   Make alignment marks between the flywheel and crankshaft using paint or a marker pen.

3   Use a flywheel holding tool or wedge

14.13b . . . and install a new one using a socket as a drift

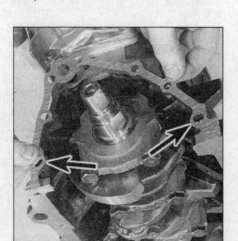

14.14 Install the new gasket over the locating dowels

14.15 When installing the oil pump, locate the inner rotor on the flats on the crankshaft

15.3 Loosen the flywheel retaining bolts with a breaker bar and socket - note the locking tool used to hold the flywheel stationary

15.6 Apply alignment marks and remove the driveplate retaining bolts

16.2 Working from below the left inner fender, carefully pry the seal out with a small screwdriver

a large screwdriver in the flywheel ring gear teeth to hold the flywheel stationary. Loosen and remove the flywheel retaining bolts and remove the flywheel (see illustration). Caution: Do not drop it - it is very heavy.

Driveplate (automatic transaxle models)

Refer to illustration 15.6

4   Remove the transaxle (see Chapter 7B).
5   Make alignment marks between the driveplate and crankshaft using paint or a marker pen.
6   Loosen and remove the retaining bolts and remove the driveplate (see illustration). Remove the spacers installed on each side of the plate.

Inspection

7   On models with a manual transaxle, examine the flywheel for scoring of the clutch face, and for wear or chipping of the ring gear teeth. If the clutch face is scored, the flywheel may be surface-ground, but replacement is

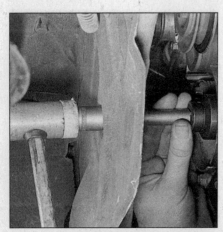

16.4 Using a socket and drift to tap the new crankshaft oil seal into the oil pump housing

preferable. Ask a dealer or automotive repair shop if machining is possible. It is possible to replace the ring gear separately, but this task should be done at a properly equipped machine shop.
8   On models with an automatic transaxle, check the torque converter driveplate carefully for signs of distortion. Look for any hairline cracks around the bolt holes or radiating outwards from the center. If any sign of wear or damage is found, the driveplate must be replaced.

Installation

9   Clean the mating surfaces of the flywheel/driveplate, spacers (if equipped) and crankshaft. Install the locating dowel if it was removed.
10   Apply thread-locking compound to the threads of the retaining bolts. Install the flywheel/driveplate, aligning the marks made previously and install the bolts. Caution: Ensure the flywheel/driveplate is installed correctly, the bolts are unequally spaced and only align in one position.
11   Hold the flywheel/driveplate stationary and tighten the retaining bolts to the torque listed in this Chapter's Specifications.
12   On manual transaxle models, install the clutch (see Chapter 8).
13   Install the transaxle (see Chapter 7A or 7B).

16   Crankshaft oil seals - replacement

Front oil seal

Refer to illustrations 16.2 and 16.4

1   Remove the timing belt, crankshaft sprocket and timing belt guide flange (see Section 7).
2   Working from below the left inner fender, note the correct installed depth of the crank-

shaft oil seal then carefully pry out the seal using a seal removal tool or small flat-bladed screwdriver (see illustration). Caution: Care must be taken to avoid damage to the oil pump housing or crankshaft. Note: If the seal is tight and cannot be pried out using a screwdriver or seal removal tool, use the method shown in illustrations 8.2a and 8.2b.
3   Clean the seal seat in the oil pump housing and polish off any burrs or raised edges which may have caused the original seal failure. If there is a groove worn in the crankshaft sealing surface (from contact with the seal), installing a new seal will probably not stop the leak.
4   Lubricate the lips of the new seal with clean engine oil and place it in position on the end of the crankshaft. Press the seal squarely into position to the previously noted depth. A hammer and a socket, which bears only on the hard outer edge of the seal can be used to tap the seal into position (see illustration). Take care not to damage the seal lips during installation and ensure that the seal lips face inwards.
5   Install the timing belt guide flange, crankshaft sprocket and the timing belt (see Section 7).

Rear oil seal

Refer to illustrations 16.7 and 16.10

Note: The preferred method for rear oil seal replacement requires removal of the oil pan and the rear oil seal retainer (see Chapter 2B). The following method may be used as an alternative, but extreme care must be taken not to damage the crankshaft sealing surface during removal and the seal must be carefully installed or an oil leak may develop.
6   Remove the flywheel/driveplate (see Section 15).
7   Carefully pry out the old oil seal out of the housing using a seal removal tool or small flat-bladed screwdriver (see illustration). Take care not to damage the surface of the crankshaft.

8   Clean the seal housing and polish off any burrs or raised edges which may have caused the original seal failure.

9   Wipe the oil seal seat clean, then dip the new seal in fresh engine oil. Place it over the crankshaft, making sure its sealing lip is facing inwards. Make sure that the oil seal lip is not damaged, it is located on the rear of the crankshaft.

10   Preferably the proper seal installation tool is required to seat the new seal in the housing, but the appropriate size metal tube or socket can be used as a drift. If the proper tool is not available, use a blunt tool and carefully drive the oil seal squarely into position slowly working around the seal **(see illustration)**. Seat the seal until it is in firm contact with the housing.

11   Install the flywheel/driveplate (see Section 15).

16.7 Use a seal removal tool to pry out the old crankshaft rear oil seal

16.10 Using a blunt tool, carefully tap the new crankshaft rear oil seal into position

17   Engine/transaxle mounts - inspection and replacement

Inspection

1   Set the parking brake and block the rear wheels. Raise the front of the vehicle and support it securely on jackstands.

2   Check the rubber on each mount to see if it is cracked, hardened or separated from the metal; replace the mount if any damage or deterioration is evident.

3   Use a torque wrench, if possible, to check that all mount fasteners are tight.

4   Using a large screwdriver or a prybar, check for wear in the mount by carefully prying against it to check for free play. When this is not possible, have a helper move the engine/transaxle back and forth, or from side to side, while you watch the mount. Some freeplay is to be expected even from new components, but excessive wear should be obvious. If excessive freeplay is found, check that the fasteners are correctly tightened, then replace worn components as described below.

Replacement
Left-hand mount

Refer to illustrations 17.7a, 17.7b and 17.7c

5   Disconnect the cable from the negative terminal of the battery.

6   Place a jack beneath the engine, with a block of wood on the jack head (if necessary, remove the splash shield to improve access to the oil pan). Raise the jack until it is supporting the weight of the engine, or, attach an engine support bar to the lifting brackets and support the weight of the engine with the bar.

7   The left-hand engine mount on 1994 and earlier models supports the timing belt end of the engine. On 1995 and later models, the left-hand side mount is at the transaxle end of the engine. On 1986 through 1989 models, the mount through-bolt has a bracket attached to its forward end which is located on two studs and held with nuts. On 1990 through 1994 models, the mount through-bolt bracket has two arms with four studs and securing nuts. Unscrew and remove the main nut from the through-bolt. On 1986 through 1989 models, unscrew the small locking nut(s), then remove

the through-bolt. Remove the bracket-to-engine mounting nuts/bolts and remove the left-hand mount bracket assembly from the engine **(see illustrations)**. Note the position of the spacers and washers.

8   Check carefully for signs of wear or damage on all components, and replace them where necessary.

9   Place the mount bracket assembly in position and tighten its retaining nuts and bolts securely. Insert the through-bolt, then install its retaining nut and main nut and tighten them securely.

10   Remove the jack from beneath the engine or the engine support bar (as applicable), and reconnect the cable to the negative terminal of the battery.

Right-hand mount

Refer to illustrations 17.13a and 17.13b

11   Apply the parking brake, then raise the front of the vehicle and support it securely on jackstands. Remove the right-hand front tire, then remove the retaining screws and the splash shield to improve access to the mount assembly. On 1986 through 1994 fuel-

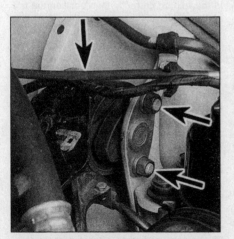

17.7a Typical left-hand engine mount through-bolt attachment points (1986 through 1990 models)

17.7b Typical left-hand engine mount bracket-to-cylinder head nuts/bolts (1991 through 1994 models)

17.7c Typical left-hand engine/transaxle mounting bracket (2008 model shown)

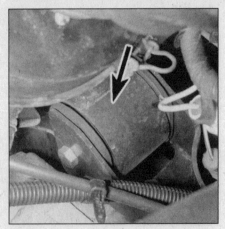

17.13a Typical right-hand engine mount at the transaxle - 1994 and earlier models

17.13b Typical right-hand engine mounting bracket (2008 model shown)

17.20 On 1986 through 1989 models, the front engine mount (roll rod) is attached to the frame and engine bracket with through-bolts (lower bracket shown)

injected models, to further improve access, remove the air cleaner housing (see Chapter 4). On 1986 through 1994 models with manual transaxle, remove the gearshift cable (see Chapter 7A). The right-hand engine mount on 1994 and earlier models supports the transaxle end of the engine. On 1995 and later models, the right-hand side mount is at the timing belt end of the engine. On 1995 and later models the mount through-bolt has a bracket attached to its forward end which is located on two studs and held with nuts.

12   Place a jack beneath the transaxle, with a block of wood on the jack head. Raise the jack until it is supporting the weight of the transaxle.

13   Loosen and remove the through-bolt and nut, then pry out the trim caps from beneath the right-hand wheelwell for access to the mount retaining bolts. Remove the bolts securing the mount to the body and remove the mount from the engine compartment. If necessary, remove the retaining nuts and bolts and remove the mount bracket (see illustrations).

14   Check carefully for signs of wear or damage on all components, and replace them where necessary.

15   If removed, install the mount bracket to the transaxle unit and tighten its retaining bolts securely.

16   Maneuver the mount into position, then tighten its retaining bolts securely and install the trim caps. Insert the through-bolt and tighten its nut securely.

17   Remove the jack from below the transaxle then install the splash shield and tire. Lower the vehicle to the ground and tighten the wheel lug nuts (see Chapter 1). Where necessary, install the air cleaner housing and gearshift control cable.

Front mount/roll rod

Refer to illustrations 17.20, 17.21a and 17.21b

18   1986 through 1989 models have a roll rod with two rubber bumpers at the front of the engine. On 1990 and later models, this was replaced by a single mount with an enlarged mount bracket.

19   Apply the parking brake, then raise the

front of the vehicle and support it securely on jackstands. If necessary, remove the retaining screws and remove the splash shield to improve access to the mount assembly.

20   On 1986 through 1989 models, unscrew and remove the through-bolts and remove the roll rod from the brackets. If necessary, unbolt the bracket from the engine (see illustration).

21   On 1990 and later models, unscrew and remove the mount through-bolt and nut, then remove the retaining bolts and the mount from the crossmember, noting how it is installed (see illustrations). If necessary, the mount bracket can then be unbolted and removed from the engine.

22   Check carefully for signs of wear or damage on all components, and replace them where necessary. On 1986 through 1989 models, the rubber bumpers can be replaced separately.

23   If removed, install the mount bracket and tighten the retaining bolts securely.

24   On 1986 through 1989 models, make sure that the rubber bumpers are located in the roll rod correctly then position the rod at the front of the engine and insert the through-bolts. Make sure the projection on the inside of the head of the lower through-bolt is inserted in the bracket slot. Tighten the nuts securely.

25   On 1990 and later models, place the mount in position and tighten its retaining bolts securely. Insert the through-bolt and tighten the nut securely.

26   Install the splash shield (if removed) and lower the vehicle to the ground.

Rear mount

Refer to illustration 17.28

27   Apply the parking brake, then raise the front of the vehicle and support it on securely on jackstands.

28   Loosen and remove the mount through-bolt and nut (see illustration), then remove the retaining bolts and mount from the

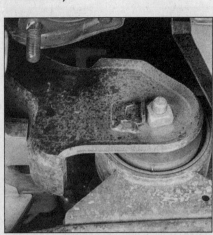

17.21a Typical front mount - 1990 through 2005 models

17.21b Typical front engine mounting bracket (2008 model shown)

17.28 Typical rear engine mounting bracket (2008 model shown)

17.33 Engine stabilizing rod - 1990 through 1994 models with manual transaxles

crossmember, noting which way it is installed. If necessary, the mount bracket can be unbolted and removed from the engine.

29   Check carefully for signs of wear or damage on all components, and replace them where necessary.

30   If removed, install the mount bracket on the engine and tighten its retaining bolts securely.

31   Maneuver the mount into position and tighten its retaining bolts securely. Insert the through-bolt and tighten its nut securely, then lower the vehicle to the ground.

Stabilizing rod (1990 through 1994 manual transaxle models)

Refer to illustration 17.33

32   Apply the parking brake, then raise the front of the vehicle and support it securely on jackstands.

33   Before removing the rod, mark its bottom to ensure correct installation; the rod is not symmetrical and the largest half of the rear mount hole must be at the bottom **(see illustration)**.

34   Loosen and remove the bolt and washers holding the stabilizing rod to the rear of the transaxle unit. Then remove the nut and

bolt holding the rod to the body and remove the stabilizing rod from underneath the vehicle, noting how it is installed.

35   Check the rod and rubber bumpers for signs of wear or damage and replace if necessary.

36   Position the rod, making sure it is installed correctly, and insert the bolt securing it to the body bracket. Place a washer on each side of the transaxle end of the rod, then screw in the mount bolt. Tighten both bolts securely, then lower the vehicle to the ground.

Notes

Chapter 2 Part B
General engine overhaul procedures

Contents

Specifications

General

Displacement
1.5L SOHC and DOHC	91.2 cubic inches (1495 cc)
1.6L DOHC	97.6 cubic inches (1599 cc)

Bore and stroke
1.5L SOHC and DOHC
Bore	2.97 inches (75.5 mm)
Stroke	3.29 inches (83.5 mm)

1.6L DOHC
Bore	3.02 inches (76.5 mm)
Stroke	3.43 inches (87.0 mm)
Cylinder compression pressure	No more than 25 percent variation between cylinders
Oil pressure (engine warm, at idle)	21 psi

Torque specifications

	Ft-lbs
Connecting rod cap nuts	25

Main bearing cap bolts
1994 and earlier models	38
1995 and later models	42

1.1 An engine block being bored. An engine rebuilder will use special machinery to recondition the cylinder bores

1.2 If the cylinders are bored, the machine shop will normally hone the engine on a machine like this

1   General information - engine overhaul

Refer to illustrations 1.1, 1.2, 1.3, 1.4, 1.5 and 1.6

Included in this portion of Chapter 2 are general information and diagnostic testing procedures for determining the overall mechanical condition of your engine.

The information ranges from advice concerning preparation for an overhaul and the purchase of replacement parts and/or components to detailed, step-by-step procedures covering removal and installation.

The following Sections have been written to help you determine whether your engine needs to be overhauled and how to remove and install it once you've determined it needs to be rebuilt. For information concerning in-vehicle engine repair, see Chapter 2A.

The Specifications included in this Part are general in nature and include only those necessary for testing the oil pressure and checking the engine compression. Refer to Chapter 2A for additional engine Specifications.

It's not always easy to determine when, or if, an engine should be completely overhauled, because a number of factors must be considered.

High mileage is not necessarily an indication that an overhaul is needed, while low mileage doesn't preclude the need for an overhaul. Frequency of servicing is probably the most important consideration. An engine that's had regular and frequent oil and filter changes, as well as other required maintenance, will most likely give many thousands of miles of reliable service. Conversely, a neglected engine may require an overhaul very early in its service life.

Excessive oil consumption is an indication that piston rings, valve seals and/or valve guides are in need of attention. Make sure that oil leaks aren't responsible before deciding that the rings and/or guides are bad. Perform a cylinder compression check to determine the extent of the work required (see Section 3). Also check the vacuum readings under various conditions (see Section 4).

Check the oil pressure with a gauge installed in place of the oil pressure sending unit and compare it to this Chapter's Specifications (see Section 2). If it's extremely low, the bearings and/or oil pump are probably worn out.

Loss of power, rough running, knocking or metallic engine noises, excessive valve train noise and high fuel consumption rates may also point to the need for an overhaul, especially if they're all present at the same time. If a complete tune-up doesn't remedy the situation, major mechanical work is the only solution.

An engine overhaul involves restoring the internal parts to the specifications of a new engine. During an overhaul, the piston rings are replaced and the cylinder walls are reconditioned (rebored and/or honed) **(see illustrations 1.1 and 1.2)**. If a rebore is done by an automotive machine shop, new oversize pistons will also be installed. The main bearings, connecting rod bearings and camshaft bearings are generally replaced with new ones and, if necessary, the crankshaft may be reground to restore the journals **(see illustration 1.3)**. Generally, the valves are serviced as well, since they're usually in less-than-perfect condition at this point. While the engine is being overhauled, other components, such as the distributor, starter and alternator, can be rebuilt as well. The end result should be similar to a new engine that will give many trouble free miles. **Note:** *Critical cooling system components such as the hoses, drivebelts, thermostat and water pump should be replaced with new parts when an engine is overhauled. The radiator should be checked carefully to ensure that it isn't clogged or leaking (see Chapter 3). If you purchase a rebuilt engine or short block, some rebuilders will not warranty their engines unless the radiator has been professionally flushed. Also, we don't recommend overhauling the oil pump - always install a new one when an engine is rebuilt.*

Overhauling the internal components on today's engines is a difficult and time-consuming task which requires a significant amount of specialty tools and is best left to a professional engine rebuilder **(see illustrations 1.4, 1.5 and 1.6)**. A competent engine rebuilder will handle the inspection of your old parts and offer advice concerning the reconditioning or replacement of the original engine;

1.3 A crankshaft having a main bearing journal ground

1.4 A machinist checks for a bent connecting rod, using specialized equipment

1.5 A bore gauge being used to check the main bearing bore

1.6 Uneven piston wear like this indicates a bent connecting rod

2.2 On early models, the oil pressure sending unit is located on the side of the engine block, near the alternator (on later models it's located on the side of the engine block, near the transaxle bellhousing)

never purchase parts or have machine work done on other components until the block has been thoroughly inspected by a professional machine shop. As a general rule, time is the primary cost of an overhaul, especially since the vehicle may be tied up for a minimum of two weeks or more. Be aware that some engine builders only have the capability to rebuild the engine you bring them while other rebuilders have a large inventory of rebuilt exchange engines in stock. Also be aware that many machine shops could take as much as two weeks time to completely rebuild your engine depending on shop workload. Sometimes it makes more sense to simply exchange your engine for another engine that's already rebuilt to save time.

2 Oil pressure check

Refer to illustration 2.2

1   Low engine oil pressure can be a sign of an engine in need of rebuilding. A "low oil pressure" indicator (often called an "idiot light") is not a test of the oiling system. Such indicators only come on when the oil pressure is dangerously low. Even a factory oil pressure gauge in the instrument panel is only a relative indication, although much better for driver information than a warning light. A better test is with a mechanical (not electrical) oil pressure gauge.
2   Locate the oil pressure sending unit on the engine block **(see illustration)**.
3   Unscrew and remove the oil pressure sending unit and screw in the hose for your oil pressure gauge. If necessary, install an adapter fitting. Use Teflon tape or thread sealant on the threads of the adapter and/or the fitting on the end of your gauge's hose.
4   Connect an accurate tachometer to the engine, according to the tachometer manufacturer's instructions.
5   Check the oil pressure with the engine running (normal operating temperature) at the specified engine speed, and compare it to this

Chapter's Specifications. If it's extremely low, the bearings and/or oil pump are probably worn out.

3 Cylinder compression check

Refer to illustration 3.6

1   A compression check will tell you what mechanical condition the upper end of your engine (pistons, rings, valves, head gaskets) is in. Specifically, it can tell you if the compression is down due to leakage caused by worn piston rings, defective valves and seats or a blown head gasket. **Note:** *The engine must be at normal operating temperature and the battery must be fully charged for this check.*
2   Disable the ignition system by unplugging the primary electrical connector from the distributor, or on models with distributorless ignition, by disconnecting the electrical connectors from the ignition coils (see Chapter 5). Also, disable the fuel system by disconnecting the fuel pump electrical connector (see Chapter 4, Section 14).
3   Clean the area around the spark plugs before you remove them (compressed air should be used, if available). The idea is to prevent dirt from getting into the cylinders as the compression check is being done.
4   Remove all of the spark plugs from the engine (see Chapter 1).
5   Block the throttle wide open.
6   Install a compression gauge in the spark plug hole **(see illustration)**.
7   Crank the engine over at least seven compression strokes and watch the gauge. The compression should build up quickly in a healthy engine. Low compression on the first stroke, followed by gradually increasing pressure on successive strokes, indicates worn piston rings. A low compression reading on the first stroke, which doesn't build up during successive strokes, indicates leaking valves or a blown head gasket (a cracked head could also be the cause). Record the highest gauge reading obtained.

8   Repeat the procedure for the remaining cylinders and compare the results to this Chapter's Specifications.
9   Add some engine oil (about three squirts from a plunger-type oil can) to each cylinder, through the spark plug hole, and repeat the test.
10   If the compression increases after the oil is added, the piston rings are definitely worn. If the compression doesn't increase significantly, the leakage is occurring at the valves or head gasket. Leakage past the valves may be caused by burned valve seats and/or faces or warped, cracked or bent valves.
11   If two adjacent cylinders have equally low compression, there's a strong possibility that the head gasket between them is blown. The appearance of coolant in the combustion chambers or the crankcase would verify this condition.
12   If one cylinder is slightly lower than the others, and the engine has a slightly rough

3.6 Use a compression gauge with a threaded fitting for the spark plug hole, not the type that requires hand pressure to maintain the seal

4.4 A simple vacuum gauge can be handy in diagnosing engine condition and performance

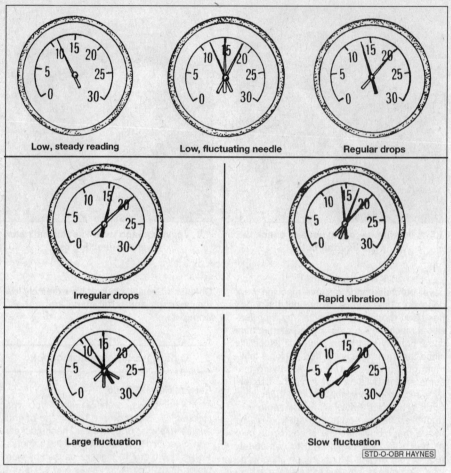

4.6 Typical vacuum gauge readings

idle, a worn lobe on the camshaft could be the cause.

13   If the compression is unusually high, the combustion chambers are probably coated with carbon deposits. If that's the case, the cylinder head(s) should be removed and decarbonized.

14   If compression is way down or varies greatly between cylinders, it would be a good idea to have a leak-down test performed by an automotive repair shop. This test will pin-point exactly where the leakage is occurring and how severe it is.

4   Vacuum gauge diagnostic checks

Refer to illustrations 4.4 and 4.6

1   A vacuum gauge provides inexpensive but valuable information about what is going on in the engine. You can check for worn rings or cylinder walls, leaking head or intake manifold gaskets, restricted exhaust, stuck or burned valves, weak valve springs, improper ignition or valve timing and ignition problems.

2   Unfortunately, vacuum gauge readings are easy to misinterpret, so they should be used in conjunction with other tests to confirm the diagnosis.

3   Both the absolute readings and the rate of needle movement are important for accurate interpretation. Most gauges measure vacuum in inches of mercury (in-Hg). The following references to vacuum assume the diagnosis is being performed at sea level. As elevation increases (or atmospheric pressure decreases), the reading will decrease. For every 1,000 foot increase in elevation above approximately 2,000 feet, the gauge readings will decrease about one inch of mercury.

4   Connect the vacuum gauge directly to the intake manifold vacuum, not to ported (throttle body) vacuum **(see illustration)**. Be sure no hoses are left disconnected during the test or false readings will result.

5   Before you begin the test, allow the engine to warm up completely. Block the wheels and set the parking brake. With the transaxle in Park, start the engine and allow it to run at normal idle speed. **Warning:** *Keep your hands and the vacuum gauge clear of the fans.*

6   Read the vacuum gauge; an average, healthy engine should normally produce about 17 to 22 in-Hg with a fairly steady needle **(see illustration)**. Refer to the following vacuum gauge readings and what they indicate about the engine's condition:

7   A low steady reading usually indicates a leaking gasket between the intake manifold and cylinder head(s) or throttle body, a leaky vacuum hose, late ignition timing or incorrect camshaft timing. Check ignition timing with a timing light and eliminate all other possible causes, utilizing the tests provided in this Chapter before you remove the timing chain cover to check the timing marks.

8   If the reading is three to eight inches below normal and it fluctuates at that low reading, suspect an intake manifold gasket leak at an intake port or a faulty fuel injector.

9   If the needle has regular drops of about two-to-four inches at a steady rate, the valves are probably leaking. Perform a compression check or leak-down test to confirm this.

10   An irregular drop or down-flick of the needle can be caused by a sticking valve or an ignition misfire. Perform a compression check or leak-down test and read the spark plugs.

11   A rapid vibration of about four in-Hg vibration at idle combined with exhaust smoke indicates worn valve guides. Perform a leak-down test to confirm this. If the rapid vibration occurs with an increase in engine speed, check for a leaking intake manifold gasket or head gasket, weak valve springs, burned valves or ignition misfire.

12   A slight fluctuation, say one inch up and down, may mean ignition problems. Check all the usual tune-up items and, if necessary, run the engine on an ignition analyzer.

13   If there is a large fluctuation, perform a compression or leak-down test to look for a weak or dead cylinder or a blown head gasket.

14   If the needle moves slowly through a wide range, check for a clogged PCV system, incorrect idle fuel mixture, throttle body or intake manifold gasket leaks.

15   Check for a slow return after revving the engine by quickly snapping the throttle open until the engine reaches about 2,500 rpm and let it shut. Normally the reading should drop

6.1 After tightly wrapping water-vulnerable components, use a spray cleaner on everything, with particular concentration on the greasiest areas, usually around the valve cover and lower edges of the block. If one section dries out, apply more cleaner

6.2 Depending on how dirty the engine is, let the cleaner soak in according to the directions and hose off the grime and cleaner. Get the rinse water down into every area you can get at; then dry important components with a hair dryer or paper towels

to near zero, rise above normal idle reading (about 5 in-Hg over) and return to the previous idle reading. If the vacuum returns slowly and doesn't peak when the throttle is snapped shut, the rings may be worn. If there is a long delay, look for a restricted exhaust system (often the muffler or catalytic converter). An easy way to check this is to temporarily disconnect the exhaust ahead of the suspected part and redo the test.

5   Engine rebuilding alternatives

The do-it-yourselfer is faced with a number of options when purchasing a rebuilt engine. The major considerations are cost, warranty, parts availability and the time required for the rebuilder to complete the project. The decision to replace the engine block, piston/connecting rod assemblies and crankshaft depends on the final inspection results of your engine. Only then can you make a cost effective decision whether to have your engine overhauled or simply purchase an exchange engine for your vehicle.

Some of the rebuilding alternatives include:

Individual parts - If the inspection procedures reveal that the engine block and most engine components are in reusable condition, purchasing individual parts and having a rebuilder rebuild your engine may be the most economical alternative. The block, crankshaft and piston/connecting rod assemblies should all be inspected carefully by a machine shop first.

Short block - A short block consists of an engine block with a crankshaft and piston/connecting rod assemblies already installed. All new bearings are incorporated and all clearances will be correct. The existing camshafts, valve train components, cylinder head and external parts can be bolted to the short

block with little or no machine shop work necessary.

Long block - A long block consists of a short block plus an oil pump, oil pan, cylinder head, valve cover, camshaft and valve train components, timing sprockets and belt and timing cover. All components are installed with new bearings, seals and gaskets incorporated throughout. The installation of manifolds and external parts is all that's necessary.

Low mileage used engines - Some companies now offer low mileage used engines which is a very cost effective way to get your vehicle up and running again. These engines often come from vehicles which have been in totaled in accidents or come from other countries which have a higher vehicle turn over rate. A low mileage used engine also usually has a similar warranty like the newly remanufactured engines.

Give careful thought to which alternative is best for you and discuss the situation with local automotive machine shops, auto parts dealers and experienced rebuilders before ordering or purchasing replacement parts.

6   Engine removal - methods and precautions

Refer to illustrations 6.1, 6.2, 6.3 and 6.4

If you've decided that an engine must be removed for overhaul or major repair work, several preliminary steps should be taken. Read all removal and installation procedures carefully prior to committing to this job.

Locating a suitable place to work is extremely important. Adequate work space, along with storage space for the vehicle, will be needed. If a shop or garage isn't available, at the very least a flat, level, clean work surface made of concrete or asphalt is required.

Cleaning the engine compartment and

engine before beginning the removal procedure will help keep tools clean and organized **(see illustrations 6.1 and 6.2)**.

An engine hoist will also be necessary. Make sure the hoist is rated in excess of the combined weight of the engine and transaxle. Safety is of primary importance, considering the potential hazards involved in removing the engine from the vehicle.

If you're a novice at engine removal, get at least one helper. One person cannot easily do all the things you need to do to remove a big heavy engine and transaxle assembly from the engine compartment. Also helpful is to seek advice and assistance from someone who's experienced in engine removal.

Plan the operation ahead of time. Arrange for or obtain all of the tools and equipment you'll need prior to beginning the job **(see illustrations 6.3 and 6.4)**. Some of

6.3 Get an engine stand sturdy enough to firmly support the engine while you're working on it. Stay away from three-wheeled models; they have a tendency to tip over more easily, so get a four-wheeled unit.

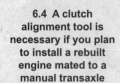

6.4 A clutch alignment tool is necessary if you plan to install a rebuilt engine mated to a manual transaxle

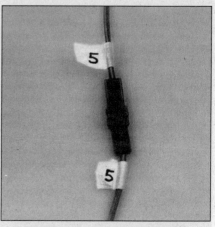

7.6 Label both ends of each wire and hose before disconnecting it

the equipment necessary to perform engine removal and installation safely and with relative ease are (in addition to a vehicle hoist) a heavy duty floor jack (preferably fitted with a transaxle jack head adapter), complete sets of wrenches and sockets as described in the front of this manual, wooden blocks, plenty of rags and cleaning solvent for mopping up spilled oil, coolant and gasoline.

Plan for the vehicle to be out of use for quite a while. A machine shop can do the work that is beyond the scope of the home mechanic. Machine shops often have a busy schedule, so before removing the engine, consult the shop for an estimate of how long it will take to rebuild or repair the components that may need work.

7   Engine - removal and installation

Warning 1: *Gasoline is extremely flammable, so take extra precautions when you work on any part of the fuel system. Don't smoke or allow open flames or bare light bulbs near the work area, and don't work in a garage where a gas-type appliance (such as a water heater or clothes dryer) is present. Since gasoline is carcinogenic, wear fuel-resistant gloves when there's a possibility of being exposed to fuel, and, if you spill any fuel on your skin, rinse it off immediately with soap and water. Mop up any spills immediately and do not store fuel-soaked rags where they could ignite. The fuel system is under constant pressure, so, if any fuel lines are to be disconnected, the fuel pressure in the system must be relieved first (see Chapter 4 for more information). When you perform any kind of work on the fuel system, wear safety glasses and have a Class B type fire extinguisher on hand.*
Warning 2: *The engine must be completely cool before beginning this procedure.*
Note: *Read through the entire sequence before beginning this procedure. The engine and transaxle must be removed as a unit, to be separated afterward on the garage floor.*

Removal

Refer to illustrations 7.6, 7.23, 7.25 and 7.26

1   Relieve the fuel system pressure (see Chapter 4).
2   Place protective covers on the fenders and cowl and remove the hood (see Chapter 11).
3   Remove the battery and the battery tray (see Chapter 5).
4   Remove the air intake duct and the air filter housing (see Chapter 4).
5   Disconnect the throttle valve cable, if equipped (see Chapter 7B). Remove the accelerator cable and the cruise control actuator cable from the throttle body, if equipped (see Chapter 4).
6   Clearly label and disconnect all vacuum lines, coolant and emissions hoses, electrical connectors, ground straps and fuel lines (for fuel line removal see Chapter 4). It's a good idea to label all vacuum lines, emissions hoses and electrical connectors with a permanent marker and tape **(see illustration)**. Take photos or sketch the locations of components and brackets, if necessary.
7   Drain the cooling system, then disconnect the heater hoses at the firewall (see Chapter 3).
8   Remove the accessory drivebelts (see Chapter 1).
9   Unbolt the power steering pump without disconnecting the hoses (see Chapter 10), set the pump aside and secure it with wire.
10   On air-conditioned models, unbolt the compressor and set it aside (see Chapter 3).
Warning: *Do not disconnect the refrigerant hoses.*
11   Unbolt the exhaust pipe from the exhaust manifold (see Chapter 2A). Also remove any exhaust pipe brackets from the engine that might be in the way.
12   Remove the engine cooling fan(s), shroud and radiator (see Chapter 3).
13   Loosen the front wheel lug nuts and the driveaxle/hub nuts. Raise the vehicle and support it securely on jackstands. **Note:** *Don't raise the vehicle any higher than necessary to perform the following steps.*

14   Remove the engine splash shields (see Chapter 2A).
15   Drain the engine oil (see Chapter 1).
16   Drain the transaxle fluid (see Chapter 1).
17   Remove the starter (see Chapter 5).
18   Remove the driveaxles (see Chapter 8).
19   If you're working a 1986 through 1989 model with a manual transaxle, disconnect the clutch cable (see Chapter 8). If you're working on a 1990 or later model with a manual transaxle, remove the clutch release cylinder (see Chapter 8).
20   If you're working on a 1986 through 1989 model with a manual transaxle, disconnect the shift rod and extension rod from the transaxle (see Chapter 7A). If you're working on a 1990 or later model, disconnect the shift cables from the transaxle (see Chapter 7A).
21   If you're working on a model with an automatic transaxle, disconnect the shift cables from the transaxle (see Chapter 7B) and disconnect the transmission fluid cooler lines from their pipes at the transaxle. Plug the lines and hoses.
22   On models with an automatic transaxle, remove the torque converter access cover from the lower bellhousing (see Chapter 7B). Mark the relationship of the torque converter to the driveplate, then remove the torque converter-to-driveplate fasteners (see Chapter 7B) and push the converter back slightly into the bellhousing.
23   Support the engine/transaxle assembly from above with a hoist **(see illustration)**. Attach the hoist chain to the lifting brackets. If no lifting brackets or hooks are present, lifting hooks may be available from your local auto parts store or dealer parts department. If not, you will have to fasten the chains to some substantial parts of the engine - ones that are strong enough to take the weight, but in locations that will provide good balance. If you're attaching a chain to a stud on the engine, or are using a bolt passing through the chain and into a threaded hole, place a washer between the nut or bolt head and the chain and tighten the nut or bolt securely. Raise the hoist slightly to take up the slack in the chain. **Warning:**

7.23 Attach the hoist chain to the engine lifting brackets

7.25 On 1986 through 1989 Excel models, it will be necessary to unbolt the brake master cylinder for clearance. Also unbolt the transaxle mounting bracket

Do not place any part of your body under the engine/transaxle when it's supported only by a hoist or other lifting device.

24 Recheck to be sure nothing except the mounts are still connecting the engine/transaxle to the vehicle. Disconnect anything still remaining on the engine and transaxle (see Chapter 7A).

25 Remove all front, side and rear engine and/or transaxle mounting bracket bolts (see Section 17 in Chapter 2A). On 1986 through 1989 Excel models, remove the brake master cylinder (see Chapter 9) and remove the engine/transaxle mounting bracket **(see illustration).**

26 Slowly raise the engine/transaxle assembly out of the vehicle. It may be necessary to tilt the front end of the engine up while pushing the transaxle end down to clear the engine compartment **(see illustration).**

27 Move the engine/transaxle assembly away from the vehicle and carefully lower the hoist until the engine/transaxle assembly is on the floor, supported by wood blocks.

28 Remove the transaxle-to-engine mounting bolts and separate the engine from the transaxle. Remove the flywheel or driveplate and mount the engine on an engine stand.

Installation

29 Installation is the reverse of removal, noting the following points:

a) *Check the rubber insulators of the engine/transaxle mounting brackets. If they're worn or damaged, replace the mounting brackets.*

b) *Attach the transaxle to the engine following the procedure described in Chapter 7.*

c) *Add coolant, oil, power steering and transaxle fluids as needed (see Chapter 1).*

d) *Run the engine and check for proper operation and leaks. Shut off the engine and recheck fluid levels.*

8 Engine overhaul - disassembly sequence

1 It's much easier to remove the external components if the engine is mounted on a portable engine stand. A stand can often be rented quite cheaply from an equipment rental yard. Before the engine is mounted on a stand, the flywheel/driveplate should be removed from the engine.

2 If a stand isn't available, it's possible to remove the external engine components with it blocked up on the floor. Be extra careful not to tip or drop the engine when working without a stand.

3 If you're going to obtain a rebuilt engine, all external components must come off first, to be transferred to the replacement engine. These components include:

Clutch and flywheel (models with manual transaxle)
Driveplate (models with automatic transaxle)
Ignition system components
Emissions-related components
Engine mounts and mount brackets
Flywheel plate (spacer plate between flywheel/driveplate and engine block)
Intake/exhaust manifolds
Fuel injection components
Oil filter
Ignition coils and spark plugs
Thermostat and housing assembly
Water pump

Note: *When removing the external components from the engine, pay close attention to details that may be helpful or important during installation. Note the installed position of gaskets, seals, spacers, pins, brackets, washers, bolts and other small items.*

4 If you're going to obtain a short block (assembled engine block, crankshaft, pistons and connecting rods), then remove the timing chain or belt, cylinder head(s), oil pan, oil pump pick-up tube, oil pump and water pump from your engine so that you can turn in your old short block to the rebuilder as a core. See *Engine rebuilding alternatives* for additional information regarding the different possibilities to be considered.

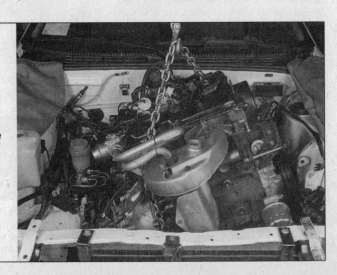

7.26 Slowly lift the engine up at an angle (1986 through 1989 Excel shown)

9.1 Before you try to remove the pistons, use a ridge reamer to remove the raised material (ridge) from the top of the cylinders

9.3 Checking the connecting rod endplay (side clearance)

9   Pistons and connecting rods - removal and installation

Removal

Refer to illustrations 9.1, 9.3 and 9.4

Note: *Prior to removing the piston/connecting rod assemblies, remove the cylinder head and oil pan (see Chapter 2A).*

1   Use your fingernail to feel if a ridge has formed at the upper limit of ring travel (about 1/4-inch down from the top of each cylinder). If carbon deposits or cylinder wear have produced ridges, they must be completely removed with a special tool **(see illustration)**. Follow the manufacturer's instructions provided with the tool. Failure to remove the ridges before attempting to remove the piston/connecting rod assemblies may result in piston breakage.

2   After the cylinder ridges have been removed, turn the engine so the crankshaft is facing up.

3   Before the connecting rods are removed, check the connecting rod endplay with feeler gauges. Slide them between the first connecting rod and the crankshaft throw until the play is removed **(see illustration)**. Repeat this procedure for each connecting rod. The endplay is equal to the thickness of the feeler gauge(s). Check with an automotive machine shop for the endplay service limit (a typical endplay limit should measure between 0.005 to 0.015 inch [0.127 to 0.381 mm]). If the play exceeds the service limit, new connecting rods will be required. If new rods (or a new crankshaft) are installed, the endplay may fall under the minimum allowable. If it does, the rods will have to be machined to restore it. If necessary, consult an automotive machine shop for advice.

4   Check the connecting rods and caps for identification marks. If they aren't plainly marked, use paint or a marker to clearly identify each rod and cap (1, 2, 3, etc., depending

on the cylinder they're associated with) **(see illustration)**.

5   Remove the connecting rod cap nuts from the number one connecting rod.

6   Remove the number one connecting rod cap and bearing insert. Don't drop the bearing insert out of the cap.

7   Remove the bearing insert and push the connecting rod/piston assembly out through the top of the engine. Use a wooden dowel to push on the connecting rod. If resistance is felt, double-check to make sure that all of the ridge was removed from the cylinder.

8   Repeat the procedure for the remaining cylinders.

9   After removal, reassemble the connecting rod caps and bearing inserts in their respective connecting rods and install the cap nuts finger tight. Leaving the old bearing inserts in place until reassembly will help prevent the connecting rod bearing surfaces from being accidentally nicked or gouged.

10   The pistons and connecting rods are

now ready for inspection and overhaul at an automotive machine shop.

Piston ring installation

Refer to illustrations 9.13, 9.14, 9.15, 9.19a, 9.19b and 9.22

11   Before installing the new piston rings, the ring end gaps must be checked. It's assumed that the piston ring side clearance has been checked and verified correct.

12   Lay out the piston/connecting rod assemblies and the new ring sets so the ring sets will be matched with the same piston and cylinder during the end gap measurement and engine assembly.

13   Insert the top (number one) ring into the first cylinder and square it up with the cylinder walls by pushing it in with the top of the piston **(see illustration)**. The ring should be near the bottom of the cylinder, at the lower limit of ring travel.

14   To measure the end gap, slip feeler

9.4 If the connecting rods and caps are not marked, mark the caps to the rods by cylinder number (for example, this would be the No. 4 connecting rod)

9.13 Install the piston ring into the cylinder then push it down into position using a piston so the ring will be square in the cylinder

9.14 With the ring square in the cylinder, measure the ring end gap with a feeler gauge

9.15 If the ring end gap is too small, clamp a file in a vise as shown and file the piston ring ends - be sure to remove all raised material

9.19a Installing the spacer/expander in the oil ring groove

gauges between the ends of the ring until a gauge equal to the gap width is found **(see illustration)**. The feeler gauge should slide between the ring ends with a slight amount of drag. A typical ring gap should fall between 0.010 and 0.020 inch [0.25 to 0.50 mm] for compression rings and up to 0.030 inch [0.76 mm] for the oil ring steel rails. If the gap is larger or smaller than specified, double-check to make sure you have the correct rings before proceeding.

15   If the gap is too small, it must be enlarged or the ring ends may come in contact with each other during engine operation, which can cause serious damage to the engine. If necessary, increase the end gaps by filing the ring ends very carefully with a fine file. Mount the file in a vise equipped with soft jaws, slip the ring over the file with the ends contacting the file face and slowly move the ring to remove material from the ends. When performing this operation, file only by pushing the

9.22 Use a piston ring installation tool to install the number 2 and the number 1 (top) rings - be sure the directional mark on the piston ring(s) is facing toward the top of the piston

ring from the outside end of the file towards the vise **(see illustration)**.

16   Excess end gap isn't critical unless it's greater than 0.040 inch (1.01 mm). Again, double-check to make sure you have the correct ring type.

17   Repeat the procedure for each ring that will be installed in the first cylinder and for each ring in the remaining cylinders. Remember to keep rings, pistons and cylinders matched up.

18   Once the ring end gaps have been checked/corrected, the rings can be installed on the pistons.

19   The oil control ring (lowest one on the piston) is usually installed first. It's composed of three separate components. Slip the spacer/expander into the groove **(see illustration)**. If an anti-rotation tang is used, make sure it's inserted into the drilled hole in the ring groove. Next, install the upper side rail in the same manner **(see illustration)**. Don't use a piston ring installation tool on the oil ring side rails, as they may be damaged. Instead, place one end of the side rail into the groove between the spacer/expander and the ring land, hold it firmly in place and slide a finger around the piston while pushing the rail into the groove. Finally, install the lower side rail.

20   After the three oil ring components have been installed, check to make sure that both the upper and lower side rails can be rotated smoothly inside the ring grooves.

21   The number two (middle) ring is installed next. It's usually stamped with a mark which must face up, toward the top of the piston. Do not mix up the top and middle rings, as they have different cross-sections. **Note:** *Always follow the instructions printed on the ring package or box - different manufacturers may require different approaches.*

22   Use a piston ring installation tool and make sure the identification mark is facing the top of the piston, then slip the ring into the middle groove on the piston **(see illustra-**

9.19b DO NOT use a piston ring installation tool when installing the oil control side rails

tion). Don't expand the ring any more than necessary to slide it over the piston.

23   Install the number one (top) ring in the same manner. Make sure the mark is facing up. Be careful not to confuse the number one and number two rings.

24   Repeat the procedure for the remaining pistons and rings.

Installation

25   Before installing the piston/connecting rod assemblies, the cylinder walls must be perfectly clean, the top edge of each cylinder bore must be chamfered, and the crankshaft must be in place.

26   Remove the cap from the end of the number one connecting rod (refer to the marks made during removal). Remove the original bearing inserts and wipe the bearing surfaces of the connecting rod and cap with a clean, lint-free cloth. They must be kept spotlessly clean.

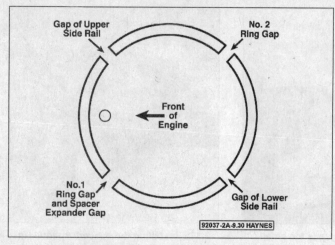

9.30 Position the piston ring end gaps as shown

9.35 Use a plastic or wooden hammer handle to push the piston into the cylinder

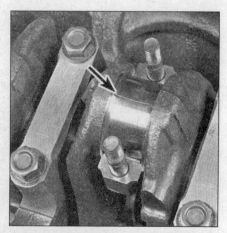

9.37 Place Plastigage on each connecting rod bearing journal parallel to the crankshaft centerline

Connecting rod bearing oil clearance check

Refer to illustrations 9.30, 9.35, 9.37 and 9.41

27   Clean the back side of the new upper bearing insert, then lay it in place in the connecting rod.

28   Make sure the tab on the bearing fits into the recess in the rod. Don't hammer the bearing insert into place and be very careful not to nick or gouge the bearing face. Don't lubricate the bearing at this time.

29   Clean the back side of the other bearing insert and install it in the rod cap. Again, make sure the tab on the bearing fits into the recess in the cap, and don't apply any lubricant. It's critically important that the mating surfaces of the bearing and connecting rod are perfectly clean and oil free when they're assembled.

30   Position the piston ring gaps at the specified intervals around the piston as shown **(see illustration)**.

31   Lubricate the piston and rings with clean engine oil and attach a piston ring compressor to the piston. Leave the skirt protruding about

1/4-inch to guide the piston into the cylinder. The rings must be compressed until they're flush with the piston.

32   Rotate the crankshaft until the number one connecting rod journal is at BDC (bottom dead center) and apply a liberal coat of engine oil to the cylinder walls.

33   With the arrow on top of the piston facing the front (timing belt end) of the engine, gently insert the piston/connecting rod assembly into the number one cylinder bore and rest the bottom edge of the ring compressor on the engine block. Install the pistons with the cavity mark(s) or arrow facing toward the timing belt end of the engine.

34   Tap the top edge of the ring compressor to make sure it's contacting the block around its entire circumference.

35   Gently tap on the top of the piston with the end of a wooden or plastic hammer handle **(see illustration)** while guiding the end of the connecting rod into place on the crankshaft journal (a pair of wooden dowels would be helpful for this). The piston rings may try to pop out of the ring compressor just before entering the cylinder bore, so keep some downward pressure on the ring compressor. Work slowly, and if any resistance is felt as the piston enters the cylinder, stop immediately. Find out what's hanging up and fix it before proceeding. Do not, for any reason, force the piston into the cylinder - you might break a ring and/or the piston.

36   Once the piston/connecting rod assembly is installed, the connecting rod bearing oil clearance must be checked before the rod cap is permanently installed.

37   Cut a piece of the appropriate size Plastigage slightly shorter than the width of the connecting rod bearing and lay it in place on the number one connecting rod journal, parallel with the journal axis **(see illustration)**.

38   Clean the connecting rod cap bearing face and install the rod cap. Make sure the mating mark on the cap is on the same side as the mark on the connecting rod **(see illustration 9.4)**.

39   Install the rod cap nuts, and tighten them to the torque listed in this Chapter's Specifications. **Note:** *Use a thin-wall socket to avoid erroneous torque readings that can result if the socket is wedged between the rod cap and the nut. If the socket tends to wedge itself between the fastener and the cap, lift up on it slightly until it no longer contacts the cap. DO NOT rotate the crankshaft at any time during this operation.*

40   Remove the fasteners and detach the rod cap, being very careful not to disturb the Plastigage.

41   Compare the width of the crushed Plastigage to the scale printed on the Plastigage envelope to obtain the oil clearance **(see illustration)**. The connecting rod oil clearance is usually about 0.001 to 0.002 inch (0.025 to 0.05 mm). Consult an automotive machine shop for the clearance specified for the rod bearings on your engine.

42   If the clearance is not as specified, the

9.41 Use the scale on the Plastigage package to determine the bearing oil clearance - be sure to measure the widest part of the Plastigage and use the correct scale; it comes with both standard and metric scales

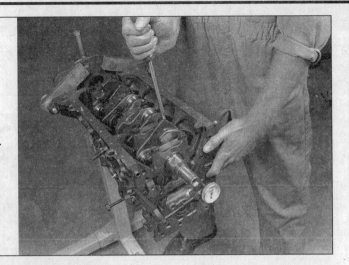

10.1 Checking crankshaft endplay with a dial indicator

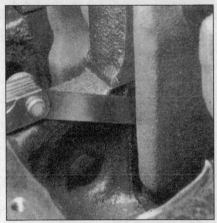

10.3 Checking the crankshaft endplay with feeler gauges at the thrust bearing journal

bearing inserts may be the wrong size (which means different ones will be required). Before deciding that different inserts are needed, make sure that no dirt or oil was between the bearing inserts and the connecting rod or cap when the clearance was measured. Also, recheck the journal diameter. If the Plasti-gage was wider at one end than the other, the journal may be tapered. If the clearance still exceeds the limit specified, the bearing will have to be replaced with an undersize bear-ing. **Caution:** *When installing a new crank-shaft always use a standard size bearing.*

Final installation

43 Carefully scrape all traces of the Plasti-gage material off the rod journal and/or bear-ing face. Be very careful not to scratch the bearing - use your fingernail or the edge of a plastic card.
44 Make sure the bearing faces are per-fectly clean, then apply a uniform layer of clean moly-base grease or engine assembly lube to both of them. You'll have to push the piston into the cylinder to expose the face of the bearing insert in the connecting rod.
45 Slide the connecting rod back into place on the journal, install the rod cap, install the nuts and tighten them to the torque listed in this Chapter's Specifications.
46 Repeat the entire procedure for the remaining pistons/connecting rods.
47 The important points to remember are:
a) *Keep the back sides of the bearing inserts and the insides of the connect-ing rods and caps perfectly clean when assembling them.*
b) *Make sure you have the correct piston/ rod assembly for each cylinder.*
c) *The arrow or mark on the piston must face the front (timing belt) of the engine.*
d) *Lubricate the cylinder walls liberally with clean oil.*
e) *Lubricate the bearing faces when install-ing the rod caps after the oil clearance has been checked.*
48 After all the piston/connecting rod assemblies have been correctly installed, rotate the crankshaft a number of times by

hand to check for any obvious binding.
49 As a final step, check the connecting rod endplay, as described in Step 3. If it was correct before disassembly and the original crankshaft and rods were reinstalled, it should still be correct. If new rods or a new crank-shaft were installed, the endplay may be inad-equate. If so, the rods will have to be removed and taken to an automotive machine shop for resizing.

---

10 Crankshaft - removal and installation

Removal

Refer to illustrations 10.1 and 10.3
Note: *The crankshaft can be removed only after the engine has been removed from the vehicle. It's assumed that the flywheel or driveplate, crankshaft pulley, timing belt or timing chain, oil pan, oil pump body, oil filter and piston/connecting rod assemblies have already been removed. The rear main oil seal retainer must be unbolted and separated from the block before proceeding with crankshaft removal.*
1 Before the crankshaft is removed, mea-sure the endplay. Mount a dial indicator with the indicator in line with the crankshaft and touching the end of the crankshaft as shown **(see illustration)**.
2 Pry the crankshaft all the way to the rear and zero the dial indicator. Next, pry the crank-shaft to the front as far as possible and check the reading on the dial indicator. The distance traveled is the endplay. A typical crankshaft endplay will fall between 0.003 to 0.010 inch (0.076 to 0.254 mm). If it is greater than that, check the crankshaft thrust surfaces for wear after it's removed. If no wear is evident, new main bearings should correct the endplay.
3 If a dial indicator isn't available, feeler gauges can be used. Gently pry the crank-shaft all the way to the front of the engine. Slip feeler gauges between the crankshaft and the front face of the thrust bearing or washer to determine the clearance **(see illustration)**.

4 Loosen the main bearing cap bolts 1/4-turn at a time each, until they can be removed by hand. Follow the reverse of the tightening sequence.
5 Remove the main bearing caps from the engine block.
6 Carefully lift the crankshaft out of the engine. It may be a good idea to have an assistant available, since the crankshaft is quite heavy and awkward to handle.

Installation

7 Crankshaft installation is the first step in engine reassembly. It's assumed at this point that the engine block and crankshaft have been cleaned, inspected and repaired or reconditioned.
8 Position the engine block with the bottom facing up.
9 Remove the original bearing inserts from the main bearing caps.
10 If they're still in place, remove the origi-nal bearing inserts from the block. Wipe the bearing surfaces of the block and main bear-ing caps with a clean, lint-free cloth. They must be kept spotlessly clean. This is critical for determining the correct bearing oil clear-ance.

Main bearing oil clearance check

Refer to illustrations 10.17 and 10.21
11 Without mixing them up, clean the back sides of the new upper main bearing inserts (with grooves and oil holes) and lay one in each main bearing saddle in the engine block. Each upper bearing (engine block) has an oil groove and oil hole in it. **Caution:** *The oil holes in the block must line up with the oil holes in the engine block inserts. The thrust washers must be installed in the correct location.* **Note:** *The thrust washers on the 1.6L SOHC are located on the 4th journal in the engine block (counting from the front). The thrust washers on the 1.6L DOHC B6, the 1.8L DOHC BP and the 1.8L T8 DOHC engines are located on the 3rd journal in the engine block. Clean the back sides of the lower main bearing inserts*

ENGINE BEARING ANALYSIS

Debris

Babbitt bearing embedded with debris from machinings

Microscopic detail of debris

Microscopic detail of gouges

Overplated copper alloy bearing gouged by cast iron debris

Aluminum bearing embedded with glass beads

Microscopic detail of glass beads

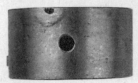

Damaged lining caused by dirt left on the bearing back

Misassembly

Result of a lower half assembled as an upper - blocking the oil flow

Excessive oil clearance is indicated by a short contact arc

Polished and oil-stained backs are a result of a poor fit in the housing bore

Result of a wrong, reversed, or shifted cap

Overloading

Damage from excessive idling which resulted in an oil film unable to support the load imposed

Damaged upper connecting rod bearings caused by engine lugging; the lower main bearings (not shown) were similarly affected

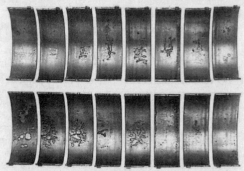

The damage shown in these upper and lower connecting rod bearings was caused by engine operation at a higher-than-rated speed under load

Misalignment

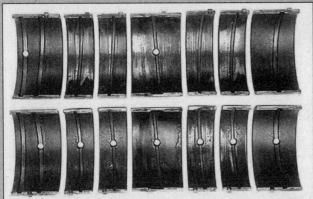

A warped crankshaft caused this pattern of severe wear in the center, diminishing toward the ends

A poorly finished crankshaft caused the equally spaced scoring shown

A tapered housing bore caused the damage along one edge of this pair

A bent connecting rod led to the damage in the "V" pattern

Lubrication

Result of dry start: The bearings on the left, farthest from the oil pump, show more damage

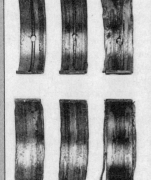

Result of a low oil supply or oil starvation

Severe wear as a result of inadequate oil clearance

Corrosion

Microscopic detail of corrosion

Corrosion is an acid attack on the bearing lining generally caused by inadequate maintenance, extremely hot or cold operation, or inferior oils or fuels

Microscopic detail of cavitation

Example of cavitation - a surface erosion caused by pressure changes in the oil film

Damage from excessive thrust or insufficient axial clearance

Bearing affected by oil dilution caused by excessive blow-by or a rich mixture

10.17 Place the Plastigage onto the crankshaft bearing journal as shown

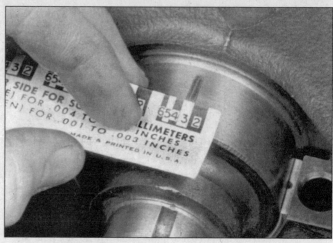

10.21 Use the scale on the Plastigage package to determine the bearing oil clearance - be sure to measure the widest part of the Plastigage and use the correct scale; it comes with both standard and metric scales

and lay them in the corresponding location in the main bearing caps. Make sure the tab on the bearing insert fits into the recess in the block. **Caution:** *Do not hammer the bearing insert into place and don't nick or gouge the bearing faces. DO NOT apply any lubrication at this time.*

12   Clean the faces of the bearing inserts in the block and the crankshaft main bearing journals with a clean, lint-free cloth.

13   Check or clean the oil holes in the crankshaft, as any dirt here can go only one way - straight through the new bearings.

14   Once you're certain the crankshaft is clean, carefully lay it in position in the cylinder block.

15   Before the crankshaft can be permanently installed, the main bearing oil clearance must be checked.

16   Cut several strips of the appropriate size of Plastigage. They must be slightly shorter than the width of the main bearing journal.

17   Place one piece on each crankshaft main bearing journal, parallel with the journal axis as shown **(see illustration)**.

18   Clean the faces of the bearing inserts in the engine block and main bearing caps. Hold the bearing inserts in place and install the main bearing caps onto the crankshaft and cylinder block. DO NOT disturb the Plastigage.

19   Apply clean engine oil to all bolt threads prior to installation, then install all bolts finger-tight. Working from the center out to the ends of the block, tighten the main bearing cap bolts, gradually and evenly, in several steps, to the torque listed in this Chapter's Specifications. DO NOT rotate the crankshaft at any time during this operation.

20   Remove the bolts in the *reverse* order of the tightening sequence and carefully lift the main bearing bridge straight up and off the block. Do not disturb the Plastigage or rotate the crankshaft.

21   Compare the width of the crushed Plasti-

gage on each journal to the scale printed on the Plastigage envelope to determine the main bearing oil clearance **(see illustration)**. Check with an automotive machine shop for the oil clearance for your engine.

22   If the clearance is not as specified, the bearing inserts may be the wrong size (which means different ones will be required). Before deciding if different inserts are needed, make sure that no dirt or oil was between the bearing inserts and the caps or block when the clearance was measured. If the Plastigage was wider at one end than the other, the crankshaft journal may be tapered. If the clearance still exceeds the limit specified, the bearing insert(s) will have to be replaced with an undersize bearing insert(s). **Caution:** *When installing a new crankshaft always install a standard bearing insert set.*

23   Carefully scrape all traces of the Plastigage material off the main bearing journals and/or the bearing insert faces. Be sure to remove all residue from the oil holes. Use your fingernail or the edge of a plastic card - don't nick or scratch the bearing faces.

Final installation

24   Carefully lift the crankshaft out of the cylinder block.

25   Clean the bearing insert faces in the cylinder block, then apply a thin, uniform layer of moly-base grease or engine assembly lube to each of the bearing surfaces. Be sure to coat the thrust faces as well as the journal face of the thrust bearing.

26   Make sure the crankshaft journals are clean, then lay the crankshaft back in place in the cylinder block.

27   Clean the bearing insert faces and apply the same lubricant to them. Clean the engine block and the mating surface of the bearing caps thoroughly. The surfaces must be free of oil residue.

28   Prior to installation, apply clean engine oil to all bolt threads, wiping off any excess,

then install all bolts finger-tight.

29   Tighten the bolts to the torque listed in this Chapter's Specifications following the correct torque sequence.

30   Recheck the crankshaft endplay with a feeler gauge or a dial indicator. The endplay should be correct if the crankshaft thrust faces aren't worn or damaged and if new bearings have been installed.

31   Rotate the crankshaft a number of times by hand to check for any obvious binding. It should rotate with a running torque of 50 in-lbs or less. If the running torque is too high, correct the problem at this time.

32   Install the new rear main oil seal (see Chapter 2A).

11   Engine overhaul - reassembly sequence

1   Before beginning engine reassembly, make sure you have all the necessary new parts, gaskets and seals as well as the following items on hand:

Common hand tools
A 1/2-inch drive torque wrench
New engine oil
Gasket sealant
Thread locking compound

2   If you obtained a short block it will be necessary to install the cylinder head, the oil pump and pick-up tube, the oil pan, the water pump, the timing belt and timing cover, and the valve cover (see Chapter 2A). In order to save time and avoid problems, the external components must be installed in the following general order:

Thermostat and housing cover
Water pump
Intake and exhaust manifolds
Fuel injection components
Emission control components
Spark plug wires and spark plugs

Ignition distributor or coils
Oil filter
Engine mounts and mount brackets
Clutch and flywheel (manual transaxle)
Driveplate (automatic transaxle)

12 Initial start-up and break-in after overhaul

Warning: *Have a fire extinguisher handy when starting the engine for the first time.*

1   Once the engine has been installed in the vehicle, double-check the engine oil and coolant levels.

2   With the spark plugs out of the engine and the ignition system and fuel pump disabled, crank the engine until oil pressure registers on the gauge or the light goes out.

3   Install the spark plugs, hook up the plug wires and restore the ignition system and fuel pump functions.

4   Start the engine. It may take a few moments for the fuel system to build up pressure, but the engine should start without a great deal of effort.

5   After the engine starts, it should be allowed to warm up to normal operating temperature. While the engine is warming up, make a thorough check for fuel, oil and coolant leaks.

6   Shut the engine off and recheck the engine oil and coolant levels.

7   Drive the vehicle to an area with minimum traffic, accelerate from 30 to 50 mph, then allow the vehicle to slow to 30 mph with the throttle closed. Repeat the procedure 10 or 12 times. This will load the piston rings and cause them to seat properly against the cylinder walls. Check again for oil and coolant leaks.

8   Drive the vehicle gently for the first 500 miles (no sustained high speeds) and keep a constant check on the oil level. It is not unusual for an engine to use oil during the break-in period.

9   At approximately 500 to 600 miles, change the oil and filter.

10   For the next few hundred miles, drive the vehicle normally. Do not pamper it or abuse it.

11   After 2,000 miles, change the oil and filter again and consider the engine broken in.

COMMON ENGINE OVERHAUL TERMS

B

Backlash - The amount of play between two parts. Usually refers to how much one gear can be moved back and forth without moving the gear with which it's meshed.

Bearing Caps - The caps held in place by nuts or bolts which, in turn, hold the bearing surface. This space is for lubricating oil to enter.

Bearing clearance - The amount of space left between shaft and bearing surface. This space is for lubricating oil to enter.

Bearing crush - The additional height which is purposely manufactured into each bearing half to ensure complete contact of the bearing back with the housing bore when the engine is assembled.

Bearing knock - The noise created by movement of a part in a loose or worn bearing.

Blueprinting - Dismantling an engine and reassembling it to EXACT specifications.

Bore - An engine cylinder, or any cylindrical hole; also used to describe the process of enlarging or accurately refinishing a hole with a cutting tool, as to bore an engine cylinder. The bore size is the diameter of the hole.

Boring - Renewing the cylinders by cutting them out to a specified size. A boring bar is used to make the cut.

Bottom end - A term which refers collectively to the engine block, crankshaft, main bearings and the big ends of the connecting rods.

Break-in - The period of operation between installation of new or rebuilt parts and time in which parts are worn to the correct fit. Driving at reduced and varying speed for a specified mileage to permit parts to wear to the correct fit.

Bushing - A one-piece sleeve placed in a bore to serve as a bearing surface for shaft, piston pin, etc. Usually replaceable.

C

Camshaft - The shaft in the engine, on which a series of lobes are located for operating the valve mechanisms. The camshaft is driven by gears or sprockets and a timing chain. Usually referred to simply as the cam.

Carbon - Hard, or soft, black deposits found in combustion chamber, on plugs, under rings, on and under valve heads.

Cast iron - An alloy of iron and more than two percent carbon, used for engine blocks and heads because it's relatively inexpensive and easy to mold into complex shapes.

Chamfer - To bevel across (or a bevel on) the sharp edge of an object.

Chase - To repair damaged threads with a tap or die.

Combustion chamber - The space between the piston and the cylinder head, with the piston at top dead center, in which air-fuel mixture is burned.

Compression ratio - The relationship between cylinder volume (clearance volume) when the piston is at top dead center and cylinder volume when the piston is at bottom dead center.

Connecting rod - The rod that connects the crank on the crankshaft with the piston. Sometimes called a con rod.

Connecting rod cap - The part of the connecting rod assembly that attaches the rod to the crankpin.

Core plug - Soft metal plug used to plug the casting holes for the coolant passages in the block.

Crankcase - The lower part of the engine in which the crankshaft rotates; includes the lower section of the cylinder block and the oil pan.

Crank kit - A reground or reconditioned crankshaft and new main and connecting rod bearings.

Crankpin - The part of a crankshaft to which a connecting rod is attached.

Crankshaft - The main rotating member, or shaft, running the length of the crankcase, with offset throws to which the connecting rods are attached; changes the reciprocating motion of the pistons into rotating motion.

Cylinder sleeve - A replaceable sleeve, or liner, pressed into the cylinder block to form the cylinder bore.

D

Deburring - Removing the burrs (rough edges or areas) from a bearing.

Deglazer - A tool, rotated by an electric motor, used to remove glaze from cylinder walls so a new set of rings will seat.

E

Endplay - The amount of lengthwise movement between two parts. As applied to a crankshaft, the distance that the crankshaft can move forward and back in the cylinder block.

F

Face - A machinist's term that refers to removing metal from the end of a shaft or the face of a larger part, such as a flywheel.

Fatigue - A breakdown of material through a large number of loading and unloading cycles. The first signs are cracks followed shortly by breaks.

Feeler gauge - A thin strip of hardened steel, ground to an exact thickness, used to check clearances between parts.

Free height - The unloaded length or height of a spring.

Freeplay - The looseness in a linkage, or an assembly of parts, between the initial application of force and actual movement. Usually perceived as slop or slight delay.

Freeze plug - See Core plug.

G

Gallery - A large passage in the block that forms a reservoir for engine oil pressure.

Glaze - The very smooth, glassy finish that develops on cylinder walls while an engine is in service.

H

Heli-Coil - A rethreading device used when threads are worn or damaged. The device is installed in a retapped hole to reduce the thread size to the original size.

I

Installed height - The spring's measured length or height, as installed on the cylinder head. Installed height is measured from the spring seat to the underside of the spring retainer.

J

Journal - The surface of a rotating shaft which turns in a bearing.

K

Keeper - The split lock that holds the valve spring retainer in position on the valve stem.

Key - A small piece of metal inserted into matching grooves machined into two parts fitted together - such as a gear pressed onto a shaft - which prevents slippage between the two parts.

Knock - The heavy metallic engine sound, produced in the combustion chamber as a result of abnormal combustion - usually detonation. Knock is usually caused by a loose or worn bearing. Also referred to as detonation, pinging and spark knock. Connecting rod or main bearing knocks are created by too much oil clearance or insufficient lubrication.

L

Lands - The portions of metal between the piston ring grooves.

Lapping the valves - Grinding a valve face and its seat together with lapping compound.

Lash - The amount of free motion in a gear train, between gears, or in a mechanical assembly, that occurs before movement can begin. Usually refers to the lash in a valve train.

Lifter - The part that rides against the cam to transfer motion to the rest of the valve train.

M

Machining - The process of using a machine to remove metal from a metal part.

Main bearings - The plain, or babbit, bearings that support the crankshaft.

Main bearing caps - The cast iron caps, bolted to the bottom of the block, that support the main bearings.

O

O.D. - Outside diameter.

Oil gallery - A pipe or drilled passageway in the engine used to carry engine oil from one area to another.

Oil ring - The lower ring, or rings, of a piston; designed to prevent excessive amounts of oil from working up the cylinder walls and into the combustion chamber. Also called an oil-control ring.

Oil seal - A seal which keeps oil from leaking out of a compartment. Usually refers to a dynamic seal around a rotating shaft or other moving part.

O-ring - A type of sealing ring made of a special rubberlike material; in use, the O-ring is compressed into a groove to provide the sealing action.

Overhaul - To completely disassemble a unit, clean and inspect all parts, reassemble it with the original or new parts and make all adjustments necessary for proper operation.

P

Pilot bearing - A small bearing installed in the center of the flywheel (or the rear end of the crankshaft) to support the front end of the input shaft of the transmission.

Pip mark - A little dot or indentation which indicates the top side of a compression ring.

Piston - The cylindrical part, attached to the connecting rod, that moves up and down in the cylinder as the crankshaft rotates. When the fuel charge is fired, the piston transfers the force of the explosion to the connecting rod, then to the crankshaft.

Piston pin (or wrist pin) - The cylindrical and usually hollow steel pin that passes through the piston. The piston pin fastens the piston to the upper end of the connecting rod.

Piston ring - The split ring fitted to the groove in a piston. The ring contacts the sides of the ring groove and also rubs against the cylinder wall, thus sealing space between piston and wall. There are two types of rings: Compression rings seal the compression pressure in the combustion chamber; oil rings scrape excessive oil off the cylinder wall.

Piston ring groove - The slots or grooves cut in piston heads to hold piston rings in position.

Piston skirt - The portion of the piston below the rings and the piston pin hole.

Plastigage - A thin strip of plastic thread, available in different sizes, used for measuring clearances. For example, a strip of plastigage is laid across a bearing journal and mashed as parts are assembled. Then parts are disassembled and the width of the strip is measured to determine clearance between journal and bearing. Commonly used to measure crankshaft main-bearing and connecting rod bearing clearances.

Press-fit - A tight fit between two parts that requires pressure to force the parts together. Also referred to as drive, or force, fit.

Prussian blue - A blue pigment; in solution, useful in determining the area of contact between two surfaces. Prussian blue is commonly used to determine the width and location of the contact area between the valve face and the valve seat.

R

Race (bearing) - The inner or outer ring that provides a contact surface for balls or rollers in bearing.

Ream - To size, enlarge or smooth a hole by using a round cutting tool with fluted edges.

Ring job - The process of reconditioning the cylinders and installing new rings.

Runout - Wobble. The amount a shaft rotates out-of-true.

S

Saddle - The upper main bearing seat.

Scored - Scratched or grooved, as a cylinder wall may be scored by abrasive particles moved up and down by the piston rings.

Scuffing - A type of wear in which there's a transfer of material between parts moving against each other; shows up as pits or grooves in the mating surfaces.

Seat - The surface upon which another part rests or seats. For example, the valve seat is the matched surface upon which the valve face rests. Also used to refer to wearing into a good fit; for example, piston rings seat after a few miles of driving.

Short block - An engine block complete with crankshaft and piston and, usually, camshaft assemblies.

Static balance - The balance of an object while it's stationary.

Step - The wear on the lower portion of a ring land caused by excessive side and back-clearance. The height of the step indicates the ring's extra side clearance and the length of the step projecting from the back wall of the groove represents the ring's back clearance.

Stroke - The distance the piston moves when traveling from top dead center to bottom dead center, or from bottom dead center to top dead center.

Stud - A metal rod with threads on both ends.

T

Tang - A lip on the end of a plain bearing used to align the bearing during assembly.

Tap - To cut threads in a hole. Also refers to the fluted tool used to cut threads.

Taper - A gradual reduction in the width of a shaft or hole; in an engine cylinder, taper usually takes the form of uneven wear, more pronounced at the top than at the bottom.

Throws - The offset portions of the crankshaft to which the connecting rods are affixed.

Thrust bearing - The main bearing that has thrust faces to prevent excessive endplay, or forward and backward movement of the crankshaft.

Thrust washer - A bronze or hardened steel washer placed between two moving parts. The washer prevents longitudinal movement and provides a bearing surface for thrust surfaces of parts.

Tolerance - The amount of variation permitted from an exact size of measurement. Actual amount from smallest acceptable dimension to largest acceptable dimension.

U

Umbrella - An oil deflector placed near the valve tip to throw oil from the valve stem area.

Undercut - A machined groove below the normal surface.

Undersize bearings - Smaller diameter bearings used with re-ground crankshaft journals.

V

Valve grinding - Refacing a valve in a valve-refacing machine.

Valve train - The valve-operating mechanism of an engine; includes all components from the camshaft to the valve.

Vibration damper - A cylindrical weight attached to the front of the crankshaft to minimize torsional vibration (the twist-untwist actions of the crankshaft caused by the cylinder firing impulses). Also called a harmonic balancer.

W

Water jacket - The spaces around the cylinders, between the inner and outer shells of the cylinder block or head, through which coolant circulates.

Web - A supporting structure across a cavity.

Woodruff key - A key with a radiused backside (viewed from the side).

Notes

Chapter 3
Cooling, heating and air conditioning systems

Contents

Specifications

General

Radiator cap pressure rating	11.3 to 15.6 psi
Refrigerant type	
1993 and earlier	R-12
1994 and later	R-134a
Refrigerant capacity	
1993 and earlier	2.0 pounds
1994 through 1999	1.5 pounds
2000 through 2002	1.3 to 1.4 pounds
2003 through 2005	1.2 to 1.3 pounds
2006 and later	1.0 to 1.2 pounds
Refrigerant oil capacity (for component replacement)	
1986 through 1989	
Receiver-drier	1.7 fluid ounces
Condenser	1.0 fluid ounces
Evaporator	1.0 fluid ounces
1990 through 1993	
Accumulator...	3.0 fluid ounces
Condenser	1.0 fluid ounces
Evaporator	1.0 fluid ounces
1994	
Accumulator...	2.6 fluid ounces
Condenser	1.0 fluid ounces
Evaporator	1.6 fluid ounces
1995 and later	
Receiver-drier	1.4 fluid ounces
Condenser	0.9 fluid ounces
Evaporator	1.4 fluid ounces

General (continued)

Thermostat
  1986 through 1999
    Opening temperature.. 190 degrees F
    Fully open at .... 212 degrees F
    Valve lift when fully open .... 0.32 inch (minimum)
  2000 through 2005
    Opening temperature.. 177 degrees F
    Fully open at .... 205 degrees F
    Valve lift when fully open .... 0.33 inch (minimum)
  2006 and later
    Opening temperature.. 180 degrees F
    Fully open at .... 203 degrees F
    Valve lift when fully open .... 0.33 inch (minimum)
Electric cooling fan switch (1994 and earlier models)
  Cut-in temperature (continuity).. 180 to 190 degrees F
  Cut-out temperature (no continuity) .... 172 degrees F
Temperature gauge sender electrical resistance*
  1986
    Sender at 176 degrees F .... 74 ohms
    Sender at 212 degrees F .... 40 ohms
  1987 through 1999
    Sender at 158 degrees F .... 90.5 to 117.5 ohms
    Sender at 239 degrees F .... 21.3 to 26.3 ohms

***Note:** On 2000 and later models, the Engine Coolant Temperature (ECT) sensor handles the temperature gauge sending unit function (see Chapter 6).*

Torque specifications   **Ft-lbs** (unless otherwise indicated)

Note: *One foot-pound (ft-lb) of torque is equivalent to 12 inch-pounds (in-lbs) of torque. Torque values below approximately 15 ft-lbs are expressed in inch-pounds, since most foot-pound torque wrenches are not accurate at these smaller values.*

Water pump bolts
  All bolts except alternator bracket-to-water pump bolt .... 120 in-lbs
  Alternator bracket-to-water pump bolt.. 18
Thermostat housing cover bolts .... 168 in-lbs

1   General information

Engine cooling system

All vehicles covered by this manual employ a pressurized engine cooling system with thermostatically controlled coolant circulation. An impeller type water pump mounted on the front (drivebelt end) of the engine block pumps coolant through the engine. The coolant flows around each cylinder and toward the rear of the engine. Cast-in coolant passages direct coolant around the intake and exhaust ports, near the spark plug areas and in close proximity to the exhaust valve guides.

A wax pellet type thermostat is located in a housing near the transaxle end of the engine. During warm up, the closed thermostat prevents coolant from circulating through the radiator. As the engine nears normal operating temperature, the thermostat opens and allows hot coolant to travel through the radiator, where it's cooled before returning to the engine.

The cooling system is sealed by a pressure type radiator cap, which raises the boiling point of the coolant and increases the cooling efficiency of the radiator. If the system pressure exceeds the cap pressure relief value, the excess pressure in the system forces the spring-loaded valve inside the cap off its seat and allows the coolant to escape through the overflow tube into a coolant reservoir. When the system cools, the excess coolant is automatically drawn from the reservoir back into the radiator.

The coolant reservoir does double duty as both the point at which fresh coolant is added to the cooling system to maintain the proper fluid level and as a holding tank for overheated coolant.

This type of cooling system is known as a closed design because coolant that escapes past the pressure cap is saved and reused.

Heating system

The heating system consists of a blower fan and heater core located in the heater box, the hoses connecting the heater core to the engine cooling system and the heater/air conditioning control panel on the dashboard. Hot engine coolant is circulated through the heater core. When the heater mode is activated, a flap door opens to expose the heater box to the passenger compartment. A fan switch on the control head activates the blower motor, which forces air through the core, heating the air.

Air conditioning system

The air conditioning system consists of a condenser mounted in front of the radiator, an evaporator mounted adjacent to the heater core, a compressor mounted on the engine, a filter-drier which contains a high pressure relief valve and the plumbing connecting all of the above components.

A blower fan forces the warmer air of the passenger compartment through the evaporator core (sort of a radiator-in-reverse), transferring the heat from the air to the refrigerant. The liquid refrigerant boils off into low pressure vapor, taking the heat with it when it leaves the evaporator.

2 Antifreeze - general information

Warning: *Do not allow antifreeze to come in contact with your skin or painted surfaces of the vehicle. Rinse off spills immediately with plenty of water. Antifreeze, if consumed, can be fatal to children and pets, so wipe up garage floor and drip pan coolant spills immediately. Keep antifreeze containers covered and repair leaks in your cooling system as soon as they are noticed.*

The cooling system should be filled with a water/ethylene glycol based antifreeze solution, which will prevent freezing down to at least -20 degrees F, or lower if local climate requires it. It also provides protection against corrosion and increases the coolant boiling point.

The cooling system should be drained, flushed and refilled at the specified intervals (see Chapter 1). Old or contaminated antifreeze solutions are likely to cause damage and encourage the formation of corrosion and scale in the system. Use distilled water with the antifreeze.

Before adding antifreeze, check all hose connections, because antifreeze tends to search out and leak through very minute

3.10a Remove the two thermostat housing cover bolts to gain access to the thermostat (1986 through 1994 models)

openings. Engines don't normally consume coolant, so if the level goes down, find the cause and correct it.

The exact mixture of antifreeze-to-water which you should use depends on the relative weather conditions. The mixture should contain at least 50 percent antifreeze, but should never contain more than 70 percent antifreeze. Consult the mixture ratio chart on the antifreeze container before adding coolant. Hydrometers are available at most auto parts stores to test the coolant. Use antifreeze which meets the vehicle manufacturer's specifications.

3 Thermostat - check and replacement

Warning: *Do not remove the radiator cap, drain the coolant or replace the thermostat until the engine has cooled completely.*

Check

1 Before assuming the thermostat is to blame for a cooling system problem, check the coolant level, drivebelt tension (see Chapter 1) and temperature gauge operation.
2 If the engine seems to be taking a long time to warm up (based on heater output or temperature gauge operation), the thermostat is probably stuck open. Replace the thermostat with a new one.
3 If the engine runs hot, use your hand to check the temperature of the upper radiator hose. If the hose isn't hot, but the engine is, the thermostat is probably stuck closed, preventing the coolant inside the engine from escaping to the radiator. Replace the thermostat. If the upper radiator hose is hot, it means that the coolant is flowing and the thermostat is open. Consult the *Troubleshooting* Section at the front of this manual for cooling system diagnosis. **Caution:** *Don't drive the vehicle without a thermostat. The computer may stay*

3.10b Thermostat housing location (1995 and later SOHC models)

in open loop and emissions and fuel economy will suffer.
4 Further testing of the thermostat can be accomplished by removing the thermostat and suspending it in a container of water. Heat the water while observing the thermostat (do not allow the thermostat to contact the sides of the container during heating). If the thermostat does not fully open as the water boils, it is defective.

Replacement

5 Disconnect the battery cable from the negative terminal of the battery.
6 Drain the cooling system (see Chapter 1). If the coolant is relatively new or in good condition (see Chapter 1), save it and reuse it.

SOHC models
Refer to illustrations 3.10a, 3.10b and 3.13
7 Follow the upper radiator hose to the engine to locate the thermostat housing.
8 Loosen the hose clamp, then detach the hose from the fitting. If it's stuck, grasp it near the end with a pair of large adjustable pliers and twist it to break the seal, then pull it off. If the hose is old or deteriorated, cut it off and install a new one.
9 If the outer surface of the large fitting that mates with the hose is deteriorated (corroded, pitted, etc.) it may be damaged further by hose removal. If it is, the thermostat housing cover will have to be replaced.
10 Remove the bolts and detach the housing cover **(see illustrations)**. If the cover is stuck, tap it with a soft-face hammer to jar it loose. Be prepared for some coolant to spill as the gasket seal is broken.
11 Note how it's installed (which end is facing up), then remove the thermostat.
12 Stuff a rag into the engine opening, then remove all traces of old gasket material and sealant from the housing and cover with a gasket scraper. Remove the rag from the opening and clean the gasket mating surfaces with lacquer thinner or acetone.
13 Install the new thermostat in the hous-

3.13 Make sure the thermostat is installed correctly - if it's installed incorrectly, the engine will overheat and damage will result

3.20 To replace the thermostat, loosen the hose clamp and pull off the radiator hose, then remove the thermostat housing cover bolts and remove the cover (typical DOHC model)

ing. Make sure the correct end faces up - the spring end is normally directed into the engine **(see illustration)**.

14   Apply a thin, uniform layer of RTV sealant to both sides of the new gasket and position it on the housing.

15   Install the cover and bolts. Tighten the bolts to the torque listed in this Chapter's Specifications.

16   Reattach the hose to the fitting and tighten the hose clamp securely.

17   Refill the cooling system (see Chapter 1).

18   Start the engine and allow it to reach normal operating temperature, then check for leaks and proper thermostat operation (as described in Steps 2 through 4).

DOHC models

Refer to illustration 3.20

19   Remove the battery (see Chapter 5) and the air filter housing (see Chapter 4).

20   Loosen the hose clamp **(see illustration)** and disconnect the radiator hose from the thermostat housing.

21   Remove the thermostat housing bolts.

22   Remove and discard the old gasket.

23   Note how the old thermostat is installed, with the jiggle valve facing up, then remove the thermostat.

24   Install the new thermostat with the jiggle valve up.

25   Installation is the reverse of removal (see Steps 12 through 18). Be sure to tighten the thermostat housing bolts to the torque listed in this Chapter's Specifications.

---

4   Radiator - removal and installation

Warning: *Wait until the engine is completely cool before beginning this procedure.*

Removal

Refer to illustrations 4.5, 4.6, 4.9a, 4.9b, 4.9c and 4.9d

1   Disconnect the cable from the negative terminal of the battery.

2   Turn the heater temperature control to the HOT position, remove the radiator drain plug, if equipped, and drain the cooling system (see Chapter 1). If the coolant is relatively new or in good condition, save it and reuse it.

3   Loosen the hose clamps, then detach the radiator hoses from the fittings. If they're stuck, grasp each hose near the end with a pair of large adjustable pliers and twist it to break the seal, then pull it off - be careful not to distort the radiator fittings! If the hoses are old or deteriorated, cut them off and install new ones.

4   Disconnect the reservoir hose from the radiator filler neck.

5   Disconnect the electrical connector(s) for the cooling fan(s) **(see illustration)**. If you can't find the electrical connector(s) for the cooling fan(s), trace the electrical wiring from the fan(s) to the connector(s). **Note:** *There is one cooling fan on models without air conditioning; there are two fans on most models with air conditioning (a few early air-conditioned models have a single fan).*

6   If the vehicle is equipped with an automatic transaxle, place a drain pan under the fittings and disconnect the fluid cooler lines from the bottom of the radiator **(see illustration)**.

7   Plug the open lines and fittings.

8   On 1986 through 1989 models, remove the grille (see Chapter 11).

9   Remove the radiator mounting bolts as follows:

a) *On 1986 through 1989 models, remove the radiator upper end and lower mounting bolts* **(see illustrations)**.

b) *On 1990 through 2005 models, remove the upper insulator bolts and remove the upper insulators from the radiator mounting posts* **(see illustration)**.

c) *On 2006 and later models, remove the fans and fan shrouds, then remove the radiator mounting bolts* **(see illustration)**.

10   Carefully lift out the radiator with the

4.5 On early models, the engine cooling fan wire harness connector is located between the radiator and battery

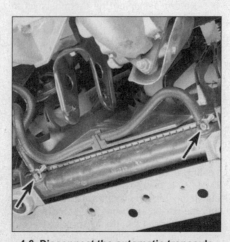

4.6 Disconnect the automatic transaxle fluid cooler lines and cap the lines and fittings (typical)

4.9a On early models, the radiator is mounted to the core support with two bolts on each side

4.9b On early models, the lower bolt on the right side of the radiator is located behind the grille

cooling fan(s) attached. Don't spill coolant on the vehicle or scratch the paint.

11   Remove the cooling fan(s) from the radiator.

12   Inspect the radiator for leaks and damage. If it needs repair, have a radiator shop or dealer service department perform the work as special techniques are required.

13   Bugs and dirt can be removed from the radiator with compressed air and a soft brush. Don't bend the cooling fins as this is done.

Installation

14   When installing the radiator, make sure that the locator pins on the underside of the radiator are correctly aligned with, and fully seated in, their insulator grommets. Installation is otherwise the reverse of the removal procedure.

15   After installation, fill the cooling system with the proper mixture of antifreeze and water. Refer to Chapter 1 if necessary.

16   Start the engine and check for leaks. Allow the engine to reach normal operating temperature, indicated by the upper radiator hose becoming hot. Recheck the coolant level and add more if required.

17   If you're working on an automatic transaxle equipped vehicle, check the transaxle fluid level and add fluid as needed.

5   Engine cooling fan - check and replacement

Check

1   On 1986 through 1994 models, the engine cooling fan is controlled by a temperature switch mounted in the bottom of the radiator. When the coolant reaches a predetermined temperature, the switch closes, turning on the fan motor. On 1986 through 1989 models, the switch completes the ground circuit for the cooling fan motor. On 1990 through 1994 models, the switch provides power to the cooling fan relay control circuit. The cooling fan relay connects the fan motor to ground

4.9c To detach the radiator from the upper crossmember on 1990 through 2005 models, remove the upper insulator brackets, then lift the radiator up to disengage the locator pins on the bottom of the radiator from their insulator grommets

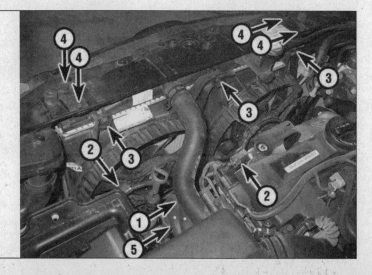

4.9d Radiator removal details (2006 and later models):

1   Disconnect the upper radiator hose
2   Disconnect the cooling fan electrical connectors
3   Remove the fan shroud retaining bolts and lift out the fans and fan shrouds
4   Remove the radiator mounting bolts and lift up the radiator far enough . . .
5   . . . to disconnect the lower radiator hose

5.8a Unplug the wiring harness and remove the four bolts (early model shown)

5.8b To detach the twin fans (most later models), remove these bolts (typical)

and the fan runs. On 1995 and later models, the cooling fan relay is controlled by the ECM. The ECM uses information provided by the Engine Coolant Temperature (ECT) sensor to operate the cooling fan.

2   First, check the fuses (see Chapter 12).

3   To test the fan motor, unplug the motor connector and use jumper wires to connect the fan directly to the battery. If the fan does not operate, replace the motor.

4   If the motor tested good and does not operate under normal conditions, the fault lies in the coolant temperature switch, cooling fan relay, the ECM or the wiring harness (as applicable).

5   Test the temperature switch by disconnecting the electrical connector and bridging the terminals of the switch harness connector with a jumper wire. Turn the ignition switch On, if the fan motor now operates, the switch is probably defective. Further testing of the switch can be accomplished by checking for continuity across the switch terminals with the coolant cold and again hot. Or remove the sensor and suspend it in a container of water

and check it while heating the water. Refer to this Chapter's Specifications for the switch operating parameters.

6   Refer to Chapter 12 and check the cooling fan relay and the wiring circuits, if necessary. On 1995 and later models, if the motor, relay and circuits are good, have the ECM (or PCM) checked by a dealership or other properly equipped repair facility.

Replacement

Refer to illustrations 5.8a, 58b, 5.9a, 5.9b and 5.10

7   Remove the radiator, with the cooling fan(s) attached, from the vehicle (see Section 4).

8   Remove the bolts and separate the fan/shroud assembly from the radiator (**see illustrations**).

9   Remove the nut and detach the fan blade assembly from the motor shaft (**see illustrations**).

10   Remove the screws and detach the fan motor from the shroud (**see illustration**).

11   Installation is the reverse of removal.

6   Coolant temperature sending unit - check and replacement

Warning: *The engine must be completely cool before removing the sending unit.*

1   On 1986 to 1989 models, the temperature gauge coolant sender is threaded into the bottom of the intake manifold, behind the distributor (**see illustration 6.3a**). On 1990 to 1994 carbureted models, a thermo switch is located below the temperature sender on the intake manifold to actuate the purge control valve of the Evaporative Emissions System, the choke breaker, and the Exhaust Gas Recirculation (EGR) valve (see Chapter 6). On 1990 and later fuel-injected models, the temperature sensor and temperature sender are located near the thermostat (**see illustration 6.3b**). For identification purposes, the engine coolant temperature (ECT) sensor has a two-pin electrical connector. The coolant temperature sender unit has a single prong for a push-on connector. Note that on 1994 and earlier models with automatic transaxles,

5.9a Hold the fan blades to keep them from turning and remove the nut (early model shown)

5.9b To detach the fan blade assembly on later models, carefully pry off the small circlip with a screwdriver (typical)

5.10 To detach the fan motor from the fan shroud, remove these screws (typical)

6.3a On 1986 through 1989 models, the coolant temperature sending unit is located in the bottom of the intake manifold, behind the distributor (distributor removed for clarity). On 1990 through 1994 models, the sending unit is threaded into the intake manifold near the thermostat cover

a coolant thermo switch used for the transaxle lock-up control circuit is located near the temperature sensor and sender.

Check

Refer to illustrations 6.3a and 6.3b

2 If the coolant temperature gauge is inoperative, check the fuses first (see Chapter 12). If the temperature indicator shows excessive temperature after running a while, see the *Troubleshooting* Section in the front of the manual.

3 If the temperature gauge indicates Hot shortly after the engine is started cold, disconnect the wire(s) at the coolant temperature sending unit **(see illustrations)**. If the gauge reading drops, replace the sending unit. If the reading remains high, the wire to the gauge or light may be shorted to ground or the gauge

6.3b On 1995 through 1999 models, the lower sensor is the temperature sender unit for the temperature gauge, while the upper sensor is the Engine Coolant Sensor (ECT) used by the ECM

is faulty. **Note:** *On 2000 and later models, the temperature sending unit function is integrated into the Engine Coolant Temperature (ECT) sensor, for which you'll need a scan tool or a code reader to diagnose (see Chapter 4).*

4 If the coolant temperature gauge fails to indicate after the engine has been warmed up (approximately 10 minutes) and the fuses checked out OK, shut off the engine. Disconnect the green/yellow wire at the sending unit and using a jumper wire, connect it to a clean ground on the engine. Turn on the ignition without starting the engine. If the gauge now indicates Hot, replace the sending unit.

5 If the gauge still does not work, the circuit may be open or the gauge may be faulty. See Chapter 12 for additional information.

6 Further testing can be accomplished by measuring the sender resistance (see Steps 7 and 8). Run the engine until it reaches normal operating temperature. Stop the engine and turn the ignition switch to the Off position.

7 Unplug the wiring from the sender unit terminal, and connect the probes of an ohmmeter between the sender terminal and a good ground point on the engine.

8 The resistance of the sender unit should be as given in this Chapter's Specifications with the coolant at the specified temperature. If the tester indicates a much different figure, then the sender is faulty and must be replaced. **Note:** *A sender unit which reads open circuit or short circuit will give a permanent full hot or full cold signal when the ignition switch is ON.*

Replacement

9 With the engine completely cool, remove the cap from the radiator to release any pressure, then replace the cap. This reduces coolant loss during sending unit replacement.

10 Disconnect the wiring harness from the sending unit.

11 Prepare the new sending unit for installation by applying sealer to the threads.

12 Unscrew the sending unit from the engine and quickly install the new one to prevent coolant loss.

13 Tighten the sending unit securely and connect the wiring harness.

14 Refill the cooling system and run the engine. Check for leaks and proper temperature gauge operation at the instrument panel.

7 Coolant reservoir - removal and installation

Refer to illustrations 7.2a, 7.2b and 7.2c

1 Lift the cap off the coolant reservoir and withdraw the overflow hose.

2 Remove the coolant reservoir-to-fender bolt and the windshield washer-to-coolant reservoir bolt **(see illustrations)** and lift the coolant reservoir out. The windshield washer reservoir can remain in place.

3 Installation is the reverse of removal.

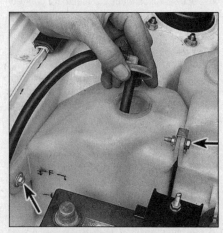

7.2a Pull out the cap and hose and remove the two bolts, then lift out the coolant reservoir (1986 to 1989 models)

7.2b Coolant reservoir and attaching bolts (1995 through 1999 models)

7.2c Typical coolant reservoir and attaching bolts (2006 and later models)

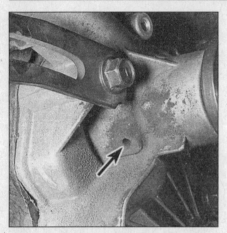

8.4 If coolant is leaking from the weep hole, the water pump must be replaced

8.5 If there is play in the shaft, replace the water pump

9.3 Loosen the water pump pulley bolts before removing the drivebelts

8   Water pump - check

Refer to illustrations 8.4 and 8.5

1   A failure in the water pump can cause serious engine damage due to overheating.

2   There are three ways to check the operation of the water pump while it's installed on the engine. If the pump is defective, it should be replaced with a new or rebuilt unit.

3   With the engine running at normal operating temperature, squeeze the upper radiator hose. If the water pump is working properly, a pressure surge should be felt as the hose is released. **Warning:** *Keep your hands away from the fan blades!*

4   The water pump is equipped with a weep or vent hole. If a failure occurs in the pump seal, coolant will leak from the hole. In most cases you'll need a flashlight to find the hole on the water pump from underneath to check for leaks **(see illustration)**.

5   If the water pump shaft bearings fail there may be a howling sound at the front of the engine while it's running. Shaft wear can

be felt if the water pump pulley is rocked up and down **(see illustration)**. Don't mistake drivebelt slippage, which causes a squealing sound, for water pump bearing failure.

9   Water pump - replacement

Refer to illustrations 9.3 and 9.7

Warning: *Wait until the engine is completely cool before beginning this procedure.*

1   Disconnect the cable from the negative terminal of the battery.

2   Drain the cooling system (see Chapter 1). If the coolant is relatively new or in good condition, save it and reuse it. Detach the radiator hose from the water pump.

3   On 1994 and earlier models, remove the left engine mount (see Chapter 2, Part A). Loosen the water pump pulley bolts **(see illustration)**.

4   Remove the drivebelts (see Chapter 1) and the pulley.

5   Remove the timing belt and tensioner (see Chapter 2A).

6   Remove the alternator bracket from the water pump.

7   Remove the bolts **(see illustration)** and detach the water pump from the engine. Note the locations of the various lengths and different types of bolts as they're removed to ensure correct installation.

8   Clean the bolt threads and the threaded holes in the engine to remove corrosion and sealant.

9   Compare the new pump to the old one to make sure they're identical.

10   Remove all traces of old gasket material from the engine with a gasket scraper.

11   Clean the engine and new water pump mating surfaces with lacquer thinner or acetone.

12   Install a new O-ring in the groove at the front end of the coolant pipe and lubricate the O-ring with coolant.

13   Apply a thin coat of RTV sealant to the engine side of the new gasket and to the gasket mating surface of the new pump, then carefully mate the gasket and the pump. Slip

a couple of bolts through the pump mounting holes to hold the gasket in place.

14   Carefully attach the pump and gasket to the engine and thread the bolts into the holes finger tight. Note that the bolt that attaches the alternator brace is longer than the other bolts.

15   Install the remaining bolts (be sure to reposition the alternator bracket at this time). Tighten them to the torque listed in this chapter's specifications in 1/4-turn increments. Don't overtighten them or the pump may be distorted.

16   Reinstall all parts removed for access to the pump.

17   Refill the cooling system and check the drivebelt tension (see Chapter 1). Run the engine and check for leaks.

10   Heater blower motor - circuit check and replacement

Check

Refer to illustration 10.3

1   If the blower motor does not operate at any speed, disconnect the electrical connector to the blower motor and connect a test light between the two terminals of the harness connector. Turn the ignition switch On and place the blower switch in the High position. The test light should glow brightly, indicating the blower motor power and ground circuits are good. If the blower motor does not operate when connected, replace the blower motor.

2   If the test light did not illuminate in Step 1, refer to the wiring diagrams at the end of Chapter 12 and determine which terminals in the blower motor harness connector are the power terminal (connected to the fuse box) and the ground terminal (grounded through the blower resistor and/or switch). Connect the test light to a good chassis ground, turn the ignition switch On, place the blower switch in the High position and probe the power terminal. If the test light does not illuminate, check the fuse, blower relay and related wiring, as applicable (see Chapter 12). If the

9.7 Remove the mounting bolts (the bolt holding the alternator brace in place is longer than the other three) (2000 model shown, other models similar)

10.3 Disconnect the electrical connector and check for continuity between each of the blower resistor terminals (typical)

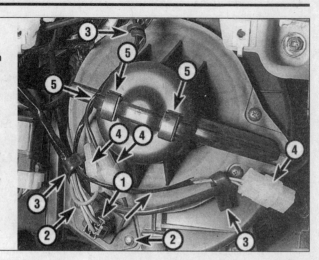

10.4a Blower motor assembly (1986 through 1989 models):

1 Blower motor resistor electrical connector
2 Blower motor resistor mounting screws
3 Wiring harness retainers
4 Electrical connectors
5 Blower motor housing clips (left clip, on left side of housing, not visible in this photo)

test light illuminates (indicating power is supplied to the blower motor), use an ohmmeter or self-powered continuity tester to check for continuity to ground at the ground terminal. If the ground circuit is open, check the circuit for continuity from the blower motor, through the blower switch to the chassis ground point.

3   If the blower motor operates at one or more speeds, but not at all speeds, disconnect the electrical connector from the blower resistor and check for continuity across the terminals of the resistor **(see illustration)**. Refer to the wiring diagrams at the end of Chapter 12 to determine which terminal is connected to the blower motor and check for continuity between that terminal and each of the other terminals in turn. Continuity should be indicated (with varying resistance values corresponding to the different blower speeds) between each terminal. If any resistor in the assembly is open, replace the blower resistor assembly. If the resistors are good, remove the control panel from the dash (see Section 17) and check for continuity between the appropriate blower switch terminals while plac-

ing the switch in each speed position. Again, use the wiring diagrams to determine the test points. Check for continuity in each individual wire from the blower resistor to the blower switch. Also check for continuity to chassis ground at the blower switch harness connector ground wire (usually a black wire). Trace the ground wire to the ground point on the chassis and repair the ground, if necessary.

Replacement
Blower motor resistor
Refer to illustrations 10.4a, 10.4b, 10.4c, 10.4d, 10.5a and 10.5b

4   On 1986 through 1989 models, the blower motor resistor is located on the front (facing toward you) lower part of the blower housing **(see illustration)**. On 1990 through 1994 models, the blower motor resistor is located on top of the upper part of the blower housing **(see illustration)**. On 1995 through 2005 models, the blower motor resistor is located on the underside of the blower housing **(see illustration)**. On 2006 and later models, the blower motor resistor is located on the lower left face of the lower part of the blower

10.4b On 1990 through 1994 models, the blower motor resistor is located on top of the upper part of the blower housing

housing **(see illustration)**.

5   Remove the glove box and, if necessary, the lower dash panel below the glove box (see Chapter 11). Disconnect the wiring connector from the resistor **(see illustration 10.4b)**. Remove the mounting screws and withdraw

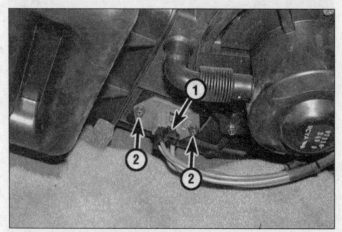

10.4c On 1995 through 2005 models, the blower motor resistor is located on the underside of the blower housing. To replace the resistor, disconnect the electrical connector (1) and remove the resistor mounting screws (2)

10.4d On 2006 and later models, the blower motor resistor is located on the lower left face of the lower part of the blower motor housing

10.5a Unscrew the blower motor mounting screws . . .

10.5b . . . and remove the blower motor resistor (1990 through 1994 model shown)

10.8a On 1992 through 1994 models, disconnect the motor cooling duct (typical)

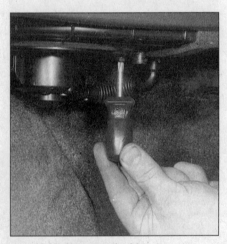

10.8b Unscrew the blower motor mounting screws . . .

10.8c . . . and withdraw the blower motor and fan assembly

the resistor **(see illustrations)**. Installation is the reverse of removal.

Heater blower motor

Refer to illustrations 10.8a, 10.8b, 10.8c, 10.8d, 10.8e and 10.9

6   Remove the lower dash panel below the glovebox and remove the glovebox (see Chapter 11).

7   Disconnect the electrical connectors and detach the wiring harness from the bottom of the blower motor **(see illustrations 10.4a, 10.4b, 10.4c or 10.4d)**.

8   On 1986 through 1989 models, remove the three clips **(see illustration 10.4a)** that secure the two halves of the blower housing, remove the housing, then remove the blower motor. On 1990 through 2002 models, remove the blower motor cooling duct, then remove the blower motor mounting flange screws and remove the blower motor from the housing **(see illustrations)**.

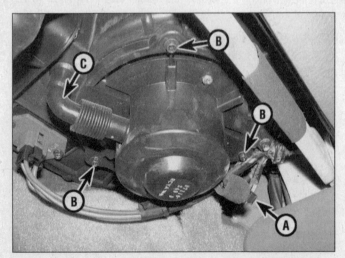

10.8d On 1995 through 2005 models, disconnect the blower motor electrical connector (A) and remove the three blower motor mounting screws (B). Pull down the blower motor assembly and remove the motor cooling duct (C)

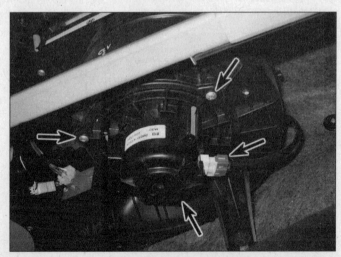

10.8e On 2006 and later models, disconnect the electrical connector, remove the three blower motor mounting screws and pull down the blower motor assembly

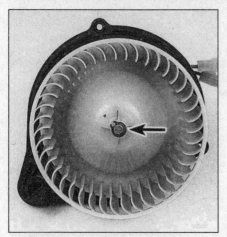

10.9 The fan is held on the motor shaft with a clip or a bolt - if a clip is used, spread the clip open and slip the fan off the shaft

11.3 Working in the engine compartment, disconnect the heater hoses from the heater core tubes located at the firewall (typical)

11.7 Remove the heater unit mounting bolts/nuts (1995 through 1999 model shown, 2000 through 2005 models similar)

9   If necessary, release the clip and detach the fan from the motor shaft (see illustration).
10   Installation is the reverse of removal. Check the operation of the blower motor before installing the glovebox.

11   Heater core - removal and installation

Warning 1: *If equipped with a Supplemental Restraint System (SRS), more commonly known as airbags, disable the airbag system before working in the vicinity of airbag system components to avoid the possibility of accidental deployment of the airbag, which could result in personal injury (see Chapter 12).*
Warning 2: *The air conditioning system is under high pressure. Do not loosen any hose fittings or remove any components until after the system has been discharged. Air conditioning refrigerant must be properly discharged into an EPA-approved recovery/recycling unit at a dealer service department or an automotive air conditioning repair facility. Always wear eye protection when disconnecting air conditioning system fittings.*
Note: *The removal and repair of the heater and related components is an involved procedure - it is recommended that the following Section is read thoroughly before beginning this procedure. Plenty of time should be allowed to complete the operation. During disassembly, make notes on the routing of all wiring and cables, and the locations of all components, to aid correct reassembly.*

Removal

Refer to illustration 11.3

1   If equipped with air conditioning, have the refrigerant discharged and recovered by a dealer service department or an automotive air conditioning repair facility.

2   Disconnect the cable from the negative terminal of the battery. Set the heater control to HOT, then drain the cooling system as described in Chapter 1.
3   Working in the engine compartment, loosen the clamps and detach the heater hoses from the heater core connection tubes at the firewall (see illustration). Identify each hose for location to ensure correct installation. On models equipped with air conditioning, disconnect the refrigerant lines from the evaporator connection tubes. On 1990 and later models, a special spring-lock coupling tool (available at most auto parts stores) is required to disconnect the lines. Remove the evaporator drain hose.

2005 and earlier models

Refer to illustrations 11.7, 11.8, 11.9a and 11.9b

4   Refer to Chapter 11 and remove the front and rear console assemblies, the lower dash panels, the glovebox and center dash bezel. Remove the air conditioning and heater control assembly (see Section 17) and the radio (see Chapter 12). On 1995 and later models, remove the entire dash panel assembly (see Chapter 11).
5   On 1986 through 1994 models, remove the center support bracket and remove the lower heating ducts. Disconnect the heater control cables or vacuum lines and electrical connectors from the heater unit, as applicable.
6   On models without air conditioning, remove the blower unit air duct. On models with air conditioning, remove the blower unit and air conditioning evaporator unit (see Section 16).
7   Remove the heater assembly mounting bolts (see illustration) and remove the heater assembly. Be prepared for some loss of coolant by placing towels or rags on the floor, but as a precaution, tilt the assembly so that the heater core tubes face upwards.
8   On 1986 through 1989 models, unbolt the inlet and outlet tubes and brackets and recover the sealing O-rings. Unscrew the retaining screws and withdraw the heater core

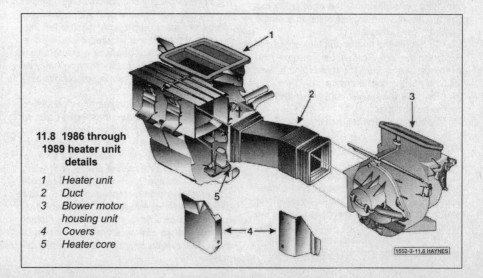

11.8 1986 through 1989 heater unit details

1   Heater unit
2   Duct
3   Blower motor housing unit
4   Covers
5   Heater core

1552-3-11.8 HAYNES

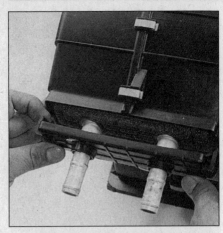

11.9a Remove the heater unit inlet and outlet tube cover (1995 through 1999 model shown, 2000 through 2005 models similar)

11.9b Pull out the heater core from the heater unit (1995 through 2005 model)

from the side of the heater assembly **(see illustration)**.

9   On 1990 through 1994 models, remove the screws and clips and separate the heater core case halves to withdraw the heater core from its location at the front of the heater unit. On 1995 through 2005 models, remove the inlet and outlet tube cover panel and slide out the heater core **(see illustrations)**. **Caution:** *The edges of the heater core fins are sharp and can cause skin abrasion or cuts.*

2006 and later models

10   Remove the instrument panel (see Chapter 11).

11   Disconnect the electrical connectors from the temperature control actuator, the mode control actuator and the evaporator temperature sensor. Also disconnect any other electrical connectors between the cowl and the coil cross bar assembly.

12   To detach the heater and blower assembly from the cowl, remove the two bolts that secure the heater and blower assembly to the cowl. To detach the cowl cross bar assembly from the cowl, remove all 12 cowl cross bar mounting bolts. Remove the cowl cross bar and the heater and blower units as a single assembly (see Chapter 11).

13   To detach the heater and blower assembly from the cowl cross bar, remove the three nuts that secure the heater and blower assembly to the cowl cross bar.

14   Remove the heater core cover and pull out the heater core.

15   Installation is the reverse of removal.

Installation

16   Install the heater core in the heater unit.

17   Install the heater and blower assembly.

18   After installing the heater and blower assembly on the cowl cross bar on 2006 and later models, install the cowl cross bar and the heater and blower units as a single assembly.

19   Reconnect all electrical harnesses and, if applicable, heater control cables and vacuum

lines. Make sure that everything is routed exactly as it was prior to disassembly.

20   Make sure that all air ducts are properly and securely connected.

21   On models with manual heater controls, reconnect the heater control cables to the heater control panel.

22   On 1986 through 2005 models, install all instrument panel trim panels that were removed (see Chapter 11). On 2006 and later models, install the instrument panel (see Chapter 11).

23   On models with manual heater controls, verify that the air mix lever slides smoothly and adjust it as necessary (see Section 17).

24   Fill the cooling system with the correct type and amount of coolant (see Chapter 1). On models with air conditioning, have the air conditioning system evacuated and recharged.

12 Air conditioning system - check and maintenance

Warning: *The air conditioning system is under high pressure. Do not loosen any hose fittings or remove any components until after the system has been discharged. Air conditioning refrigerant must be properly discharged into an EPA-approved recovery/recycling unit at a dealer service department or an automotive air conditioning repair facility. Always wear eye protection when disconnecting air conditioning system fittings.*
Caution: *Two different types of air conditioning refrigerant are used on the models covered by this manual. 1993 and earlier models use R-12 refrigerant, while 1994 and later models use the non-ozone-depleting R-134a refrigerant. The R-134a refrigerant and its lubricating oil are not compatible with the R-12 system and under no circumstances should the two different types of refrigerant or lubricating oil be intermixed. The system charging fittings are different so that accidental connection of the unlike system charging hoses cannot be made.*

Note: *Because of Federal regulations proposed by the Environmental Protection Agency, R-12 refrigerant is no longer available to the home mechanic. Models with R-12 systems should be serviced by a dealership or other properly equipped repair facility.*

1   The following maintenance checks should be performed on a regular basis to ensure that the air conditioner continues to operate at peak efficiency.

a) *Check the compressor drivebelt. If it's worn or deteriorated, replace it (see Chapter 1).*
b) *Check the drivebelt tension and, if necessary, adjust it (see Chapter 1).*
c) *Check the system hoses. Look for cracks, bubbles, hard spots and deterioration. Inspect the hoses and all fittings for oil bubbles and seepage. If there's any evidence of wear, damage or leaks, replace the hose(s).*
d) *Inspect the condenser fins for leaves, bugs and other debris. Use a fin comb or compressed air to clean the condenser.*
e) *Make sure the system has the correct refrigerant charge.*

2   It's a good idea to operate the system for about 10 minutes at least once a month, particularly during the winter. Long term non-use can cause hardening, and subsequent failure, of the seals.

3   Because of the complexity of the air conditioning system and the special equipment necessary to service it, in-depth troubleshooting and repairs are not included in this manual. However, simple checks and component replacement procedures are provided in this Chapter.

4   The most common cause of poor cooling is simply a low system refrigerant charge. If a noticeable drop in cool air output occurs, one of the following quick checks will help you determine if the refrigerant level is low.

5   Warm the engine up to normal operating temperature.

6   Place the air conditioning temperature selector at the coldest setting and put the blower at the highest setting. Open the doors (to make sure the air conditioning system doesn't cycle off as soon as it cools the passenger compartment).

7   After the system reaches operating temperature, feel the two pipes connected to the evaporator at the firewall. The pipe (thinner tubing) leading from the condenser outlet to the evaporator should be warm, and the evaporator outlet line (the thicker tubing that leads back to the compressor) should be cold. If the two pipes are the same temperature (or close to the same temperature), the system charge is low.

8   If the system is equipped with a sight glass (on top of the receiver-drier), check for the presence of air bubbles in the refrigerant. If the refrigerant passing through the sight glass looks foamy, the system charge is low.

9   Further inspection or testing of the system is beyond the scope of the home mechanic and should be left to a professional.

12.11 If you have a 1994 or later model, R-134a refrigerant and recharge kits are available from auto parts stores - follow the instructions that come with the recharge kit

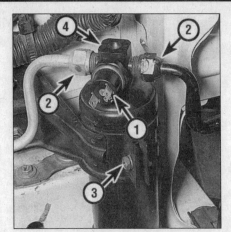

13.2a Typical 1986 through 1989 receiver-drier and related components

1   Pressure switch
2   Refrigerant lines
3   Clamp bolt
4   Sight glass

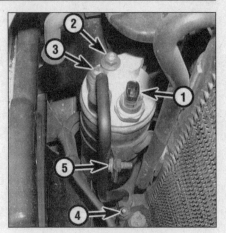

13.2b Typical 1995 through 1999 receiver-drier and related components:

1   Electrical connector (already disconnected)
2   Liquid line fitting nut
3   Liquid line fitting nut
4   Liquid line fitting nut (doesn't apply to all models)
5   Mounting bracket nut

Adding refrigerant (1994 and later models only)

Refer to illustration 12.11

Caution: *Make sure any refrigerant, refrigerant oil or replacement component your purchase is designated as compatible with environmentally-friendly R-134a systems.*

10   1993 and earlier models use R-12 refrigerant. Because of federal restrictions on the sale of R-12 refrigerant, it isn't practical for refrigerant to be added by the home mechanic. When the system needs recharging, take the vehicle to a dealer service department or professional air conditioning shop for evacuation, leak testing and recharging. On 1994 and later models using R-134a refrigerant, make sure any refrigerant, oil or replacement component is designated for R-134a systems.

11   Buy an R-134a automotive charging kit at an auto parts store **(see illustration)**. A charging kit includes a can of refrigerant, a tap valve and a short section of hose that can be attached between the tap valve and the system low side service valve. Because one can of refrigerant may not be sufficient to bring the system charge up to the proper level, it's a good idea to buy an additional can. **Warning:** *Never add more than two cans of refrigerant to the system.*

12   Hook up the charging kit by following the manufacturer's instructions. **Warning:** *DO NOT hook the charging kit hose to the system high side!* The fittings on the charging kit are designed to fit **only** on the low side of the system.

13   Back off the valve handle on the charging kit and screw the kit onto the refrigerant can, making sure first that the O-ring or rubber seal inside the threaded portion of the kit is in place. **Warning:** *Wear protective eyewear when dealing with pressurized refrigerant cans.*

14   Remove the dust cap from the low-side charging and attach the quick-connect fitting on the kit hose.

15   Warm up the engine and turn on the air conditioning. Keep the charging kit hose away from the fan and other moving parts. **Note:** *The charging process requires the compressor to be running. If the clutch cycles off, you can put the air conditioning switch on High and leave the car doors open to keep the clutch on and compressor working.*

16   Turn the valve handle on the kit until the stem pierces the can, then back the handle out to release the refrigerant. You should be able to hear the rush of gas. Add refrigerant to the low side of the system, keeping the can upright at all times, but shaking it occasionally. Allow stabilization time between each addition. **Note:** *The charging process will go faster if you wrap the can with a hot-water-soaked shop rag to keep the can from freezing up.*

17   If you have an accurate thermometer, you can place it in the center air conditioning duct inside the vehicle and keep track of the output air temperature. A charged system that is working properly should cool down to approximately 40-degrees F. If the ambient (outside) air temperature is very high, say 110 degrees F, the duct air temperature may be as high as 60 degrees F, but generally the air conditioning is 30-40 degrees F cooler than the ambient air.

18   When the can is empty, turn the valve handle to the closed position and release the connection from the low-side port. Replace the dust cap.

19   Remove the charging kit from the can and store the kit for future use with the piercing valve in the UP position, to prevent inadvertently piercing the can on the next use.

13   Air conditioning accumulator or receiver-drier - removal and installation

Warning: *The air conditioning system is under high pressure. Do not loosen any hose fittings or remove any components until after the system has been discharged. Air conditioning refrigerant must be properly discharged into an EPA-approved recovery/recycling unit at a dealer service department or an automotive air conditioning repair facility. Always wear eye protection when disconnecting air conditioning system fittings.*

1   The accumulator or receiver-drier acts as a reservoir and filter/dehumidifier for the refrigerant. 1986 through 1989 models and 1995 and later models both use a receiver-drier, while 1990 through 1994 models use an accumulator. The receiver-drier on 1986 through 1989 models is located at the left (drivers side) of the condenser. On 1995 through 1999 models, it's located at the right (passenger side) of the condenser. On 2000 and later models, the receiver-driver function is integrated into the condenser assembly. A vertical tube on the left side of the condenser carries the dessicant bag that filters and dehumidifies the refrigerant. The accumulator (1990 through 1994 models) is mounted on the left side of the firewall. Have the system discharged and recovered by a dealership or other properly equipped repair facility.

1986 through 1999 models
Removal

Refer to illustrations 13.2a and 13.2b

2   Unplug the electrical connector from the pressure switch **(see illustrations)**.

13.10 To replace the dessicant in the receiver-drier on 2000 and later models, you have to remove the condenser

13.12 Remove the threaded plug from the receiver-drier with an Allen wrench . . .

13.13 . . . remove the filter from the receiver-drier . . .

3   Detach the two refrigerant lines from the receiver-drier. **Note:** *On 1990 through 1994 models (with an accumulator), a special spring-lock coupling tool (available at most auto parts stores) is required to disconnect the refrigerant lines.*
4   Immediately cap the open fittings to prevent the entry of dirt and moisture.
5   Unbolt the accumulator or receiver-drier and lift it out of the engine compartment.

Installation
6   Install new O-rings on the lines and lubricate them with clean refrigerant oil.
7   Installation is the reverse of removal. **Note:** *Do not remove the sealing caps until you are ready to reconnect the lines. Do not mistake the inlet (marked IN) and the outlet (marked OUT) connections. Install new fitting O-rings.*
8   If a new receiver-drier is installed, add the proper amount (and type) of refrigerant oil to the system (see this Chapter's Specifications).
9   Have the system evacuated, recharged and leak tested.

2000 and later models
Refer to illustrations 13.10, 13.12, 13.13 and 13.14
10   On these models, the receiver-drier is an integral part of the condenser assembly **(see illustration).** Unlike conventional receiver-drier setups, you don't replace this type of receiver-driver, because it cannot be removed; you simply replace the dessicant bag inside.
11   Remove the condenser (see Section 15).
12   Using an Allen wrench, unscrew the threaded plug from the lower end of the receiver-drier **(see illustration). Caution:** *Do NOT use an impact wrench to unscrew this plug. Doing so might crack the dessicant tube housing.*
13   Remove the filter from the dessicant tube **(see illustration).**
14   Using long needle-nose pliers, pull out

the old dessicant bag **(see illustration).**
15   Using a flashlight, inspect the dessicant tube for any residual crumbled dessicant. Use compressed air to blow out any residual dessicant in the receiver-drier.
16   Inspect the filter. If it's clogged, try cleaning it very carefully with an old toothbrush and some clean solvent. This filter must be spotless. If you can't clean it, then replace it. You might be able to replace the filter by itself; or you might have to purchase a new condenser.
17   Lubricate a new O-ring and install it on a new plug (do NOT re-use the old plug). Install the dessicant bag in the tube, then immediately screw on the new plug. **Caution:** *If you leave the new dessicant bag outside its protective wrapping for any length of time, it will absorb moisture in the air and its effectiveness will be compromised.*
18   Installation is the reverse of removal.
19   Have the air conditioning system evacuated, recharged and leak tested.

---

14   Air conditioning compressor - removal and installation

Warning: *The air conditioning system is under high pressure. Do not loosen any hose fittings or remove any components until after the system has been discharged. Air conditioning refrigerant must be properly discharged into an EPA-approved recovery/recycling unit at a dealer service department or an automotive air conditioning repair facility. Always wear eye protection when disconnecting air conditioning system fittings.*

Removal
Refer to illustrations 14.6 and 14.7
1   Have the system discharged and recovered by a dealership or other properly equipped repair facility.
2   On 1986 through 1989 models, the com-

13.14 . . . and remove the dessicant bag with needle-nose pliers

pressor and its mounting bracket are bolted to the lower left rear side of the engine block. On 1990 through 1994 models, the compressor and its mounting bracket are bolted to the lower right front side of the engine block. On 1995 through 2002 models, the compressor and its mounting bracket are bolted to the lower right rear side of the engine block. On 2003 and later models, the compressor is bolted directly (no mounting bracket) to the lower right rear side of the engine block.
3   Remove the compressor drivebelt (see Chapter 1).
4   Set the parking brake and block the rear tires. Raise the front of the vehicle and support it securely on jackstands. Remove the under-vehicle splash shield, if equipped.
5   Disconnect the electrical connector from the compressor clutch.
6   Detach the refrigerant lines from the compressor **(see illustration)** and immediately cap the open fittings to prevent the entry of dirt and moisture.
7   Remove the mounting bolts **(see illustration)** and lower the compressor from the

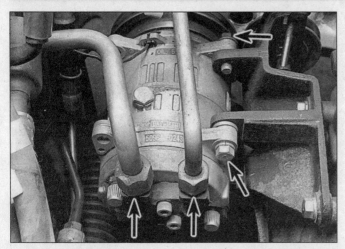

14.6 Air conditioning compressor viewed from above, showing refrigerant line fittings and upper mounting bolts (typical)

14.7 Air conditioning compressor lower mounting bolts (typical)

engine compartment. Note the location and thickness of any shims or spacers and reinstall them in the same location. **Note:** *Keep the compressor level during handling and storage. If the compressor seized or you find metal particles in the refrigerant oil, the system must be flushed out by an air conditioning technician and the accumulator or receiver-drier must be replaced.*

Installation

8   If you are installing a new compressor, refer to the compressor manufacturer's instructions for adding refrigerant oil to the system.
9   Prior to installation, turn the center of the clutch six times to disperse any oil that has collected in the head.
10   Install the compressor in the reverse order of removal. Install new fitting O-rings.

Tighten the compressor mounting bolts securely.
11   Have the system evacuated, recharged and leak tested.

15   Air conditioning condenser - removal and installation

Warning: *The air conditioning system is under high pressure. Do not loosen any hose fittings or remove any components until after the system has been discharged. Air conditioning refrigerant must be properly discharged into an EPA-approved recovery/recycling unit at a dealer service department or an automotive air conditioning repair facility. Always wear eye protection when disconnecting air conditioning system fittings.*

Removal

Refer to illustrations 15.3a, 15.3b, 15.4 and 15.6

1   Have the system discharged and recovered by dealership or other properly equipped repair facility.
2   On 1986 through 1994 models, remove the radiator grille (see Chapter 11). On 1990 through 1994 models, remove the radiator (see Section 4). On 1995 through 2002 models, remove the two upper radiator mounting bracket bolts and remove the fresh air inlet duct.
3   Disconnect the refrigerant lines from the condenser. Be sure to use a back-up wrench to avoid twisting the lines **(see illustration)**. **Note:** *On 1990 through 1994 models, a special spring-lock coupling tool (available at most auto parts stores) is required to disconnect the refrigerant lines* **(see illustration)**.

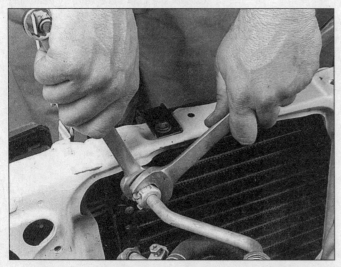

15.3a Use a back-up wrench to avoid twisting the lines

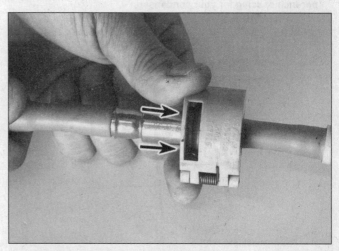

15.3b To separate the refrigerant line fittings on 1990 through 1994 models, use a spring-lock coupling device. Install the tool on the fitting, push it toward the female side of the fitting until you can see the fitting through the window in the tool, then pull the lines apart

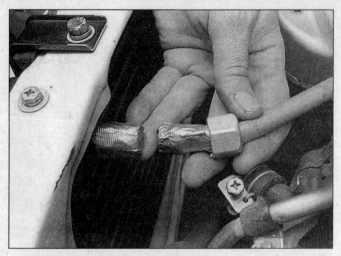

15.4 Immediately seal off the ends - tape works well

15.6 Remove the bolts and center brace and lift out the condenser (1986 through 1989 models)

15.7 Straighten and clean the fins of the condenser with a fin comb. Use the side of the tool with the correct number of fins-per-inch spacing for your condenser

4   Immediately cap the open fittings to prevent the entry of dirt and moisture (see illustration).
5   Drain the engine coolant and remove the radiator and fan assembly (see Section 4).
6   Unbolt the condenser (see illustration) and lift it out of the vehicle. Store it upright to prevent oil loss.

Installation

Refer to illustration 15.7

7   If reusing the condenser, straighten the condenser fins using a fin comb (see illustration) and blow out the debris with compressed air. **Caution:** *Use a face shield and goggles if using compressed air to clean the condenser.*
8   Installation is the reverse of removal.
9   If a new condenser was installed, add the proper amount (and type) of refrigerant oil to the system (see this Chapter's Specifications).

10   Have the system evacuated, recharged, and leak tested.

16   Air conditioning and heater control assembly - removal, installation and cable adjustment

Removal and installation

Refer to illustrations 16.4a, 16.4b, 16.4c, 16.5a and 16.5b

1   Disconnect the cable from the negative terminal of the battery.
2   Remove the center trim bezel surrounding the control assembly (see Chapter 11).
3   Remove the glove compartment and the covers on the sides of the console under the dash.
4   Disconnect the control cables at the ends opposite from the control by detaching

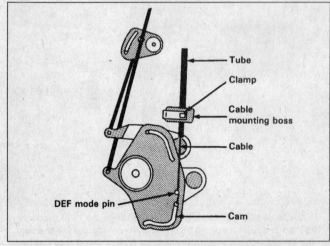

16.4a Mode control cable mounting details (1986 through 1989 manual lever type)

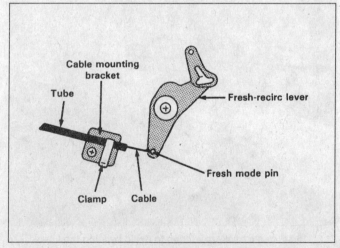

16.4b Fresh-recirc cable mounting details (1986 through 1989 manual lever type)

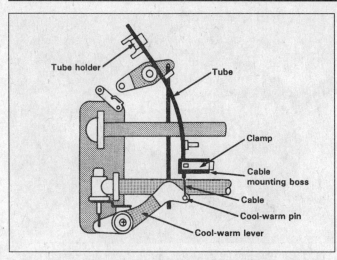

16.4c Temperature cable mounting details (1986 through 1989 manual lever type)

16.5a Heater control mounting screw locations (1986 through 1989 manual lever type heater control unit shown)

the cable clamps and separating the cables from the pins on the operating levers **(see illustrations)**.

5   Remove the control mounting screws **(see illustrations)**. On the vacuum rotary switch controls (1990 and later models), detach the vacuum tubes. Mark them to ensure correct reassembly.

6   Carefully remove the unit from the dash.

7   Installation is the reverse of removal.

Cable adjustment

Refer to illustrations 16.8, 16.9 and 16.10

Defrost-vent cable (1986 through 1989 manual lever type)

8   Set the control to defrost **(see illustration)**. Move the lever all the way back, connect the cable to the lever and reinstall the clamp.

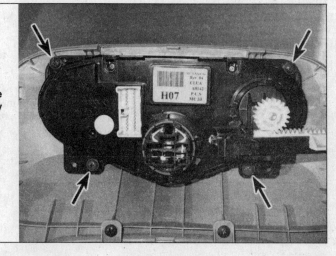

16.5b On 1990 and later models, remove the control assembly retaining screws to detach it from the trim bezel (2008 model shown, other models similar)

Fresh-recirc cable - (1986 through 1989 manual lever type)

9   Set the control in the outside-air position **(see illustration)**. Move the lever all the way back, connect the cable to the lever and reinstall the clamp.

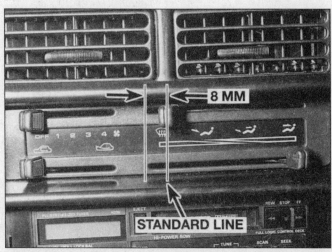

16.8 Mode control in the defrost position for cable adjustment - manual lever type

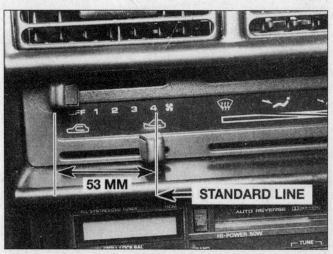

16.9 Fresh-recirc control in the outside air position for cable adjustment (1986 through 1989 manual lever type)

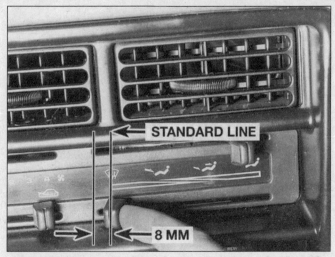

16.10 Place the temperature lever all the way to the left for cable adjustment (1986 through 1989 manual lever type)

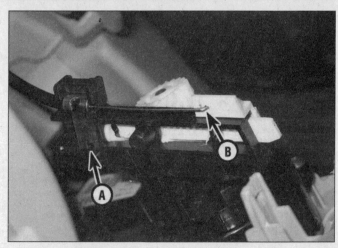

16.11 On 1990 and later models, move the air mix control lever or knob all the way to the full HOT position, then pry off the cable clip (A) and disconnect the end of the wire (B) from the control mechanism. When installing the cable, make sure that the control lever or knob is still in the full HOT position

Temperature control cable (1986 through 1989 manual lever type)

10   Set the control to the left position **(see illustration)**. Move the water valve lever to the highest position, connect the cable to the lever and reinstall the clamp.

Air mix cable - 1990 and later models

Refer to illustration 16.11

11   Set the air mix control lever or rotary knob to the HOT position. Rotate the air mix door shaft to the left and connect the cable. Slide the cable housing back to remove the slack (without moving the control lever) and connect the cable housing to the clamp.

Chapter 4
Fuel and exhaust systems

Contents

Specifications

Carbureted fuel system

Electrical and power steering load idle-up speed	
1986 models	
Canada	
Manual transaxle	900 ± 10 rpm
Automatic transaxle	950 ± 10 rpm
USA	850 rpm
1987 and later models	850 ± 100 rpm
Air conditioner load idle-up speed (1988 through 1993 models)	875 ± 25 rpm
Solenoid valve resistance (approximate) (1986 and 1987 models)*	
Idle-up control solenoid valve	40 ohms
Deceleration solenoid valve (DSV)	49.7 ohms
Enrichment solenoid valve (ESV)	49.7 ohms
Jet mixture solenoid valve (JSV)	49.7 ohms
Bowl vent valve (BVV)	80 ohms
Throttle position sensor	
Resistance (approximate)	
Closed throttle	1.2 K-ohms
Wide open throttle	4.9 K-ohms
Dash pot adjustment engine speed	1800 rpm
Choke valve-to-bore clearance (1988 through 1993 models)**	0.055 to 0.063 inch
Fast idle speed (1988 and later models)	
Manual transaxle	2800 rpm
Automatic transaxle	2700 rpm
Choke heater resistance (approximate) (1988 through 1993 models)	6 ohms at 68 degrees F
Fuel pump pressure	3.0 to 5.0 psi at 2500 rpm

*Specifications not available for 1988 and later models
**Engine idling, vacuum hose detached

Fuel injection system

Fuel pressure
    1990 through 1994
        Vacuum line disconnected from fuel pressure regulator.............. 46 to 49 psi
        Vacuum line connected to fuel pressure regulator...................... 39 psi
    1995 through 1999
        Vacuum line disconnected from fuel pressure regulator.............. 43 to 45 psi
        Vacuum line connected to fuel pressure regulator...................... 37 psi
    2000 and later .... 49 to 50 psi
Throttle position sensor resistance
    1994 and earlier .... 3,500 to 6,500 ohms
    1995 and later .... 700 to 3,000 ohms
Idle Speed Control (ISC) actuator resistance
    1994 and earlier .... 5 to 35 ohms at 68 degrees F
    1995 and later .... 10.5 to 14 ohms at 68 degrees F
Air Flow Sensor (AFS) output voltage (1994 and earlier)...................... 2.7 to 3.2 volts
Mass Air Flow (MAF) sensor output voltage (1995 and later)
    At idle .... 0.7 to 1.1 volt
    At 3,000 rpm... 1.3 to 2.0 volts
Engine Coolant Temperature (ECT) sensor and Intake Air Temperature (IAT) sensor resistance
    At 32 degrees F... 5,000 to 6,000 ohms
    At 68 degrees F... 2,000 to 3,000 ohms
    At 104 degrees F... 1,000 to 1,300 ohms
    At 140 degrees F... 500 to 650 ohms
    At 176 degrees F... 300 to 400 ohms
Fuel injector resistance.. 13 to 16 ohms at 68 degrees F
Crankshaft Position (CKP) sensor resistance (1995 and later).............. 480 to 595 ohms at 68 degrees F
Knock sensor resistance (1995 and later SOHC only)........................... 5 Megohms at 68 degrees F
Oxygen sensor heater resistance (hot) .... 30 ohms (minimum)

Torque specifications   **Ft-lb** (unless otherwise indicated)

Note: *One foot-pound (ft-lb) of torque is equivalent to 12 inch-pounds (in-lbs) of torque. Torque values below approximately 15 foot-pounds are expressed in inch-pounds, because most foot-pound torque wrenches are not accurate at these smaller values.*

Carburetor mounting bolts .... 168 in-lbs
Oxygen sensor
    1994 and earlier models.. 33
    1995 and later models... 40
Fuel pressure regulator
    1994 and earlier models.. 84 in-lbs
    1995 and later models... 48 in-lbs
Temperature sensor
    1994 and earlier models.. 19
    1995 and later models... 156 in lbs
Knock sensor attachment bolt 15
Throttle position sensor .... 24 in-lbs
Throttle body to intake plenum .... 156 in lbs
High pressure hose to fuel filter.. 22
High pressure hose to fuel tank... 26

1   General information

Refer to illustrations 1.2a, 1.2b and 1.2c

The models covered by this manual were manufactured with two different types of fuel systems - a Feedback Carburetor (FBC) system or a Multi-Port fuel Injection (MFI) system. 1986 through 1989 models are equipped with the FBC carburetor system. 1990 through 1993 models were available with either the FBC carburetor system or the MFI system, depending on market (USA, Canada, etc.). All 1994 and later models feature an updated fuel injection system.

Carbureted models

The fuel system consists of a fuel tank, two fuel filters (one in-tank and one in the engine compartment), a fuel pump, an air cleaner assembly and a two-barrel carburetor **(see illustrations)**.

The fuel pump is a mechanical type mounted on the cylinder head. The pump is driven off the camshaft by a pushrod.

The Feedback Carburetor (FBC) system is controlled by a computer which monitors changes in engine operation with various information sensors, compares this data to parameters stored in its memory and alters fuel delivery accordingly by means of actuators installed on the carburetor. Refer to Chapter 6 for more information.

Fuel-injected models

The multi-port fuel injection system consists of a fuel tank, two fuel filters (one in the tank and one in the fuel feed line), an electric fuel pump, a fuel pressure regulator, a fuel rail, injectors at each intake valve port, and an air cleaner assembly.

The fuel pump supplies pressurized fuel to the injectors. The regulator allows excess fuel to return to the fuel tank to maintain the pressure at a set limit. The fuel pump is located inside the fuel tank. The fuel pressure regulator is located at the fuel rail (1999 and earlier models) or integral with the fuel pump (2000 and later models).

This computerized fuel control system uses various input sensors to feed information to the Electronic Control Module (ECM). The ECM uses the various sensor inputs to determine the amount of time to hold the injectors open. Refer to Section 13 for more information.

Exhaust system

All vehicles are equipped with an exhaust manifold, a catalytic converter, the connecting pipe between the converter and a main muffler assembly (the rear part of the exhaust pipe and the muffler itself). The exhaust system is suspended from the underside of the vehicle and insulated from vibration by a series of rubber hangers.

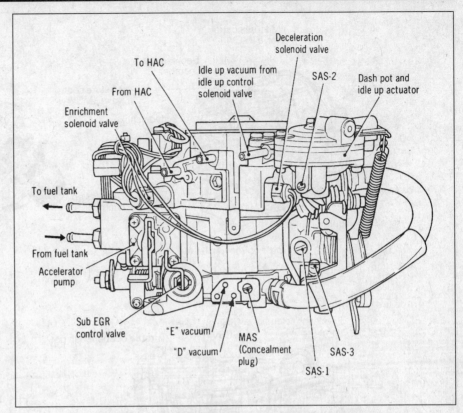

1.2a Feedback carburetor components (1986 and 1987 models)

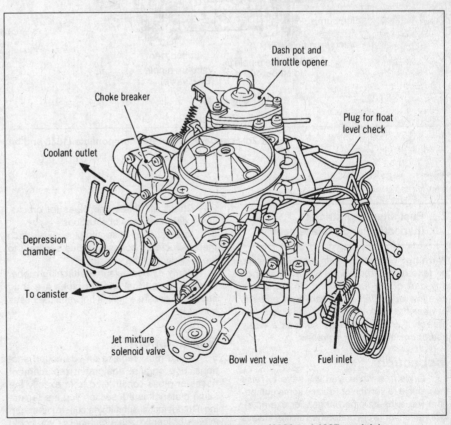

1.2b Feedback carburetor components (1986 and 1987 models)

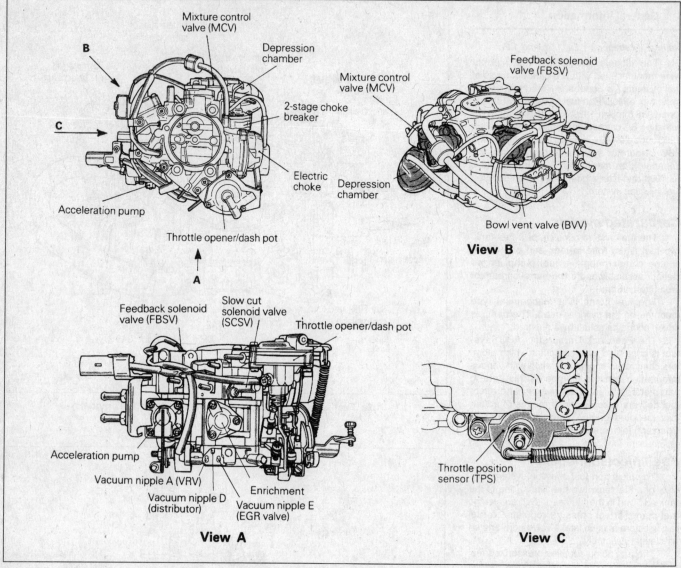

1.2c Feedback carburetor components (1988 and later models)

2 Fuel lines and fittings - inspection and replacement

Warning: *Gasoline is extremely flammable, so take extra precautions when working on any part of the fuel system. Do not smoke or allow open flames or bare light bulbs in or near the work area. Also, don't work in a garage if a gas appliance such as a water heater or clothes dryer is present.*

Inspection

1   Once in a while, you will have to raise the vehicle to service or replace some component (an exhaust pipe hanger, for example). Whenever you work under the vehicle, always inspect the fuel lines and fittings for possible damage or deterioration.

2   Check all hoses and pipes for cracks, kinks, deformation or obstructions.
3   Make sure all hose and pipe clips attach their associated hoses or pipes securely to the underside of the vehicle.
4   Verify all hose clamps attaching rubber hoses to metal fuel lines or pipes are snug enough to assure a tight fit between the hoses and pipes.

Replacement

5   If you must replace any damaged sections, use original equipment replacement hoses or pipes constructed from exactly the same material as the section you are replacing. Do not install substitutes constructed from inferior or inappropriate material or you could cause a fuel leak or a fire.
6   Always, before detaching or disassem-

bling any part of the fuel line system, note the routing of all hoses and pipes and the orientation of all clamps and clips to assure that replacement sections are installed in exactly the same manner.
7   Before detaching any part of the fuel system, be sure to relieve the fuel tank pressure by removing the fuel filler cap.
8   While you're under the vehicle, it's a good idea to check the following related components:

a)   *Check the condition of the fuel filter - make sure that it's not clogged or damaged (see Chapter 1).*
b)   *Inspect the evaporative emission control system. Verify that the overfill limiter, the fuel check valve and the purge control valve are operating properly (see Chapter 6).*

3.4 Check the fuel pump breather hole; if any gas or oil is leaking out, replace the pump (intake manifold removed for clarity)

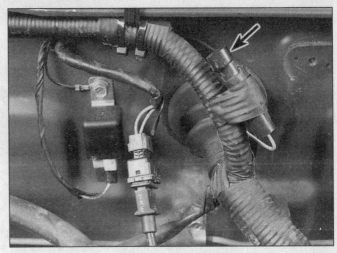

3.19 Using a fused jumper wire, apply battery voltage to the fuel pump test connector (typical)

3   Fuel pump - check

Warning: *Gasoline is extremely flammable, so take extra precautions when working on any part of the fuel system. Do not smoke or allow open flames or bare light bulbs in or near the work area. Also, don't work in a garage if a gas appliance such as a water heater or clothes dryer is present.*

1   If you suspect insufficient fuel delivery, first inspect all fuel lines to ensure that the problem is not simply a leak in a line (see Section 2).

2   If there are no leaks evident in the fuel lines, inspect the fuel pump.

Carbureted models (mechanical fuel pump)

Refer to illustration 3.4

3   Remove the air cleaner (see Section 8).

4   Locate the fuel pump (see Section 4), on the rear side of the cylinder head, between the left and right intake manifold runners **(see illustration)**.

5   Note whether there is any fuel or oil leaking from the breather hole. If there is, either the oil seal or the diaphragm in the fuel pump is defective. Replace the fuel pump if leakage is noted (see Section 4).

Fuel pump output check

6   Hook up a remote starter switch in accordance with the manufacturer's instructions. If you don't have a remote starter switch, you will need an assistant to help you with this and the following procedure.

7   Follow the fuel outlet hose from the pump to the carburetor and detach it at the carburetor (see Section 4).

8   Detach the wires from the ignition coil primary terminals (see Chapter 5).

9   Place a metal or approved gasoline con-

tainer under the open end of the fuel pump outlet hose.

10   Direct the fuel pump outlet hose into the container while cranking the engine for a few seconds with the remote starter (or while an assistant cranks the engine with the ignition key).

11   If fuel is emitted in well defined spurts, the pump is operating satisfactorily. If fuel dribbles or trickles out the hose, the pump is defective. Replace it (see Section 4).

Inlet valve check

12   Detach the inlet hose from the fuel pump.

13   Attach a vacuum gauge to the inlet fitting.

14   Crank the engine with a remote starter switch (or have an assistant crank it with the ignition key).

15   A fairly steady vacuum, uninterrupted by alternating blowback pulses (sudden pulses of pressure), should be evident.

16   If blowback is evident, the fuel pump inlet valve is not seating properly. Replace the pump (see Section 4).

17   Replace the wires on the ignition coil primary terminals.

Fuel-injected models (electric fuel pump)
Preliminary check

Refer to illustration 3.19

18   Depending on the symptom, the fuel pump and its related circuit have several items that must be checked in order to pinpoint the exact problem.

19   If the vehicle won't start, remove the fuel filler cap, turn the ignition key On and listen for the sound of the fuel pump. **Note:** *The ECM controls the operation of the fuel pump relay and turns the fuel pump off after several seconds (if the vehicle does not start). Cycle the ignition key On and Off several times to*

determine if the fuel pump is operating. If the sound of the fuel pump operating cannot be heard, turn the ignition key Off and using a fused jumper wire, apply battery voltage to the fuel pump test connector **(see illustration)**. Listen for the sound from the electric fuel pump. If there is no sound from the fuel pump, pinch the fuel hose from the fuel filter to check if pressure is felt. If the fuel pump is obviously not operating, disconnect the fuel pump connector and using a test light or voltmeter, check for battery power at the appropriate terminal in the wiring connector with battery power applied to the test connector. Check for continuity to ground at the black wire terminal. If power and ground are available and the fuel pump does not operate when connected, replace the fuel pump.

20   If the fuel pump runs with power applied to the test connector, but does not run under normal conditions, check the fuel pump relay, fuse and fusible link (see Chapter 12). If the fuel pump, relay and related circuits are all good the fuel pump control circuitry inside the ECM may be defective, have the ECM checked by a dealership or other properly equipped repair facility. If the vehicle starts but has poor driveability, check the fuel pressure (see Step 21).

Fuel pressure check
1990 through 1999 models

Refer to illustrations 3.22a, 3.22b, 3.22c and 3.22d

Note: *When reconnecting the fuel line always use new sealing washers. Check to make sure the bolt does not have stripped threads. This procedure requires a special fuel pressure gauge and fittings. If the special tools are not available, have the test performed by a dealer service department or other properly equipped repair facility.*

21   Relieve the fuel system pressure (see Section 14).

3.22a To install a fuel pressure gauge, remove the fuel filter union-bolt

3.22b A special fitting (available at automobile parts stores) is required to install a fuel pressure gauge

3.22c Install the special fitting on the fuel filter in place of the union-bolt

3.22d Install a fuel pressure gauge onto the special fitting

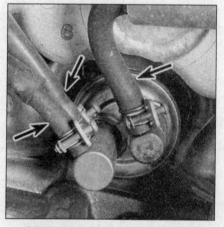

4.5 Working from under the intake manifold side of the engine, detach the fuel inlet, outlet and return hoses from the fuel pump

22   Disconnect the fuel hose between the fuel filter and the fuel rail and install a fuel pressure gauge **(see illustrations)**.
23   Using a fused jumper wire, apply battery voltage to the fuel pump test connector **(see illustration 3.19)**. Check for leakage around the gauge connections.
24   Read and record the fuel pressure on the gauge. Compare your reading with the value listed in this Chapter's Specifications.
25   If the fuel pressure is low, check for a restricted fuel line or fuel filter. Replace the fuel filter if necessary. Pinch the fuel return line shut and watch the gauge. If the pressure rises sharply, replace the fuel pressure regulator (see Section 17). If the pressure doesn't rise and there is no restriction in the fuel feed line, the fuel pump is defective.
26   If the fuel pressure is high, check for a restriction in the fuel return line. If the line is unrestricted, replace the fuel pressure regulator (see Section 17).
27   Disconnect the test connector jumper wire from the battery while observing the gauge. The pressure should hold steady for several minutes. If the pressure drops to near

zero suddenly, the check valve in the fuel pump is defective, replace the fuel pump. If the pressure immediately begins to drop slowly, check for a leak in the fuel line, fuel rail or fuel injectors. Before disconnecting the fuel pressure gauge and removing the adapter, relieve the fuel system pressure (see Section 14).

2000 and later models
28   The manufacturer recommends that you tee into the fuel system at the mounting flange between the fuel supply line and the fuel rail. To do so, you will need to obtain a special fuel pressure gauge adapter (09353-38000 or equivalent), and a fuel pressure gauge equipped with a Schrader valve fitting.
29   With the pressure gauge and adapter connected between the fuel rail and the fuel line, turn the ignition key to the On position and check for leaks at the adapter and gauge. If there are no leaks, start the engine and note the reading on the gauge, comparing your reading with the pressure listed in this Chapter's Specifications.
30   If the fuel pressure is not within specifi-

cations, check the following:
a) *If the pressure is lower than specified, check for a restriction in the fuel system. One likely cause is a clogged fuel filter or inlet strainer at the base of the fuel pump/fuel level sensor module in the left fuel tank. A faulty pump or fuel pressure regulator could also be the cause. The pressure regulator is part of the fuel pump assembly (see Section 4).*
b) *If the fuel pressure is higher than specified, replace the fuel pressure regulator, which is part of the fuel pump assembly (see Section 4).*

31   Before disconnecting the fuel pressure gauge and removing the adapter, relieve the fuel system pressure (see Section 14).

4   Fuel pump - removal and installation

Warning: *Gasoline is extremely flammable, so take extra precautions when working on any part of the fuel system. Do not smoke or allow open flames or bare light bulbs in or near the work area. Also, don't work in a garage where a gas appliance such as a water heater or clothes dryer is present.*

Carbureted models (mechanical fuel pump)

Refer to illustrations 4.5 and 4.6
1   Disconnect the cable from the negative terminal of the battery.
2   Remove the fuel tank filler cap to relieve fuel tank pressure.
3   Remove the air cleaner assembly (see Section 8).
4   Apply the parking brake and place blocks behind the rear wheels. Raise the front of the vehicle and support it with jackstands.
5   Working from underneath the rear (intake manifold side) of the engine, detach the fuel inlet, outlet and return hoses **(see illustration)** from the pump.

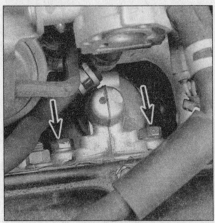

4.6 Working from above, remove the fuel pump bolts, then carefully break the pump loose with your hand and detach it, along with the two gaskets and the insulator - note that the insulator is sandwiched between the two gaskets

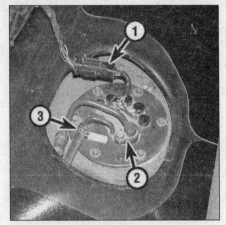

4.16 Fuel pump mounting details

1   *Electrical connector*
2   *High pressure line flange bolt*
3   *Fuel return hose clamp (1999 and earlier models)*

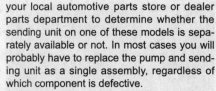

your local automotive parts store or dealer parts department to determine whether the sending unit on one of these models is separately available or not. In most cases you will probably have to replace the pump and sending unit as a single assembly, regardless of which component is defective.

22   Check the hoses and pipes for cracks or other damage.

23   Check the fuel tank for deformation, corrosion, or other damage. Check inside the fuel tank for dirt or any foreign material.

24   Check the in-tank fuel filter for damage or restriction. Check the two-way valve by blowing lightly into the inlet and then the outlet side. If air passes through after a slight resistance, the two-way valve is good.

25   Installation is the reverse of removal. Securely tighten all fittings and electrical connectors.

6   Working from above, remove the fuel pump mounting bolts **(see illustration)**.

7   Carefully break the fuel pump loose with your hand - do not use a pry bar - and remove the pump, gaskets and insulator. Note that the insulator is sandwiched between the two gaskets.

8   Using a scraper, remove the old gasket material from the insulator, the pump (if it will be reused), and the pump mating surface on the cylinder head.

9   Inspect the condition of the fuel inlet, outlet and return hoses. If they're damaged or worn, replace them (see Section 2).

10   Installation is the reverse of removal. Be sure to use new gaskets.

Fuel-injected models (electric fuel pump)

Refer to illustrations 4.16, 4.18 and 4.20

11   Relieve the fuel system pressure (see Section 14).

12   Disconnect the negative battery cable.

13   On 1994 and earlier models, remove the fuel tank from the vehicle (see Section 6). On 1995 and later models, remove the rear seat cushion for access to the fuel pump.

14   On 1994 and earlier models, remove the nuts from the fuel pump cover and lift the fuel pump assembly from the tank.

15   On 1995 and later models, remove the fuel pump access cover screws and remove the fuel pump access cover.

16   Disconnect the fuel pump/fuel level sending unit electrical connector **(see illustration)**.

17   Disconnect the fuel supply line fitting and, on 1999 and earlier models, loosen the fuel return hose clamp and disconnect the return hose **(see illustration 4.16)**.

18   On 1990 through 1994 models and on 2000 and later models, remove the fuel pump mounting flange screws **(see illustration)**.

19   On 1995 through 1999 models, unscrew the threaded retainer that secures the fuel pump mounting flange to the fuel tank. You can buy a special tool for this job or you can use very large water pump pliers. If you use water pump pliers, be very careful not to damage the retainer.

20   Remove the fuel pump from the fuel tank **(see illustration)**. As you're pulling the pump/fuel level sending unit assembly out of the tank, you'll have to angle it properly to avoid damaging the float arm for the sending unit.

21   On 1990 through 1994 models, the fuel level sending unit is a separate component installed in the fuel tank the same way as the fuel pump; so this unit can be replaced separately from the fuel pump. On 1995 and later models, the fuel level sending unit is an integral component of the fuel pump. Check with

5   In-tank fuel filter/drain plug (1989 and earlier models) - removal and installation

Refer to illustrations 5.3a, 5.3b and 5.5

Warning: *Gasoline is extremely flammable, so take extra precautions when working on any part of the fuel system. Do not smoke or allow open flames or bare light bulbs in or near the work area. Also, don't work in a garage if a gas appliance such as a water heater or clothes dryer is present. Have a fire extinguisher handy.*

Note: *Although it's not a regularly scheduled maintenance item, occasionally cleaning the in-tank fuel filter will prevent it's becoming clogged. You can also use this procedure anytime you need to drain the fuel tank (for example, before you remove it). Since you will be draining the fuel tank in this procedure, make sure the tank is nearly empty before beginning.*

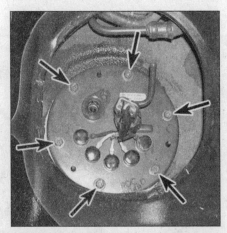

4.18 The fuel pump/fuel level sending unit assembly on 1990 through 1994 models, and 2000 and later models, is retained by screws (1995 through 1999 models are secured by a threaded retainer ring)

4.20 To remove the fuel pump/fuel level sending unit assembly from the fuel tank, first lift it straight up, then angle it so as not to damage the float arm

5.3a The drain plug is located on the bottom of the fuel tank

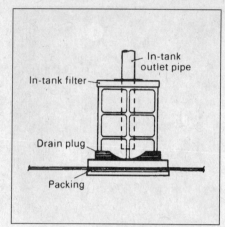

5.3b To prevent damage to the in-tank fuel filter during removal and installation, be sure to pull the plug/filter assembly straight down until it clears the in-tank outlet pipe

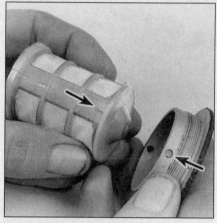

5.5 When installing a new in-tank fuel filter, be sure to press down on the new filter until the claws of the filter fit snugly into the locking holes in the plug

1   Disconnect the cable from the negative terminal of the battery.
2   Raise the rear of the vehicle and support it securely on jackstands. Place blocks in front of the front wheels.
3   Place an approved gasoline container under the drain plug. Unscrew the plug and pull it straight down so it will clear the fuel tank outlet pipe **(see illustrations)**.
4   Thoroughly clean the filter with a brush and solvent.
5   If the filter is damaged, replace it by pulling the old filter out of the drain plug and pressing in the new filter until it's claws fit snugly into the locking holes in the plug **(see illustration)**.
6   Carefully slide the filter up over the fuel tank outlet pipe and tighten the drain plug securely.
7   Use a funnel to pour the drained fuel back into the fuel tank.
8   Reconnect the negative battery terminal.

6   Fuel tank - removal and installation

Warning: *Gasoline is extremely flammable, so take extra precautions when working on any part of the fuel system. Do not smoke or allow open flames or bare light bulbs in or near the work area. Also, don't work in a garage if a gas appliance is present. While performing any work on the fuel tank it is advisable to wear safety glasses and to have a dry chemical (Class B) fire extinguisher on hand. If you spill any fuel on your skin, rinse it off immediately with soap and water.*

Removal and installation

Refer to illustrations 6.5 and 6.7

1   On fuel injected models, relieve the fuel system pressure (see Section 14). Remove the fuel tank filler cap to relieve fuel tank pressure.

2   Disconnect the cable from the negative terminal of the battery.
3   If equipped, remove the fuel tank drain plug and allow the fuel to drain in an approved gasoline container. On later models, use a siphoning kit (available at most auto parts stores) to siphon the fuel into an approved gasoline container.
4   Raise the vehicle and support it securely on jackstands.
5   Disconnect the fuel hoses or lines and the vapor return line **(see illustration)**. Clearly label the three lines and the fittings. Be sure to plug the hoses to prevent leakage and contamination of the fuel system.
6   Support the fuel tank with a floor jack. Place a wood block between the jack head and the fuel tank to protect the tank.
7   Remove the fuel tank strap bolts and the fuel tank protector (if equipped) **(see illustration)**
8   Swing the fuel tank retaining straps down

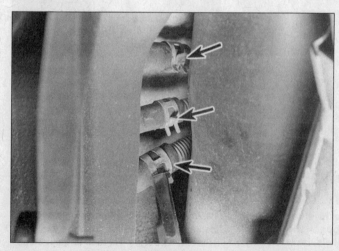

6.5 Clearly label, then detach the fuel feed, return and vapor lines (typical)

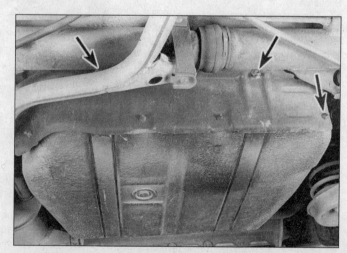

6.7 Remove the fuel tank strap bolts and the protector (if equipped) and swing the straps down out of the way (typical)

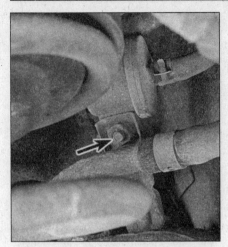

6.12 The overfill limiter valve is located on the upper left side of the fuel tank - to replace it, detach the mounting bolt (arrow) and both hoses

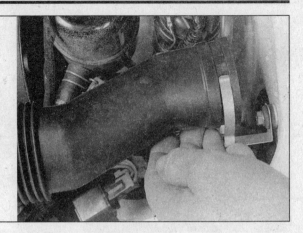

8.3 On carbureted models, you don't have to detach the cold air snorkel from the air cleaner assembly - just detach the snorkel mouth from the bracket on the wall of the engine compartment

until they are out of the way.

9   On 1994 and earlier models, lower the tank enough to disconnect the electrical connector from the fuel gauge sending unit, which is located on the upper right side of the fuel tank.

10   Remove the tank from the vehicle.

11   Installation is the reverse of removal.

Overfill limiter (two-way) valve replacement

Refer to illustration 6.12

Note: *The overfill limiter valve is located on the fuel tank. If it is defective, you can replace it using the following procedure.*

12   Remove the overfill limiter mounting bolt (**see illustration**).

13   Detach the vapor hoses from the limiter and remove it.

14   Installation is the reverse of removal.

7   Fuel tank cleaning and repair - general information

1   All repairs to the fuel tank or filler neck should be carried out by a professional who has experience in this critical and potentially dangerous work. Even after cleaning and flushing of the fuel system, explosive fumes can remain and ignite during repair of the tank.

2   If the fuel tank is removed from the vehicle, it should not be placed in an area where sparks or open flames could ignite the fumes coming out of the tank. Be especially careful inside garages where a gas-type appliance is located, because it could cause an explosion.

8   Air cleaner assembly - removal and installation

Carbureted models

Refer to illustrations 8.3, 8.4, 8.6, 8.7, 8.8 and 8.9

Warning: *Gasoline is extremely flammable, so take extra precautions when working on*

any part of the fuel system. Do not smoke or allow open flames or bare light bulbs in or near the work area. Also, don't work in a garage where a gas appliance such as a water heater or clothes dryer is present.

1   Disconnect the cable from the negative terminal of the battery.

2   Remove the air cleaner cover and filter element (see Chapter 1). **Note:** *Always inspect the filter element for contamination or moisture when you remove it.*

3   Detach the cold air snorkel from its clip (**see illustration**).

4   Detach the small and large breather hoses from the air cleaner (**see illustration**).

5   Remove the two 12 mm flange nuts that attach the air cleaner to the rocker arm cover bracket studs (**see illustration 8.4**).

6   If your vehicle is a 1986 or 1987 model, detach the small canister mounted on the firewall behind the air cleaner from its clamp (**see illustration**) and set it aside. **Caution:** *Don't pull any of the vacuum hoses loose from this canister or you will have a vacuum leak when you reinstall the air cleaner assembly.*

7   Disconnect the electrical connector

8.4 Although you don't really need to remove the air cleaner cover and filter element to remove the air cleaner assembly, now is a good time to inspect the filter (see Chapter 1) - remove the large and small breather hoses (arrows) - also remove the two 12 mm flange nuts (arrows) to detach the air cleaner assembly from the rocker arm cover bracket studs

8.6 If your vehicle is a 1986 or 1987 model, detach the vacuum canister and set it aside (being careful not to detach any of the vacuum hoses attached to it)

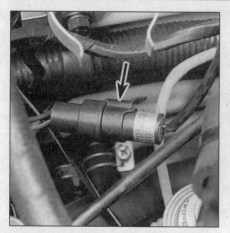

8.7 If your vehicle is a 1986 or 1987 model, disconnect this electrical connector located underneath the vacuum canister you removed in the last step

8.8 Raise the air cleaner slightly and detach it from the heat riser tube (as they get older, these heat riser tubes have a tendency to fall off, so it's a good idea to put it aside in some place where you can find it when you reinstall the air cleaner)

8.9 Raise the left side of the air cleaner and detach this small vacuum hose from its clamp, then detach it from the underside of the case

(see illustration) located under the canister mounting clamp (not used on 1987 and 1988 vehicles).

8   Raise the air cleaner slightly and detach it from the heat riser tube **(see illustration)**.

9   Raise the left side of the air cleaner assembly and detach the small vacuum hose **(see illustration)** from the underside of the case.

10   Remove the air cleaner assembly.

11   Installation is the reverse of removal.

Fuel-injected models

Refer to illustration 8.15

12   Disconnect the cable from the negative terminal of the battery.

13   Unclamp the air intake tube from the air cleaner cover. Remove the air cleaner cover and air filter element (see Chapter 1). **Note:** *Always inspect the filter element for con-*

tamination or moisture when you remove it. Replace the element if necessary.

14   On 1994 and earlier models, remove the two bolts that attach the resonator to the air cleaner housing. Remove the resonator.

15   Remove the bolts that attach the air cleaner housing to the inner fender panel. Remove the air cleaner assembly **(see illustration)**.

16   Remove the air cleaner housing from the engine compartment.

17   Installation is the reverse of removal.

9   Throttle cable - removal and installation

Warning: *Gasoline is extremely flammable, so take extra precautions when working on any part of the fuel system. Do not smoke or*

allow open flames or bare light bulbs in or near the work area. Also, don't work in a garage where a gas appliance such as a water heater or clothes dryer is present.

Removal

Refer to illustrations 9.2, 9.3a, 9.3b, 9.4a, 9.4b and 9.5

1   On carbureted models, remove the air cleaner assembly (see Section 8).

2   Loosen the throttle cable adjusting nut **(see illustration)**.

3   Detach the throttle cable from the throttle lever **(see illustrations)**.

4   Detach the throttle cable from the accelerator pedal **(see illustrations)**.

5   Detach the throttle cable guide from the firewall **(see illustration)**.

6   From outside the vehicle, pull the throttle cable through the firewall.

8.15 Remove the three air cleaner housing mounting bolts (other bolt not visible) (typical 1995 and later model shown)

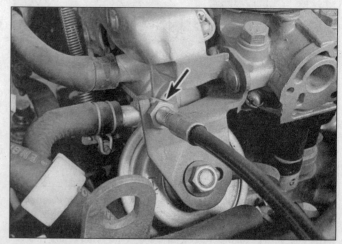

9.2 To detach the throttle cable from the bracket, loosen the adjusting nut - typical

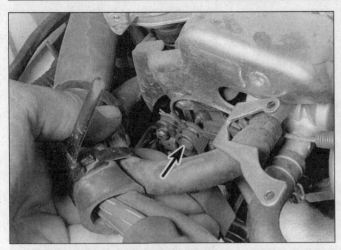

9.3a On carbureted models, to detach the throttle cable from the throttle lever, rotate the lever to place slack in the cable, then push the cable plug toward the carburetor (there is a gap on the carburetor side of the lever where the cable can slide free)

9.3b On fuel-injected models, remove the throttle cable from the throttle body linkage

Installation

7   Installation is the reverse of removal. Don't leave any sharp bends in the cable.

8   After installing the cable, adjust free play as follows:

a) *Run the engine until it reaches normal operating temperature. Verify the idle speed is correct and adjust it if necessary (see Chapter 1).*

b) *Verify that the throttle cable has no slack in it.*

c) *If the cable is slack, adjust it as follows:*

d) *Turn the adjusting nut counterclockwise until the throttle lever is free.*

e) *Remove any sharp bends from the accelerator cable.*

f) *Loosen the locknut and turn the throttle cable adjusting nut clockwise to the point at which the throttle lever just begins to move, then back off the adjusting nut one turn and tighten the locknut securely.*

10 Carburetor - on-vehicle check, adjustment and component replacement

Warning: *Gasoline is extremely flammable, so take extra precautions when working on any part of the fuel system. Do not smoke or allow open flames or bare light bulbs in or near the work area. Also, don't work in a garage where a gas appliance such as a water heater or clothes dryer is present.*

Note: *If your vehicle's engine is hard to start or does not start at all, has an unstable idle or poor driveability and you suspect the carburetor is malfunctioning, it's best to first take the vehicle to a dealer service department that has the Feedback Carburetor equipment necessary to diagnose this highly complicated system. The following procedures are intended to help the home mechanic verify proper opera-*

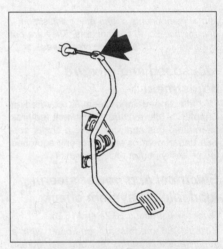

9.4a Remove the trim panel under the dash to access the top of the accelerator pedal . . .

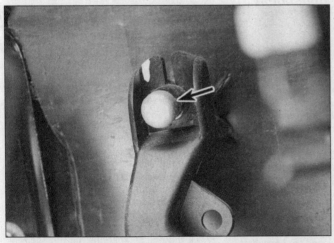

9.4b . . . and detach the throttle cable from the accelerator pedal (arrow)

9.5 To detach the throttle cable from the firewall, remove the two mounting bolts and separate the guide from the firewall

10.2a Inspect the idle-up actuator hose (1) for cracks and deterioration - remove it from the vacuum-fitting before testing the actuator; take out the two screws (2) to remove the actuator. Adjust the actuator with the adjustment screw (3)

10.2b Inspect the hoses and wiring harness connected to the idle-up actuator (1) - to detach the solenoid mounting bracket from the engine, take out the two bolts (2)

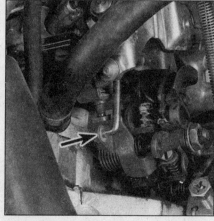

10.11 To detach the idle-up actuator rod from the free lever, pull the rod in the direction indicated by the arrow

tion of components, make minor adjustments, and replace some components. They are not intended as troubleshooting procedures.

Idle speed and mixture adjustment

1   Idle speed adjustment is covered in Chapter 1. Idle mixture adjustment requires an infrared gas analyzer. Have a dealer service department or other properly equipped repair facility perform this procedure.

Electrical and power steering load idle-up system check

Refer to illustrations 10.2a and 10.2b

Note: *1986 models are equipped with a throttle opener system; 1987 and later models are equipped with an idle-up system. These two systems are highly similar and, for sim-*

10.23 To adjust the idle-up actuator for proper idle speed under an air conditioning load, turn the throttle adjusting screw (arrow) until the tachometer indicates the specified speed

plicity, are both referred to below as idle-up-systems.

2   Inspect the vacuum hoses and the idle-up control solenoid harness - make sure they're properly connected **(see illustrations)**.

3   Detach the vacuum hose from the fitting on the idle-up actuator/dashpot **(see illustration 10.2a)**.

4   Attach a vacuum pump to the idle-up actuator/dashpot vacuum fitting.

5   Hook up a tachometer in accordance with the manufacturer's instructions.

6   Start the engine and allow it to idle.

7   Apply 11.8 in-Hg vacuum with the vacuum pump. Engine speed should increase.

8   If engine speed does not increase, replace the idle-up actuator/dashpot, as described below. Stop the engine and remove the vacuum pump.

Idle-up actuator/dashpot replacement and adjustment

Replacement

Refer to illustration 10.11

9   Remove the throttle return spring from the throttle lever.

10   Remove the two idle-up actuator/dashpot attaching screws **(see illustration 10.2a)**.

11   Detach the idle-up actuator rod from the free lever **(see illustration)** and remove the idle-up actuator.

12   Install the new idle-up actuator/dashpot and reattach the vacuum hose.

13   Adjust the idle-up actuator/dashpot as described below.

Adjustment

Note: *The following procedure adjusts the idle-up actuator control of the idle speed when electric or power steering loads are applied.*

14   Make sure that the curb idle speed is set as specified in Chapter 1. If it's not, readjust

the idle speed to the specified speed before proceeding.

15   Unbolt the solenoid mounting bracket from the transaxle end of the cylinder head **(see illustration 10.2b)**. Remove the electrical connector from the bottom of the idle-up control solenoid. Using jumper wires, connect one of the solenoid's terminals to the positive terminal of the battery and the other solenoid terminal to the negative terminal of the battery. This applies intake manifold vacuum to the idle-up actuator, which activates the actuator.

16   Open the throttle slightly - until engine speed reaches about 2000 rpm - then slowly close it.

17   Note the indicated engine speed. Adjust it, if necessary, to the specified rpm with the throttle opener adjustment screw **(see illustration 10.2a)**.

18   Repeat Step 16 above and check the engine speed again.

19   Remove the jumper wire you attached in Step 15 and reattach the wire harness.

Idle-up air conditioning load actuator adjustment

Refer to illustration 10.23

Note: *The following procedure adjusts the idle-up actuator's control of the idle speed when an air conditioning load is applied.*

20   Hook up a tachometer in accordance with the manufacturer's instructions.

21   Start the engine.

22   Turn on the air conditioner switch. This opens the solenoid valve, which allows intake manifold vacuum to move the actuator to its full open position. Note the indicated engine speed and compare your reading to the specified rpm.

23   If the engine speed is out of specification, adjust it with the throttle adjusting screw **(see illustration)**.

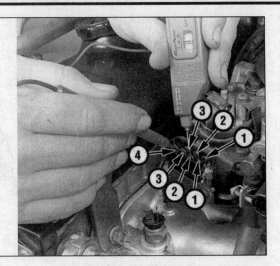

10.28 To check the mixture solenoid valve coils, unplug the connector and measure the resistance across the indicated pairs of terminals with an ohmmeter (for the bowl vent valve, measure between the indicated terminal and the negative post of the battery), then compare your readings with the specified resistance for each coil:

1 Jet mixture solenoid valve
2 Enrichment solenoid valve
3 Deceleration solenoid valve
4 Bowl vent valve

10.30 Before you can remove the deceleration, enrichment or jet mixture solenoid valves, you must detach the wire harness from the carburetor body at the locations indicated by arrows

Idle-up control solenoid valve check

24 Set the ignition switch in the Off position.
25 Remove the solenoid bracket from the transaxle end of the cylinder head and detach the electrical connector from the idle-up control solenoid (see illustration 10.2b).
26 Check the solenoid valve coil with an ohmmeter. Compare your reading with the specified resistance. If the indicated resistance is not as specified, there is an open or short in the solenoid coil. Replace it.

Deceleration, enrichment, jet mixture solenoid valves and bowl vent valve check (1986 and 1987 models) and replacement

Refer to illustrations 10.28, 10.30, 10.31a, 10.31b, 10.31c and 10.33

27 Unplug the solenoid valve connector.

28 Check each solenoid valve coil with an ohmmeter between the indicated ter-minals (see illustration). Compare your readings with the specified resistance. For the bowl vent valve, measure between the indicated terminal and the negative post of the battery. If the indicated resistance for any solenoid valve is not as specified, there's an open or short in it. Replace it (proceed to the next step). If there's a problem with the bowl vent valve, proceed to Step 33.
29 To remove the deceleration solenoid valve, you will need to remove the idle-up actuator (see illustration 10.2a).
30 Detach the wire harness (see illustration).
31 Remove the deceleration solenoid valve, enrichment solenoid valve or jet mixture solenoid valve (see illustrations) from the float cover.
32 Install the new solenoid valve and reattach the connector.
33 If your vehicle is a 1986 or 1987 model, detach the BVV wire harness terminal blade from the solenoid control valve electrical con-

10.31a Location of the deceleration solenoid valve

10.31b Location of the enrichment solenoid valve

10.31c Location of the jet mixture solenoid valve

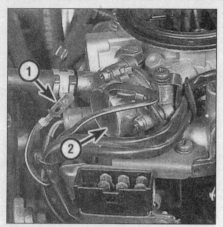

10.33 On 1986 and 1987 vehicles, detach the terminal blade (1) from the solenoid control valve connector by depressing the tang next to the terminal blade with a small screwdriver and pulling the blade out the bottom of the connector - to remove the bowl vent solenoid and valve assembly (2), take out the three mounting screws

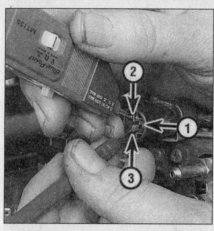

10.37 To check the throttle position sensor, unplug the connector and measure the resistance between terminals 2 and 3

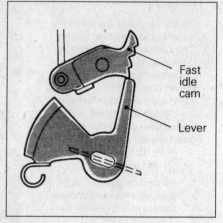

10.40 Verify the fast idle cam is released (the lever must not be resting on the cam)

nector **(see illustration)**. If it's a 1988 and later model, simply unplug the BVV harness connector.

34   Remove the screws and detach the bowl vent solenoid and valve assembly from the float chamber cover **(see illustration 10.33)**.

35   Install the new bowl vent valve assembly on the float chamber cover and connect the harness.

Throttle Position Sensor (TPS) check and adjustment

Refer to illustrations 10.37, 10.40, 10.42 and 10.45

Check

36   Unplug the TPS connector.
37   Check the resistance between term-inals 2 and 3 with an ohmmeter **(see illustration)**.
38   Verify that the resistance changes smoothly as the throttle valve is slowly turned from a closed position to wide open. Note your readings and compare them to the specified resistance. If the resistance does not change smoothly, replace the sensor. If it is not within specifications, try adjusting the sensor. If you cannot adjust the sensor to specifications, replace the sensor. Be sure to adjust the new sensor.

Adjustment (1986 and 1987 models)

39   Warm up the engine.
40   Loosen the throttle cable (see Section 9) and verify the fast idle cam is released **(see illustration)**.
41   Stop the engine.
42   Back off (turn counterclockwise) the speed adjusting screws (SAS-1 and SAS-2) **(see illustration)** until the throttle valve is fully closed. Count the number of turns required

by each screw to close the throttle valve and record these figures.

43   Attach a digital voltmeter between terminals 2 and 3 of the TPS connector **(see illustration 10.37)**. **Note:** *Don't disconnect the TPS connector from the main wire harness.*

44   Turn the ignition switch to On (don't start the engine), measure the TPS output voltage and compare your reading to the specified output voltage.

45   If the output voltage is incorrect, loosen the TPS adjusting screw and adjust the output voltage by turning the adjusting screw **(see illustration)**.

46   Turn the ignition switch to Off.
47   Retighten (turn clockwise) the SAS-1 and SAS-2 screws the same number of turns that you backed them off in Step 42 above.
48   Adjust the throttle cable free play (see Section 9).
49   Start the engine and verify the idle speed is within specifications (see Chapter 1).

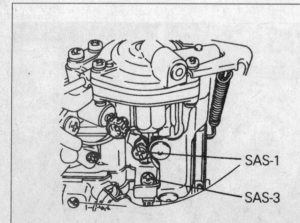

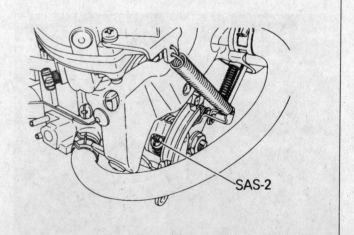

10.42 Back off the speed adjusting screws (SAS-1 and SAS-2) until the throttle valve is fully closed - be sure to count the number of turns (down to 1/4 -turn) so you can later return the screws to the same positions

10.45 To adjust the TPS output voltage on 1986 and 1987 models, turn the adjusting screw (arrow) until the output voltage is correct

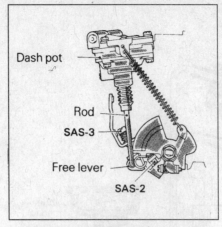

10.51 With the engine idling, open the throttle valve until the free lever contacts SAS-3

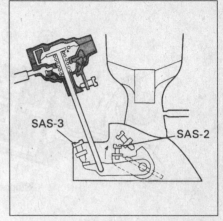

10.52 Close the throttle valve until SAS-2 contacts the free lever and note the indicated idle speed at that point

Dash pot check and adjustment (1988 and later models)

Refer to illustrations 10.51 and 10.52

50   Before checking the dash pot:

a) *Start the engine and warm it up (coolant temperature must be between 176 and 203-degrees F).*

b) *Turn off all lights and electrical accessories. Make sure that the cooling fan is off.*

c) *Place the transmission in Neutral (manual transaxle) or Park (automatic transaxle).*

d) *If the vehicle has power steering, make sure that the wheel are pointed straight ahead.*

51   With the engine idling, open the throttle valve the full stroke of the rod until the free lever contacts SAS-3 **(see illustration)**.

52   Close the throttle valve until the SAS-2 contacts the free lever **(see illustration)** and note the indicated engine idle speed at that moment.

53   If the indicated idle speed is not as spec-ified, adjust the dash pot setting by turning SAS-3.

54   Release the free lever and verify that the engine returns to its idle speed slowly.

Electric choke system check (1988 and later models)

Refer to illustrations 10.55 and 10.57

Note: *The carburetor on all models has a tamperproof choke. The choke related parts are factory adjusted, so no further adjustments should be necessary unless you rebuild the carburetor, or a smog inspection indicates that choke related parts need to be adjusted.*

55   Verify that the alignment marks on the electric choke and bimetal assembly are lined up **(see illustration)**.

a) *If they are misaligned in a clockwise direction, the engine will start better but the plugs are probably sooty.*

b) *If they are misaligned in a counterclockwise direction, the engine will be hard to start and will be more likely to stall.*

56   Make sure that the engine coolant temperature is below 50-degrees F.

57   Start the engine and place your hand on the electric choke body to check the operation of the choke valve and fast idle cam **(see illustration)**.

a) *The choke valve should open as the choke body temperature rises.*

b) *The fast idle cam should release as the engine coolant temperature rises and the choke opener operates.*

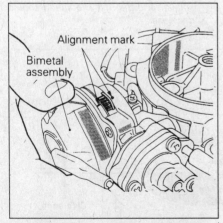

10.55 Verify that the alignment marks on the electric choke and bimetal assembly line up properly

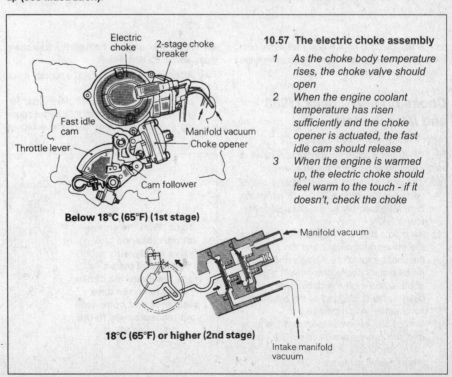

10.57 The electric choke assembly

1   *As the choke body temperature rises, the choke valve should open*

2   *When the engine coolant temperature has risen sufficiently and the choke opener is actuated, the fast idle cam should release*

3   *When the engine is warmed up, the electric choke should feel warm to the touch - if it doesn't, check the choke*

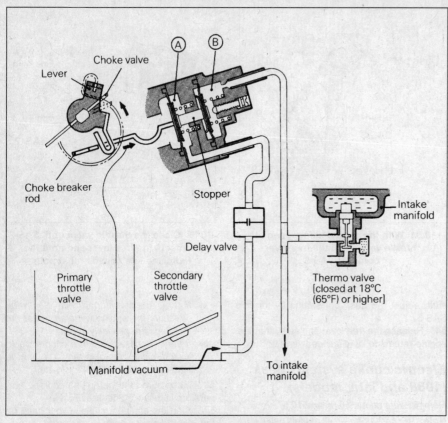

10.59 The choke breaker system

1   *Choke valve is fully closed when the engine is off*
2   *Choke valve opens slowly and slightly (about 0.059-inch) after the engine is started*
3   *Once the engine is warmed up and idling, the choke valve should not move when the yellow-striped vacuum hose is detached*
4   *After the engine temperature exceeds 65-degrees F and vacuum hose is reattached, with engine idling, push choke valve closed with your finger - it should have a slightly larger opening than in 2 above (about 0.118-inch)*

58   If the electric choke body remains cool even after the engine is warmed up, check the choke heater (see below).

Choke breaker check (1988 and later models)

Refer to illustrations 10.59 and 10.62

59   While the engine coolant temperature is below 65-degrees F **(see illustration)**:

a)   *The choke should be fully closed before you start the engine. If it isn't, either the bimetal assembly or the linkage operation is faulty.*

b)   *After you start the engine (fully depress the accelerator pedal) and run it at idle, the choke should open slowly and slightly (immediately after starting), with a gap of about 0.059-inch If it doesn't, either the delay valve is clogged or the diaphragm for chamber A is ruptured.*

c)   *Detach the yellow-striped vacuum hose and run the engine at idle. The choke valve shouldn't move. If it does, the thermo valve is faulty.*

60   After the engine coolant temperature goes above 65-degrees F:

a)   *Attach the yellow striped vacuum hose and run the engine at idle.*

b)   *Lightly close the choke valve with your finger. It should stop at a slightly larger opening than it did in Step 59b above (about 0.118-inch). If it doesn't, either the thermo valve is faulty or the diaphragm for chamber B is ruptured* **(see illustration 10.59)**.

61   After inspecting the choke breaker system, detach the vacuum hose from the choke breaker and make the following check.

62   With the engine idling, close the choke valve lightly with your finger until the choke valve stops. Measure the choke valve-to-bore clearance **(see illustration)** and compare your measurement to the specification.

63   If the clearance is not as specified, take the vehicle to the dealer to have the internal choke linkage adjusted or the bimetal assembly replaced.

Fast idle check and adjustment (1988 and later models)

Refer to illustrations 10.70, 10.71 and 10.73

64   Start the engine and warm up the coolant to between 176 and 203-degrees F.

65   Make sure that all lights, the cooling fan and all electrical accessories are off.

66   Place the transmission in Neutral (manual transaxle) or Park (automatic transaxle).

67   If the vehicle is equipped with power steering, make sure that the wheels are pointed straight ahead.

68   Remove the air cleaner assembly (see Section 8).

69   Hook up a tachometer in accordance with the manufacturer's instructions.

70   Detach the white-striped vacuum hose from the choke opener **(see illustration)**.

71   Set the lever on the second highest step of the fast idle cam **(see illustration)**.

72   Start the engine and check the fast idle speed. Compare your reading with the specified value.

73   If the fast idle speed is out of specification, adjust it with the fast idle adjusting screw **(see illustration)**.

a)   *If you turn the fast idle screw in a clockwise direction, the valve opening will be larger and the fast idle speed should increase.*

b)   *If you turn the fast idle screw counterclockwise, the valve opening will be smaller and the fast idle speed should decrease.*

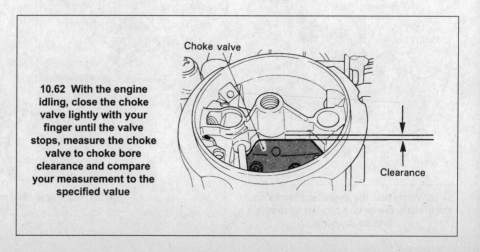

10.62 With the engine idling, close the choke valve lightly with your finger until the valve stops, measure the choke valve to choke bore clearance and compare your measurement to the specified value

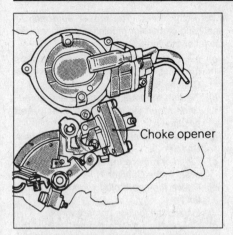

10.70 Detach the white-striped vacuum hose from the choke opener

Choke heater inspection (1988 and later models)

Refer to illustration 10.74

74   Unplug the electric choke heater connector and check the heater with an ohmmeter **(see illustration)**. It should indicate about 6 ohms.

75   If the resistance is not as specified, replace the bimetal assembly (electric choke body).

11   Carburetor - removal and installation

Warning: *Gasoline is extremely flammable so take extra precautions when working on any part of the fuel system. Do not smoke or allow open flames or bare light bulbs in or near the work area. Also, don't work in a garage if a gas appliance such as a water heater or clothes dryer is present.*

Removal

1   Remove the fuel filler cap to relieve fuel tank pressure.

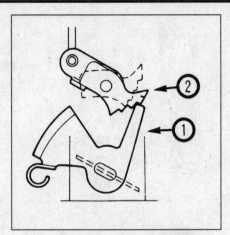

10.71 Set the lever (1) on the second highest step of the fast idle cam (2)

2   Remove the air cleaner assembly (see Section 8).
3   Disconnect the throttle cable from the throttle lever (see Section 9).
4   If the vehicle is equipped with an automatic transmission, disconnect the TV cable from the throttle lever (see Chapter 7B).
5   Clearly label all vacuum hoses and fittings, then disconnect the hoses.
6   Disconnect the fuel line from the carburetor.
7   Label the wires and terminals, then unplug all wire harness connectors.
8   Remove the mounting bolts and detach the carburetor from the intake manifold. The bolts extend all the way through the carburetor. Remove the carburetor mounting gasket. Stuff a shop rag into the intake manifold opening.

Installation

9   Use a gasket scraper to remove all traces of gasket material and sealant from the intake manifold (and the carburetor, if it's being reinstalled), then remove the shop rag from the manifold openings. Clean the mating surfaces with lacquer thinner or acetone.

10   Place a new gasket on the intake manifold.
11   Position the carburetor on the gasket and install the mounting fasteners.
12   To prevent carburetor distortion or damage, tighten the fasteners in a criss-cross pattern, 1/4-turn at a time, to the torque listed in this Chapter's Specifications.
13   The remaining installation steps are the reverse of removal.
14   Check and, if necessary, adjust the idle speed (see Chapter 1).
15   If the vehicle is equipped with an automatic transmission, refer to Chapter 7B for the TV cable adjustment procedure.
16   Start the engine and check carefully for fuel leaks.

12   Carburetor - diagnosis and overhaul

Refer to illustrations 12.8a, 12.8b and 12.8c
Warning: *Gasoline is extremely flammable, so take extra precautions when working on any part of the fuel system. Do not smoke or allow open flames or bare light bulbs in or near the work area. Also, don't work in a garage if a gas appliance such as a water heater or clothes dryer is present.*

Diagnosis

1   A thorough road test and check of carburetor adjustments should be done before any major carburetor service work. Specifications for some adjustments are listed on the Vehicle Emissions Control Information (VECI) label found in the engine compartment.
2   Carburetor problems usually show up as flooding, hard starting, stalling, severe backfiring and poor acceleration. A carburetor that's leaking fuel and/or covered with wet looking deposits definitely needs attention.
3   Some performance complaints directed at the carburetor are actually a result of loose, out-of-adjustment or malfunctioning engine or electrical components. Others develop when vacuum hoses leak, are disconnected or are

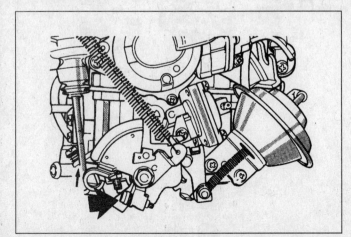

10.73 If the fast idle speed is out of specification, adjust it with the fast idle adjusting screw (arrow)

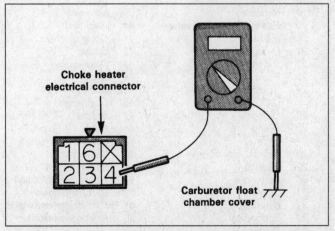

10.74 To check the electric choke heater, unplug the connector and check the resistance of the heater with an ohmmeter

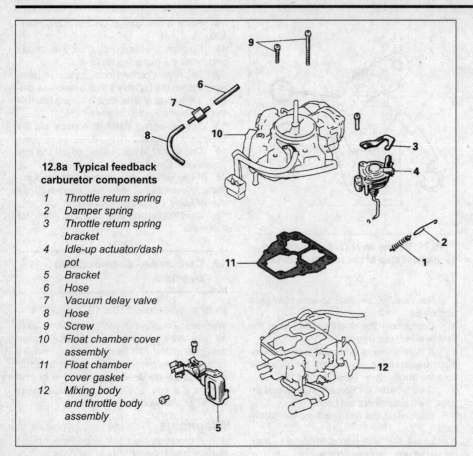

12.8a Typical feedback carburetor components

1 Throttle return spring
2 Damper spring
3 Throttle return spring bracket
4 Idle-up actuator/dash pot
5 Bracket
6 Hose
7 Vacuum delay valve
8 Hose
9 Screw
10 Float chamber cover assembly
11 Float chamber cover gasket
12 Mixing body and throttle body assembly

incorrectly routed. The proper approach to analyzing carburetor problems should include the following items:

a) Inspect all vacuum hoses and actuators for leaks and correct installation (see Chapters 1 and 6).
b) Tighten the intake manifold and carburetor mounting nuts/bolts evenly and securely.
c) Perform a cylinder compression test (see Chapter 2).
d) Clean or replace the spark plugs as necessary (see Chapter 1).
e) Check the spark plug wires (see Chapter 1).
f) Inspect the ignition primary wires.
g) Check the ignition timing (follow the instructions printed on the Vehicle Emissions Control Information label).
h) Check the fuel pump pressure/volume (see Chapter 4).
i) Check the heat control valve in the air cleaner for proper operation (see Chapter 1).
j) Check/replace the air filter element (see Chapter 1).
k) Check the PCV system (see Chapter 6).
l) Check/replace the fuel filter (see Chapter 1). Also, the strainer in the tank could be restricted.
m) Check for a plugged exhaust system.
n) Check EGR valve operation (see Chapter 6).

12.8b Typical feedback carburetor float chamber cover assembly components

13	Pin	35	Body
14	Float	36	Spring
15	Needle valve	37	Diaphragm
16	Needle valve seat	38	Valve
17	O-ring	39	Mixture control valve (MCV) assembly
18	Packing		
19	Retainer	40	Gasket
20	Feedback solenoid valve (FBSV)	41	Cover
		42	Spring
21	O-ring	43	Diaphragm
22	O-ring	44	Body
23	Retainer	45	Spring
24	Slow cut solenoid valve (SCSV)	46	Diaphragm
		47	Bracket
25	O-ring	48	Cover
26	O-ring	49	Spring
27	Plate	50	Diaphragm
28	Bimetal assembly	51	Body
29	Packing	52	Main air jet (primary)
30	Connector	53	Pilot jet (primary)
31	Cover	54	Pilot jet (secondary)
32	Diaphragm	55	Float chamber cover
33	Spring seat		
34	Spring		

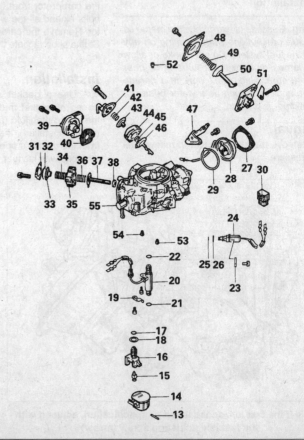

o) *Check the choke-it should be completely open at normal engine operating temperature (see Chapter 1).*

p) *Check for fuel leaks and kinked or dented fuel lines (see Chapters 1 and 4)*

q) *Check accelerator pump operation with the engine off (remove the air cleaner cover and operate the throttle as you look into the carburetor throat - you should see a stream of gasoline enter the carburetor).*

r) *Check for incorrect fuel or bad gasoline.*

s) *Check the valve clearances and cam- shaft lobe lift (see Chapters 1 and 2)*

t) *Have a dealer service department or repair shop check the electronic engine and carburetor controls.*

4   Diagnosing carburetor problems may require that the engine be started and run with the air cleaner off. While running the engine without the air cleaner, backfires are possible. This situation is likely to occur if the carburetor is malfunctioning, but just the removal of the air cleaner can lean the fuel/air mixture enough to produce an engine backfire. **Warning:** *Do not position any part of your body, especially your face, directly over the carburetor during inspection and servicing procedures. Wear eye protection!*

Overhaul

5   Once it's determined that the carburetor needs an overhaul, several options are available. If you're going to attempt to overhaul the carburetor yourself, first obtain a good quality carburetor rebuild kit (which will include all necessary gaskets, internal parts, instructions and a parts list). You'll also need some special solvent and a means of blowing out the internal passages of the carburetor with air.

6   An alternative is to obtain a new or rebuilt carburetor. They are readily available from dealers and auto parts stores. Make absolutely sure the exchange carburetor is identical to the original. A tag is usually attached to the top of the carburetor or a number is stamped on the float bowl. It will help determine the exact type of carburetor you have. When obtaining a rebuilt carburetor or a rebuild kit, make sure the kit or carburetor matches your application exactly. Seemingly insignificant differences can make a large difference in engine performance.

7   If you choose to overhaul your own carburetor, allow enough time to disassemble it carefully, soak the necessary parts in the cleaning solvent (usually for at least one-half day or according to the instructions listed on the carburetor cleaner) and reassemble it, which will usually take much longer than disassembly. When disassembling the carburetor, match each part with the illustration in the carburetor kit and lay the parts out in order on a clean work surface. Overhauls by inexperienced mechanics can result in an engine which runs poorly or not at all. To avoid this, use care and patience when disassembling the carburetor so you can reassemble it correctly.

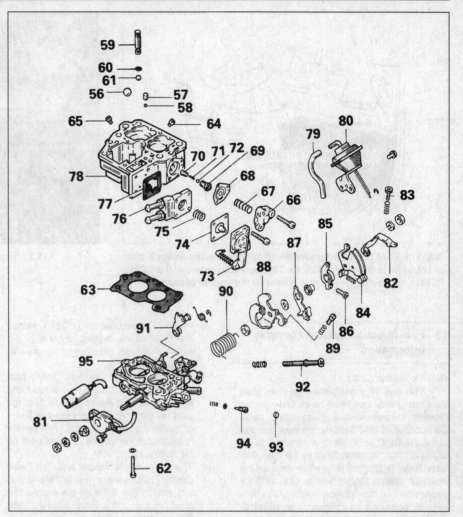

12.8c Typical feedback carburetor mixing chamber/throttle body assembly components

56	Steel ball	76	Pump body
57	Weight	77	Gasket
58	Ball	78	Mixing body
59	Plug	79	Vacuum hose
60	O-ring	80	Depression chamber
61	Ball	81	Throttle position sensor (TPS)
62	Screw	82	Lever
63	Gasket	83	Adjusting screw
64	Main jet (primary)	84	Throttle Lever
65	Main jet (secondary)	85	Cam follower
66	Cover	86	Fast idle adjusting screw
67	Spring	87	Free lever
68	Diaphragm	88	Abutment plate
69	Enrichment jet valve	89	Idle speed adjusting screw (SAS-2)
70	Enrichment jet	90	Spring
71	Spring	91	Secondary lever
72	Ball	92	Idle speed adjusting screw (SAS-1)
73	Pump cover assembly	93	Plug
74	Diaphragm	94	Mixture adjusting screw (MAS)
75	Spring	95	Throttle body

8   Because carburetor designs are constantly modified by the manufacturer in order to meet increasingly more stringent emissions regulations, it isn't feasible to include a step-by-step overhaul of each type. You'll receive a detailed, well illustrated set of instructions with any carburetor overhaul kit; they will apply in a more specific manner to the carburetor on your vehicle. Exploded views of the carburetors are included here **(see illustrations)**.

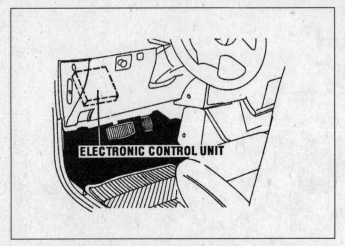

13.1 The ECM is located under the dashboard on the driver's side of the vehicle (through 2005; on 2006 and later models, the ECM/PCM is located in the left rear corner of the engine compartment)

15.2 Location of Check Engine Light (typical)

13   Fuel injection system - general information

Refer to illustration 13.1

The engine management system (fuel injection/ignition) as fitted to all fuel-injected models incorporates a closed-loop catalytic converter and various emission control components. The system is referred to as Multi-port Fuel Injection (MFI) by the manufacturer. Refer to Chapter 6 for information on the emission control system and to Chapter 5 for information on the ignition system. The fuel system operates as follows **(see illustrations)**:

The fuel pump (which is immersed in the fuel tank) supplies fuel from the tank to the fuel rail, via a filter located in the engine compartment. Fuel supply pressure is controlled by the pressure regulator on the end of the fuel rail. When the optimum operating pressure of the fuel system is exceeded, the regulator allows excess fuel to return to the tank.

The electrical control system consists of the Electronic Control Module (ECM), along with the following sensors:

a) *The 1994 and earlier MFI system uses a Karman vortex type air flow sensor to detect the air flow rate and to send an intake air volume signal to the ECM. The 1995 and later MFI system uses a hot film type Mass Air Flow sensor (MAF) to determine the volume of air and provide a signal to the ECM.*

b) *Throttle position sensor (TPS) (also contains the idle position switch) - informs the ECM of the throttle position, and the rate of throttle opening/closing.*

c) *Engine Coolant Temperature (ECT) sensor - informs the ECM of engine temperature.*

d) *Intake Air Temperature (IAT) sensor - informs the ECM of the temperature of the air passing through the intake manifold.*

e) *Heated Oxygen Sensor (HOS) - informs the ECM of the oxygen content of the exhaust gases (explained in greater detail in Chapter 6).*

f) *Manifold Absolute Pressure (MAP) sensor - this sensor is uses on the 1994 and earlier system. It informs the ECM of the load on the engine (expressed in terms of intake manifold vacuum). The sensor is located in the engine compartment on the bulkhead.*

g) *The crank angle sensor and Top Dead Center (TDC) sensor (inside the distributor) inform the ECM of the crankshaft position and the engine speed (1986 through 1994 models).*

h) *The Camshaft Position (CMP) sensor informs the PCM of the camshaft position (1995 and later models).*

i) *The Crankshaft Position (CKP) sensor informs the PCM of the crankshaft position (1995 and later models).*

j) *The PCM-controlled Idle Speed Control Actuator (ISCA) controls the idle speed (1995 and later models).*

k) *Vehicle speed sensor (contained in the speedometer assembly) - informs the ECM of the vehicle speed.*

l) *Power steering pressure switch (contained in the power steering pump) - informs the ECM when the power steering pump is under load.*

m) *The knock sensor signals the PCM to control spark timing (1995 and later models).*

n) *When the conditions are right, the PCM-controlled Evaporative Emissions (EVAP) canister purge valve controls the flow of evaporative emissions from the EVAP canister into the engine (1995 and later models).*

All the above signals are analyzed by the ECM, which selects the fuelling response appropriate to those values. The ECM controls the fuel injectors (varying the pulse width - the length of time the fuel injectors are held open - to provide the optimum air/fuel mixture to the cylinders, as appropriate). The mixture is constantly varied by the ECM, to provide the best setting for cranking, starting (with either a hot or cold engine), warm-up, idle, cruising, and acceleration. The injector is a small, precision solenoid valve. As the ECM outputs an injection signal to each fuel injector, the coil built into the injector pulls the needle valve back and fuel is sprayed through the nozzle into the intake manifold. The amount of fuel injected is controlled by the ECM by varying the injection pulse duration.

The ECM also has full control over the engine idle speed, via the idle speed control servo which bypasses the throttle valve. When the throttle valve is closed, the ECM controls the opening of the servo, which in turn regulates the amount of air entering the manifold, and so controls the idle speed.

The ECM also controls the exhaust and evaporative emission control systems, which are described in detail in Chapter 6.

If there is an abnormality in any of the readings obtained from either the coolant temperature sensor, the intake air temperature sensor or the oxygen sensor, the ECM enters its back-up mode. In this event, it ignores the abnormal sensor signal, and assumes a pre-programmed value which will allow the engine to continue running (albeit at reduced efficiency). If the ECM enters this back-up mode, the warning light on the instrument panel will come on, and the relevant fault code will be stored in the ECM memory.

If the warning light comes on, a check of the problem should be done at the earliest opportunity. See Section 15 for checking trouble codes stored in the ECM to help determine the fault. Additional testing of the engine management system is suggested at a dealer or repair shop. **Note:** *Only unleaded fuel is to be used. The use of leaded fuel will damage the catalytic converter.*

14   Fuel pressure relief procedure

Note: *Refer to the* **Warning** *in Section 2 before proceeding.*
Warning: *The following procedure will merely relieve the pressure in the fuel system - remember that fuel will still be present in the system components and take precautions accordingly before disconnecting any of them.*

1   The fuel system referred to in this Section is defined as the tank-mounted fuel pump, the fuel filter, the fuel injectors, the fuel rail and the pressure regulator, and the metal pipes and flexible hoses of the fuel lines between these components. All these contain fuel which will be under pressure while the engine is running or while the ignition is switched on. The pressure will remain for some time after the ignition has been switched off, and it must be relieved in a controlled fashion when any of the system components are disturbed for servicing work.
2   Remove the rear seat cushion (1985 through 1990 models and 1995 and later models) or remove the spare wheel (1991 through 1994 models), then remove the fuel pump access cover and disconnect the fuel pump electrical connector (this will disable the fuel pump).
3   Start the engine and allow it to run until it stalls, indicating that the fuel pressure present in the fuel lines/rail assembly has been released, then switch off the engine.
4   Reconnect the fuel pump wiring and install the seat cushion or rear wheel, as applicable.

15   Fuel injection system testing - general information

Refer to illustration 15.2
1   If a fault occurs in the fuel injection system or related systems, first ensure that all the system wiring connectors are securely connected and free of corrosion. Ensure that the fault is not due to poor maintenance; check that the air filter element is clean, the spark plugs are in good condition and correctly gapped, the cylinder compression pressures are correct, the ignition timing is correct, and that the engine breather hoses are clear and undamaged.
2   A diagnostic connector is incorporated in the engine management circuit, located in the fusebox on 1994 and earlier models or at the lower dash area on 1995 and later models. The CHECK ENGINE light, located on the instrument panel **(see illustration)**, illuminates if a failure is detected and a trouble code is stored in the ECM memory. The system can be accessed and the stored trouble codes obtained on some models (see Chapter 6). A special electronic diagnostic tester (scan tool) can be plugged in to the diagnostic connector and will locate the fault quickly

16.6 Disconnect the vacuum hose(s) from the throttle body

16.7 Remove the coolant hoses connected to the throttle body

and simply, alleviating the need to test all the system components individually, which is a time-consuming operation that also carries a risk of damaging the ECM. If the checks described in the following Sections fail to reveal the cause of the problem, the vehicle should be taken to a dealer or repair shop for testing.

16   Throttle body - removal and installation

Removal
Refer to illustrations 16.6 and 16.7
1   Disconnect the cable from the negative terminal of the battery.
2   Loosen the throttle body air intake duct retaining clamp and remove the air intake duct from the throttle body.
3   Disconnect the accelerator cable from the throttle cam. On 1994 and earlier automatic transaxle models, also disconnect the kickdown cable.
4   For 1995 and later automatic transaxle models, disconnect the idle switch electrical connector. Remove the idle switch if the throttle body is going to be cleaned in solvents.
5   Disconnect the wiring from the throttle position sensor and the idle speed control motor assembly as applicable.
6   On 1994 and earlier models, disconnect vacuum hose(s) from the throttle body, marking the hose(s) for later reassembly **(see illustration)**.
7   Remove the retaining screws/nuts and remove the throttle body from the intake manifold. Remove the gasket and discard it; a new one must be used on reassembly. On 1995 and later models remove the coolant hoses connected to the throttle body, marking the hoses for later reassembly **(see illustration)**.
Note: *Do not remove or adjust the throttle valve set screw.*

Installation
8   Ensure that the mating surfaces are clean and dry, position the new gasket, and install the throttle body, tightening its retaining bolts to the torque listed in this Chapter's Specifications.
9   Reconnect the vacuum hose(s) and wiring and connect the accelerator cable to the throttle cam. On 1994 and earlier automatic transaxle models, reconnect the kickdown cable. On 1995 and later automatic transaxle models, reinstall the idle switch.
10   Reconnect the air intake duct and tighten the clamp, then reconnect the battery.
11   Reconnect any coolant hoses where necessary and tighten the clips.
12   Adjust the accelerator cable as described in Section 3 and, where necessary, the kickdown cable as described in Chapter 7B. Check the engine coolant level and fill if necessary.

17   Fuel injection system components - check and replacement

Warning: *Gasoline is extremely flammable, so take extra precautions when working on any part of the fuel system. Do not smoke or allow open flames or bare light bulbs in or near the work area. Also, don't work in a garage if a gas appliance such as a water heater or clothes dryer is present.*

Fuel rail and injectors
Refer to illustrations 17.2 17.4, 17.5a, 17.5b, 17.6a, 17.6b and 17.7
Note: *If a faulty injector is suspected, try an injector-cleaning treatment before removal of injectors.*
1   Relieve the fuel system pressure as described in Section 14, then disconnect the cable from the negative terminal of the battery.
2   Position a rag beneath the fuel rail to catch any spilled fuel. Remove the fuel sup-

17.2 Remove the two nuts and detach the fuel supply line from the fuel rail

17.4 Release the injector wiring connector clip (arrow) and remove the injector wiring connectors

17.5a Unbolt the fuel rail and remove it from the engine intake manifold with the injectors attached

ply line from the fuel rail **(see illustration)**. Disconnect the fuel return hose from the fuel pressure regulator (1994 and earlier) or the steel tubing line which runs the length of the fuel rail (1995 and later).

3   Disconnect the vacuum hose from the fuel pressure regulator.

4   Release the retaining clips on the injector electrical connectors and disconnect the connectors from the four injectors **(see illustration)**.

5   Remove the fuel rail retaining bolts then carefully ease the fuel rail and injector assembly from the intake manifold and remove it from the vehicle. On 1994 and earlier models, remove the insulator spacers which are located between the fuel rail and intake manifold. Remove the injector seals from the intake manifold and discard them; they must be replaced whenever they are disturbed **(see illustrations)**.

6   Slide out the retaining clip(s) and remove the injector(s) from the fuel rail. Remove the upper O-ring and rubber seal from each injector and discard; all removed O-rings and seals must be replaced with new ones **(see illustrations)**.

7   Refitting is a reversal of the removal procedure, noting the following:

a) Test the injector electrical resistance using an ohmmeter between the two ter-

minals of the injector **(see illustration)**. Resistance should be as listed in this Chapter's Specifications. If not within this range of resistance, replace the individual injectors.

b) Install new O-rings and seals to all injectors.

c) Apply a light coat of engine oil to the O-ring and seal to aid installation then ease the injectors and fuel rail into position ensuring that the O-ring is in its correct position.

d) On 1994 and earlier models, ensure that the insulator spacers are correctly positioned between the fuel rail and manifold before tightening the retaining bolts to the torque listed in this Chapter's Specifications.

e) Fit a new O-ring seal to the feed hose fitting groove on 1994 and earlier models, or new union-bolt washers on 1995 and later models if removed from the fuel rail, and tighten the fitting retaining bolt(s) securely.

f) On completion, start the engine and check for fuel leaks.

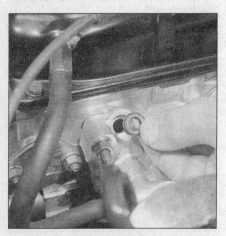

17.5b Remove the injector seals and O-rings from the intake manifold (typical)

17.6a Slide out the retaining clip . . .

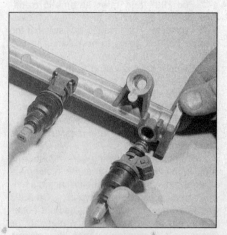

17.6b . . . then ease the injector out of the fuel rail and remove its upper O-ring and seal

17.7 Check the injector resistance using an ohmmeter connected to the injector terminals

17.8 Attach a hand vacuum pump to the fuel pressure regulator vacuum port - plug the disconnected vacuum hose

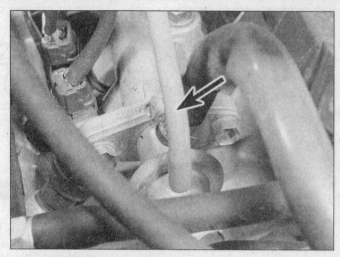

17.9a Disconnect the vacuum line from the fuel pressure regulator

Fuel pressure regulator

Refer to illustrations 17.8, 17.9a, 17.9b, 17.9c and 17.10

Note: *This procedure applies to 1999 and earlier models only. On 2000 and later models, the fuel pressure regulator is an integral component of the fuel pump assembly (see Section 4).*

Note: *Check the vacuum source and vacuum hose for proper vacuum with the engine running before checking the fuel pressure regulator. Also check the vacuum hose for the presence of fuel; if raw fuel is noted in the vacuum hose, replace the fuel pressure regulator.*

8   Install a fuel pressure gauge to the fuel system (see Section 8). Disconnect the fuel pressure regulator vacuum line, plug the hose and attach a hand vacuum pump to the regulator port **(see illustration)**. Start the engine and note the fuel pressure at idle. Apply vacuum to the fuel pressure regulator with the hand vacuum pump and note the fuel pressure again. When vacuum is applied to the regulator the fuel pressure should decrease approximately 5 to 7 psi. If there is no difference in pressure with or without vacuum applied, replace the fuel pressure regulator.

9   Relieve the fuel system pressure as described in Section 14 then disconnect the battery negative cable. Disconnect the vacuum hose from the fuel pressure regulator. On 1994 and earlier models, loosen the hose clamp and disconnect the fuel return hose from the fuel pressure regulator. On 1995 through 1999 models, loosen the union-bolt and disconnect the return line fitting from the fuel pressure regulator **(see illustrations)**.

10   Remove the retaining screws and withdraw the pressure regulator from the end of the fuel rail **(see illustration)**.

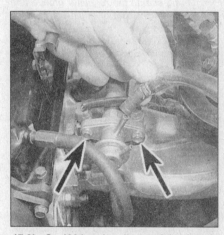

17.9b On 1994 and earlier models, detach the return hose from the fuel pressure regulator

17.9c On 1995 through 1999 models, remove the union-bolt and detach the return line fitting from the fuel pressure regulator

17.10 Remove the fuel pressure regulator from the end of the fuel rail - replace the O-ring seal

17.12a Using an ohmmeter, measure the resistance of the throttle position sensor

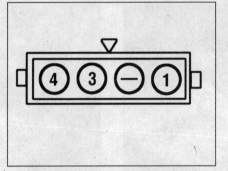

17.12b Throttle Position Sensor terminal identification - 1994 and earlier models

11   Installation is the reverse of removal, noting the following:
   a) On 1994 and earlier models, fit the new O-ring seal to the regulator groove and apply a light coat of engine oil to ease installation.
   b) On 1995 and later models, install new union-bolt washers at the return line fitting.
   c) Tighten the regulator screws to the torque listed in this Chapter's Specifications and reconnect the fuel return hose and vacuum hose.

Throttle Position Sensor (TPS)

Refer to illustrations 17.12a, 17.12b, 17.12c and 17.15

Note: *The following check procedure applies only to 1995 and earlier models. The OBD-II system on 1996 and later models requires a code reader or scan tool to obtain diagnostic trouble codes, and a scan tool for diagnosis. Refer to the* Haynes OBD-II and Electronic Engine Management Systems *manual for diagnosing the information sensors and output actuators.*

12   Disconnect the electrical connector from the TPS. On 1994 and earlier models, con-

nect an ohmmeter to terminals 1 and 4 and compare your measurement to this Chapter's Specifications; then reconnect the ohmmeter across terminals 1 and 3 and slowly open the throttle from closed to fully open, checking that the resistance value changes smoothly and proportionately (use an analog ohmmeter for this check). On 1995 models, connect an ohmmeter to terminals 2 and 3 and compare your measurement to this Chapter's Specifications; then reconnect the ohmmeter to terminals 1 and 3 and slowly open the throttle and check that the resistance value changes smoothly and proportionately **(see illustrations)**. If the TPS resistance is beyond the specifications or does not change smoothly, replace the TPS.

13   Disconnect the cable from the negative terminal of the battery.

14   Disconnect the wiring from the throttle position sensor.

15   Loosen and remove the retaining screws from the throttle position sensor. Disengage the sensor from the throttle valve spindle and remove it from the vehicle **(see illustration)**.

16   Reconnect the negative cable to the battery.

17   Engage the sensor with the throttle valve spindle and lightly tighten the retaining screws.

18   Connect the wiring connector to the TPS and by backprobing the connector, connect a voltmeter to terminals 1 and 3 **(see illustra-**

tions 17.12b and 17.12c).

19   Switch on the ignition (but do not start the engine).

20   If necessary, loosen the retaining screws and rotate the TPS until the meter reads 0.48 to 0.52 volt.

21   Tighten the screws securely. **Note:** *Not all models are equipped with an adjustable TPS. If the mounting screw holes are not slotted, the TPS is not adjustable.*

Electronic Control Module (ECM)

Caution: *Make sure your body is electrically grounded to the vehicle body when removing or attaching the ECM connectors to prevent serious damage to electronic components in the unit.*

22   On 2005 and earlier models, the ECM is located under the left end of the instrument panel. On 2006 and later models, the ECM is located in the left rear corner of the engine compartment, behind the air filter housing.

23   2005 and earlier models: At the left end of the dashboard, remove the dashboard cover retaining screws and remove the covers (see Chapter 11).

24   Disconnect the wiring, remove the retaining screws and remove the ECM from the vehicle.

25   Installation is the reverse of removal.

Idle Speed Control (ISC) actuator

Refer to illustrations 17.26a, 17.26b, 17.26c and 17.27

Note: *The check procedure applies only to 1995 and earlier models. The OBD-II system on 1996 and later models requires a code reader or scan tool to obtain diagnostic trouble codes, and a scan tool for diagnosis. Refer to the* Haynes OBD-II and Electronic Engine Management Systems *manual for diagnosing the information sensors and output actuators.*

26   On 1990 through 1994 models, the Idle Speed Control (ISC) servo is bolted to the

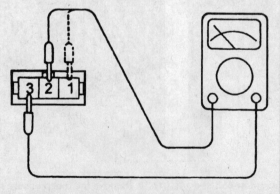

17.12c Throttle Position Sensor terminal identification - 1995 models - check the sensor resistance with the ohmmeter connected to terminals 2 and 3, then connect the meter to terminals 1 and 3 and test for resistance change as the throttle is opened

17.15 Disconnect the wiring connector, remove the retaining screws and carefully remove the throttle position sensor from the throttle body (typical)

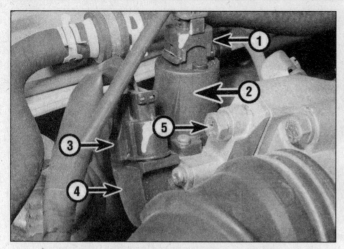

17.26a Idle Speed Control (ISC) servo details (1990 through 1994 models)

1 *Electrical connector*
2 *ISC motor*
3 *Electrical connector*

4 *Motor position sensor*
5 *Mounting bolt (lower bolt not visible)*

17.26b Idle Speed Control (ISC) actuator - 1995 through 1999 models

1 *Idle Speed Control (ISC) actuator*
2 *Electrical connector*

3 *Inlet hose*
4 *Outlet hose*
5 *Rubber insulator*

throttle body **(see illustration)**. On 1995 through 1999 models, the Idle Speed Control (ISC) actuator is located above the valve cover, in front of the intake plenum, and is mounted on a metal bracket with a rubber insulator **(see illustration)**. On 2000 through 2005 models, the ISC actuator is bolted to the throttle body **(see illustration)**. On 2006 and later models, the ISC actuator is bolted to the intake manifold plenum, near the throttle body.

27 The ISC resistance can be checked without removing the ISC. On 1994 and earlier models, disconnect the connector and measure the resistances across the two terminals of the ISC. On 1995 models, there are two sets of coils in the actuator, disconnect the connector and measure the resistance of each coil in turn **(see illustration)**.

28 Compare your measurements with the values listed in this Chapter's Specifications.

If the ISC actuator coils are open or shorted, replace the ISC actuator.

29 If the ISC actuator is defective, replace it **(see illustration 17.26a, 17.26b or 17.26c)**.

30 Installation is the reverse of removal.

Air Flow Sensor (AFS) (1994 and earlier models)

Refer to illustration 17.32

31 The AFS sensor is located in the air filter housing. It detects air flow rate and sends it to the ECM as the intake air volume. The ECM then uses this air volume signal to determine the basic fuel injection pulse duration. **Note:** *The barometric pressure sensor and the intake air temperature sensors are incorporated within the AFS sensor.*

32 To check the AFS sensor, disconnect the harness connector. Connect a voltmeter to terminals 3 (+) and 6 (-) **(see illustration)**.

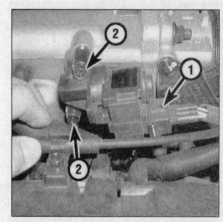

17.26c Idle Speed Control Actuator (ISCA) - 2000 through 2005 models

1 *Electrical connector*
2 *Mounting screws*

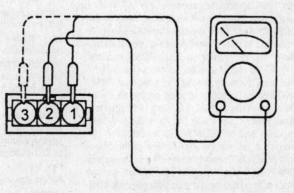

17.27 On 1995 models, measure the resistance of ISC actuator across terminals 1 and 2, then across terminals 2 and 3 - each measurement should be within specifications

3	2	1
6	5	4

43015-4-17.32 HAYNES

17.32 Air flow sensor terminal identification (1994 and earlier models)

17.35a Engine Coolant Temperature (ECT) sensor location (1995 and later models)

17.35b On 2006 and later models, the ECT sensor is located on the left rear part of the cylinder head, next to the heater hose pipes

17.38a Intake Air Temperature (IAT) sensor location (1995 through 1999 models)

Start the engine, warm it up to operating temperature and check the air flow sensor output voltage at idle. The output voltage should be between 2.7 and 3.2 volts. Next connect the voltmeter to terminal 5 (+) and 6 (-). Start the engine (at operating temperature), allow it to idle and not the voltage reading on the meter. Slowly cover the air cleaner intake opening with your hand, the voltage should decrease as the intake air pressure falls. If the sensor does not respond as described, replace the air flow sensor. **Note:** *Refer to the procedure described below to check the intake air temperature sensor portion of the air flow sensor.*
33   To remove the sensor, open the air filter housing, disconnect the wiring connector, and detach the AFS sensor from the housing.
34   Installation is the reverse of removal.

Engine Coolant Temperature (ECT) sensor

Refer to illustrations 17.35a and 17.35b
Note: *The check procedure applies only to 1995 and earlier models. The OBD-II system on 1996 and later models requires a code reader or scan tool to obtain diagnostic trouble codes, and a scan tool for diagnosis. Refer to the Haynes OBD-II and Electronic Engine Management Systems manual for diagnosing the information sensors and output actuators.*
35   The ECM uses the Engine Coolant Temperature (ECT) sensor to determine the engine coolant temperature. On 1994 and earlier models, the ECT is mounted in the intake manifold near the thermostat housing. On 1995 through 2005 models, the ECT is mounted in the thermostat housing **(see illustration)**. On 2006 and later models, the ECT sensor is located on the left rear part of the cylinder head, just to the right of the heater hose pipes **(see illustration)**.
36   To check the ECT, drain the cooling system and remove the sensor. Suspend the sensor in a container of water and heat the water on a stove while monitoring the water

temperature with a cooking thermometer. Do not allow the sensor to touch the sides or bottom of the container. Connect an ohmmeter to the sensor terminals and measure the resistance of the sensor as the water is heated. Compare your measurements with the values listed in this Chapter's Specifications. Replace the sensor if the measured resistance varies greatly from the specified resistance values.
37   Installation is the reverse of removal. Be sure to tighten the ECT sensor to the torque listed in this Chapter's Specification.

Intake Air Temperature (IAT) sensor

Refer to illustration 17.38
Note: *The check procedure applies only to 1995 and earlier models. The OBD-II system on 1996 and later models requires a code reader or scan tool to obtain diagnostic trouble codes, and a scan tool for diagnosis. Refer to the Haynes OBD-II and Electronic Engine Management Systems manual for diagnosing the information sensors and output actuators.*
38   The ECM uses the Intake Air Temperature (IAT) sensor to determine the temperature of the air entering the intake system. On 1994 and earlier models, the IAT sensor is incorporated into the air flow sensor. On 1995 through 1999 models, the IAT sensor is mounted in the cleaner housing **(see illustration)**. On 2000 through 2002 SOHC models, the IAT sensor is an integral component of the Mass Air Flow/Intake Air Temperature (MAF/IAT) sensor, which is located on the air intake duct, near the air filter housing **(see illustration 17.47)**. On 2003 through 2005 DOHC models, and on 2005 SOHC models, the IAT sensor is an integral component of the Manifold Absolute Pressure/Intake Air Temperature (MAP/IAT) sensor, which is located on the front side of the intake manifold **(see illustration)**. On 2006 and later models, the IAT sensor is an integral component of the MAF/IAT

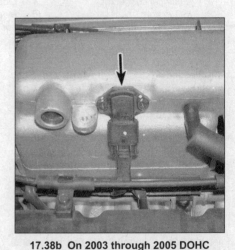

17.38b On 2003 through 2005 DOHC models, the Manifold Absolute Pressure/ Intake Air Temperature (MAP/IAT) sensor is located on the front of the intake manifold. To remove the MAP/IAT sensor from the intake manifold, disconnect the electrical connector and remove the two sensor mounting screws

sensor, which is located in the air intake duct.
39   To check the resistance of the IAT sensor, disconnect the wiring connector from the IAT sensor or air flow sensor as applicable and remove the cover from the air cleaner housing. On 1994 and earlier models, connect an ohmmeter to terminals 4 and 6 of the air flow sensor **(see illustration 17.32)** On 1995 models, connect the ohmmeter to the two terminals of the IAT sensor. Measure the resistance of the IAT sensor as you heat the sensor with a heat gun or hair dryer. Compare your measurements with the values listed in this Chapter's Specifications. Replace the sensor if the measured resistance varies greatly from the specified resistance values.
40   Installation is the reverse of removal.

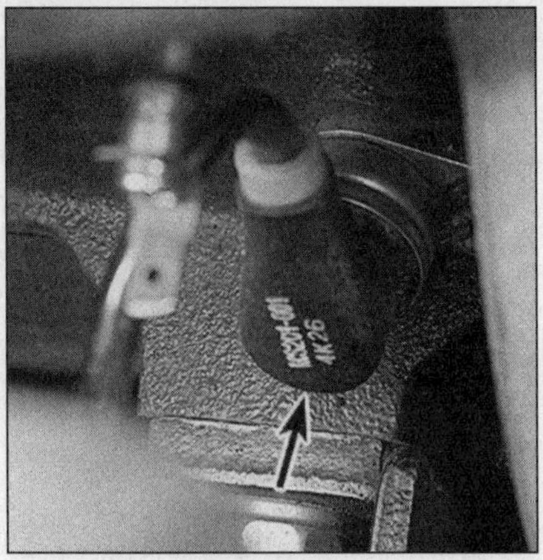

17.41 Crankshaft Position (CKP) sensor location (1995 models)

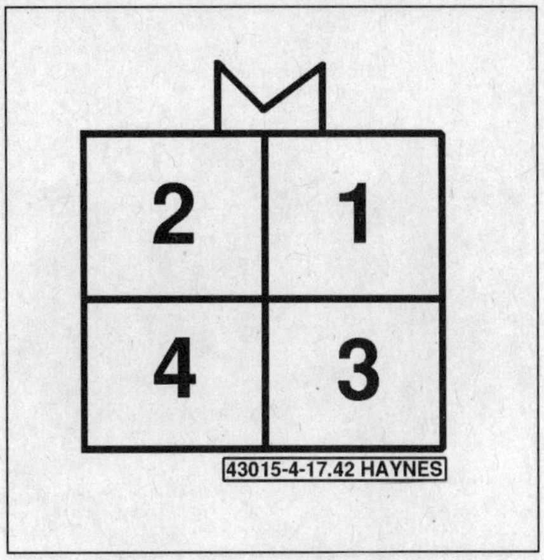

17.42 Crankshaft Position sensor (CKP) terminal identification (1994 and earlier models)

Crankshaft Position (CKP) sensor

Refer to illustrations 17.41, 17.42 and 17.43

Note: *The check procedure applies only to 1995 and earlier models. The OBD-II system on 1996 and later models requires a code reader or scan tool to obtain diagnostic trouble codes, and a scan tool for diagnosis. Refer to the* Haynes OBD-II and Electronic Engine Management Systems *manual for diagnosing the information sensors and output actuators.*

41 The crankshaft position sensor detects engine RPM and the position of the crankshaft. The CKP is incorporated in the distributor body in 1994 and earlier models - if faulty, the complete distributor assembly will have to be replaced (see Chapter 5). On 1995 and later models the CKP is located on the front of the engine block near the transaxle bellhousing **(see illustration)**.

42 To check the CKP sensor on 1994 and earlier models, detach the ignition coil wire from the distributor and ground it on the engine block so the engine will not start. Using suitable probes, backprobe the distributor connector terminals 2 (+) and 1(-) and connect a voltmeter **(see illustration)**. Crank the engine and note the voltage. The voltage should fluctuate from zero to approximately 5 volts if the sensor is functioning properly.

43 On 1995 models, disconnect the wiring connector from the sensor and measure the resistance between terminals 2 and 3 of the sensor **(see illustration)**. Compare your measurement with the value listed in this Chapter's Specifications. Replace the sensor if the measured resistance varies greatly from the specified resistance value.

Vehicle Speed Sensor (VSS)

Refer to illustrations 17.44a and 17.44b

Note: *The check procedure applies only to 1990 through 1999 models. The vehicle speed sensor on 2000 and later models, which is located on the transaxle, requires a code reader or scan tool to obtain diagnostic trouble codes, and a scan tool for diagnosis. Refer to the* Haynes OBD-II and Electronic Engine Management Systems *manual for diagnosing the vehicle speed sensor on these models..*

44 The vehicle speed sensor is incorporated in the speedometer unit inside the instrument cluster **(see illustrations)**. Removal and installation procedures for the instrument cluster are given in Chapter 12.

17.43 Crankshaft Position sensor (CKP) terminal identification (1995 models)

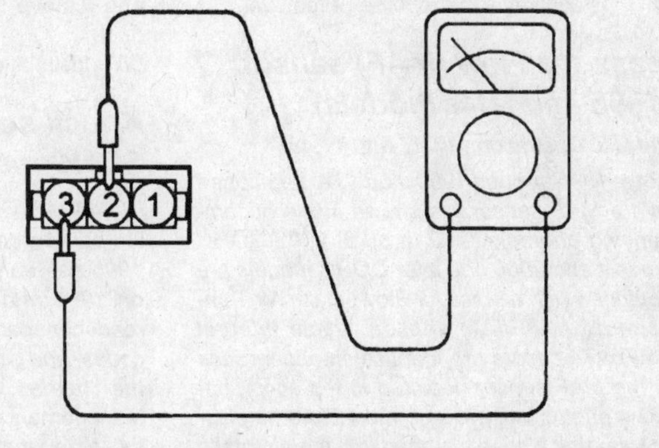

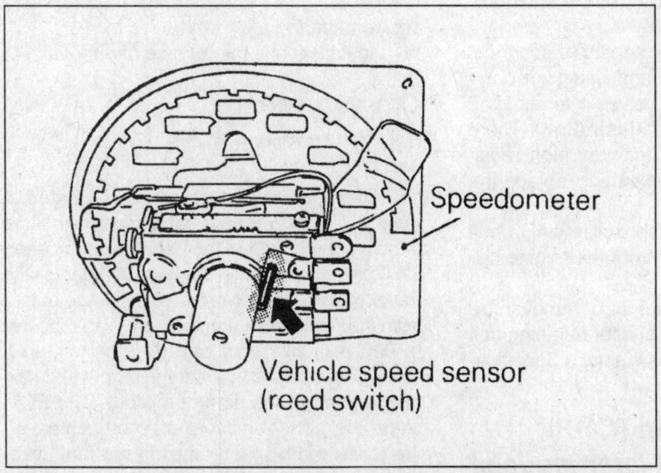

17.44a On 1990 through 1999 models, the Vehicle Speed Sensor (VSS) is located on the rear of the speedometer; it sends the vehicle speed signal to the ECM (early model shown)

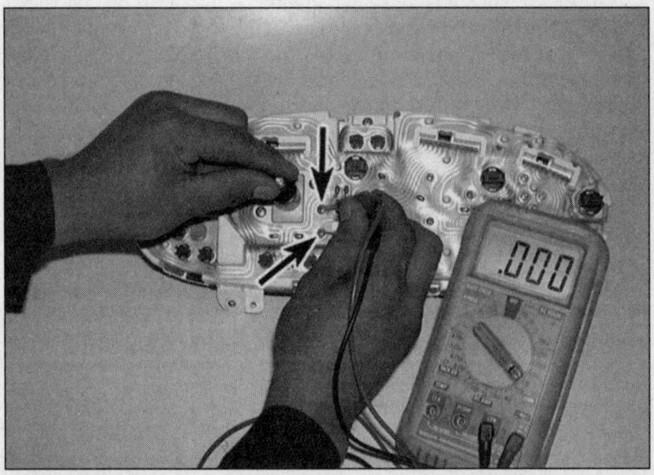

17.44b To test the Vehicle Speed Sensor (VSS), hook up an ohmmeter to the test terminals, then rotate the speedometer drive (later model shown)

17.47 Mass Air Flow (MAF) sensor location (1995 models)

17.48 Check the MAF sensor output voltage at terminal 1 (MAF sensor removed for clarity)

17.51 The knock sensor (arrow) is mounted on the side of the engine cylinder block

45   To check the Vehicle Speed Sensor on 1990 through 1999 models, remove the instrument cluster. Connect an ohmmeter to the sensor terminals and rotate the speedometer. The sensor should pulse on (continuity) and off (no continuity) four times per revolution. If the sensor is defective, replace the speedometer.
46   Installation is the reverse of removal.

Mass Air Flow (MAF) sensor (1995 and later models)

Refer to illustrations 17.47 and 17.48

Note: *1995 through 1999 models are equipped with a MAF sensor (as shown in the accompanying photos). 2000 through 2002 SOHC models and 2006 and later DOHC models are equipped with a Mass Air Flow/Intake Air Temperature (MAF/IAT) sensor. These integral MAF/IAT sensors are identical in appearance to the MAF sensor depicted in the accompanying photos and are also mounted on a plastic tube that's hose-clamped into the air intake duct assembly.*

47   The MAF sensor is located in the intake duct between the air cleaner housing and the throttle body **(see illustration)**.
48   The MAF sensor may be checked without removal. Without disconnecting the wiring connector to the sensor, backprobe the sensor terminal 1 using a suitable probe and

connect a voltmeter **(see illustration)**. Check the output voltage at both idle and 3,000 rpm. Compare your measurement with the values listed in this Chapter's Specifications. If the MAF sensor output voltage varies greatly from the specified values, replace the MAF sensor.
49   To remove the MAF sensor, disconnect the wiring connector, loosen the hose clamps and remove the MAF sensor from the intake duct.
50   Installation is the reverse of removal.

Knock sensor (1995 and later SOHC models)

Refer to illustrations 17.51 and 17.52

Note: *The check procedure applies only to 1995 and earlier models. The OBD-II system on 1996 and later models requires a code reader or scan tool to obtain diagnostic trouble codes, and a scan tool for diagnosis. Refer to the* Haynes OBD-II and Electronic Engine Management Systems *manual for diagnosing the information sensors and output actuators.*

51   The knock sensor is mounted on the side of the engine cylinder block, below the intake manifold **(see illustration)**.
52   To check the knock sensor, disconnect the electrical connector and using an ohmmeter, check resistance between terminals 2 and 3 at the sensor **(see illustration)**. There should be no continuity (or very high resistance). If continuity is indicated, replace the knock sensor.
53   Remove the knock sensor retaining bolt and withdraw the sensor from the engine cylinder block.
54   Installation is the reverse of removal. Be sure to tighten the knock sensor retaining bolt to the torque listed in this Chapter's Specifications.

Camshaft Position (CMP) sensor (1995 and later models)

Refer to illustrations 17.55a, 17.55b and 17.56

Note: *The check procedure applies only to 1995 and earlier models. The OBD-II system*

on 1996 and later models requires a code reader or scan tool to obtain diagnostic trouble codes, and a scan tool for diagnosis. Refer to the Haynes OBD-II and Electronic Engine Management Systems *manual for diagnosing the information sensors and output actuators.*

55   The CMP senses the TDC point of the number one cylinder piston during its compression stroke and signals the ECM. On 1995 through 2005 models, the CMP is located on the engine at the end of the cylinder head near the ignition coil assembly **(see illustration)**. On 2006 and later models, it's located at the left end of the cylinder head **(see illustration)**.
56   Check the CMP sensor without disconnecting the wiring connector. Using a suitable probe, backprobe the wiring connector terminal 2 **(see illustration)**. Connect a voltmeter and measure the sensor output voltage while cranking the engine. The sensor output voltage should fluctuate between zero and 5 volts as the engine is cranked. If the sensor does not operate as described, replace the sensor.
57   Disconnect the wiring connector, remove the mounting bolt and withdraw the CMP sensor from the cylinder head.
58   Installation is the reverse of removal.

Oxygen sensor

Refer to illustrations 17.59a, 17.59b and 17.59c

59   The oxygen sensor, which is located in the exhaust pipe **(see illustrations)**, monitors the oxygen content of the exhaust gas stream. The oxygen content in the exhaust reacts with the oxygen sensor to produce a voltage output from 100 millivolts (high oxygen, lean mixture) to 900 millivolts (low oxygen, rich mixture). The ECM monitors this voltage output to determine optimum the air/fuel mixture. The ECM alters the air/fuel mixture ratio by controlling the pulse width (open time) of the fuel injectors. A mixture of 14.7 parts air to 1 part fuel is the ideal ratio for minimizing exhaust emissions, thus allowing the catalytic converter to operate at maximum efficiency. It is this ratio

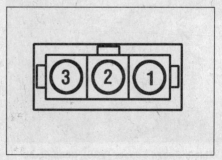

17.52 Knock sensor terminal identification

17.55a Camshaft position sensor location (1995 through 2005 models)

17.55b On 2006 and later models, the CMP sensor is located at the left end of the cylinder head, next to the intake camshaft

of 14.7 to 1 which the ECM and the oxygen sensor attempt to maintain at all times.

60   The oxygen sensor must be hot to operate properly (approximately 600-degrees F). During the initial warm-up period, the ECM operates in open loop mode - that is, it controls fuel delivery in accordance with a programmed default value instead of feedback information from the oxygen sensor.

61   The proper operation of the oxygen sensor depends on four conditions:

   a) *Electrical* - The low voltages and low currents generated by the sensor depend upon good, clean connections which should be checked whenever a malfunction of the sensor is suspected or indicated.

   b) *Outside air supply* - The sensor is designed to allow air circulation to the internal portion of the sensor. Whenever the sensor is removed and installed or replaced, make sure the air passages are not restricted.

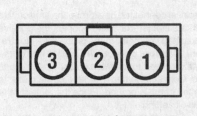

17.56 Camshaft position sensor terminal identification - 1995 and later models

   c) *Proper operating temperature* - The ECM will not react to the sensor signal until the sensor reaches approximately 600-degrees F. This factor must be taken into consideration when evaluating the performance of the sensor.

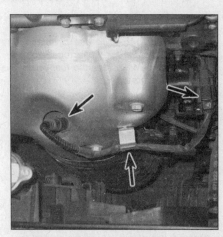

17.59a On 1990 through 1993 and 2000 and later models, the oxygen sensor is on the exhaust manifold (this is the upstream oxygen sensor)

17.59b On 1994 through 1999 models, the upstream oxygen sensor is located under the engine, on the exhaust pipe leading to the catalytic converter

17.59c On OBD-II models, the downstream oxygen sensor is located after the catalytic converter

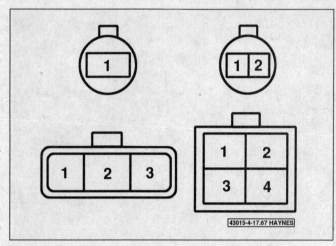

17.64 Oxygen sensor electrical connector terminal identification - on one, two and three wire connectors, probe terminal no. 1; on a four wire connector probe terminal no. 1 (1994 and earlier) or no. 2 (1995 models)

17.69 Remove and install oxygen sensors with a special oxygen sensor socket, which has a slot in one side for the sensor harness (available at auto parts stores)

d) *Unleaded fuel* - *The use of unleaded fuel is essential for proper operation of the sensor. Make sure the fuel you are using is of this type.*

62   In addition to observing the above conditions, special care must be taken whenever the sensor is serviced.

a) *The oxygen sensor has a permanently attached pigtail and connector which should not be removed from the sensor. Damage or removal of the pigtail or connector can adversely affect operation of the sensor.*
b) *Grease, dirt and other contaminants should be kept away from the electrical connector and the louvered end of the sensor.*
c) *Do not use cleaning solvents of any kind on the oxygen sensor.*
d) *Do not drop or roughly handle the sensor.*
e) *The silicone boot must be installed in the correct position to prevent the boot from being melted and to allow the sensor to operate properly.*

Check

Refer to illustration 17.64
Note: *The following check procedure applies only to 1995 and earlier models. The OBD-II system on 1996 and later models requires a code reader or scan tool to obtain diagnostic trouble codes, and a scan tool for diagnosis. Refer to the* Haynes OBD-II and Electronic Engine Management Systems *manual for diagnosing the information sensors and output actuators.*

63   The sensor can be checked with a high-impedance digital voltmeter. Warm up the engine to normal operating temperature, then turn the engine off. Locate the oxygen electrical connector by following the wiring harness from the sensor up to the connector.
64   Without disconnecting the oxygen sensor

electrical connector, backprobe the sensor wire with a suitable probe and connect the positive lead of the voltmeter to the probe **(see illustration)**. **Caution:** *Don't let the sensor wire or the voltmeter lead touch the exhaust pipe or manifold.* Connect the negative lead of the meter to a good chassis ground. Place the meter to the millivolt setting.
65   Start the engine and monitor the voltage output of the sensor. When the engine is cold the sensor should produce a steady voltage of approximately 100 to 200 millivolts. After a period of approximately two minutes the engine should reach operating temperature and the voltage should begin to fluctuate between 100 and 900 millivolts. This indicates the system has reached closed loop and the computer is controlling fuel delivery. If the system fails to reach closed loop mode in a reasonable amount of time, the sensor may be defective or a fuel system problem could be the cause. If the voltage is fixed (or fluctuating very slowly), create a rich condition by opening the accelerator sharply and snapping it shut and then a lean condition by disconnecting a vacuum hose, if the sensor voltage does not respond quickly with the proper voltage fluctuations, the sensor is probably defective.

Replacement

Refer to illustration 17.69
Note: *Because oxygen sensors are located in the exhaust pipe, they may be too tight to remove when the engine is cold. If you find an oxygen sensor difficult to loosen, start and run the engine for a minute or two, then shut it off. Be careful not to burn yourself during the following procedure.*
66   Disconnect the cable from the negative terminal of the battery.
67   If necessary, raise the vehicle and place it securely on jackstands.
68   Disconnect the electrical connector from the sensor.

69   Note the position of the silicone boot, if equipped, and carefully unscrew the sensor from the exhaust pipe with an oxygen sensor socket **(see illustration)**, which you can buy at automotive parts stores. **Caution:** *Excessive force may damage the threads.*
70   Anti-seize compound must be used on the threads of the sensor to facilitate future removal. The threads of a new sensor will already be coated with this compound, but if an old sensor is removed and reinstalled, recoat the threads.
71   Install the sensor and tighten it to the torque listed in this Chapter's Specifications.
72   Reconnect the electrical connector of the pigtail lead to the main engine wiring harness.
73   Lower the vehicle and reconnect the cable to the negative terminal of the battery.

---

18   Exhaust system - general information, removal and installation

Warning: *Inspection and repair of exhaust system components should be done only after the exhaust system is cool. Make sure the vehicle is securely supported on jackstands.*

General information

Refer to illustration 18.2
1   The exhaust system consists of the front pipe, the catalytic converter, and the tailpipe section which incorporates the main muffler. If any of the components are incorrectly installed, excessive noise and vibration will be transmitted to the body, and possible exhaust gas leakage can occur which can be dangerous to passengers. **Note:** *Regular inspections of the exhaust system to keep is safe is recommended. Look for damaged or bent parts, open seams, holes, loose connections,*

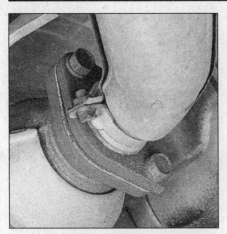

18.2 Exhaust components are typically connected using flanged joints

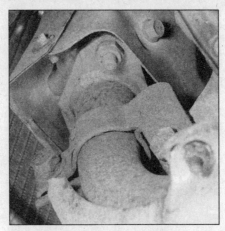

18.6 Exhaust front pipe connection to the exhaust manifold (typical)

18.9 Exhaust system tailpipe mounting and flange joint to the catalytic converter (typical)

excessive corrosion or other defects which could allow exhaust fumes to enter the vehicle. Damaged or deteriorated parts should be replaced with new parts.

2   The exhaust system sections are joined by flanged joints **(see illustration)** which are secured by nuts or bolts. The exhaust system is supported by brackets, hangers and clamps. The system is suspended throughout its length by rubber mountings.

Removal

Refer to illustrations 18.6, 18.9, 18.12a, 18.12b and 18.12c

Note: *If the exhaust system components are extremely corroded or rusted together, have a muffler repair shop remove the corroded sections. An alternative is to use a hacksaw if the parts are to be replaced with new parts. If you have a source of compressed air, pneumatic cutting chisels can be used. Wear safety goggles and leather work gloves to protect your eyes and hands.*

3   The exhaust sections can be removed individually, or alternatively, the complete system can be removed as a unit. **Caution:** *Make sure the exhaust system and especially the catalytic converter is cool before working on the system.*

4   To remove the system or part of the system, first raise the front and/or rear of the car, and securely support it on jackstands. Alternatively, position the car over an inspection pit, or on car ramps.

Front pipe

5   Where applicable, disconnect the oxygen sensor wiring.

6   Remove the nuts securing the front pipe flange joint to the manifold, and the single bolt securing the front pipe to its mounting bracket **(see illustration)**. Separate the flange joint, and recover the gasket.

7   Support the front pipe then loosen and remove the bolts securing the front pipe flange joint to the tailpipe or catalytic converter and recover the flange gasket.

8   Release the front pipe from the rubber mounting and remove it from the vehicle.

Catalytic converter

Note: *On some models the front catalytic converter is incorporated into the exhaust manifold (see Chapter 2A).*

9   Support the underfloor catalytic converter, then loosen and remove the bolts and nuts securing the front and tailpipe flange joints to the catalytic converter **(see illustration)**. Remove the catalytic converter from under the vehicle and recover the front gasket.

Tailpipe

10   Where applicable, disconnect the wiring from the oxygen sensor at the front of the tailpipe.

11   Loosen and remove the bolts/nuts securing the tailpipe flange joint to the front pipe/catalytic converter and separate the joint.

12   Support the tailpipe then loosen and remove the bolts and nuts securing the tailpipe to its mounting brackets and rubbers. Remove the tailpipe from the vehicle and recover the spacer from the mounting rubber **(see illustrations)**.

18.12a Exhaust tailpipe center mounting . . .

18.12b . . . right-hand rear mounting . . .

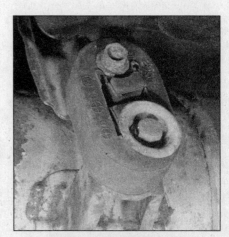

18.12c . . . and left-hand rear mounting (typical)

Complete system

13   Where applicable, disconnect the wiring from the oxygen sensor either on the front pipe or tailpipe.

14   Remove the nuts securing the front pipe flange joint to the manifold, and the bolts from the mounting bracket. Separate the flange joint, and collect the gasket.

15   Support the exhaust system then loosen and remove the nuts and bolts securing the tailpipe to the mounting bracket and rubbers. Release the front pipe from the mounting rubber, then remove the complete exhaust sys-tem from underneath the vehicle and recover the spacers from the rubber mountings.

Installation

16   Each section is installed by reversing the removal sequence, noting the following:

a) *Ensure that all traces of corrosion have been removed from the flanges, and renew all necessary gaskets.*

b) *Inspect the rubber mountings for signs of damage or deterioration, and renew as necessary.*

c) *Prior to tightening the exhaust system fasteners, ensure that all rubber mount-ings are correctly located, and that there is adequate clearance between the exhaust system and vehicle underbody. Ensure that all fasteners are tightened. Ensure that the oxygen sensor wiring is correctly routed and in no danger of touching the hot exhaust/engine.*

d) *Be sure there is sufficient clearance between the catalytic converter and the underbody - install all factory shields to protect the underbody or other compo-nents from the high temperature of the catalytic converter.*

Chapter 5
Engine electrical systems

Contents

Specifications

Charging system
System type	12-volt, negative ground
Charging voltage	12.5 to 14.7 volts
Regulator/alternator brush length	0.18 inch

Ignition system
System type	
1994 and earlier	Breakerless electronic ignition
1995 and later	Distributorless ignition system
Firing order	1-3-4-2
Distributor air gap	0.03 inch
Ignition timing	
1994 and earlier	5-degrees BTDC at 700 rpm
1995 and later	Not adjustable

Ignition system (continued)

Ignition coil resistance (approximate, at 68 degrees F)

    1994 and earlier

        Carbureted models

Primary windings	1.1 to 1.3 ohms
Secondary windings	11.6 to 15.8 K-ohms

        Fuel injected models

Primary windings	0.72 to 0.88 ohms
Secondary windings	10.3 to 13.9 K-ohms

    1995 through 2001

Primary windings	0.45 to 0.55 ohms
Secondary windings	10.3 to 13.9 K-ohms

    2002 and later

Primary windings	0.78 to 0.96 ohms
Secondary windings	11.05 to 14.95 K-ohms
Ballast resistor (carbureted models)	1.2 to 1.6 ohms

Torque specifications   Ft-lb (unless otherwise indicated)

Note: *One foot-pound (ft-lb) of torque is equivalent to 12 inch-pounds (in-lbs) of torque. Torque values below approximately 15 ft-lbs are expressed in inch-pounds, since most foot-pound torque wrenches are not accurate at these smaller values.*

Distributor mounting nut	108 in-lbs

1   General information

The engine electrical systems include all ignition, charging and starting components. Because of their engine-related functions, these components are discussed separately from chassis electrical accessories such as the lights, the instruments, etc. (see Chapter 12).

Be very careful when working on engine electrical components. They are easily damaged if checked, connected or handled improperly. The alternator is driven by a drive-belt which could cause serious injury if you become entangled in it with the engine running. Both the starter and alternator are connected directly to the battery and could arc and cause a fire if mishandled, overloaded or shorted out.

Never leave the ignition switch on for long periods of time with the engine off.

Don't disconnect the battery cables while the engine is running. Correct polarity must be maintained when connecting battery cables from another source, such as another vehicle, or during jump starting. Always disconnect the negative cable first and hook it up last or the battery may be shorted by the tool being used to loosen the cable clamps.

Additional safety related information on the engine electrical systems can be found in *Safety first!* near the front of this manual. It should be referred to before beginning any operation in this Chapter.

There are two different distributors used on 1990 to 1994 models. The distributor used in conjunction with the Feedback Carburetor (FBC) system is equipped with vacuum advance and has many internal components. The distributor used on the 1990 to 1994 models equipped with multi-point fuel injection (MPI) system is less complicated and has an electronic advance system.

2   Battery - emergency jump starting

Refer to the *Booster battery (jump) starting* procedures at the front of this manual.

3   Battery - removal and installation

Refer to illustrations 3.1 and 3.4

1   Disconnect the negative cable then the positive cable from the battery **(see illustration)**. **Caution:** *Always disconnect the negative battery cable first and hook it up last or the battery may be shorted by the tool being used to loosen the cable clamps.*

2   Remove the nuts and bolts and the battery hold down clamp.

3   Lift out the battery. Special battery lifting straps that attach to the battery posts are

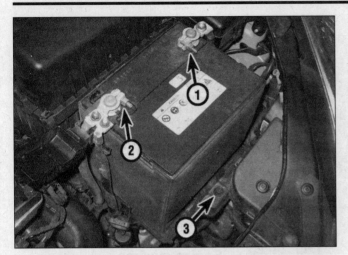

3.1 To remove the battery; 1) detach the cable from the negative terminal, 2) detach the cable from the positive terminal, 3) remove the nuts and detach the clamp (typical)

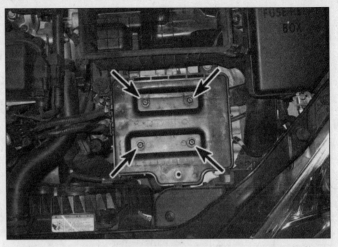

3.4 To remove the battery tray, remove these mounting bolts

available at auto parts stores. Lifting the battery is much easier if you use one.

4   If the battery tray is damaged or must be removed for access to other components, remove the mounting bolts and lift it out **(see illustration)**.

5   If you are replacing the battery, make sure that you get one that's identical, with the same dimensions, amperage rating, cold cranking rating, etc.

6   Installation is the reverse of removal.

4   Battery cables - check and replacement

1   Periodically inspect the entire length of each battery cable for damage, cracked or burned insulation and corrosion. Poor battery cable connections can cause starting problems and decrease engine performance.

2   Check the cable-to-terminal connections for cracks, loose wire strands and corrosion. The presence of white, fluffy deposits under the insulation at the cable terminal connection is a sign that the cable is corroded and should be replaced. Check the terminals for distortion, missing mounting hardware and corrosion.

3   When removing the cables, **always disconnect the negative cable first and hook it up last** or the battery may be shorted by the tool used to loosen the cable clamps. Even if only the positive cable is being replaced, be sure to disconnect the negative cable from the battery first.

4   Disconnect and remove the old cables. Make sure the new cables are the same length and diameter as the originals.

5   If you are replacing either or both of the old cables, take them with you when buying new cables. It is important that you replace the cables with identical parts. Cables have characteristics that make them easy to identify: positive cables are usually red, larger in

diameter and have a larger diameter battery post clamp; ground cables are usually black, smaller in diameter and have a slightly smaller diameter clamp for the negative post.

6   Clean the threads of the relay or ground connection with a wire brush to remove rust and corrosion. Apply a light coat of battery terminal corrosion inhibitor, or petroleum jelly to the threads to prevent future corrosion.

7   Attach the cables to the relay or ground connection and tighten the mounting nut/bolt securely.

8   Before connecting a new cable to the battery, make sure that it reaches the battery post without having to be stretched. Clean the battery posts thoroughly and apply a light coat of battery corrosion inhibitor, or petroleum jelly to prevent corrosion.

9   Connect the positive cable first, followed by the negative cable.

5   Ignition system - general information and precautions

1   The ignition system is designed to ignite the fuel/air charge entering each cylinder at the exact moment for maximum efficiency. It does this by producing a high voltage spark between the electrodes of each spark plug.

2   The ignition system includes the ignition switch, the battery, the igniter, the coil, the primary (low voltage) and secondary (high voltage) wiring circuits, the distributor and the spark plugs.

3   When working on the ignition system, take the following precautions:

a)   *Do not keep the ignition switch on for more than 10 seconds if the engine will not start.*

b)   *Always connect a tachometer in accordance with the manufacturer's instructions. Some tachometers may be incompatible with this ignition system. Consult a*

dealer service department before buying a tachometer for use with this vehicle.

c)   *Never allow the ignition coil terminals to touch ground. A grounded coil could result in damage to the igniter and/or the ignition coil.*

d)   *Do not disconnect the battery when the engine is running.*

e)   *Make sure that the igniter is properly grounded.*

Carbureted models

4   A breakerless electronic ignition system is on carbureted models. The system consists of the ignition coil and the distributor which is driven off the camshaft. The distributor contains a toothed rotor mounted on its shaft, and the igniter unit attached to its body. The system operates as follows. When the ignition is switched on but the engine is not running, the igniter unit is inoperative and no current flows through the ignition system primary circuit. As the crankshaft rotates, the rotor moves through the magnetic field created by the igniter unit. When the rotor teeth are correctly positioned, a small AC voltage is created. The igniter unit uses this voltage to switch on the ignition system primary circuit. As the rotor teeth move out of alignment, the AC voltage changes, and the igniter unit switches off the primary circuit. This causes a high voltage to be induced in the coil secondary windings, which travels down the coil lead to the distributor and onto the correct spark plug. The system incorporates a ballast resistor mounted on the side of the ignition coil.

Fuel-injected models
1990 through 1994

5   On 1994 and earlier fuel injection models, the ignition system is integrated with the fuel system, to form a fuel/ignition system controlled by the Electronic Control Module (ECM) (see Chapter 4). The distributor con-

7.2 On early models, the ignition coil and ballast resistor assembly is located in the left front corner (driver's side) of the engine compartment, immediately behind the air cleaner intake

tains a crank angle sensor, which informs the ECM of engine speed and crankshaft position, and a TDC sensor which informs the ECM of the position of no. 1 cylinder piston. Based on this information, and the information received from its other sensors, the ECM then calculates the correct ignition timing setting, and switches the power transistor unit on and off accordingly. This causes a high voltage to be induced in the coil secondary windings, which travels to the correct spark plug. The ignition coil and power transistor are both located on the intake manifold.

1995 and later

6   1995 and later models are equipped with a Distributorless Ignition System (DIS). 1995 through 2002 SOHC models and 2001 through 2005 DOHC models use a coil pack mounted on the left end of the cylinder head. 1995 through 1997 DOHC models use two coil-over-plug type ignition coils, with spark plug wires leading to the remaining two cylinders. 2006 and later DOHC models use an individual coil-over plug type ignition coil for each cylinder.

7   This ignition system does not have any moving parts (no distributor) and all engine timing and spark distribution is handled electronically. During engine operation, the ECM receives signals from the crankshaft position sensor to determine the proper spark advance and firing sequence of the ignition coils.

6   Ignition system - check

Warning: *Because of the high voltage produced by the electronic ignition system, extreme care must be taken when working on the ignition system.*

1   The components of electronic ignition systems are very reliable; most problems are likely to be caused by loose or dirty connections, or to "tracking" of high voltage due to dirt, dampness or damaged insulation, than the failure of any of the system's components. Check the wiring thoroughly before blaming

an electrical component, and methodically eliminate all other possibilities before deciding that a component is faulty.

2   Checking for spark by holding the live end of a spark plug or coil lead a short distance away from the engine is not recommended; there is a risk of a powerful electric shock, and the ignition coil or power transistor unit may be damaged. For the same reason, never try to "diagnose" misfires by pulling off one spark plug lead at a time.

Engine will not start

3   If the engine will not turn over, or turns very slowly, check the battery and starter motor. Connect a voltmeter across the battery terminals (meter positive probe to battery positive terminal), then disconnect the ignition coil lead from the distributor cap and ground it to the engine. Note the voltage reading obtained while turning over the engine with the starter for (no more than) ten seconds. If the reading is less than approximately 9.5 volts, check the battery, starter motor and charging system as described in this Chapter.

4   If the engine turns over normally but will not start, check the high voltage circuit with a "calibrated ignition tester" (available at most auto parts stores). Disconnect the spark plug wire from any spark plug and attach it to the calibrated ignition tester. Clip the tester to a bolt or metal bracket on the engine, crank the engine and watch the end of the tester to see if consistent, bright, well-defined sparks occur. If the sparks occur, voltage is reaching the spark plugs, so they should be checked first. If no spark occurs, check the spark plug leads. On 1994 and earlier models, check the distributor cap and the rotor (see Chapter 1).

5   If there is spark, check the carburetor or fuel injection system (see Chapter 4).

6   If there is still no spark, check the voltage at the ignition coil "+" terminal; it should be the same as the battery voltage (at least 11.7 volts). If the voltage at the coil is more than 1 volt less than that at the battery, check the power feed through the fuse box and igni-

tion switch to the battery, including its ground until the problem is found.

7   If the circuit to the ignition coil is functional, check the coil primary and secondary winding resistance (see Section 7); replace the coil if faulty, but be careful to check the condition of the wiring connections, to ensure that the problem is not due to dirty or loose connectors.

8   If the ignition coil is in good condition, the problem is probably in the distributor, igniter unit, sensor unit, power transistor, crankshaft position sensor or ECM, as applicable. See Chapter 4 for information and testing of the sensors. Testing of the ECM should be performed by a dealer or other properly equipped repair shop.

Engine misfires

9   An irregular misfire suggests either a loose connection or intermittent problem on the primary circuit, or an high voltage problem.

10   With the ignition switch off, check the system, ensuring that all connections are clean and securely fastened. If the proper equipment is available, check the primary (low voltage) circuit as described above.

11   Check that the ignition coil, the spark plug leads and the distributor cap are clean and dry. Check the continuity of the leads and the spark plugs (by substitution, if necessary), then check the distributor cap and rotor (see Chapter 1).

12   Regular misfiring is usually due to a faulty distributor cap, spark plug leads or spark plugs. Use a calibrated ignition tester (see Step 4) to check if spark is present at all spark plug leads.

13   If spark is not present on a particular lead, the problem is in that lead, the distributor cap (1994 and earlier) or the ignition coil (1995 and later). If spark is present on all leads, the problem is the spark plugs; check and replace them if there is any doubt about their condition.

14   If no spark is present, check the ignition coil; its secondary windings may be breaking down under load.

7   Ignition coil, ballast resistor and power transistor - check and replacement

1994 and earlier models
Carbureted models

Refer to illustrations 7.2, 7.4a and 7.4b

1   Disconnect the cable from the negative terminal of the battery.

2   On early models the ignition coil is located in the front left-hand corner of the engine compartment **(see illustration)**. On later models it is located on the left-hand side of the engine by the distributor. The ballast resistor is mounted on the coil. Prior to coil removal, make sure that the ignition is off.

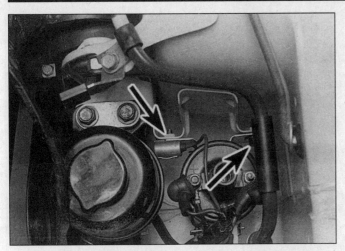

7.4a Ignition coil clamp bolts on an early carbureted model

7.4b To remove the ballast resistor, detach the leads at both ends, loosen the clamp screw and slide the resistor out

3   Note the location of the coil primary (low voltage) wiring then disconnect it from the coil. Disconnect the high voltage lead from the coil.

4   Unscrew the coil clamp bolts then remove the coil. On early models it is necessary to unscrew the ballast resistor clamp screw and move the resistor to one side (see illustrations).

Fuel injected models

Refer to illustration 7.5

5   The ignition coil and power transistor are located on the intake manifold (see illustration). Remove the upper intake manifold (see Chapter 4B).

6   Detach the high voltage lead from the coil. Disconnect the wiring connectors from the ignition coil and power transistor, remove the mounting bolts and remove the units from the intake manifold.

Testing

Refer to illustrations 7.7a, 7.7b and 7.9

7   Using an ohmmeter, measure the resistance across the primary ("+" to "-" terminals) and secondary ("+" to high voltage lead terminal) windings (see illustrations). Compare the results obtained to those given in this Chapter's Specifications. Note that the resistance of the coil windings will vary slightly according to the coil temperature. Check that there is no continuity between the high voltage lead terminal and the coil body. If the coil is defective, replace it.

8   To test the ballast resistor (carbureted models only), disconnect the wiring terminals from the resistor and measure the resistance across the two terminals. Compare your readings with the values listed in this Chapter's Specifications. If the ballast resistor is defective, replace it.

9   To test the power transistor (fuel injected

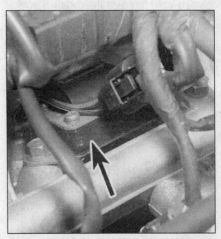

7.5 On 1990 through 1994 fuel-injected models, the ignition coil is located on the intake manifold

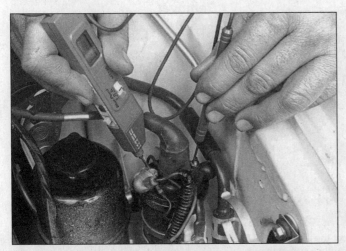

7.7a To test the coil, measure the primary resistance . . .

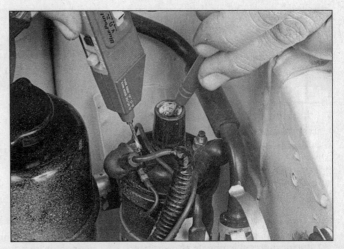

7.7b . . . then measure the secondary resistance and compare the readings to the specified values - if the indicated resistance is incorrect, replace the coil

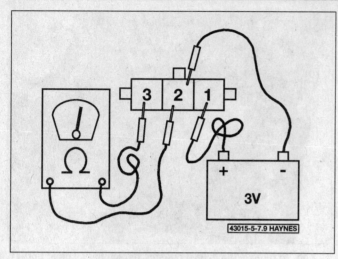

7.9 Power transistor test details

7.10 On 1995 through 2002 SOHC models and 2000 through 2005 DOHC models, the ignition coil pack is mounted at the left end of the cylinder head

models only), connect the negative terminal of a 3-volt power source to terminal no. 2 of the power transistor electrical connector (**see illustration**). Connect an ohmmeter to terminals 2 and 3. Momentarily connect and disconnect the positive terminal of the 3-volt power source to terminal no. 1 while observing the ohmmeter. When power is connected continuity should be indicated on the meter and no continuity when the power is disconnected. If the power transistor fails to operate as described, replace it.

1995 through 2002 SOHC and 1995 through 2005 DOHC models

Refer to illustrations 7.10 and 7.13

10   On SOHC models and later DOHC engines, the ignition coil assembly is mounted at the left (drivers) side of the cylinder head (**see illustration**). On 1995 through 1997 DOHC models, two separate ignition coils are mounted under a cover in the center of the valve cover.

11   On SOHC models, label and detach the spark plug leads from the coil assembly. Disconnect the wiring connector, remove the mounting bolts and remove the coil.

12   On DOHC models, remove the cover over the coils, disconnect the wiring connectors and remove the coil mounting bolts. Detach the spark plug lead and carefully pull the coil straight up.

13   Using an ohmmeter, measure the resistance of the primary windings at the coil wiring connector (**see illustration**). On SOHC models, measure across terminals 3 and 2, then 3 and 1 in turn to check both coils in the assembly. On DOHC models, measure across terminals 1 and 2 of each coil.

14   Measure the resistance of the secondary windings across the two spark plug lead towers of each coil.

15   Compare the results obtained to those given in this Chapter's Specifications. Replace

the coil assembly (SOHC) or individual coil (DOHC) if defective.

2006 and later models

Refer to illustration 7.18

Note: *These models have four coil-over-plug ignition coils.*

16   Remove the engine cover.

17   If you're removing the ignition coil for cylinder No. 3 or No. 4, remove the engine harness cover bolts and remove the harness cover. Push the harness aside.

18   Disconnect the electrical connector from the ignition coil (**see illustration**).

19   Remove the ignition coil mounting bolt and remove the coil.

20   Installation is the reverse of removal.

---

8   Distributor - removal and installation

Removal

Refer to illustrations 8.6a, 8.6b, 8.8a and 8.8b

1   Disconnect the cable from the negative terminal of the battery.

2   Position no. 1 cylinder at TDC on its compression stroke (see Chapter 2A).

3   Detach the coil lead from the distributor cap.

4   On carbureted models, detach the vacuum hose(s) from the advance unit.

5   If you're removing the spark plug wires from the cap, look for a raised "1" on the distributor cap. This marks the location for the number one cylinder spark plug wire terminal. If the cap does not have a mark for the number one terminal, locate the number one spark plug and trace the wire back to the terminal on the cap and apply a mark. Label all the spark plug wires and detach them from the distributor cap.

6   Release the retaining clips and remove the distributor cap (**see illustrations**). If you've left the spark wires attached, posi-

7.13 Ignition coil terminal identification (1995 through 1999 models shown; later models have two terminals)

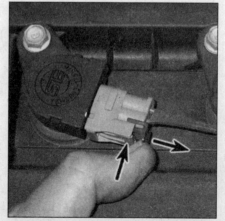

7.18 To disconnect the electrical connector from the ignition coil, pull out the locking tab, then depress the release tab (2006 and later models)

8.6a The distributor is mounted at the left (drivers) side of the cylinder head

8.6b Release the distributor cap retaining clips

tioning the cap clear of the distributor body. Remove the cap seal from the distributor.

7   Follow the distributor wiring harness back to the connector and disconnect it.

8   Check the distributor flange and cylinder head for alignment marks. If no marks are visible, use a scribe or marker pen, to mark the relationship of the distributor body to the cylinder head. Make a mark on the edge of the distributor base directly below the rotor tip and in line with it **(see illustrations)**.

9   Remove the distributor hold down nut and washer, then pull the distributor straight out to remove it. **Caution:** *DO NOT turn the crankshaft while the distributor is out of the engine, or the alignment marks will be useless.* Remove the O-ring from the end of the distributor body and discard it; a new one must be used when the distributor is reinstalled.

10   If necessary, remove the rotor.

11   If necessary, remove the vacuum diaphragm (see Section 10) and the igniter (see Section 11).

Installation

Refer to illustration 8.15

Note: *If the crankshaft has been moved while the distributor is out, the number one piston must be repositioned at TDC. This can be done by feeling for compression pressure at the number one plug hole as the crankshaft is turned. Once compression is felt, align the notch in the drivebelt pulley with the T on the timing scale.*

12   On carburetor models, if the vacuum diaphragm unit has been removed, reinstall it making sure its pushrod is engaged with the base pin, and securely tighten its retaining screws. Install the igniter unit, making sure its wiring is correctly reconnected, and lightly tighten its retaining screws. Align one of the rotor teeth with the igniter pick-up lug and set the air gap (see section 13) before tightening the igniter retaining screws.

13   Press the rotor firmly onto the distributor shaft.

14   Lubricate the new O-ring with engine oil, and install it in the groove in the distributor body. Examine the distributor cap seal for wear or damage, and replace if necessary.

15   Position the rotor slightly to the side of the mark made on the distributor prior to removal; in this position the punch mark on the side of the distributor drive gear will align with the cut-out on the base of the distributor housing **(see illustration)**.

16   Align the marks on the distributor body and cylinder head then insert the distributor, while rotating the rotor slightly to ensure that the camshaft and drive gear engage correctly.

17   Align the mark on the distributor flange with the center of the mounting stud or alternately align the marks made prior to removal. Install the washer and nut, and tighten loosely.

18   Ensure that the seal is correctly located in its groove, then install the cap assembly on the distributor and lock it in position with the retaining clips.

19   Reconnect the distributor wiring, and on carburetor models, reconnect the vacuum hose(s) to the diaphragm unit.

8.8a Mark the distributor flange in relation to the cylinder head before loosening the mounting nut

8.8b Before removing the distributor, paint or scribe an alignment mark on the edge of the distributor base inline with the rotor tip

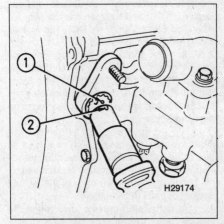

8.15 Align the punch mark on the drive gear (1) with the cut-out (2) on the distributor base

9.1 Crankshaft pulley notch (1) and timing belt cover timing marks (2)

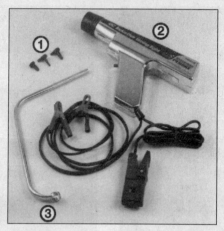

9.3 Tools needed to check and adjust the ignition timing

10.4 To detach the vacuum unit from the distributor, remove the two screws (arrows) . . .

20   Attach the spark plug wires to the plugs (if removed).
21   Connect the cable to the negative terminal of the battery.
22   Check, and if necessary, adjust the ignition timing (see Section 9), then tighten the distributor hold down nut.

9   Ignition timing - check and adjustment

Refer to illustrations 9.1 and 9.3
Note: *The following procedure applies to 1994 and earlier models. 1995 and later models are equipped with a distributorless ignition system and timing is not adjustable. If the information on your vehicle's VECI label differs from this procedure, use the information on the VECI label.*
1   The timing marks are on the timing belt cover, which align with a notch on the crankshaft pulley rim **(see illustration)**. The marks on the timing belt cover are spaced at intervals of 5-degrees, with TDC marked with a "T." The marks to the left of the "T" are Before Top Dead Center (BTDC) and the marks to the right are After Top Dead Center (ATDC). The ignition timing is checked as follows.
2   Start the engine, warm it up to normal operating temperature, and switch it off. The timing check and adjustment must be made with all electrical accessories, including the electric cooling fan and air conditioning compressor switched off.
3   Connect the timing light to the no. 1 cylinder (nearest the timing belt) plug lead as described in the timing light manufacturer's instructions **(see illustration)**. Make sure that the timing light wires are clear of the moving and/or hot parts of the engine.
4   On carbureted models, disconnect the vacuum hose from the distributor and plug the hose. On fuel injected models, connect a jumper lead between the battery negative (ground) terminal and the ignition timing adjustment connector terminal (see Chap-

1   **Vacuum plugs** - *Vacuum hoses will, in most cases, have to be disconnected and plugged. Molded plugs in various shapes and sizes are available for this*
2   **Inductive pick-up timing light** - *Flashes a bright concentrated beam of light when the number one spark plug fires. Connect the leads according to the instructions supplied with the light*
3   **Distributor wrench** - *On some models, the hold-down bolt for the distributor is difficult to reach and turn with a conventional wrench or socket. A special wrench like this must be used*

ter 1). On early models, this connector is located near the bulkhead on the left-hand side of the intake manifold, but on later models it is located near the battery on the right-hand side of the cylinder head.
5   Start the engine, allowing it to idle at the specified speed, and point the timing light at the crankshaft pulley. The pulley notch should be aligned with the correct point on the timing belt cover scale (see this Chapter's Specifications for the correct timing setting).
6   If adjustment is necessary, loosen the distributor hold down nut, then slowly rotate the distributor body until the crankshaft pulley notch is correctly positioned. Turning the distributor counterclockwise will advance the ignition timing and turning it clockwise will retard the ignition timing. **Warning:** *Avoid touching the spark plug leads, and keep loose clothing, long hair, etc., away from the moving parts of the engine.* When the marks are correctly aligned, hold the distributor firmly, and tighten its hold down nut securely. Recheck that the timing marks are still correctly aligned and, if necessary, repeat the adjustment procedure.
7   When the timing is correctly set, increase the engine speed, and check that the pulley mark advances beyond the beginning of the timing reference marks, and returns to the specified mark when the engine is allowed to idle; this indicates that the distributor advance mechanism is functioning.
8   When the ignition timing is correct, stop

the engine and disconnect the timing light. Connect the vacuum hose to the distributor or remove the jumper from the timing adjustment connector.

10   Vacuum advance unit - replacement

Refer to illustrations 10.4 and 10.5
Note: *This procedure applies to carbureted models only.*
1   Remove the distributor (see Section 8)
2   Carefully clamp the distributor in a bench vise. Pad the jaws of the vise to avoid damage to the housing. Do not overtighten the vise - the distributor is an aluminum casting and will crack if squeezed too hard.
3   Pull the rotor off the shaft (see Chapter 1).
4   Remove two vacuum unit mounting screws **(see illustration)**.
5   Remove the controller link from the pin on the breaker base **(see illustration)**, then detach the vacuum unit.
6   Installation is the reverse of removal.

10.5 . . . tilt the unit down and detach the arm from the pin on the breaker base (arrow)

11.2a Disconnect the two wiring connectors from the igniter . . .

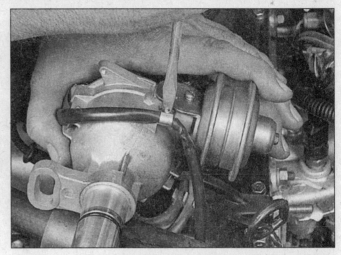

11.2b . . . and remove the wiring clip screw to release the wiring

11 Igniter - replacement

Refer to illustrations 11.2a, 11.2b and 11.3

Note: *This procedure applies to carbureted models only.*

1   Remove the distributor (see Section 8). Remove the rotor.
2   Disconnect the wiring connectors from the igniter **(see illustrations)**.
3   Remove the two igniter mounting screws, detach the black ground wire from the igniter and remove the igniter **(see illustration)**.
4   Installation is the reverse of removal. Be sure to connect one end of the ground wire to the igniter mounting screw and the other end to the breaker plate.
5   Adjust the air gap (see Section 13) before reinstalling the distributor.

12 Centrifugal advance mechanism - removal and installation

Note: *This procedure applies to carbureted models only.*

Removal

Refer to illustrations 12.3, 12.4, 12.5, 12.6a, 12.6b and 12.7

1   Remove the distributor (see Section 8) and detach the vacuum advance unit (see Section 10).
2   Remove the igniter (see Section 11).
3   Remove the signal rotor shaft screw and breaker plate screws **(see illustration)**.
4   Remove the signal rotor shaft and breaker plate assembly **(see illustration)**.
5   If you're replacing either the signal rotor or the signal rotor shaft, pull the two apart. If

11.3 To detach the igniter, remove the two mounting screws (arrows) (one of them also holds the ground wire in place)

12.3 Remove the screws (arrows) to detach the signal rotor shaft and breaker plate

12.4 Pull the signal rotor shaft/breaker plate assembly off the distributor shaft

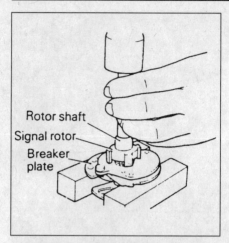

12.5 If you can't pull the signal rotor off the shaft, support the breaker plate assembly, then gently tap the shaft out of the signal rotor with a soft-face hammer

12.6a Using a pair of needle-nose pliers, remove the two spring retainers . . .

12.6b . . . and the two governor springs

12.7 Remove the two governor weights

you're unable to pull the rotor off the shaft, support the breaker plate assembly and gently tap the shaft out of the signal rotor with a soft-face hammer **(see illustration)**.
6   Using a pair of needle-nose pliers, remove the two spring retainers, then remove the two governor springs **(see illustrations)**.
7   Remove the two governor weights **(see illustration)**.

Installation

Refer to illustrations 12.10, 12.11 and 12.13

8   Apply a small amount of lightweight grease to the pivot pins, then install the governor weights.
9   Attach the governor springs and spring retainers.
10   Lubricate the shaft with lightweight grease, then slide the signal rotor shaft onto the distributor shaft. Make sure the pins on the

governor weights are aligned with the slots in the signal rotor shaft arm **(see illustration)**. Don't forget to install the screw.
11   Install the breaker plate in the housing. Make sure the breaker plate tab fits into the groove in the housing **(see illustration)**.
12   Tighten the two breaker plate screws.
13   If you disassembled the signal rotor/signal rotor shaft assembly to replace either part, push the signal rotor onto the shaft. The flat face of the signal rotor must face up (the four projections must protrude down). Be sure to match the flat side of the signal rotor bore with the machined flat on the signal rotor shaft **(see illustration)**. If you try to assemble it without matching the two flat surfaces, you will damage the rotor and/or the shaft.
14   Install the igniter (see Section 11).
15   Adjust the air gap (see Section 13).
16   The remainder of installation is the reverse of removal.

12.10 Make sure the governor weight pins (arrows) fit into the slots in the signal rotor shaft arm (apply a small amount of lightweight grease to the pins)

12.11 The projection on the breaker plate must fit into the groove in the distributor housing (arrows)

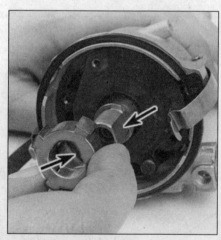

12.13 When you press the signal rotor onto the rotor shaft, be sure to align the flats (arrows)

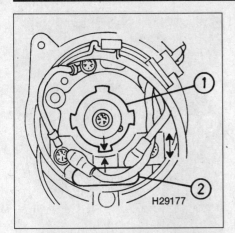

13.1 The air gap is the clearance between the rotor (1) and igniter pick-up (2)

13.2 To adjust the air gap, loosen the igniter mounting screws, insert a brass feeler gauge of the specified thickness between the igniter and one of the signal rotor projections, push the igniter against the gauge and tighten the mounting screws

13 Air gap - adjustment

Refer to illustrations 13.1 and 13.2

Note: *This procedure applies to carbureted models only.*

1 Any time you replace the igniter - or remove it in order to get at the signal rotor or centrifugal advance mechanism - be sure to adjust the air gap before reinstalling the distributor cap **(see illustration)**.

2 Loosen the igniter mounting screws. Place a brass (non-magnetic) feeler gauge of the specified thickness (see this Chapter's Specifications) between one of the four projections on the signal rotor and the igniter **(see illustration)**.

3 Gently push the igniter toward the signal rotor until it's a snug - not tight - fit against the feeler gauge.

4 Tighten the igniter mounting screws.

5 Check the adjustment by noting the amount of drag on the feeler gauge when

you pull it out of the gap between the signal rotor and the igniter. You should feel a slight amount of drag. If you feel excessive drag on the gauge, the gap is probably too small. If you don't feel any drag on the gauge when you pull it out, the air gap is too large.

14 Sensor unit - replacement

Refer to illustration 14.4

Note: *This procedure applies to 1994 and earlier fuel injected models only.*

1 Remove the distributor (see Section 8).

2 Carefully clamp the distributor in a bench vise. Pad the jaws of the vise to avoid damage to the housing. Do not overtighten the vise - the distributor housing is an aluminum

casting and will crack if squeezed too hard.

3 Pull the rotor off the shaft (see Chapter 1).

4 Remove the packing rubber then lift off the cover **(see illustration)**.

5 Remove the screw and the rotor shaft.

6 Carefully remove the disc from the slot in the pickup unit, then remove the spacer.

7 Detach the lead wire connector.

8 Remove the three screws and remove the plate and sensor unit.

9 Assembly is the reverse of disassembly. Install the disc into the slot in the sensor unit aligned with the spacer. Install the cover and align the indention with the housing notch.

15 Charging system - general information and precautions

The charging system includes the alternator, an integral voltage regulator, the battery, a fusible link and the wiring between all the components. The charging system supplies electrical power for the ignition system, the lights, the radio, etc. The alternator is driven by a drivebelt at the front of the engine.

The purpose of the voltage regulator is to limit the alternator's voltage to a preset value. This prevents power surges, circuit overloads, etc., during peak voltage output.

The fusible link is a short length of insulated wire integral with the engine compartment wiring harness. The link is four wire gauges smaller in diameter than the circuit it protects. Production fusible links and their identification flags are identified by the flag center. See Chapter 12 for additional information about fusible links.

The charging system doesn't normally require periodic maintenance. However, the drivebelt, battery and wires and connections should be inspected at specified intervals (see Chapter 1).

The dashboard warning light should

14.4 Distributor and related components (1994 and earlier fuel-injected models)

1 Breather
2 Distributor cap
3 Carbon contact
4 Rotor
5 Packing
6 Cover
7 Rotor shaft
8 Disc
9 Spacer
10 Plate
11 Sensor unit
12 Bearing
13 Distributor shaft
14 Distributor housing
15 Lead wire
16 O-ring
17 Drive gear
18 Roll pin

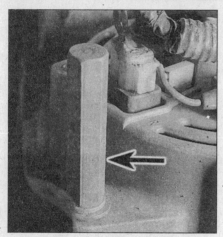

17.5a Alternator lower mounting bolt (early models)

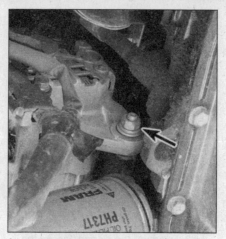

17.5b Alternator lower mounting bolt (later models)

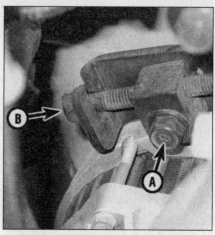

17.5c Alternator upper mounting bolt (A) and adjustment bolt (B) typical

come on when the ignition key is turned to Start, then go off immediately. If it remains on, there is a malfunction in the charging system (see Section 16).

Be very careful when making electrical connections to a vehicle equipped with an alternator and note the following:

a) *When reconnecting wires to the alternator from the battery, be sure to note the polarity.*

b) *Before using arc welding equipment to repair any part of the vehicle, disconnect the wires from the alternator and the battery terminals.*

c) *Never start the engine with a battery charger connected.*

d) *Always disconnect both battery leads before using a battery charger.*

e) *The alternator is driven by a drivebelt which could cause serious injury if your hands, hair or clothes become entangled in it with the engine running.*

f) *The alternator is connected directly to the battery, and could arc or cause a fire if overloaded or shorted out.*

g) *Wrap a plastic bag over the alternator and secure it with rubberbands before steam cleaning the engine.*

16 Charging system - check

Note: *Refer to the warnings given in "Safety first!" and in Section 1 of this Chapter before starting work.*

1   If a malfunction occurs in the charging circuit, don't automatically assume that the alternator is causing the problem. First check the following items:

a) *Check the drivebelt tension and condition (see Chapter 1). Replace it if it's worn or deteriorated.*

b) *Make sure the alternator mounting and adjustment bolts are tight.*

c) *Inspect the alternator wiring harness and the connectors at the alternator and voltage regulator. They must be in good condition and tight.*

d) *Check the fusible link (if equipped) located between the starter solenoid and the alternator. If it's burned, determine the cause, repair the circuit and replace the link (the vehicle won't start and/or the accessories won't work if the fusible link blows). Sometimes a fusible link may look good, but still be bad. If in doubt, remove it and check for continuity.*

e) *Start the engine and check the alternator for abnormal noises (a shrieking or squealing sound indicates a bad bearing).*

f) *Check the specific gravity of the battery electrolyte. If it's low, charge the battery (doesn't apply to maintenance free batteries).*

g) *Make sure the battery is fully charged (one bad cell in a battery can cause overcharging by the alternator).*

h) *Disconnect the battery cables (negative first, then positive). Inspect the battery posts and the cable clamps for corrosion. Clean them thoroughly if necessary (see Chapter 1). Reconnect the cable to the positive terminal.*

i) *With the key off, connect a test light between the negative battery post and the disconnected negative cable clamp.*

   1) *If the test light does not illuminate (or illuminates dimly), reattach the clamp and proceed to the next step.*

   2) *If the test light illuminated brightly, there is a short in the electrical system of the vehicle. The short must be repaired before the charging system can be checked.*

   3) *Disconnect the alternator wiring harness.*

    (a) *If the light goes out, the alternator is bad.*

    (b) *If the light stays on, pull each fuse until the light goes out (this will tell you which component is shorted).*

2   Using a voltmeter, check the static battery voltage with the engine off. If should be approximately 12-volts.

3   Start the engine and check the battery voltage again. It should now be greater than the voltage measured in Step 2, but not greater than approximately 15 volts.

4   Turn on the headlights. The voltage should drop, and then come back up, if the charging system is working properly.

5   If the voltage reading is more than the specified charging voltage, replace the voltage regulator (see Section 18). If the voltage is the same as, or less than, the static battery voltage, the alternator diode(s), stator or rectifier may be bad or the voltage regulator may be malfunctioning.

17 Alternator - removal and installation

Removal

Refer to illustrations 17.5a, 17.5b, 17.5c, 17.6a and 17.6b

1   Disconnect the cable from the negative terminal of the battery.

2   On 1994 and earlier models, if the vehicle is equipped with air conditioning, remove the left (driver's side) electric cooling fan (see Chapter 3).

3   On some models with power steering, it will be necessary to unbolt the power steering pump to access the alternator (see Chapter 10). On these models, do not disconnect the power steering lines from the pump unless you have to. Just push the power steering pump out of the way to provide sufficient clearance to unbolt and remove the alternator. On some later models you will also have to remove the power steering pump bracket.

4   Raise the vehicle and support it securely on jackstands. Remove the left (1994 and earlier) or right (1995 and later) front wheel, then remove the splash shield.

5   Loosen the alternator lower mounting pivot bolt, then loosen the upper adjustment lockbolt and back off the adjustment bolt until the alternator can be swiveled towards the engine enough to release the drivebelt from the alternator pulley **(see illustrations)**.

17.6a If you have difficulty detaching the electrical connectors from the back of the alternator while it's still bolted to the engine . . .

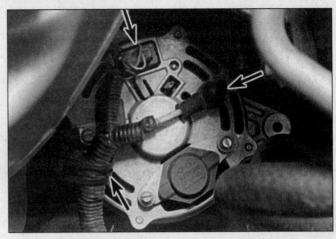

17.6b . . . remove the alternator, then detach the connectors, open the wire harness clip and lift the alternator out

6   Remove the rubber covers (where used) from the alternator terminals, then unscrew the retaining nut and disconnect the wiring from the rear of the alternator **(see illustrations)**.

7   Unscrew the alternator upper and lower mounting bolts and washers, then pull the alternator away from its mounting brackets.

Installation

8   If you are replacing the alternator, take the old one with you when purchasing a new unit. Make sure the new/rebuilt unit looks identical to the old alternator. Look at the terminals - they should be the same in number, size and location as the terminals on the old alternator. Finally, look at the identification numbers - they will be stamped into the housing or printed on a tag attached to the housing. Make sure the numbers are the same on both alternators.

9   Many new/rebuilt alternators do not have a pulley installed, so you may have to switch the pulley from the old unit to the new/rebuilt one. When buying an alternator, find out the shop's policy regarding pulleys - some shops will perform this service free of charge.

10   Installation is the reverse of removal. Tension the auxiliary drivebelt (see Chapter 1) and tighten the alternator mounting bolts securely. **Note:** *If the alternator is suspect, it should be removed from the vehicle and taken to an automotive shop for testing. Most automotive shops can supply and install brushes at a reasonable cost. However, check on the cost of repairs before proceeding as it may be more economical to obtain a new or rebuilt alternator.*

18   Voltage regulator/alternator brushes - replacement

Refer to illustrations 18.2, 18.3 and 18.4

Note 1: *This procedure applies to 1986 through 1988 models only. On 1989 and later models, complete disassembly of the alternator is required to replace the voltage regulator/ brush assembly - replace the alternator with a new or remanufactured unit.*

Note 2: *If you are replacing the brushes (but not the regulator itself), the following procedure requires that you unsolder the old brush leads from the regulator and solder the new ones into place. Unless you are skilled with a soldering gun, have this procedure performed by someone who is. If you overheat and damage the regulator, you could end up spending a lot more money than necessary.*

1   Remove the alternator (see Section 17).

2   Remove the voltage regulator mounting screws **(see illustration)**.

3   Remove the regulator/brush holder assembly and measure the length (see this Chapter's Specifications) of the brushes **(see illustration)**. If they are less than specified, replace them. **Note:** *If you're simply replacing the voltage regulator, skip the next step - the new regulator assembly includes a new set of brushes so the following step is unnecessary.*

18.2 To detach the voltage regulator/brush holder assembly, remove the two mounting screws (arrows) and pull the regulator/ brush holder straight out

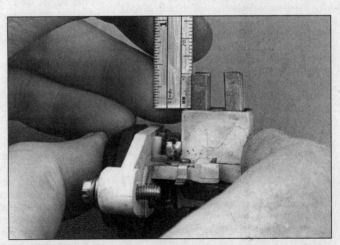

18.3 Measure the brushes with a small ruler - if they're shorter than 0.18 in, install new ones

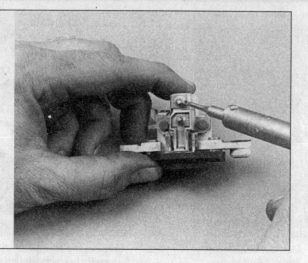

18.4 To detach worn brushes from the voltage regulator/brush holder assembly, carefully unsolder the brush leads and extract each brush and lead from the holder

4   Unsolder the brush wiring connections **(see illustration)** and remove the brushes and springs.
5   Installation is the reverse of removal. Be sure to solder the new brush leads properly.

19 Starting system - general information and precautions

The function of the starting system is to turn over the engine quickly enough to allow it to start.

The starting system consists of the battery, the starter motor, the starter solenoid and the wires connecting them. The solenoid is mounted directly on the starter motor.

The solenoid/starter motor assembly is installed on the lower part of the engine, next to the transmission bellhousing.

When the ignition key is turned to the Start position, the starter solenoid is actuated through the starter control circuit. The starter solenoid then connects the battery to the starter. The battery supplies the electrical energy to the starter motor, which does the actual work of cranking the engine.

The starter motor on a vehicle equipped with a manual transmission can only be operated when the clutch pedal is depressed; the starter on a vehicle equipped with an automatic transmission can only be operated when the transmission selector lever is in Park or Neutral.

Always observe the following precautions when working on the starting system:

a) *Excessive cranking of the starter motor can overheat it and cause serious damage. Never operate the starter motor for more than 30 seconds at a time without pausing to allow it to cool for at least two minutes.*
b) *The starter is connected directly to the battery and could arc or cause a fire if mishandled, overloaded or shorted out.*
c) *Always detach the cable from the negative terminal of the battery before working on the starting system.*

20 Starter motor - testing in vehicle

Note: *Refer to the precautions given in "Safety first!" and in Section 1 of this Chapter before starting work. Before diagnosing starter problems, make sure the battery is fully charged.*

1   If the starter motor does not turn when the switch is operated, make sure that the shift lever is in Neutral or Park (automatic transmission) or that the clutch pedal is depressed (manual transmission).
2   Make sure that the battery is charged and that all cables, both at the battery and starter solenoid terminals, are clean and secure.
3   To check the battery, switch on the headlights. If they dim after a few seconds, indicating that the battery is discharged - recharge or replace the battery. If the headlights glow brightly, operate the ignition switch and observe the lights. If they dim, this indicates that current is reaching the starter motor, and the problem is in the starter motor. If the lights continue to glow brightly (and no clicking sound can be heard from the starter motor solenoid), this indicates a problem in the circuit or solenoid - see following paragraphs. If the starter motor turns slowly when operated, but the battery is in good condition, this indicates the starter motor is faulty, or there is considerable resistance somewhere in the circuit.
4   If a problem in the circuit is suspected, disconnect the battery leads (including the ground connection to the body), the starter/ solenoid wiring and the engine/transmission ground strap. Thoroughly clean the connections, reconnect the leads and wiring, then use a voltmeter or test light to check that full battery voltage is available at the battery positive lead connection to the solenoid, and that the ground is sound. Smear petroleum jelly around the battery terminals to prevent corrosion - corroded connections are among the most frequent causes of electrical system problems.
5   If the starter motor spins but the engine is not cranking, the clutch in the starter motor is slipping and the starter motor must be replaced.

6   If, when the switch is actuated, the starter motor does not operate at all but the solenoid clicks, then the problem is either the battery, the main solenoid contacts or the starter motor (or the engine is seized).
7   If the solenoid plunger cannot be heard when the switch is actuated, the battery is bad, the fusible link is burned (the circuit is open) or the solenoid is defective.
8   To check the solenoid, connect a jumper between the battery (+) and the ignition switch wire terminal (the small terminal) on the solenoid. If the starter motor now operates, the solenoid is OK and the problem is in the ignition switch, neutral start switch or the wiring.
9   If the starter motor still does not operate, remove the starter/solenoid assembly for disassembly, testing and repair.
10   If the starter motor cranks the engine at an abnormally slow speed, make sure that the battery is charged and that all terminal connections are tight. If the engine is partially seized, or has the wrong viscosity oil in it, it will crank slowly.
11   Run the engine until normal operating temperature is reached, then disconnect the coil wire from the distributor cap and ground it on the engine.
12   Connect a voltmeter positive lead to the positive battery post and connect the negative lead to the negative post.
13   Crank the engine and take the voltmeter readings as soon as a steady figure is indicated. Do not allow the starter motor to turn for more than 30 seconds at a time. A reading of 9 volts or more, with the starter motor turning at cranking speed, is normal. If the reading is 9 volts or more but the cranking speed is slow, the motor is faulty. If the reading is less than 9 volts and the cranking speed is slow, the solenoid contacts are probably burned, the starter motor is bad, the battery is discharged or there is a bad connection.

21 Starter motor - removal and installation

Refer to illustrations 21.7 and 21.9
Note: *On some vehicles, it may be necessary to remove the exhaust pipe(s) or frame crossmember to access the starter motor. In extreme cases it may even be necessary to unbolt the mounts and raise the engine slightly to get the starter out.*
1   Disconnect the cable from the negative terminal of the battery.
2   On fuel-injected models, remove the air cleaner assembly (see Chapter 4).
3   On 1990 through 1994 models, remove the Exhaust Gas Recirculation (EGR) valve, if equipped (see Chapter 6).
4   On 1990 through 1999 models, disconnect the speedometer cable from the transaxle and set it aside.
5   On some models it will be necessary to disconnect the shift cable (see Chapter 7) and set it aside.

21.7 Disconnect the electrical connector (A) from the spade terminal on the starter solenoid, then remove the nut (B) and disconnect the battery cable from the B+ terminal (typical)

21.9 Starter motor mounting bolts (typical)

6   Raise the vehicle and support it securely on jackstands.

7   Unscrew the nut and disconnect the battery cable from the starter motor. Disconnect the wiring from the solenoid **(see illustration)**.

8   Where applicable on later models, remove the EGR valve (see Chapter 4).

9   Remove the starter motor mounting bolts **(see illustration)**, supporting the starter motor as the bolts are removed, and remove the starter motor.

10   Installation is the reverse of removal, tighten the mounting bolts securely.

22   Starter solenoid - removal and installation

Refer to illustrations 22.3 and 22.4

1   Disconnect the cable from the negative terminal of the battery.

2   Remove the starter motor (see Section 21).

3   Disconnect the large starter motor lead

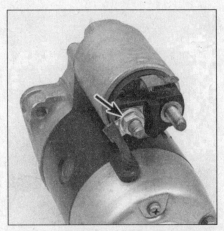

22.3 To separate the solenoid from the starter motor, remove the nut and detach the lead . . .

from the solenoid terminal **(see illustration)**.

4   Remove the screws which secure the solenoid to the starter motor **(see illustration)**.

22.4 . . . remove the solenoid mounting screws and pull the solenoid straight off the starter flange

5   Pull the solenoid from the starter motor body flange.

6   Installation is the reverse of removal.

Notes

Chapter 6
Emissions and engine control systems

Contents

1   General information

To prevent pollution of the atmosphere from incompletely burned and evaporating gases, and to maintain good driveability and fuel economy, a number of emission control systems and devices are incorporated. They include the:

Positive Crankcase Ventilation (PCV) system
Evaporative emission control system
Heated Air Intake (HAI) system
Jet air system
Exhaust Gas Recirculation (EGR) system
Secondary air supply system
Catalytic converter
Deceleration devices
Electronic Control Module (ECM)
Fuel injection system (later models)

The Sections in this Chapter include general descriptions, checking procedures within the scope of the home mechanic and component replacement procedures (when possible) for each of the systems listed above.

Before assuming that an emissions control system is malfunctioning, check the fuel and ignition systems carefully. The diagnosis of some emission control devices requires specialized tools, equipment and training. If checking and servicing become too difficult or if a procedure is beyond your ability, consult a dealer service department. Remember, the most frequent cause of emissions problems is simply a loose or broken vacuum hose or wire, so always check the hose and wiring connections first.

This doesn't mean, however, that emission control systems are particularly difficult to maintain and repair. You can quickly and easily perform many checks and do most of the regular maintenance at home with common tune-up and hand tools. **Note:** *Because of a Federally mandated extended warranty which covers the emission control system compo-nents, check with your dealer about warranty coverage before working on any emissions-related systems. Once the warranty has expired, you may wish to perform some of the component checks and/or replacement proce-dures in this Chapter to save money.*

Pay close attention to any special pre-cautions outlined in this Chapter. It should be noted that the illustrations of the various systems may not exactly match the system installed on your vehicle because of changes made by the manufacturer during production or from year-to-year.

A Vehicle Emissions Control Informa-tion label is located in the engine compart-ment. This label contains important emissions specifications and adjustment information, as well as a vacuum hose schematic with emissions components identified. When ser-vicing the engine or emissions systems, the VECI label in your particular vehicle should always be checked for up-to-date informa-tion.

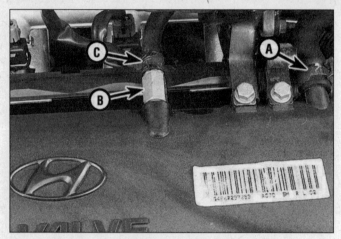

2.2a Positive Crankcase Ventilation (PCV) system details - SOHC models

A   *Fresh air hose (from intake duct)*
B   *PCV valve*
C   *Crankcase ventilation hose (to intake manifold)*

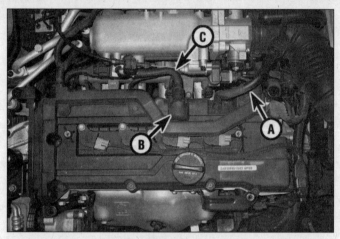

2.2b Positive Crankcase Ventilation (PCV) system details - DOHC models

A   *Fresh air hose (from intake duct)*
B   *PCV valve*
C   *Crankcase ventilation hose (to intake manifold)*

2   Positive Crankcase Ventilation (PCV) system

Description

Refer to illustrations 2.2a and 2.2b

1   The Positive Crankcase Ventilation (PCV) system reduces hydrocarbon emissions by scavenging crankcase vapors. It does this by circulating fresh air from the air cleaner through the crankcase, where it mixes with blow-by gases, before being drawn through a PCV valve into the intake manifold.

2   The PCV system consists of the PCV valve and two hoses, one of which connects the air intake duct to the crankcase and the other (containing the PCV valve) which connects the crankcase to the intake manifold **(see illustrations)**. The fresh air inlet hose connects the intake air duct to a pipe on the valve cover. The PCV valve is located in the valve cover, and the PCV hose connects the PCV valve to the intake manifold. **Note:** *If you are servicing the PCV system on a 1986 through 1990 model, refer to Section 38 in Chapter 1.*

3   To maintain idle quality, the PCV valve restricts the flow when the intake manifold vacuum is high. If abnormal operating conditions (such as piston ring problems) arise, the system is designed to allow excessive amounts of blow-by gases to flow back through the crankcase vent tube into the air cleaner to be consumed by normal combustion.

Check

4   There is no scheduled inspection interval for the PCV valve or the PCV system hoses on 1991 and later models. But, over time the PCV system might become less efficient as an oil residue of sludge builds up inside the PCV valve and the hoses. One symptom of a clogged PCV system is leaking seals. When crankcase vapors can't escape, pressure builds inside the bottom end and eventually causes crankshaft seals to leak. So anytime that you're changing the oil, the air filter, the spark plugs, etc. it's a good idea to pull off the PCV hoses and inspect them and clean them out. If they're cracked, torn or deteriorated, replace them. **Note:** *If you are servicing the PCV system on a 1986 through 1990 model, refer to Section 38 in Chapter 1.*

Component replacement

5   Remove the PCV fresh air inlet hose.
6   Remove the PCV crankcase ventilation hose.
7   Remove the PCV valve from the valve cover.
8   Inspect the condition of the hoses. If they're clogged and/or dirty, blow them out with compressed air and wipe them off, then inspect them more carefully. If they're cracked, torn or deteriorated, replace them.
9   Inspect the condition of the PCV valve. If it's clogged, clean it with fresh solvent, then blow it out with compressed air. If you cannot remove the residue from the inside of the PCV valve, replace it.
10   Installation is the reverse of removal.

3   Evaporative emission control system

Warning: *Gasoline is extremely flammable, so take extra precautions when working on any part of the fuel system. Don't smoke or allow open flames or bare light bulbs in or near the work area. Also, don't work in a garage in which a natural gas appliance such as a water heater or clothes dryer is present.*

General description

Refer to illustrations 3.3, 3.4, 3.5a, 3.5b, 3,5c, 3.6, 3.8 and 3.9

1   The evaporative emission control system is designed to prevent the escape of fuel vapors from the fuel system into the atmosphere.

2   The evaporative emission control system consists of a canister, a bowl vent valve, a purge control valve, an overfill limiter, a thermo valve, a fuel check valve and a specially designed fuel filler cap. The purpose of each of these components, and how to check them, is described briefly in this Section.

Canister

3   When the engine is inoperative, fuel vapors generated inside the fuel tank and the carburetor float chamber are absorbed and stored in the canister. When the engine is running, the fuel vapors absorbed in the canister are drawn into the intake manifold through the purge control valve and an orifice **(see illustration)**. The 1997 DOHC engine model and later SOHC models have a new configuration evaporative canister which is square in shape with a Canister Close Valve (CCV) and a two way valve mounted on the canister to control vapor flow.

Bowl vent valve (carbureted models)

4   The bowl vent valve controls the carburetor bowl vapors. When the engine is running, intake vacuum acts on a diaphragm to close the bowl vent valve so that the bowl is connected to an air vent **(see illustration)**. During engine operation, the diaphragm is kept open by a solenoid valve - even when intake manifold vacuum falls to a value equal to atmospheric pressure - as long as the ignition key is turned on. When the key is turned

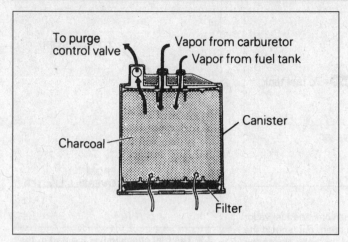

3.3 The canister absorbs and stores fuel system vapors when the engine is off - when it's started, the vapors are routed through a series of valves and lines into the intake manifold

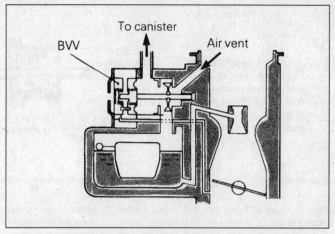

3.4 The bowl vent valve controls carburetor float bowl vapors - when the engine is on, the bowl vent valve closes to connect the float bowl to the carburetor air vent - when the key is off, the bowl vent valve opens to allow fuel vapors to flow to the canister

off, the solenoid valve closes, the bowl vent valve opens to connect the carburetor bowl to the canister, allowing fuel vapors to migrate to the canister where they are stored until the next time the key is turned on.

Purge control valve

5   The carbureted engine purge control valve **(see illustration)** is closed during idle to prevent vaporized fuel from entering the intake manifold. At higher engine speeds, the purge control valve opens. 1990 and later fuel-injected models employ a computer-controlled, solenoid-actuated purge control valve **(see illustrations)**.

Thermo valve (carbureted models)

6   The thermo valve **(see illustration)**, which monitors the engine coolant temperature at the intake manifold, closes the purge control valve when the engine coolant temperature is lower than the pre-set temperature.

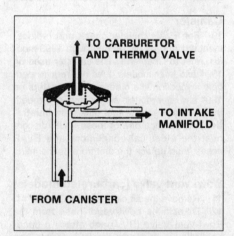

3.5a The carbureted engine purge control valve is closed during idle to prevent vaporized fuel from entering the intake manifold

3.5b On 1995 through 1999 models, the purge control solenoid valve is located under the air filter housing and engine compartment fuse and relay box (air filter housing removed for clarity)

3.5c On 2000 and later models, the purge control solenoid is located between the throttle body/intake manifold assembly and the firewall

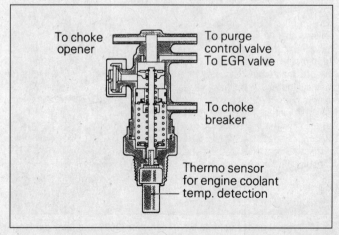

3.6 The carbureted engine thermo valve closes the purge control valve during engine warm-up and opens the purge control valve after the coolant temperature rises above a pre-set value

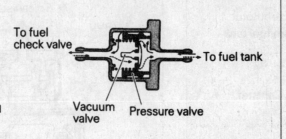

3.8 The overfill limiter contains two valves: the pressure valve opens when fuel tank internal pressure builds up; the vacuum valve opens when fuel tank internal pressure is low

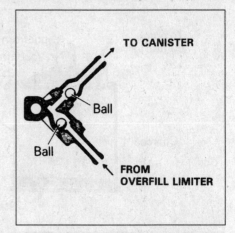

3.9 The fuel check valve, located in the fuel vapor line between the canister and the overfill limiter, prevents fuel leaks in the event of a vehicle rollover

This reduces CO and HC emissions under engine warm-up conditions. The thermo valve opens the purge control valve when the engine coolant temperature is above the pre-set temperature. The thermo valve also controls the choke breaker, EGR valve and choke opener.

Fuel filler cap
7   The fuel filler cap is equipped with a vacuum relief valve to prevent the escape of fuel vapor into the atmosphere.

Overfill limiter
8   The overfill limiter (see illustration) consists of two valves:
  a) *The pressure valve, which opens when fuel tank internal pressure exceeds normal pressure.*
  b) *The vacuum valve, which opens when fuel tank internal pressure is lower than normal pressure.*

Fuel check valve
9   The fuel check valve (see illustration), which is connected in the fuel vapor line between the canister and the overfill limiter (it's mounted in the engine compartment on the firewall), prevents fuel leaks in the event of a vehicle rollover. The valve contains two

balls. Under normal conditions, the fuel vapor passage in the valve is open, but, should the vehicle roll over, one of the balls closes the fuel passage, preventing fuel leakage.

Check
Refer to illustrations 3.10, 3.12, 3.14 and 3.15

Canister
10   For EVAP canister check and replacement procedures on 1986 through 1993 models, refer to Chapter 1. The canister used on 1994 and later models does not require periodic inspection like older units. Canisters on 1994 and later models are located underneath the vehicle, near the fuel tank (see illustration). To replace one of these units, disconnect the electrical connectors and EVAP hoses, then detach the unit from its mounting bracket.

Bowl vent valve (carbureted models)
11   Remove the air cleaner (see Chapter 4).
12   Detach the bowl vapor hose from the Bowl Vent Valve (BVV) and attach a hand-held vacuum pump to the BVV fitting (see illustration).
13   Apply a vacuum of 3 in-Hg to the BVV.

With the engine operating, it should hold vacuum. With the engine off, it should leak vacuum.

Purge control valve (carbureted models)
14   Remove the purge control valve (see illustration).
15   Attach a hand-held vacuum pump to the vacuum fitting on the valve (see illustration).
16   Blow in air lightly from the canister side. The valve's operating vacuum should be more than 1.4 in-Hg.

Purge control valve (fuel-injected models)
17   Disconnect the purge control solenoid valve electrical connector (see illustration 3.5b).
18   Using an ohmmeter across both terminals of the connector on the solenoid side,

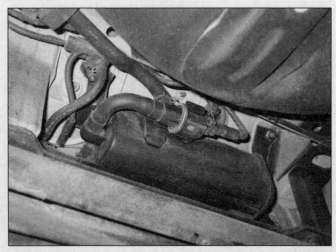

3.10 Typical under-vehicle EVAP canister (2006 and later canister shown, other units similar)

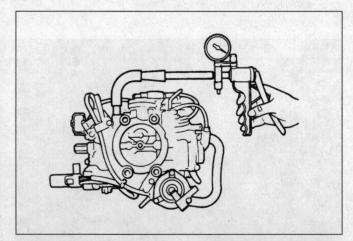

3.12 To check the carburetor bowl vent valve (BVV), detach the vapor hose from the BVV, attach a hand-held vacuum pump to the fitting and apply a vacuum to the BVV - with the engine operating, the BVV should hold vacuum - with the engine off, it should leak vacuum

3.14 On carbureted engines, purge the control valve is located on top of the canister. To remove it, detach the two hoses

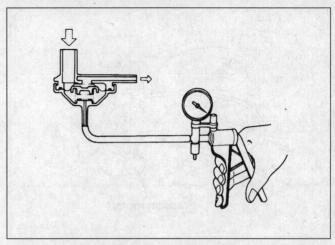

3.15 To check the carbureted engine purge control valve, attach a hand-held vacuum pump to the vacuum fitting and blow in air lightly from the canister side - you should not be able to blow air through the valve at a vacuum less than 1.4 in-Hg

check resistance of the solenoid coil. For 1990 to 1994 models, 36 to 44 ohms should be measured. For 1995 models, 45 ohms should be measured. For 1996 and later models, 26 ohms should be measured. **Note:** *These resistance values are approximate.*

19   Disconnect the small vacuum line from the solenoid valve. Connect a hand-held vacuum pump to the solenoid where the small vacuum line was removed. Apply vacuum to the purge control solenoid valve.

20   With the purge control solenoid valve electrical connector disconnected, and with vacuum applied to the purge control solenoid valve, vacuum should be held by the valve if it is operating properly.

21   Then apply battery voltage (12 volts) directly to the solenoid terminals. With battery voltage applied, the vacuum should be released by the purge control solenoid valve if it is operating properly.

22   Disconnect the battery voltage from the solenoid.

23   If the purge control solenoid valve is operating properly, reconnect the electrical connector.

24   If defective, replace the purge control solenoid valve.

Fuel filler cap

25   Inspect the gasket on the underside of the cap for deformation and deterioration. If damage is evident, replace the cap.

4   Heated Air Intake (HAI) system (carbureted models)

General description

Refer to illustration 4.2

1   All carbureted models are equipped with a Heated Air Intake (HAI) system to permit a leaner air/fuel ratio, which reduces HC and

CO emissions, improves warm-up characteristics and minimizes carburetor icing.

2   The air cleaner is equipped with an air control valve inside the snorkel to regulate the temperature of intake air, which is admitted to the carburetor through the fresh air duct, the heat cowl and air duct, or through both routes **(see illustration)**.

3   The air control valve is operated by a vacuum motor. A temperature sensor in the air cleaner controls when the vacuum motor receives intake manifold vacuum. When intake air is below about 86-degrees F, the temperature sensor allows intake manifold vacuum to the vacuum motor. This draws the air control valve up and causes hot air to be drawn through the heat cowl and air duct. When intake air is

above about 113-degrees F, the temperature sensor does not allow vacuum to the vacuum motor and the air control valve remains down. This causes cold air to be drawn through the fresh air duct. When intake air temperature is between about 86-degrees F and 113-degrees F, the air control valve is partially open and intake air is a blend of air drawn through both routes.

Check

Refer to illustrations 4.5 and 4.8

Note: *For information on checking the thermostatically controlled air cleaner for proper operation, refer to Chapter 1.*

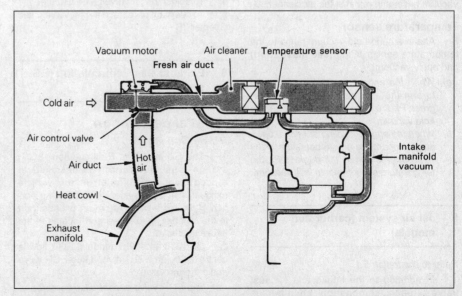

4.2 The Heated Air Intake (HAI) system - when the engine is cold, the temperature sensor allows intake manifold vacuum to the vacuum motor, which opens the air control valve, allowing hot air to be drawn into the air cleaner through the heat cowl and air duct

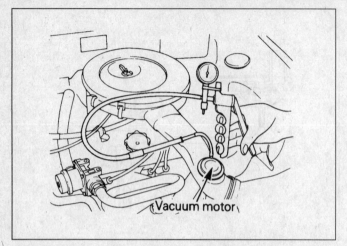

4.5 To check the air control valve and vacuum motor, remove the air cleaner, detach the vacuum hose from the vacuum motor, attach a hand-held vacuum pump to the valve and apply vacuum - the air valve inside the air cleaner snorkel should move up at a vacuum greater than 7.6 in-Hg

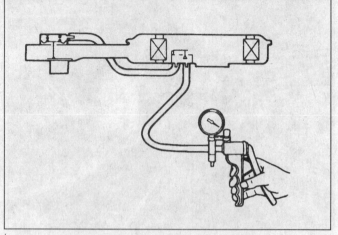

4.8 To check the temperature sensor, attach a hand-held vacuum pump to the temperature sensor and apply vacuum - when the engine is cold, the temperature sensor should hold vacuum; when the engine is at normal operating temperature, the sensor should leak vacuum

Air control valve and vacuum motor

4   Remove the air cleaner (see Chapter 4).

5   Detach the vacuum hose from the air control valve and attach a hand-held vacuum pump to the valve fitting **(see illustration)**.

6   Apply vacuum with the vacuum pump. Note the readings and look down the snorkel of the air cleaner to observe the position of the air control valve. Under 3.6 in-Hg, the air control valve should be down all the way. Over 7.6 in-Hg, the air control valve should be up all the way. If either does not happen, the vacuum motor, the air control valve, or the linkage that connects the two is faulty.

7   Detach the vacuum pump, reattach the vacuum hose, and reinstall the air cleaner.

Temperature sensor

8   Attach a hand-held vacuum pump to the temperature sensor fitting **(see illustration)** and apply vacuum.

a) *When the engine is cold (the temperature in the air cleaner is below 86-degrees F), the temperature sensor should hold vacuum.*

b) *When the engine is idling at normal operating temperature (the temperature in the air cleaner is above 113-degrees F), the temperature sensor should leak vacuum.*

5   Jet air system (carbureted models)

Refer to illustration 5.1

1   In addition to the intake and exhaust valves, each combustion chamber is equipped with a smaller jet valve **(see illustration)** which allows a super lean mixture to be admitted into the combustion chamber

during the intake stroke. This super lean mixture swirls as it enters the combustion chamber. The swirl continues throughout the compression stroke and improves flame propagation after ignition, assuring efficient combustion.

2   Air is admitted through intake openings located near the primary throttle valve of the carburetor, then routed to the jet valve via a passage through the intake manifold and cylinder head, where it is drawn through the jet valve opening into the combustion chamber.

3   The jet valve is operated by a forked rocker arm which also activates the intake valve (they share the same cam lobe). This design ensures that the intake and jet valve open simultaneously.

4   To adjust the jet valves, see Chapter 1.

5   To overhaul or replace the jet valves, see Chapter 2B.

6   Exhaust Gas Recirculation (EGR) system

General description

Refer to illustration 6.1

1   The Exhaust Gas Recirculation (EGR) system **(see illustration)** is designed to reduce oxides of nitrogen in the vehicle exhaust. The EGR system recirculates a portion of the exhaust gas from an exhaust port in the cylinder head into a port located in the intake manifold.

2   On 1986 and 1987 models, EGR flow is controlled by an EGR valve, a sub-EGR valve and a thermo valve.

a) *The EGR valve is controlled by carburetor vacuum in response to throttle valve opening; EGR flow is suspended at idle and during wide open throttle conditions.*

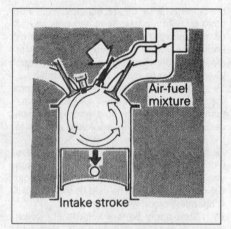

5.1 The jet valve (arrow) allows a super lean mixture to be admitted into the combustion chamber during the intake stroke

b) *The vacuum applied to the EGR valve is controlled by a thermo valve, which senses engine temperature. The thermo valve interrupts the vacuum signal to the EGR valve during warm-up when less NOx is generated and less EGR promotes better driveability.*

c) *The sub-EGR valve (not shown in illustration 6.1) opens and closes with the throttle valve via a linkage to regulate EGR flow through the EGR valve in response to the throttle valve position.*

3   On 1988 and 1989 models, the EGR system operates similarly, except no sub-EGR valve is used and a vacuum regulator valve (VRV) is used to modulate the vacuum signal to the EGR valve. On 1990 and later FBC carbureted models and fuel-injected models (except California), the EGR valve operates similarly to that described for 1988 and 1989 models. California fuel-injected models have

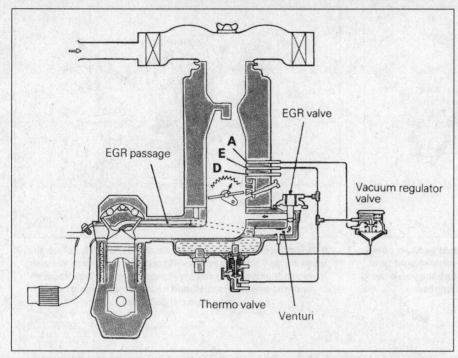

6.1 The Exhaust Gas Recirculation (EGR) system - 1988 and 1989 system shown

an EGR temperature sensor to signal the ECM if abnormal conditions are detected, and a control solenoid valve to port EGR vacuum to the throttle body.

Check

1986 and 1987 models

Refer to illustrations 6.13 and 6.16

EGR system

4   Check all EGR system vacuum hoses for proper routing and installation.
5   Start the engine when it's cold and run it at idle speed.

6   Verify that an increase in engine speed from idle to 2500 rpm doesn't cause the EGR valve to operate. If the EGR valve operates, replace the thermo valve.
7   Warm up the engine until coolant temperature reaches about 185 to 205-degrees F.
8   Verify that an increase in engine speed from idle to 2500 rpm causes the EGR valve to operate. It if doesn't operate, the problem may lie in the thermo valve or the EGR valve. Check them, as described below.

Thermo valve

9   Detach the green striped hose from the thermo valve.

10   Attach a vacuum pump to the thermo valve and apply vacuum. If vacuum does not hold, the thermo valve is defective. Replace it.
11   Detach the vacuum pump from the thermo valve and reattach the green striped hose to the thermo valve.

EGR valve

12   Detach the green striped hose from the vacuum fitting on the carburetor and attach a vacuum pump to the end of the hose.
13   While pulling the sub-EGR valve open by hand **(see illustration)**, apply 9.4 in-Hg vacuum with the hand pump.

  a) *If the idle speed becomes unstable, the EGR valve is operating properly.*
  b) *If the idle speed remains unchanged, the EGR valve is not operating. Replace it.*

14   Detach the vacuum pump and reattach the green striped hose to the carburetor.
15   Detach the yellow striped hose from the EGR valve.
16   Attach a vacuum pump to the EGR valve vacuum fitting from which you disconnected the yellow striped hose **(see illustration)**.
17   While pulling the sub-EGR valve open by hand **(see illustration 6.13)**, apply 6.6 in-Hg vacuum with the vacuum pump.

  a) *If the idle speed becomes unstable, the EGR valve is operating properly.*
  b) *If the idling speed remains unchanged, the valve is not operating. Replace the EGR valve.*

18   Detach the vacuum pump from the EGR valve and reattach the yellow striped hose to the EGR valve.

1988 through 1994 models

Refer to illustrations 6.20, 6.24 and 6.27

Note: *1995 and later models are not equipped with an EGR system.*

EGR valve

19   Remove the EGR valve and check it for sticking, carbon deposits or other damage.

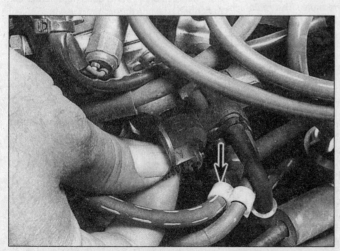

6.13 When checking the EGR valve on 1986 and 1987 models, you must pull the sub-EGR valve open by hand

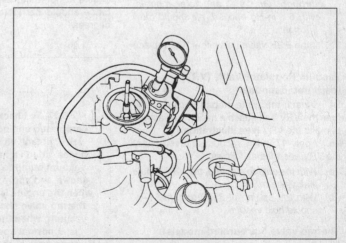

6.16 On 1986 and 1987 models, attach a hand-held vacuum pump to the EGR valve and apply vacuum - if the idle speed becomes unstable, the EGR valve is OK; if the idle speed remains unchanged, replace the EGR valve

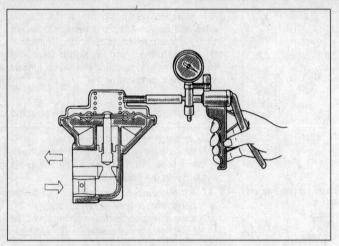

6.20 On 1988 and 1989 models, attach a hand-held vacuum pump to the EGR valve and apply vacuum - the EGR valve should hold vacuum; you should also be able to blow through the valve (as indicated by arrows) when vacuum is applied

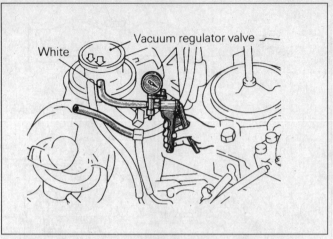

6.24 To check the Vacuum Regulator Valve (VRV), detach the white-striped hose from the VRV, attach a hand-held vacuum pump to it and apply vacuum - the VRV should leak vacuum with the engine stopped and should hold vacuum with the engine at 3500 rpm

If necessary, clean the valve with solvent to ensure tight valve seat contact.

20   Attach a hand-held vacuum pump to the vacuum fitting on the EGR valve **(see illustration)**.

21   On 1988 and 1989 models, apply a vacuum of 22 in-Hg and verify that the EGR valve holds vacuum. On 1990 and later FBC carbureted models, apply a vacuum of 19.8 in-Hg and verify that the EGR valve holds vacuum.

22   With vacuum applied, blow air into one passage of the EGR:

a) *On 1988 and 1989 models, with 2.6 in-Hg applied, air should not blow through. On 1990 and later models, with 2.4 in-Hg applied, air should not blow through.*

b) *On 1988 and 1989 models, with 7.28 in-Hg applied, air should not blow through. On 1990 and later models, with 6.8 in-Hg applied, air should blow through*

23   If the EGR valve fails either test, replace it.

Vacuum Regulator Valve (VRV) (carbureted models)

24   Detach the white-striped vacuum hose from the VRV and attach a hand-held vacuum pump to the VRV **(see illustration)**.

25   Apply 17 in-Hg vacuum and verify that the VRV operates as follows:

a) *With the engine stopped, the VRV should leak vacuum.*

b) *With the engine at 3500 rpm, the VRV should hold vacuum.*

Thermo valve (carbureted models)

26   Detach all vacuum hoses from the thermo valve. Be sure to note where each is attached so you can return it to its proper location.

27   Attach a hand-held vacuum pump to the indicated fitting **(see illustration)** and apply vacuum to verify that the thermo valve operates as follows:

a) *Below approximately 145-degrees F, the thermo valve should leak vacuum.*

b) *Above approximately 145-degrees F, the thermo valve should hold vacuum.*

EGR temperature sensor (California fuel-injected models)

28   Disconnect the sensor electrical connector at the EGR valve.

29   Using an ohmmeter, measure the resistance of the sensor across the two terminals of the connector.

30   The sensor resistance should be approximately 60 to 83 K-ohms at 122 degrees F. Check the sensor resistance again with the engine at operating temperature. The resistance should be 11 to 14 K-ohms at 212 degrees F.

31   If the sensor resistance values are incorrect, replace the sensor.

EGR control solenoid valve (California fuel-injected models)

32   Disconnect the green-striped vacuum hose from the solenoid valve and attach a hand-held vacuum pump the valve fitting.

33   Disconnect the electrical connector from the solenoid valve.

34   Using fused jumper wires, connect the solenoid valve terminals to the positive and negative battery terminals.

35   Apply vacuum to the valve, the valve should hold vacuum with battery voltage applied to the solenoid. Vacuum should be released when the battery is disconnected.

36   If the solenoid valve does not operate as described, replace the solenoid valve.

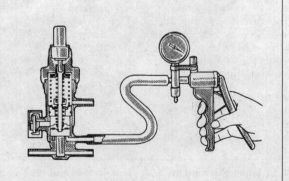

6.27 To check the carbureted engine thermo valve, detach all vacuum hoses, attach a hand-held vacuum pump to the port shown and apply vacuum- when the engine is cold, the thermo valve should leak vacuum; when the engine is at normal operating temperature, the valve should hold vacuum

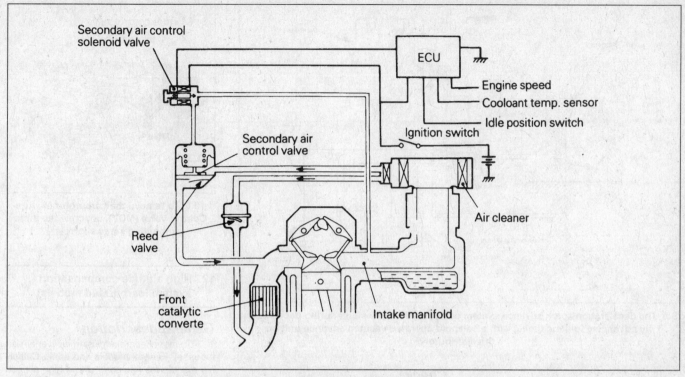

7.1 Secondary air supply system (1986 Federal system shown)

7 Secondary air supply system (carbureted models)

Refer to illustrations 7.1 and 7.3

General description

1   The secondary air supply system **(see illustration)** delivers air to the front catalytic converter through a reed valve to promote further oxidation of exhaust emissions during engine warm-up, deceleration and heavy engine loads. The reed valve is actuated by vacuum generated by exhaust pulsation.
2   The system is controlled by the secondary air control valve, a solenoid valve and the vehicle's Electronic Control Module (ECM).

Check

3   Remove the secondary air control valve **(see illustration)**.
4   Blow air into the fitting where the air cleaner hose was connected. Air shouldn't flow through the valve.
5   Attach a hand-held vacuum pump to the secondary air control valve fitting **(see illustration 7.3)**.
6   Apply a vacuum of 5.9 in-Hg and blow into the valve:
   a) *You should be able to blow air through the valve from the fitting where the air cleaner hose was attached.*
   b) *You should not be able to blow air through the threaded hole where the exhaust manifold tube was attached.*

7   If the secondary air control valve does not perform as described, replace it.

8 Catalytic converter

Note: *Because of a Federally mandated extended warranty which covers emissions-related components such as the catalytic converter, check with a dealer service department before replacing the converter at your own expense.*

General description

1   The catalytic converter is an emission control device added to the exhaust system to reduce pollutants from the exhaust gas stream. Early models are equipped with two catalytic converters; one at the exhaust manifold and one under the vehicle. Later models have only one converter, either integral with the exhaust manifold or in the exhaust system under the vehicle.

Check

2   The test equipment for a catalytic converter is expensive and highly sophisticated. If you suspect that the converter on your vehicle is malfunctioning, take it to a dealer service department or an authorized emissions inspection facility for diagnosis and repair. Trouble code readout (see Section 14) may indicate some converter problems.
3   Whenever the vehicle is raised for servicing of underbody components, check the converter for leaks, corrosion, dents and other

damage. Check the welds/flange bolts that attach the front and rear ends of the converter to the exhaust system. If damage is discovered, the converter should be replaced.

Replacement

4   Converter replacement requires removal of the exhaust manifold (see Chapter 2A) or a portion of the exhaust system (see Chapter 4).

7.3 To remove the secondary air control valve, detach the hose from the air cleaner (1) (already removed in photograph), unscrew the threaded fitting for the metal tube to the exhaust (2), remove the vacuum hose (3) and unscrew the mounting bolts (4) - when checking the valve, remove the vacuum hose (3)

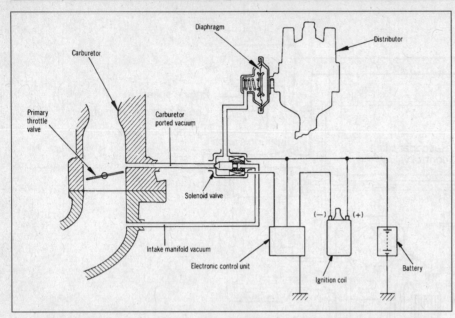

9.1   The deceleration spark advance system decreases HC emissions during deceleration by advancing ignition timing with a solenoid operated vacuum advance unit on the distributor

9   Deceleration devices (1986 and 1987 models)

Deceleration spark advance system

Refer to illustration 9.1

1   Ignition timing is advanced during deceleration by a vacuum advance unit on the distributor (**see illustration**). This unit normally has carburetor ported vacuum applied to it, but when the vehicle is decelerating, the Electronic Control Module (ECM) sends a signal to a solenoid valve which opens to apply the higher vacuum from the intake manifold. This advances the ignition timing, reducing HC emissions.

Dash pot

2   The carburetor is equipped with a dash pot which slows the rate at which the throttle valve closes to its normal idling position, thereby reducing HC emissions.
3   For further information on the dash pot, refer to Chapter 4.

10   Mixture Control Valve (MCV) (1988 and later carbureted models)

Refer to illustration 10.6

General description

1   When the throttle is closed suddenly during deceleration or shifting, the remaining fuel in the intake manifold causes a temporarily over-rich mixture. To prevent this, the mixture control valve (MCV) temporarily supplies air from another passage to correct the air-fuel ratio and reduce HC emissions.

Check

2   Remove the air cleaner (see Chapter 4).
3   Warm up the engine.
4   Open and close the throttle valve quickly and note the presence or absence of air suction noise.
   a) *Immediately after opening the throttle and closing it abruptly, the MCV should open and you should hear air suction noise (a hissing sound).*
   b) *After the engine returns to idle, the hissing sound should disappear.*

Replacement

5   Remove the carburetor (see Chapter 4).
6   Unscrew the three mounting screws (**see illustration**) and remove the MCV assembly.
7   Installation is the reverse of removal.

11   Idle-up system (carbureted models)

1   The Idle-up system consists of a dash pot assembly, a solenoid valve, a blower motor switch, a tail light switch and an oil pump pressure switch in the power steering system.
2   When the blower motor, tail light switch or oil pump switch is turned on during engine idle, the solenoid valve is opened, allowing vacuum from the intake manifold to act on the dash pot. This vacuum acting on the dash pot opens the throttle valve slightly via the idle-up lever on the throttle shaft. Thus, engine idle speed increases whenever power steering or electrical loads are high.
3   For further information on the idle-up system, see Chapter 4.

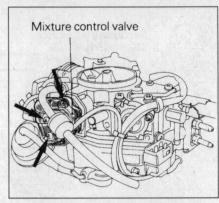

10.6   To remove the carburetor Mixture Control Valve (MCV), unscrew the three mounting screws (arrows)

12   High altitude compensation system (carbureted models)

General description

1   To meet Federal emission laws at all altitudes, all Federal models and some California models are equipped with a high altitude compensation system. This system consists of a high altitude compensator (HAC) valve, a vacuum switching valve (Federal models), a check valve and a distributor equipped with a high altitude vacuum advance device.
2   At high altitude, the system maintains the air-fuel mixture at its sea level ratio by supplying additional air into the carburetor. The system also supplies additional vacuum to the high altitude vacuum advance device on the distributor to compensate for high altitude.

Check

Refer to illustrations 12.3, 12.4 and 12.5

3   Remove the HAC valve (**see illustration**) and look for deformation and cracks.

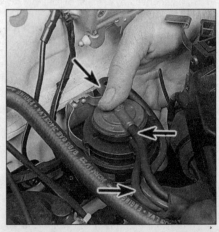

12.3   To remove the carburetor High Altitude Compensator (HAC) valve, detach the vacuum hoses (arrows) and unclip it from the bracket on the firewall

12.4 Remove the HAC air filter, clean it with compressed air, inspect it and, if necessary, replace it

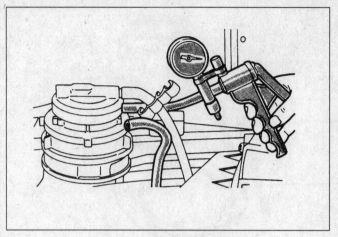

12.5 Checking the HAC valve

Replace the HAC valve if either of these conditions exists.

4   Clean the air filter in the HAC valve **(see illustration)** and reinstall the valve.

5   At altitudes below 3900 feet:

a) *Detach the vacuum hose from the HAC lower fitting and attach a hand-held vacuum pump to it **(see illustration)**.*

b) *Apply vacuum with the pump. The HAC valve should leak vacuum. If it doesn't, replace the valve. Reattach the vacuum hose to the lower fitting.*

c) *Detach the vacuum hose from the HAC valve upper fitting and attach a hand-held vacuum pump to it.*

d) *Apply vacuum. The HAC valve should hold vacuum. If it doesn't, replace the valve.*

6   At altitudes above 3900 feet:

a) *Detach either vacuum hose from the HAC valve and attach a hand-held vacuum pump to the fitting.*

b) *Apply vacuum. The HAC valve should hold vacuum. If it doesn't, replace the valve.*

13 Feedback carburetor (FBC) system

Refer to illustration 13.2

General description

1   The feedback carburetor (FBC) system consists of four components or groups of components:

a) *Information sensors*
b) *Electronic Control Module (ECM)*
c) *Output actuators*
d) *Feedback carburetor*

2   Two systems are used on the vehicles covered by this manual. The original system is installed on 1986 and 1987 models; the newer system is used on 1988 and later carbureted models. Although similar in operation, the two systems differ in the number and type of sensors and actuators used **(see illustration)**.

Information sensors

3   Both systems use information sensors to monitor various engine operating conditions and relay this data to the computer. They include:

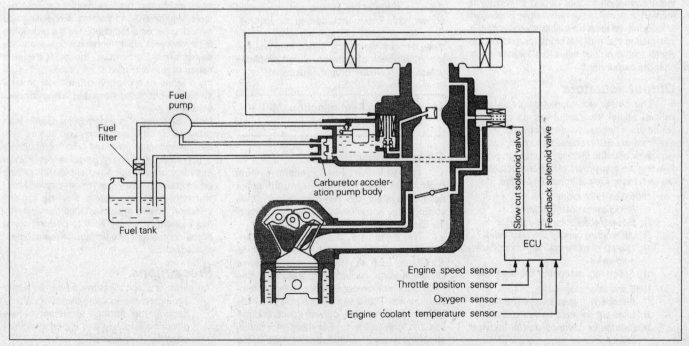

13.2 Typical feedback carburetor system

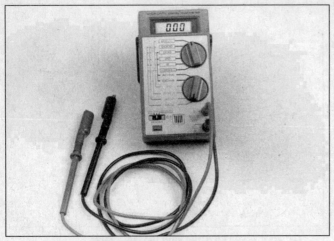

14.4 Digital multimeters can be used for testing all types of circuits; because of their high impedance, they are much more accurate than analog meters for measuring voltage in low-voltage circuits

14.5 Scanners like these from Actron and AutoXray are powerful diagnostic aids - they can tell you just about anything that you want to know about your engine management system

a) *Exhaust oxygen sensor*
b) *Coolant temperature sensor*
c) *Engine speed sensor*
d) *Throttle position sensor*
e) *Closed throttle (idle) switch*
f) *Intake air temperature sensor (not used on newer system)*

Electronic Control Module (ECM)

4   The ECM, which is located under the dash, just forward of the console, processes the constant information it receives from the above listed information sensors, compares this information to the values stored in its memory, calculates the new values necessary to maintain an ideal air-fuel ratio, converts this information into a digital signal and sends this signal to the output actuators located on or near the carburetor.

Output actuators

5   The output actuators (mainly solenoid valves) adjust the carburetor as operating conditions change. When energized by signals from the ECM, actuators turn on, turn off, reroute or alter the intensity of vacuum signals affecting the adjustment of devices installed on the carburetor. Output actuators include:

a) *1986 and 1987 models:*
   1) *Enrichment solenoid valve*
   2) *Deceleration solenoid valve*
   3) *Jet mixture control solenoid valve*
   4) *Idle-up (throttle opener) control solenoid valve*
   5) *Secondary air control solenoid valve*
b) *1988 and later models:*
   1) *Feedback solenoid valve (FBSV)*
   2) *Slow cut solenoid valve (SCSV)*
   3) *Distributor advance control solenoid valve*

4) *Distributor cold advance control solenoid valve*
5) *Throttle opener control solenoid valve*
6) *Air conditioner power relay*
7) *Mixture heater relay*

Feedback carburetor

6   Because of the complexity of the feedback carburetor system and because of the special electronic instrument needed to check and troubleshoot the entire system, servicing the system is beyond the scope of this manual.

7   Where possible, the procedures for checking some of the components described above have been included in Chapter 4. However, because of the interrelationship of these devices, we do not recommend that you tackle feedback carburetor related problems unless you have the proper equipment.

---

14   Multi-Port Fuel Injection (MFI) - self-diagnosis system

General information

1   The Multi-Port Fuel Injection system controls the fuel injection system, the spark advance system, the self-diagnosis system, cooling fans, and other systems by means of the Electronic Control Module (ECM).

2   The ECM receives signals from various sensors which monitor changing engine operations such as intake air volume, intake air temperature, coolant temperature, engine RPM, acceleration/deceleration, exhaust temperature etc. These signals are utilized by the ECM to determine the correct injection duration and ignition timing. For more information about the sensors and actuators used in the fuel injection system, refer to Chapter 4.

3   Before assuming the fuel and ignition systems are malfunctioning, first ensure that all the system wiring connectors are securely connected and free of corrosion. Ensure that the fault is not due to poor maintenance; check that the air cleaner filter element is clean, the spark plugs are in good condition and correctly gapped, the cylinder compression pressures are correct, the ignition timing is correct, and that the engine breather hoses are clear and undamaged, referring to Chapters 1, 2 and 5 for further information. The emission system and the fuel system are closely interrelated but can be checked separately. The diagnosis of some of the fuel and emission control devices requires specialized tools, equipment and training. If checking and servicing become too difficult or if a procedure is beyond your ability, consult a dealer service department. Remember, the most frequent cause of fuel and emissions problems is simply a loose or broken vacuum hose or wire, so always check the hose and wiring connections first.

Note: *Because of a federally mandated warranty which covers the emission control system components (and any other components which have a primary purpose other than emission control but have significant effects on emissions), check with your dealer about warranty coverage before working on any emission related systems. Once the warranty has expired, you may wish to perform some of the component checks and/or replacement procedures.*

Precautions

a) *Always disconnect the power by either turning off the ignition switch or disconnecting the battery terminals before disconnecting any fuel injection system electrical connectors.*

14.7 Simple code readers are an economical way to extract trouble codes when the CHECK ENGINE light comes on

14.9a On 1995 models and 2000 through 2005 models, the Data Link Connector (DLC) is located under the left side of the dash (1995 model shown)

b) *When installing a battery, be particularly careful to avoid reversing the positive and negative cables.*

c) *Do not subject fuel injection or emission related components or the ECM to severe impact during removal or installation.*

d) *Do not be careless during troubleshooting. Even slight terminal contact can invalidate a testing procedure and even damage one of the numerous transistor circuits.*

e) *Never attempt to work on the ECM or open the cover. The ECM is protected by an extended warranty that will be nullified if you tamper with it.*

f) *If you are inspecting electronic control system components during rainy weather, make sure water does not enter any part. When washing the engine compartment, do not spray these parts or their connectors with water.*

Diagnostic tool information

Refer to illustrations 14.4, 14.5 and 14.7

4   A digital multimeter is necessary for checking fuel injection and emission-related components **(see illustration)**. A digital volt-ohmmeter is preferred over the older style analog multimeter for several reasons. An analog multimeter cannot display the measured values precisely enough. When working with electronic circuits which are often very low voltage, this accurate reading is most important. Another reason for the digital multimeter is the high-impedance circuitry. Most digital multimeters are equipped with a high resistance internal circuitry (10 million ohms). Because a voltmeter is hooked up in parallel with the circuit when testing, it is vital that none of the voltage being measured should be allowed to travel the parallel path set up by

the meter itself. This dilemma does not show itself when measuring greater voltages (9 to 12 volt circuits) but if you are measuring a low voltage circuit such as the oxygen sensor signal voltage, a fraction of a volt may be a significant amount when diagnosing a problem. Obtaining the diagnostic trouble codes is one exception where using an analog voltmeter is necessary.

5   Hand-held scanners are the most powerful and versatile tools for analyzing engine management systems used on later model vehicles **(see illustration)**.

6   Before purchasing a scan tool, make sure it's compatible with your vehicle. Prior to 1996, vehicle manufacturers had different ways to access the self-diagnostic system. Beginning with the 1996 model year, any generic OBD-II scan tool should work with any OBD-II vehicle.

7   Another type of code reader, which is far less expensive, is available at most auto parts stores **(see illustration)**. These tools simplify the procedure for extracting codes from the engine management computer by simply plugging into the diagnostic connector.

Self-diagnosis system

Refer to illustrations 14.9a, 14.9b, 14.10a and 14.10b

8   The self-diagnosis trouble code system is useful to diagnose malfunctions in major sensors and actuators of the engine control system. A diagnostic connector called a Data Link Connector is incorporated in the engine management circuit, located in the fuse box on 1994 and earlier models and at the lower left dash area on 1995 and later models. A CHECK ENGINE Light, located on the instrument panel **(see Chapter 4, illustration 15.2)**, illuminates if a failure is detected. The Data Link Connector (diagnostic connector)

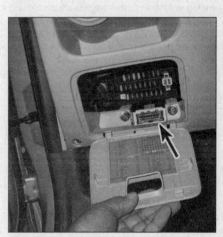

14.9b On 1996 through 1999 models and 2006 and later models, the Data Link Connector (DLC) is located inside the receptacle at the left end of the dash. On 2006 and later models, this receptacle also houses the interior fuses (2008 model shown)

can be accessed to locate the circuit or system which is experiencing the fault, alleviating the need to test all the system components individually, which is a time-consuming operation that also carries a risk of damaging the ECM.

9   Locate the Data Link Connector (DLC). On 1995 models, the DLC is located under the left end of the dash **(see illustration)**. On 1996 through 1999 models, it's located inside the storage receptacle at the left end of the dash. On 2000 through 2005 models, it's located under the dash, just to the left of the steering column. On 2006 and later models, it's located inside the fuse box receptacle at the left end of the dash **(see illustration)**.

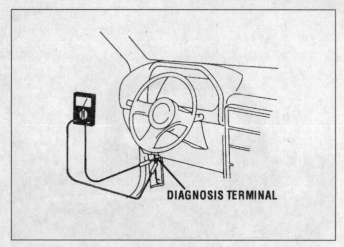

14.10a An analog voltmeter is connected to the self-diagnosis terminal to read trouble codes - 1986 through 1994 models

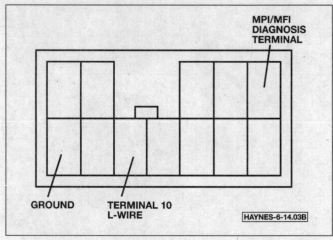

14.10b Data Link Connector terminals for trouble code readout

10   On 1994 and earlier models, connect an analog voltmeter to the diagnosis terminal and the ground terminal **(see illustrations)**. Turn the ignition key ON (do not start the engine) - the pulse groups give a two-digit trouble code after three seconds delay time. Watch the needle on the voltmeter carefully. The needle will move up and back to zero. The first pattern is always extended (slow), indicating the first digit of the code. After the extended deflection(s) will come fast deflection(s) indicating the second digit of the code. The voltmeter will continue to deflect (pulse) signals until the entire code has been released by the ECM. For example, if there is a problem with the vehicle speed sensor, the meter will indicate two slow deflections followed by four fast deflections, or Code 24. Refer to the code chart for a complete list of diagnostic codes.

11   On 1995 models, turn the ignition key ON

(do not start the engine) and using a jumper wire, connect terminal 10 **(see illustration 14.10b)** to ground for 2.5 to 7 seconds; then remove the jumper wire - the pulse groups give a four-digit trouble code. If no fault is stored in the ECM, the code 4444 will display. The trouble code repeats continuously until you check for additional trouble codes as follows: To check for additional trouble codes, reconnect the jumper wire for 2.5 to 7 seconds, then remove the jumper wire and check the next code. The last output will be code 3333, indicating that you are finished with the diagnostic test mode.

12   On 1996 and later models, a scan tool is required to read the trouble codes. Connect the scan tool to the data link connector and follow the tool manufacturers instructions to obtain the trouble codes.

13   If any faults are detected, record the

trouble code. After the tests have been performed and the repairs completed, erase the memory by disconnecting the negative battery cable for 15 seconds or more.

14   Because of the complexity of the Multi-Port Fuel Injection system and because of the special electronic instrument needed to check and troubleshoot the entire system, servicing the system is beyond the scope of this manual. Where possible, the procedures for checking some of the components described above have been included in Chapter 4. However, because of the inter-relationship of these devices, we do not recommend that you tackle MFI system related problems unless you have the proper equipment. If these checks fail to reveal the cause of the problem, the vehicle should be taken to a dealer service department or other repair shop for testing.

SELF-DIAGNOSIS SYSTEM TROUBLE CODES - 1986 through 1994 models

Code	Circuit or system
9	Normal - system functioning properly
11	Oxygen sensor (front)
12	Air flow sensor
13	Air temperature sensor
14	Throttle position sensor
15	Motor position sensor
21	Engine coolant temperature

Code	Circuit or system
22	Crankshaft position sensor
23	Camshaft (TDC) position sensor
24	Vehicle speed sensor
25	Barometric pressure sensor
41	Fuel injector
42	Fuel pump
43	EGR system
59	Oxygen sensor (rear)

SELF DIAGNOSIS SYSTEM TROUBLE CODES - 1995 models

Code	Circuit or system
2222	Start diagnosis
3333	End diagnosis
4444	No fault
1233, 1234, 1169, 4133, 3241, 3242, 3243	ECM failure
3153	Throttle position sensor
3128	Oxygen sensor
3146	Intake air temperature sensor
3145	Engine coolant temperature sensor
3137	Battery/alternator
3232	Crankshaft position sensor
3222	Camshaft position sensor
3112	No. 1 cylinder injector failure
3234	No. 2 cylinder injector failure
3116	No. 3 cylinder injector failure
3235	No. 4 cylinder injector failure
4151, 4152, 4153	Air/fuel ratio lean or rich
3159	Vehicle speed sensor
3135	EVAP canister purge solenoid valve

SELF DIAGNOSIS SYSTEM TROUBLE CODES - 1995 models (continued)

Code	Circuit or system
3211	Knock sensor (SOHC)
3117	Mass airflow sensor
3149	Air conditioning switch or relay
3114, 3112	Idle speed control

SELF DIAGNOSIS SYSTEM TROUBLE CODES - 1996 and later models

Code	Circuit or system
P0011	A Camshaft Position (CMP) sensor, timing too advanced or system performance
P0012	A Camshaft Postion (CMP) sensor, timing too retarded
P0016	Crankshaft Position (CKP) sensor, camshaft position correlation
P0030	Oxygen sensor heater control circuit malfunction (bank 1, sensor 1)
P0031	Oxygen sensor heater circuit, low voltage (bank 1, sensor 1)
P0032	Oxygen sensor heater circuit, high voltage (bank 1, sensor 1)
P0036	Oxygen sensor heater control circuit malfunction (bank 1, sensor 2)
P0037	Oxygen sensor heater circuit, low voltage (bank 1, sensor 2)
P0038	Oxygen sensor heater circuit, high voltage (bank 1, sensor 2)
P0068	Manifold Absolute Pressure (MAP) or Mass Air Flow (MAF) sensor, throttle position correlation
P0075	Intake valve control solenoid circuit
P0076	Intake valve control solenoid circuit, low
P0077	Intake valve control solenoid circuit, high
P0100	Mass Air Flow (MAF) sensor circuit
P0101	Mass Air Flow (MAF) sensor circuit, range or performance problem
P0102	Mass Air Flow (MAF) sensor circuit, low input
P0103	Mass Air Flow (MAF) sensor circuit, high input
P0106	Manifold Absolute Pressure (MAP) sensor or BARO sensor, abnormal pressure
P0107	Manifold Absolute Pressure (MAP) sensor circuit, low input
P0108	Manifold Absolute Pressure (MAP) sensor circuit, range too high
P0111	Intake Air Temperature (IAT) sensor circuit, range or performance problem

Code	Circuit or system
P0112	Intake Air Temperature (IAT) sensor circuit, low input
P0113	Intake Air Tempertature (IAT) sensor circuit, high input
P0115	Engine Coolant Temperature (ECT) sensor circuit
P0116	Engine Coolant Temperature (ECT) sensor circuit, range or performance problem
P0117	Engine Coolant Temperature (ECT) sensor circuit, low input
P0118	Engine Coolant Temperature (ECT) sensor circuit, high input
P0121	Throttle Position Sensor (TPS) or Accelerator Pedal Position (APP) sensor circuit, voltage doesn't agree with MAF voltage
P0121	Throttle Position Sensor (TPS) or Accelerator Pedal Position (APP) sensor circuit, range or performance problem
P0122	Throttle Position Sensor (TPS) or Accelerator Pedal Position (APP) sensor circuit, low input
P0123	Throttle Position Sensor (TPS) or Accelerator Pedal Position (APP) sensor circuit, high input
P0124	Throttle Position Sensor (TPS) or Accelerator Pedal Position (APP) sensor circuit, intermittent
P0125	Insufficient coolant temperature for closed loop fuel control
P0128	Coolant thermostat (coolant temperature below thermostat regulating temperature)
P0130	Oxygen sensor circuit malfunction (sensor 1)
P0131	Oxygen sensor circuit, low voltage (sensor 1)
P0132	Oxygen sensor circuit, high voltage (sensor 1)
P0133	Oxygen sensor circuit, slow response (sensor 1)
P0134	Oxygen sensor circuit, no activity detected (sensor 1)
P0135	Oxygen sensor heater circuit malfunction (sensor 1)
P0136	Oxygen sensor circuit malfunction (sensor 2)
P0137	Oxygen sensor circuit, low voltage (sensor 2)
P0138	Oxygen sensor circuit, high voltage (sensor 2)
P0139	Oxygen sensor circuit, slow response (sensor 2)
P0140	Oxygen sensor circuit, no activity detected (sensor 2)
P0141	Oxygen sensor heater circuit malfunction (sensor 2)
P0171	System too lean
P0172	System too rich
P0201	Cylinder 1, injector malfunction
P0202	Cylinder 2, injector malfunction

SELF DIAGNOSIS SYSTEM TROUBLE CODES - 1996 and later models (continued)

Code	Circuit or system
P0203	Cylinder 3, injector malfunction
P0204	Cylinder 4, injector malfunction
P0230	Fuel pump relay or fuel pump relay circuit, malfunction
P0231	Fuel pump secondary circuit, low
P0232	Fuel pump secondary circuit, high
P0261	Injector circuit, cylinder 1, low input
P0262	Injector circuit, cylinder 1, high input
P0264	Injector circuit, cylinder 2, low input
P0265	Injector circuit, cylinder 2, high input
P0267	Injector circuit, cylinder 3, low input
P0268	Injector circuit, cylinder 3, high input
P0270	Injector circuit, cylinder 4, low input
P0271	Injector circuit, cylinder 4, high input
P0300	Random misfire detected
P0301	Misfire detected in cylinder 1
P0302	Misfire detected in cylinder 2
P0303	Misfire detected in cylinder 3
P0304	Misfire detected in cylinder 4
P0325	Knock sensor circuit malfunction
P0326	Knock sensor 1 circuit, range or performance problem
P0327	Knock sensor 1 circuit, low input
P0328	Knock sensor 1 circuit, high input
P0335	Crankshaft Position (CKP) sensor A circuit, no signal or circuit malfunction
P0336	Crankshaft Position (CKP) sensor A circuit, range or performance problem
P0337	Crankshaft Position (CKP) sensor A circuit, low input
P0338	Crankshaft Position (CKP) sensor A circuit, high input
P0339	Crankshaft Position (CKP) sensor A circuit
P0340	Camshaft Position (CMP) sensor A circuit malfunction (single sensor)
P0341	Camshaft Position (CMP) sensor A circuit, range or performance problem (single sensor)

Code	Circuit or system
P0342	Camshaft Position (CMP) sensor A circuit, low input
P0343	Camshaft Position (CMP) sensor A circuit, high input
P0420	Catalyst system efficiency below threshold
P0421	Warm-up catalyst efficiency below threshold
P0441	Evaporative emissions (EVAP) system, incorrect purge flow
P0442	Evaporative emissions (EVAP) system, small leak detected
P0443	Evaporative emissions (EVAP) system, purge control valve circuit malfunction
P0444	Evaporative emissions (EVAP) system, purge control valve circuit open
P0445	Evaporative emissions (EVAP) system, purge control valve circuit shorted
P0446	Evaporative emissions (EVAP) system, canister close valve permanently closed or vent control circuit
P0447	Evaporative emissions (EVAP) system, ventilation control valve circuit shorted to ground
P0448	Evaporative emissions (EVAP) system, ventilation control valve circuit shorted to battery voltage
P0449	Evaporative emissions (EVAP) system, vent valve or solenoid circuit
P0450	Evaporative emissions (EVAP) system, pressure sensor or switch
P0451	Evaporative emissions (EVAP) system, fuel tank pressure sensor, signal not plausible
P0452	Evaporative emissions (EVAP) system, fuel tank pressure sensor, signal low
P0453	Evaporative emissions (EVAP) control system, fuel tank pressure sensor, signal high
P0455	Evaporative emissions (EVAP) system, incorrect purge flow
P0456	Evaporative emissions (EVAP) system, very small leak detected
P0457	Evaporative emissions (EVAP) system, leak detected (fuel tank filler cap loose or off)
P0458	Evaporative emissions (EVAP) system, purge control valve circuit high
P0459	Evaporative emissions (EVAP) system, purge control valve circuit low
P0461	Fuel level sensor A circuit, range or performance problem
P0462	Fuel level sensor A circuit, low input
P0463	Fuel level sensor A circuit, high input
P0496	Evaporative emissions (EVAP) system, high purge flow
P0497	Evaporative emissions (EVAP) system, low purge flow
P0498	Evaporative emissions (EVAP) system, vent valve control circuit low
P0499	Evaporative emissions (EVAP) system, vent valve control circuit high
P0501	Vehicle Speed Sensor (VSS) circuit, range or performance problem

SELF DIAGNOSIS SYSTEM TROUBLE CODES - 1996 and later models (continued)

Code	Circuit or system
P0502	Vehicle Speed Sensor (VSS) circuit, low input
P0503	Vehicle Speed Sensor (VSS) circuit, erratic, intermittent or high input
P0505	Idle air control system
P0506	Idle air control system, idle rpm lower than expected
P0507	Idle air control system, idle rpm higher than expected
P0532	Air conditioning refrigerant pressure sensor A circuit, low input
P0533	Air conditioning refrigerant pressure sensor A circuit, high input
P0560	System voltage
P0561	System voltage unstable
P0562	System voltage too low
P0563	System voltage too high
P0605	Powertrain Control Module (PCM), Read Only Memory (ROM) error or PCM failure
P0624	Fuel cap warning light control circuit
P0630	Vehicle Identification Number (VIN) not programmed into PCM, or incompatible
P0642	Sensor reference voltage A circuit, low
P0643	Sensor reference voltage A circuit, high
P0645	Air conditioning clutch relay control circuit
P0646	Air conditioning clutch relay control circuit, low
P0647	Air conditioning clutch relay control circuit, high
P0650	Malfunction Indicator Light (MIL) control circuit
P0700	Transmission Control Module (TCM) Malfunction Indicator Light (MIL) request
P0707	No input signal
P0708	Transaxle Range (TR) switch, more than two input signals
P0711	Fluid temperature sensor, rationality check
P0712	Fluid temperature sensor, open circuit
P0713	Fluid temperature sensor, short circuit
P0716	Input speed sensor malfunction
P0717	Pulse generator A, open circuit; or input speed sensor, open or short circuit
P0722	Pulse generator B, open circuit; or output speed sensor, open or short circuit

Code	Circuit or system
P0727	lignition pulse pickup cable, open circuit
P0731	Shifting to first geat does not match engine speed
P0732	Shifting to second gear does not match engine speed
P0733	Shifting to third gear does not match engine speed
P0734	Shifting to fourth gear does not match engine speed
P0740	Defect in damper clutch system
P0741	Torque Converter Clutch (TCC) stuck in OFF position
P0742	Torque Converter Clutch (TCC) control solenoid valve, short circuit; or damper clutch stuck in ON position
P0743	Torque Converter Clutch (TCC) control solenoid valve, open circuit
P0745	Pressure control solenoid valve A, open or short circuit
P0747	Pressure control solenoid valve, open circuit
P0748	Pressure control solenoid valve circuit, short circuit
P0750	Shift control solenoid valve A, open or short circuit
P0752	Shift control solenoid valve A, open circuit
P0753	Shift control solenoid valve, short circuit
P0755	Shift control solenoid valve B, open or short circuit
P0757	Shift control solenoid valve B, open circuit
P0758	Shift control solenoid valve B, short circuit
P0760	Shift control solenoid valve C, open or short circuit
P0765	Pressure control solenoid valve, short circuit
P0775	Pressure control solenoid valve B, open or short circuit

Notes

Chapter 7 Part A
Manual transaxle

Contents

Specifications

Torque specifications
Ft-lbs (unless otherwise indicated)

Note: *One foot-pound (ft-lb) of torque is equivalent to 12 inch-pounds (in-lbs) of torque. Torque values below approximately 15 ft-lbs are expressed in inch-pounds, since most foot-pound torque wrenches are not accurate at these smaller values.*

Bellhousing cover	72 in-lbs
Drain and filler plugs	See Chapter 1
Shift rod set screw	24
Starter motor bolt	21
Transaxle-to-engine bolts	
8 x 14 mm	84 to 108 in-lbs
8 x 20 mm	132 to 192 in-lbs
8 x 60 mm	22 to 25
10 x 40 mm	31 to 40
10 x 55 mm	16 to 23
10 x 65 mm	31 to 40
Transaxle mounting bracket-to-transaxle bolts	52
Transaxle mounting bracket-to-body bolts	72

1 General information

The vehicles covered by this manual are equipped with either a four or five speed manual transaxle or a three speed automatic transaxle. Information on the manual transaxle is included in this Part of Chapter 7. Service procedures for the automatic transaxle are contained in Chapter 7, Part B.

The manual transaxle is a compact, two piece, lightweight aluminum alloy housing containing both the transmission and differential assemblies.

Because of the complexity, unavailability of replacement parts and special tools required, internal repair of the manual transaxle by the home mechanic is not recommended. For readers who wish to tackle a transaxle rebuild, exploded views and a brief *Manual transaxle overhaul - general information* section are provided. The bulk of information in this Chapter is devoted to removal and installation procedures.

2 Manual transaxle shift assembly - removal and installation

1989 and earlier models
Refer to illustrations 2.5a and 2.5b
1 Remove the shift knob (if required) and center console.
2 On models so equipped, remove the rear heat floor duct.
3 On early models, remove the shift

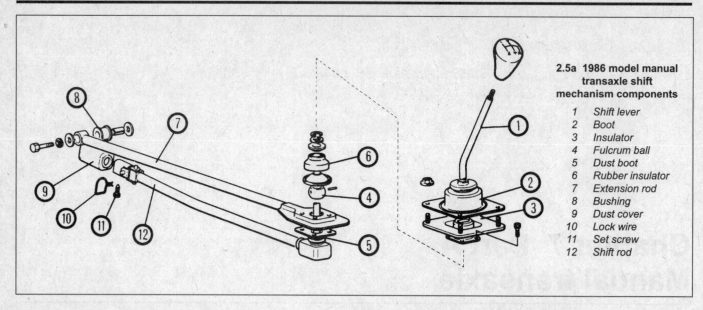

2.5a 1986 model manual transaxle shift mechanism components

1   Shift lever
2   Boot
3   Insulator
4   Fulcrum ball
5   Dust boot
6   Rubber insulator
7   Extension rod
8   Bushing
9   Dust cover
10 Lock wire
11 Set screw
12 Shift rod

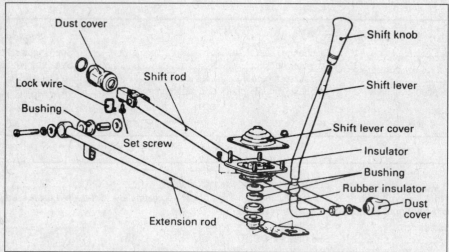

2.5b 1987 through 1989 model manual transaxle shift mechanism components

assembly bracket nuts.

4   Raise the vehicle and support it securely on jackstands.

5   Disconnect the extension rod from the transaxle (see illustrations).

6   Remove the lock wire from the shift rod set screw. Loosen (early models) or remove (later models) the set screw and detach the shift rod from the transaxle.

7   On early models, remove the heat shield from the body for clearance when removing the shift assembly.

8   Remove the extension rod and shift lever assembly by lowering it from the vehicle.

9   Installation is the reverse of removal.

1990 and later models
Refer to illustrations 2.11, 2.17a and 2.17b

10   Remove the center console (see Chapter 11).

11   Remove the pins securing the shift cables to the shift lever assembly (see illustration).

12   Unbolt the shift lever assembly and remove it.

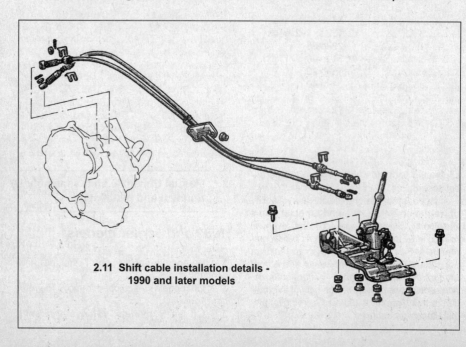

2.11 Shift cable installation details - 1990 and later models

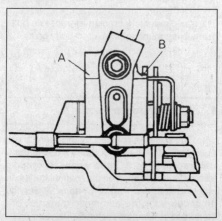

2.17a Dimensions A and B on both sides of the shift lever must be equal

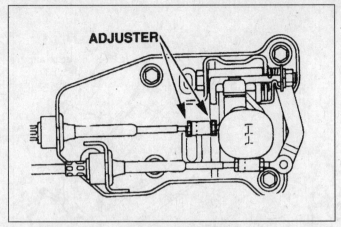

2.17b Adjust the cable length by turning the adjuster nuts

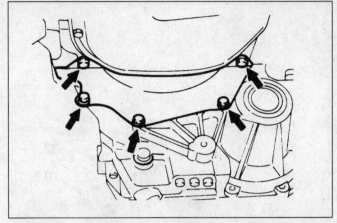

3.12 Remove the bolts (arrows) and detach the bellhousing cover for access to the lower transaxle-to-engine bolts

13   Unbolt the retainer from the bulkhead.

14   Raise the vehicle and support it securely on jackstands.

15   Remove the pins securing the shift cables to the transaxle assembly.

16   Remove the shift cable assembly.

17   Installation is the reverse of removal. Make sure the shifter operates freely and selects all gears. If not, the cable lengths can be adjusted at the shift lever ends **(see illustrations)**.

3   Manual transaxle - removal and installation

Removal

Refer to illustration 3.12

1   Disconnect the cable from the negative terminal of the battery.

2   Raise the vehicle and support it securely on jackstands.

3   Drain the transaxle lubricant (see Chapter 1).

4   On 1995 and later models, remove the air cleaner assembly from the engine.

5   On 1995 and later models, remove the windshield wiper motor mounting bolts, and move the wiper motor upwards, but do not remove the wiper motor.

6   On 1994 and earlier models, disconnect the shift and clutch linkage from the transaxle. On 1995 and later models, remove the shift select cable and shift cable, and remove the clutch release cylinder and connecting tubing from the transaxle.

7   Detach the speedometer cable and wire harness connectors from the transaxle.

8   Remove the exhaust system components as necessary for clearance.

9   Support the engine from above with an engine hoist or an engine support fixture. The engine must remain supported at all times while the transaxle is out of the vehicle!

10   Disconnect the driveaxles from the transaxle (see Chapter 8).

11   Remove the starter motor.

12   Support the transaxle with a jack, then remove the bolts securing the transaxle to the engine. You'll have to remove the bellhousing cover to gain access to the lower transaxle-to-engine bolts **(see illustration)**.

13   Remove the transaxle mount nuts and bolts. Unbolt and remove the transaxle mount bracket. On 1995 and later models, remove the engine support center member and front and rear motor mount roll stoppers (see Chapter 2).

14   Make a final check that all wires and hoses have been disconnected from the transaxle. Then carefully pull the transaxle and jack away from the engine.

15   Once the input shaft is clear, lower the transaxle and remove it from under the vehicle.

16   With the transaxle removed, the clutch components are now accessible and can be inspected. In most cases, new clutch components should be routinely installed when the transaxle is removed.

Installation

17   If removed, install the clutch components (see Chapter 8).

18   With the transaxle secured to the jack with a chain, raise it into position behind the engine, then carefully slide it forward, engaging the input shaft with the clutch disc splines. Do not use excessive force to install the transaxle - if the input shaft does not slide into place, readjust the angle of the transaxle so it is level and/or turn the input shaft so the splines engage properly with the clutch plate hub.

19   Install the transaxle-to-engine bolts. Tighten the bolts securely.

20   Install the transaxle mount bracket and the mount nuts or bolts.

21   Install the chassis and suspension components which were removed. Tighten all nuts and bolts to the torque listed in the Chapter 10 Specifications.

22   Remove the jack supporting the transaxle

and the engine hoist or support fixture.

23   Install the various items removed previously, referring to Chapter 8 for installation of the driveaxles.

24   Make a final check that all wires, hoses, linkages and the speedometer cable have been connected and that the transaxle has been filled with lubricant to the proper level (see Chapter 1). On 1995 and later models, fill and bleed the clutch hydraulic system and check clutch operation.

25   Connect the cable to the negative terminal of the battery. Road test the vehicle for proper operation and check for leaks.

4   Manual transaxle overhaul - general information

Refer to illustrations 4.4a and 4.4b

Overhauling a manual transaxle is a difficult job for the do-it-yourselfer. It involves the disassembly and reassembly of many small parts. Numerous clearances must be precisely measured and, if necessary, changed with select fit spacers and snap-rings. As a result, if transaxle problems arise, it can be removed and installed by a competent do-it-yourselfer, but overhaul should be left to a transmission repair shop. Rebuilt transaxles may be available - check with your dealer parts department and auto parts stores. At any rate, the time and money involved in an overhaul is almost sure to exceed the cost of a rebuilt unit.

Nevertheless, it's not impossible for an inexperienced mechanic to rebuild a transaxle if the special tools are available and the job is done in a deliberate step-by-step manner so nothing is overlooked.

The tools necessary for an overhaul include internal and external snap-ring pliers, a bearing puller, a slide hammer, a set of pin punches, a dial indicator and possibly a hydraulic press. In addition, a large, sturdy workbench and a vise or transaxle stand will be required.

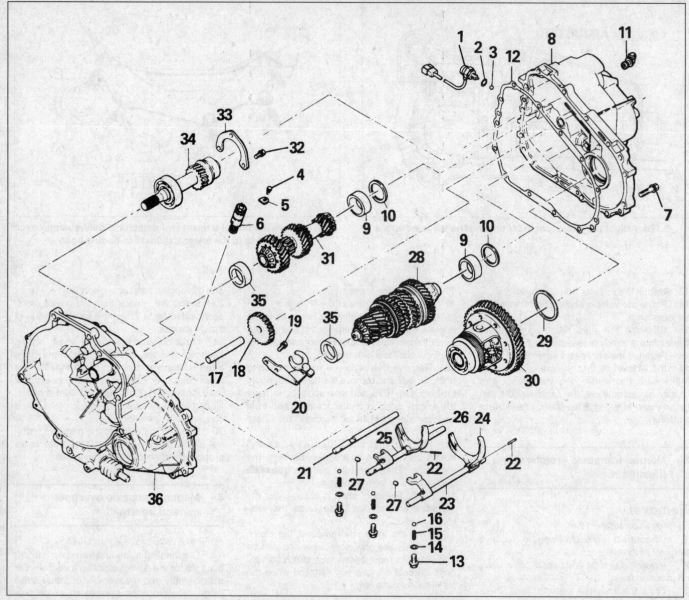

4.4a Typical four-speed transaxle components

1	Back-up light switch	13	Poppet plugs	25	3rd/4th shift rail
2	Gasket	14	Gasket	26	3rd/4th shift fork
3	Steel ball	15	Poppet springs	27	Interlock plungers
4	Bolt	16	Poppet balls	28	Output shaft assembly
5	Locking plate	17	Reverse idler gear shaft	29	Spacer
6	Speedometer gear assembly	18	Reverse idler gear	30	Differential assembly
7	Bolt	19	Bolts	31	Intermediate gear assembly
8	Transaxle case	20	Reverse shift lever assembly	32	Bolts
9	Outer bearing race	21	Reverse shift rail	33	Bearing retainer
10	Spacers	22	Spring pins	34	Input shaft assembly
11	Breather	23	1st/2nd shift rail	35	Bearing outer race
12	Gasket	24	1st/2nd shift fork	36	Clutch housing

During disassembly of the transaxle, make careful notes of how each piece comes off, where it fits in relation to other pieces and what holds it in place (**see illustrations**).

Before taking the transaxle apart for repair, it will help if you have some idea what area of the transaxle is malfunctioning. Certain problems can be closely tied to specific areas in the transaxle, which can make component examination and replacement easier.

Refer to the *Troubleshooting* section at the front of this manual for information regarding possible sources of trouble.

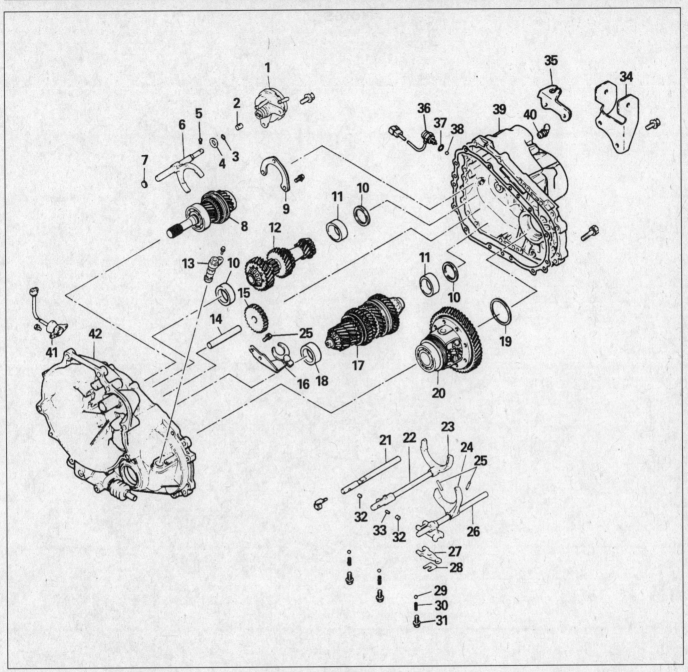

4.4b Typical five-speed transaxle components

1	5th gear actuator	15	Reverse idler gear	29	Poppet ball
2	Collar	16	Reverse shift gear	30	Poppet spring
3	O-ring	17	Output shaft assembly	31	Plug
4	Seat	18	Outer bearing race	32	Interlock plunger
5	Locking plate	19	Spacer	33	Interlock plunger
6	Select rail fork assembly	20	Differential assembly	34	Transaxle bracket
7	Seat	21	Reverse shift rail	35	Clutch cable bracket
8	Input shaft assembly	22	1st/2nd shift rail	36	Back-up light switch
9	Bearing retainer	23	1st/2nd shift fork	37	Gasket
10	Spacer	24	3rd/4th shift fork	38	Steel ball
11	Bearing outer race	25	Spring pin	39	Transaxle case
12	Intermediate gear assembly	26	3rd/4th shift rail	40	Breather
13	Speedometer gear assembly	27	5th gear lug	41	5th gear actuator switch
14	Reverse idler gear shaft	28	Selector spacer	42	Clutch housing

Notes

Chapter 7 Part B
Automatic transaxle

Contents

Specifications

Shift lever assembly adjusting sleeve-to-lever end clearance
    1989 and earlier .... 0.677 to 0.705 inch
    1990 and later .... 0.598 to 0.625 inch
Throttle valve (TV) cable clearance (1989 and earlier) .... 0.02 to 0.06 inch

Torque specifications

Ft-lbs (unless otherwise indicated)

Note: *One foot-pound (ft-lb) of torque is equivalent to 12 inch-pounds (in-lbs) of torque. Torque values below approximately 15 ft-lbs are expressed in inch-pounds, since most foot-pound torque wrenches are not accurate at these smaller values.*

Torque converter-to-driveplate bolts
    1989 and earlier 27
    1990 through 1994 55
    1995 and later 37
Torque converter cover bolts
    8 mm x 14 .... 84 to 108 in-lbs
    8 mm x 20 .... 11 to 16
Drain plug .... See Chapter 1
Throttle valve lower cable bracket bolt .... 120 in-lbs
Fluid pan bolts .... 96 in-lbs
Starter motor bolts 21

1   General information

All vehicles covered in this manual come equipped with either a four or five speed manual transaxle or an automatic transaxle. 1989 and earlier automatic transaxle models are equipped with a three-speed automatic transaxle. 1990 and later automatic transaxle models are equipped with an electrically controlled four-speed automatic transaxle. All information on the automatic transaxle is included in this Part of Chapter 7. Information for the manual transaxle can be found in Part A of this Chapter.

Due to the complexity of the automatic transaxle and the need for specialized equipment to perform most service operations, this Chapter contains only general diagnosis, routine maintenance, adjustment and removal and installation procedures.

If the transaxle requires major repair work, it should be left to a dealer service department or an automotive or transmission repair shop. You can, however, remove and install the transaxle yourself and save the expense, even if the repair work is done by a transmission shop.

2   Diagnosis - general

Note: *Automatic transaxle malfunctions may be caused by four general conditions: poor engine performance, improper adjustments, hydraulic malfunctions or mechanical malfunctions. Diagnosis of these problems should always begin with a check of the easily repaired items: fluid level and condition (see Chapter 1), shift linkage adjustment and throttle·linkage adjustment. Next, perform a road test to determine if the problem has been corrected or if more diagnosis is necessary. If the problem persists after the preliminary tests and corrections are completed, additional diagnosis should be done by a dealer service department or transmission repair shop. Refer to the Troubleshooting section at the front of this manual for transaxle problem diagnosis.*

Preliminary checks

1   Drive the vehicle to warm the transaxle to normal operating temperature.
2   Check the fluid level as described in Chapter 1:
   a) *If the fluid level is unusually low, add enough fluid to bring the level within the designated area of the dipstick, then check for external leaks.*
   b) *If the fluid level is abnormally high, drain off the excess, then check the drained fluid for contamination by coolant. The presence of engine coolant in the automatic transmission fluid indicates that a failure has occurred in the internal radiator walls that separate the coolant from the transmission fluid (see Chapter 3).*
   c) *If the fluid is foaming, drain it and refill the transaxle, then check for coolant in the fluid or a high fluid level.*
3   Check the engine idle speed. **Note:** *If the engine is malfunctioning, do not proceed with the preliminary checks until it has been repaired and runs normally.*
4   Check the throttle valve cable for freedom of movement. Adjust it if necessary (see Section 6). **Note:** *The throttle valve cable may function properly when the engine is shut off and cold, but it may malfunction once the engine is hot. Check it cold and at normal engine operating temperature.*
5   Inspect the shift control cable (see Section 5). Make sure that it's properly adjusted and that the linkage operates smoothly.

Fluid leak diagnosis

6   Most fluid leaks are easy to locate visually. Repair usually consists of replacing a seal or gasket. If a leak is difficult to find, the following procedure may help.
7   Identify the fluid. Make sure it's transmission fluid and not engine oil or brake fluid (automatic transmission fluid is a deep red color).
8   Try to pinpoint the source of the leak. Drive the vehicle several miles, then park it over a large sheet of cardboard. After a minute or two, you should be able to locate the leak by determining the source of the fluid dripping onto the cardboard.
9   Make a careful visual inspection of the suspected component and the area immediately around it. Pay particular attention to gasket mating surfaces. A mirror is often helpful for finding leaks in areas that are hard to see.
10   If the leak still cannot be found, clean the suspected area thoroughly with a degreaser or solvent, then dry it.
11   Drive the vehicle for several miles at normal operating temperature and varying speeds. After driving the vehicle, visually inspect the suspected component again.
12   Once the leak has been located, the cause must be determined before it can be properly repaired. If a gasket is replaced but the sealing flange is bent, the new gasket will not stop the leak. The bent flange must be straightened.
13   Before attempting to repair a leak, check to make sure that the following conditions are corrected or they may cause another leak. **Note:** *Some of the following conditions cannot be fixed without highly specialized tools and expertise. Such problems must be referred to a transmission shop or a dealer service department.*

Gasket leaks

14   Check the pan periodically. Make sure the bolts are tight, no bolts are missing, the gasket is in good condition and the pan is flat (dents in the pan may indicate damage to the valve body inside).
15   If the pan gasket is leaking, the fluid level or the fluid pressure may be too high, the vent may be plugged, the pan bolts may be too tight, the pan sealing flange may be warped, the sealing surface of the transaxle housing may be damaged, the gasket may be damaged or the transaxle casting may be cracked or porous. If sealant instead of gasket material has been used to form a seal between the pan and the transaxle housing, it may be the wrong sealant.

Seal leaks

16   If a transaxle seal is leaking, the fluid level or pressure may be too high, the vent may be plugged, the seal bore may be damaged, the seal itself may be damaged or improperly installed, the surface of the shaft protruding through the seal may be damaged or a loose bearing may be causing excessive shaft movement.
17   Make sure the dipstick tube seal is in good condition and the tube is properly seated. Periodically check the area around the speedometer gear or sensor for leakage. If transmission fluid is evident, check the O-ring for damage. Also inspect the side gear shaft oil seals for leakage.

Case leaks

18   If the case itself appears to be leaking, the casting is porous and will have to be repaired or replaced.
19   Make sure the oil cooler hose fittings are tight and in good condition.

Fluid comes out vent pipe or fill tube

20   If this condition occurs, the transaxle is overfilled, there is coolant in the fluid, the case is porous, the dipstick is incorrect, the vent is plugged or the drain back holes are plugged.

Self-diagnosis system (1990 through 1995 models)
Refer to illustration 2.22

21   On 1990 through 1995 models, the automatic transaxle shift points are electronically controlled by the Transaxle Control Module (TCM). The system can detect automatic transaxle problems associated with the fluid temperature sensor, speed sensors, shift control solenoids, pressure control solenoids, damper clutch solenoid, shift synchronizer, ignition pulse signal, throttle position sensor and transaxle range switch. Transaxle operating problems detected by the control module will cause the Check Engine light on the dashboard to light, and the computer will store a trouble code. Obtaining the trouble code readout may direct you to the component or area at fault, but final diagnosis and repair should be performed by a dealer service department or qualified repair shop.
22   Trouble codes can be obtained using a scan tool (see Chapter 6) or with an analog voltmeter connected to the Data Link Connector (DLC) located near the fuse box on 1990 through 1994 models. If using the analog voltmeter method, connect the positive voltmeter lead to the Data Link Connector terminal 6 and

the other lead to ground, then use a jumper wire and ground terminal 10 **(see illustration)**. Turn the ignition ON. If a transaxle trouble code is stored in the TCM, the voltmeter needle will deflect quickly indicating the first digit of the trouble code, then pause, then another quick series of pulses indicating the second digit, then pause, then another quick series of pulses indicating the last digit (if applicable). Trouble codes for the transaxle are as follows:

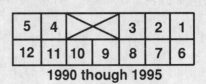

1990 though 1995

2.22 Data Link Connector terminal identification

43015-7b-2.22 HAYNES

Transaxle Trouble Codes

1990 through 1995 models	Trouble area
11, 12, 13	Throttle position sensor or circuit
5	Fluid temperature sensor or circuit
21, 22	Kickdown servo switch or circuit
23	Ignition pulse pickup circuit
24	Idle switch or circuit (check adjustment)
31, 32	Speed sensor A or B or circuit
41, 42, 43, 44	Shift control solenoid valve A or B or circuit
45, 46	Pressure control solenoid or circuit
47, 48, 49	Damper clutch control solenoid, circuit or damper clutch
51, 52, 53, 54	Indicated gear position does not match engine speed (defective speed sensor or transaxle slippage)

Transaxle Trouble Codes (1996 and later models)

23   On these OBD-II compliant models, refer to the Diagnostic Trouble Codes (DTCs) in Chapter 6. The transaxle DTCs begin with P0700.

3   Oil seal replacement

Refer to illustrations 3.4 and 3.6

1   Oil leaks frequently occur due to wear of the driveaxle oil seals, and/or the speedometer drive gear O-ring. Replacement of these seals is relatively easy, since the repairs can usually be performed without removing the transaxle from the vehicle.
2   The driveaxle oil seals are located at the sides of the transaxle, where the driveaxles are attached. If leakage at the seal is suspected, raise the vehicle and support it securely on jackstands. If the seal is leaking, lubricant will be found on the sides of the transaxle.
3   Refer to Chapter 8 and remove the driveaxles.

4   Using a screwdriver or pry bar, carefully pry the oil seal out of the transaxle bore **(see illustration)**.

3.4 Insert the tip of a large screwdriver (arrow) behind the oil seal and very carefully pry it out

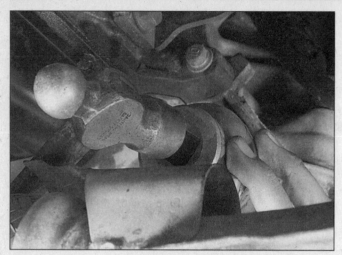

3.6 Apply a thin layer of grease to the outer edge of the new seal and carefully tap it into the bore with a large socket and a hammer

4.1 Pry on the transaxle mount with a large screwdriver to check for movement

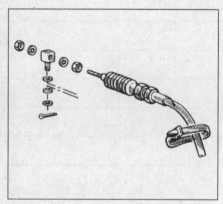

5.2 On 1989 and earlier models, the shift cable is attached to the lever on the transaxle by a cotter pin and washers and to the bracket by a spring clip or two large nuts (one on either side of the bracket). On 1990 and later models, the shift cable is attached by a pin, washer, and spring clip pin

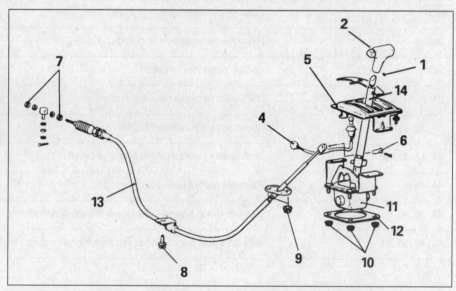

5.5a Shift linkage components - 1989 and earlier models

1	Handle set screw	8	Cable mounting bolt
2	Handle	9	Cable mounting bracket nuts
3	Console (not shown)	10	Selector lever assembly mounting nuts
4	Shift indicator light bulb	11	Selector lever assembly
5	Indicator panel	12	Gasket
6	Bolt	13	Shift cable
7	Shift cable adjusting nuts	14	Selector lever

5   If the oil seal cannot be removed with a screwdriver or pry bar, a special oil seal removal tool (available at auto parts stores) will be required.

6   Using a large section of pipe or a large deep socket as a drift, install the new oil seal **(see illustration)**. Drive it into the bore squarely and make sure it's completely seated.

7   Install the driveaxle(s). Be careful not to damage the lip of the new seal.

8   The speedometer cable and driven gear housing is located on the transaxle housing. Look for lubricant around the cable housing to determine if the O-ring is leaking.

9   Disconnect the speedometer cable from the transaxle.

10   Install a new O-ring on the driven gear housing and reinstall the speedometer cable assembly.

4   Transaxle mount - check and replacement

Refer to illustration 4.1

1   Insert a large screwdriver or pry bar between the mount and transaxle bracket and pry it back and forth **(see illustration)**.

2   The transaxle bracket should not move away from the mount. If it does, replace the mount.

3   To replace a mount, support the transaxle with a jack, remove the nut and through bolt and the bracket-to-transaxle bolts, then detach the mount. It may be necessary to lower the transaxle slightly to provide enough clearance to remove the mount.

4   Installation is the reverse of removal.

5   Shift cable - removal, installation and adjustment

Removal

Refer to illustrations 5.2, 5.5a and 5.5b

1   Disconnect the negative cable from the battery. On carbureted models, remove the air

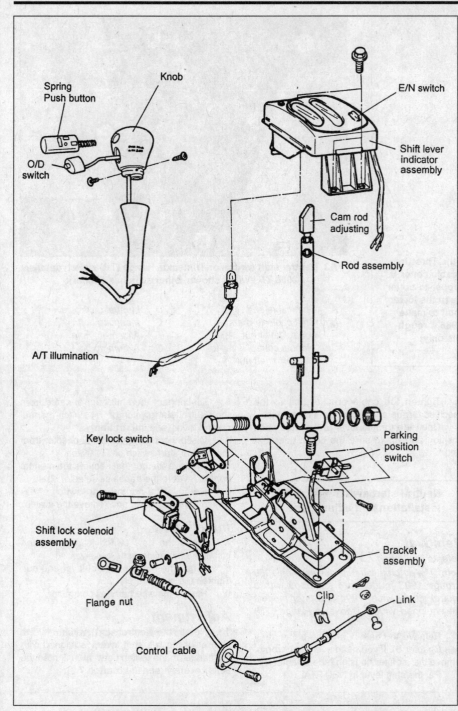

Spring
Push button

Knob

O/D switch

A/T illumination

Key lock switch

Shift lock solenoid assembly

Flange nut

Control cable

E/N switch

Shift lever indicator assembly

Cam rod adjusting

Rod assembly

Parking position switch

Bracket assembly

Clip

Link

5.5b Shift linkage components (typical 1990 and later models)

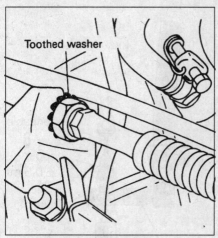

Toothed washer

5.9 Make sure the toothed washer is installed as shown so the cable won't slip (1994 and earlier models)

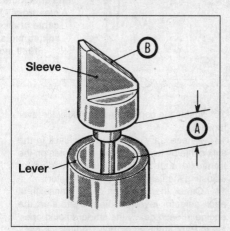

Sleeve

Lever

5.11 Turn the shift lever sleeve to achieve the specified clearance to the end of the lever (A) - the angled face (B) must face the driver's side of the vehicle after adjustment

cleaner assembly.

2   Working in the engine compartment, disconnect the shift cable at the bracket and transaxle lever **(see illustration)**.

3   Raise the vehicle and support it securely on jackstands.

4   Working under the vehicle, remove the shift cable assembly mounting bolt and nuts.

5   Remove the selector lever assembly mounting nuts **(see illustrations)**.

6   Working inside the vehicle, remove the handle set screw on 1989 and earlier models,

or two handle screws on 1990 and later models. On 1989 and earlier models, grasp the selector lever handle, press the lockout button in and pull up sharply to remove the handle. On 1990 and later models, disconnect the overdrive switch connector, drive out the three small connector pins, and then remove the handle. For all models, remove the shift lever indicator and center console (see Chapter 11). Disconnect the shift cable and remove the selector lever assembly.

7   Remove the shift cable from under the

vehicle by removing the bolts at the passenger compartment firewall.

Installation
Refer to illustration 5.9

8   Install the selector lever assembly. Tighten the mounting nuts securely.

9   Install the shift cable and connect it to the firewall, transaxle and selector lever. On 1994 and earlier models, make sure the toothed washer is correctly positioned on the transaxle mounting bracket **(see illustration)**.

Adjustment
Refer to illustration 5.11

10   Place the selector lever in Neutral.

11   Turn the lever adjusting sleeve to achieve the specified sleeve-to-lever end clearance listed in this Chapter's Specifications. Make sure the angled surface of the sleeve faces the driver's side after adjustment **(see illustration)**. Apply a small dab of multi-purpose grease to the outer edge and the angled surface of the sleeve.

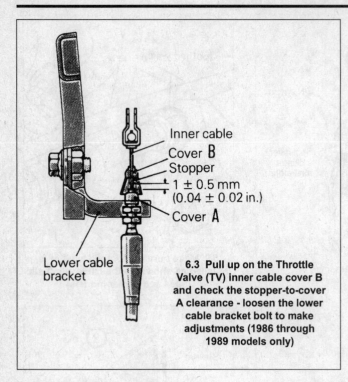

Inner cable
Cover B
Stopper
1 ± 0.5 mm
(0.04 ± 0.02 in.)
Cover A

Lower cable bracket

6.3 Pull up on the Throttle Valve (TV) inner cable cover B and check the stopper-to-cover A clearance - loosen the lower cable bracket bolt to make adjustments (1986 through 1989 models only)

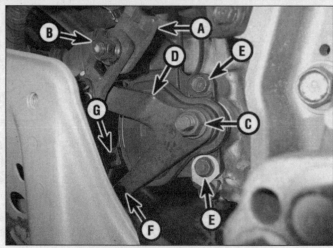

7.3 Neutral start switch or Transaxle Range (TR) switch details (2008 TR switch shown, other switches similar):

A Shift cable end
B Shift cable-to-manual control lever nut
C Manual control lever-to-selector shaft nut
D Manual control lever
E Mounting bolts
F Alignment hole
G Alignment hole

12 Install the console and the selector lever handle.
13 If necessary, eliminate any slack in the shift cable by turning the adjusting nuts on the transaxle shift cable (1989 and earlier) or adjusting the flange nut (1990 and later).
14 Check the operation of the transaxle in each selector lever position (try to start the engine in each gear - the starter should operate in Park and Neutral only). Adjust the Neutral start switch if necessary (see Section 7).

6 Throttle Valve (TV) cable - check and adjustment

Refer to illustration 6.3
Note: *This procedure applies to 1989 and earlier models only.*
1 The throttle valve (TV) cable adjustment is very important to proper transaxle operation. The cable positions a valve inside the transaxle which controls shift speed, shift quality and part throttle downshift sensitivity. If the cable is adjusted too short, early shifts and slippage between shifts may occur. If the cable is adjusted too long, shifts may be delayed and part throttle downshifts may be erratic.
2 Start and run the engine until it reaches normal operating temperature. Make sure the choke is off and the carburetor throttle lever is at the normal curb idle position (if applicable). Turn off the engine.
3 Pull up on the cable cover B **(see illustration)** to expose the stopper and cover A, then loosen the lower cable bracket bolt.
4 Move the lower cable until the stopper is the specified distance from cover A.

5 Tighten the cable bracket bolt to the specified torque and recheck the clearance.
6 Open the throttle lever to the wide open position and make sure the cable does not bind.

7 Neutral start switch - removal, installation and adjustment

Removal
Refer to illustration 7.3
Note: *The automatic transaxles used on 1986 through 1993 models are equipped with a neutral start switch; 1994 and later models are equipped with a Transaxle Range (TR) switch.*
1 Remove the battery and the battery tray (see Chapter 5). If you need even more room, remove the air filter housing (see Chapter 4).
2 Put the shift lever in NEUTRAL.

3 Disconnect the shift control cable from the neutral start switch or TR switch manual control lever **(see illustration)**.
4 Disconnect the electrical connector from the neutral start switch or TR switch.
5 Remove the nut that secures the manual control lever to the transaxle selector shaft.
6 Remove the neutral start switch or TR switch mounting bolts and remove the switch.

Installation
7 Place the new switch in position and install the mounting bolts loosely.
8 Install the manual control lever and nut. Tighten the nut securely.
9 Plug in the wire harness connector.

Adjustment
10 Rotate the Neutral start switch until the shorter of the two shift levers is aligned with the flange on the switch body, then tighten the bolts securely **(see illustration 7.3)**.

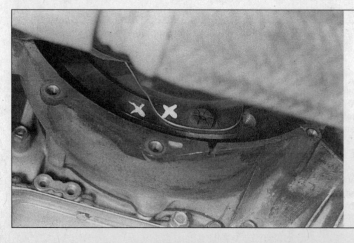

8.5 Mark the driveplate and the torque converter with white paint so they can be reinstalled in the same relationship

11   Check the operation of the transaxle in each selector lever position (try to start the engine in each gear - the starter should operate in Park and Neutral only). Readjust the switch if the engine starts in any other gears.

8   Automatic transaxle - removal and installation

Removal

Refer to illustration 8.5

1   Disconnect the negative cable from the battery. Remove the air cleaner assembly.

2   Raise the vehicle and support it securely on jackstands.

3   Drain the transaxle fluid (see Chapter 1). Disconnect the transaxle cooler hoses and plug the hoses and fittings.

4   Remove the torque converter cover.

5   Mark the torque converter and the driveplate with white paint so they can be installed in the same position **(see illustration)**.

6   Remove the torque converter-to-driveplate bolts. Turn the crankshaft pulley bolt for access to each bolt.

7   Remove the starter motor (see Chapter 5).

8   Disconnect the driveaxles from the transaxle (see Chapter 8).

9   Disconnect the speedometer cable.

10   Disconnect the electrical connectors from the transaxle and position the wire harness aside.

11   On models so equipped, disconnect the vacuum hose(s).

12   Remove any exhaust components which will interfere with transaxle removal (see Chapter 4).

13   On 1989 and earlier models, disconnect the TV cable from the carburetor.

14   Disconnect the shift cable from the transaxle (see Section 5).

15   Support the engine using a hoist from above or a jack and a block of wood under the oil pan to spread the load. Support the transaxle with a jack - preferably a special jack made for this purpose. Safety chains will help steady the transaxle on the jack.

16   Remove any chassis or suspension components which will interfere with transaxle removal.

17   On 1990 and later models, remove the center member.

18   Remove the nuts and bolts and detach the transaxle mount and bracket.

19   Remove the bolts securing the transaxle to the engine.

20   Lower the transaxle slightly and disconnect and plug the transaxle cooler lines.

21   Move the transaxle back to disengage it from the engine block dowel pins and make sure the torque converter is detached from the driveplate. Secure the torque converter to the transaxle so it will not fall out during removal. Lower the transaxle from the vehicle.

Installation

22   Prior to installation, make sure that the torque converter hub is securely engaged in the pump.

23   With the transaxle secured to the jack, raise it into position. Be sure to keep it level so the torque converter does not slide out.

24   Turn the torque converter to align the bolt holes with the holes in the driveplate. The white paint mark on the torque converter and the driveplate made in Step 5 must align.

25   Move the transaxle forward carefully until the dowel pins and the torque converter are engaged.

26   Install the transaxle-to-engine bolts. Tighten them securely. Install the transaxle mount.

27   Install the torque converter-to-driveplate bolts. Tighten the bolts to the specified torque.

28   Install the any suspension and chassis components which were removed. Tighten the bolts and nuts to the specified torque.

29   Remove the jacks supporting the transaxle and the engine.

30   The remainder of installation is the reverse of removal.

31   Adjust the shift linkage (see Section 5).

32   Fill the transaxle (see Chapter 1), run the vehicle and check for fluid leaks.

Notes

Chapter 8
Clutch and driveaxles

Contents

Specifications

Clutch
Pedal freeplay... See Chapter 1
Clutch disc lining minimum thickness...................... 0.012 inch above rivet heads

Torque specifications   **Ft-lbs**
Note: *One foot-pound (ft-lb) of torque is equivalent to 12 inch-pounds (in-lbs) of torque. Torque values below approximately 15 ft-lbs are expressed in inch-pounds, since most foot-pound torque wrenches are not accurate at these smaller values.*
Pressure plate-to-flywheel bolts .... 180 in-lbs
Driveaxle hub nut.. 185
Wheel lug nuts.. See Chapter 1

1   General information

The information in this Chapter deals with the components from the rear of the engine to the drive wheels, except for the transaxle, which is dealt with in the previous Chapter. For the purposes of this Chapter, these components are grouped into two categories; clutch and driveaxles. Separate Sections within this Chapter offer general descriptions and checking procedures for components in each of the two groups.

Since nearly all the procedures covered in this Chapter involve working under the vehicle, make sure it's securely supported on sturdy jackstands or on a hoist where the vehicle can be easily raised and lowered.

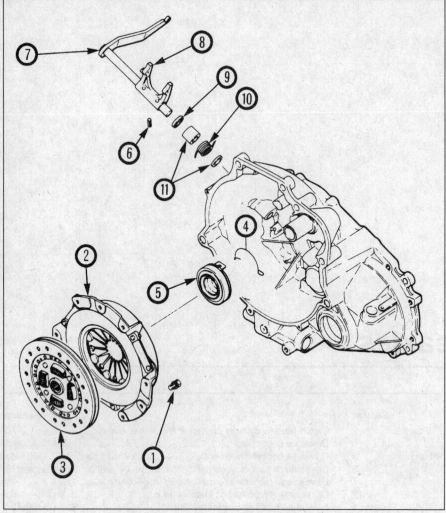

2.1 Clutch and related components (typical)

1 Pressure plate-to-flywheel bolt (6)
2 Pressure plate assembly
3 Clutch disc
4 Release bearing retaining clip
5 Release bearing
6 Spring pin
7 Clutch release shaft
8 Clutch release fork
9 Seal
10 Return spring
11 Spacers

2   Clutch - description and check

Refer to illustration 2.1

1   All vehicles with a manual transaxle use a single dry plate, diaphragm spring type clutch **(see illustration)**. The clutch disc has a splined hub which allows it to slide along the splines of the transaxle input shaft. The clutch and pressure plate are held in contact by spring pressure exerted by the diaphragm in the pressure plate.

2   All 1986 through 1989 and some 1990 through 1993 models are equipped with a cable-actuated clutch release system that includes the clutch pedal, the clutch release cable, the clutch release fork and the clutch release bearing. Some 1990 through 1993 and all 1994 and later models are equipped with a hydraulic release system that consists of the clutch pedal, the clutch master cylinder,

the clutch release cylinder, the hydraulic line between the master cylinder and release cylinder, the relase fork and the release bearing.

3   When pressure is applied to the clutch pedal to release the clutch, the clutch cable or hydraulic system moves the outer end of the clutch release fork. As the fork pivots, the shaft fingers push against the release bearing. The release bearing pushes against the fingers of the diaphragm spring of the pressure plate assembly, which in turn releases the clutch plate.

4   Terminology can be a problem when discussing the clutch components because common names are in some cases different from those used by the manufacturer. For example, the driven plate is also called the clutch plate or disc, the clutch release bearing is sometimes called a throwout bearing, the release cylinder is sometimes called the release lever.

5   Other than to replace components with obvious damage, some preliminary checks should be performed to diagnose clutch problems.

 a) *On 1989 and earlier models, the first check should be of the clutch cable adjustment. If there is too much slack in the cable, the clutch won't release completely, making gear engagement difficult or impossible. Refer to Section 5 for the adjustment procedure.*

 b) *On 1990 and later models, the first check should be the fluid level in the clutch master cylinder. If the fluid level is low, add fluid as necessary and inspect the hydraulic system for leaks. If the master cylinder reservoir has run dry, bleed the system as described in Section 8 and retest the clutch operation.*

 c) *To check "clutch spin down time," run the engine at normal idle speed with the transaxle in Neutral (clutch pedal up - engaged). Disengage the clutch (pedal down), wait several seconds and shift the transaxle into Reverse. Assuming that the transaxle is in good condition, no grinding noise should be heard. A grinding noise would most likely indicate a problem in the pressure plate or the clutch disc.*

 d) *To check for complete clutch release, run the engine (with the parking brake applied to prevent movement) and hold the clutch pedal approximately 1/2-inch from the floor. Shift the transaxle between 1st gear and Reverse several times. If the shift is rough, component failure is indicated, or as stated above, the cable is out of adjustment.*

 e) *Visually inspect the pivot bushing at the top of the clutch pedal to make sure there is no binding or excessive play.*

 f) *A clutch pedal that is difficult to operate is most likely caused by a faulty clutch cable. Check the cable where it enters the housing for frayed wires, rust and other signs of corrosion. If it looks good, lubricate the cable with penetrating oil. If pedal operation improves, the cable is worn out and should be replaced.*

3   Clutch components - removal, inspection and installation

Warning: *Dust produced by clutch wear and deposited on clutch components is hazardous to your health. DO NOT blow it out with compressed air and DO NOT inhale it. DO NOT use gasoline or petroleum-based solvents to remove the dust. Brake system cleaner should be used to flush the dust into a drain pan. After the clutch components are wiped clean with a rag, dispose of the contaminated rags and cleaner in a covered, marked container.*

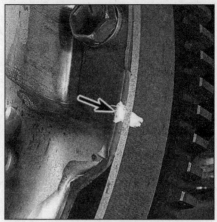

3.5 Make an index mark across the pressure plate and flywheel (just in case you're going to reuse the same pressure plate)

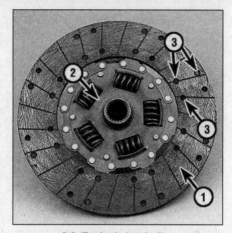

3.9 Typical clutch disc

1 **Lining** - this will wear down in use
2 **Marks** - "Flywheel Side" or something similar
3 **Rivets** - secure the lining and will damage the pressure plate if allowed to contact it

Removal

Refer to illustration 3.5

1   Access to the clutch components is normally accomplished by removing the transaxle, leaving the engine in the vehicle. If, of course, the engine is being removed for major overhaul, then check the clutch for wear and replace worn components as necessary. However, the relatively low cost of the clutch components compared to the time and trouble spent gaining access to them warrants their replacement anytime the engine or transaxle is removed, unless they are new or in near perfect condition. The following procedures are based on the assumption the engine will stay in place.

2   Referring to Chapter 7 Part A, remove the transaxle from the vehicle. Support the engine while the transaxle is out. Preferably, an engine hoist should be used to support it from above. However, if a jack is used underneath the engine, make sure a piece of wood is positioned between the jack and oil pan to spread the load. **Caution:** *The pickup for the oil pump is very close to the bottom of the oil pan. If the pan is bent or distorted in any way, engine oil starvation could occur.*

3   The clutch fork and release bearing can remain attached to the transaxle housing for the time being.

4   To support the clutch disc during removal, install a clutch alignment tool through the clutch disc hub.

5   Carefully inspect the flywheel and pressure plate for indexing marks. The marks are usually an X, an O or a white letter. If they cannot be found, scribe marks yourself so the pressure plate and the flywheel will be in the same alignment during installation **(see illustration)**.

6   Turning each bolt only 1/4-turn at a time, loosen the pressure plate-to-flywheel bolts. Work in a criss-cross pattern until all spring pressure is relieved. Then hold the pressure plate securely and completely remove the bolts, followed by the pressure plate and clutch disc.

Inspection

Refer to illustrations 3.9, 3.11a and 3.11b

7   Ordinarily, when a problem occurs in the clutch, it can be attributed to wear of the clutch driven plate assembly (clutch disc). However, all components should be inspected at this time.

8   Inspect the flywheel for cracks, heat checking, grooves and other obvious defects. If the imperfections are slight, a machine shop can machine the surface flat and smooth, which is highly recommended regardless of the surface appearance. Refer to Chapter 2, Part A for the flywheel removal and installation procedure.

9   Inspect the lining on the clutch disc. There should be at least 1/16-inch of lining above the rivet heads. Check for loose rivets, distortion, cracks, broken springs and other obvious damage **(see illustration)**. As mentioned above, ordinarily the clutch disc is routinely replaced, so if in doubt about the condition, replace it with a new one.

10 The release bearing should also be replaced along with the clutch disc (see Section 4).

11 Check the machined surfaces and the diaphragm spring fingers of the pressure plate **(see illustrations)**. If the surface is grooved or otherwise damaged, replace the pressure

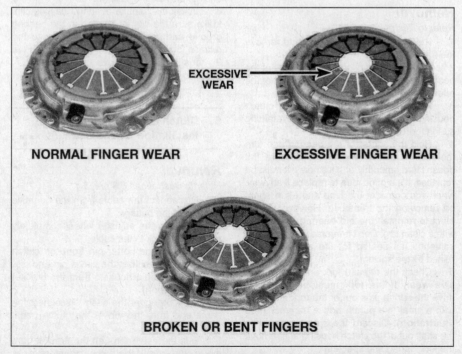

NORMAL FINGER WEAR EXCESSIVE WEAR EXCESSIVE FINGER WEAR

BROKEN OR BENT FINGERS

3.11a Replace the pressure plate if the fingers are worn excessively, broken or bent

3.11b Also examine the pressure plate friction surface for score marks, cracks and evidence of overheating (blue discolored areas)

3.13 Center the clutch disc in the pressure plate with a clutch alignment tool

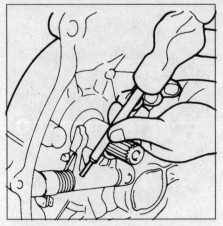

4.5 Drive out the spring pins with a small pin punch and hammer - use new pins for reassembly

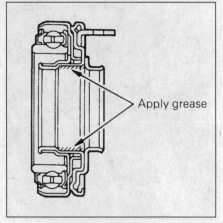

4.7 Pack the inner groove of the release bearing with high-temperature grease

plate. Also check for obvious damage, distortion, cracking, etc. Light glazing can be removed with emery cloth. If a new pressure plate is required, new and factory-rebuilt units are available.

Installation

Refer to illustration 3.13

12   Before installation, clean the flywheel and pressure plate machined surfaces with brake system cleaner, lacquer thinner or acetone. It's important that no oil or grease is on these surfaces or the lining of the clutch disc. Handle the parts only with clean hands.

13   Position the clutch disc and pressure plate against the flywheel with the clutch held in place with an alignment tool **(see illustration)**. Make sure it's installed properly (most replacement clutch plates will be marked "flywheel side" or something similar - if not marked, install the clutch disc with the damper springs toward the transaxle).

14   Tighten the pressure plate-to-flywheel bolts only finger tight, working around the pressure plate.

15   Center the clutch disc by ensuring the alignment tool extends through the splined hub and into the pocket in the crankshaft. Wiggle the tool up, down or side-to-side as needed to center the disc. Tighten the pressure plate-to-flywheel bolts a little at a time, working in a crisscross pattern to prevent distorting the cover. After all of the bolts are snug, tighten them to the torque listed in this Chapter's Specifications. Remove the alignment tool.

16   Using high-temperature grease, lubricate the inner groove of the release bearing (refer to Section 4). Also place grease on the release lever contact areas and the transaxle input shaft bearing retainer.

17   Install the clutch release bearing as described in Section 4.

18   Install the transaxle and all components removed previously and tighten all fasteners, (see Chapter 7, Part A).

4   Clutch release bearing, fork and shaft - removal and installation

Warning: *Dust produced by clutch wear and deposited on clutch components is hazardous to your health. DO NOT blow it out with compressed air and DO NOT inhale it. DO NOT use gasoline or petroleum-based solvents to remove the dust. Brake system cleaner should be used to flush the dust into a drain pan. After the clutch components are wiped clean with a rag, dispose of the contaminated rags and cleaner in a labeled, covered container.*

Removal

Refer to illustration 4.5

1   Refer to Chapter 7, Part A, and remove the transaxle.

2   Using a pair of pliers, pull the ends of the bearing retaining clip (or return clip) out of the release fork **(see illustration 2.1)**.

3   Remove the bearing from the clutch housing. Be careful not to lose the retaining spring (or return clip).

4   Hold the center of the bearing and turn the outer portion while applying pressure. If it doesn't turn smoothly or if it's noisy, it must be replaced. It's a good idea to replace it anyway, when you consider the time and effort spent on removing the transaxle. However, if you elect to reinstall the old bearing, wipe it off with a clean rag. Don't immerse the bearing in solvent - it's sealed for life and would be ruined by the solvent.

5   Check the release fork ends for excessive wear. If the fork must be replaced, drive the spring pins out of the fork and shaft with a small pin punch and a hammer **(see illustration)**. Discard the spring pins, slide the shaft out of the clutch housing and remove the fork, spring and spacers.

Installation

Refer to illustration 4.7

6   Lubricate the release shaft bore in the clutch housing with high temperature grease, slide the shaft part way into the housing and place the spacers, spring and fork in position. Continue to slide the shaft through the components and align the spring pin holes. Insert new spring pins and drive them into position.

7   Lubricate the release fork ends with a small amount of high temperature grease (don't overdo it). Pack the groove in the inner diameter of the release bearing with the same grease **(see illustration)** and position it against the release fork.

8   Install the release bearing retaining clip. Make sure the clip is secured in the bearing groove and the ends are inserted into the release fork properly.

9   Install the transaxle (see Chapter 7, Part A).

5   Clutch cable - removal, installation and adjustment

Removal

Refer to illustrations 5.3 and 5.4

1   Disconnect the cable from the negative terminal of the battery.

2   Unscrew the adjuster wheel completely to produce slack in the cable.

3   Remove the cotter pin from the clutch release lever, pull out the clevis pin and disconnect the cable housing from the bracket **(see illustration)**.

4   Working under the dash, disconnect the cable end from the top of the clutch pedal **(see illustration)**.

5   Pull the cable through the firewall from the engine side. If the rubber grommet sticks in the firewall, pry it out with a screwdriver.

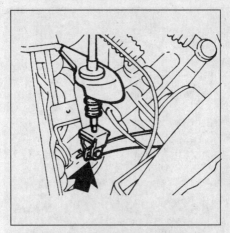

5.3 The clutch cable is secured to the release shaft lever by a clevis pin and cotter pin - once they're removed, the cable housing and grommet can be pulled (or pried, if necessary) out of the bracket

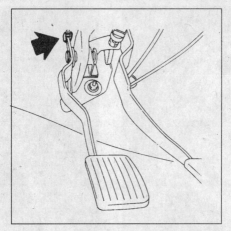

5.4 Unhook the cable end from the top of the clutch pedal

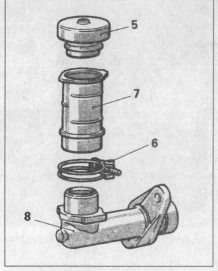

7.4 Clutch master cylinder and reservoir (hydraulically actuated clutch models)

    5   Cap
    6   Clamp
    7   Reservoir
    8   Master cylinder

Installation and adjustment

6   When installing the cable, lightly lubricate the ends with multipurpose grease. Install the cable by reversing the removal procedure, then adjust the clutch pedal freeplay by following the procedure in Chapter 1.

6   Clutch release cylinder - removal and installation

1   Disconnect the negative cable from the battery.
2   Raise the vehicle and support it securely on jackstands.
3   Loosen the bleed plug on the release cylinder (it's bolted to the transaxle) and place a drain pan under the bleed plug. Apply the clutch pedal several times to force the hydraulic brake fluid out of the system. Continue to apply the clutch pedal until all fluid is expelled. Tighten the bleed plug securely. **Caution:** *Don't allow hydraulic brake fluid to come into*

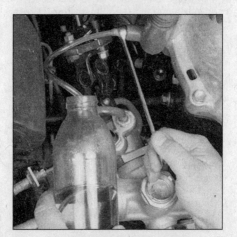

8.5 Clutch hydraulic system bleeding setup

contact with paint, as it will damage the finish
4   Disconnect the hydraulic line at the release cylinder. Have a small can and rags handy, as some residual fluid will be spilled as the line is removed.
5   Remove the snap-ring and remove the clevis pin. Disconnect the pushrod from the transaxle lever.
6   Unbolt the release cylinder from the clutch housing and remove the release cylinder.
7   Installation is the reverse of the removal procedure. Tighten the clutch release cylinder mounting bolts securely. Bleed the system (see Section 8).

7   Clutch master cylinder - removal and installation

Refer to illustration 7.4
1   Disconnect the negative cable from the battery.
2   Raise the vehicle and support it securely on jackstands.
3   Loosen the bleed plug on the release cylinder and place a drain pan under the bleeding plug. Apply the clutch pedal several times to force the hydraulic brake fluid out of the system. Continue to apply the clutch pedal until all fluid is expelled. Tighten the bleed plug securely. **Caution:** *Don't allow hydraulic brake fluid to come into contact with paint as it will damage the finish.*
4   Disconnect the hydraulic line at the master cylinder **(see illustration)**. Have a small can and rags handy, as some residual fluid will be spilled as the line is removed.
5   Working inside the vehicle, remove the cotter pin, washer and clevis pin. Disconnect the pushrod from the clutch pedal.
6   Working in the engine compartment, remove the nuts securing the master cylinder to the firewall and remove the master cylinder. Installation is the reverse of removal. Tighten

the clutch master cylinder mounting bolts/nuts securely. Be sure to bleed the system (see Section 8).

8   Clutch hydraulic system - bleeding

Refer to illustration 8.5
1   The hydraulic system should be bled to remove all air whenever any part of the system has been removed or if the fluid level has been allowed to fall so low that air has been drawn into the master cylinder. The procedure is very similar to bleeding a brake system.
2   Fill the master cylinder with new brake fluid conforming to DOT 3 specifications. **Caution:** *Do not re-use any of the fluid coming from the system during the bleeding operation or use fluid which has been inside an open container for an extended period of time.*
3   Raise the vehicle and place it securely on jackstands to gain access to the release cylinder, which is located on the side of the clutch housing.
4   Remove the dust cap which fits over the bleed plug and push a length of plastic hose over the plug. Place the other end of the hose into a clear container partially filled with brake fluid. The hose end must be in the fluid at the bottom of the container.
5   Have an assistant depress the clutch pedal and keep it depressed. Open the bleeder valve on the release cylinder **(see illustration)**, allowing fluid to flow through the hose. Close the bleed valve when your assistant signals that the clutch pedal is at the bottom of its travel. Once closed, have your assistant release the pedal.

10.1 With the vehicle on the ground, loosen the driveaxle hub nut

10.4a If the driveaxle won't slide out of the hub easily, a puller can be used to push it out - DO NOT hammer on the end of the driveaxle to force it out!

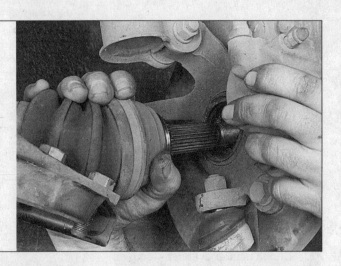

10.4b Pull out on the steering knuckle and remove the driveaxle from the hub splines

6   Continue this process until all air is evacuated from the system, indicated by a solid stream of fluid being ejected from the bleed plug each time with no air bubbles in the hose or container. Keep a close watch on the fluid level inside the clutch master cylinder reservoir - if the level drops too low, air will be sucked back into the system and the process will have to be started all over again.

7   Install the dust cap and lower the vehicle. Check carefully for proper operation before placing the vehicle in normal service.

9   Driveaxles - general information and inspection

Power is transmitted from the transaxle to the wheels through a pair of driveaxles. The inner end of each driveaxle is splined to the differential. The outer ends of the driveaxles are splined to the axle hubs and locked in place by an axle nut.

The inner ends of the driveaxles are equipped with sliding double offset joints (1994 and earlier) or tri-pot joints (1995 and later), which are capable of both angular and axial motion. Each inner joint assembly consists of an inner race, ball bearing and cage assembly (double offset joint) or a tripot spider bearing assembly (1995 and later models) and an outer race (housing) in which the inner bearing assembly is free to slide in and out as the driveaxle moves up and down with the wheel. The inner joints are replaceable.

Each outer joint, which consists of ball bearings running between an inner race and an outer cage, is capable of angular but not axial movement. The outer joints are neither rebuildable nor removable. Should one of them fail, a new driveaxle/outer joint assembly must be installed.

The boots should be periodically inspected for damage, leaking lubricant and cuts. Damaged CV joint boots must be replaced immediately or the joints can be damaged. Boot replacement involves removal of the driveaxle (see Section 10). **Note:** *Some auto parts stores carry "split" type replacement boots, which can be installed without removing the driveaxle from the vehicle. This is a convenient alternative; however, it's rec-* ommended that the driveaxle be removed and the CV joint disassembled and cleaned to ensure that the joint is free from contaminants such as moisture and dirt, which will accelerate CV joint wear. The most common symptom of worn or damaged CV joints, besides lubricant leaks, is a clicking noise in turns, a clunk when accelerating from a coasting condition or vibration at highway speeds.

To check for wear in the CV joints and driveaxle shafts, grasp each axle (one at a time) and rotate it in both directions while holding the CV joint housings, inspecting for movement, indicating worn or damaged CV joints. Also check the driveaxle shafts for cracks, dents, twisting and bending.

10   Driveaxles - removal and installation

Removal
Refer to illustrations 10.1, 10.4a, 10.4b and 10.6

1   Remove the wheel cover and loosen the driveaxle hub nut **(see illustration)**. Loosen the wheel lug nuts, raise the front of the vehicle and support it securely on jackstands. Remove the front wheel.

2   Remove the driveaxle hub nut. To prevent the hub from turning, brace a screwdriver across two of the wheel studs, then remove the nut.

3   On 1994 and earlier models, remove the two balljoint-to-lower arm bolts/nuts and separate the lower arm from the balljoint (refer to Chapter 10 if necessary). On 1995 and later models, detach the lower arm balljoint from the strut/knuckle assembly, detach the steering tie-rod, and detach the stabilizer bar (see Chapter 10).

4   Press the driveaxle from the hub with a puller, then pull out on the steering knuckle and remove the outer end of the driveaxle from the hub splines **(see illustrations)**.

10.6 Be careful when prying the inner end of the axle out of the transaxle (the seal is very close to the edge of the joint and could be damaged if the prybar is inserted too far)

10.7 Always replace the circlip on the inner CV joint stub shaft before reinstalling the driveaxle

5   Before removing the driveaxle from the transaxle, drain the transaxle fluid (see Chapter 1).

6   Carefully insert a prybar between the transaxle case at the case rib and the Constant Velocity (CV) driveaxle joint and pry while supporting the CV joints **(see illustration)**. Do not insert the prybar too deep (no more than 1/4-inch) to prevent damage to the differential oil seal. **Note:** *On 1995 and later models with an automatic transaxle, it may be necessary to remove the differential cover and use a flat tipped screwdriver to pry against the end of the driveaxle (inside the differential gearset) to push the driveaxle out of the transaxle housing. Do not pull on the driveaxle as this will damage the inner joint.*

Installation
Refer to illustration 10.7

7   Pry the old circlip from the inner end of the driveaxle and install a new one **(see illustration)**. Lubricate the differential seal with multi-purpose grease, raise the driveaxle into position while supporting the CV joints and insert the splined end of the inner CV joint into the differential side gear. Seat the shaft into the side gear by pushing firmly on the driveaxle.

8   Apply a light coat of multi-purpose grease to the outer CV joint splines, pull out on the strut/steering knuckle assembly and install the stub axle in the hub.

9   Connect the balljoint to the lower arm (see Chapter 10).

10   Install the hub nut using a new large washer underneath it. Lock the brake disc so that it cannot turn and tighten the hub nut securely.

11   Grasp the inner CV joint housing (not the driveaxle) and pull out to make sure that the axle has seated securely in the transaxle.

12   Install the wheel and lower the vehicle.

13   Tighten the hub nut to the specified torque and install the wheel cover.

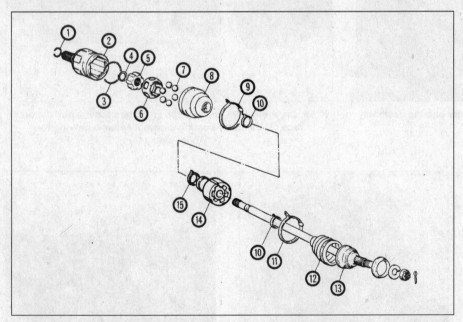

11.1 Typical driveaxle and CV joint components

1	Circlip (always replace)	9	Boot clamp
2	Inner CV joint outer race	10	Boot clamp
3	Wire ring ball retainer	11	Boot clamp
4	Snap-ring	12	Outer boot
5	Inner race	13	Outer CV joint and axle assembly
6	Cage	14	Dynamic damper (left side only)
7	Balls	15	Dynamic damper clamp
8	Inner boot		

11 Driveaxle boot replacement

Inner CV joint and boot
Disassembly
Refer to illustrations 11.1, 11.3, 11.4, 11.5a, 11.5b, 11.6, 11.7, 11.9, 11.10a and 11.10b

1   Remove the driveaxle from the vehicle (see Section 10) **(see illustration)**.

2   Mount the driveaxle in a vise. The jaws of the vise should be lined with wood or rags to prevent damage to the axleshaft.

3   Pry the boot clamp retaining tabs up with

11.3 Pry the boot clamp retaining tabs up with a small screwdriver and slide the clamps off the boot

11.4 On 1986 through 1994 and some 1995 models, pry the wire ring ball retainer out of the outer race . . .

a small screwdriver and slide the clamps off the boot **(see illustration)**.

4   On 1986 through 1994 and some 1995 models, slide the boot back and pry the wire ring ball retainer from the outer race **(see illustration)**.

5   Pull the outer race off the inner bearing assembly **(see illustrations)**.

6   Remove the snap-ring from the groove in the axleshaft with a pair of snap-ring pliers **(see illustration)**.

7   Mark the inner race and cage to ensure that they are reassembled with the correct sides facing out **(see illustration)**.

8   Slide the inner bearing assembly off the axleshaft.

9   On On 1986 through 1994 and some 1995 models, use a screwdriver or piece of wood to pry the balls from the cage **(see illustration)**. Be careful not to scratch the inner race, the balls or the cage.

11.5a . . . then slide the outer race off the inner bearing assembly

11.5b On some 1995 and all 1996 and later models, pull the outer race off the inner bearing assembly after removing the boot clamps

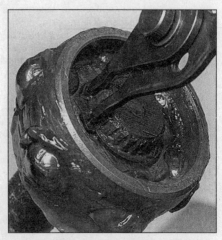

11.6 Remove the snap-ring from the end of the axle

11.7 Place match marks on the inner race and cage to identify which side must face the end of the shaft during reassembly

11.9 On 1986 through 1994 and some 1995 models, pry the balls out of the cage with a screwdriver - be careful not to nick or scratch them

11.10a Align the lands of the inner race with the windows of the cage . . .

11.10b . . . then remove the inner race from the cage

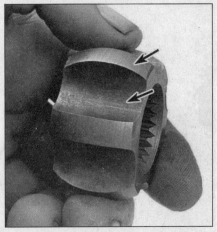

11.11a Check the inner race lands and grooves for pitting and score marks

10 Align the inner race lands with the cage windows and pull the race out of the cage **(see illustrations)**.

Inspection

Refer to illustrations 11.11a, 1.11b and 11.11c

11 Clean the components with solvent to remove all traces of grease. On 1994 and earlier models, inspect the cage and races for pitting, score marks, cracks and other signs of wear and damage. Shiny, polished spots are normal and will not adversely affect CV joint performance **(see illustrations)**. On some 1995 and all 1996 and later models, inspect the rollers and needle bearings for wear or damage **(see illustration)**.

Reassembly

Refer to illustrations 11.13, 11.14, 11.17, 11.20, 11.21a and 11.21b

12 On 1994 and earlier models, insert the inner race into the cage. Verify that the matchmarks are on the same side. However, it's not necessary for them to be in direct alignment with each other.

13 Press the balls into the cage windows with your thumbs **(see illustration)**.

14 Wrap the axleshaft splines with tape to avoid damaging the boot. Slide the small boot clamp and boot onto the axleshaft, then remove the tape **(see illustration)**.

15 Install the inner bearing assembly on the axleshaft with the previously applied marks facing the axleshaft end.

16 Install the snap-ring in the groove. Make sure it's completely seated by pushing on the inner race and cage assembly.

17 Fill the outer race and boot with the specified type and quantity of CV joint grease (normally included with the new boot kit). Pack the inner race and cage assembly with grease, by hand, until grease is worked completely

11.11b Check the cage for cracks, pitting and score marks (shiny spots are normal and don't affect operation)

11.11c On some 1995 and all 1996 and later models, make sure the rollers turn smoothly and check the bearings for wear or damage

11.13 On 1994 and earlier models, press the balls into the cage through the windows using thumb pressure only

11.14 Wrap the splined area of the axle with tape to prevent damage to the boot when installing it

11.17 Pack the inner race and cage assembly full of CV joint grease

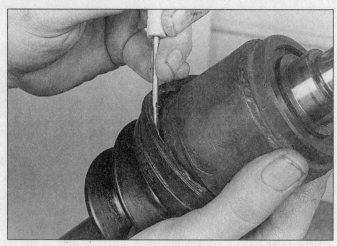

11.20 Equalize the pressure inside the boot by inserting a small, dull screwdriver between the boot and the outer race

11.21a To install the new clamps, bend the tang down . . .

11.21b . . . and fold the tabs over to hold it in place

11.28 After the old grease has been rinsed away and the solvent has been blown out with compressed air, rotate the outer joint housing through its full range of motion and inspect the bearing surfaces for wear and damage - if any of the balls, the race or the cage look damaged, replace the driveaxle and outer joint assembly

into the assembly **(see illustration)**.

18   Slide the outer race over the inner bearing assembly. On 1994 and earlier models, install the wire ring retainer.

19   Wipe any excess grease from the axle boot groove on the outer race. Seat the small diameter of the boot in the recessed area on the axleshaft. Push the other end of the boot onto the outer race and position the CV joint mid-way through its (in-and-out) travel.

20   With the axle set to the proper length, equalize the pressure in the boot by inserting a dull screwdriver between the boot and the outer race **(see illustration)**. Don't damage the boot with the tool.

21   Install the boot clamps **(see illustrations)**.

22   Install a new circlip on the inner CV joint stub axle **(see illustration 10.7)**.

23   Install the driveaxle as described in Section 10.

Outer CV joint and boot
Disassembly

24   Following Steps 1 through 10, remove the inner CV joint from the axleshaft and disassemble it.

25   If the left driveaxle outer CV joint is being serviced, mark the position of the dynamic damper on the shaft, then pry open the dynamic damper clamp and slide the damper off the axleshaft.

26   Remove the outer CV joint boot clamps, using the technique described in Step 3. Slide the boot off the axleshaft.

Inspection
Refer to illustration 11.28

27   Thoroughly wash the inner and outer CV joints in clean solvent and blow them dry with compressed air, if available. **Note:** *Because the outer joint cannot be disassembled, it is*

difficult to wash away all the old grease and to rid the bearing of solvent once it's clean. But it is imperative that the job be done thoroughly, so take your time and do it right.

28   Bend the outer CV joint housing at an angle to the driveaxle to expose the bearings, inner race and cage **(see illustration)**. Inspect the bearing surfaces for signs of wear. If the bearings are damaged or worn, replace the driveaxle.

Reassembly

29   Slide the new outer boot onto the driveaxle. It's a good idea to wrap vinyl tape around the splines of shaft to prevent damage to the boot **(see illustration 11.14)**. When the boot is in position, add the specified amount of grease (included in the boot replacement kit)

to the outer joint and the boot (pack the joint with as much grease as it will hold and put the rest into the boot). Slide the boot on the rest of the way and install the new clamps **(see illustrations 11.21a and 11.21b)**.

30   If you are overhauling the left driveaxle, install the dynamic damper. Position it the same distance from the outer CV joint housing that it was in before removal. Attach the damper clamp.

31   Proceed to clean and reassemble the inner CV joint by following Steps 11 through 22, then install the driveaxle as outlined in Section 10.

12 Clutch pedal - removal and installation

Refer to illustration 12.3

1   Disconnect the cable from the negative battery terminal.

2   On 1989 and earlier models, loosen the clutch cable adjuster wheel (see Chapter 1) and unhook the end of the cable from the top of the clutch pedal (under the dash). On 1990 and later models, remove the pin and pull out the clevis pin from the master cylinder push-rod.

3   Remove the pedal shaft nut and washers, then slide the pedal off the shaft **(see illustration)**. Wipe the old grease off the shaft.

4   Remove the bushings from the pedal and inspect them for wear. Install new ones if

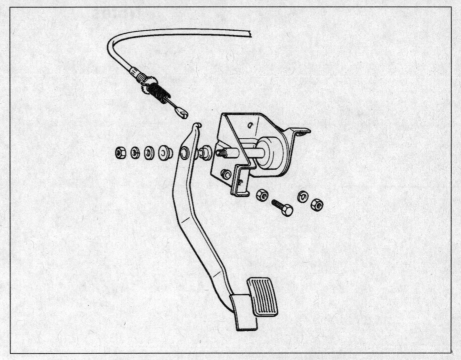

12.3 Typical clutch pedal and related components

necessary. When installing the bushings in the pedal, lubricate them with multi-purpose grease. Also lubricate the hook at the top of the clutch pedal.

5   Install the clutch pedal by reversing the removal procedure, then adjust the freeplay as outlined in Chapter 1.

Notes

Chapter 9 Brakes

Contents

Specifications

General

Brake fluid type	See Chapter 1
Power brake booster pushrod-to-master cylinder piston clearance	
1989 and earlier models	0.016 to 0.031 inch
1990 and later models (with 20 in-Hg vacuum applied to booster)	0.0 inch
Brake pedal height	
1986 through 1989	7.2 to 7.4 inches
1990 through 1996	6.4 to 6.6 inches
1997 through 2002	N/A
2003 through 2005	6.2 to 6.4 inches
2006 and later	6.5 inches
Clearance between brake pedal and brake light switch	0.020 to 0.040 inch
Brake pedal freeplay	
1986 through 1991	0.4 to 0.6 inch
1992 and later	0.1 to 0.3 inch
Brake pedal reserve height (distance between firmly depressed pedal and floor, with carpet removed)	
1986 through 1989	At least 1.6 inches
1990 through 1996 and 1999 through 2002	At least 2.8 inches
1997 and 1998	See brake pedal stroke below
2003 and later	N/A
Brake pedal stroke (distance that pedal travels when firmly depressed)	
1986 through 1996 and 1999 through 2002	See brake pedal reserve height above
1997 and 1998	5.7 inches
2003 and later	N/A
Parking brake lever travel	6 to 7 clicks

Front brakes

Minimum brake pad thickness	See Chapter 1
Disc minimum thickness	Refer to the dimension cast into the disc
Disc runout (maximum)	
1994 and earlier models	0.006 inch
1995 and later models	0.002 inch

Rear brakes

Minimum brake shoe lining thickness	See Chapter 1
Drum maximum diameter	Refer to the dimension cast into the drum
Drum out-of-round	0.0006 inch

Torque specifications

Ft-lbs (unless otherwise indicated)

Note: *One foot-pound (ft-lb) of torque is equivalent to 12 inch-pounds (in-lbs) of torque. Torque values below approximately 15 ft-lbs are expressed in inch-pounds, since most foot-pound torque wrenches are not accurate at these smaller values.*

Front brake caliper	
Fixed (Sumitomo) caliper	
Caliper-to-steering knuckle bolts	43 to 58
Caliper inner-to-outer (bridge) bolts	58 to 69
Floating caliper	
Caliper mounting bolt(s)	16 to 23
Caliper mounting bracket-to-steering knuckle bolts	
2003 and earlier models	48 to 54
2004 and 2005 models	51 to 62
2006 and later models	62 to 68
Caliper pin-to-mounting bracket (2003 and earlier models)	26 to 32
Rear brake caliper	
Caliper mounting bolts	16 to 23
Caliper mounting bracket-to-hub carrier bolts	62 to 68
Brake hose inlet fitting-to-caliper bolt	18 to 22
Disc-to-hub bolts (1988 and earlier models with fixed calipers)	36 to 43
Wheel cylinder mounting bolts	
1986 through 1988 models	72 to 108 in-lbs
1989 and later models	108 to 144 in-lbs
Brake backing plate-to-axle flange bolts	
1986 through 1990 models	22 to 29
1991 and later models	37 to 43
Rear wheel bearing nut	See Chapter 10
Master cylinder-to-brake booster nuts	70 to 108 in-lbs
Brake booster-to-firewall nuts	70 to 108 in-lbs
Brake pedal support-to-firewall nuts	70 to 108 in-lbs
Wheel lug nuts	See Chapter 1

2.5 Always wash the brakes with brake cleaner before disassembling anything; don't use compressed air or a brush

2.6a Pry the pad protector off of the pad retaining pins

2.6b Before removing anything, wash the brake assembly with brake cleaner and allow it to dry. Remember - NEVER blow off the brake dust with compressed air - brake dust is a health hazard!

1   General information

The vehicles covered by this manual are equipped with hydraulically operated front and rear brake systems. The front brakes are disc type and the rear brakes are either disc or drum type. Both the front and rear brakes are self adjusting. The front disc brakes automatically compensate for pad wear, while the rear drum brakes incorporate an adjustment mechanism which is activated when the parking brake is applied and released and the brake pedal is pumped, alternately.

Hydraulic system

The hydraulic system consists of two separate, diagonally split circuits. The master cylinder has separate reservoirs for the two circuits and in the event of a leak or failure in one hydraulic circuit, the other circuit will remain operative. A visual warning of low fluid level is given by a warning light activated by a float switch in the master cylinder reservoir.

Proportioning valve

A proportioning valve, located in the engine compartment below the master cylinder, regulates outlet pressure to the rear brakes after a predetermined rear input pressure has been reached, preventing early rear wheel lock-up under heavy brake loads. The valve is also designed to assure full pressure to one brake system should the other system fail.

Power brake booster

The power brake booster, utilizing engine manifold vacuum and atmospheric pressure to provide assistance to the hydraulically operated brakes, is mounted on the firewall in the engine compartment.

Parking brake

The parking brake operates the rear brakes only, through a cable. It's activated by a lever mounted in the center console.

Anti-lock Brake System (ABS)

1995 and later models feature an ABS system for increased braking safety. See Section 16 for description and system information.

Service

After completing any operation involving disassembly of any part of the brake system, always test drive the vehicle to check for proper braking performance before resuming normal driving. When testing the brakes, perform the tests on a clean, dry, flat surface. Conditions other than these can lead to inaccurate test results.

Test the brakes at various speeds with both light and heavy pedal pressure. The vehicle should stop evenly without pulling to one side or the other. Avoid locking the brakes because this slides the tires and diminishes braking efficiency and control of the vehicle.

Tires, vehicle load and front end alignment are factors which also affect braking performance.

Servicing of ABS braking systems and components, other than routine checks, should be performed by a dealer service department or other qualified repair shop due to the ABS system's complexity and critical safety requirements.

2   Disc brake pads - replacement

Refer to illustration 2.5

Warning: Disc brake pads must be replaced on both front wheels at the same time - never replace the pads on only one wheel. Also, the dust created by the brake system is harmful to your health. Never blow it out with compressed air and don't inhale any of it. An approved filtering mask should be worn when working on the brakes. Do not, under any circumstances, use petroleum based solvents to clean brake parts. Use brake system cleaner only!

Note: This procedure applies to front and rear disc brakes.

1   Remove the cap from the brake fluid reservoir (see Chapter 1) and siphon off about two-thirds of the fluid from the reservoir. Failing to do this could result in the reservoir overflowing when the caliper pistons are pressed into their bores.

2   If you're working on the front brakes, apply the parking brake. Loosen the wheel lug nuts, raise the vehicle and support it securely on jackstands. Place blocks behind the wheels at the opposite end of the vehicle.

3   Remove the wheels. Work on one brake assembly at a time, using the assembled brake for reference, if necessary.

4   Inspect the brake disc carefully as outlined in Section 4. If machining is necessary, follow the information in that Section to remove the disc, at which time the pads can be removed from the calipers as well.

5   Before disassembling the brake, wash it thoroughly with brake system cleaner and allow it to dry **(see illustration)**. Be sure to position a drain pan under the brake to catch the residue. **Warning:** *Do not use compressed air or a brush to remove the brake dust.*

1986 through 1988 models with Sumitomo calipers

Refer to illustrations 2.6a through 2.6k

6   To replace the pads on Sumitomo calipers, follow **illustrations 2.6a through 2.6k**, being sure to stay in order and read the caption with each illustration. Then proceed to Step 13.

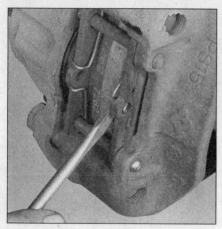

2.6c Pry the center of the M-clip out of the outer brake pad . . .

2.6d . . . then pull the ends of the clip out of the pad retaining pins

2.6e Using a pair of pliers, pull the K spring off of the inner brake pad and out from under the retaining pins

2.6f Pull out both pad retaining pins

2.6g Using a C-clamp (or a pair of large pliers), push the inner brake pad towards the inside of the caliper, which will bottom the caliper piston in its bore, making room for the new pads

2.6h Pull the brake pads straight out of the caliper

2.6i If the anti-squeal shim hasn't stuck to the brake pad, remove it from the caliper

2.6j Before installing the new brake pads, it's a good idea to apply an anti-squeal compound to the pad backing plates, following label instructions

2.6k Install the new pads and clips, referring, if necessary, to the assembled brake on the other side of the car. When installing the M-clip, insert one end into the hole in one of the retaining pins, then rotate the other retaining pin so its hole is properly angled to insert the other end of the clip. Push the center of the clip into the hole in the brake pad

2.7 Using a large C-clamp, push the piston back into the caliper - note that one end of the clamp is on the back side of the caliper and the other end (screw end) is pressing on the outer brake pad

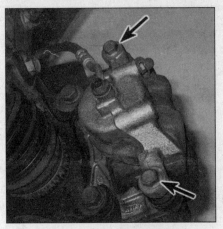

2.8a Remove the caliper lower mounting bolt . . .

2.8b . . . then swing the caliper up for access to the pads

1986 through 1988 models with Tokico calipers, and all 1989 and later models

Refer to illustrations 2.7, 2.8a, 2.8b, 2.9a, 2.9b and 2.11

7   Push the piston back into the bore to provide room for the new brake pads. A C-clamp can be used to accomplish this **(see illustration)**. As the piston is depressed to the bottom of the caliper bore, the fluid in the master cylinder will rise. Make sure it doesn't overflow. If necessary, drain off some of the fluid.

8   Remove the caliper lower mounting bolt **(see illustration)** and swing the caliper up far enough to allow removal of the brake pads **(see illustration)**. Secure it in the raised position with a piece of wire.

9   Pull the brake pads out of the caliper mounting bracket **(see illustration)**. Remove the spring clips from each end of the caliper mounting bracket, noting their installed positions **(see illustration)**. Inspect each clip for

distortion, replacing it if necessary.

10   Apply a coat of anti-squeal compound to the backing plates of the brake pads, following label instructions **(see illustration 2.6j)**.

11   Place the spring clips on the caliper mounting bracket. Clip the anti-squeal shim(s) onto the new pad(s) **(see illustration)** and insert the pads into the caliper mounting bracket.

12   Swing the caliper body down over the pads and install the lower mounting bolt, tightening it to the specified torque.

All models

13   After replacing the pads, firmly depress the brake pedal a few times to bring the pads into contact with the disc. The pedal should be firm and at normal height above the floorpan. Check the brake fluid level and add some, if necessary (see Chapter 1).

14   Check for fluid leakage and make sure the brakes operate normally before driving in traffic.

3   Disc brake caliper - removal and installation

Warning: *Dust created by the brake system is harmful to your health. Never blow it out with compressed air and don't inhale any of it. An approved filtering mask should be worn when working on the brakes. Do not, under any circumstances, use petroleum-based solvents to clean brake parts. Use brake system cleaner only.*

Note: *Always replace the calipers in pairs - never replace just one of them.*

Note: *This procedure applies to front and rear disc brakes.*

Front calipers
Removal

1   Remove the cap from the brake fluid reservoir, siphon off about two-thirds of the fluid into a container and discard the fluid. Brake

2.9a Remove the brake pads from the caliper mounting bracket

2.9b Remove the lower and upper anti-rattle springs

2.11 Clip the anti-squeal shim(s) to the new pad(s)

3.5 If you're removing a Sumitomo caliper, remove the caliper mounting bolts (A) to detach the caliper from the steering knuckle. Don't loosen the caliper inner-to-outer (bridge) bolts (B)

3.6 On 1986 through 1988 models with Tokico calipers and all 1989 and later models, remove the inlet fitting bolt

fluid will damage paint, so be careful not to spill any.

2   Apply the parking brake. Loosen the wheel lug nuts, raise the vehicle and support it securely on jackstands. Remove the front wheels.

1986 through 1988 models with Sumitomo calipers

Refer to illustration 3.5

3   Remove the brake pads from the caliper following the procedure in Section 2.

4   Loosen the hose fitting at the frame bracket and remove the hose securing clip (see Section 9). The brake hose can now be unscrewed from the caliper. Plug the end of the hose to prevent excessive fluid loss.

5   Remove the two mounting bolts and lift the caliper from the vehicle steering knuckle **(see illustration)**.

1986 through 1988 models with Tokico calipers and all 1989 and later models

Refer to illustration 3.6

6   Disconnect the brake line from the caliper by removing the inlet fitting bolt **(see illustration)**. Plug the end of the line to prevent excessive brake fluid loss.

7   If you're working on a 2005 or earlier model, remove the caliper lower mounting bolt **(see illustration 2.8a)**, swing the caliper up until it clears the disc, then slide it off the upper pin. If you're working on a 2006 or later model, remove both caliper mounting bolts and pull the caliper from its mounting bracket.

Installation

8   On Sumitomo calipers, slide the caliper over the disc, aligning the threaded holes in the torque plate with the holes in the steering knuckle. Install the mounting bolts, tightening them to the specified torque. The brake hose and pads can now be installed.

9   If you're working on a 2005 or earlier model, clean and lubricate the caliper pin with

high-temperature disc brake grease. Ensure the brake pads are in place, then slide the caliper upper mounting hole over the pin and pivot the caliper into place. Install the lower mounting bolt, tightening it to the torque listed in this Chapter's Specifications. Connect the brake hose, using new sealing washers on each side of the inlet fitting, then tighten the inlet fitting bolt to the torque listed in this Chapter's Specifications.

10   If you're working on a 2006 or later model, make sure the brake pads are in place, then position the caliper over the brake disc and pads. Install the caliper mounting bolts, tightening them to the torque listed in this Chapter's Specifications. Connect the brake hose, using new sealing washers on each side of the inlet fitting, then tighten the inlet fitting bolt to the torque listed in this Chapter's Specifications.

11   Bleed the brakes following the procedure in Section 10.

12   Install the wheels and lower the vehicle. Tighten the lug nuts to the torque specified in Chapter 1.

13   Firmly depress the brake pedal a few times to bring the pads into contact with the disc. Check the brake fluid level and add some, if necessary (see Chapter 1).

14   Inspect the caliper for fluid leaks and check brake operation before driving the vehicle in traffic.

Rear calipers

Removal

15   Release the parking brake and remove the clip from the parking brake cable on the back side of the caliper assembly.

16   Separate the parking brake cable from the lever on the caliper.

17   Unscrew the inlet fitting bolt and detach the brake line from the caliper. Plug the fitting to prevent fluid loss and contamination.

18   Remove the caliper mounting bolts.

19   Pivot the caliper back and slide it off.

Installation

20   Install the caliper by reversing the removal procedure. Remember to replace the sealing washers on either side of the brake line fitting with new ones, and tighten the inlet fitting bolt and caliper mounting bolts to the torque values listed in this Chapter's Specifications.

21   Bleed the brake system (see Section 10).

22   Install the wheels and lug nuts. Lower the vehicle and tighten the lug nuts to the torque listed in the Chapter 1 Specifications.

---

4   Brake disc - inspection, removal and installation

Inspection

Refer to illustrations 4.2, 4.4a, 4.4b, 4.5a and 4.5b

1   Loosen the wheel lug nuts, raise the vehicle and support it securely on jackstands. Remove the wheel.

2   Remove the brake caliper as outlined in Section 3. It's not necessary to disconnect the brake hose. After removing the caliper, suspend it out of the way with a piece of wire **(see illustration)**.

3   Visually inspect the disc surface for scoring and other damage. Light scratches and shallow grooves are normal after use and may not always be detrimental to brake operation, but deep scoring (over 0.015-inch) requires disc removal and refinishing by an automotive machine shop. Be sure to check both sides of the disc. If pulsating has been noticed during application of the brakes, suspect disc runout.

4   To check disc runout, place a dial indicator at a point about 1/2-inch from the outer edge of the disc **(see illustration)**. Set the indicator to zero and turn the disc. The difference between the highest and lowest indicator reading should not exceed the specified

4.2 Suspend the caliper with a piece of wire whenever you have to move it - don't let it hang by the brake hose!

4.4a Check the disc runout with a dial indicator - if the reading exceeds the maximum allowable runout limit, the disc will have to be machined or replaced

4.4b Using a swirling motion, remove the glaze from the disc with emery cloth or sandpaper

4.5a The minimum allowable disc thickness is stamped on the edge of the disc

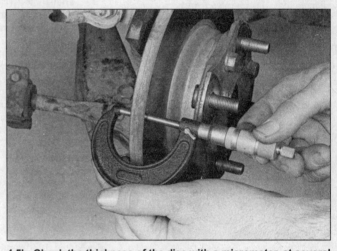

4.5b Check the thickness of the disc with a micrometer, at several points around the outer edge

allowable runout maximum. If it does, the disc should be refinished by an automotive machine shop. **Note:** *Professionals recommend resurfacing of brake discs regardless of the dial indicator reading (to produce a smooth, flat surface that will eliminate brake pedal pulsations and other undesirable symptoms related to questionable discs). At the very least, if you elect not to have the discs resurfaced, deglaze them with sandpaper or emery cloth (use a swirling motion to ensure a non-directional finish)* **(see illustration)**.

5   It is absolutely critical that the disc not be machined to a thickness under the specified minimum allowable thickness. This thickness is stamped onto the edge of the disc **(see illustration)**. The disc thickness can be checked with a micrometer **(see illustration)**.

Removal and installation
1986 through 1999 models
Note: *On these models, the brake disc is sandwiched between the hub and the steering knuckle, so you can't remove it like you would on a conventional setup.*

6   Remove the brake caliper (see Section 3) and suspend it out of the way. **Note:** *Don't disconnect the hose from the caliper.*

7   On 1986 through 1988 models with Tokico calipers, and all 1989 through 1999 models, remove the caliper mounting bracket **(see illustration 4.12)**.

8   Remove the hub and steering knuckle assembly (see Chapter 10).

9   Special tools are required to remove and install the hub and disc and to adjust the hub bearing preload, so this is not a job for a do-it-yourselfer. Take the hub and steering knuckle assembly to an automotive machine shop or other repair facility with the necessary tools.

10   Installation is the reverse of removal.

2000 and later models
Refer to illustration 4.12

11   Remove the brake caliper (see Section 3) and suspend it out of the way. **Note:** *Don't disconnect the hose from the caliper.*

12   Remove the caliper bracket **(see illustration)**.

13   Remove the brake disc from the hub.

14   Installation is the reverse of removal.

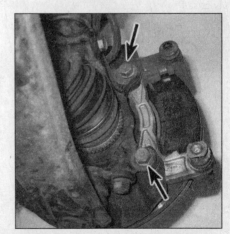

4.12 Caliper mounting bracket bolts

All models

15   Install the wheel, then lower the vehicle to the ground. Depress the brake pedal a few times to bring the brake pads into contact with the disc. Bleeding of the system will not be necessary unless the brake hose was disconnected from the caliper. Check the operation of the brakes carefully before placing the vehicle into normal service.

5   Drum brake shoes - replacement

Warning: *Drum brake shoes must be replaced on both wheels at the same time - never replace the shoes on only one wheel. Also, the dust created by the brake system is harmful to your health. Never blow it out with compressed air and don't inhale any of it. An approved filtering mask should be worn when working on the brakes. Do not, under any circumstances, use petroleum based solvents to clean brake parts. Use brake system cleaner only!*
Caution: *Whenever the brake shoes are replaced, the shoe-to-shoe automatic adjuster (if equipped) and hold-down springs should also be replaced. Due to the continuous heating/cooling cycle that the springs are subjected to, they lose their tension over a period*

5.4a Before removing any internal drum brake components, wash them off with brake cleaner and allow them to dry - position a drain pan under the brake to catch the residue - DO NOT USE COMPRESSED AIR TO BLOW THE BRAKE DUST FROM THE PARTS!

of time and may allow the shoes to drag on the drum and wear at a much faster rate than normal.
1   Loosen the wheel lug nuts, raise the rear of the vehicle and support it securely on jackstands. Block the front wheels to keep the vehicle from rolling.
2   Release the parking brake.
3   Remove the wheel and brake drum (see Chapter 1, Section 32, for the brake drum removal procedure) on 1994 and earlier models. On 1995 and later models, remove the wheel and follow the procedure described

below. **Note:** *All four rear brake shoes must be replaced at the same time, but to avoid mixing up parts, work on only one brake assembly at a time.*

1986 through 1988 models

Refer to illustrations 5.4a through 5.4w

4   Refer to the accompanying illustrations **(5.4a through 5.4w)** for the inspection and replacement of the brake shoes. Be sure to stay in order and read the caption under each illustration. Then proceed to Step 32.

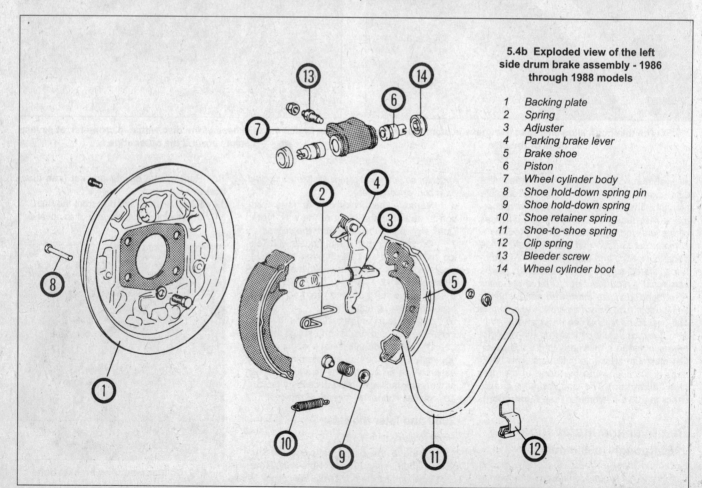

5.4b Exploded view of the left side drum brake assembly - 1986 through 1988 models

1   Backing plate
2   Spring
3   Adjuster
4   Parking brake lever
5   Brake shoe
6   Piston
7   Wheel cylinder body
8   Shoe hold-down spring pin
9   Shoe hold-down spring
10 Shoe retainer spring
11 Shoe-to-shoe spring
12 Clip spring
13 Bleeder screw
14 Wheel cylinder boot

5.4c Pry the clip spring off the anchor point at the bottom of the brake shoes

5.4d Using a pair of needle-nose pliers, unhook the shoe retainer spring from the bottom of the shoes

5.4e Pry the shoe-to-shoe spring out from the holes in the brake shoes

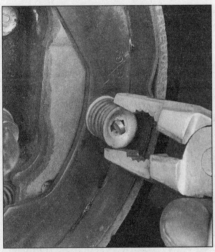

5.4f Remove the shoe hold-down springs from each brake shoe - this is done by pushing the retainer cap down, turning it 90-degrees to align the slot with the pin and then releasing it

5.4g Remove the shoes and adjuster from the backing plate as an assembly

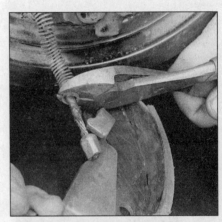

5.4h Disconnect the parking brake cable from the parking brake lever. This is most easily accomplished by pulling the spring back on the cable with a pair of diagonal cutting pliers and gripping the cable lightly with the pliers, then disengaging the cable from the lever - be careful not to nick the cable

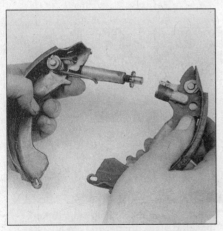

5.4i Separate the trailing shoe (the one with the parking brake lever attached) from the leading shoe

5.4j Pry the C-clip off of the parking brake lever pivot pin (there's a clip on each side, but only remove the one on the side opposite the lever)

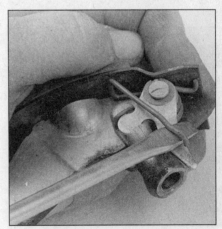

5.4k Pry the spring off the adjuster actuator . . .

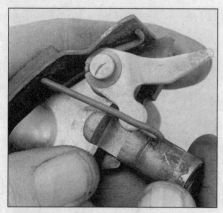

5.4l . . . then remove the end of the adjuster strut

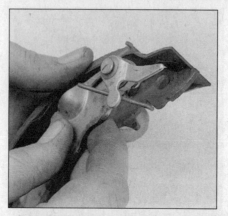

5.4m Separate the parking brake lever from the trailing shoe. Transfer the lever to the new trailing shoe and secure it in place with the C-clip, crimping it closed with pliers. Attach the end of the adjuster to the shoe and pry the spring back over the actuator (reverse steps k and l)

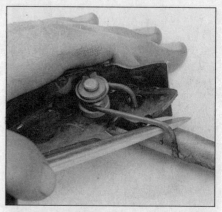

5.4n Pry the spring on the adjuster screw up and over the screw

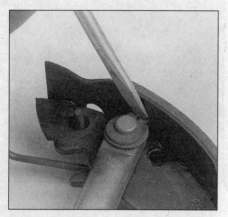

5.4o Pry off the C-clip from the back side of the leading shoe, then remove the adjuster screw

5.4p Clean the adjuster screw and apply multi-purpose grease to the threads and end. Attach the adjuster to the new leading shoe and secure it by crimping the C-clip shut around the pivot pin. Pry the spring over the adjuster so it's positioned on the under side

5.4q Apply a LIGHT coat of multi-purpose grease to the brake shoe contact areas on the backing plate. Don't overdo it, though, as grease on the friction surface of the shoes will ruin them

5.4r Attach the parking brake cable to the parking brake lever, once again holding the spring back on the cable with a pair of diagonal cutting pliers

5.4s Position the trailing shoe on the backing plate and install the hold-down spring - make sure the shoe engages properly with the wheel cylinder

5.4t Mount the leading shoe to the backing plate, connecting the adjuster screw with its other end (on the trailing shoe). Install the hold-down spring and ensure the shoe is properly engaged with the wheel cylinder

5.4u Insert one end of the shoe-to-shoe spring into its hole, then push the other end into its corresponding hole - make sure the ends are pushed in completely

5.4v Connect the shoe retainer spring across the bottom of each shoe - it must be installed behind the anchor, as shown

5.4w Hook the clip spring under the shoe anchor, then pull it up over the top of the anchor far enough for the tang on the anchor (arrow) to snap into the slot in the clip

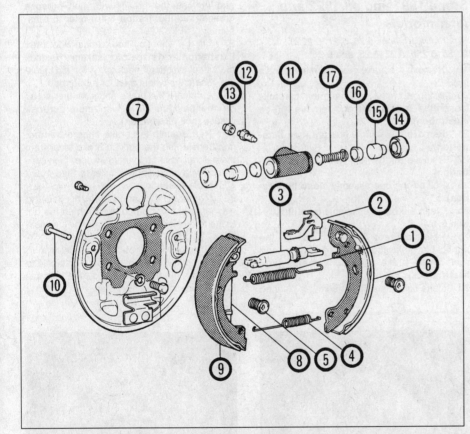

5.6a Exploded view of drum brake assembly - 1989, 1990 and some 1991 models

1	*Automatic adjuster spring*	9	*Shoe and lining assembly - trailing*
2	*Adjuster lever*	10	*Shoe hold-down spring pin*
3	*Adjuster*	11	*Wheel cylinder body*
4	*Shoe-to-shoe spring*	12	*Bleeder screw*
5	*Shoe hold-down spring*	13	*Bleeder screw cap*
6	*Shoe, lining and pin assembly -*	14	*Boot*
	leading	15	*Piston*
7	*Backing plate*	16	*Wheel cylinder cup*
8	*Parking lever and pin assembly*	17	*Spring and expander cup assembly*

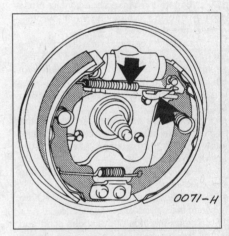

5.6b Unhook the adjuster spring, then remove the spring and lever (arrows)

1989, 1990 and some 1991 models

Refer to illustrations 5.6a, 5.6b and 5.17

5   Clean the brake assembly (**see illustration 5.4a**).

6   Using a pair of pliers, grip the automatic adjuster spring, unhook it from the adjuster lever, then remove the spring and lever (**see illustrations**).

7   Spread the shoes apart and remove the adjuster.

8   Grip the shoe-to-shoe spring with a pair of pliers and unhook it.

9   Remove the hold-down springs from each shoe, using the technique shown in **illustration 5.4f**.

10   Remove the leading shoe from the brake backing plate, then unhook the parking brake cable from the parking brake lever.

11   Clean the adjuster screw and lubricate its threads with multi-purpose grease (**see illustration 5.4p**).

5.17 Make sure the slotted ends of the adjuster slide over the slots in the shoes

5.20 Tap the spindle cap off for access to the spindle hub nut

12   Lubricate the brake shoe contact areas on the backing plate with multi-purpose grease (see illustration 5.4q).
13   Transfer the parking brake lever from the old trailing shoe to the new one. It will be necessary to pry the C-clip from the lever pivot pin and crimp it into position once the lever is attached to the new shoe (see illustration 5.4j).
14   Connect the parking brake lever to the parking brake cable and position the trailing shoe against the backing plate. Install the holddown spring.
15   Place the leading shoe on the backing plate and install the holddown spring.
16   Connect the shoe-to-shoe spring between the bottom of the two shoes.
17   Spread the tops of the shoes apart and install the adjuster. Make sure the slotted ends of the adjuster slide over the slots in the shoes (see illustration).
18   Install the adjuster lever and automatic adjuster spring. Proceed to Step 32.

Some 1991 and all 1992 and later models

Refer to illustrations 5.20, 5.21, 5.22, 5.23, 5.25a, 5.25b, 5.27, 5.28, and 5.31

19   Remove the brake drum from the spindle hub.
20   Using a chisel and hammer, carefully loosen the spindle cap and remove it (see illustration).
21   Remove the spindle hub nut (see illustration).
22   Remove the bearing washer (see illustration).
23   Pull off the hub assembly (see illustration).
24   Clean the brake assembly (see illustration 5.4a).
25   Refer to Steps 5 through 18 and the applicable illustrations, where similar, and replace the brake shoe components (see illustrations).
26   Make sure the adjuster screw is cleaned

and lubricate the threads with multi-purpose grease (see illustration 5.4p) prior to reassembly.
27   Lift the wheel cylinder rubber boot (see illustration) and inspect for leakage. Replace the wheel cylinder if necessary. If it isn't leaking, reseat the wheel cylinder rubber boot.
28   Lubricate the brake shoe contact areas on the backing plate with multi-purpose grease (see illustration).
29   Reassemble the brake shoe assembly, first transferring the parking brake lever from the old trailing shoe to the new one, then continuing with reassembly, similar to Step 4 and applicable illustrations.
30   Reinstall the spindle hub, bearing washer, and spindle hub nut. Tighten the nut to the torque listed in this Chapter's Specifications.
31   On models without a self-locking nut, stake the hub nut into the slot in the spindle to prevent the nut from loosening (see illustration). Proceed to the next Step.

5.21 Remove the spindle hub nut with a socket

5.22 Pull out the hub bearing washer

5.23 Pull off the hub assembly

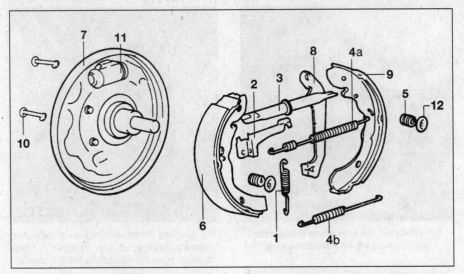

5.25b Begin the brake shoe disassembly by removing the lower shoe return spring with pliers

5.25a Exploded view of rear brake assembly - some 1991 and all 1992 and later models

1	Automatic adjuster spring	6	Leading shoe
2	Adjuster lever	7	Backing plate
3	Adjuster	8	Parking brake lever
4a	Shoe-to-shoe spring - upper	9	Trailing shoe
4b	Shoe-to-shoe spring - lower (2006 and later models have a shorter spring)	10	Hold-down spring pin
		11	Wheel cylinder
5	Shoe hold-down spring*	12	Hold-down spring retainer*

*2006 and later models have flat, spring steel retainers

All models

Refer to illustration 5.32

32 Before reinstalling the drum it should be checked for cracks, score marks, deep scratches and hard spots, which will appear as small discolored areas. If the hard spots cannot be removed with sandpaper or emery cloth or if any of the other conditions listed above exist, the drum must be taken to an automotive machine shop for resurfacing.

Note: *Professionals recommend resurfacing the drums whenever a brake job is done. Resurfacing will eliminate the possibility of out-of-round drums. If the drums are worn so much that they can't be resurfaced without exceeding the maximum allowable diameter (cast into the drum)* **(see illustration),** *then new ones will be required. At the very least, if you elect not to have the drums resurfaced, remove the glazing from the surface with sandpaper or emery cloth using a swirling motion.*

5.27 Pull back the wheel cylinder rubber boot to check for leakage

33 Install the brake drum and, on 1994 and earlier models, adjust the rear wheel bearings (see Chapter 1).

5.28 Lubricate the brake shoe contact points on the backing plate

5.31 Stake the spindle hub nut after installation to prevent it from loosening (models without a self-locking nut)

5.32 The maximum allowable diameter is cast into the drum

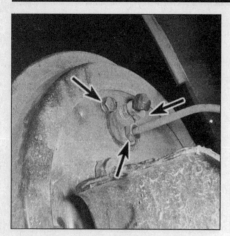

6.4 Unscrew the brake line fitting, then remove the two wheel cylinder mounting bolts (typical)

7.4 Unscrew the brake line fitting tube nuts (arrows) with a flare nut wrench

7.6 Unplug the brake fluid level indicator electrical connector, then remove the two master cylinder mounting nuts (arrows)

34 Mount the wheel, install the lug nuts, then lower the vehicle. Tighten the lug nuts to the torque listed in the Chapter 1 Specifications.
35 Alternately cycle the parking brake lever and pump the brake pedal several times to adjust the brake shoes to the drum.
36 Check brake operation before driving the vehicle in traffic.

6   Wheel cylinder - removal and installation

Note: *Never replace only one wheel cylinder - always replace both of them at the same time.*

Removal

Refer to illustration 6.4

1 Raise the rear of the vehicle and support it securely on jackstands. Block the front wheels to keep the vehicle from rolling.
2 Remove the brake shoe assembly (see Section 5).
3 Remove all dirt and foreign material from around the wheel cylinder.
4 Unscrew the brake line fitting from the inner side of the brake backing plate **(see illustration)**. Use a flare nut wrench, if available, to prevent rounding off the corners of the fitting. Don't pull the brake line away from the wheel cylinder.
5 Remove the wheel cylinder mounting bolts from the inner side of the brake backing plate.
6 Detach the wheel cylinder from the brake backing plate and place it on a clean workbench. Immediately plug the brake line to prevent fluid loss and contamination. **Note:** *If the brake shoe linings are contaminated with brake fluid, install new brake shoes.*

Installation

7 Apply a thin coat of RTV sealant to the backing plate where the wheel cylinder seats, place the cylinder in position and install the mounting bolts.

8 Connect the brake line and tighten the fitting, then tighten the wheel cylinder bolts. Install the brake shoe assembly.
9 Bleed the brakes (see Section 10).
10 Check brake operation before driving the vehicle in traffic.

7   Master cylinder - removal and installation

Note: *Before deciding to overhaul the master cylinder, check on the availability and cost of a new or factory rebuilt unit and also the availability of a rebuild kit.*

Removal

Refer to illustrations 7.4 and 7.6

1 The master cylinder is located in the engine compartment, mounted to the power brake booster.
2 Remove as much fluid as you can from the reservoir with a syringe.
3 Place rags under the fluid fittings and prepare caps or plastic bags to cover the ends of the lines once they are disconnected. **Caution:** *Brake fluid will damage paint. Cover all body parts and be careful not to spill fluid during this procedure.*
4 Loosen the tube nuts at the ends of the brake lines where they enter the master cylinder **(see illustration)**. To prevent rounding off the flats on these nuts, the use of a flare nut wrench, which wraps around the nut, is preferred.
5 Pull the brake lines slightly away from the master cylinder and plug the ends to prevent contamination.
6 Disconnect the electrical connector at the master cylinder, then remove the two nuts attaching the master cylinder to the power booster **(see illustration)**. Pull the master cylinder off the studs and out of the engine compartment. Again, be careful not to spill the fluid as this is done.

Installation

Refer to illustration 7.8

7 Bench bleed the master cylinder before installing it. Mount the master cylinder in a vise, with the jaws of the vise clamping on the mounting flange.
8 Attach a pair of master cylinder bleeder tubes to the outlet ports of the master cylinder **(see illustration)**.
9 Fill the reservoir with brake fluid of the recommended type (see Chapter 1).
10 Using a large Phillips screwdriver, slowly push the pistons into the master cylinder **(see illustration 7.8)** to expel the air from the pressure chamber into the reservoir. Because the tubes are submerged in fluid, air can't be drawn back into the master cylinder when you release the pistons.
11 Repeat the procedure until no more air bubbles are present.
12 Remove the bleed tubes, one at a time, and install plugs in the open ports to prevent

7.8 The best way to bleed air from the master cylinder before installing it on the vehicle is with a pair of bleed tubes that direct brake fluid back into the reservoir during bleeding

9.4a Pry the spring clip off the brake hose fitting

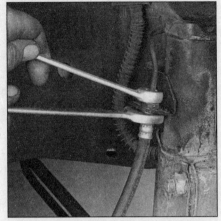

9.4b A backup wrench must be used to keep the hose from turning, otherwise the steel brake line will twist - if available, use a flare nut wrench.on the line fitting to prevent rounding off the corners

fluid leakage and air from entering. Install the reservoir cap.

13 Install the master cylinder over the studs on the power brake booster and tighten the attaching nuts only finger tight at this time.

14 Thread the brake line fittings into the master cylinder. Since the master cylinder is still a bit loose, it can be moved slightly for the fittings to thread in easily. Be careful not to strip the threads as the fittings are tightened.

15 Fully tighten the mounting nuts and the brake line fittings.

16 Fill the master cylinder reservoir with fluid, then bleed the brake system as described in Section 10. Test the operation of the brake system carefully before placing the vehicle into normal service.

8 Proportioning valve - removal and installation

Note: *This procedure applies to 1986 through 1999 models with a separate proportioning valve. On 2000 and later models with ABS, there is no proportioning valve.*

1999 and earlier models

Removal

1 Although special test equipment is necessary to properly diagnose a proportioning valve malfunction, you can remove and install it if it has been diagnosed as being faulty.

2 The proportioning valve is located either below the master cylinder or on the firewall. Using a flare nut wrench to avoid rounding off the tube nuts, unscrew the tube nuts at the ends of the brake lines where they enter the valve. Gently pull the lines away from the valve and plug the ends of the lines or wrap plastic bags tightly around them to prevent excessive leakage and brake system contamination.

3 Remove the mounting nut from the center of the valve and maneuver the valve out from the brake lines.

Installation

4 Position the valve on the bracket and insert the brake lines into the holes. Screw all of the tube nuts into the valve by hand, being careful not to cross thread them. Install the mounting nut and tighten it securely.

5 Tighten the tube nuts securely, again using the flare nut wrench.

6 Bleed the entire brake system as described in Section 10.

2000 and later models

7 Using a flare-nut wrench, unscrew the brake lines from the proportioning valve(s) on the master cylinder.

8 Unscrew the proportioning valves from the master cylinder.

9 Installation is the reverse of removal.

10 Bleed the brake system as described in Section 10.

9 Brake lines and hoses - inspection and replacement

Refer to illustrations 9.4a and 9.4b

1 About every six months the flexible hoses which connect the steel brake lines with the rear brakes and front calipers should be inspected for cracks, chafing of the outer cover, leaks, blisters, and other damage (see Chapter 1).

2 Replacement steel and flexible brake lines are commonly available from dealer parts departments and auto parts stores. Do not, under any circumstances, use anything other than genuine steel lines or approved flexible brake hoses as replacement items.

3 When installing the brake line, leave at least 3/4-inch clearance between the line and any moving or vibrating parts.

4 When disconnecting a hose and line, first remove the spring clip. Then, using an open end wrench to hold the hose and a flare nut wrench to hold the tube, unscrew the fitting **(see illustrations)**. Use the wrenches in the same manner when reconnecting the hose and line, then install a new clip. **Note:** *Make sure the tube passes through the center of its grommet.*

5 When disconnecting two hoses, use open end wrenches on the hose fittings. When connecting two hoses, make sure they are not bent, twisted or strained.

6 Steel brake lines are usually retained along their span with clips. Always remove these clips completely before removing a fixed brake line. Always reinstall these clips, or new ones if the old ones are damaged, when replacing a brake line, as they provide support and keep the lines from vibrating, which can eventually break them.

10 Brake system bleeding

Refer to illustration 10.8

Warning: *Wear eye protection when bleeding the brake system. If the fluid comes in contact with your eyes, immediately rinse them with water and seek medical attention.*

Note: *Bleeding the hydraulic system is necessary to remove any air that manages to find its way into the system when it's been opened during removal and installation of a hose, line, caliper or master cylinder.*

1 It will probably be necessary to bleed the system at all four brakes if air has entered the system due to low fluid level, or if the brake lines have been disconnected at the master cylinder.

2 If a brake line was disconnected only at a wheel, then only that caliper or wheel cylinder must be bled.

3 If a brake line is disconnected at a fitting located between the master cylinder and any of the brakes, that part of the system served by the disconnected line must be bled.

4 Remove any residual vacuum from the brake power booster by applying the brake several times with the engine off.

5 Remove the master cylinder reservoir cover and fill the reservoir with brake fluid. Reinstall the cover. **Note:** *Check the fluid level often during the bleeding operation and add fluid as necessary to prevent the fluid level from falling low enough to allow air bubbles into the master cylinder.*

6 Have an assistant on hand, as well as a supply of new brake fluid, a clear container partially filled with clean brake fluid, a length of plastic or vinyl tubing to fit over the bleeder screw and a wrench to open and close the bleeder screw.

7 Beginning at the left rear wheel, loosen the bleeder screw slightly, then tighten it to a point where it is snug but can still be loosened quickly and easily.

8 Place one end of the tubing over the bleeder screw and submerge the other end in

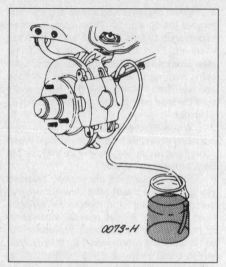

10.8 When bleeding the brakes, a hose is connected to the bleeder screw at the caliper or wheel cylinder and then submerged in brake fluid. Air will be seen as bubbles in the tube and container. All air must be expelled before moving on to the next wheel

brake fluid in the container (**see illustration**).
9   Have your assistant push down on the brake pedal and hold the pedal firmly depressed.
10   While the pedal is held depressed, open the bleeder screw just enough to allow a flow of fluid to occur. Watch for air bubbles to exit the submerged end of the tube. When the fluid flow slows after a couple of seconds, tighten the screw and have your assistant release the pedal.
11   Repeat Steps 9 and 10 until no more air is seen leaving the tube, then tighten the bleeder screw and proceed to the right front wheel, the right rear wheel and the left front wheel, in that order, and perform the same procedure. Be sure to check the fluid in the master cylinder reservoir frequently.
12   Never use old brake fluid. It contains moisture which will deteriorate the brake system components.
13   Refill the master cylinder with fluid at the end of the operation.
14   Check the operation of the brakes. The pedal should feel solid when depressed, with no sponginess: If necessary, repeat the entire process. **Warning:** *Do not operate the vehicle if you are in doubt about the effectiveness of the brake system.*

---

11   Power brake booster - check, removal and installation

Check

1   Depress the pedal and start the engine. If the pedal goes down slightly, operation is normal.
2   Depress the brake pedal several times with the engine running and make sure that

11.7 Remove the cotter pin and clevis pin, then unscrew the booster mounting nuts (typical)

there is no change in the pedal reserve distance.
3   Start the engine and turn it off after one or two minutes. Depress the brake pedal several times slowly. If the pedal goes down farther the first time but gradually rises after the second or third depression, the booster is air tight.
4   Depress the brake pedal while the engine is running, then stop the engine with the pedal depressed. If there is no change in the pedal reserve travel after holding the pedal for 30 seconds, the booster is air tight.

Removal

Refer to illustration 11.7

5   Power brake booster units should not be disassembled. They require special tools not normally found in most automotive repair stations or shops. They are fairly complex and because of their critical relationship to brake performance it is best to replace a defective booster unit with a new or rebuilt one.

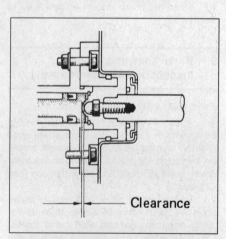

11.14a The booster pushrod-to-master cylinder piston clearance must be as specified - if there is interference between the two, the brakes may drag; if there is too much clearance, there will be excessive brake pedal travel

6   To remove the booster, first remove the brake master cylinder as described in Section 7. Pull the proportioning valve and bracket forward, being careful not to kink the lines.
7   Locate the pushrod clevis connecting the booster to the brake pedal (**see illustration**). This is accessible from the interior in front of the passenger's seat, under the dash.
8   Remove the clevis pin cotter pin with pliers and pull out the clevis pin.
9   Holding the clevis with pliers, disconnect the clevis locknut with a wrench.
10   Disconnect the hose leading from the engine to the booster. Be careful not to damage the hose when removing it from the booster fitting.
11   Remove the four nuts and washers holding the brake booster to the firewall (**see illustration 11.7**).
12   Slide the booster straight out from the firewall until the studs clear the holes, and pull the booster, brackets and gaskets from the engine compartment area.

Installation

Refer to illustrations 11.14a, 11.14b, 11.14c, 11.14d and 11.15

13   Installation procedures are basically the reverse of those for removal. Tighten the clevis locknut securely and the booster mounting nuts to the specified torque.
14   If a new power brake booster unit is being installed, check the pushrod clearance (**see illustration**). **Note:** *When checking the pushrod clearance on 1990 and later models, connect a hand-held vacuum pump to the vacuum port on the booster and apply a vacuum of 20 in-Hg.*
a)   *Measure the distance that the pushrod protrudes from the master cylinder mounting surface on the front of the power brake booster, including the gasket (if equipped) (**see illustration**). This is "dimension A."*

11.14b Measure the distance that the pushrod protrudes from the master cylinder mounting surface on the power brake booster

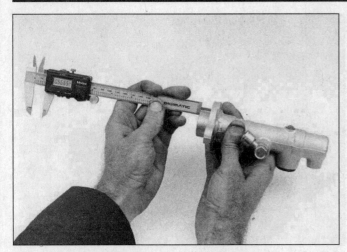

11.14c Measure the distance from the mounting flange to the end of the master cylinder

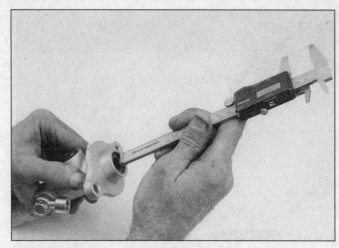

11.14d Measure the distance from the piston pocket to the end of the master cylinder

b) *Measure the distance from the mounting flange to the end of the master cylinder* **(see illustration)**. *This is "dimension B."*

c) *Measure the distance from the end of the master cylinder to the bottom of the pocket in the piston* **(see illustration)**. *This is "dimension C."*

d) *Subtract measurement B from measurement C, then subtract measurement A from the difference between B and C. This the pushrod clearance.*

e) *Compare your calculated pushrod clearance to the pushrod clearance listed in this Chapter's Specifications. If necessary, adjust the pushrod length to achieve the correct clearance.*

15   To adjust the pushrod length, hold the serrated part of the pushrod with a pair of pliers and turn the pushrod end with a wrench **(see illustration)**. Recheck the clearance.

Repeat this step as often as necessary until the clearance is correct.

16   After the final installation of the master cylinder and brake hoses and lines, the brake pedal height and freeplay must be adjusted and the system must be bled. See the appropriate Sections of this Chapter for the procedures.

12   Parking brake - adjustment

Refer to illustrations 12.2, 12.3 and 12.4

1   Pull the parking brake lever up as far as possible, counting the number of clicks as you go. The travel should be five to seven clicks. If you are able to raise the lever higher, the parking brake might not hold the vehicle on an incline. If the travel is less than specified, the automatic adjusters on the rear brakes could be rendered useless. If the parking brake

lever travel is not five to seven clicks, adjust the parking brake, as described below.

2   On models without an access panel at the bottom of the rear of the center console, remove the center console (see Chapter 11). On models with an access panel, carefully pry out the panel **(see illustration)**.

3   On 1989 and earlier models, turn the cable adjusting nuts on the equalizer until the specified lever travel is obtained **(see illustration)**. Tighten the nuts evenly to avoid over-adjusting one cable, leaving the other slack. On 1990 and later models, turn the single cable adjustment nut on the equalizer until the specified lever travel is obtained.

4   If necessary, adjust the parking brake indicator light switch so the brake light on the instrument panel is off when the parking brake lever is all the way down. To adjust the switch, loosen the switch mounting screw (directly in front of the lever quadrant teeth) and move the

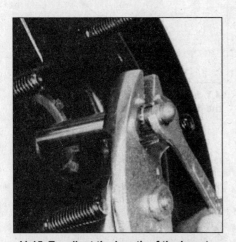

11.15 To adjust the length of the booster pushrod, hold the serrated portion of the rod with a pair of pliers and turn the adjusting screw in or out, as necessary, to achieve the desired setting

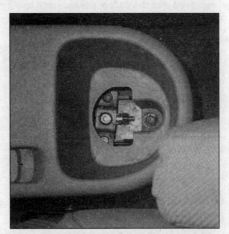

12.2 On models with an access panel in the center console, pry out the panel for access to the parking brake cable adjuster

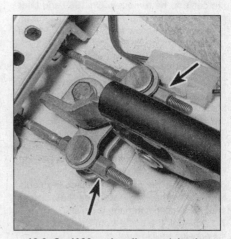

12.3 On 1989 and earlier models, the parking brake cable adjusting nuts are located under the center console. When adjusting the cables, turn each adjusting nut an equal amount to obtain the correct lever travel

12.4 To adjust the parking brake light switch, loosen the mounting screw and, with the handle in the released position, move the switch as necessary to turn the light off. Tighten the mounting screw

13.6 Pry off the parking brake E-clip, then push the cable through the backing plate (1989 and earlier models shown; later models have a U-shaped spring clip)

switch up or down, as necessary **(see illustration)**. After the switch has been adjusted, tighten the screw securely.

5   Check to make sure the rear brakes don't drag when the vehicle is driven.

13   Parking brake cables - replacement

Refer to illustrations 13.6 and 13.8

Note: *This procedure applies to both the right and left cables.*

1   Remove the center console (see Chapter 11).

2   On 1986 through 1989 models, completely unscrew the cable adjusting nut from the cable to be removed. On 1989 and later models, turn the single cable adjusting nut on the equalizer to allow slack in the cable to be removed.

3   Loosen the rear wheel lug nuts on the side of the vehicle on which the cable is to be removed. Raise the rear of the vehicle and support it securely on jackstands. Place blocks in front of the front wheels. Remove the wheel.

4   Remove the brake drum and shoes, following the procedure outlined in Section 5.

5   Unhook the cable end from the parking brake lever on the brake shoe.

6   Remove the clip that secures the cable to the brake backing plate **(see illustration)** and pull the cable through the plate.

7   Unhook the cable from the clips on the suspension trailing arm.

8   Remove the rear seat cushion. Lift up the carpet, unscrew the cable clamp bolt and free the cable from the clamp **(see illustration)**. Pull the cable and grommet through the floorpan into the interior.

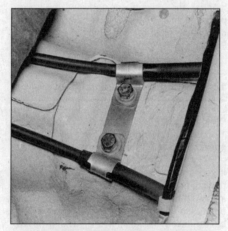

13.8 The rear seat cushion must be removed and the carpet peeled back to gain access to the cable clamp bolts - you only need to remove the bolt that holds the cable being replaced

9   Installation is the reverse of the removal procedure. After the cable is installed, adjust the parking brake (see Section 12).

14   Brake pedal height and freeplay - adjustment

Brake pedal height and brake light switch adjustment

Refer to illustrations 14.1 and 14.4

1   The brake pedal height is the measured distance that the pedal sits off the floor **(see illustration)**. Measure the pedal height from the top of the brake pedal pad to the floor. If the pedal height is not within the specified

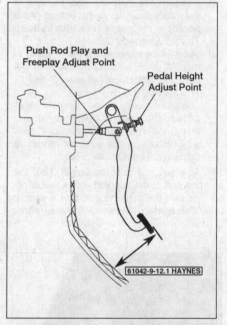

14.1 Measure the brake pedal height from the pedal pad to the floor (typical setup)

range listed in this Chapter's Specifications, adjusted it as follows.

2   The brake pedal height and the gap between the brake pedal and the brake light switch are somewhat interrelated; you can't always adjust one without having to adjust the other. So, loosen the brake light switch locknut, then turn the switch counterclockwise until there's enough gap between the switch plunger and the brake pedal arm to allow you to adjust the pedal height as necessary.

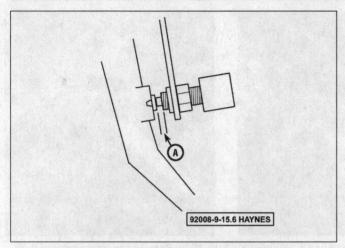

14.4 To adjust the brake light switch, loosen the locknut and rotate the switch until the plunger distance (A) is within the range listed in this Chapter's Specifications

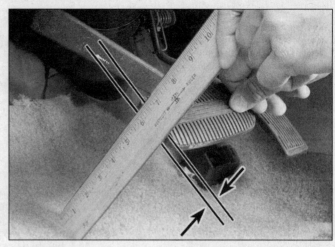

14.5 Brake pedal freeplay is the distance that the brake pedal travels before the piston inside the master cylinder is actuated

3   To adjust the brake pedal height, loosen the locknut on the pedal height adjusting bolt, then turn the adjusting bolt to raise or lower the pedal height as necessary. When the pedal height is correct, tighten the pedal height adjusting bolt locknut.
4   To adjust the brake light switch, simply turn the switch in or out until the gap between the switch and the brake pedal arm (see illustration) is within the specified clearance listed in this Chapter's Specifications, then tighten the switch locknut.

Brake pedal freeplay

Refer to illustration 14.5
5   The brake pedal freeplay (see illustration) is the distance that the pedal can be depressed before it starts to push against the piston inside the master cylinder and apply braking force. If the pedal freeplay is not within the specified range listed in this Chapter's Specifications, adjust it.
6   To adjust brake pedal freeplay, loosen the locknut on the brake pushrod (see illustration 14.1), then turn the pushrod to adjust the pedal freeplay to the specified range. When the freeplay is within the specified range, retighten the locknut.

Brake pedal reserve height

Note: *This specification doesn't apply to all years (see this Chapter's Specifications).*
7   The brake pedal reserve height is the measured distance between the brake pedal and the floor when the pedal is firmly and fully depressed. If you have adjusted brake pedal height and freeplay correctly, the brake pedal reserve height should be fine as long as the brake system itself if functioning correctly. If the pedal reserve is too low, there could be air in the system or a brake fluid leak, an auto-

matic adjuster could be malfunctioning, or the clearance between the booster pushrod and the master cylinder might be excessive. Troubleshoot the brake system, fix the problem, then measure the pedal reserve height again.

Brake pedal stroke

Note: *This specification doesn't apply to all years (see this Chapter's Specifications).*
8   The brake pedal stroke is the measured distance that the brake pedal travels from its unapplied position to its lowest position when the pedal is firmly and fully depressed. Measuring the brake pedal stroke is another way to determine whether the brake system itself is functioning well. If the pedal stroke is excessive, there is air in the system or there's a brake fluid leak, or an automatic adjuster is malfunctioning, or the clearance between the push rod and the master cylinder is excessive. Troubleshoot the brake system, fix the problem, then measure the pedal stroke again.

15   Brake light switch - removal, installation and adjustment

Refer to illustration 15.2
1   Remove the lower dash panel trim under the steering column (see Chapter 11).
2   Locate the brake light switch, which is mounted at the top of the left side brake pedal support (see illustration 14.4 and the accompanying illustration). Follow the switch wiring to the electrical connector and unplug it.
3   Unscrew the locknut on the switch and unscrew the switch from its bracket.
4   Installation is the reverse of removal. To adjust the switch, refer to Section 14.

16   Parking brake shoes - inspection and replacement

Refer to illustrations 16.4, 16.5a through 16.5u, 16.7a and 16.7b
Warning 1: *Dust created by the brake system is hazardous to your health. Never blow it out with compressed air and don't inhale any of it. An approved filtering mask should be worn when working on the brakes. Do not, under any circumstances, use petroleum-based solvents to clean brake parts. Use brake system cleaner only!*
Warning 2: *Parking brake shoes must be replaced on both wheels at the same time - never replace the shoes on only one wheel.*
1   Remove the rear brake discs (see Section 5).
2   Inspect the thickness of the lining material on the shoes. If the lining has worn down to 1/32-inch or less, the shoes must be replaced.

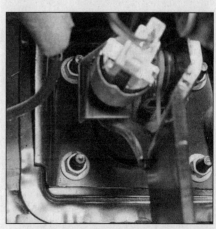

15.2 Typical 1995 and later model brake light switch

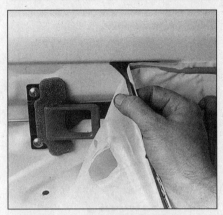

12.7 Be very careful when removing the plastic watershield - don't tear or distort it

12.11 To detach the trim panel for the inside door handle, remove this screw

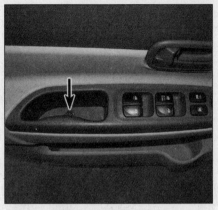

12.12 To detach the switch panel, remove this screw

7   For access to the inner door, peel back the plastic watershield, taking care not to tear it **(see illustration)**.
8   Prior to installation of the door panel, make sure to reinstall any clips in the panel which may have come out during the removal procedure and remain in the door itself. Place the watershield in position and press it in place.
9   Plug in any electrical connectors and place the panel in position in the door. Press the door panel into place until the clips are seated and install any retaining screws and armrest/door pulls. Install the manual regulator window crank.

Newer models

Refer to illustrations 12.11, 12.12, 12.13, 12.14, 12.15 and 12.16

10   Disconnect the cable from the negative battery terminal (see Chapter 5).
11   Remove the inside handle retaining screw **(see illustration)**.
12   Remove the switch panel retaining screw **(see illustration)**.
13   Remove the trim panel for the outside

12.13 Using a trim removal tool, carefully pop loose the trim panel for the outside mirror

mirror **(see illustration)**.
14   Remove the trim plug for the retaining screw near the upper end of the rear edge of the trim panel **(see illustration)**, then remove the trim panel retaining screw.

12.14 Remove this trim plug near the top of the rear edge of the door trim panel and remove the trim panel retaining screw

15   Using a trim removal tool, carefully pop loose the clips that secure the trim panel to the door **(see illustration)**.
16   Remove the trim panel and disconnect the electrical connectors **(see illustration)**.

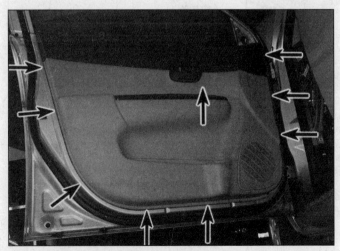

12.15 Carefully pop loose the door trim panel clips

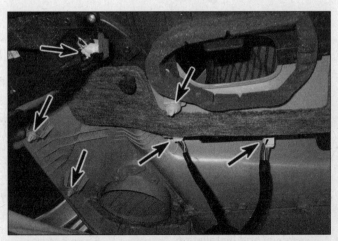

12.16 Remove the door trim panel and disconnect the electrical connectors. In this photo you can see some of the trim panel retaining clips; make sure none stick in the door

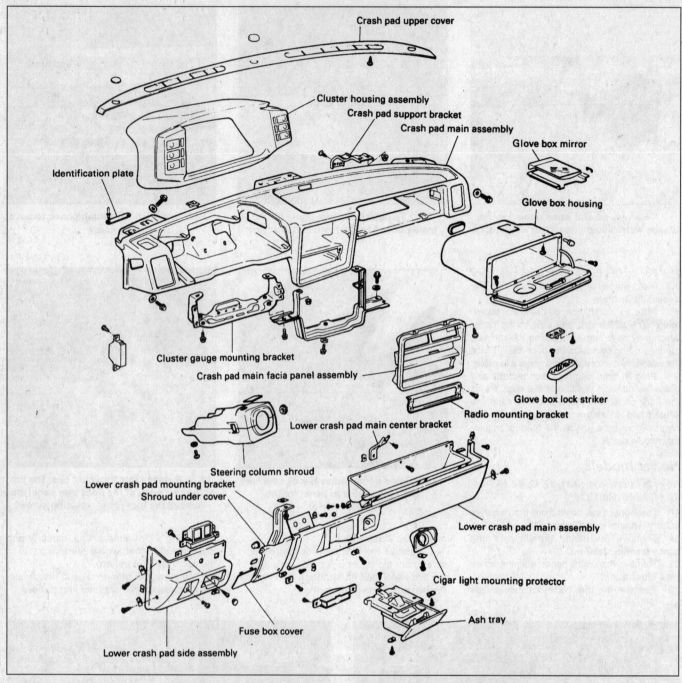

Crash pad upper cover

Cluster housing assembly
Crash pad support bracket
Crash pad main assembly

Glove box mirror

Identification plate

Glove box housing

Cluster gauge mounting bracket

Crash pad main facia panel assembly

Lower crash pad main center bracket

Glove box lock striker
Radio mounting bracket

Steering column shroud

Lower crash pad mounting bracket
Shroud under cover

Lower crash pad main assembly

Cigar light mounting protector

Ash tray

Fuse box cover

Lower crash pad side assembly

13.1 Dashboard and related components (1986 through 1989 models)

17   If you're going to service the door lock mechanism, the inside or outside door handle, or the window glass or window regulator, carefully remove the watershield (see illustration 12.7).
18   Installation is the reverse of removal.

13 Dashboard and trim panels - removal and installation

Warning: *If equipped with a Supplemental Restraint System (SRS), more commonly known as airbags, disable the airbag system before working in the vicinity of airbag system components to avoid the possibility of accidental deployment of the airbag, which could result in personal injury (see Chapter 12).*

1986 through 1989 models
Refer to illustrations 13.1, 13.3 and 13.13

Knee bolster
1   Remove the retaining screws (including the two hood release handle mounting screws), lower the assembly, unplug the electrical connector and remove the lower dashboard side assembly (see illustration).
2   Installation is the reverse of removal.

Steering column lower cover
3   Remove the two retaining screws (see illustration).
4   Swing the cover down and detach it from the dashboard.

Lower dashboard assembly
5   Remove the center console (see Section 15).
6   Remove the retaining screws, detach the

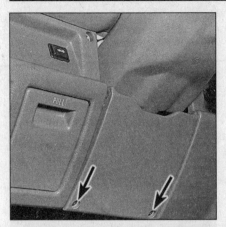

13.3 Remove the two cover retaining screws (arrows)

13.13 Remove the screws and pry off the radio trim bezel

assembly, lower it sufficiently for access to the electrical connectors and unplug them **(see illustration 13.1)**.

7   Remove the assembly.

8   Installation is the reverse of removal.

Instrument cluster bezel

9   Remove the retaining screws.

10   Pull the bezel away from the dash and disconnect the electrical connectors.

11   Installation is the reverse of removal.

Center bezel assembly

12   Remove the screws at the top of the assembly.

13   Pry off the radio cover for access to the two lower retaining screws **(see illustration)**. Remove the screws and pull the bezel away from the dash.

14   Installation is the reverse of removal.

Dashboard main assembly

15   Remove all previously described components attached to the dashboard main assembly and the glove box **(see illustration 13.1)**. Remove the steering wheel and the steering column covers (see Section 14).

16   Remove the instrument cluster and the radio (see Chapter 12). Remove the air conditioning and heater control panel (see Chapter 3).

17   Remove the screw covers and the screws from the upper cover at the base of the windshield.

18   Remove the screws from the mounting brackets. Carefully remove the dashboard from the vehicle.

19   Installation is the reverse of removal.

1990 to 1994 models

Refer to illustration 13.21

Knee bolster

20   Remove the hood release handle mounting screws.

21   Remove the screws, pull the panel away from the dash **(see illustration)**. Disconnect any electrical connectors and remove the panel from the vehicle.

22   Installation is the reverse of removal.

Center trim bezel

23   Remove the screws and remove the center trim bezel.

24   Installation is the reverse of removal.

Lower dashboard assembly

25   Remove the screws and remove the glove box assembly. Remove the center trim bezel.

26   Remove the retaining screws and remove the assembly from the dash.

27   Installation is the reverse of removal.

Instrument cluster bezel

28   Remove the retaining screws and pull the bezel from the retaining clips.

29   Installation is the reverse of removal.

Dashboard main assembly

30   Remove all previously described components attached to the dashboard main assembly **(see illustration 13.21)**. Remove the instrument cluster and the radio (see Chapter 12). Remove the air conditioning and heater control panel (see Chapter 3). Remove the steering column cover (see Section 14). Remove the center console (see Section 15).

31   Remove the front speaker grilles and the speakers. Remove the dashboard mounting screws in the speaker openings. Carefully pry the clock assembly from the dash. Remove the mounting screw in the clock opening.

32   Remove the retaining screws in the instrument cluster opening, at each end of the dashboard and at the center support bracket. Carefully pull the dashboard main assembly toward the rear and remove it from the vehicle.

33   Installation is the reverse of removal.

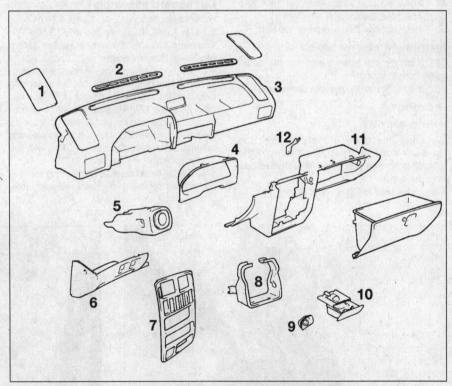

13.21 Dashboard and related components - 1990 through 1994 models

1	*Speaker grille*	*7*	*Center trim bezel*
2	*Dashboard upper cover*	*8*	*Dashboard center support bracket*
3	*Dashboard main assembly*	*9*	*Cigar lighter bezel*
4	*Instrument cluster bezel*	*10*	*Ash tray*
5	*Steering column cover*	*11*	*Lower dashboard assembly*
6	*Knee bolster*	*12*	*Lower dashboard bracket*

13.34 With the ashtray removed, remove the center panel trim mounting screws (1995 through 2005 models)

13.39 Unsnap the glove box stop(s) (arrow), then remove the mounting screws and remove the glove box (1995 through 2005 models)

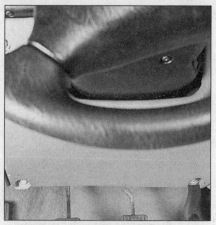

13.41 Remove the lower steering column cover retaining screws (1995 through 2005 models)

1995 through 2005 models

Center trim bezel

Refer to illustration 13.34

34   Remove the ashtray and remove the bezel mounting screws **(see illustration)**.
35   Pull the bezel away from the dash and disconnect the electrical connectors.
36   Installation is the reverse of removal.

Instrument cluster bezel

37   Remove the screws and pull the bezel away from the dash
38   Installation is the reverse of removal.

Glovebox

Refer to illustration 13.39

39   Open the glove box and unsnap the glove box stop **(see illustration)**. Remove the mounting screws and remove the glove box from the dash.
40   Installation is the reverse of removal.

Lower steering column cover

Refer to illustration 13.41

41   Remove the screws and pull the lower cover away from the dash **(see illustration)**.
42   Installation is the reverse of removal.

Dashboard assembly

Refer to illustration 13.44, 13.46, 13.47a, 13.47b, 13.48, 13.49, 13.50a and 13.50b
Warning: *Disable the airbag system before beginning this procedure (see Chapter 12).*
43   Remove all previously described components attached to the dashboard assembly. Remove the instrument cluster and the radio (see Chapter 12). Remove the air conditioning and heater control panel (see Chapter 3). Remove the steering wheel and the steering column cover (see Section 14). Remove the center console (see Section 15).
44   Lift the hood release handle and remove the screws retaining the hood release cable/

lever assembly to the dash **(see illustration)**.
45   Reach through the glove box opening and unclip the heater cable from the bracket. Disconnect the electrical connector to the passenger airbag module (if equipped).
46   Remove the screw covers in the glove box opening to access the dash panel mounting bolts **(see illustration)**. Remove the bolts.
47   Remove the kick panel retaining screws, remove both kick panels and remove the lower dashboard mounting bolts at each end of the dash **(see illustrations)**.
48   Remove the windshield A-pillar trim panels **(see illustration)**.
49   Remove the dashboard mounting bolts at each upper corner **(see illustration)**.
50   Remove the lower dashboard mounting bolts at the center of the dash panel and at the heater/radio control opening **(see illustrations)**.

13.44 Lift the hood release handle and remove the screws (1995 through 2005 models)

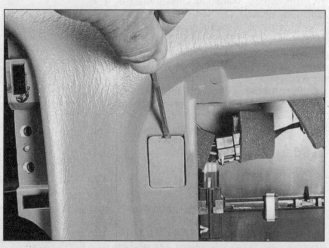

13.46 Remove the screw covers in the glove box opening to access the dash panel mounting bolts (1995 through 2005 models)

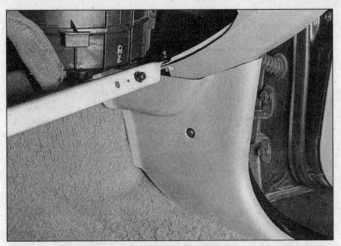

13.47a Remove the kick panel retaining screws and remove the kick panels on both sides (1995 through 2005 models)

13.47b Remove the lower dashboard mounting bolts at each end of the dash (1995 through 2005 models)

51   With the help of an assistant, carefully pull the dash panel toward the rear of the vehicle. Disconnect any remaining wiring harness retainers or connectors still attached to the dash and remove the assembly from the vehicle.

52   Installation is the reverse of removal. Securely tighten all mounting bolts and screws. Make sure all the wiring connectors and cables are fitted correctly, and check the function of all the electrical components after reconnecting.

2006 and later models
Instrument cluster trim panel
Refer to illustration 13.54

53   On models with an adjustable steering column, move the steering wheel to its lowest position.

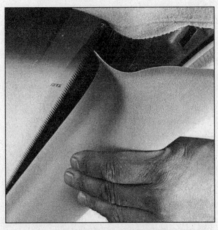

13.48 Carefully remove the windshield A-pillar trim panels (1995 through 2005 models)

13.49 Remove the upper corner dashboard mounting bolts from each end (1995 through 2005 models)

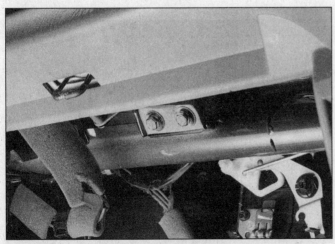

13.50a Remove the mounting bolts under the dashboard (1995 through 2005 models)

13.50b Make sure all the mounting bolts are removed and the dashboard is ready for removal from the vehicle (1995 through 2005 models)

13.54 To detach the instrument cluster trim panel, remove these two screws (2006 and later models)

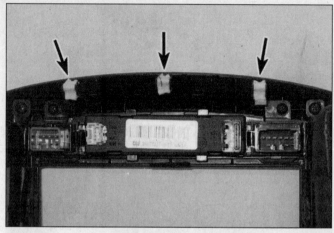

13.58 The center trim panel is secured to the instrument panel by six clips (three upper clips shown)

54   Remove the two screws that secure the instrument cluster trim panel **(see illustration)**.
55   Grasp the instrument cluster trim panel firmly and carefully pull off the panel. The cluster trim panel is secured by two clips located at the lower left and right corners of the panel, so pull on the lower part of the panel to disengage these two clips.
56   Pull out the cluster trim panel and disconnect the electrical connector for the trip sensor.
57   Installation is the reverse of removal.

Center trim panel

Refer to illustration 13.58

58   The center trim panel is secured to the instrument panel by clips along the upper and lower edges of the panel **(see illustration)**. Carefully pry it loose with a trim removal tool.
59   Disconnect the electrical connectors from the backside of the panel.
60   Installation is the reverse of removal.

Instrument panel end covers

Refer to illustration 13.61

61   Carefully pry the end cover off with a trim

removal tool **(see illustration)**.
62   Installation is the reverse of removal.

Glove box

63   Disengage the stops from the glove box **(see illustration 13.39)**.
64   Remove the glove box mounting bolts and remove the glove box.
65   When installing the glove box, make sure that the catches are properly engaged.

Knee bolster trim panel

Refer to illustration 13.68

66   Remove the left end cover **(see illustration 13.61)**.
67   Open and remove the fuse box cover.
68   Remove the knee bolster retaining screws **(see illustration)**.
69   Disengage the knee bolster locator clips and remove the knee bolster.
70   Installation is the reverse of removal.

Instrument panel

71   Remove the instrument cluster trim panel (see Step 53).

72   Remove the center trim panel (see Steps 58 and 59).
73   Remove the end covers (see Step 61).
74   Remove the glove box (see Steps 63 and 64).
75   Remove the steering column covers (see Section 14).
76   Remove the front door sill trim plates.
77   Disconnect the electrical connector for the passenger's side airbag (see Chapter 12). **Warning:** *Do NOT disconnect this connector until you have disconnected the battery and read Section 17 in Chapter 12.*
78   Remove the heater and air conditioning control assembly (see Chapter 3), then remove the instrument cluster and the radio (see Chapter 12).
79   Remove the instrument panel mounting bolts and nuts and remove the instrument panel:

a) *There are two bolts at each end of the instrument panel, behind the end covers (see illustration 13.61).*
b) *There is a bolt in the center of the instrument cluster recess.*

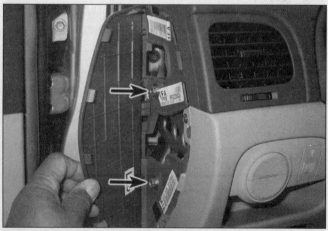

13.61 To remove the end cover from either end of the instrument panel, carefully pry it off. Two of the instrument panel bolts are shown here (2006 and later models)

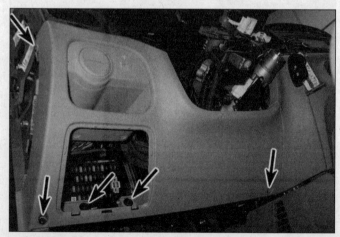

13.68 To detach the knee bolster trim panel, remove these fasteners (2006 and later models)

c) There is a nut in the center of the instrument panel, in the middle of the recess for the radio.

d) There are three bolts above the recess for the glove box and another bolt in lower left corner of the glove box recess.

e) There is one bolt at each lower corner of the instrument panel

80   Installation is the reverse of removal.

14 Steering column covers - removal and installation

Older models

Warning: *If equipped with a Supplemental Restraint System (SRS), more commonly known as airbags, disable the airbag system before working in the vicinity of airbag system components to avoid the possibility of accidental deployment of the airbag, which could result in personal injury (see Chapter 12).*

1   Remove the steering wheel (see Chapter 10).
2   Remove the retaining screws on the lower side of the steering column.
3   Carefully pry the halves of the cover apart. Unplug any electrical connectors and remove the cover halves from the steering column.
4   Installation is the reverse of removal.

Newer models

Refer to illustrations 14.5 and 14.6

5   Remove the retaining screw from the lower steering column cover **(see illustration)**.

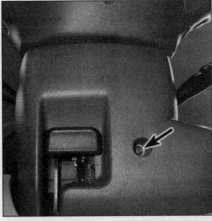

14.5 To detach the lower steering column cover, remove this retaining screw

6   To remove the other two screws, turn the steering wheel to the left to access the left screw and to the right to access the right screw **(see illustration)**.
7   Remove the upper and lower steering column covers.
8   Installation is the reverse of removal.

15 Center console - removal and installation

Warning: *If equipped with a Supplemental Restraint System (SRS), more commonly known as airbags, disable the airbag system before working in the vicinity of airbag system components to avoid the possibility of acci-*

14.6 To access the right retaining screw for the upper steering column cover, turn the steering wheel to the right. To access the left retaining screw, turn the wheel to the left

dental deployment of the airbag, which could result in personal injury (see Chapter 12).

1986 through 1989 models

Refer to illustration 15.3

1   Disconnect the cable from the negative terminal of the battery.
2   Remove the shift knob or handle.
3   Remove the retaining screws **(see illustration)**. If necessary, move the seats forward for access to the rear screws.
4   Detach the console and lift it from the vehicle.
5   Installation is the reverse of removal.

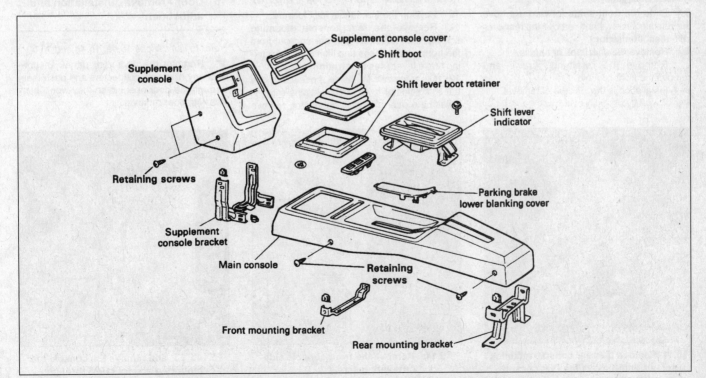

15.3 Center console and related components (1986 through 1989 models)

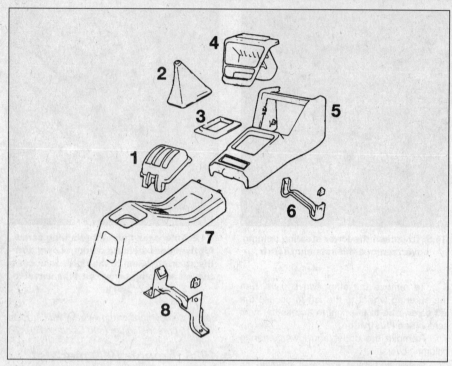

15.6 Center console and related components (1990 through 1994 models)

1   *Shift indicator (automatic transaxle)*
2   *Shift lever boot (manual transaxle)*
3   *Shift lever boot retainer*
4   *Front console storage box*

5   *Front console*
6   *Front console mounting bracket*
7   *Rear console*
8   *Rear console mounting bracket*

1990 through 1994 models

Refer to illustration 15.6

6   Slide the front seats forward. Remove the retaining screws and remove the rear console **(see illustration)**.
7   Remove the shift knob or handle.
8   Remove the retaining screws and remove the front console.
9   Installation is the reverse of removal.

1995 through 1999 models

Refer to illustrations 15.11, 15.14a and 15.14b

10   Position the front seats fully forward.
11   Remove the rear console mounting screws, then withdraw the rear console from the front location pegs and lift it over the parking brake lever **(see illustration)**.
12   On automatic transaxle models, remove the shift selector lever knob retaining screws, detach the overdrive shift connector, remove

the three connector pins with a small punch, and then remove the shift selector knob.
13   On manual transaxle models, unscrew the shift knob from the shaft.
14   Remove the front console side and rear mounting screws, then lift the front console from the floor and disconnect the wiring from the power window switch, if equipped **(see illustrations)**.
15   Installation is the reverse of removal.

2000 through 2005 models

16   Remove the two rear console mounting screws (one on each side), then pull off the rear console.
17   Remove the shift control lever (see Chapter 7B).
18   Remove the four front console mounting screws (two at the front, one on each side, and two at the rear).
19   Lift up the front console and disconnect the electrical connectors.
20   Installation is the reverse of removal.

2006 and later models

21   Remove the front seats (see Section 22).
22   Pry out the small trim piece ahead of the shift lever and disconnect the electrical connector.
23   Remove the parking brake cover.
24   Remove the console side covers.
25   Remove the three console mounting bolts and remove the console.
26   Installation is the reverse of removal.

---

16   Door - removal, installation and adjustment

Refer to illustrations 16.4a, 16.4b and 16.5

1   Remove the door trim panel. Disconnect any electrical connectors and push them through the door opening so they won't interfere with door removal.

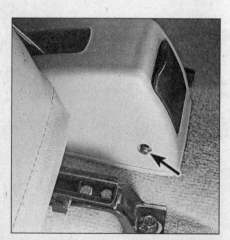

15.11 Remove the rear console retaining screws and remove the rear console (1995 through 1999 models)

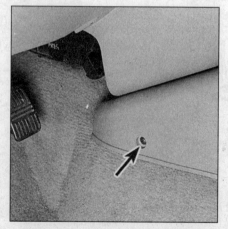

15.14a Remove the front console side mounting screws . . .

15.14b . . . and remove the console rear mounting screws (1995 through 1999 models)

16.4a If the door is equipped with a door stop strut, remove the strut bolt

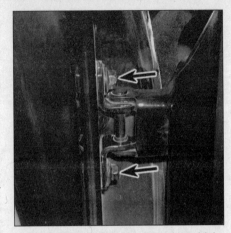

16.4b To detach the door from the vehicle, remove the hinge bolts

16.5 To adjust the door lock striker, loosen the retaining screws just enough to move the striker in the desired direction when you tap it with a hammer

2   Place a floor jack under the door or have an assistant on hand to support it when the hinge bolts are removed. **Note:** *If a jack is being used, place a rag between it and the door to protect the door's painted surfaces.*

3   Mark around the hinge-to-door bolts so you can return the door to its proper adjustment when installing it.

4   Remove the door stop strut bolt and the hinge-to-door bolts and carefully lift off the door **(see illustrations)**. Installation is the reverse of removal.

5   Following installation of the door, check that it is in proper alignment and adjust it, if necessary, as follows **(see illustration)**:

a) *Up-and-down and forward-and-backward adjustments are made by loosening the hinge-to-body bolts and moving the door, as necessary. A special offset tool may be required to reach some of the bolts.*

b) *The door lock striker can also be adjusted both up-and-down and sideways to provide a positive engagement with the locking mechanism. This is done by loosening the retaining screws and moving the striker, as necessary.*

17 Trunk lid - removal, installation and adjustment

Refer to illustration 17.7

1   Open the trunk lid and cover the edges of the trunk compartment with pads or cloths to protect the painted surfaces when the lid is removed.

2   Disconnect any cable or electrical connectors which are attached to the trunk lid and would interfere with removal.

3   Scribe or paint alignment marks around the hinge bolt mounting flanges.

4   While an assistant supports the lid, remove the lid-to-hinge bolts on both sides and lift off the lid.

5   Installation is the reverse of removal. **Note:** *When reinstalling the trunk lid, align the lid-to-hinge bolts with the marks made during removal.*

6   After installation, close the lid and check that it is in proper alignment with the surrounding panels. Front and rear and side-to-side adjustments of the lid are controlled by the position of the lid-to-hinge bolts in their

slots. To adjust, loosen the lid-to-hinge bolts, reposition the lid and retighten the bolts.

7   The height of the lid in relation to the surrounding body panels when closed can be adjusted by loosening the striker bolts, repositioning the striker and tightening the bolts **(see illustration)**.

18 Liftgate - removal, installation and adjustment

Refer to illustrations 18.3, 18.4, 18.8a and 18.8b

1   Open the liftgate and cover the upper body area around the opening with pads or cloths to protect the painted surfaces when the liftgate is removed.

2   Disconnect any cables, hoses or electrical connectors which would interfere with removal of the liftgate.

3   Paint or scribe around the hinge bolts **(see illustration)**.

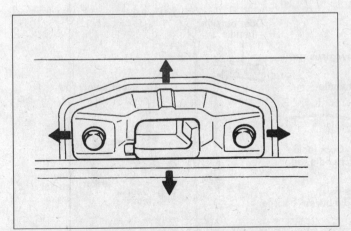

17.7 After loosening the bolts, you can move the striker to adjust the trunk lid position (early models shown)

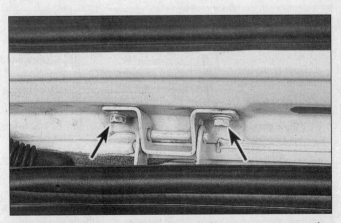

18.3 Paint or scribe around the hinge bolts so you can return the liftgate to the same position when you install it - there's a hinge on each side of the liftgate, so make sure you mark the bolts on each of them

18.4 Use a small screwdriver to pry up on the lock, and then detach the support strut end from the liftgate

18.8a To adjust the engagement of the liftgate, loosen the three liftgate latch mounting bolts . . .

18.8b . . . and/or the lock striker screws and move the components as necessary

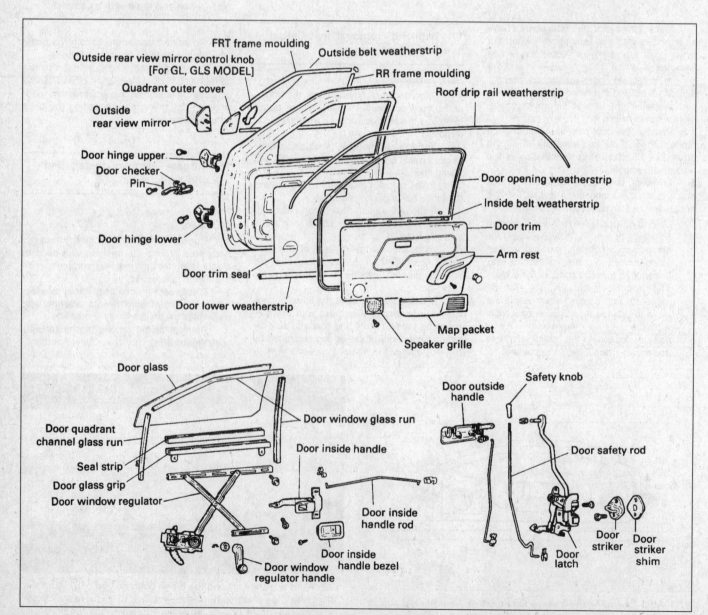

19.3a Front door and related components (1986 through 1989 models)

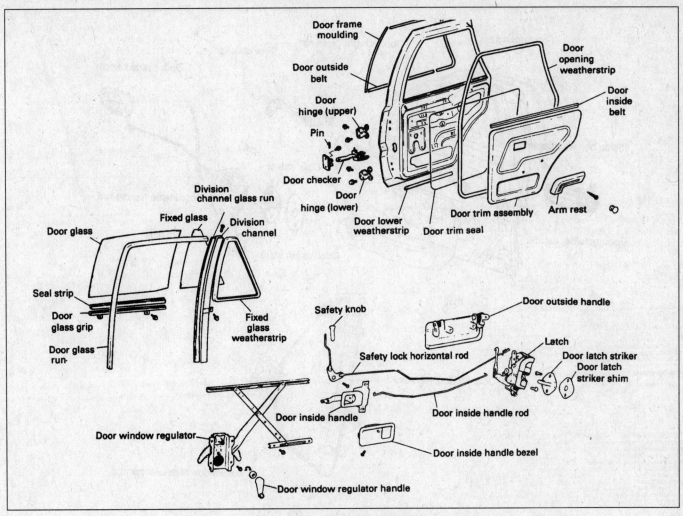

19.3b Rear door and related components (1986 through 1989 models)

4   While an assistant supports the liftgate, detach the support struts **(see illustration)**.
5   Remove the hinge bolts and detach the liftgate from the vehicle.
6   Installation is the reverse of removal.

7   After installation, close the liftgate and check that the door is in proper alignment with the surrounding panels. Adjustments to the liftgate are made by moving the position of the hinge bolts in their slots. To adjust, loosen the

hinge bolts and reposition them either side-to-side or front-to-rear the desired amount and retighten the bolts **(see illustration 18.3)**.
8   The engagement of the liftgate can be adjusted by loosening the latch mounting bolts and/or the lock striker screws, repositioning the latch and/or striker and tightening the screws **(see illustrations)**.

19   Door latch, lock cylinder and handle - removal and installation

1   Remove the door trim panel and watershield (see Section 12).
2   Remove the door window glass and on 2006 and later models, the rear channel (see Section 20).

Door latch

Refer to illustrations 19.3a, 19.3b, 19.3c and 19.3d

3   Reach in through the door service hole and disconnect the door safety rod and the door inside handle rod from the latch **(see illustrations)**. It might be difficult to discon-

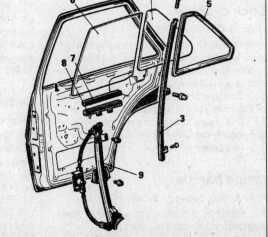

19.3c Typical 1990 through 1994 door components (rear door shown, front door similar)

3   *Division channel*
4   *Fixed glass*
5   *Weatherstrip*
6   *Door glass*
7   *Pad*
8   *Glass run*
9   *Regulator*

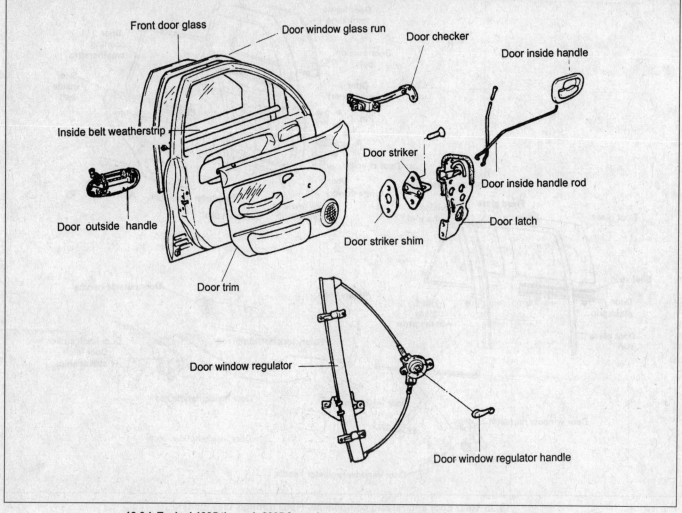

19.3d   Typical 1995 through 2005 front door components (2006 and later models similar)

nect the rods from the latch mechanism on later model vehicles. If so, disconnect the rods from the inside handle mechanism instead. Then you can disconnect both rods from the

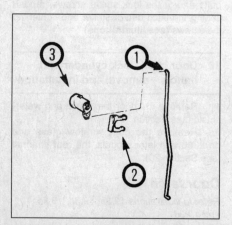

19.6   Disconnect the lock cylinder rod (1) from the lock cylinder, then use pliers to slide the retaining clip (2) off the lock cylinder (3) (1994 and earlier models)

latch after you detach it from the door and work it closer to the service hole.

4   Remove the door latch retaining screws from the end of the door. Remove the door latch.

5   Installation is the reverse of removal.

Lock cylinder

Refer to illustration 19.6

Note: *On 1995 and later models the lock cylinder is an integral part of the outside door handle. Refer to Steps 12 through 14 for the outside handle removal procedure.*

6   Disconnect the lock cylinder rod from the lock cylinder **(see illustration)**.

7   Use pliers to slide the retaining clip off and remove the lock cylinder from the door.

8   Installation is the reverse of removal.

Inside handle

Refer to illustrations 19.9a and 19.9b

9   Remove the retaining screw(s) **(see illustrations)** and pull out the handle.

10   Disconnect the rods or cables from the

handle mechanism. On models with rods, disconnect the L-shaped end of each rod by simply rotating the handle assembly to the correct angle so that the rod slips out. On models with cables, rotate the cable end to disengage it from the inside handle mechanism.

11   Installation is the reverse of removal. On front doors, before tightening the retaining screws, adjust the position of the handle assembly so the handle stroke travel is approximately 45-degrees **(see illustration 19.9a).**

Outside door handle

Refer to illustrations 19.12 and 19.13

12   Disconnect the lock rod and outside handle rod from the door handle **(see illustration)**.

13   Remove the outside door handle retaining bolts **(see illustration)**.

14   Slide the outside handle base (the part with the key lock cylinder in it) forward, then remove the outside door handle.

15   Installation is the reverse of removal.

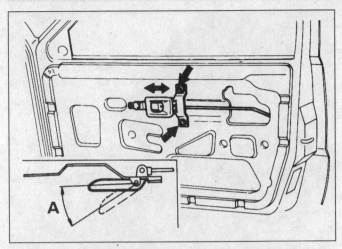

19.9a Remove the inside handle retaining screws (1986 through 1989 models)

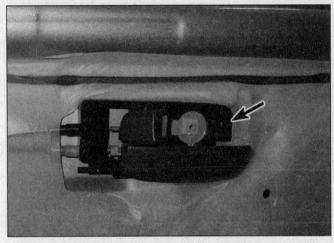

19.9b To detach the inside door handle on most 1990 and later models, simply remove the mounting screw(s)

20 Door window glass - removal and installation

Refer to illustrations 20.5a, 20.5b, and 20.7

1 Remove the door trim panel and watershield (see Section 12).
2 Lower the window glass.
3 On rear doors, remove the retaining screws, pull the glass run and division channel out of the door and remove the fixed glass assembly **(see illustration 19.3b)**.
4 Scribe or paint marks on the two window channel-to-regulator bolts and remove them.
5 On front doors, use a screwdriver to pry out the trim strips at the top of the door **(see illustration)**. Remove the window glass by tilting it to detach the glass from the glass channel studs and then sliding the glass up and out of the door **(see illustration)**.
6 If necessary, remove the regulator retain-

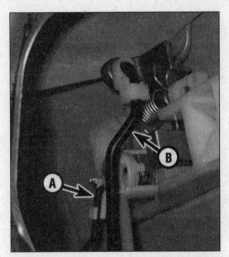

19.12 Disconnect the lock rod (A) and the outside handle rod (B)

19.13 To detach the outside handle, remove these two bolts

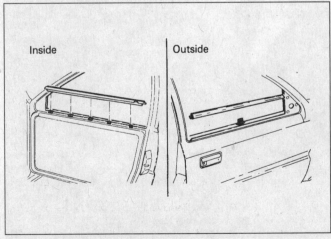

20.5a On front doors, pry out the trim strips before removing the glass

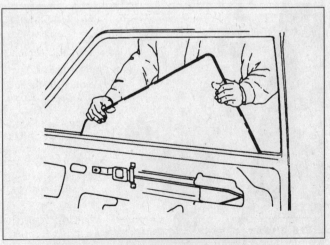

20.5b Tilt the door glass as shown when lifting it out of the opening

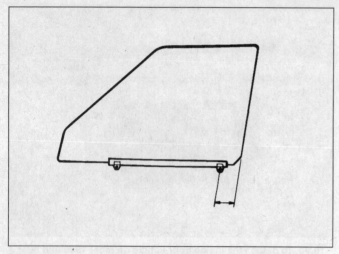

20.7 Make sure to install the glass in the channel with the same distance between the rear bolt hole and the edge of the glass as when removed

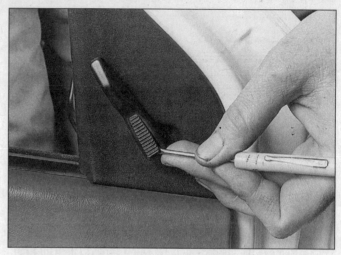

21.1 Use a small screwdriver to pry off the mirror adjusting lever cover

21.2a Remove the screw and adjusting lever . . .

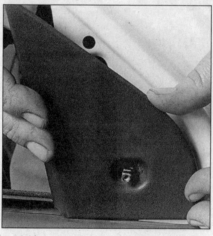

21.2b . . . and rotate the trim cover off

ing bolts and then slide the regulator out of the opening in the door.

7   Installation is the reverse of removal. On front doors, if the glass has been removed from the channel, make sure to reinstall it with the rear edge of the glass the same distance from the rear channel bolt hole as when the glass was removed **(see illustration)**.

21   Outside mirrors - removal and installation

Manually-adjusted mirrors

Refer to illustrations 21.1, 21.2a, 21.2b and 21.3

1   Use a screwdriver to pry off the adjusting lever trim cover **(see illustration)**.

2   Remove the screw and adjusting lever

21.3 The mirror is retained by three screws

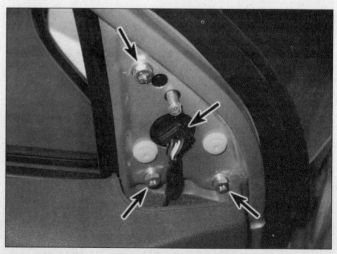

21.6 To remove a power mirror, disconnect the electrical connector, then remove the mirror mounting bolts

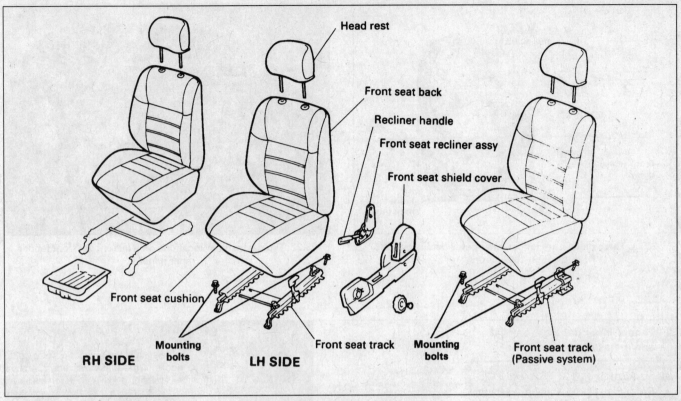

22.1a Typical front seat installation details

and lift off the mirror trim cover (see illustrations).

3   Remove the three retaining screws and lift off the mirror (see illustration).

4   Installation is the reverse of removal.

Power mirrors

Refer to illustration 21.6

5   Remove the triangular-shaped trim piece (see illustration 12.13).

6   Disconnect the electrical connector (see illustration).

7   Remove the mirror mounting bolts and remove the mirror.

8   Installation is the reverse of removal.

22   Seats - removal and installation

Refer to illustrations 22.1a, 22.1b and 22.1c

1   On front seats, remove the mounting bolts, unplug any electrical connectors and lift the seat(s) from the vehicle (see illustration). To remove the rear seat cushion or the fixed rear seat back, remove the bolts retaining the seat the body and lift the seat up. To remove a folding rear seat back, fold the seat down, remove the hinge bracket-to-body bolts and remove the seat (see illustrations).

2   Installation is the reverse of removal. Tighten the mounting bolts securely.

22.1b To remove the rear seat cushion or a fixed rear seat back, remove the bolts that attach the two seat retaining loops to the body then lift the seat up

22.1c To remove a folding rear seat back, fold down the seat back, remove the side bracket mounting bolts and slide the seat back off the center mounting bracket

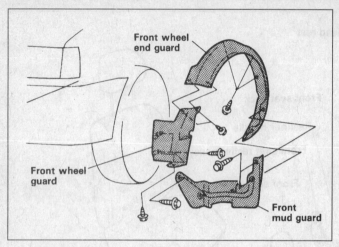

23.2a Three-piece front fender inner panel details on 1986 through 1994 models

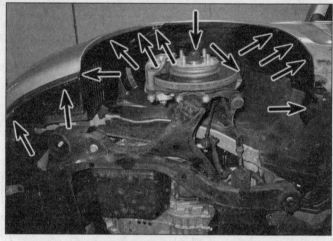

23.2b Typical fastener locations on a late-model front fender inner panel

23 Fender inner panels - removal and installation

Refer to illustrations 23.2a, 23.2b and 23.2c

1　Raise the vehicle, support it securely and remove the wheel(s).
2　Remove the bolts and lower the panel(s) from the fenderwell **(see illustration)**.
3　Installation is the reverse of removal.

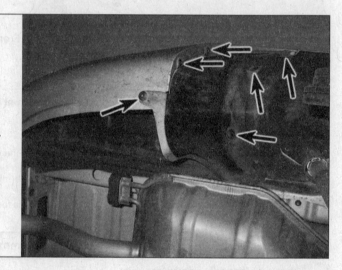

23.2c Typical fastener locations on a late-model rear fender inner panel

24 Seat belt check

1　Check the seat belts, buckles, latch plates and guide loops for any obvious damage or signs of wear.
2　Check that the seat belt reminder light comes on when the key is turned to the On or Start positions. A chime should also sound.
3　The seat belts are designed to lock up during a sudden stop or impact, yet allow free movement during normal driving. Check that the retractors return the belt against your chest while driving and rewind the belt fully when the buckle is unlatched.

4　If any of the above checks reveal problems with the seat belt system, replace parts as necessary.

Chapter 12
Chassis electrical system

Contents

1   General information

The electrical system is a 12-volt, negative ground type. Power for the lights and all electrical accessories is supplied by a lead/acid-type battery which is charged by the alternator.

This Chapter covers repair and service procedures for the various electrical components not associated with the engine. Information on the battery, alternator, distributor and starter motor can be found in Chapter 5.

It should be noted that when portions of the electrical system are serviced, the cable should be disconnected from the negative battery terminal to prevent electrical shorts and/or fires.

2   Electrical troubleshooting - general information

A typical electrical circuit consists of an electrical component, any switches, relays, motors, fuses, fusible links or circuit breakers related to that component and the wiring and connectors that link the component to both the battery and the chassis. To help you pinpoint an electrical circuit problem, wiring diagrams are included at the end of this Chapter.

Before tackling any troublesome electrical circuit, first study the appropriate wiring diagrams to get a complete understanding of what makes up that individual circuit. Trouble spots, for instance, can often be narrowed down by noting if other components related to the circuit are operating properly. If several components or circuits fail at one time, chances are the problem is in a fuse or ground connection, because several circuits are often routed through the same fuse and ground connections.

Electrical problems usually stem from simple causes, such as loose or corroded connections, a blown fuse, a melted fusible link or a bad relay. Visually inspect the condition of all fuses, wires and connections in a problem circuit before troubleshooting it.

If testing instruments are going to be utilized, use the diagrams to plan ahead of time where you will make the necessary connections in order to accurately pinpoint the trouble spot.

The basic tools needed for electrical troubleshooting include a circuit tester or voltmeter (a 12-volt bulb with a set of test leads can also be used), a continuity tester, which includes a bulb, battery and set of test leads, and a jumper wire, preferably with a circuit breaker incorporated, which can be used to bypass electrical components. Before attempting to locate a problem with test instruments, use the wiring diagram(s) to decide where to make the connections.

Voltage checks

Voltage checks should be performed if a circuit is not functioning properly. Connect one lead of a circuit tester to either the negative battery terminal or a known good ground. Connect the other lead to a connector in the circuit being tested, preferably nearest to the battery or fuse. If the bulb of the tester lights, voltage is present, which means that the part of the circuit between the connector and the battery is problem free. Continue checking the rest of the circuit in the same fashion. When you reach a point at which no voltage is present, the problem lies between that point and the last test point with voltage. Most of the time the problem can be traced to a loose connection. **Note:** *Keep in mind that some circuits receive voltage only when the ignition key is in the Accessory or Run position.*

3.1a Pull down the hinged cover for access to the fuses (1986 through 1989 models)

3.1b On 1990 through 2005 models, the interior fuse box is located behind the left kick panel

Finding a short

One method of finding shorts in a circuit is to remove the fuse and connect a test light or voltmeter in its place to the fuse terminals. There should be no voltage present in the circuit. Move the wiring harness from side to side while watching the test light. If the bulb goes on, there is a short to ground somewhere in that area, probably where the insulation has rubbed through. The same test can be performed on each component in the circuit, even a switch.

Ground check

Perform a ground test to check whether a component is properly grounded. Disconnect the battery and connect one lead of a self-powered test light, known as a continuity tester, to a known good ground. Connect the other lead to the wire or ground connection being tested. If the bulb goes on, the ground is good. If the bulb does not go on, the ground is not good.

Continuity check

A continuity check is done to determine if there are any breaks in a circuit - if it is passing electricity properly. With the circuit off (no power in the circuit), a self-powered continuity tester can be used to check the circuit. Connect the test leads to both ends of the circuit (or to the "power" end and a good ground), and if the test light comes on the circuit is passing current properly. If the light doesn't come on, there is a break somewhere in the circuit. The same procedure can be used to test a switch, by connecting the continuity tester to the power in and power out sides of the switch. With the switch turned On, the test light should come on.

Finding an open circuit

When diagnosing for possible open circuits, it is often difficult to locate them by sight because oxidation or terminal misalignment are hidden by the connectors. Merely wiggling

a connector on a sensor or in the wiring harness may correct the open circuit condition. Remember this when an open circuit is indicated when troubleshooting a circuit. Intermittent problems may also be caused by oxidized or loose connections.

Electrical troubleshooting is simple if you keep in mind that all electrical circuits are basically electricity running from the battery, through the wires, switches, relays, fuses and fusible links to each electrical component (light bulb, motor, etc.) and to ground, from which it is passed back to the battery. Any electrical problem is an interruption in the flow of electricity to and from the battery.

3   Fuses - general information

Refer to illustrations 3.1a, 3.1b, 3.1c and 3.3

The electrical circuits of the vehicle are protected by a combination of fuses, circuit breakers and fusible links. On 1986 through 1989 models, the main fuse box is located at the left side of the dashboard under a cover **(see illustration)**. On 1990 through 2005 models, the main fuse box is located under a cover in the driver's side kick panel **(see illustration)**. On 2006 and later models, the fuse and relay box is located at the left end of the instrument panel **(see illustration)**. Note that all of the covers for the interior fuse and relay boxes include a fuse and relay guide on their backside.

Each of the fuses is designed to protect a specific circuit, and the various circuits are identified on the fuse panel itself.

Miniaturized fuses are employed in the fuse block in the passenger compartment. These compact fuses, with blade terminal design, allow fingertip removal and replacement. If an electrical component fails, always check the fuse first. The best way to check the fuses is with a test light. Check for power at the exposed terminal tips of each fuse. If power is present at one side of the fuse but

not the other, the fuse is blown. A blown fuse can also be identified by visually inspecting it **(see illustration)**.

Be sure to replace blown fuses with the correct type. Fuses of different ratings are physically interchangeable, but only fuses of the proper rating should be used. Replacing a fuse with one of a higher or lower value than specified is not recommended. Each electrical circuit needs a specific amount of protection. The amperage value of each fuse is molded into the fuse body.

If the replacement fuse immediately fails, don't replace it again until the cause of the problem is isolated and corrected. In most cases, this will be a short circuit in the wiring caused by a broken or deteriorated wire.

4   Fusible links - general information

Refer to illustrations 4.3a, 4.3b, 4.3c, 4.3d and 4.3e

Some circuits are protected by fusible links. The links are used in circuits which are not ordinarily fused, such as the ignition circuit.

On 1986 through 1989 models, the fusible links are housed separately from the other engine compartment fuses and relays. On 1990 and later models, the fusible links are located inside the engine compartment fuse and relay box. On 1986 models, check the continuity of a suspect fusible link to determine whether it's burned out. On 1987 and later models, you can visually inspect a fusible link just like you would inspect a fuse **(see illustration 3.3)**.

To replace a fusible link, first disconnect the negative cable from the battery. Disconnect the burned out link and replace it with a new one (available from most auto parts stores) **(see illustrations)**. Always determine the cause for the overload which melted the fusible link before installing a new one.

3.1c On 2006 and later models, the interior fuse and relay box is located at the left end of the instrument panel

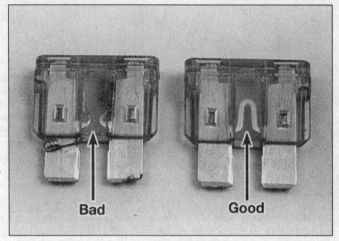

3.3 When a fuse blows, the element between the terminals melts

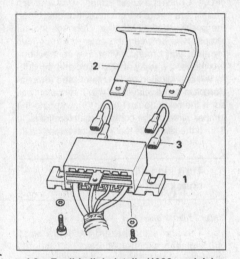

4.3a Fusible link details (1986 models):

1 *Fusible link housing*
2 *Cover*
3 *Fusible link*

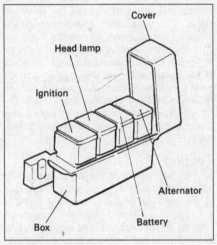

4.3b On later models, the fusible links are similar to large fuses (1987 through 1989 models shown)

4.3c On 1990 through 1994 models, the fusible links are located in the underhood fuse and relay box . . .

4.3d . . . and at the battery terminal

4.3e Typical underhood fuse and relay box - note the fuse/fusible link and relay designations are printed on the cover

5.2a On 1987 through 1989 models, the relays for the horn, headlights and tail lights are located on the firewall in the engine compartment

5.2b Typical 1995 and later model underhood relay box (an additional relay box is mounted under the dash)

5.2c On 2006 and later models, most of the interior relays are located on the backside of the interior fuse box. To access them, disconnect the negative battery cable, remove the knee bolster trim panel (see Chapter 11), then remove these two nuts and pull off the fuse box

5   Relays - general information

Refer to illustrations 5.2a, 5.2b, 5.2c and 5.5

1   Several electrical accessories in the vehicle use relays to transmit the electrical signal to the component. If the relay is defective, the component will not operate properly.

2   The various relays are grouped together in several locations under the dash, adjacent to the component, or in the engine compartment for convenience in the event of needed replacement **(see illustrations)**. If a faulty relay is suspected, it can be removed and tested using the following procedure. Defective relays must be replaced as a unit.

Testing

3   It's best to refer to the wiring diagram for the circuit to determine the proper hook-ups for the relay you're testing. However, if you're not able to determine the correct hook-up from the wiring diagrams, you may be able to determine the test hook-ups from the information that follows.

4   On most relays, two of the terminals are the relay's control circuit (they connect to the relay coil which, when energized, closes the large contacts to complete the circuit). The other terminals are the power circuit (they are connected together within the relay when the control-circuit coil is energized).

5   Most relays are marked as an aid to help you determine which terminals are the control circuit and which are the power circuit. Connect an ohmmeter to the two terminals of the power circuit. Connect a fused jumper wire between one of the two control circuit terminals and the positive battery terminal. Connect another jumper wire between the other control circuit terminal and ground. When the connections are made, the relay should click and continuity will be indicated on the meter **(see illustration)**. On some relays, polarity may be critical, so, if the relay doesn't click, try swapping the jumper wires on the control circuit terminals.

6   If the relay fails the above test, replace it.

6   Turn signal/hazard flasher - check and replacement

Refer to illustration 6.5

1   The turn signal/hazard flasher, a small black plastic canister shaped unit located under the dash in the wiring harness, flashes the turn signals.

2   When the flasher unit is functioning properly, and audible click can be heard during its operation. If the turn signals fail on one side or the other and the flasher unit does not

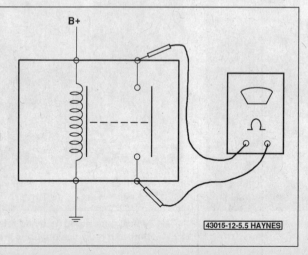

5.5 To test a typical four-terminal normally open relay, connect an ohmmeter to the two terminals of the power circuit - the meter will indicate no continuity until battery power and ground are connected to the two terminals of the control circuit, then the relay will click and continuity will be indicated

B+

43015-12-5.5 HAYNES

6.5 On 2006 and later models, the turn signal/hazard flasher relay is located on the backside of the interior fuse and relay box

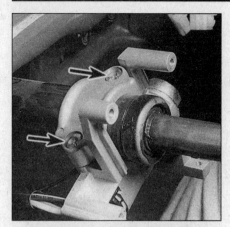

7.5 Drill out the heads of the special screws (arrows) retaining the ignition switch clamp - use a screw extractor or a hammer and punch to unscrew them

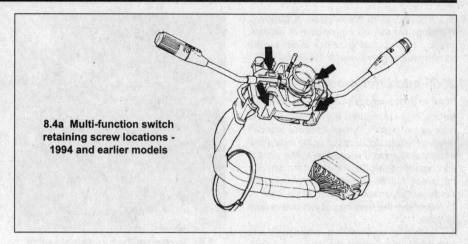

8.4a Multi-function switch retaining screw locations - 1994 and earlier models

make its characteristic clicking sound, a faulty turn signal bulb is indicated.

3   If both turn signals fail to blink, the problem may be due to a blown fuse, a faulty flasher unit, a broken switch or a loose or open connection. If a quick check of the fuse box indicates that the turn signal fuse has blown, check the wiring for a short before installing a new fuse.

4   On 2005 and earlier models, the turn signal/hazard flasher unit is located on the interior fuse and relay box, which is located under the left end of the dash. To access this fuse and relay box, remove the kick panel (see Chapter 11). Refer to the fuse and relay guide on the cover to identify the location of the flasher unit.

5   On 2006 and later models, the flasher unit (see illustration) is located on the backside of the interior fuse and relay box (it faces toward the firewall). On these models, disconnect the cable from the negative terminal of the battery, remove the knee bolster trim panel (see Chapter 11), remove the fuse and relay box mounting nuts (see illustration 5.2c), pull off the box and flip it over.

6   To replace the flasher, simply pull it out of the fuse block or wiring harness.

7   Make sure that the replacement unit is identical to the original. Compare the old one to the new one before installing it.

8   Installation is the reverse of removal.

7 Ignition switch and lock cylinder - removal and installation

Refer to illustration 7.5

Warning: *If equipped with a Supplemental Restraint System (SRS), more commonly known as airbags, disable the airbag system before working in the vicinity of airbag system components to avoid the possibility of accidental deployment of the airbag, which could result in personal injury (see Section 18).*

1   Disconnect the cable from the negative terminal of the battery.

2   Remove the steering wheel (see Chapter 10).

3   Remove the lower dash panel and steering column cover (see Chapter 11).

4   Disconnect the switch electrical connector.

5   Drill out the heads of the special screws securing the clamp bracket to the ignition switch assembly (see illustration). Remove the screws with a screw extractor. It may be necessary to use a punch and hammer to turn the screws in a counterclockwise direction if they are stuck.

6   Separate the ignition switch from the clamp and remove it.

7   Installation is the reverse of removal. When installing the new screws, tighten them until their heads break off.

8 Steering column switches - removal and installation

Warning: *If equipped with a Supplemental Restraint System (SRS), more commonly known as airbags, disable the airbag system before working in the vicinity of airbag system components to avoid the possibility of accidental deployment of the airbag, which could result in personal injury (see Section 18).*

1   Park the vehicle with the front wheels in the straight-ahead position. Disconnect the cable from the negative terminal of the battery.

2005 and earlier models

Refer to illustrations 8.4, 8.5a and 8.5b

2   Remove the steering wheel (see Chapter 10).

3   Remove the lower dash panel and steering column cover (see Chapter 11).

4   On 1994 and earlier models, remove the switch retaining screws (see illustration). Trace the wiring harness down the steering column to the connector. Cut the wiring tie-strap (if equipped), disconnect the connector and slide the switch up off the column.

5   On 1995 through 2005 models, disconnect the electrical connector, remove the three multi-function switch mounting screws, then slide the switch assembly off the steering column (see illustrations).

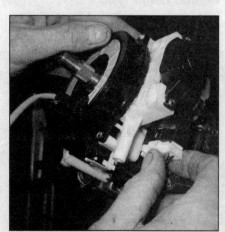

8.5a To remove the multi-function switch assembly on 1995 through 2005 models, disconnect the electrical connectors from the turn signal switch and from the windshield wiper/washer switch (shown) . . .

8.5b . . . then remove the three switch retaining screws and slide the switch assembly off the steering column (typical 2000 through 2005 unit shown; 1995 through 1999 units similar)

6   Installation is the reverse of removal.
Warning: *On models equipped with airbags, center the clockspring before installing the steering wheel (see Chapter 10, Section 15).*

2006 and later models

Refer to illustrations 8.8a and 8.8b

Note: *On these models, it's not necessary to remove the steering wheel, because you can remove the turn signal switch or the windshield wiper/washer switch separately. The photos accompanying this Section depict the turn signal switch, but the procedure for removing the windshield wiper/washer switch is identical.*

7   Remove the steering column covers (see Chapter 11).
8   Using a screwdriver, disengage the switch locking tab and pull out the switch **(see illustrations)**.
9   Installation is the reverse of removal.

---

9   Radio and speakers - removal and installation

Warning: *If equipped with a Supplemental Restraint System (SRS), more commonly known as airbags, disable the airbag system before working in the vicinity of airbag system components to avoid the possibility of accidental deployment of the airbag, which could result in personal injury (see Section 18).*

Radio

Refer to illustration 9.4

1   Disconnect the cable from the negative terminal of the battery.
2   On 2000 through 2005 models, remove the glove box (see Chapter 11), then disconnect the heater control cables under the glove box area.
3   Remove the center trim panel (see Chapter 11).
4   Remove the radio mounting screws or bolts **(see illustration)**.
5   Pull out the radio, reach behind it and

8.8a To remove the turn signal switch (shown) or the windshield wiper/washer switch, on 2006 and later models, insert a screwdriver through this slot to depress the locking lug . . .

8.8b . . . and pull out the switch. When installing the switch, make sure that the locking lug snaps into place at the slot

disconnect the electrical connector and the antenna lead.
6   Installation is the reverse of removal.

Door speakers

Refer to illustration 9.8

7   Remove the door trim panel (see Chapter 11).
8   Remove the speaker mounting screws, pull out the speaker and disconnect the electrical connector from the speaker **(see illustration)**.

---

10   Headlight bulb - replacement

---

1   Disconnect the cable from the negative terminal of the battery.

Sealed beam type

2   Remove the radiator grille (see Chapter 11).

3   Remove the headlight retainer screws, taking care not to disturb the adjustment screws.
4   Remove the retainer and pull the headlight out far enough to disconnect the connector.
5   Remove the headlight.
6   To install the headlight, plug the connector in, place the headlight in position and install the retainer and screws. Tighten the screws securely.
7   Install the radiator grille.

Halogen bulb type

Refer to illustrations 10.8, 10.9 and 10.10

Warning: *The halogen gas filled bulbs are under pressure and may shatter if the surface is scratched or the bulb is dropped. Wear eye protection and handle the bulbs carefully, grasping only the base whenever possible. Do not touch the surface of the bulb with your fingers because the oil from your skin could cause it to overheat and fail prematurely. If you do touch the bulb surface, clean it with rubbing alcohol.*

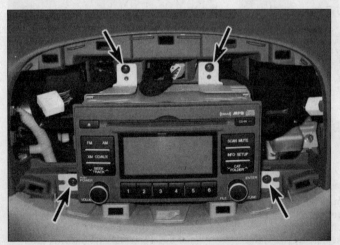

9.4 Radio mounting screws (2006 and later models shown, others similar)

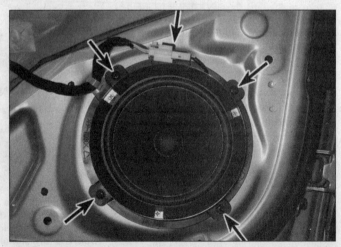

9.8 To detach a speaker from the door, disconnect the electrical connector and remove the mounting screws

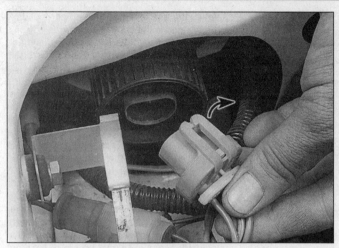

10.8 Pry up on the locking tab and disconnect the connector from the headlight bulb

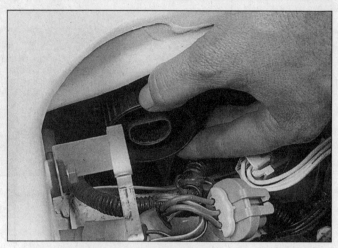

10.9 Turn the bulb retainer counterclockwise to unlock the bulb assembly from the housing

8   Open the hood. Disconnect the electrical connector **(see illustration)**.
9   Reach behind the headlight assembly, grasp the retainer and turn it counterclockwise **(see illustration)**.
10   Withdraw the bulb assembly from the housing **(see illustration)**.
11   Install the bulb in the headlight assembly.
12   Install the retainer and turn it clockwise to lock it in place.
13   Plug in the electrical connector.

11   Headlight housing - removal and installation

1986 and 1987 models

1   Refer to Steps 1 through 7 in Section 10.

1988 and later models

Refer to illustration 11.8

2   On 1988 through 1994 models, remove the grille (see Chapter 11).

3   On 1988 through 1999 models, remove the front turn signal housing.
4   On 2000 through 2005 models, remove the front bumper cover upper mounting bolt.
5   On 2006 and later models, remove the front bumper cover (see Chapter 11).
6   If you're removing the left headlight housing on 2006 and later models, remove the battery (see Chapter 5); if you're removing the right headlight housing on these models, remove the power steering fluid reservoir and set it aside (don't disconnect the power steering fluid hoses).
7   Disconnect the electrical connector from the headlight housing **(see illustration 10.8)**. **Note:** *On some models, depending on what's located directly behind the headlight that you are removing, it might be difficult to disconnect the electrical connector from the headlight housing. If so, just wait and do it after you unbolt the headlight housing.*
8   Remove the headlight housing mounting bolts **(see illustration)**.
9   Pull out the headlight housing. If you

were unable to disconnect the electrical connector(s) before, do so now.
10   Installation is the reverse of removal.

12   Headlights - adjustment

Refer to illustrations 12.3, 12.6a, 12.6b and 12.6c

Note: *It is very important to have the headlights adjusted correctly. If adjusted incorrectly they could blind the driver of an oncoming vehicle and cause a serious accident or seriously reduce your ability to see the road. The headlights should be checked for proper aim every 12 months and any time a new headlight is installed or front end body work is performed. It should be emphasized that the following procedure is only an interim step which will provide temporary adjustment until the headlights can be adjusted by a properly equipped shop.*

1   On 1986 through 1994 models, headlights have two adjusting screws, one on the top controlling up and down movement

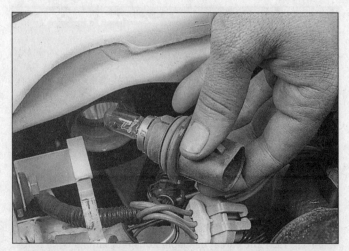

10.10 Withdraw the bulb assembly straight out of the housing

11.8 To detach the headlight housing on 2006 and later models, remove these bolts (earlier models similar)

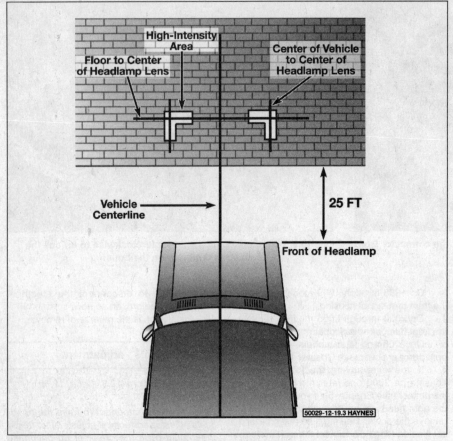

12.3 Headlight adjustment details

and one on the side controlling left and right movement. On 1995 and later models, both adjusters are on top.

2　There are several methods of adjusting the headlights. The simplest method requires an open area with a blank wall and a level surface in front of the wall.

3　Attach masking tape vertically to the wall in reference to the vehicle centerline and the centerlines of both headlights **(see illustra-tion)**.

4　Position a horizontal tape line in reference to the centerline of all the headlights. **Note:** *It may be easier to position the tape on the wall with the vehicle parked only a few inches away.*

5　Adjustment should be made with the vehicle parked 25 feet from the wall, sitting level, the gas tank half-full and no unusually heavy load in the trunk or cargo area.

6　Starting with the low beam adjustment, position the high intensity zone so it is two inches below the horizontal line and two inches to the side of the headlight vertical line and away from oncoming traffic. Adjustment on sealed beam equipped models is made by turning the top adjusting screw clockwise to raise the beam and counterclockwise to lower the beam **(see illustration)**. The adjusting screw on the side should be used in the same manner to move the beam left or right. On 1988 and 1989 bulb-type head-lights, the upper adjusting screw moves the headlight assembly right or left and the lower one moves it up and down **(see illustration)**. On 1990 through 1992 models, the vertical adjuster screw is located on top of the front edge of the headlight housing, near the upper inner corner of the housing; the horizontal adjuster screw is also located on the front edge of the housing, near the lower outer cor-ner. On 1993 and 1994 models, both of the adjusters can be accessed through holes in the top of the headlight housing and the upper radiator crossmember, respectively. On 1995 models, one adjustment hole is on top and the other, near the upper inner corner of the headlight housing, faces forward. On 1996 and later models, both adjustment holes are located above the headlight housing. On 1996 through 2005 models, the inner hole is for vertical adjustment and the outer hole is for horizontal adjustment. However, the manu-facturer doesn't recommend trying to per-form horizontal adjustment yourself at home on these models; if the headlights on these models need horizontal adjustment, it should be done by a dealer service department. On 2006 and later models, only vertical adjust-ment is possible **(see illustration)**.

7　With the high beams on, the high inten-sity zone should be vertically centered with the exact center just below the horizontal line. **Note:** *It may not be possible to position the headlight aim exactly for both high and low*

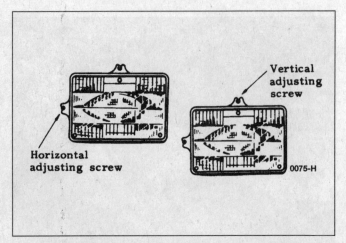

12.6a Sealed beam headlight adjusting screw locations

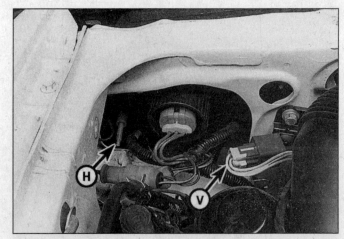

12.6b On 1994 and earlier headlight housings with halogen bulbs, the upper adjusting screw (H) moves the beam horizontally and the lower screw (V) moves the beam vertically

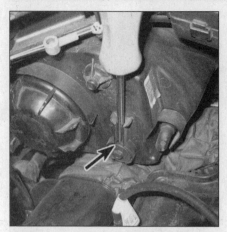

12.6c On later models, the headlight adjusters are small gears that are turned by the tip of a Phillips screwdriver. This is the vertical adjuster screw on a 2006 and later model

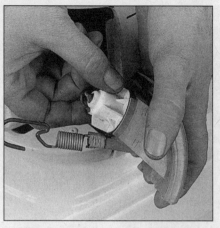

13.3a On 1994 and earlier models, the front parking light bulb is accessible after releasing the spring and rotating the housing out of the fender. On 1995 and later models, first detach and remove the parking/turn signal light assembly

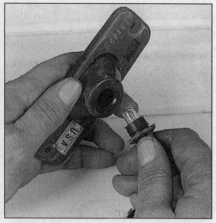

13.3b Pull the holder out of the side marker housing for access to the bulb

beams. If a compromise must be made, keep in mind that the low beams are the most used and have the greatest effect on driver safety.

8   Have the headlights adjusted by a dealer service department or service station at the earliest opportunity.

13   Bulb replacement

Refer to illustrations 13.3a, 13.3b, 13.4a and 13.4b

1   The lenses of many lights are held in place by screws, which makes it a simple procedure to gain access to the bulbs.

2   On some lights, the lenses are held in place by clips. On these lights, the lenses can either be removed by unsnapping them or by using a small screwdriver to pry them off.

3   Several types of bulbs are used. Some are removed by pushing in and turning coun-

terclockwise **(see illustrations)**. Others can simply be unclipped from the terminals or pulled straight out of the socket.

4   To gain access to the instrument panel illumination lights **(see illustrations)**, the instrument cluster will have to be removed as described in Section 15.

14   Wiper motors - removal and installation

1   Disconnect the cable from the negative terminal of the battery.

Windshield wiper motor
1986 through 1989 models

Refer to illustrations 14.2, 14.3, and 14.4

2   Disconnect the washer hoses **(see illustration)**.

13.4a Remove the switch housing from the cluster and turn the holder counterclockwise for access to the bulb

13.4b After removing the instrument cluster, turn the bulb holders, lift them out and withdraw the bulbs

14.2 Disconnect the washer hoses

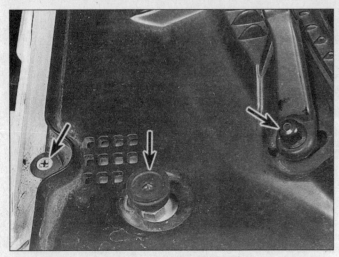

14.3 Remove the wiper arms and the cowl trim panel retaining screws (not all screws visible)

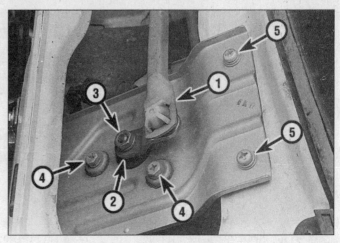

14.4 Windshield wiper motor details (1986 through 1989 models)

1	Link rod	4	Wiper motor mounting bolts (one bolt not visible)
2	Crank arm	5	Upper mounting bracket screws
3	Crank arm nut		

3   Remove the wiper arms and the cowl trim retaining screws or clips **(see illustration)**, then detach the trim for access to the motor.

4   Separate the link rod from the wiper motor crank arm **(see illustration)**, then unscrew the crank arm nut and remove the crank arm. Loosen, but don't remove, the three wiper motor mounting bolts. Remove the two upper motor mounting bracket screws and the lower mounting bracket screws, remove the mounting bracket and motor as a single assembly and disconnect the electrical connector.

5   Remove the three motor mounting bolts and separate the motor from its mounting bracket. Install the new motor on the mounting bracket and tighten the bolts securely. Install the crank arm and tighten the nut securely

6   Install the motor and mounting bracket

and tighten the upper and lower mounting bracket screws securely, then retighten the motor mounting bolts and the crank arm nut. Installation is otherwise the reverse of removal.

1990 through 2005 models

Refer to illustration 14.9

7   Follow Steps 1 through 3.

8   Working in the cowl area, separate the link rod from the wiper motor crank arm. Unscrew the crank arm nut and remove the crank arm from the wiper motor shaft.

9   Remove the wiper motor mounting bolts **(see illustration)**. Disconnect the electrical connector and remove the assembly from the vehicle.

10   Installation is the reverse of removal.

2006 and later models

Refer to illustrations 14.11, 14.12a, 14.12b and 14.13

11   Remove the trim caps for the windshield wiper arm retaining nuts **(see illustration)**, unscrew the wiper arm retaining nuts and remove the wiper arms.

12   Remove the cowl trim panel **(see illustrations)** and disconnect the windshield washer fluid line.

13   Disconnect the electrical connector from the windshield wiper motor, then remove the windshield wiper motor/linkage assembly retaining bolts **(see illustration)**.

14   To remove the windshield wiper motor/linkage assembly from the cowl area, move it to the right (toward the passenger side of the vehicle) to disengage the rubber mounting insulator.

14.9 Wiper motor details (typical 1990 and later model)

1   *Electrical connector*
2   *Mounting bolts (lower bolt not visible)*

14.11 Remove the trim caps for the windshield wiper arm retaining nuts and remove the nuts, then remove the windshield wiper arms

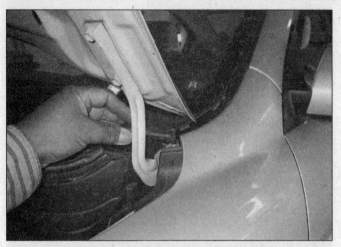

14.12a To detach the cowl trim panel, remove the small trim pieces from each rear corner of the cowl . . .

14.12b . . . then disengage these fasteners and remove the cowl

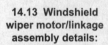
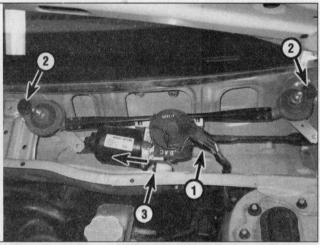

14.13 Windshield wiper motor/linkage assembly details:

1 Electrical connector
2 Mounting bolts
3 Mounting insulator

14.18a Lift the cover up for access to the rear window wiper retaining nut - typical

15   Remove the crank arm retaining nut and separate the crank arm from the wiper motor.
16   Remove the wiper motor mounting bolts.
17   Installation is the reverse of removal. Be sure to tighten the wiper motor mounting bolts and the crank arm nut securely.

Rear window wiper motor

Refer to illustrations 14.18a, 14.18b, 14.19 and 14.20

18   Remove the spindle nut and wiper arm **(see illustration)**. Note the order in which the wiper spindle washers are arranged for installation **(see illustration)**.

19   Open the liftgate and remove the trim panel **(see illustration)**.

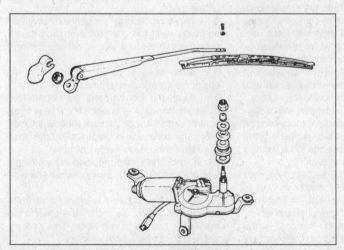

14.18b Rear window wiper components - typical

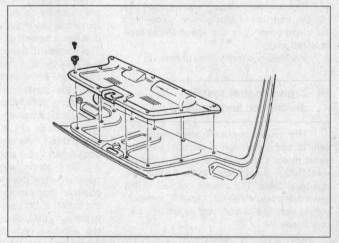

14.19 Liftgate trim panel details - typical

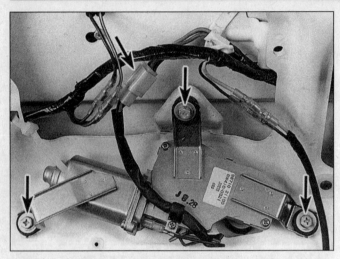

**14.20 Disconnect the connector, remove the mounting screws
and lower the wiper motor from the liftgate**

15.4a Remove the instrument cluster retaining screws - typical

20   Disconnect the electrical connector, remove the three mounting screws and lower the motor from the liftgate **(see illustration)**.
21   Installation is the reverse of removal.

15   Instrument cluster - removal and installation

Refer to illustrations 15.4a and 15.4b

Warning: *If equipped with a Supplemental Restraint System (SRS), more commonly known as airbags, disable the airbag system before working in the vicinity of airbag system components to avoid the possibility of accidental deployment of the airbag, which could result in personal injury (see Section 18).*
1   Disconnect the cable from the negative terminal of the battery.
2   Remove the steering wheel, if necessary (see Chapter 10).
3   Remove the steering column cover and the cluster housing (see Chapter 11).
4   Remove the retaining screws, then pull out the instrument cluster and disconnect the wiring connectors and speedometer **(see illustrations)**.
5   Installation is the reverse of removal.

16   Cruise control system - description and check

The cruise control system maintains vehicle speed through a vacuum actuated servo motor located in the engine compartment, which is connected to the throttle linkage by a cable. The system consists of the servo motor, clutch switch, brake light switch, control switches, a relay and associated vacuum hoses.
Diagnosis can usually be limited to simple checks of the wiring and vacuum connections for minor faults which can be easily repaired. These include:
a) *Inspecting the cruise control actuating switches and wiring for broken wires or loose connections.*
b) *Checking the cruise control fuse.*
c) *Checking the hoses in the engine compartment for tight connections, cracked hoses and obvious vacuum leaks. The cruise control system is operated by vacuum so it is critical that all vacuum switches, hoses and connections be secure.*
d) *Check the brake light switch and clutch switch for proper operation.*

17   Power window system - description and check

1   The power window system consists of the control switches, the motors (regulators), glass mechanisms and associated wiring.
2   Power windows are wired so they can be lowered and raised from the master control switch by the driver or by remote switches located at the individual windows. Each window has a separate motor which is reversible. The position of the control switch determines the polarity and therefore the direction of operation. Some systems are equipped with relays that control current flow to the motors.
3   Some vehicles are equipped with a separate circuit breaker for each motor in addition to the fuse or circuit breaker protecting the whole circuit. This prevents one stuck window from disabling the whole system.
4   The power window system will only operate when the ignition switch is ON. In addition, many models have a window lockout switch at the master control switch which, when activated, disables the switches at the rear windows and, sometimes, the switch at the passenger's window also. Always check

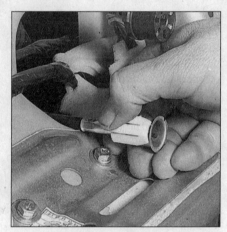

15.4b On 1986 through 1999 models, squeeze the clip together to disconnect the cable from the speedometer (cluster removed for clarity)

these items before troubleshooting a window problem.
5   These procedures are general in nature, so if you can't find the problem using them, take the vehicle to a dealer service department.
6   If the power windows don't work at all, check the fuse or circuit breaker.
7   If only the rear windows are inoperative, or if the windows only operate from the master control switch, check the rear window lockout switch for continuity in the unlocked position. Replace it if it doesn't have continuity.
8   Check the wiring between the switches and fuse panel for continuity. Repair the wiring, if necessary.
9   If only one window is inoperative from the master control switch, try the other control switch at the window. **Note:** *This doesn't apply to the driver's door window.*
10   If the same window works from one

switch, but not the other, check the switch for continuity.

11   If the switch tests OK, check for a short or open in the wiring between the affected switch and the window motor.

12   If one window is inoperative from both switches, remove the trim panel from the affected door and check for voltage at the motor while the switch is operated.

13   If voltage is reaching the motor, disconnect the glass from the regulator (see Chapter 11). Move the window up and down by hand while checking for binding and damage. Also check for binding and damage to the regulator. If the regulator is not damaged and the window moves up and down smoothly, replace the motor. If there's binding or damage, lubricate, repair or replace parts, as necessary.

14   If voltage isn't reaching the motor, check the wiring in the circuit for continuity between the switches and motors. You'll need to consult the wiring diagram for the vehicle. Some power window circuits are equipped with relays. If equipped, check that the relays are grounded properly and receiving voltage from the switches. Also check that each relay sends voltage to the motor when the switch is turned on. If it doesn't, replace the relay.

18   Airbag system - general information

Description

1   1995 and later models are equipped with a Supplemental Restraint System (SRS), more commonly known as an airbag. All models have two airbags, one for the driver and one for the front seat passenger. The SRS system is designed to protect the driver and passenger) from serious injury in the event of a head-on or frontal collision.

2   The SRS system consists of an SRS unit - which contains an impact sensor, safing sensor, self-diagnosis circuit and a back-up power circuit - located under the dash, in front of the floor console, an airbag assembly in the center of the steering wheel and a second airbag assembly for the front seat passenger, located in the top of the dashboard above the glove box.

Operation

3   For the airbag(s) to deploy, the impact and safing sensors must be activated. When this condition occurs, the circuit to the airbag inflator is closed and the airbag inflates. If the battery is destroyed by the impact, or is too low to power the inflator, a back-up power unit inside the SRS unit provides power.

Self-diagnosis system

4   A self-diagnosis circuit in the SRS unit displays a light when the ignition switch is turned to the On position. If the system is operating normally, the light should go out after about six seconds. If the light doesn't come on, or doesn't go out after six seconds, or if it comes on while you're driving the vehicle, there's a malfunction in the SRS system. Have it inspected and repaired as soon as possible. Do not attempt to troubleshoot or service the SRS system yourself. Even a small mistake could cause the SRS system to malfunction when you need it.

Servicing components near the SRS system

5   Nevertheless, there are times when you need to remove the steering wheel, radio or service other components on or near the dashboard. At these times, you'll be working around components and wire harnesses for the SRS system. Do not disconnect the connectors for these wires. And do not use electrical test equipment on SRS wires. *ALWAYS DISABLE THE SRS SYSTEM BEFORE WORKING NEAR THE SRS SYSTEM COMPONENTS OR RELATED WIRING*.

Disabling the SRS system

Warning: *Anytime you are working in the vicinity of airbag wiring or components, DISABLE THE SRS SYSTEM.*

6   Turn the Ignition key to the Lock position.

7   Disconnect the cable from the negative battery terminal.

8   Wait one minute for the back-up power supply to be depleted.

Enabling the SRS system

9   Turn the ignition key to the Lock position.

10   Reattach the negative battery cable.

11   Turn the ignition key On and verify the airbag warning light goes out.

19   Wiring diagrams - general information

Since it isn't possible to include all wiring diagrams for every year covered by this manual, the following diagrams are those that are typical and most commonly needed.

Prior to troubleshooting any circuits, check the fuse and circuit breakers (if equipped) to make sure they are in good condition. Make sure the battery is properly charged and has clean, tight cable connections (see Chapter 1).

When checking the wiring system, make sure that all connectors are clean, with no broken or loose pins. When disconnecting a connector, do not pull on the wires, only on the connector housings themselves.

Notes

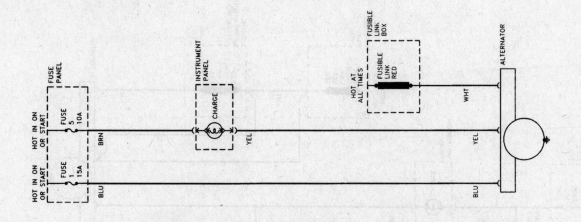

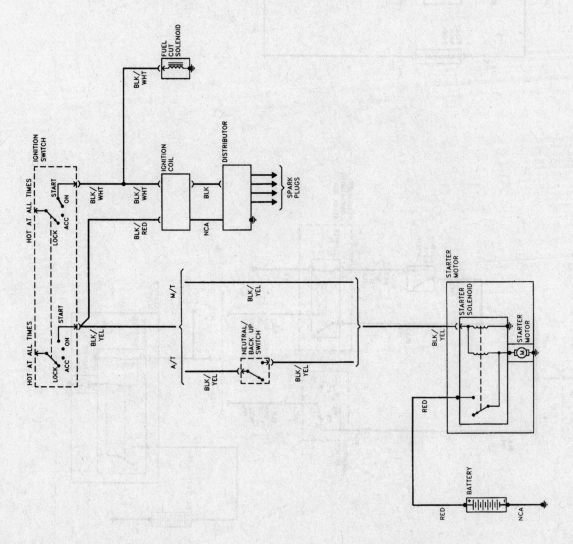

Starting, charging and ignition systems - 1986 through 1989 models

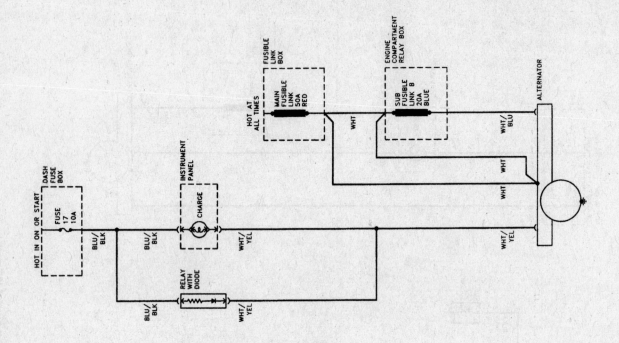

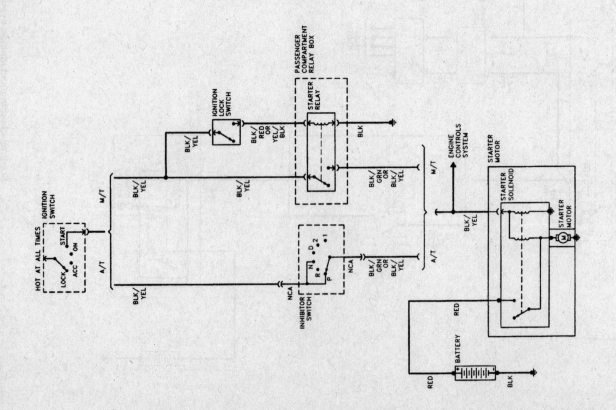

Starting and charging systems - 1990 through 1994 models

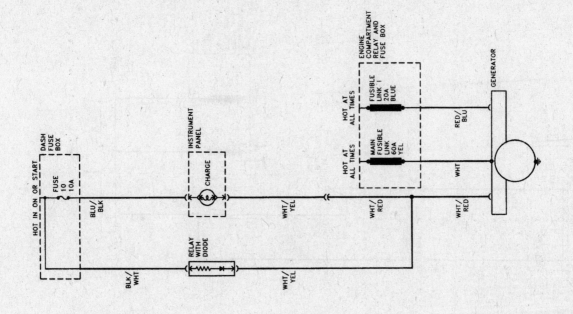

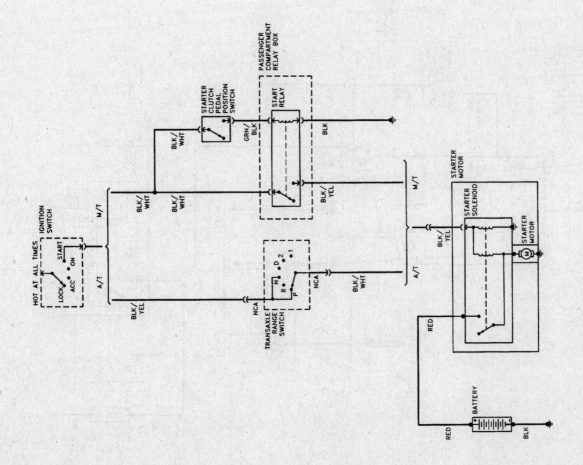

Starting and charging systems - 1995 and 1996 models

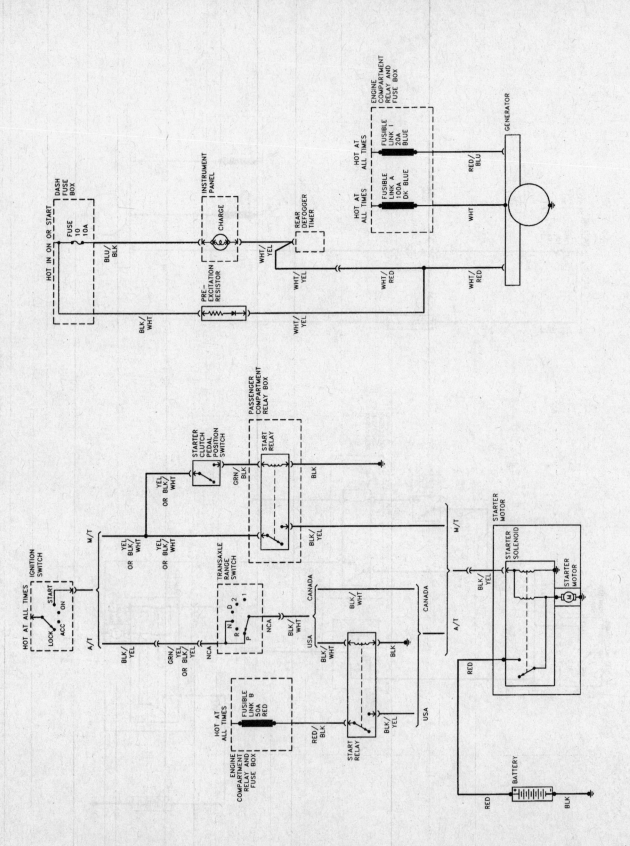

Starting and charging systems - 1997 and later models

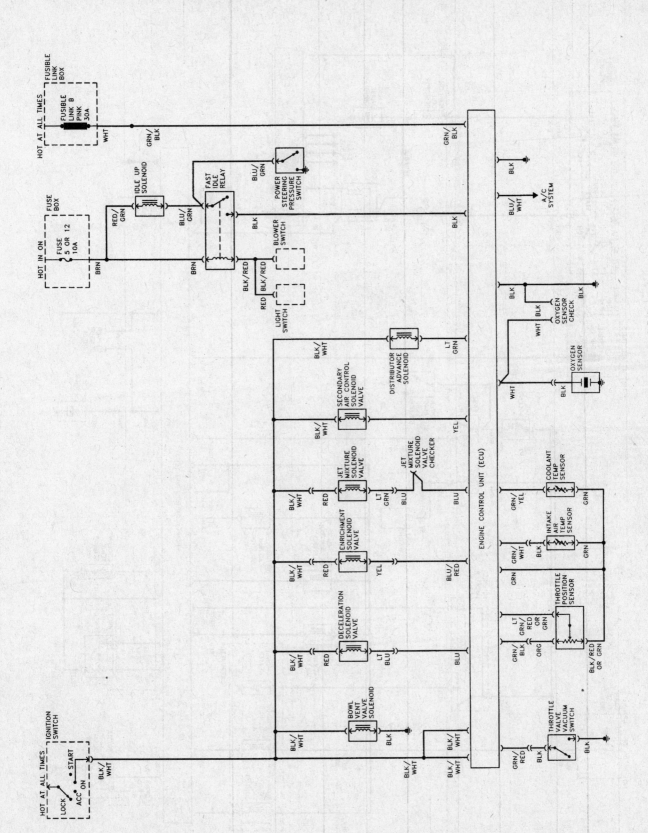

Emissions and engine control systems - 1986 through 1989 models

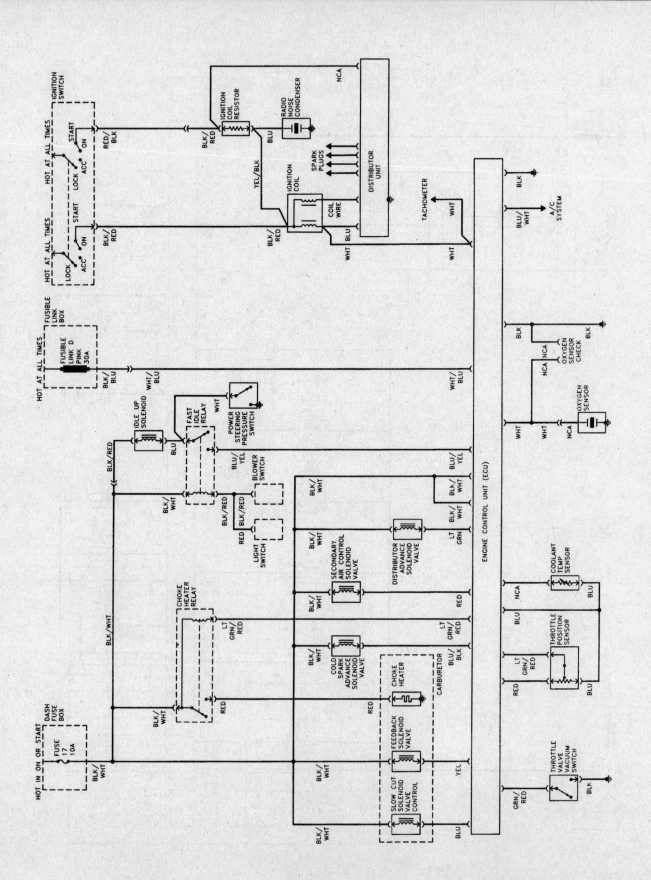

Emissions and engine control systems - 1990 through 1994 carbureted models

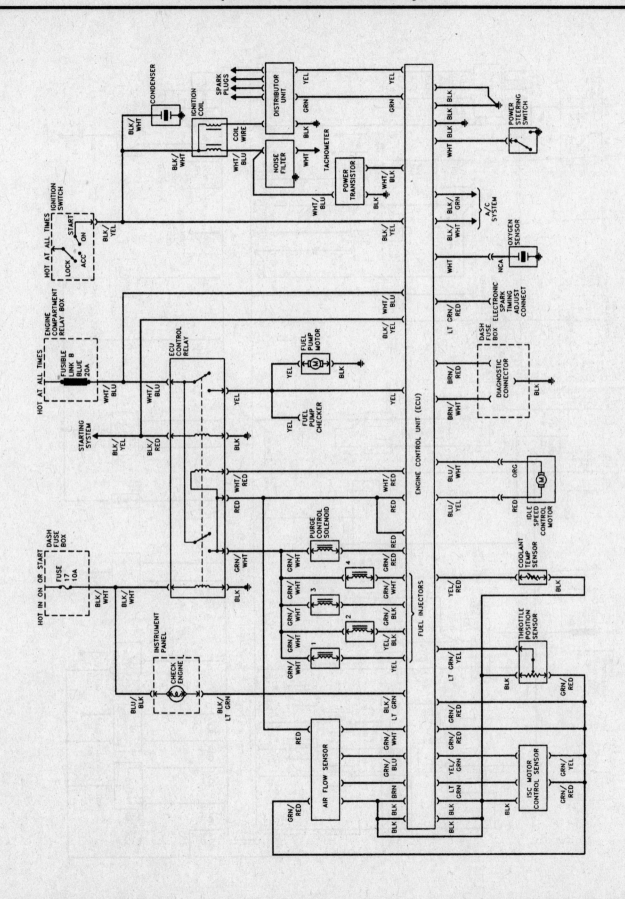

Emissions and engine control systems - 1990 through 1994 fuel-injected models

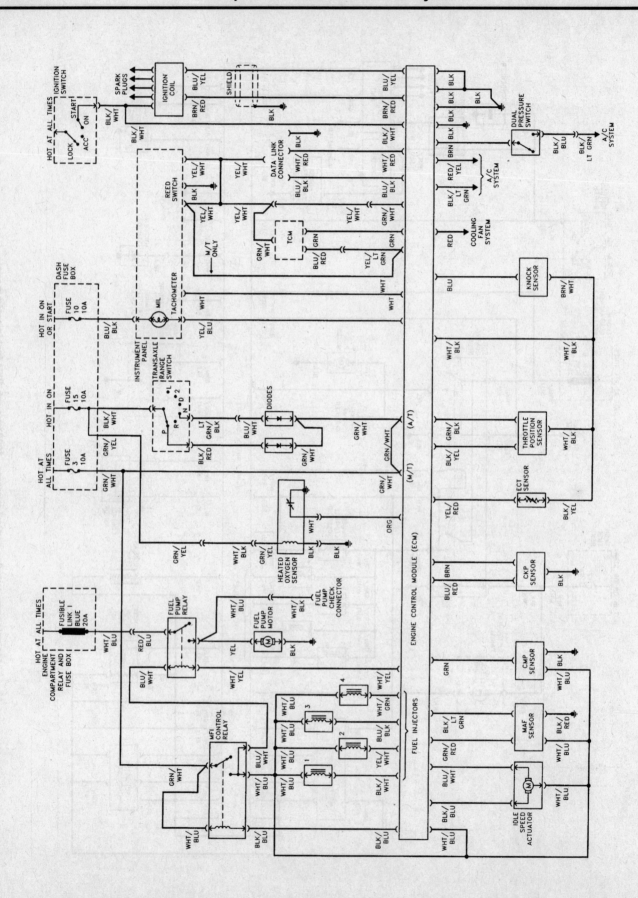

Emissions and engine control systems - 1995 model

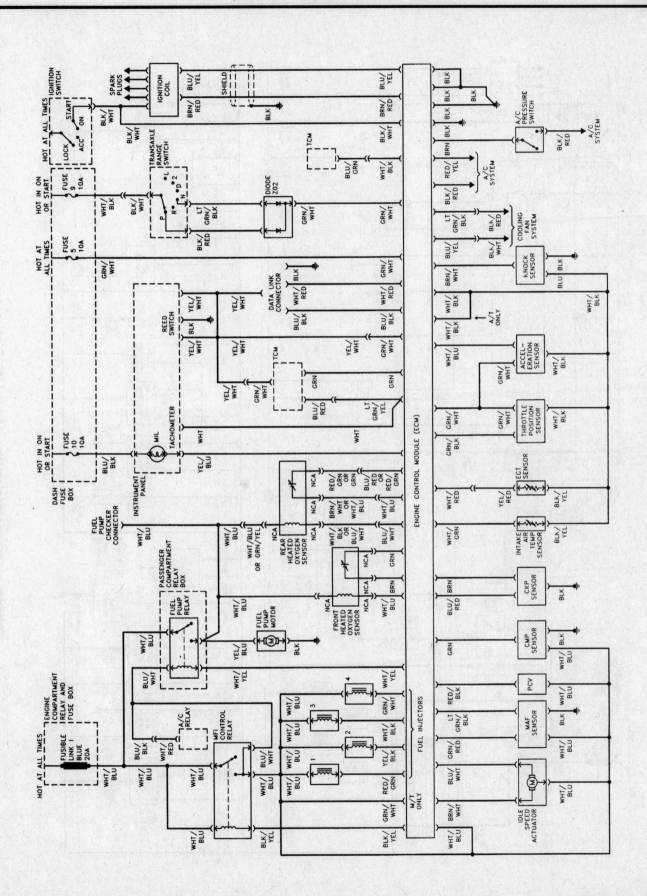

Emissions and engine control systems - 1996 and 1997 SOHC models

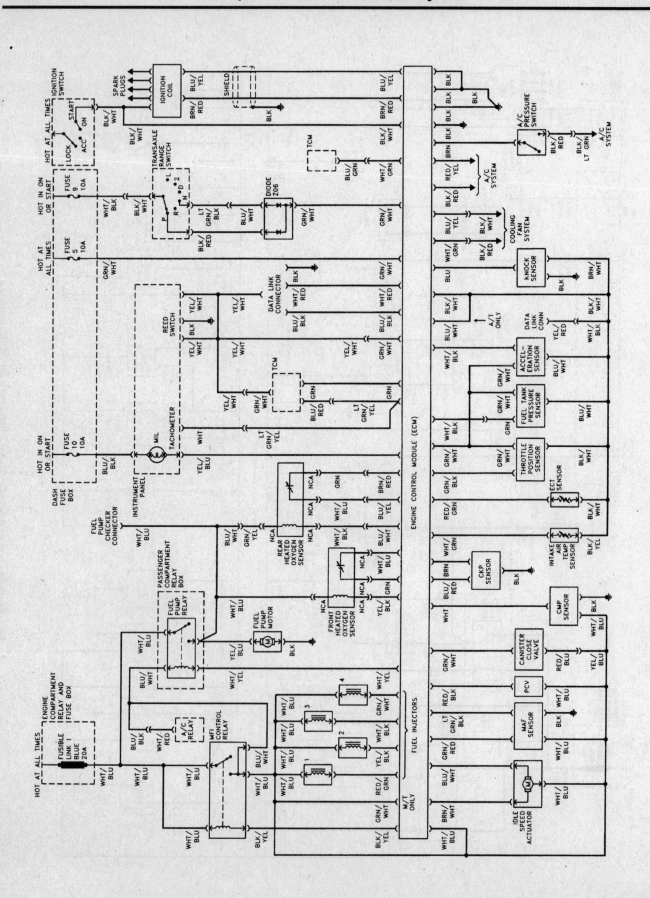

Emissions and engine control systems - 1996 and 1997 DOHC models

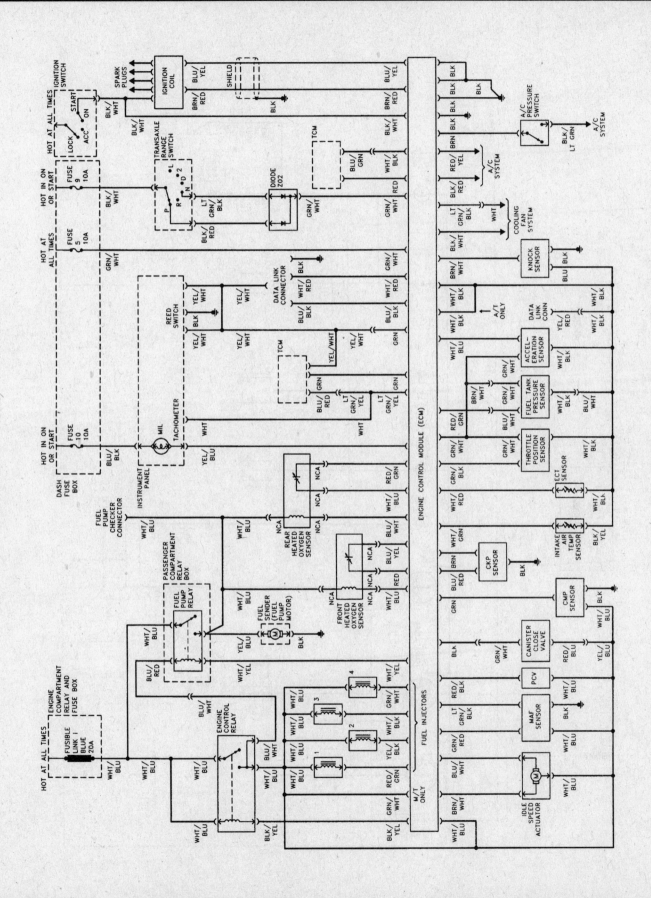

Emissions and engine control systems - 1998 model

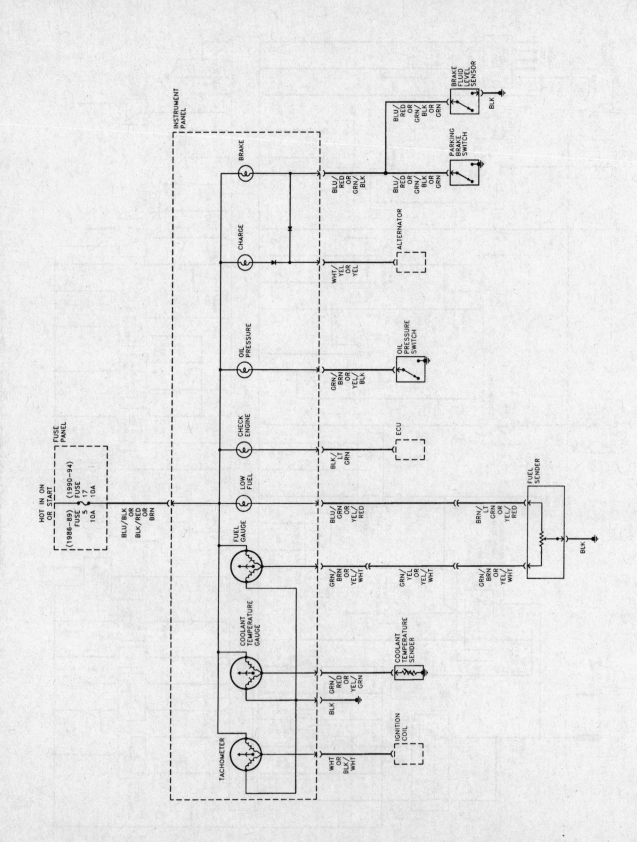

Gauges and warning lights system - 1986 through 1994 models

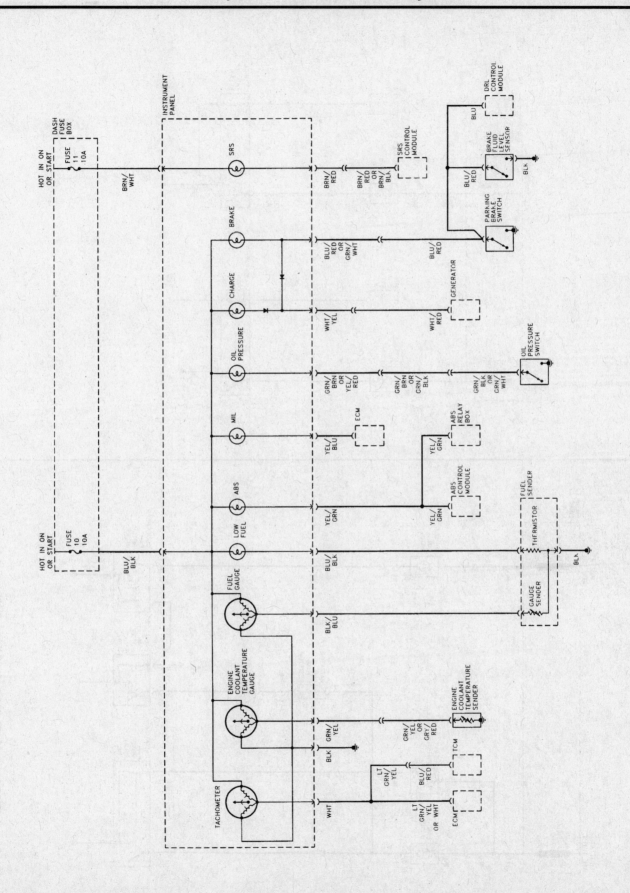

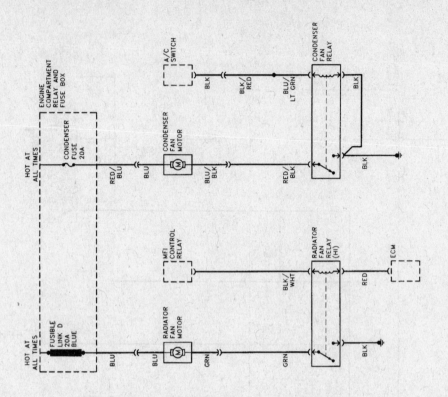

Engine cooling fan system - 1995 model

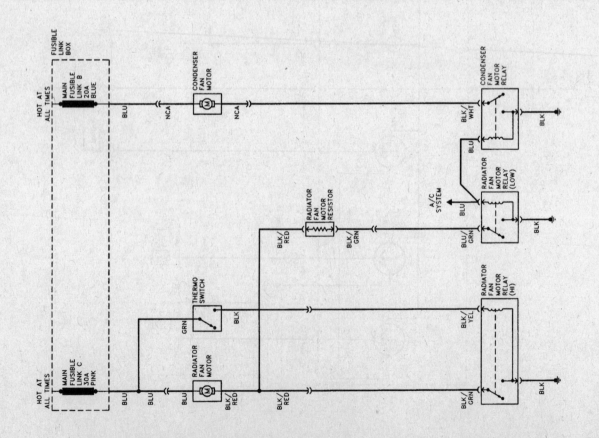

Engine cooling fan system - 1990 through 1994 models

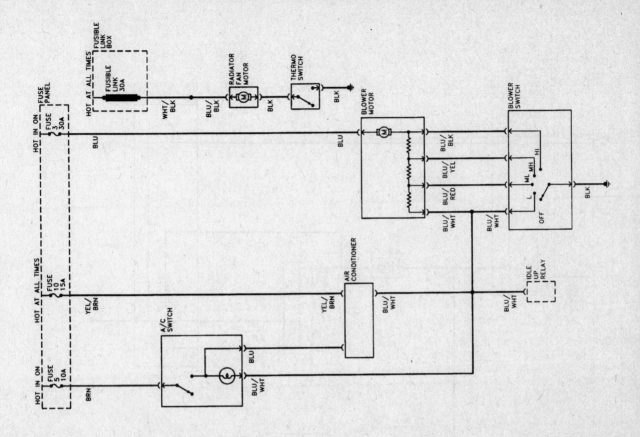

Heating and air conditioning system (includes engine cooling fan system) - 1986 through 1989 models

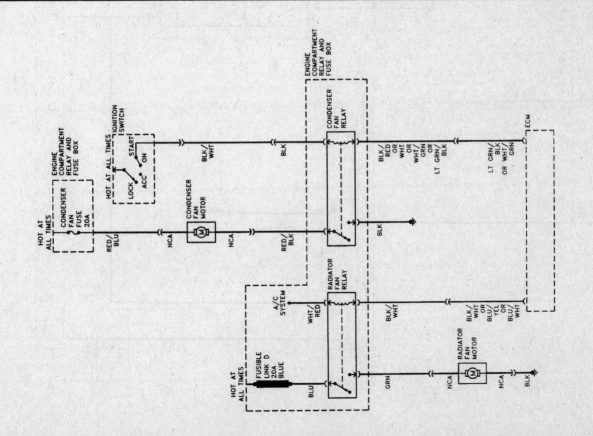

Engine cooling fan system - 1996 and later models

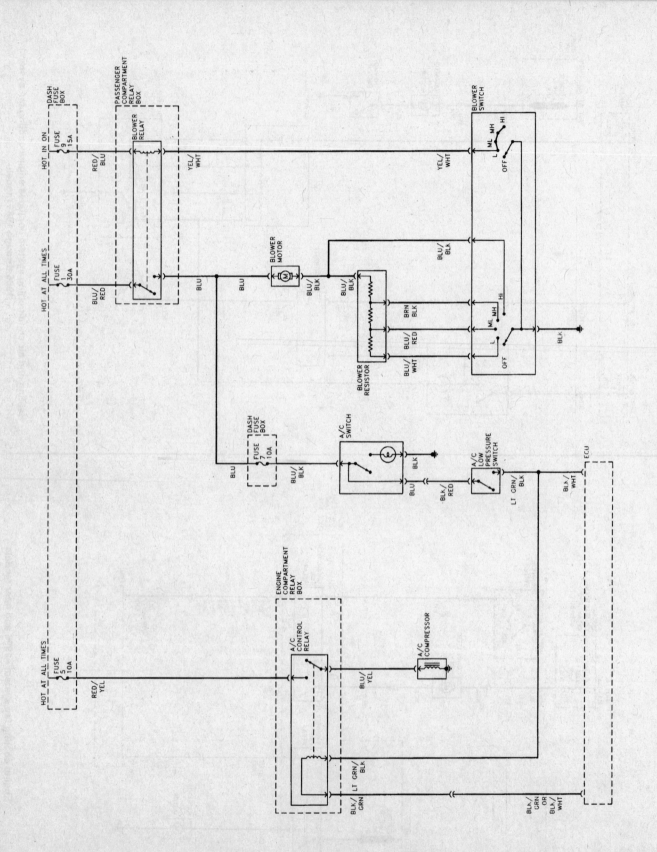

Heating and air conditioning system - 1990 through 1994 models

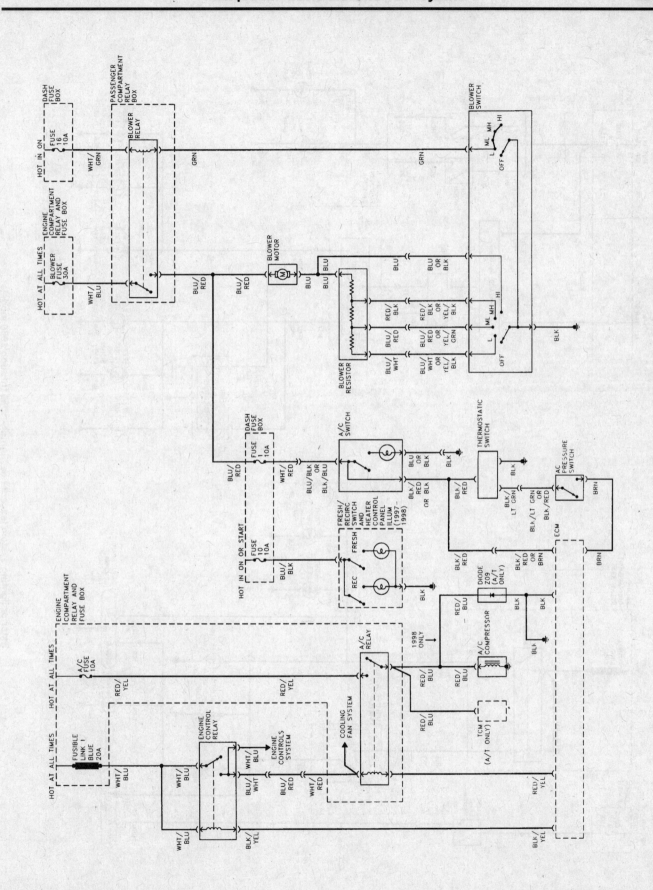

Heating and air conditioning system - 1995 and later models

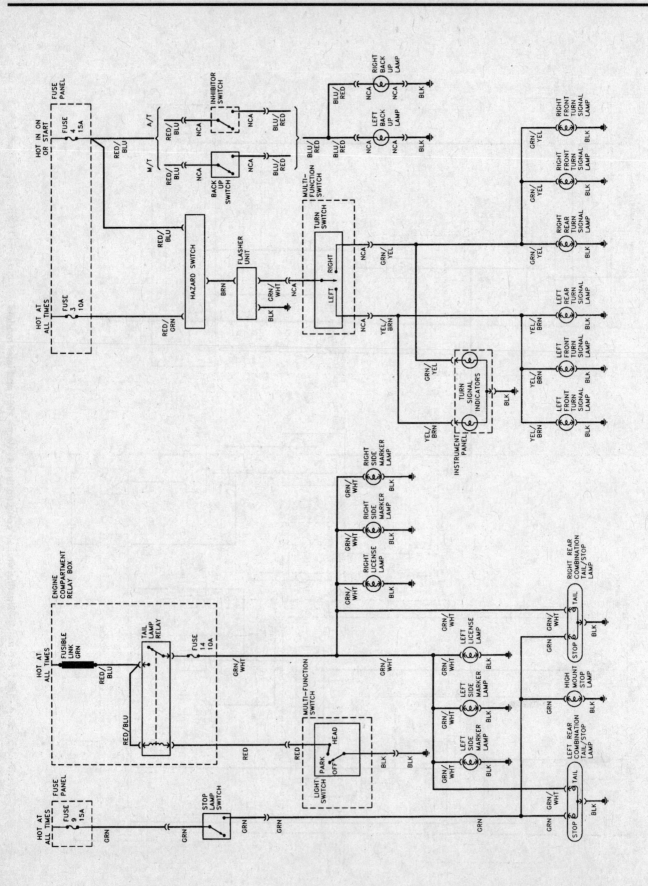

Exterior lighting system (except headlights) - 1986 through 1989 models

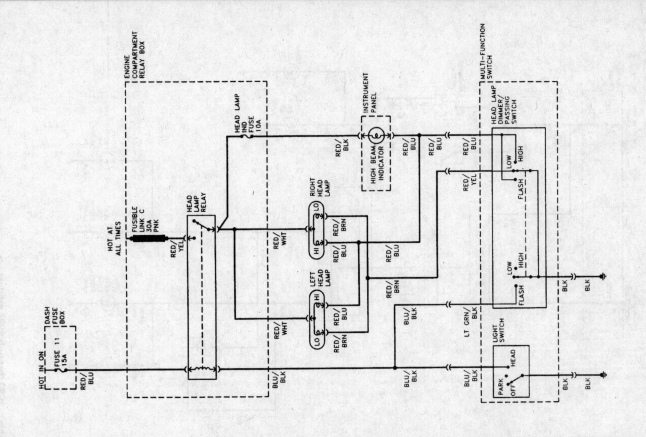

Headlight system - 1990 through 1994 models

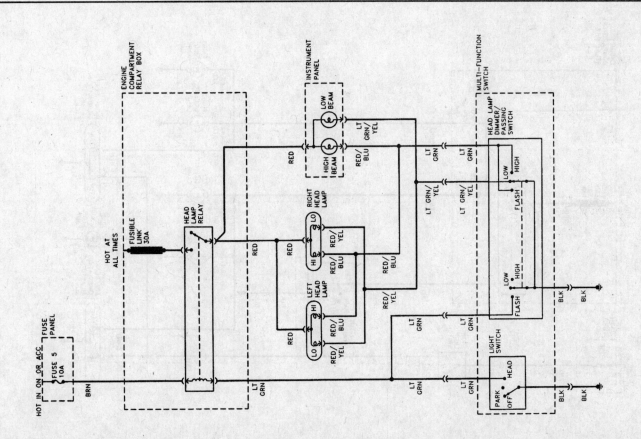

Headlight system - 1986 through 1989 models

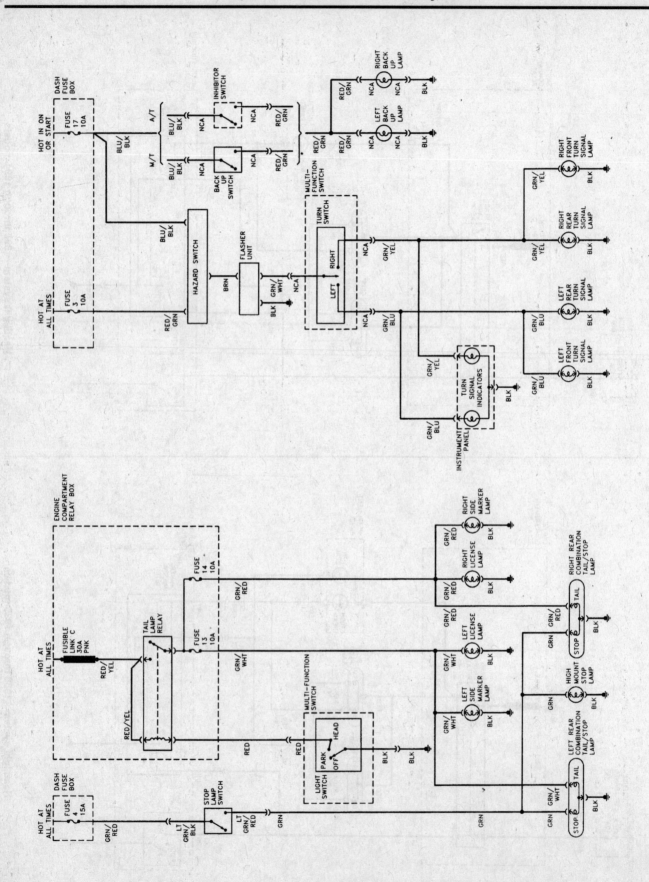

Exterior lighting system (except headlights) - 1990 through 1994 models

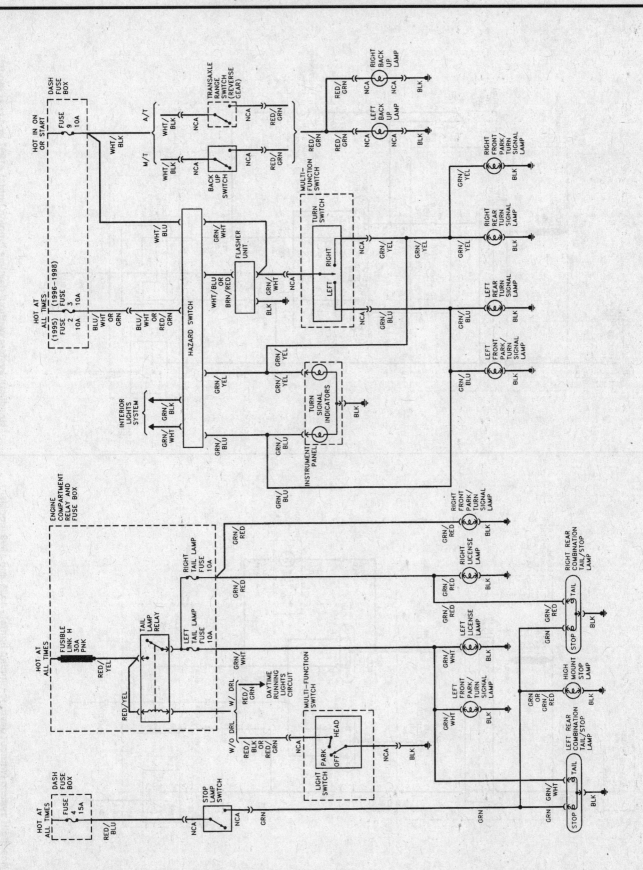

Exterior lighting system (except headlights and fog lights) - 1995 and later models

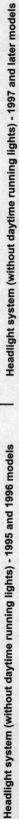

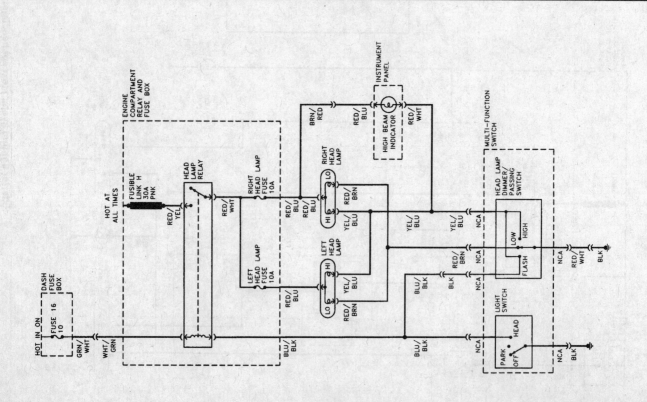

Headlight system (without daytime running lights) - 1997 and later models

Headlight system (without daytime running lights) - 1995 and 1996 models

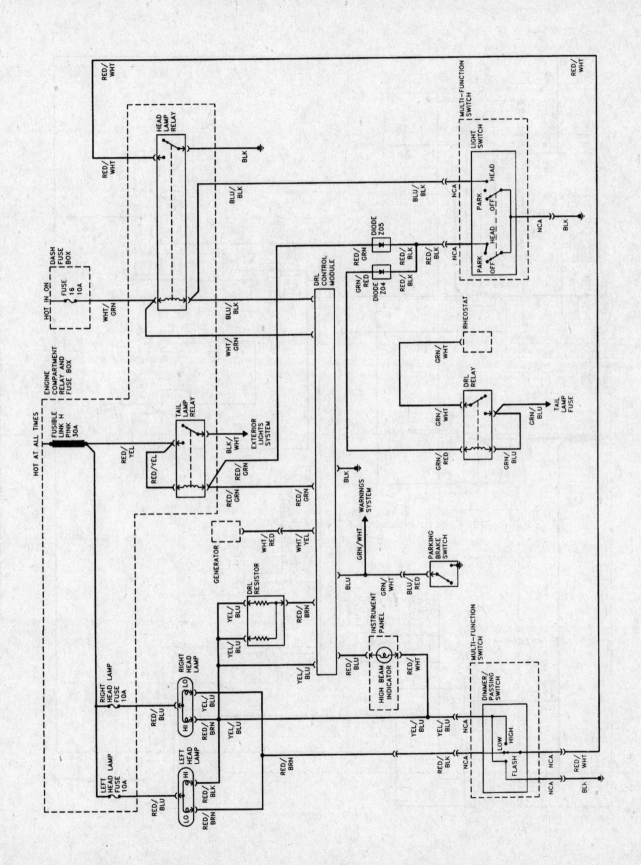

Headlight system (with daytime running lights) - 1995 and 1996 models

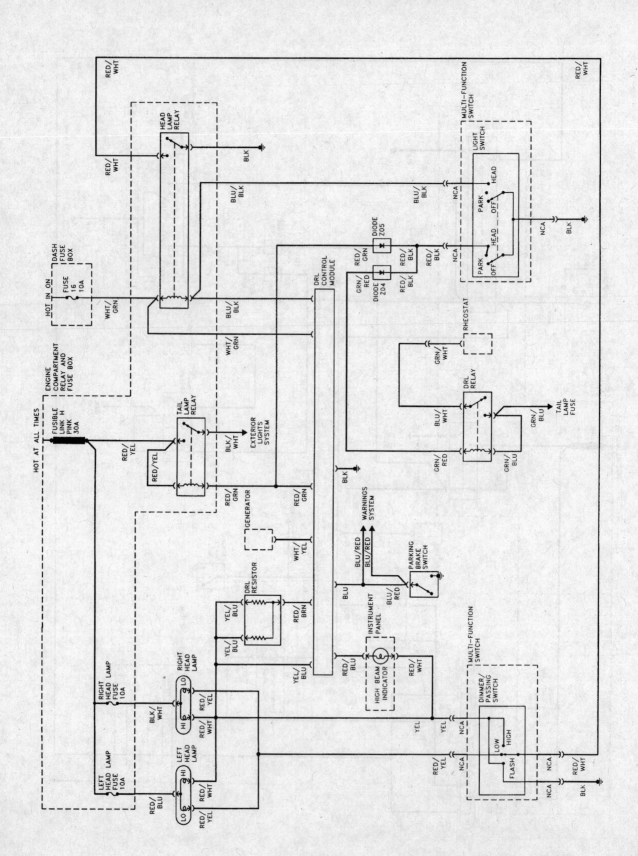

Headlight system (with daytime running lights) - 1997 and later models

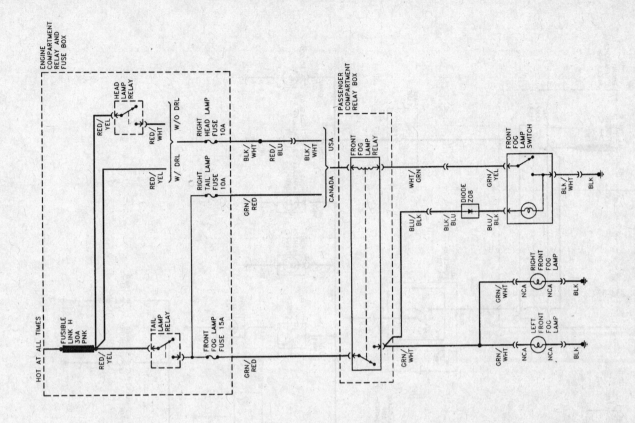

Fog light system - 1998 model

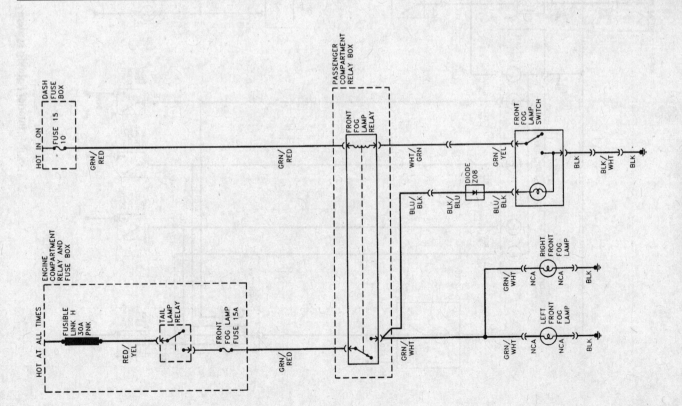

Fog light system - 1997 model

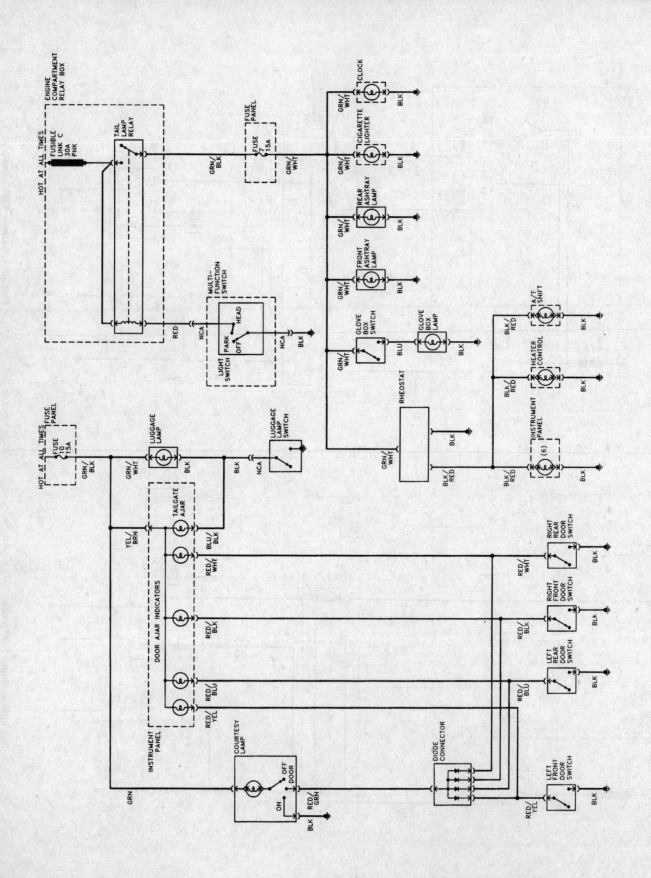

Interior lighting system - 1986 through 1989 models

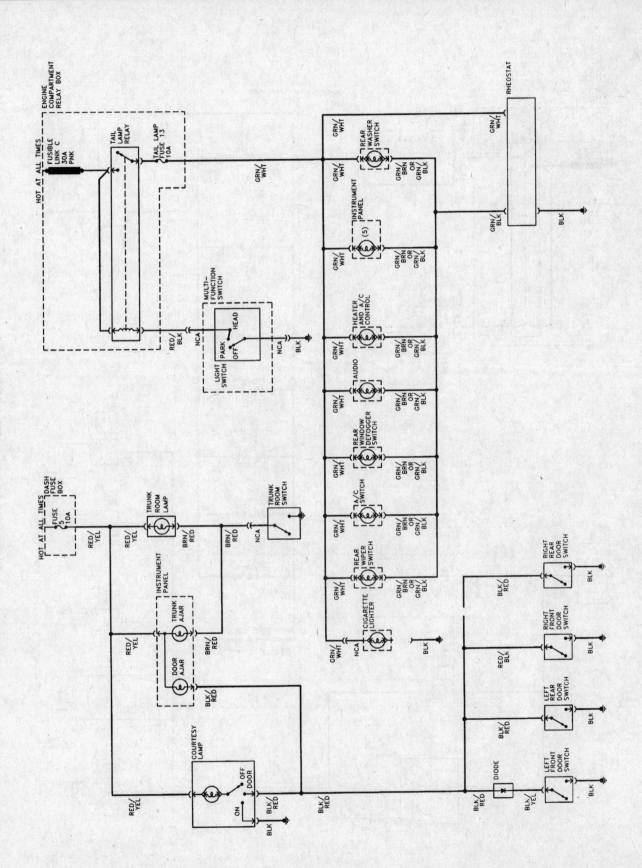

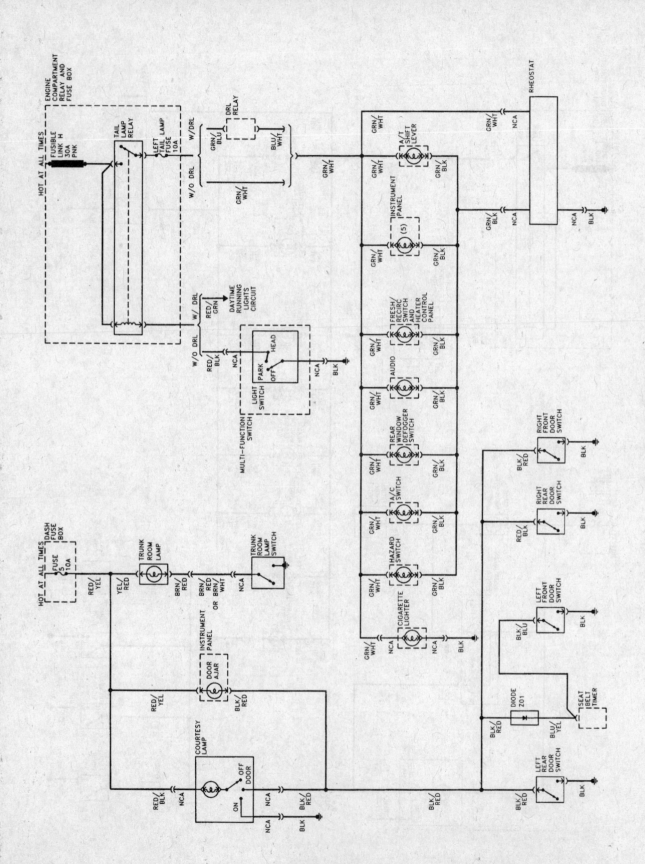

Interior lighting system - 1995 and later models

Power window system - 1997 and later models

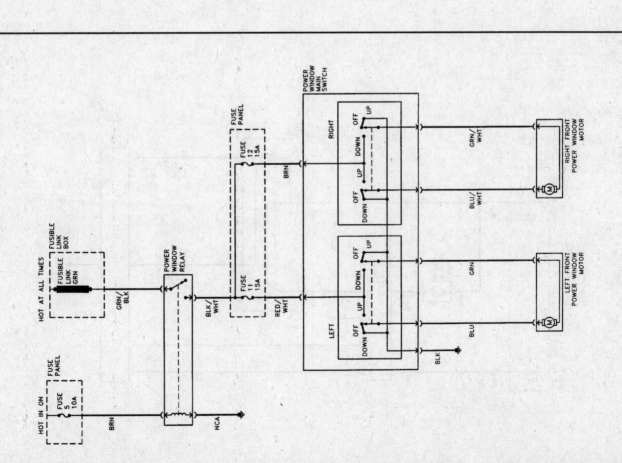

Power window system - 1996 and earlier models

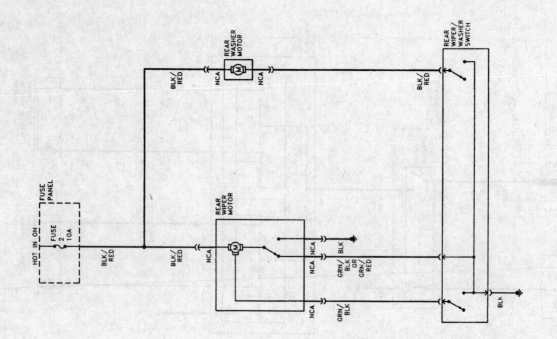

Rear wiper and washer system - 1986 through 1989 models

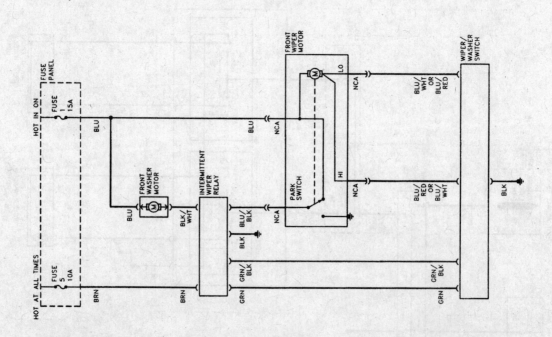

Windshield wiper and washer system - 1986 through 1989 models

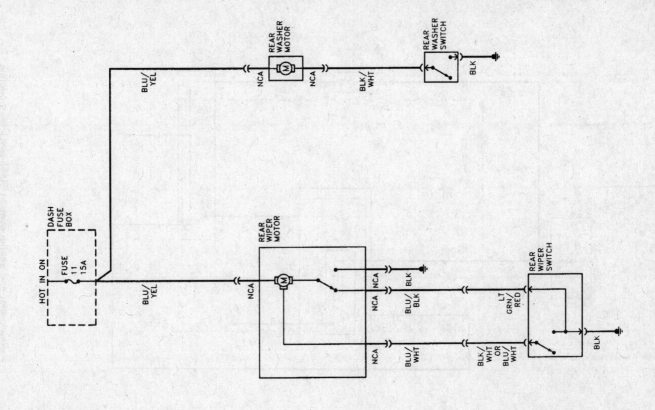

Rear wiper and washer system - 1990 through 1994 models

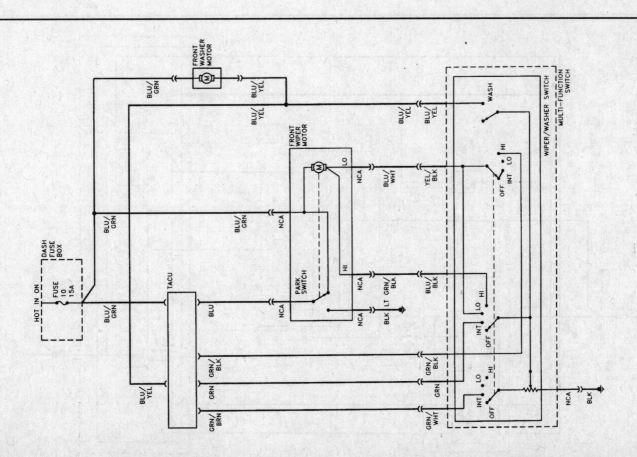

Windshield wiper and washer system - 1990 through 1994 models

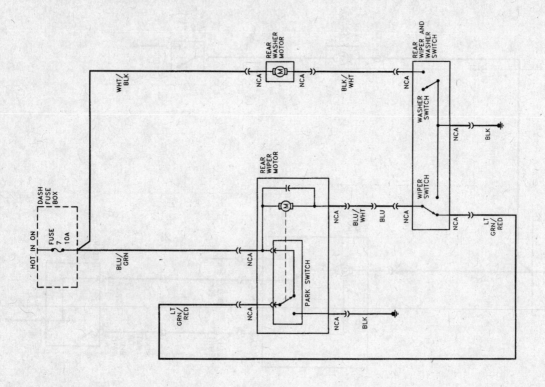

Rear wiper and washer system - 1995 and later models

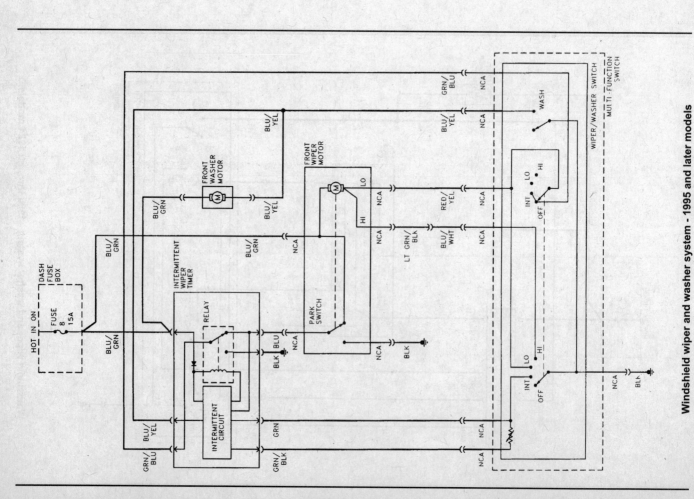

Windshield wiper and washer system - 1995 and later models

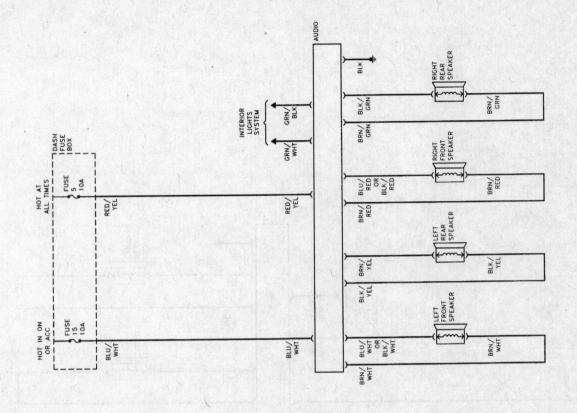

Typical audio system - 1990 through 1994 models

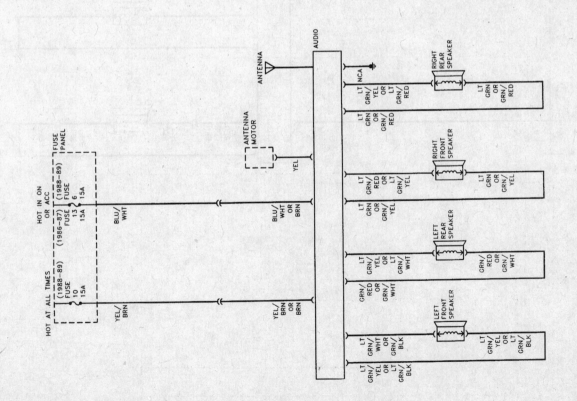

Typical audio system - 1986 through 1989 models

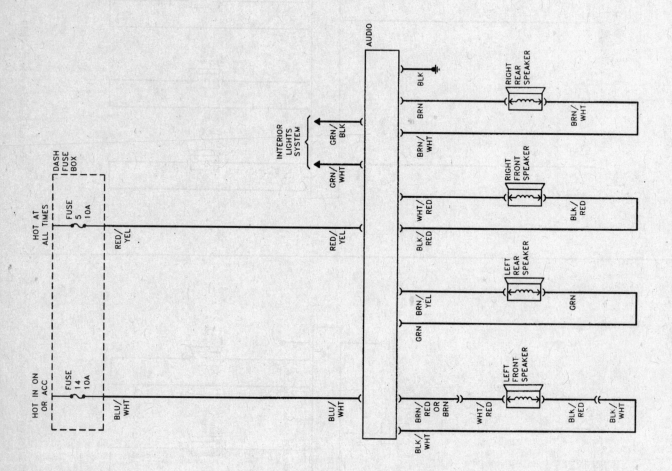

Typical audio system - 1995 and later models

Notes

Notes

Index

Notes

Haynes Automotive Manuals

NOTE: If you do not see a listing for your vehicle, consult your local Haynes dealer for the latest product information.

ACURA
- 12020 **Integra** '86 thru '89 & **Legend** '86 thru '90
- 12021 **Integra** '90 thru '93 & **Legend** '91 thru '95
  - **Integra** '94 thru '00 - *see HONDA Civic (42025)*
  - **MDX** '01 thru '07 - *see HONDA Pilot (42037)*
- 12050 **Acura TL** all models '99 thru '08

AMC
- **Jeep CJ** - *see JEEP (50020)*
- 14020 **Mid-size models** '70 thru '83
- 14025 **(Renault) Alliance & Encore** '83 thru '87

AUDI
- 15020 **4000** all models '80 thru '87
- 15025 **5000** all models '77 thru '83
- 15026 **5000** all models '84 thru '88
  - **Audi A4** '96 thru '01 - *see VW Passat (96023)*
- 15030 **Audi A4** '02 thru '08

AUSTIN-HEALEY
- **Sprite** - *see MG Midget (66015)*

BMW
- 18020 **3/5 Series** '82 thru '92
- 18021 **3-Series** incl. Z3 models '92 thru '98
- 18022 **3-Series** incl. Z4 models '99 thru '05
- 18023 **3-Series** '06 thru '10
- 18025 **320i** all 4 cyl models '75 thru '83
- 18050 **1500 thru 2002** except Turbo '59 thru '77

BUICK
- 19010 **Buick Century** '97 thru '05
  - **Century** (front-wheel drive) - *see GM (38005)*
- 19020 **Buick, Oldsmobile & Pontiac Full-size** (Front-wheel drive) '85 thru '05
  - **Buick** Electra, LeSabre and Park Avenue; **Oldsmobile** Delta 88 Royale, Ninety Eight and Regency; **Pontiac** Bonneville
- 19025 **Buick, Oldsmobile & Pontiac Full-size** (Rear wheel drive) '70 thru '90
  - **Buick** Estate, Electra, LeSabre, Limited, **Oldsmobile** Custom Cruiser, Delta 88, Ninety-eight, **Pontiac** Bonneville, Catalina, Grandville, Parisienne
- 19030 **Mid-size Regal & Century** all rear-drive models with V6, V8 and Turbo '74 thru '87
  - **Regal** - *see GENERAL MOTORS (38010)*
  - **Riviera** - *see GENERAL MOTORS (38030)*
  - **Roadmaster** - *see CHEVROLET (24046)*
  - **Skyhawk** - *see GENERAL MOTORS (38015)*
  - **Skylark** - *see GM (38020, 38025)*
  - **Somerset** - *see GENERAL MOTORS (38025)*

CADILLAC
- 21015 **CTS & CTS-V** '03 thru '12
- 21030 **Cadillac Rear Wheel Drive** '70 thru '93
  - **Cimarron** - *see GENERAL MOTORS (38015)*
  - **DeVille** - *see GM (38031 & 38032)*
  - **Eldorado** - *see GM (38030 & 38031)*
  - **Fleetwood** - *see GM (38031)*
  - **Seville** - *see GM (38030, 38031 & 38032)*

CHEVROLET
- 10305 **Chevrolet Engine Overhaul Manual**
- 24010 **Astro & GMC Safari Mini-vans** '85 thru '05
- 24015 **Camaro V8** all models '70 thru '81
- 24016 **Camaro** all models '82 thru '92
- 24017 **Camaro & Firebird** '93 thru '02
  - **Cavalier** - *see GENERAL MOTORS (38016)*
  - **Celebrity** - *see GENERAL MOTORS (38005)*
- 24020 **Chevelle, Malibu & El Camino** '69 thru '87
- 24024 **Chevette & Pontiac T1000** '76 thru '87
  - **Citation** - *see GENERAL MOTORS (38020)*
- 24027 **Colorado & GMC Canyon** '04 thru '10
- 24032 **Corsica/Beretta** all models '87 thru '96
- 24040 **Corvette** all V8 models '68 thru '82
- 24041 **Corvette** all models '84 thru '96
- 24045 **Full-size Sedans** Caprice, Impala, Biscayne, Bel Air & Wagons '69 thru '90
- 24046 **Impala SS & Caprice and Buick Roadmaster** '91 thru '96
  - **Impala** '00 thru '05 - *see LUMINA (24048)*
- 24047 **Impala & Monte Carlo** all models '06 thru '11
  - **Lumina** '90 thru '94 - *see GM (38010)*
- 24048 **Lumina & Monte Carlo** '95 thru '05
  - **Lumina APV** - *see GM (38035)*
- 24050 **Luv Pick-up** all 2WD & 4WD '72 thru '82
  - **Malibu** '97 thru '00 - *see GM (38026)*
- 24055 **Monte Carlo** all models '70 thru '88
  - **Monte Carlo** '95 thru '01 - *see LUMINA (24048)*
- 24059 **Nova** all V8 models '69 thru '79
- 24060 **Nova and Geo Prizm** '85 thru '92
- 24064 **Pick-ups** '67 thru '87 - Chevrolet & GMC
- 24065 **Pick-ups** '88 thru '98 - Chevrolet & GMC

- 24066 **Pick-ups** '99 thru '06 - Chevrolet & GMC
- 24067 **Chevrolet Silverado & GMC Sierra** '07 thru '12
- 24070 **S-10 & S-15 Pick-ups** '82 thru '93, **Blazer & Jimmy** '83 thru '94,
- 24071 **S-10 & Sonoma Pick-ups** '94 thru '04, including **Blazer, Jimmy & Hombre**
- 24072 **Chevrolet TrailBlazer, GMC Envoy & Oldsmobile Bravada** '02 thru '09
- 24075 **Sprint** '85 thru '88 & **Geo Metro** '89 thru '01
- 24080 **Vans - Chevrolet & GMC** '68 thru '96
- 24081 **Chevrolet Express & GMC Savana** Full-size Vans '96 thru '10

CHRYSLER
- 10310 **Chrysler Engine Overhaul Manual**
- 25015 **Chrysler Cirrus, Dodge Stratus, Plymouth Breeze** '95 thru '00
- 25020 **Full-size Front-Wheel Drive** '88 thru '93
  - **K-Cars** - *see DODGE Aries (30008)*
  - **Laser** - *see DODGE Daytona (30030)*
- 25025 **Chrysler LHS, Concorde, New Yorker, Dodge Intrepid, Eagle Vision,** '93 thru '97
- 25026 **Chrysler LHS, Concorde, 300M, Dodge Intrepid,** '98 thru '04
- 25027 **Chrysler 300, Dodge Charger & Magnum** '05 thru '09
- 25030 **Chrysler & Plymouth Mid-size** front wheel drive '82 thru '95
  - **Rear-wheel Drive** - *see Dodge (30050)*
- 25035 **PT Cruiser** all models '01 thru '10
- 25040 **Chrysler Sebring** '95 thru '06, **Dodge** Stratus '01 thru '06, **Dodge** Avenger '95 thru '00

DATSUN
- 28005 **200SX** all models '80 thru '83
- 28007 **B-210** all models '73 thru '78
- 28009 **210** all models '79 thru '82
- 28012 **240Z, 260Z & 280Z** Coupe '70 thru '78
- 28014 **280ZX** Coupe & 2+2 '79 thru '83
  - **300ZX** - *see NISSAN (72010)*
- 28018 **510 & PL521 Pick-up** '68 thru '73
- 28020 **510** all models '78 thru '81
- 28022 **620 Series Pick-up** all models '73 thru '79
  - **720 Series Pick-up** - *see NISSAN (72030)*
- 28025 **810/Maxima** all gasoline models '77 thru '84

DODGE
- **400 & 600** - *see CHRYSLER (25030)*
- 30008 **Aries & Plymouth Reliant** '81 thru '89
- 30010 **Caravan & Plymouth Voyager** '84 thru '95
- 30011 **Caravan & Plymouth Voyager** '96 thru '02
- 30012 **Challenger/Plymouth Saporro** '78 thru '83
- 30013 **Caravan, Chrysler Voyager, Town & Country** '03 thru '07
- 30016 **Colt & Plymouth Champ** '78 thru '87
- 30020 **Dakota Pick-ups** all models '87 thru '96
- 30021 **Durango** '98 & '99, **Dakota** '97 thru '99
- 30022 **Durango** '00 thru '03 **Dakota** '00 thru '04
- 30023 **Durango** '04 thru '09, **Dakota** '05 thru '11
- 30025 **Dart, Demon, Plymouth Barracuda, Duster & Valiant** 6 cyl models '67 thru '76
- 30030 **Daytona & Chrysler Laser** '84 thru '89
  - **Intrepid** - *see CHRYSLER (25025, 25026)*
- 30034 **Neon** all models '95 thru '99
- 30035 **Omni & Plymouth Horizon** '78 thru '90
- 30036 **Dodge and Plymouth Neon** '00 thru '05
- 30040 **Pick-ups** all full-size models '74 thru '93
- 30041 **Pick-ups** all full-size models '94 thru '01
- 30042 **Pick-ups** full-size models '02 thru '08
- 30045 **Ram 50/D50 Pick-ups & Raider and Plymouth Arrow Pick-ups** '79 thru '93
- 30050 **Dodge/Plymouth/Chrysler RWD** '71 thru '89
- 30055 **Shadow & Plymouth Sundance** '87 thru '94
- 30060 **Spirit & Plymouth Acclaim** '89 thru '95
- 30065 **Vans - Dodge & Plymouth** '71 thru '03

EAGLE
- **Talon** - *see MITSUBISHI (68030, 68031)*
- **Vision** - *see CHRYSLER (25025)*

FIAT
- 34010 **124 Sport Coupe & Spider** '68 thru '78
- 34025 **X1/9** all models '74 thru '80

FORD
- 10320 **Ford Engine Overhaul Manual**
- 10355 **Ford Automatic Transmission Overhaul**
- 11500 **Mustang** '64-1/2 thru '70 Restoration Guide
- 36004 **Aerostar Mini-vans** all models '86 thru '97
- 36006 **Contour & Mercury Mystique** '95 thru '00
- 36008 **Courier Pick-up** all models '72 thru '82
- 36012 **Crown Victoria & Mercury Grand Marquis** '88 thru '10
- 36016 **Escort/Mercury Lynx** all models '81 thru '90
- 36020 **Escort/Mercury Tracer** '91 thru '02

- 36022 **Escape & Mazda Tribute** '01 thru '11
- 36024 **Explorer & Mazda Navajo** '91 thru '01
- 36025 **Explorer/Mercury Mountaineer** '02 thru '10
- 36028 **Fairmont & Mercury Zephyr** '78 thru '83
- 36030 **Festiva & Aspire** '88 thru '97
- 36032 **Fiesta** all models '77 thru '80
- 36034 **Focus** all models '00 thru '11
- 36036 **Ford & Mercury Full-size** '75 thru '87
- 36044 **Ford & Mercury Mid-size** '75 thru '86
- 36045 **Fusion & Mercury Milan** '06 thru '10
- 36048 **Mustang** V8 all models '64-1/2 thru '73
- 36049 **Mustang II** 4 cyl, V6 & V8 models '74 thru '78
- 36050 **Mustang & Mercury Capri** '79 thru '93
- 36051 **Mustang** all models '94 thru '04
- 36052 **Mustang** '05 thru '10
- 36054 **Pick-ups & Bronco** '73 thru '79
- 36058 **Pick-ups & Bronco** '80 thru '96
- 36059 **F-150 & Expedition** '97 thru '09, **F-250** '97 thru '99 & **Lincoln Navigator** '98 thru '09
- 36060 **Super Duty Pick-ups, Excursion** '99 thru '10
- 36061 **F-150** full-size '04 thru '10
- 36062 **Pinto & Mercury Bobcat** '75 thru '80
- 36066 **Probe** all models '89 thru '92
  - **Probe** '93 thru '97 - *see MAZDA 626 (61042)*
- 36070 **Ranger/Bronco II** gasoline models '83 thru '92
- 36071 **Ranger** '93 thru '10 & **Mazda Pick-ups** '94 thru '09
- 36074 **Taurus & Mercury Sable** '86 thru '95
- 36075 **Taurus & Mercury Sable** '96 thru '05
- 36078 **Tempo & Mercury Topaz** '84 thru '94
- 36082 **Thunderbird/Mercury Cougar** '83 thru '88
- 36086 **Thunderbird/Mercury Cougar** '89 thru '97
- 36090 **Vans** all V8 Econoline models '69 thru '91
- 36094 **Vans** full size '92 thru '10
- 36097 **Windstar Mini-van** '95 thru '07

GENERAL MOTORS
- 10360 **GM Automatic Transmission Overhaul**
- 38005 **Buick Century, Chevrolet Celebrity, Oldsmobile Cutlass Ciera & Pontiac 6000** all models '82 thru '96
- 38010 **Buick Regal, Chevrolet Lumina, Oldsmobile Cutlass Supreme & Pontiac Grand Prix** (FWD) '88 thru '07
- 38015 **Buick Skyhawk, Cadillac Cimarron, Chevrolet Cavalier, Oldsmobile Firenza & Pontiac J-2000 & Sunbird** '82 thru '94
- 38016 **Chevrolet Cavalier & Pontiac Sunfire** '95 thru '05
- 38017 **Chevrolet Cobalt & Pontiac G5** '05 thru '11
- 38020 **Buick Skylark, Chevrolet Citation, Olds Omega, Pontiac Phoenix** '80 thru '85
- 38025 **Buick Skylark & Somerset, Oldsmobile Achieva & Calais and Pontiac Grand Am** all models '85 thru '98
- 38026 **Chevrolet Malibu, Olds Alero & Cutlass, Pontiac Grand Am** '97 thru '03
- 38027 **Chevrolet Malibu** '04 thru '10
- 38030 **Cadillac Eldorado, Seville, Oldsmobile Toronado, Buick Riviera** '71 thru '85
- 38031 **Cadillac Eldorado & Seville, DeVille, Fleetwood & Olds Toronado, Buick Riviera** '86 thru '93
- 38032 **Cadillac DeVille** '94 thru '05 & **Seville** '92 thru '04 **Cadillac DTS** '06 thru '10
- 38035 **Chevrolet Lumina APV, Olds Silhouette & Pontiac Trans Sport** all models '90 thru '96
- 38036 **Chevrolet Venture, Olds Silhouette, Pontiac Trans Sport & Montana** '97 thru '05
  - **General Motors Full-size Rear-wheel Drive** - *see BUICK (19025)*
- 38040 **Chevrolet Equinox** '05 thru '09 **Pontiac Torrent** '06 thru '09
- 38070 **Chevrolet HHR** '06 thru '11

GEO
- **Metro** - *see CHEVROLET Sprint (24075)*
- **Prizm** - '85 thru '92 *see CHEVY (24060)*, '93 thru '02 *see TOYOTA Corolla (92036)*
- 40030 **Storm** all models '90 thru '93
- **Tracker** - *see SUZUKI Samurai (90010)*

GMC
- **Vans & Pick-ups** - *see CHEVROLET*

HONDA
- 42010 **Accord CVCC** all models '76 thru '83
- 42011 **Accord** all models '84 thru '89
- 42012 **Accord** all models '90 thru '93
- 42013 **Accord** all models '94 thru '97
- 42014 **Accord** all models '98 thru '02
- 42015 **Accord** '03 thru '07
- 42020 **Civic 1200** all models '73 thru '79
- 42021 **Civic 1300 & 1500 CVCC** '80 thru '83
- 42022 **Civic 1500 CVCC** all models '75 thru '79

(Continued on other side)

Haynes North America, Inc., 861 Lawrence Drive, Newbury Park, CA 91320-1514 • (805) 498-6703 • http://www.haynes.com

Haynes Automotive Manuals (continued)

NOTE: If you do not see a listing for your vehicle, consult your local Haynes dealer for the latest product information.

42023 **Civic** all models '84 thru '91
42024 **Civic & del Sol** '92 thru '95
42025 **Civic** '96 thru '00, **CR-V** '97 thru '01, **Acura Integra** '94 thru '00
42026 **Civic** '01 thru '10, **CR-V** '02 thru '09
42035 **Odyssey** all models '99 thru '10
 Passport - see ISUZU Rodeo (47017)
42037 **Honda Pilot** '03 thru '07, **Acura MDX** '01 thru '07
42040 **Prelude CVCC** all models '79 thru '89

HYUNDAI
43010 **Elantra** all models '96 thru '10
43015 **Excel & Accent** all models '86 thru '09
43050 **Santa Fe** all models '01 thru '06
43055 **Sonata** all models '99 thru '08

INFINITI
 G35 '03 thru '08 - see NISSAN 350Z (72011)

ISUZU
 Hombre - see CHEVROLET S-10 (24071)
47017 **Rodeo, Amigo & Honda Passport** '89 thru '02
47020 **Trooper & Pick-up** '81 thru '93

JAGUAR
49010 **XJ6** all 6 cyl models '68 thru '86
49011 **XJ6** all models '88 thru '94
49015 **XJ12 & XJS** all 12 cyl models '72 thru '85

JEEP
50010 **Cherokee, Comanche & Wagoneer Limited** all models '84 thru '01
50020 **CJ** all models '49 thru '86
50025 **Grand Cherokee** all models '93 thru '04
50026 **Grand Cherokee** '05 thru '09
50029 **Grand Wagoneer & Pick-up** '72 thru '91
 Grand Wagoneer '84 thru '91, Cherokee & Wagoneer '72 thru '83, Pick-up '72 thru '88
50030 **Wrangler** all models '87 thru '11
50035 **Liberty** '02 thru '07

KIA
54050 **Optima** '01 thru '10
54070 **Sephia** '94 thru '01, **Spectra** '00 thru '09, **Sportage** '05 thru '10

LEXUS
 ES 300/330 - see TOYOTA Camry (92007) (92008)
 RX 330 - see TOYOTA Highlander (92095)

LINCOLN
 Navigator - see FORD Pick-up (36059)
59010 **Rear-Wheel Drive** all models '70 thru '10

MAZDA
61010 **GLC Hatchback** (rear-wheel drive) '77 thru '83
61011 **GLC** (front-wheel drive) '81 thru '85
61012 **Mazda3** '04 thru '11
61015 **323 & Protegé** '90 thru '03
61016 **MX-5 Miata** '90 thru '09
61020 **MPV** all models '89 thru '98
 Navajo - see Ford Explorer (36024)
61030 **Pick-ups** '72 thru '93
 Pick-ups '94 thru '00 - see Ford Ranger (36071)
61035 **RX-7** all models '79 thru '85
61036 **RX-7** all models '86 thru '91
61040 **626** (rear-wheel drive) all models '79 thru '82
61041 **626/MX-6** (front-wheel drive) '83 thru '92
61042 **626, MX-6/Ford Probe** '93 thru '02
61043 **Mazda6** '03 thru '11

MERCEDES-BENZ
63012 **123 Series Diesel** '76 thru '85
63015 **190 Series** four-cyl gas models, '84 thru '88
63020 **230/250/280** 6 cyl sohc models '68 thru '72
63025 **280 123 Series** gasoline models '77 thru '81
63030 **350 & 450** all models '71 thru '80
63040 **C-Class:** C230/C240/C280/C320/C350 '01 thru '07

MERCURY
64200 **Villager & Nissan Quest** '93 thru '01
 All other titles, see FORD Listing.

MG
66010 **MGB** Roadster & GT Coupe '62 thru '80
66015 **MG Midget, Austin Healey Sprite** '58 thru '80

MINI
67020 **Mini** '02 thru '11

MITSUBISHI
68020 **Cordia, Tredia, Galant, Precis & Mirage** '83 thru '93
68030 **Eclipse, Eagle Talon & Ply. Laser** '90 thru '94
68031 **Eclipse** '95 thru '05, **Eagle Talon** '95 thru '98
68035 **Galant** '94 thru '10
68040 **Pick-up** '83 thru '96 & **Montero** '83 thru '93

NISSAN
72010 **300ZX** all models including Turbo '84 thru '89
72011 **350Z & Infiniti G35** all models '03 thru '08
72015 **Altima** all models '93 thru '06
72016 **Altima** '07 thru '10
72020 **Maxima** all models '85 thru '92
72021 **Maxima** all models '93 thru '04
72025 **Murano** '03 thru '10
72030 **Pick-ups** '80 thru '97 **Pathfinder** '87 thru '95
72031 **Frontier Pick-up, Xterra, Pathfinder** '96 thru '04
72032 **Frontier & Xterra** '05 thru '11
72040 **Pulsar** all models '83 thru '86
 Quest - see MERCURY Villager (64200)
72050 **Sentra** all models '82 thru '94
72051 **Sentra & 200SX** all models '95 thru '06
72060 **Stanza** all models '82 thru '90
72070 **Titan pick-ups** '04 thru '10 **Armada** '05 thru '10

OLDSMOBILE
73015 **Cutlass** V6 & V8 gas models '74 thru '88
 For other OLDSMOBILE titles, see BUICK, CHEVROLET or GENERAL MOTORS listing.

PLYMOUTH
 For PLYMOUTH titles, see DODGE listing.

PONTIAC
79008 **Fiero** all models '84 thru '88
79018 **Firebird** V8 models except Turbo '70 thru '81
79019 **Firebird** all models '82 thru '92
79025 **G6** all models '05 thru '09
79040 **Mid-size Rear-wheel Drive** '70 thru '87
 Vibe '03 thru '11 - see TOYOTA Matrix (92060)
 For other PONTIAC titles, see BUICK, CHEVROLET or GENERAL MOTORS listing.

PORSCHE
80020 **911** except Turbo & Carrera 4 '65 thru '89
80025 **914** all 4 cyl models '69 thru '76
80030 **924** all models including Turbo '76 thru '82
80035 **944** all models including Turbo '83 thru '89

RENAULT
 Alliance & Encore - see AMC (14020)

SAAB
84010 **900** all models including Turbo '79 thru '88

SATURN
87010 **Saturn** all S-series models '91 thru '02
87011 **Saturn Ion** '03 thru '07
87020 **Saturn** all L-series models '00 thru '04
87040 **Saturn VUE** '02 thru '07

SUBARU
89002 **1100, 1300, 1400 & 1600** '71 thru '79
89003 **1600 & 1800** 2WD & 4WD '80 thru '94
89100 **Legacy** all models '90 thru '99
89101 **Legacy & Forester** '00 thru '06

SUZUKI
90010 **Samurai/Sidekick & Geo Tracker** '86 thru '01

TOYOTA
92005 **Camry** all models '83 thru '91
92006 **Camry** all models '92 thru '96
92007 **Camry, Avalon, Solara, Lexus ES 300** '97 thru '01
92008 **Toyota Camry, Avalon and Solara and Lexus ES 300/330** all models '02 thru '06
92009 **Camry** '07 thru '11
92015 **Celica Rear Wheel Drive** '71 thru '85
92020 **Celica Front Wheel Drive** '86 thru '99
92025 **Celica Supra** all models '79 thru '92
92030 **Corolla** all models '75 thru '79
92032 **Corolla** all rear wheel drive models '80 thru '87
92035 **Corolla** all front wheel drive models '84 thru '92
92036 **Corolla & Geo Prizm** '93 thru '02
92037 **Corolla** models '03 thru '11
92040 **Corolla Tercel** all models '80 thru '82
92045 **Corona** all models '74 thru '82
92050 **Cressida** all models '78 thru '82
92055 **Land Cruiser** FJ40, 43, 45, 55 '68 thru '82
92056 **Land Cruiser** FJ60, 62, 80, FZJ80 '80 thru '96
92060 **Matrix & Pontiac Vibe** '03 thru '11
92065 **MR2** all models '85 thru '87
92070 **Pick-up** all models '69 thru '78
92075 **Pick-up** all models '79 thru '95
92076 **Tacoma, 4Runner, & T100** '93 thru '04
92077 **Tacoma** all models '05 thru '09
92078 **Tundra** '00 thru '06 & **Sequoia** '01 thru '07
92079 **4Runner** all models '03 thru '09
92080 **Previa** all models '91 thru '95
92081 **Prius** all models '01 thru '08
92082 **RAV4** all models '96 thru '10
92085 **Tercel** all models '87 thru '94
92090 **Sienna** all models '98 thru '09
92095 **Highlander & Lexus RX-330** '99 thru '07

TRIUMPH
94007 **Spitfire** all models '62 thru '81
94010 **TR7** all models '75 thru '81

VW
96008 **Beetle & Karmann Ghia** '54 thru '79
96009 **New Beetle** '98 thru '11
96016 **Rabbit, Jetta, Scirocco & Pick-up** gas models '75 thru '92 & Convertible '80 thru '92
96017 **Golf, GTI & Jetta** '93 thru '98, **Cabrio** '95 thru '02
96018 **Golf, GTI, Jetta** '99 thru '05
96019 **Jetta, Rabbit, GTI & Golf** '05 thru '11
96020 **Rabbit, Jetta & Pick-up** diesel '77 thru '84
96023 **Passat** '98 thru '05, **Audi A4** '96 thru '01
96030 **Transporter 1600** all models '68 thru '79
96035 **Transporter 1700, 1800 & 2000** '72 thru '79
96040 **Type 3 1500 & 1600** all models '63 thru '73
96045 **Vanagon** all air-cooled models '80 thru '83

VOLVO
97010 **120, 130 Series & 1800 Sports** '61 thru '73
97015 **140 Series** all models '66 thru '74
97020 **240 Series** all models '76 thru '93
97040 **740 & 760 Series** all models '82 thru '88
97050 **850 Series** all models '93 thru '97

TECHBOOK MANUALS
10205 **Automotive Computer Codes**
10206 **OBD-II & Electronic Engine Management**
10210 **Automotive Emissions Control Manual**
10215 **Fuel Injection Manual** '78 thru '85
10220 **Fuel Injection Manual** '86 thru '99
10225 **Holley Carburetor Manual**
10230 **Rochester Carburetor Manual**
10240 **Weber/Zenith/Stromberg/SU Carburetors**
10305 **Chevrolet Engine Overhaul Manual**
10310 **Chrysler Engine Overhaul Manual**
10320 **Ford Engine Overhaul Manual**
10330 **GM and Ford Diesel Engine Repair Manual**
10333 **Engine Performance Manual**
10340 **Small Engine Repair Manual,** 5 HP & Less
10341 **Small Engine Repair Manual,** 5.5 - 20 HP
10345 **Suspension, Steering & Driveline Manual**
10355 **Ford Automatic Transmission Overhaul**
10360 **GM Automatic Transmission Overhaul**
10405 **Automotive Body Repair & Painting**
10410 **Automotive Brake Manual**
10411 **Automotive Anti-lock Brake (ABS) Systems**
10415 **Automotive Detailing Manual**
10420 **Automotive Electrical Manual**
10425 **Automotive Heating & Air Conditioning**
10430 **Automotive Reference Manual & Dictionary**
10435 **Automotive Tools Manual**
10440 **Used Car Buying Guide**
10445 **Welding Manual**
10450 **ATV Basics**
10452 **Scooters 50cc to 250cc**

SPANISH MANUALS
98903 **Reparación de Carrocería & Pintura**
98904 **Manual de Carburador Modelos Holley & Rochester**
98905 **Códigos Automotrices de la Computadora**
98906 **OBD-II & Sistemas de Control Electrónico del Motor**
98910 **Frenos Automotriz**
98913 **Electricidad Automotriz**
98915 **Inyección de Combustible** '86 al '99
99040 **Chevrolet & GMC Camionetas** '67 al '87
99041 **Chevrolet & GMC Camionetas** '88 al '98
99042 **Chevrolet & GMC Camionetas Cerradas** '68 al '95
99043 **Chevrolet/GMC Camionetas** '94 al '04
99048 **Chevrolet/GMC Camionetas** '99 al '06
99055 **Dodge Caravan & Plymouth Voyager** '84 al '95
99075 **Ford Camionetas y Bronco** '80 al '94
99076 **Ford F-150** '97 al '09
99077 **Ford Camionetas Cerradas** '69 al '91
99088 **Ford Modelos de Tamaño Mediano** '75 al '86
99089 **Ford Camionetas Ranger** '93 al '10
99091 **Ford Taurus & Mercury Sable** '86 al '95
99095 **GM Modelos de Tamaño Grande** '70 al '90
99100 **GM Modelos de Tamaño Mediano** '70 al '88
99106 **Jeep Cherokee, Wagoneer & Comanche** '84 al '00
99110 **Nissan Camioneta** '80 al '96, **Pathfinder** '87 al '95
99118 **Nissan Sentra** '82 al '94
99125 **Toyota Camionetas y 4Runner** '79 al '95

Over 100 Haynes motorcycle manuals also available

7-12